Anglican Toryism in Upper Canada
– The Critical Years, 1812-1840 –

Robert W. Passfield

Rock's Mills Press
Oakville, Ontario
2020

Published by

Rock's Mills Press

www.rocksmillspress.com

Copyright © 2019 by Robert W. Passfield.
All rights reserved. Published by arrangement with the author.

No part of this book may be reproduced, stored in a retrieval system, or transmitted by any means without the written permission of the author.

For information, including Library and Archives Canada Cataloguing in Publication data, please contact the publisher at customer.service@rocksmillspress.com.

Cover Design: Craig Passfield

The Cross conveys the adherence of the Anglican Tories to the timeless beliefs and values of the Christian religion, and the St. Edward's Crown symbolizes the loyalty of the Tories to the Sovereign which was the basis of the unity of the British Empire.

Author's website: www.passrob.com

ISBN-13 (casebound): 978-1-77244-181-9
ISBN-13 (paperback): 978-1-77244-182-6

Dedication

To the memory of the Anglican Tories of the Province of Upper Canada

> May historians come to treat the Anglican Tories of Upper Canada with the respect and understanding that they deserve, and may Canadians come to know and appreciate the outstanding contribution of the Upper Canadian Anglican Tories to Canada in the laying of the foundations for a future nation, in ensuring its survival while in embryo, and in the forming of the distinct political culture of English Canada.
>
> Robert W. Passfield

Table of Contents

Preface ix
Acknowledgements xv
Introduction 1
1. The War of 1812 15
2. The American Threat 63
3. The Exclusion of Aliens 99
4. A Spiritually-independent Clergy 149
5. The Politics of Religion 187
6. Defending the Constitution 243
7. Revolt of the Radicals 287
Conclusion 343
Bibliography 427
Appendix A: Egerton Ryerson & the English Moderate Tories . . 443
Appendix B: The 'Young Tories' of Upper Canada 460
Appendix C: Terminology 465
Index 477

Illustrations

1. "Portrait of the Reverend John Strachan", artist unknown, n.d. [ca. 1820]. The Trinity Art Collection, Trinity College, University of Toronto. Gift of the Reverend Henry W. Davies. Page viii.

2. Sketch Map of the "Districts of Upper Canada, ca. 1815", prepared by Ken W. Watson, 2018. Page 2.

3. "The Battle of Queenston, Octr 13th 1812, which ended in complete Victory on the part of the British, having captured 927 Men, killed or wounded about 500. Taken 1400 Stand of Arms, a six Pounder, and a Stand of Colours". Drawn by Major James Dennis, British Army, and engraved by Thomas Sutherland, 1836, John Ross Robertson Collection, Toronto Reference Library. Page 16.

4. "The Honourable John Macaulay", by George Théodore Berthon, pastel on paper, 1857, Agnes Etherington Art Centre, Queen's University. Gift of Miss Charlotte Macaulay Abbot, 1973. Page 64.

5. John Beverley Robinson, portrait by Francis Hoppner Meyer, 1842, Archives of Ontario. Page 100.

6. "View of King St., looking E. from Toronto St.", lithograph by Thomas Young, 1834, John Ross Robertson Collection, Toronto Reference Library. Page 150.

7. "Reverend Egerton Ryerson, portrait by William Gush; Engraved by Thomas A. Dean, 1838", Toronto Public Library. Page 188.

8. "Front St. W. looking n. w. from Front & Simcoe Sts., Toronto, Ont.", 1834, watercolour painting by John George Howard, Toronto Reference Library, JRR 826. Page 244.

9. Map of "Toronto & Environs,1837" in Read & Stagg, eds., *The Rebellion of 1837 in Upper Canada, A Collection of Documents* (Toronto: The Champlain Society/Ontario Heritage Foundation, 1985), f 129. Page 288.

"Portrait of the Reverend John Strachan", artist unknown, n.d., Trinity College, University of Toronto. A true Christian, gifted teacher and administrator, the Rev. John Strachan was the de facto chief minister of the Province of Upper Canada during the 1820s and an éminence grise during the 1830s. He was a member of the Executive Council and Legislative Council, and the fountainhead of Upper Canadian Anglican Toryism.

Preface

This book is a supplement to an earlier publication by the author –*The Upper Canadian Anglican Tory Mind, A Cultural Fragment* (2018)– that reconstructed the ideas, beliefs, and principles of the Upper Canadian Anglican Tories with respect to the British constitution, religion and education, and their Christian worldview. That earlier study was undertaken to determine whether the Tories of Upper Canada were simply Old Whigs, as had been asserted in Canadian historiography, or were true philosophical Tories who adhered to Anglican theology and political philosophy as set forth by Richard Hooker (1554-1600), the Anglican divine, in his eight-volume work –*The Lawes of Ecclesiastical Politie*– produced at the time of the English Reformation. An underlying assumption – a subsidiary theme --was that "ideas influence actions', and that a reconstruction of the Tory mind would permit historians to attain a better understanding of the reason why the Upper Canadian Tories took the particular positions that they did on the major political issues of their day.

That earlier study had taken on a broader significance, for the author personally, when he began to think about a comment made by a British exchange student who was taking a Canadian history course in the M.A. programme at McMaster University. At that time, the author had asked the student: "What do you think of Canadian history"? He had replied: "It's hollow at the core. It's a history of political agitations and protest movements".

It was a startling statement, but upon reflection the author came to a similar conclusion. The history of Upper Canada, and of Canadian history more generally, was written from the viewpoint of political agitators and outgroups who were attacking the governing establishment, and who were espousing Lockean-liberal values in the pursuit of their own partisan self-interests. In truth, as interpreted in the historical works of liberal-Whig historians, Canadian history was 'hollow at the core', and the Canada that they portrayed – where English Canada was concerned – lacked a soul. There was no clearly defined national culture in their historical works. In response, the author came to view his study as laying the groundwork for a Tory history of Canada that would restore its soul, and that would bring recognition to the true founders and defenders of what became the Dominion of Canada: viz. the Tories of the British North American provinces. It was decidedly an ambitious undertaking, and perhaps somewhat naïve in the aspirations that it gave rise to, but inspiring nonetheless.

In pursuing the research for that original study, it became clear to the author that the Upper Canadian Anglican Tories were true philosophical conservatives who had evolved a unique variant of English Anglican Toryism. The political thought of the Tories of Upper Canada was an amalgam of a political philosophy that embodied a Christian worldview, a theory of the union of church and state, and a concept of natural law as forged by the Anglican divine, Richard Hooker, at the time of the English Reformation; the Old Tory concept of the sovereignty of God exercised through the King – God's Vicegerent -- the supremacy of law, and the 'historic rights of Englishmen'; and the 18th Century English Tory concept of the balanced British Constitution that grew out of the Glorious Revolution of 1688 and was distinctly different from 18th Century Whig parliamentarianism.

It was a Tory political philosophy that in Upper Canada was leavened by a belief in a meritocracy based on social mobility through education. Public offices, the National Church clergy, and the professions were to be filled with well-educated 'gentlemen' of a strong Christian moral character, well versed in science and the useful arts. To that end, the Tories believed in a 'national system' of education that would be open to all ranks of society, and that would be under the direction of the established Church of England to ensure Christian moral values were inculcated in the youth of the province. Government bursaries were to be provided for 'the clever poor' who excelled in the common school. The bursaries were intended to enable such God-gifted individuals to proceed to the District Grammar School, and beyond to a projected university (King's College University) and to ultimately take their proper place in the natural hierarchical social order in keeping with their God-given talents and abilities, and application.

The present book carries forward the concept that 'ideas influence actions'. It does so through an examination of the response of the Anglican Tories to several major public issues of their day, and through setting forth an explanation for their actions in keeping with the tenets of their political philosophy: viz. the principles, values, beliefs and worldview of the Anglican Tory mind. The chapters of the book focus on the critical years, 1812-1840, when the Anglican Tories were defending the cultural values and institutions of the Loyalist asylum of Upper Canada, and were engaged in a veritable struggle for survival against an external threat posed by the imperialism of the United States and its democratic republican ideology, and an internal political threat posed by democratic radicals and evangelical sectarians espousing American political ideas and religious beliefs. In that struggle, the Anglican Tories strove to ensure the sustainability of their traditional Church-State polity through the maintenance of the balanced British Constitution, the extension of the ministrations of the established Church of England, and the teaching of the youth of the province in a 'national system' of education under the direction of the Established Church.

In their efforts to ensure the survival of the Province of Upper Canada, which had been established as an asylum for the Loyalists of the American Revolution, the Tories expressed the cultural and political values that they shared with the Loyalists of the American Revolution. The Loyalists were men, and their families, who were driven out of the new United States of America for their expressed loyalty to the Crown. It was a loyalty that was based on a reverence for the traditional social and political order under a monarchical form of government, a fervent belief in the unity of the British Empire under the Crown, and an adherence to the moral values and worldview of a Christian society in opposition to the novel secular democratic republicanism of the leading American revolutionaries.

Secondarily, this book analyzes the ideas and character of the politicized 'outgroups' who were assailing the Tory establishment from within the province, and the threat posed externally – both militarily and ideologically -- by the new American democratic republic on the borders of Upper Canada. In doing so, this study yields a deeper understanding of the ideological struggle, a veritable 'battle of ideas', in which the Anglican Tories were engaged in Upper Canada following the close of the War of 1812.

In Upper Canada, the politicized 'outgroups' were united under the umbrella of a Reform Party in striving to foster political unrest and to overthrow of the Tory establishment. Among the opposition groups were democratic radicals, evangelical sectarians, liberal-Whig secularists and, as of the early 1830s, egalitarian democratic republicans who were principally from the non-Loyalist American areas of settlement.

More particularly, in carrying forward the concept that 'ideas influence actions', each chapter of the present study focuses on the Tory response to a particular threat to the survival of the Loyalist asylum of Upper Canada, its institutions, and the Tory governing establishment: viz. The War of 1812 (American imperialism); The America Threat (the spread of the democratic republican ideology into Upper Canada); The Exclusion of Aliens (the growing political threat posed by American immigrant aliens); A Spiritually-independent Clergy (the radical threat to confiscate the clergy reserves land endowment of the established Church of England); the Politics of Religion (the evangelical sectarian threat); Defending the Constitution (the House of Assembly threat to the balance of the constitution); and the Rebellion of 1837 (an attempted coup d'état by the egalitarian democratic republicans).

The Conclusion, which is written in the form of an essay, sets forth the insights gained by the author into the politics of Upper Canada, the character and ideological origins of each of the four 'outgroups' who were attacking the Tory establishment, the political events that brought about the demise of the Upper Canadian Anglican Tories as a governing elite, and ultimately the impact of the implementation of the principle of responsible government on political behavior.

It is the contention of this book that the particular response of the Upper Canadian Tories to the military, ideological, political and religious forces that threatened the survival of the Loyalist Province of Upper Canada illustrates clearly the theme that 'ideas influence actions'. The book highlights the extent to which the Tories were responsible for the survival of Upper Canada in preserving the Province from conquest, as well as cultural assimilation by the American behemoth, and attests to the strict adherence of the Anglican Tory leadership to their Christian principles, values and beliefs, in maintaining the rule of law and exercising the virtue of mercy when under duress.

In each and every conflict, whether under an external military attack, an ideological threat, an internal political disorder, or an attempted coup d'état by revolutionaries in arms, it was the Upper Canadian Anglican Tories who were in the forefront in defending the Loyalist Asylum of Upper Canada and the traditional conservative values upon which it was founded. They could do no less as they were philosophical conservatives who adhered to the traditional values, beliefs and principles of Anglican Toryism, and were imbued with a sense of duty to defend the traditional Christian order in a situation where their 'ideas influenced their actions'.

Preface

Background

With the success of the American Revolution (1776-1783), upwards of 70,000 Loyalist refugees who had fought for the Crown and the Unity of Empire and/or had publicly declared their loyalty to the King, were forced to flee the newly-established United States of America. They fled principally to Britain, the British colonies of Nova Scotia and New Brunswick, the British West Indies, and Spanish Florida. A much smaller number fled northward to the Province of Quebec, a province that had been created by the Proclamation Act of 1763, following the British conquest of the French colonies of New France.

As of the signing of the Peace of Paris (1783) – that recognized the independence of the new United States of America – almost 8,000 Loyalist refugees had migrated to the western part of the Province of Quebec. They settled along the north shore of the Upper St. Lawrence River, along the shores of the Bay of Quinte on Lake Ontario, and in the wilderness north of the lower Great Lakes in the Niagara Peninsula, in the Grand River Valley, along the Thames River, and at Long Point on Lake Erie. In 1791, the Province of Upper Canada was created by the British government by dividing the Province of Quebec into two provinces: Lower Canada and Upper Canada. (1)

The new province was an English Crown colony. The Constitution of the new Province -- the Constitutional Act of 1791 – was a transcript of the British Constitution with the executive in the hands of a Lt. Governor appointed by the Crown, a balanced legislature comprising the Lt. Governor, an appointed Legislative Council, and a House of Assembly elected on a 40-shilling property franchise, and an appointed judiciary administering the law 'at the pleasure of the Crown'. An established Church, the Church of England, constituted an integral part of the Constitution under the union of Church and State in providing religious services and moral guidance, and the clerics of the established Church were expected to serve as teachers in a 'national' education system that the Anglican Tories were bent on establishing.

There were no direct taxes or tithes imposed in the Province of Upper Canada. The provincial government was supported by financial grants from the British government, by revenues raised from duties imposed on imports and, to a minor extent, from licenses and fees paid by commercial establishments. In the Constitution, a provision was made for the established Church of England to be supported by a land endowment – one-seventh of the land reserved in each surveyed township – with the lots of the Clergy Reserves to be leased to gain revenues for the payment of clerical salaries and the erection of churches and parsonages. (2)

In establishing the Province of Upper Canada, the intention of the British government was to establish a sanctuary wherein Loyalist refugees -- who were driven out of the new American democratic republic -- could continue to live in a traditional conservative society as befit British subjects. It was a colony wherein the Loyalists would enjoy 'the historic rights of Englishmen' under the British Crown, the benefits of the balanced British Constitution, the ministrations of the established Church of England (if desired), the rule of law and equality before the law, religious toleration, and paternal government, while continuing to live within the British Empire. As such, the new Province of Upper Canada was founded upon a conscious rejection of the democratic republicanism of the newly-independent United States of America which was based on a Lockean liberalism that embodied inalienable natural rights, individualism, limited laissez-faire government, and a secular worldview.

Notes:

1. On the Loyalist refugees, see: Christopher Moore, *The Loyalists, Revolution, Exile, Settlement* (Toronto: Macmillan of Canada, 1984); Mary Beacock Fryer, *Loyal She Remains, A Pictorial History of Ontario* (Toronto: United Empire Loyalists' Association of Canada, 1984), 73-93 & 97-127; and Maya Jasanoff, *Liberty's Exiles, American Loyalists in the Revolutionary War* (New York: Alfred A. Knopf, 2011).

2. See "The Government of Upper Canada" in Aileen Dunham, *Political Unrest in Upper Canada, 1815-1836* (Toronto: McClelland & Stewart, 1969), 29-46.

Erratum

In his earlier work, (2018), the author repeatedly referred to 'the alliance of church and state', which is an error. In the British Constitution, and the Anglican Tory political philosophy, there was a complete fusion or 'union of church and state', which is the proper phrase that ought to have been employed by the author. The church and state were not separate bodies joined in an alliance; they were integral, and interrelated, parts of the constitution.

Acknowledgements

The present study, *Anglican Toryism in Upper Canada, The Critical Years, 1812-1840*, has evolved in a rather *ad hoc* manner. Long after he retired from his position as a public historian with the Canadian government, the author decided to revisit the draft chapters of his abortive Ph. D. dissertation on 'The Upper Canadian Tory Mind'. The draft chapters and research notes had remained in basement storage since his days as a history graduate student, some forty years earlier, but his new intention was to produce a finished manuscript for potential publication in a book format. However, in copy editing the original dissertation chapters on the ideas of the Upper Canadian Anglican Tories, the author decided to expand upon a subsidiary theme that "ideas influence actions'. In doing so, three additional chapters were researched and written that focused on: the politics of religion in the Province of Upper Canada; the Tory defence of the constitution against assaults by the House of Assembly; and the Tory response to a rebellion in December 1837.

Once the three new chapters were inserted into the copy-edited chapters of the earlier dissertation manuscript, the projected book – entitled 'The Upper Canadian Anglican Tory Mind, a Cultural Fragment -- had two related themes: an intellectual history main theme, with chapters focusing on the constitutional, religious and educational ideas of the Anglican Tories and their worldview; and a political history subsidiary theme focusing on 'ideas influence actions' with chapters setting forth the Tory response to the major political issues of their day. Both themes were united within an overarching framework of the setting forth and defending of the traditional conservative values, beliefs and principles of the Upper Canadian Anglican Tories in the Loyalist asylum of Upper Canada in the two decades or more after the War of 1812.

What appeared initially to the author as a good idea, in rounding out the treatment of Upper Canadian Anglican Toryism, proved ultimately to be a major misstep. When fully-edited and formatted, the resultant manuscript constituted a massive tome of twenty chapters and upwards of 1,000 pages. It was obvious that in the writing of the original dissertation chapters, as well as in the working up of the three new additional chapters, the author had fallen into the pitfall of trying to develop the subsidiary theme that 'ideas influence actions' to its full extent. In that endeavor, he had been, and was, motivated by a deep desire to write a 'great work' on Upper Canadian Anglican Toryism that would be substantial, unsurpassed in its breadth of treatment, and a standard reference work. Be that as it may, major cuts had to be made.

Faced with such an inordinately massive manuscript, the author decided to divide the study into two separate books. The first -- on the Upper Canadian Anglican Tory Mind -- would focus strictly on the ideas of the Tories; whereas the second book would focus on the subsidiary political theme that 'ideas influence actions'. The enlarged manuscript lent itself to such a division as each chapter was complete within itself with an introductory paragraph and a conclusion that related the chapter directly to one or the other of the two existing themes.

In addition to removing the three new political chapters from the enlarged work, it was decided that three chapters of the original dissertation text ought to be removed as well, owing to their strong political content: viz. a chapter on the military and ideological struggle faced by the Tories during the War of 1812; a chapter on the Tory effort to combat the ideological threat posed by American immigrant aliens; and a chapter on the Tory defence of the clergy reserves land endowment of the established Church of England.

In sum, six chapters -- which focused on the 'ideas influence actions' subsidiary theme -- were removed from the expanded manuscript. They form the content of this present book together with a reprint of another original dissertation chapter on 'The American Threat'.

The American threat chapter sets forth the geopolitical and ideological circumstance in which the Upper Canadian Tories found themselves in seeking to conserve and strengthen the Loyalist Asylum of Upper Canada in the post-War of 1812 period. In that respect, the American Threat chapter provides a background context for the Tory response to the major political issues of their day as related in this present book: whereas, in the earlier Anglican Tory Mind book, the American Threat chapter provided a background context for a deeper understanding of the Tory effort to expound publicly on their ideas and to inculcate them into the population at large and, in particular, the youth of the Province.

Acknowledgements

The Conclusion to this present book is not a conclusion *per se*, but rather an essay that sets forth the insights that the author has gained into the politics of Upper Canada through his earlier research and study, and through the new research which was undertaken into the ideological origins of the several 'outgroups' who were attacking the Tory establishment. The analysis of the composition and nature of the several opposition groups -- who were aligned under the umbrella of the Reform Party of Upper Canada -- yields a better understanding of the nature of the ideological challenges that the Tories faced in the fields of politics, religion, and education, in defending the traditional institutions and conservative political culture of the Loyalist asylum of Upper Canada. Ultimately, the Anglican Tories failed to maintain themselves as a governing elite. They were defeated by external forces beyond their control, but they did succeed in preventing Upper Canada from becoming thoroughly Americanized and gave Upper Canada a national vision and purpose that was realized in the founding of the Dominion of Canada in 1867.

This present work on the Anglican Tory effort to maintain, strengthen, and defend the Loyalist Asylum of Upper Canada is based primarily on the extant published writings and archival records of four prominent Upper Canadian Anglican Tories: a Loyalist, Richard Cartwright Jr. (1759-1815) of Kingston, Upper Canada; the Rev. John Strachan (1778-1867) of the established Church of England in Upper Canada; and two of his former students, who were the sons of Loyalists: John Beverley Robinson (1791-1863) of York (Toronto), and John Macaulay (1792-1857) of Kingston. All four of these men were prominent High Church Anglican Tories, and members of the political, religious and social elite of the Province. They held influential positions in various public offices and played a leading role in the politics of Upper Canada.

The four chapters extracted from the original text of the abortive Ph.D. dissertation are based on primary sources, with the historical context strengthened by a subsequent insertion of material from secondary historical sources; whereas the three new chapters are based on secondary historical sources supplemented extensively by material from published primary sources.

The analysis of the ideas of the opponents of the Tory establishment is based on primary sources – an examination of the published writings of the malcontents – while the analysis of the political character and behavior of the politicized 'outgroups' is based on secondary works in history and political science.

There are three appendices to this publication:

Appendix A: "Egerton Ryerson & the English moderate Tories" is a reprint, with commentary, of an article by Ryerson that astonished his contemporaries when published in October 1833;

Appendix B: "The 'young Tories' of Upper Canada", identifies many of the leading members of the Tory governing establishment who were educated by the Rev. John Strachan; and

Appendix C: "Terminology", identifies the different politicized groups in Upper Canada, expands on the concept of 'democracy' held by the Reformers, and comments on the terms 'Outgroups', 'Family Compact', 'liberal-Whig', and 'Whig history'.

The publication of this present book, *Anglican Toryism in Upper Canada, The Critical Years, 1812-1840*, together with the earlier book, *The Upper Canadian Anglican Tory Mind, A Cultural Fragment* (2018), brings full circle the study of the Upper Canadian Tory Mind as it evolved from the original concept as set forth by the author forty years ago while in the History Graduate School at McMaster University. These two published works are the product of almost three years of research, thought, and writing as a history graduate student and -- after a forty-year hiatus -- of a further three years of work as a retired public historian in copy-editing and preparing for publication a greatly enlarged treatment of the two themes present in the undertaking of the projected Ph. D. dissertation.

The completion of this odyssey brought to mind a comment that was made to the author, many years ago, by the late Professor G.R. Elton of Cambridge University, the renowned English historian of Tudor England. During a brief meeting with history graduate students at McMaster University -- while on a lecture tour in Canada -- Professor Elton asked the author: "What is your thesis subject"? The author replied that he was

Acknowledgements

going to prepare a thesis on the political thought of the Upper Canadian Tories in focusing on their ideas pertaining to the constitution, religion, and education, and their worldview. Professor Elton responded abruptly: "That's a subject for a mature historian, not a graduate student". It was a warning that the author ought to have heeded, often wished that he had, but now has few regrets that he did not.

Forty years later, in taking up that unfinished task, the author was motivated by a feeling that he owed a debt -- as an historian -- to the Upper Canadian Anglican Tories to restore an historical memory of their existence, ideas, and achievements to Canadians.

One can only hope that the two Tory books, in combination, will fulfill their intended purpose over time. However, if not, some consolation can be found in the thought of the poet, Robert Browning, on life and art:

> Ah, but a man's reach should exceed his grasp,
> Or, what's a heaven for?
>
> *Andrea del Sarto* (1855)

On a strictly personal level, I would like to thank my brother, John Passfield, for his encouragement and insightful comments during the preparation of this work. I am indebted as well to my nephew, Craig Passfield, for the design and preparation of the book covers, and to a good friend, Ken Watson, who prepared the sketch map of the Districts of Upper Canada, circa 1815, which has been reproduced in both Tory books.

Once again, a debt of gratitude is owed to Susan James for her understanding and support as my retirement years continue to be devoted to a demanding muse – Clio – in the research and writing of historical works.

Any errors, omissions or misconceptions in the present work are solely the responsibility of the author.

Robert W. Passfield
Ottawa, Ontario
March 2019

Introduction

'Ideas Influence Actions'

The Tory National Policy

The Tory Governing Elite

The Tory Legacy: Canadian Historiography

"I have difficulty imagining that anyone can be a historian without realizing that history itself is part of the life of the mind; hence I have been compelled to insist that the mind of man is the basic factor in human history."

Perry Miller

Errand into the Wilderness (1964), Preface, ix.

"For history, the object to be discovered is not the mere event, but the thought expressed in it. To discover that thought is already to understand it. ... The cause of the event ... means the thought in the mind of the person [or persons] by whose agency the event came about; and this is not something other than the event, it is the inside of the event itself."

R.G. Collingwood

The Idea of History
(1963 ed.), 214-215.

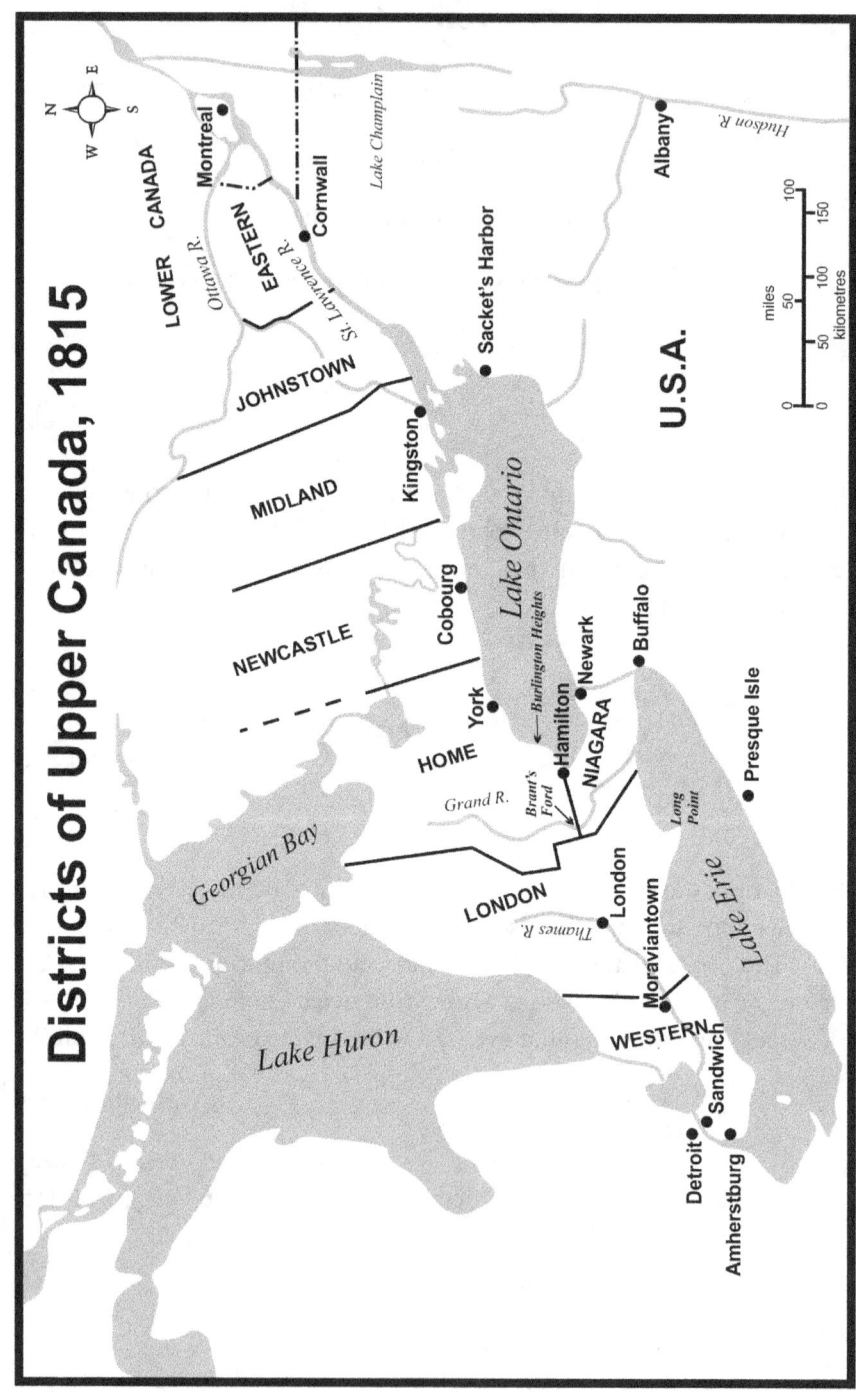

Sketch Map of the "Districts of Upper Canada, ca. 1815", prepared by Ken W. Watson, 2018.

Introduction

In their political behavior, the leading Anglican Tories of Upper Canada showed a remarkable consistency with respect to their stand on the major political issues of their day. It was a product of the fact that the leading Tories shared a common faith in being adherents of the Church of England. Moreover most, but not all, of the leading tories shared a common education in being former students of the Rev. John Strachan; they had a common moral character forged during their attendance at his Cornwall District Grammar School (1803-1811): a boarding school where the social and political elite of the province sent their sons to be educated. Hence, their political behavior was governed by a conscious body of beliefs, values and principles, that found expression in a national policy designed to strengthen the national character and defences of the Province of Upper Canada. The Tory values that gave rise to the National Policy fostered an economic nationalism that was to have a major impact on the political and economic development of 19th Century Canada.

'Ideas Influence Actions'

This study rests upon an assumption, which has been made by intellectual historians, that the understanding of the history of a period, "its politics or public events", is dependent upon an awareness of the climate of opinion of the time: "the peculiar mixture of ideas and values that made up the mind of [an] age". It is a conviction that the actions of individuals and of peoples proceed in relation to a specific set of assumptions and ideas; and that events take place within a conjunction of peculiar historical circumstances. Hence, it is from the manifold interaction of ideas and circumstances that the history of a period ought to be assessed and written. (1)

In an age of ideological diversity -- such as was the situation in Upper Canada wherein there was a veritable 'battle of ideas' among politicized groups – historians must strive to understand the respective ideologies of the protagonists. In sum, the achievement of an historical understanding depends upon the recognition that:

> "If ideas in politics more than elsewhere are the children of political needs, none-the-less, is it true, that the actual world

is the result of men's thought. The existing arrangement of political forces is dependent at least as much upon ideas, as it is upon men's perception of their interests." (2)

Hence, ideas play a critical role in history, regardless of whether one fully accepts the assertion of the American intellectual historian, Perry Miller, that "the mind of man is the basic factor in human history". (3) In sum, the actions of men are not merely an arbitrary response to various events or contingencies. Their response to events, and even their interpretation of the circumstances to which they were responding, is determined by the intellectual framework of their mind: their worldview, their religion, and their political philosophy which embrace the basic values, beliefs, and principles that form their character and outlook. (4)

The Tory National Policy

In educating the sons of the social and political elite of Upper Canada -- at the Cornwall District Grammar School in the decade prior to the War of 1812 -- the Rev. John Strachan aspired to have his pupils achieve a future prominence in the public life and professions of the Province of Upper Canada. In the postwar decade, that aspiration was realized as the young Tory 'gentlemen' entered the professions and public life and, in comprising a well-educated elite in a pioneer society, they soon rose rapidly to positions of prominence in their respective fields. Once in positions of power and influence, the 'young Tories' – under the leadership of the Rev. John Strachan and his protégé, John Beverley Robinson – sought to implement policies to guide the development of the young Province of Upper Canada, and to lay the foundations for a future nation within the British Empire.

Immediately following the close of the War of 1812, Strachan and Robinson devised a comprehensive national policy to guide the development of the Province of Upper Canada. They called on the provincial government to implement the various aspect of their national policy, while trying to convince the British government to render its full support. The National Policy was intended to defend the existing order, to safeguard the province, and to strengthen its "British national character". In presenting arguments in support of the proposed programme, the Tories drew upon their fundamental principles, values and beliefs.

In calling on the province and the British government to implement their National Policy, the Anglican Tories revealed what they saw as threatening the existing institutions of the province and the social order, and their view of the purpose and efficacy of the institutions that they were defending. The National Policy was formulated in response to the events of their time, and the circumstance in which the Tories found themselves, but drew on the deeper governing principles, beliefs, and values of the Anglican Tory mind. (5)

The National Policy was born at a time when the Province of Upper Canada had narrowly escaped being overrun -- during the War of 1812 -- by a new revolutionary power, the United States of America. It was a republic that showed unmistakable signs of becoming even more powerful in the future, and that appeared to be committed to an extension of its democratic republicanism over the entire North American continent by force of arms. The future existence of the Province of Upper Canada appeared to depend on the implementation of a unified plan of government action to develop the resources of the province and to maximize its strength and population.

To that end, the leading Tories had a very definite conception of what a 'national policy' should comprehend. In a succession of memoranda and lengthy letters -- which were submitted to the Colonial Office at intervals throughout the decade following the termination of the War of 1812, and at times of crisis thereafter -- the Tories elaborated on their ideas in detail. Over a period of two decades, they were to show a striking degree of consistency in the policies which they put forward as being necessary to the very survival of the province. The policies, which they advocated, constituted practical solutions to political problems that plagued the Province of Upper Canada.

The Tories argued that a concerted plan of action would be beneficial not only to the Province of Upper Canada, but also to the Mother Country upon whose unstinted aid and support the prescribed measures were dependent for their ultimate success. The Tories were convinced that the growing power of the United States, and its expansionist nature, made it impossible for the Province of Upper Canada to survive without a commitment from Great Britain to use its military and naval power in defence of the colony. However, the National Policy programme was designed not only to prepare Upper Canada to resist foreign aggression in the form of American expansionism, but also to counteract an ideological threat: viz. the impact that the American democratic-republican ideas were having within the Province of Upper Canada.

A primary aim of the National Policy was to maintain, strengthen, and build a specific type of society in Upper Canada, and ultimately in British North America at large: viz. one having a "British national character". The experience of the war years, recent historical events, and the bias of the education which they had received, all combined to establish a fundamental dichotomy in the Upper Canadian Tory mind. For the Anglican Tories, the aggressive and acquisitive American national character, and the democratic secular polity of the United States which they viewed as a 'mobocracy', represented what they deplored in any people or in any society. In contrast, the British national character was viewed as the ideal for sustaining a polity based on 'peace, order and good government'. England was regarded as 'the good society' incarnate which Upper Canada should strive to emulate.

What the Anglican Tories sought to create in Upper Canada was a society modeled on that of England. The Province of Upper Canada was to have a well-ordered polity which would be peopled by subjects of the Crown who possessed:

> The character of a perfect British citizen, who knows his rank, his place, his value, his duties, and his rights; and who will not step out of his own sphere unless he can do so in a constitutional manner – one to whom self-denial is as dear a privilege as the protection of his person and property, because the detail of that virtue among his fellow citizens is how own security.

The Tories of Upper Canada were aware that England had shortcomings, but these were attributed to human frailties rather than to any imperfections in her institutions. From the vantage point of Upper Canada, it seemed that in England:

> The comforts, the Knowledge and the virtues of social life have been carried to the highest perfection. The lofty sense of

independence among her people, their truthful and vigorous morality, their sober and rational piety and the impartial decorous and laudable administration of their laws, are all matters of joyful admiration.

The policies that the Tories wanted to see adopted as part of a national policy were aimed at establishing a foundation for the development of the Province of Upper Canada in keeping with what they thought the Province was, and ought to be. They believed that Upper Canada was founded as an asylum for the Loyalists of the American Revolution. It was an asylum where the Loyalists could continue to live as members of the British Empire, to be governed by British institutions, and to enjoy the unsurpassed benefits of British subjects and of British civilization.

As expressed by John Beverley Robinson:

> It should now be felt that we, in this generation, are laying the foundation of a social system, which is to extend its avails upon millions who will soon succeed. The responsibility upon us is great, & upon the measure in which we discharge our obligations, the very happiness of those who are to come afterwards may very well depend.

For the Anglican Tories, the Province of Upper Canada was an integral part of 'the national family' of Great Britain and had as much of a claim to belong and to receive the benefits of her government as any county of England. Upper Canadians, as British subjects, were entitled to the same rights and security as British subjects in the United Kingdom. Thus, the Upper Canadian Tories did not hesitate to request the aid of Great Britain in support of their proposed national policy measures.

The National Policy programme covered all areas of 'national life', including politics, religion, and education, as well as immigration, defence, and the economic development of the province. It involved the maintenance of the existing constitution -- the Constitutional Act of 1791 -- and the strengthening and extension of the Church of England which was held to be the established National Church of Upper Canada. A national system of education was to be established which would be open to all, but under the aegis of the provincial government and the direction of the Established Church. British emigration, particularly of men of means and good character, was to be encouraged to increase the population; whereas the influx of American settlers was to be curtailed until the national character was sufficiently formed to permit American immigrants to be safely absorbed.

Changes were to be made in the laws which governed the naturalization of foreigners to ensure that all public positions, including the positions governed by election as well as by appointment, would be kept in the hands of 'the loyal' for the immediate future. For the Tories, 'the loyal' were the bona fide Loyalist settlers, British immigrant settlers, and the men who had fought in the defence of Upper Canada during the recently concluded War of 1812, or individuals who had otherwise distinguished themselves in opposing the American invaders. Those who were to be excluded from public positions, were recent immigrants – primarily American settlers -- who had yet to become naturalized British subjects or had refused to take the Oath of Allegiance to the King. Many of the pre-war American settlers in Upper Canada had been disaffected during the War and were viewed as being democratic republicans in their political beliefs. During the War, many of the pre-war American settlers had refused to fight in defence of the province against the American invading armies, some had joined the American invaders, and most had refused to support the war effort in defence of Upper Canada.

As part of the National Policy, the Tories advocated that the colonies of British North America be incorporated into a general political confederation under the Crown to foster the development of closer ties, both tangible and intangible, with the mother country. The proposed union of the British North American colonies was envisaged as involving some form of imperial federation, which together with existing imperial trade preferences, would strengthen the Imperial tie by promoting the development of a common national feeling. It was held that in time, the British connection of Upper Canada would be thoroughly fixed through the sharing of a common character and outlook embodied in the British national character.

The French Canadians of the Province of Lower Canada were to be peaceably assimilated to the British national character in the proposed new general confederation of the British North American colonies. It was to be done by extending to French Canadians the benefits of a provincial education system – with bilingual teachers to be found among the Scots immigrants -- and by the opening of public offices to those who availed themselves of the opportunity to learn English. In the meantime, the representatives of the French Canadians in the elected House of Assembly of the proposed confederation government would be unable to block legislation aimed at promoting the economic development of the provinces or to oppose British emigration to the North American colonies. Where Upper Canada was concerned, various measures were proposed to foster the economic development of the province, and to establish essential war industries. The Tories also supported the plans prepared by the British military for strengthening the militia and the defences of Upper Canada. (6)

The various measures advocated in the National Policy programme were interrelated and mutually sustaining. They could not be separated, one from another, without endangering the whole. Ultimately, the National Policy was a product of the Tory Mind: viz. of their worldview, their political philosophy, the circumstance in which they found themselves within the Province of Upper Canada, and their commitment to preserving the Loyalist asylum of Upper Canada and the traditional values on which it was founded.

The implementation of the National Policy is not the subject of this present study, but it does reveal the national vision that the Tories were striving to realize, and that gave a cohesiveness, direction, and clear sense of purpose to their response to the political challenges and public issues of their day.

The Tory Governing Elite

Much of Tory politics in the post-war period was focused on the implementation of their National Policy to guide the development of the Province of Upper Canada. The Rev. John Strachan, and his former public and protégé, John Beverley Robinson, were not only responsible for the formulation of that policy, but were instrumental in securing provincial acts to further the national policy objectives and were unflagging in their efforts to secure the aid of the British government in support of the various national policy initiatives. In many ways, the National Policy consisted of a setting forth -- in a unified programme -- of several initiatives that

Richard Cartwright – an Anglican Loyalist, and close friend and associate of the young Rev. John Strachan -- had urged on the provincial government in the years prior to the War of 1812 to protect the 'national interest' of the Province of Upper Canada. The National Policy of the Tories was an embodiment of the governing principles of the Anglican Tory mind and, as such, the initiatives of the national policy programme received strong support from John Macaulay, a High Church Tory, the son of a Loyalist, and yet another former pupil of the Rev. John Strachan.

When the Rev. John Strachan entered public life following the War of 1812, it was to promote the interests of the Established Church of England and to defend the traditional social, religious, and political order. In that endeavour, he counted upon, and for the most part received, the support of the young men whom he had educated in his Cornwall District Grammar School (1803-1811) at Cornwall, Upper Canada. His former pupils were the sons of the leading Loyalists and prominent British immigrants whose families comprised the political, social, and economic elite of the province. Indeed, a significant number of his former pupils, who were among the most highly-educated young men in the province, were just entering the professions, the government, the Church, and public life in the immediate postwar period.

Within two years of the August 1818 arrival of a new governor in Upper Canada -- Lt. Governor, Major General Sir Peregrine Maitland – the members of a distinctive provincial Tory elite were becoming well established in the provincial government, in the judiciary at all levels, and in education. And they would remain in positions of power and influence until the demise of the Province of Upper Canada in February 1841. For the most part, the governing elite of the Province of Upper Canada comprised the Rev. John Strachan and his protégé John Beverley Robinson -- who provided the leadership in articulating a response to critical issues and challenges – and the young Anglican Tories who were educated by the Rev. John Strachan. They held public offices together with other tories who shared their principles and values in being defenders of the traditional order, inclusive of several prominent young Presbyterians and Scots Roman Catholics who had been educated by the Rev. John Strachan.

For two decades, the provincial Anglican Tory elite struggled to implement the national policy programme in the face of a belligerent opposition comprised of several 'outgroups' who were aligned in the House of Assembly under the umbrella of the Reform Party. Among the opposition groups were democratic radicals, evangelical sectarians, liberal-Whig secularists, and, as of the early 1830s, egalitarian democratic republicans. In seeking to implement their national policy programme, the governing Tories were also plagued by the indifference of the British government and, after the coming to power in November 1830 of a liberal-Whig reform party in Britain, by the outright hostility of the Colonial Department towards the Anglican Tories of Upper Canada.

This study is intended to yield a better understanding of the nature of Upper Canadian Anglican Toryism through a setting forth of the positions that the Tories took on the major public issues of their day in the context of the ideas that they expressed in support of the positions taken. It is the contention of this work that a study of the Tory efforts to realize their ideas in action will not only illustrate the theme that 'ideas influence actions' but will yield a deeper meaning and significance to the principles, values and beliefs to which the Tories adhered.

The Upper Canadian Anglican Tories judged men by their actions and sought always to act in keeping with what they regarded as an eternal moral order and eternal verities. The Christian principles and beliefs which governed their lives and political behavior embodied for them "the complete teaching for all men everywhere". (7)

The Tory Legacy: Canadian Historiography

Although liberal-Whig historians in the writing of the history of Upper Canada have dismissed, and often disparaged, the religious, social and political views of the Upper Canadian Tories, the national policy objectives and economic nationalism of the Tories has received some recognition for its influence on the Canadian psyche and the economic development of Canada. The late Professor S.F. Wise of Carleton University has written extensively on the conservative contribution to the political and economic development of Canada. However, in the published works of Professor Wise, 'tory' and 'conservative' were treated as interchangeable terms.

In several publications, Professor Wise stressed that it was conservatives -- following the close of the War of 1812 – who provided "the leadership in economic and political nationalism" which was to sustain Canada throughout the better part of the nineteenth century. (8) It was the conservatives who were "acutely conscious of the military, economic and political menace of the United States", and who -- out of a concern for the survival of their distinct values -- formulated and pursued policies which transcended purely local interests to meet the dangers that were inherent in the peculiar position of Upper Canada. These 'national policies' were invested with "a special sense of mission" which the conservatives imparted to succeeding generations of Canadians during the developmental projects of the canal building era and, subsequently, during the railway construction era of the 1850s.

Ultimately, as argued by Professor Wise, "it was precisely this kind of developmental strategy, in the hands of a second generation of Upper Canadian conservatives, that was central to the scheme for the union of the British North American provinces in the 1860's and for the cementing of that union in the post-Confederation era." (9)

Moreover, the economic development policies of the Upper Canadian conservatives were directly related to the "total structure of conservative values" which, in turn, came to inform the tone, feeling, and character of Canadian politics as the Reformers came to share the earlier Tory rejection of democratic radicalism and republicanism. Professor Wise maintains that it was the fundamental attitudes and political values of the Upper Canadian tories, moderated somewhat over time, which by the 1850s permeated the bulk of the population of Upper Canada. (10) Furthermore, Professor Wise has argued that the conservative value system and outlook, and the 'nationalist assumptions' which it embodied, also provided the goals, as well as the means, for carrying forward Confederation and the nation-building efforts of Sir John A. Macdonald. (11)

Despite the important role which Tory conservatism has played in fostering the development of Canada, no Canadian historian or political scientist has attempted to write a history of Upper Canada focused on the national policies and achievements of the Tory governing establishment.

Notes

Introduction

This Introduction consists of a re-working of a draft Introduction that the author prepared years ago for his abortive Ph.D. dissertation. That original draft Introduction was reproduced more recently as the Introduction to *The Upper Canadian Anglican Tory Mind, A Cultural Fragment* (2018). Herein, it has been re-structured and only partially reproduced to provide a framework for this study of the political actions of the Tories of Upper Canada.

1. R.N. Stromberg, *An Intellectual History of Modern Europe* (New York: Appleton-Century-Crofts, 1966), 1.

2. J.N. Figgis, *Studies of Political Thought from Gerson to Grotius, 1414-1625* (Cambridge: Cambridge University Press, 1956 (First ed., 1907), as quoted by Stromberg, 1-2.

3. Perry Miller, *Errand into the Wilderness* (Cambridge, Mass.: Harvard University Press), 1956, ix.

4. Alan Heimert, *Religion and the American mind, From the Great Awakening to the Revolution* (Cambridge, Mass.: Harvard University Press, 1966), 21.

5. There are numerous references to the need for 'a national policy', and what such a policy should comprise, in the various letters and reports produced by Strachan and Robinson. On "the three great pillars of the body politic", see the *Kingston Chronicle*, 31 December 1831, "One of the People" [Rev. Adam Hood Burwell].

6. The economic development and defence policy components of the Tory national policy are not treated in this study. The quotations are from the *Kingston Chronicle*, [Rev. A.H. Burwell], "One of the People", 28 May 1831; PAO, Strachan Sermons, Box E, Psalm 29:11, "Lord Will Give Strength", 4 November 1855, 4-5; and PAO, Robinson Papers, Charges to the Grand Juries,1829-1841, John Beverley Robinson, "Charge to the Grand Jury", Toronto, 1 April 1834, 9, respectively.

7. There are excellent online biographical entries, with extensive bibliographies, for the leading Anglican Tories of this study, in the *Dictionary of Canadian Biography*: viz. *DCB*, IX, G. M. Craig, "Strachan, John" & and Robert E. Saunders, "Robinson, Sir John Beverley"; *DCB*, V, George Rawlyk and Janice Potter, "Cartwright, Richard"; and *DCB*, VIII, Robert Lochiel Fraser, "Macaulay (McAulay), John". The quoted phrase is from George Grant (*Lament for a Nation*, 95), and the point being made is dependent upon an understanding of

Grant's discussion of the difference between ancient and modern philosophy. As Christians, the Anglican Tories did not forsake revealed religion or the traditional view of the Christian cosmos and teleology, and they did not believe that human reason alone was the ultimate arbitrator of truth, virtue or goodness. In contrast, Lockean-liberalism is a man-centred, individualistic and rationalistic, modern political philosophy.

For the Upper Canadian Anglican Tories, the highest political embodiment of Toryism was the unity of church and state. They proclaimed themselves to be 'Tories' based on their adherence to Christian moral values and their belief in an established church within a church-state polity. Moreover, they continued to oppose secular liberalism long after the demise of Upper Canada in February 1841. See PAO, Strachan Papers, reel 6, 61, John Macaulay to J.B. Robinson, 22 February 1850; PAO, Robinson Papers, Robinson Letterbook 1814-62, J.B. Robinson to Strachan, 8 April 1851; and PAO, Strachan Letterbook 1844-49, reel 12, Strachan to Robert Gillespie, 2 February 1848.

8. S. F. Wise, "Conservatism and Political Development: The Canadian Case", *The South Atlantic Quarterly*, LXIX, 1970, 226-243; and S.F. Wise, "Upper Canada and the Conservative Tradition" in Edith Firth, ed., *Profiles of a Province, Studies in the History of Ontario* (Toronto: The Ontario Historical Society, 1967), 20-33.

9. Wise, 'Conservative Tradition', 30; and Wise, "Conservatism and Political Development', 241-242. The quotation is from page 242.

10. Wise, 'Conservative Tradition', 30-32. For a related commentary, see: S.F. Wise, "The Annexation Movement and Its Effect on Canadian Opinion, 1837-67", in S.F. Wise & R.C. Brown, *Canada Views the United States, Nineteenth-century Political Attitudes* (Toronto: Macmillan, 1967), 94 & 95. In this work, Wise comments that the democratic radicalism of men such as William Lyon Mackenzie and Louis-Joseph Papineau represented only a small minority of Canadians by mid-century. "However much the fortunes of nineteenth-century radicalism have attracted the interest and sympathy of later historians, the Canadian radical tradition is so episodic in character that it may scarcely be said to have existed". While the present author does not agree with the argument that the radicals had little real historical impact, he does think that Canadian historians have been highly biased in their focus on the democratic radicals, as well as the Reformers more generally, in the writing of Canadian history.

8. Wise, "Conservatism and Political Development', 242. See also, Wise, 'Conservative Tradition', 31.

Chapter One

The War of 1812

View of the United States

View of Upper Canada

The Internal American Threat

Disaffection, Sedition & Treason

The Impact of the War

A Proclamation

INHABITANTS of CANADA! ... The Army under my command, has invaded your country & the Standard of the UNION now waves over the Territory of CANADA. ... I tender to you the invaluable blessings of Civil, Political, and Religious Liberty & their necessary result, individual and general prosperity; ....

...Remain at your homes. ...Raise not your hands against your Brethren. ....

If contrary to your own interest, & the just expectation of my Country, you should take part in the approaching contest [on the side of Great Britain] you will be considered & treated as enemies & the horrors & calamities of war will stalk before you.

Brigadier-General William Hull, Commander
Northwestern Army of the United States, 12 July 1812.

[Once the United States declared war on Great Britain, Thomas Jefferson – the former President of the United States --expressed his belief that Canada could be easily conquered by the American Army.]

"Our present enemy [Great Britain] will have the sea to herself, while we shall be equally predominate on land, and shall strip her of all her possessions on this continent ...."

Thomas Jefferson, Monticello, to Tadeusz Kosciuszko,
June 28, 1812.

"The Battle of Queenston, Oct'r 13th 1812", Major James Dennis, British Army, 1836, Toronto Reference Library. The Battle of Queenston Heights was a decisive engagement that repelled a threatening American conquest of Upper Canada, raised the morale of the loyal Upper Canadians, and enabled the Anglican Tories to rouse the Province of Upper Canada to resist further American military invasions during the War of 1812.

Chapter One

The War of 1812

On June 18, 1812, the United States declared war on Great Britain. Almost immediately the Americans launched an attack aimed at the conquest of the Province of Upper Canada while Britain was engaged in a life and death struggle in Europe with Imperial France under the dictatorship of Napoleon Bonaparte. For the Upper Canadian Tories, the invasion by American troops was viewed as a second coming of the American Revolution. Once again, the Loyalists and their families were under attack for their loyalty to the Crown and the unity of Empire, and, once again, they faced the threat of dispossession and the loss of everything that they valued.

With the outbreak of the War, the leading Tories appealed to Upper Canadians to have the courage to defend the province and, in doing so, revealed their view of the political character of the United States which differed dramatically from that of the Province of Upper Canada. For the Tories, it was a war in which the United States was betraying "the cause of humanity" in aligning itself with Napoleonic France. In sum, the United States was held to be denying everything which should have bound her to the side of Great Britain: interest, affection and virtue; consanguinity; language; the English common law; and similar manners, habits and opinions. (Such was the public stance of the Tories; they refrained from mentioning that in their view the manners and public character of the United States were sinking fast into decline.)

View of the United States

In their appeals to Upper Canadians, the Tories maintained that a vast majority of Americans did not want war; and that the most enlightened and best-informed men in the United States – the Federalists -- would shortly attain control of the American government and re-establish peace with Great Britain. Opponents of the war in the United States were quoted to sustain an argument that the ruling democratic faction in the United States had been misled by 'infatuation or madness', or were even bribed by the French tyrant Napoleon, to act contrary to the best interests and professed ideals of the United States.

Instead of professing friendship to all men, and support for the liberty and independence of mankind, the democratic governing faction had allied the United States with the military dictatorship of France, the enemy of "all just and rational freedom". Statements by members of Congress, and resolutions of state legislatures, were cited by the Tories in support of their contention that the American declaration of war was totally unprovoked.

The Upper Canadian Tories sought to secure the support of the non-Loyalist American settlers in Upper Canada by linking the republican democratic administration in the United States directly with Napoleon.

> This war, on the part of the United States includes an alliance with the French usurper, whose dreadful policy has destroyed all that was great & good, venerable and holy on the Continent of Europe. The government of this bloody Tyrant penetrates into everything -- it crushes individuals as well as nations; fetters thoughts as well as motives, and delights in destroying forever all that is fair and just in opinion and sentiments. It is evidently this Tyrant who now directs the Rulers of America. (1)

For the Tories, the War of 1812 appeared in large measure as a continuation, or refighting, of the American Revolution. They observed that the Loyalists, who had suffered at the hands of rebels for their loyalty to the King, were being attacked in a most vindictive manner by the Democrats, their implacable enemies, who now controlled the Government of the United States. In public pronouncements, the Upper Canadian Tories appealed directly to the Loyalists to once again come forward in 'the old cause'. In such appeals, the Tories played upon the memories and fears of the old Loyalists -- which they shared -- that should the province succumb to invasion, it was the Loyalists would suffer abuse, degradation, and persecution, for their adherence to the Crown and the unity of the British Empire. Indeed, several leading members of Congress had already called for all Loyalists in Canada to be deprived of their property and possessions.

Both the Loyalists, as well as the American settlers who might disapprove of developments in the United States or even those who preferred American ideals and principles of government, were admonished that Upper Canada had nothing to gain and everything to lose by an American conquest. There was a real danger of being plundered by a host of undisciplined and unprincipled vagabonds, and American rule was nothing to desire. Upper Canadians were cautioned in viewing the United States, to be aware that "the advantages of a Government are not to be estimated from theory, but from its practical effects."

In seeking to enlighten Upper Canadians with respect to the reality of American government and politics, as distinct from the ideal conception of democratic republicanism, the Tories enunciated their view of the United States. It was viewed as a country that was rent by the violence of faction and agitated by political discord, where the intrigues of demagogues pervaded every state and dictated every public measure. In the United States, party feuds and factions had invaded all areas of life, including the judiciary, and impaired the happiness and tranquility of domestic life.

Anarchy and disorder awaited Upper Canada if she failed to repulse the aggression of the revolutionary state on her borders. It was a republic that had not only formed a monstrous connection with "the most powerful military despot who ever oppressed the world", but already showed unmistakable signs of evolving in the same direction. It was observed that:

> the conjuncture is perhaps not far distant, when the collision of factions contending for power shall produce explosions similar to those which have deluged other Republics with the blood of their best citizens, and which have ended in their subjection to some ambitious leader. (2)

Thus, for the Upper Canadian Tories, the war being waged in defence of Upper Canada was no more a purely military struggle than the war being waged in Europe against Napoleonic France. The Tories were acutely conscious that they were engaged in an ideological conflict, a veritable battle for the mind of Upper Canada.

View of Upper Canada

The Tories were aware of the many benefits that the Province of Upper Canada had received, and was receiving, from the British government, and they maintained that Upper Canadians were bound by duty, honour, and gratitude to fight for Britain. Moreover, it was in the best interests of Upper Canadians to do so. In their writings and public statements, the Tories emphasized that Upper Canada had been the beneficiary - through her connection with the mother country - of all the advantages that a civil society could possess. Among the most cherished was a constitution -- closely modeled on that of Great Britain -- that supported mild and equitable laws which, under the administration of a respectable judiciary supported and maintained by the Crown, guaranteed to Upper Canadians all the liberties, civil and religious rights, possessed by free-born British subjects.

Not only did Upper Canadians enjoy the most perfect security of person and property, safe from all anarchy, despotism and oppression, but their condition of life was second to none among the peoples of the world. They were not taxed to support the administration of government and had received their land from the Crown at little or no cost, free of all encumbrances. Every man, under the British monarchical system of government and the rule of law which it sustained, possessed a real independence. In Upper Canada, it did not matter what social position an individual occupied:

> he may be poor, ... he feels himself independent, and he bows not to the proud and the haughty, the rich or the powerful, for they dare not molest him.

Upper Canadians were the beneficiaries of a system of government which had bestowed the blessings of order and tranquility upon them through uniting liberty with security, by means of a representative form of government that permitted the people – or, more correctly, their elected representatives - to enact the laws which governed them. They were blessed as well with an impartial judiciary which in administrating the laws ensured to all men the peaceable enjoyment of their rights, while safeguarding them from injustice and the violence of the mob.

It was a government that was based upon a recognition of the right of those in authority to govern, and the necessity on the part of the subject to yield a reasonable and prompt obedience to legitimate authority. Such a duty was in no sense contrary to the enjoyment of a rational liberty under:

> a constitution of free and equal laws, secured on the one hand against the arbitrary will of the sovereign, and the licentiousness of the people on the other.

As a means of maintaining the existing system of government in the face of the American invasion threat, parents were encouraged to inculcate into their children:

> a proper resignation and obedience to the laws, a due deference and homage for superiors, and for those who are publicly entrusted with the administration of the province. (3)

Upper Canadians were told that not only did they have much worth fighting to preserve in their superior system of government and the practical benefits that it bestowed upon them, but their very duty, as men and as Christians, demanded that they do so. The Tories believed that in defending Upper Canada from its American transgressors, they were fighting a defensive war in a Christian cause. They did not hesitate to appeal to the Christian conscience of Upper Canadians, and to invoke the aid of the Almighty in defence of the province. Thus, Upper Canadians were encouraged to put their faith in God, and to conduct themselves as Christian soldiers in defending their families, friends, and property from violation at the hands of "lawless and desperate plunderers".

Upper Canadians were admonished that a true Christian would put aside all private interests and fears for his personal safety, and motivated by honour, reverence for his religion and loyalty to his Sovereign, would fight for the good of his country. The true Christian would act always from the best patriotic motives and, secure in the knowledge of the justice of his cause, would not fear death. Man was "born to die", and it was for God, in His wisdom and goodness, to decide when a man's time had come. Upper Canadians were exhorted to emulate the example of Christ and the Christian martyrs who willingly suffered death for the Christian religion, and the countless British patriots who sacrificed their lives over the centuries to oppose tyranny and oppression in defence of their constitutional privileges.

To those who might question the equating of religion with patriotism, it was pointed out that far from being contrary to Christian principles, Christianity actually embraced patriotism, because:

> The Christian soldier loves his country. Were patriotism a determination to support our country when in the wrong,

were it an inclination to do evil to promote her advantage, then might we admit it to be a narrow and illiberal prejudice; but the patriotism for which we plead, is an ardent and fixed disposition to promote our country's good by all the lawful means in our power; to sacrifice life, fortune, and everything that we hold most dear, for its security and defence; not to seek its aggrandizement by the depression of other nations, or by doing anything inconsistent with justice, piety and virtue. It is that warm affection which a good man feels for the happiness of his kindred and friends, extended to the society of which he is a member. (4)

The Upper Canadian Tories had several reasons for seeking to appeal to the Christian beliefs of their society, and to equate them in wartime with the defence of the province. On the one hand, there was a critical need to unite Upper Canadians in a common cause, and to motivate them to fight. The Tories were aware that religion gave an energy to any common activity, which nothing else could impart to the same degree. Moreover, they were convinced that the habits of diligence, industry, and disinterestedness which religion engendered, were the best protection of any state. In their view, the Christian had no private interests to serve above all else and was dedicated to the good of his country.

On the other hand, the appeal to Christians and Christian principles was based on a sincere belief that in defending Upper Canada from an American invasion, Upper Canadians were contributing to the struggle being waged in Europe to preserve "the civilized and Christian world". It was a world-defining struggle against the onslaught of America's ally, Napoleon Bonaparte, who aimed at obliterating all virtue, religion, and true liberty from the face of the earth.

The Upper Canadian Tories continually stressed that Upper Canada was fighting a just war because she was engaged in defending her own territory. The province had not sought war, but it was attacked by the Americans. Their great object – as the Rev. John Strachan for one believed -- was to gain possession of the Province of Upper Canada so that the United States might exercise a decisive control over the Indians

-- who threatened their settlement frontier -- and prevent all British aid to the embattled Indians.

The Upper Canadian Tories held that "all defensive wars are just"; and that Upper Canada was fighting for a limited objective: the preservation of her own polity and independence free of foreign domination. Thus, her cause was compatible with Christianity.

Christianity did not preclude the defending of oneself from aggression, but rather its teachings limited the aims of such a resistance. In effect, the Christian:

> seeks not the destruction of his enemy, but his return to justice and humanity. The end proposed by all wars is peace; and as soon as this can be obtained on equitable terms by the friend of the Gospel, he wars no longer. (5)

Despite the extensive efforts of the leading Tories of the province to instill patriotism, and a will to fight to preserve Upper Canada as an integral part of the British Empire, there was a great deal of disaffection in evidence among the American settlers in Upper Canada throughout the War of 1812. It was so extensive that the very survival of the province was constantly in jeopardy.

To the Tories, the question raised by the war was not whether British power would ultimately prevail in the struggle. It was whether Upper Canada would fall to the Americans and become thoroughly Americanized before the conclusion of the War. The Tories had been consciously striving for years to influence the British government to take steps to preserve and safeguard the British national character and constitutional principles of Upper Canada against American democratic republicanism. Now, with the war underway, they were only too well aware that should the province be overrun by the Americans, for a couple of years, the Loyalists would suffer oppression and their influence would be destroyed. Even if the province should be restored to Great Britain at the termination of hostilities, the character of the province would have become thoroughly Americanized in the interim, beyond rectification.

Thus, Richard Cartwright, the Rev. John Strachan, and the young Tories of the province whom Strachan had schooled and who were just coming of age upon the outbreak of war, threw themselves into the military contest. They did so with the same energy that had characterized Cartwright and Strachan in the ideological struggle prior to the war. (6)

The Internal American Threat

Behind all of the Tory rhetoric and arguments of a political, religious, military, and ideological nature that were promulgated to inspire Upper Canadians to actively resist an American invasion, was a deep awareness of the political character and national composition of the population of the province. The Tories were acutely conscious of the large number of American settlers in the province, and the leading Tories had always feared that should Great Britain become involved in a war with the United States, the American settlers might well become disaffected.

Right up to the American declaration of the war in June 1812, the Upper Canadian Tories had continued to voice their concern to the British government about the developing character of the province, and their great unease respecting the indiscriminate influx of American immigrants into the province. Not only was it evident that the American settlers were retaining their ideas of equality and insubordination, but some were heard to openly express their hostility towards the British monarchical form of government.

The Americans had been permitted to settle in Upper Canada in such numbers that as of the first decade of the 19th Century, almost three-fifths of the population of the province consisted of non-Loyalist Americans. For the old Loyalists, the presence of American settlers in such numbers was a threat to the British national character of the Loyalist province. They expressed their apprehension that their children were in danger of imbibing principles which were very different those which had induced their parents to fight for the King, the British Constitution, and the unity of the British Empire.

In assessing the strength of Upper Canada in the immediate pre-war years, not only the old Loyalists, but the new Lt. Governor of the Province, Sir Francis Gore -- a retired British Army officer – were aware that a definite distinction would have to be made between the Loyalists and their descendants, and the American immigrant settlers. It was believed that the non-Loyalist Americans, who had entered the province in recent years, had done so simply to obtain cheap land and were "without any predilection for His Majesty's Government". A good many of the American settlers were openly declaring that they would not fight "against their countrymen", and American emissaries were entering the province in what was viewed as an effort "to alienate the minds of His Majesty's subjects".

In such circumstances, the authorities in Upper Canada became worried about the loyalty of the militia, and approached the Legislature to support the government in taking steps to discourage disaffection and encourage the loyal. Thus, in the spring of 1812, Major-General Isaac Brock, the military commander and interim civil administrator of the province - with Sir Francis Gore absent on a visit to England – had approached the Legislature to secure a strengthening of the Militia Act. What he requested were amendments requiring that all militiamen take an oath abjuring any foreign allegiance; that a provision be made for the occasional suspension of habeas corpus; and that a right be granted to the military commander to invoke martial law when, and if required, during any wartime emergency.

The proposed Militia Act amendments were intended to strengthen the hand of the military governor in dealing with disaffection among the American settlers, and any future acts of sedition and/or treason in wartime. However, much to the surprise and alarm of Major-General Brock, the influence of the American settlers and their elected representatives in the House of Assembly was so great that the opposition succeeded in preventing the passage of the proposed legislation. (7)

In the United States, the American government was fully cognizant of disaffection among the American settlers in Upper Canada and deliberately set out to exploit it. Less than a month after the June 12th American declaration of war, an American army of 2,000 men under the command of Brigadier-General William Hull crossed into Upper Canada from Detroit. The invasion force captured the small Loyalist settlement of Sandwich (near Windsor) in the Western District of Upper

Canada – a district in which there were many American settlers. General Hull immediately circulated a proclamation that combined a national and ideological appeal to American settlers with threats of punishment for any Upper Canadians who might dare to oppose his army.

The Americans presented themselves, in the Proclamation of July 12th, as the bearers of civil, political and religious liberty. Upper Canadians were assured that it was this spirit of liberty which had carried the United States through in her struggle for independence; and that the same spirit was responsible for the individual and general prosperity which the United States was experiencing. Upper Canadians were encouraged to throw off the "tyranny and oppression" under which they were supposedly suffering. They were promised that their persons, property and rights would be protected, and were counseled to:

> Raise not you're your hands against your brethren, many of your forefathers fought for the freedom & *Independence* we now enjoy. Being children therefore of the same family with us and heirs to the same Heritage, the arrival of an army of Friends must be hailed by you with a Cordial welcome.

The Loyalists, and other British subjects in Upper Canada, who rejected that revolutionary, democratic republican heritage, were not to be spared. Assurances were given that those who refused to accept the proffered peace, liberty, and security, and chose to resist the American invasion force, would be "treated as enemies, and the horrors and calamities of war will stalk before you." (8)

The impact of the American invasion and of General Hull's Proclamation upon the public mind of Upper Canada was far worse than the Tories could have imagined, despite their long-held fears. Major-General Brock estimated that a total of five hundred militiamen deserted in the Western District alone, while in another threatened area – the Niagara Peninsula - the majority of the population was reported as:

> either indifferent to what is passing or so completely American as to rejoice in the prospect of a change of Government.

A general gloom had quickly enveloped the loyal population of the province, and the belief that the province must inevitably succumb infected all ranks of society. Even the most fervently loyal to the Crown and the British constitution were completely discouraged from making any exertion at all on behalf of the government. Indeed, ever mindful of the suffering that the loyal had brought down upon themselves during the American Revolution, even the magistrates -- of whom many were Loyalists – were found to be shirking the carrying out of the duties of their office. No action was being taken against individuals who were going about the province preaching sedition and fostering disaffection.

Militia officers neglected their duty, and the House of Assembly in its first wartime session (27 July- 3 August 1812) refused to respond to a renewal of the earlier request from Major-General Brock for the passing of legislation to strengthen the militia and to grant the military commander the authority to invoke martial law and suspend habeas corpus, when and if required. Moreover, the House of Assembly even declined to release surplus monies in the treasury for the defence of the province.

The whole province seemed to be seized by a virtual paralysis of authority, and a debilitating fear which moved Brock to comment that: "Everything shows as if a certainty existed of a change taking place soon". In such circumstances, he could only take solace in the belief that the arrival of British troop reinforcements might yet avert a threatening calamity. Once assured of British troop support, the hope was that many of the loyal would become active in defence of the province.

What Major-General Brock clearly realized, and what the leading Tories were aware of given their interpretation of the course of the American Revolution, was that the presence of British troops was needed to protect and encourage the loyal to serve in defence of the province. The loyal population needed to receive some concrete assurance of the willingness of Great Britain to seriously defend Upper Canada. Once given active leadership, and a hope that the war could be won, many were expected to come forward in support of the His Majesty's Provincial Government. On the other hand, in lacking such encouragement and protection, it was believed that many of the loyal would invariably acquiesce in an American conquest, regardless of their loathing of American principles. They would not fight and suffer persecution in a hopeless cause. (9)

The main concern of the government in the crisis, and of the Tory elite who rallied to its support, was to give encouragement to the loyal and to overawe the disaffected. To that end, the magnitude of the problem of disaffection was purposely downplayed, and the loyalty of the militia was praised in all public pronouncements. Moreover, the support of the House of Assembly for the war effort was greatly exaggerated.

Since the Tories remained convinced that the real struggle was for the mind of Upper Canada, they were anxious to secure the detention and punishment of all subversives who were seeking to seduce the people from their allegiance through threats and falsehoods. What they wanted was the enactment of stricter laws against sedition, and for the loyal magistrates to enforce the existing laws.

The Upper Canadian Tories were only too conscious of the means by which the American revolutionaries had undermined, and then overthrown, the legitimate colonial governments during the American rebellion. Hence, there was a critical need to restrain and control the disaffected, and to warn Upper Canadians of the methods of such people. The Tories were convinced that they faced "more danger from the private machinations of their foes than from their open attacks."

Individuals who might contemplate joining the enemy were warned of the consequences. If they violated their oath of allegiance, they would be guilty of treason for which they would forfeit their life and their property. And, should they managed to escape from the Province, they would never be allowed to return. American settlers were warned that treacherous would be swiftly punished, and the loyal were assured that they would be rewarded for their loyalty. (10)

The Upper Canadian Tories did not expect to receive much support from the American settlers who had but recently come into the province as their "inclination, tho' in the main good, would naturally lean against us". The Rev. John Strachan, in his speeches and sermons, addressed his appeals to the Loyalists and their descendants and identified the defence of the province with their cause. The Loyalist families were called upon to show the same spirit that had motivated them in the past to fight for the Unity of Empire, the King and the Constitution, and to once again come to the defence of their patriotic principles against men who sought to promote discontent and rebellion.

The Loyalists were reminded that during the American Revolution they had resisted the efforts of "wicked and designing men" who tried to turn them against the government through slandering those in authority and concocting imaginary grievances. Now they were called upon to stand once again in the good cause against:

> the same enemy who once already, aided by the mistaken lenity of our Mother Country and the misconduct of her Commanders, were able to drive us from our native homes and possessions to this province, a people ... who now envy us the habitations which through the blessings of our parent state and our own industry, we have gained from the wilderness.

This time though the Loyalists and their descendants were assured that in defending their asylum, they would receive the vigorous aid of the British government to ensure that they would not again experience defeat:

> Great Britain will not now consider Americans as perverse children who may be reclaimed, but as her most malignant foes. Her commanders will not, as formerly, temporize & raise hosts of enemies by their misconduct and delays but they will hasten to punish them with all the rigour of war. (11)

Such threats and exhortations were all to no avail while the military situation remained totally discouraging. However, in General Brock, the Tories had a man of their own mettle to retrieve the situation. Brock ordered an attack on the American northwest outpost at Fort Michilimackinac, which proved highly successful, and won over the Indians of the Northwest to the side of the British, and then prepared to drive the American army of General Hull back across the Detroit River.

With the militia of the Western District wracked by desertions, the flank companies of the York militia were called out. They responded under the command of several of the leading young Tories of the province. With a small force of British regulars and over 250 men of the York militia, Major-General Brock advanced to Sandwich, where he found the American army had withdrawn to Detroit. At Sandwich, Brock managed to assemble a field force of 300 regulars and 400 militia (including the York militia flank companies), along with a 600-man force of Indian allies and crossed the Detroit River to attack Fort Detroit. That show of force, and the threat of turning the Indians loose on the Detroit frontier, led to the capitulation of Fort Detroit (15 August 1812). Brigadier-General Hull surrendered his entire Army and ceded the Michigan Territory to Britain.

The Upper Canadian Tories did not fail to note the momentous effect of Brock's successful offensive strategy on the province. The marching of lines of American prisoners eastward, under the guard of the York militia companies, was a startling spectacle that drew much attention in Upper Canada. It strengthened the resolve of the waverers among the settlers to continue to support the provincial government, gave encouragement to the loyal, and kept the American settlers from renouncing their allegiance to the Crown.

Thereafter, the successful repulse of a large-scale American attack on the Niagara frontier at Queenston -- which cost Major-General Brock his life -- did much to rouse the province out of its torpor, and greatly encouraged the Tories in their exertions. In the Battle of Queenston Heights (13 October 1812) a combined force of British regulars and the loyal Upper Canadian militia and their Indian allies, managed to defeat an invasion force of 1300 Americans (600 regulars and 700 New York militia). The British forces took 958 American prisoners, and inflicted losses of almost 200 killed or wounded, in driving the American invasion force back across the Niagara River. The Rev. John Strachan observed at that time:

> We trust in God & the justice of our cause. The Province is wonderfully animated, and with a few more troops we have nothing to fear, but there is some reason to apprehend that we shall be overpowered by numbers before any succours can reach us.

The situation of the province remained perilous; yet, to the dismay of the Tories, the British forces failed to take the offensive to keep the Americans off-balance. Thereafter, throughout the war, the Tories were highly critical of the defensive strategy adopted by the Commander-in-Chief/Governor-in-Chief of the British North American Provinces, Lt. General, Sir George Prevost.

The implementation of a purely defensive strategy was held to be a mistake. As viewed by the Tories, the American character was such that "every concession renders them more arrogant and raises their demands". Only the carrying of the war into the United States, and the fear of defeat, would induce the Americans to accept a peace which they would never consider on the grounds of moderation and justice. Secondly, a defensive policy, in failing to prosecute the war on American soil, would discourage the loyal by reminding them of the torpid policy pursued by the British army during the American rebellion.

In numerous appeals, which they addressed to the British Army military commanders, the Tories continuously praised the exploits of the late Major-General Brock, criticized the defensive policy of Lt. General Prevost, and lauded the fighting qualities of the inferior ranks. They called for the defensive forces of the province to be concentrated at key strategic points, rather than being dispersed to cover the whole province, and for the British forces to go on the offensive against the Americans. It was argued that despite shortcomings,

> the means at the disposal of the Governor General [at Quebec] were Sufficient, if vigorously & judiciously employed, not only to defend the Canadas but to carry the war into the Enemy's territory. (12)

In seeking to further the war effort, the Tories continually strove to strengthen the militia of Upper Canada, and they praised its contribution to the war effort on every public occasion. Thus, the Rev. John Strachan was instrumental in founding the Loyal and Patriotic Society of Upper Canada in December 1812. Its stated aim was to furnish aid to the families of militiamen who were suffering distress and/or members of the militia who were disabled by their wounds, and to bestow medals in recognition of their meritorious service. It was an initiative that had a military purpose, in addition to its humanitarian purpose, in seeking to encourage the resolve of the militia to continue to resist the enemy.

In support of that initiative, the Rev. Strachan took the occasion -- in reprinting a speech which he had given earlier (22 November 1812) -- to publicly claim for the militia a pre-eminent role in the survival of Upper Canada:

> It will be told by the future Historian, that the Province of Upper Canada, without the assistance of men or arms, except a handful of regular troops, repelled its invaders, slew or took them all prisoners, and captured from its enemies the greater part of the arms by which it was defended. And never, surely, was greater activity shewn in any country, than our militia have exhibited, ...
> ... They have twice saved the country.

That the role of the militia should be so exaggerated at that time was perfectly understandable. Every means was needed to increase and sustain the morale of the militia for the fighting yet to come. The leading Tories in York (the capital of the province), were particularly proud of the role which the York Militia had played under Major-General Brock in the offensive against General Hull at Detroit and in the Battle of Queenston Heights.

In the former case, 260 militiamen – the officers of whom were former students of the Rev. John Strachan -- had volunteered to accompany Brock's force of 40 regulars from York to engage Hull's invasion force at a time when the militia in American-settled areas in the Western and London districts, were deserting in droves. The Tories sincerely believed that had the York Militia flank companies not responded to Brock's call, then Hull's army would not have been defeated, and the cause of Upper Canada would have been lost beyond recall.

Similarly, the York militia was directly involved at a crucial stage in the Battle of Queenston Heights. A flank company of the York Militia, under the command of young John Beverley Robinson, had participated in the final counterattack by British troops and Indians that had pushed the Americans off their commanding position on the Queenston Heights, and had turned the course of the battle.

Nonetheless, the Tory leaders were acutely aware of their utter dependence upon British troops for their survival and ultimate victory. Indeed, at the time, they were anxiously awaiting the arrival of British troop reinforcements. However, they believed, and said so, that the York militia by its valour at a desperate time had saved Upper Canada. Indeed, had the York militia failed to respond to Brock's call, the leading Tories believed that the province would have succumbed to the combined American military and ideological offensive of the 1812 campaign. There would have been no actively loyal population left for British troops to defend, nor any loyal militia units willing to fight alongside the British regulars in defence of the province.

In being conscious of the failure of the British Army to make proper use of the loyal volunteers during the American Revolution, and the political and military repercussions of that failure, the Upper Canadian Tories were alarmed to note the same tendency prevailing among British Army officers after the death of Brock. The militia was generally neglected, and its usefulness disparaged by several British officers who maintained that "nobody can fight well but a regular soldier". That attitude had to be counteracted. The Tories continued to praise the militia, and to encourage the loyal to act in defence of the province through providing them with an active leadership.

This was not to say that the Tory elite was unaware of the shortcomings of the militia units. They were unable to furnish a protracted military service because of the necessity of tending to their farms and families, particularly during the fall harvest of crops. However, the Tories maintained that, if properly led, the militiamen were viewed as being capable of making a major contribution to the military strength of Upper Canada. They were excellent riflemen, and it was recommended that they be deployed with the regular forces and their Indian allies, for patrol duties and to fight in engagements. To overcome some of the difficulties which were faced in trying to keep militia forces in regular service, the Tory supporters of the Crown managed to secure -- with the aid of John Beverley Robinson, the newly-appointed Acting/Attorney General -- a Legislative Act (March 1813) that provided financial support for an Incorporated Militia to be raised for regular army service. (13)

The Problems of Disaffection, Sedition & Treason

In addition to seeking to counteract the American ideological appeal, and to strengthen the morale and effective fighting strength of the militia, the Tories were anxious that the provincial government take steps to deal with a persistent problem of disaffection. It was widespread amongst the American settlers, but initially did not result in any open acts of aggression against the provincial authorities and defenders of Upper Canada. However, during the 1813 summer campaign sedition became a serious problem, and a new threat emerged as American victories gave rise to a disturbing number of cases of outright treason among the American settlers of Upper Canada.

It was a period that witnessed a series of decisive defeats for the British forces that were engaged in defending Upper Canada, interspersed with victories in several crucial smaller engagements that staved off, but did not remove, the prospect of a complete defeat. In such a situation, there was a growing fear on the part of the Tories that British troops would be withdrawn to Kingston, and that Upper Canada would be abandoned to its fate. During the 1813 summer campaign, American invasion armies managed to occupy two large areas of the province.

In April 1813, having attained a temporary naval supremacy on Lake Ontario, the U.S. Navy transported an American army of 1,700 men from Sacket's Harbor, New York, for an attack on York (Toronto). The lightly defended provincial capital was quickly captured, the deserted homes were looted, and public buildings were burned. In addition, during a three-day occupation of April 28-30, a large quantity of naval guns and stores which were intended for the support of the Royal Navy Squadron on Lake Erie, were taken from the York naval yard.

A month later, in May 1813, an American Army of 3,000 men was transported across Lake Ontario to attack Fort George in the Niagara Peninsula. The outnumbered defending forces under Brigadier-General John Vincent were forced to abandon the fort and withdraw to Burlington Heights to re-group, which resulted in the Niagara Peninsula being overrun and occupied by the American forces. A further American advance towards Burlington Heights was halted by British troops after fierce fighting at the Battle of Stoney Creek (6 June 1813), and a further probe in force by an American force was defeated by Britain's Indian allies at the Battle of Beaver Dams (24 June 1813).

On the Lake Erie Front, the destruction of the Royal Navy squadron on Lake Erie, in September 1813 by an American naval force, cut off all reinforcements and provisions from being forwarded along the lake to the British Army Right Division at Fort Detroit and Fort Amherstburg. Faced with a desperate situation, the British forces, under the command of Major-General Henry Procter, commenced a retreat up the Thames River towards the British Centre Division at Burlington Heights. The victorious Lake Erie squadron of the U.S. Navy immediately transported an American Army of 5,500 men across Lake Erie from Ohio. Detroit was re-occupied by the American North-West Army under the command of Major-General William Henry Harrison and, in Upper Canada, Sandwich (Windsor) and Amherstburg were overrun, and the retreating British force was pursued up the Thames River.

At the Battle of Moraviantown (5 October 1813), Major-General Proctor and his Indian allies under Tecumseh were totally defeated, and the town looted and burned by the Kentucky mounted riflemen who spearheaded Harrison's army. The Indians at Detroit made peace with the Americans, and the loyal militia units of the western districts were disbanded. The Western and London districts of Upper Canada came under the control of the American invasion forces, while the Americans continued to occupy much of the Niagara Peninsula. (14)

Throughout the summer of 1813, the Tories were thoroughly alarmed to note that with each success of American arms the militias in the threatened areas suffered heavily from desertions, large numbers of men readily surrendered to the American invading armies to secure their parole, and a significant number of American settlers openly expressed their support for the American cause. Moreover, the war effort was greatly hampered when settlers in other areas of American settlement in Upper Canada, were emboldened to refuse to sell food and forage to the military forces defending the province.

What was even more disturbing was the number of renegade settlers in Upper Canada – mostly American settlers -- who came forward to supply the American invaders with information and guidance in their advances into the province. Appalled by the vehemence of the disaffected in denouncing the Loyalists families in the American-occupied areas, and by the pillaging and destruction of the private property of the Loyalist families by American raiding parties in the areas of the province devoid of British troops, the leading Tories re-doubled their earlier actions to counteract what they saw as a growing evil.

Earlier in the year, just prior to the American seizure of York (Toronto), the Rev. John Strachan was instrumental in organizing a meeting of the magistrates and judges which drafted, and unanimously approved, a public declaration calling for the immediate adoption of measures to preserve order and prevent anarchy. The intention was to provide support and encouragement for the loyal, and to overawe the wavering and the disaffected.

The Declaration of the York Magistrates (April 1813), had sought to remind Upper Canadians that it was "high treason to aid, assist, counsel or comfort the enemy", and to encourage the loyal to come forward and denounce traitors in their midst. Moreover, it called upon all of those who abhorred anarchy to provide aid and support for the civil authorities and the judiciary in maintaining law and order.

Even earlier, in October-November 1812, following in the wake of the outstanding military victories of Major-General Brock at Detroit and at Queenston Heights, the Executive Council of Upper Canada had attempted to deal with the problem of disaffection. An Act was passed to the effect that all American citizens resident in Upper Canada who refused to take the oath of allegiance, were to be deported. British subjects who engaged in treasonous activities, including American settlers who had taken the oath of allegiance to the Crown, were to be prosecuted at law.

All American citizens who declined to swear the oath of allegiance and claimed exemption from military service in defence of Upper Canada, were ordered to report by January 1, 1813, to local alien boards, which were established at Niagara, York, and Kingston. The boards were empowered to examine into the citizenship of individuals who appeared before them, and to issue passports to bona fide citizens of the United States to facilitate their exit from the province. Prominent Tories were appointed to the three boards, including Richard Cartwright who sat on the Kingston alien board.

In the changed circumstances of the summer of 1813, all efforts to deport American citizens, and to prosecute disloyal British subjects, broke down. In many areas where disaffection was rife, magistrates failed to conduct investigations and prosecutions. It was reported that in the face of American military successes, it was "beyond the power of the well-disposed to repress and keep down the turbulence" of the disaffected. However, it was noted that where British troops were present, there was an obvious change in the manner and language of the people in the disaffected areas.

The immediate response of the leading Tories, in witnessing at first hand the treasonable activities committed by the disloyal individuals during the American occupation of York in April 1813, was to call for the establishment of a permanent British garrison in the provincial capital, which would be capable of "confirming the loyal and overawing the disaffected". (15)

During the summer of 1813, the Tories found that their situation was becoming perilous, and concluded that "the numbers of persons publicly known and avowedly . . . enemies of the government & country" could not be allowed to remain free of prosecution. It was felt necessary to set an example for the disaffected by taking the worst offenders into custody and bringing them to trial. However, the problem for the government of Upper Canada, which shared the Tories assessment of the situation, was whether to proceed by civil process or by martial law.

The leading Tories of York were convinced that the crisis required extraordinary measures. In August 1813, the Executive Council responded by recommending to the Acting/Lt. Governor and military commander, Major- General De Rottenburg, that a regular army force be stationed at York, and charged with the duty of maintaining order and arresting persons "justly suspected of any treasonable practice".

Both the Rev. John Strachan and John Beverley Robinson, the latter in his position as Acting/Attorney General, strongly supported the Executive Council recommendation. Although they admitted that the proposal to have the military arrest and detain men who were suspected of engaging in seditious activities was "in the abstract ... illegal," they believed that such a measure was justified to save the country. It was a situation in which the civil administration of justice was unable to function properly to protect the public, maintain law and order, and to deal with acts of sedition and outright treason.

Despite possessing a deep and abiding respect for the law, and an abhorrence of employing irregular means to maintain order, the Tories were convinced of the necessity of detaining the openly disaffected. In defence of the proposed system of military detention, they could only plead that:

> The present crisis demands measures to be taken with the disaffected much stronger than any that can be warranted by the common law, and they will excite the gratitude of all the loyal.

Earlier, in July 1813, the Tories had planned to deal with sedition through the courts. In York, a Committee had been appointed to take dispositions from the public to record the disloyal conduct of individuals who were engaging in seditious activities. Once the evidence of guilt was found to be beyond question, the intention was that the justices of the peace issue warrants for the apprehension, detention, and trial of the men concerned. The aim was to keep the worst of the men who were openly disaffected from continuing to engage in sedition, and/or from going over to join the American invading forces.

The York Committee was composed of members of the local Tory elite: Thomas Ridout, the Rev. John Strachan, John Beverley Robinson, Alexander Wood, William Allen, and Duncan Cameron. It reported, on 16 August 1813, the names of individuals on whom sufficient evidence had been received to establish their guilt beyond dispute. However, in the interim, a second American landing in force at York, and a brief occupation of July 31st- August 1st, had led to a change of mind. The Tories concluded that the civil process would be insufficient to deal with the disaffection problem. They had witnessed some residents of York and the surrounding American settlement areas coming forward to provide aid and information to the enemy during the American occupation of the provincial capital. Such actions raised a serious question as to whether juries would be able to reach a verdict in sedition cases where disaffection was rife.

From that time forward, the Tories called for the military to arrest individuals guilty of sedition, and to transport them to Quebec for incarceration for the duration of the war. Acting/Attorney General Robinson suggested that a Committee of Information be appointed from among the most respectable gentlemen of the provincial capital to furnish the local military commander with an unprejudiced report of the seditious activities of the most notorious offenders.

He recommended that the Committee of Information consist of the same men who had served on the earlier York Committee, with the addition of the appointment of his brother, Peter Robinson, a York militia captain. The mandate of the Committee of Information would be the same as the earlier York Committee; although now it was proposed that individuals preaching sedition, or engaging in seditious activities, be apprehended and incarcerated by the military, rather than brought before a Justice of the Peace. (16)

During the summer of 1813, treason emerged as a critical problem on a scale that completely eclipsed the earlier fears of the Tories concerning the state of disaffection in the province. During the American occupation of the Niagara Peninsula, a disturbing number of renegade American settlers had joined the invading American forces and proceeded to engage in a predatory form of warfare in plundering the private property of the Loyalist settlers. Among the traitors were several prominent opposition members of the House of Assembly.

In July 1813, Joseph Willcocks -- a disappointed Irish-immigrant office seeker, and leader of the opposition in the House of House of Assembly -- turned traitor and joined the American army of occupation at Niagara. It was Willcocks who had been instrumental earlier in the House of Assembly in blocking the efforts of Major-General Brock to strengthen the Militia Act to deal with disaffection and sedition. Now Willcocks declared that his purpose was to facilitate the annexation of Upper

Canada to the United States and, subsequently, he raised a mounted company of Upper Canadian volunteers to fight alongside the American invasion army.

The 'Company of Canadian Volunteers' soon had a fighting strength of over 130 men, who were recruited from among the American settlers in the Niagara District and the Thames River settlements. The company was incorporated into the American Army and placed under the command of Willcocks, who was charged with policing the American-occupied Niagara area. Led by 'Colonel' Willcocks, the Volunteers plundered the settlements and the farms of known Loyalists throughout the Niagara District. Loyal militia officers were arrested and transported to prisons in the United States, and flour, pork, salt and forage were seized from the farms of the loyal settlers for the support of the American Army of occupation.

In the Western District, the American Northwestern Army withdrew back to Detroit after its decisive victory at the Battle of Moraviantown, and left a force of 400 regulars and 1300 Ohio militia to occupy Sandwich and Amherstburg. A proclamation was issued by General Harrison that promised security of person and property to the settlers under the American occupation, but that promise had soon proved worthless. Faced with a shortage of provisions, the American military garrison at Detroit sent foraging parties into Upper Canada that stripped the farms around Sandwich and Amherstburg of wheat, flour, livestock, horses, sleighs and wagons.

The Tory fear of impending defeat and dispossession was only relieved in the late fall of 1813 with the receipt of reports of several major victories which were achieved by the British forces elsewhere. On the St. Lawrence Front, two large American armies were defeated in their advance on Montreal, and in Europe a major defeat was inflicted on the armies of Napoleon Bonaparte.

In early October 1813, the Americans had launched a two-pronged attack against Montreal. According to the American invasion plan, a 7,000-man American army under Major-General James Wilkinson was to proceed in a gunboat flotilla from Sacket's Harbor, New York, and descend the St. Lawrence River towards Montreal to join up with a 4,000-man American army under Major- General Wade Hampton, which was to approach Montreal overland from Lake Champlain along the Chateauguay River.

At the Battle of Châteauguay (26 October 1813), a force of Canadian Voltigeurs, Select Embodied Militia, and Sedentary Militia -- composed almost entirely of French-Canadians under the command of Lieutenant-Colonel Charles de Salaberry, with English-Canadians militia units in reserve -- managed to inflict a defeat on Hampton's advancing army, which resulted in its withdrawing back into the United States. And on the St. Lawrence Front, British pursuit troops from Kingston caught up with and thoroughly defeated the 4,000-man rearguard of Wilkinson's army in the Battle of Crysler's Farm (11 November 1813), which resulted in the withdrawal of Wilkinson's army into winter quarters in the United States.

The news of the decisive victories over the American invading armies at Châteauguay and Crysler's Farm was soon followed by the receipt of news that the Grande Armée of Napoleon Bonaparte had suffered a severe defeat in its invasion of Russia, and that Napoleon was in full retreat. The Tories praised the patriotism of the Russians in defending their country and called upon the militia of Upper Canada to emulate the Russian success. Upper Canadians were assured that France has suffered a devastating defeat and, with her resources wasted, it was only a matter of time until Napoleon would be defeated and the full force of Great Britain brought to the aid of a beleaguered Upper Canada.

In the western and London districts, the situation remained particularly grim. Following on the withdrawal of British troops and the disbanding of the district militias, detachments of American troops had occupied the settlements and were forcing the settlers to swear oaths of neutrality. Renegade settlers, mounted on stolen horses, were plundering the homes of the loyal residents, rustling cattle, and kidnapping militia officers. However, there was an encouraging development.

On their own initiative, a volunteer force of loyal militia of the 1st Norfolk Regiment under Lt. Col. Henry Bostwick – a member of an Anglican Loyalist family from Massachusetts – surprised a band of renegade Upper Canadians who were plundering farms in the London

District. The marauders were surrounded in a house on Nanticoke Creek (11 November 1813) and, in the ensuring firefight, five marauders were killed and sixteen captured.

In the late fall of 1813, there was cause for hope that the war might be won, and Upper Canada preserved; however, the war in the Niagara region soon took a savage turn. At Niagara, the American regular troops had been withdrawn in early October and conveyed to Sacket's Harbor to join Wilkinson's Army for the descent on Montreal. Fort George was left in the hands of 1,000 volunteers of the New York Militia under the command of Brigadier-General George McClure – an Irish immigrant/ American republican from Bath, New York, who was bent on plundering "tories". The renegade 'Canadian Volunteers', under the command of Joseph Willcocks, remained responsible for policing the American-occupied areas of the Niagara District.

When a British regular force marched against Fort George from Burlington Heights, McClure burned Fort George (10 December 1813), and Willcocks led his men in pillaging and torching the village of Newark (Niagara-on-the-Lake) during the retreat of the New York militia across the Niagara River to Buffalo. Ninety-two homes, two churches, the jail, the courthouse and a public library were burned to the ground. Newark was left a burned out, smoking ruin with its 400 inhabitants turned out of doors in a snowstorm at mid-winter.

The war immediately entered a new phase of incendiary warfare as the British forces retaliated under their new commander, Lieutenant-General Gordon Drummond. British troops, accompanied by Upper Canadian militia and Indian allies crossed the Niagara River, seized Fort Niagara from the Americans in a surprise assault, and burned the towns of Lewiston, Buffalo, Black Rock, and the Indian village of Tuscarora. Both the American military and Lt. General Prevost, the Commander of the British forces, denounced the resort to incendiary warfare, which shocked the public in both the United States and the Canadian provinces.

The outrage expressed by Upper Canadians against the renegades Joseph Willcocks and Benajah Mallory -- two former leading members of the opposition in the House of Assembly – and against the 'Canadian Volunteers' under their command who burned Newark, when coupled with the success of the British Army assault on the New York frontier towns, brought about a change in the outlook of the House of Assembly. The provincial government of Upper Canada had no difficulty in securing the passage of legislation to deal with acts of treason.

In the legislative session of February 1814, three acts were readily passed to facilitate the arrest, detention, and trial of persons who were engaging in treasonable acts. Richard Cartwright introduced bills in the Legislative Council for the more speedy and effectual punishment of treason, and for the declaration of certain persons as aliens and the vesting of their estates in His Majesty. Another leading wartime supporter of the government, Robert Nichol, the Quarter-Master General of Militia, introduced into the House of Assembly a bill to empower His Majesty, for a limited time, to secure and detain such persons as His Majesty shall suspect of a treasonable adherence to the enemy. In effect, the latter act provided for a suspension of habeas corpus in the detention of traitors. (17)

Armed with the new powers, the provincial government was empowered to apprehend and detain suspected traitors for trial by the judiciary. Almost immediately, John Beverley Robinson, in his capacity as Acting/Attorney General, proceeded to prepare indictments against several traitors. The indictments were easy to draw up. The names of the renegades who had joined the American forces were well known. Their actions in looting and destroying the properties of the loyal, and their acts of pillaging private property, had been witnessed by their victims to whom the perpetrators were well known. The difficulty was to apprehend and bring the offenders to justice.

The aim of the prosecution was to carry out a long-held desire on the part of the provincial government, and its Tory supporters, to punish treason by holding public trials and imposing sentences that would serve as an example to deter others from joining the American invasion forces. To that end, it was essential that the accused be tried openly under the rule of law.

Earlier, out of a dire necessity, the Tories had been willing to countenance a proposal that the military arrest traitors and transport them to Quebec for incarceration and trial by a military tribunal. However, once legislation was passed to enable the provincial government to detain traitors for trial in the civil courts, the Tories opposed any resort to the arrest and trial of civilians by the military in treason cases. The fear expressed was that:

> Executions of Traitors by military power would have comparatively very little influence: the people would consider them as arbitrary Acts of punishment, but would not acknowledge them as the natural effects of Justice.

To achieve the impact desired on the public mind, it was essential that the common course of justice be followed through trial by jury. However, that was a course that posed a potential difficulty as John Beverley Robinson pointed out. For in the Home District:

> as in the District of Niagara, and indeed in those inhabited by Emigrants from the United States, the Jurors ... are in general very indifferent to the honour, or interests of government. Indeed, if they are not wholly indifferent, their bias is the other way.

To ensure convictions, and because it was felt that the punishment of a few traitors would suffice as a potent example for the province, only the most notorious traitors were proceeded against at law. A total of fifty men were indicted; most of whom had joined the American forces or had fled to the United States and were conducting plundering raids against Upper Canada.

After many delays and difficulties, a total of nineteen men – all of whom had been captured by the loyal militia in the act of conducting raids against Upper Canadian settlements -- were brought to trial. The trials were held in Ancaster, Upper Canada, over the period May 23-June 21, 1814. Fifteen men were found guilty of treason by a jury of their peers and were sentenced to death. Several traitors, who were well-known members of the 'Canadian Volunteers' -- such as its commander Joseph Willcocks, and its second-in-command, Benajah Mallory -- were also convicted of treason and sentenced to death in absentia.

Neither the provincial government nor the prosecutor John Beverley Robinson, the Acting/Attorney General, had any desire to impose the full force of the law. Robinson recommended that only one or two of the convicted traitors be executed, but the final decision on their fate was reserved for the pleasure of the Crown represented by the Acting/Lt. Governor/military commander, Lt. General Gordon Drummond.

The trial period was a difficult and dangerous time for the government and the judiciary. No sooner were the Ancaster trials concluded than an American army, under Major-General Jacob Brown, crossed the Niagara River and captured Fort Erie (3 July 1814). The invading army comprised 2,700 regulars, 800 militia, and 60 members of the 'Canadian Volunteers'. It marched along the Niagara Portage Road and defeated a British force under the command of Major-General Phineas Riall at the Battle of Chippawa (5 July 1814). However, despite the threat which was posed by an American Army advancing across the Niagara Peninsula with the intent of attacking Burlington Heights, the sentence of the civil court was carried out with respect to the worst offenders. Eight of the men, who were convicted of treason at the Ancaster assize, were hanged on 20 July 1814 at Burlington Heights.

The public hangings marked the successful issue of a long and difficult struggle by the Upper Canadian Tories in seeking to encourage the judiciary to enforce the law of the land. To the Tory mind, the hanging of the convicted traitors was necessary to impress upon those who might be inclined to join the American invaders that acts of treason would be punished to the full extent of the law.

On the other hand, little could be done to punish the renegade American settlers who had already joined the 'Canadian Volunteers'. For the better part of a month, while the Americans were in control of a large area of the Niagara Peninsula, the 'Canadian Volunteers' were employed as foragers for the American army. As of the summer of 1814, however, they ceased to focus their foraging on the farms of the known Loyalists and began to engage in an indiscriminate plundering of the farms and villages in the American-occupied area of the Niagara District. When a party of foragers were fired upon and driven off by a local militia force (men of the Lincoln county militia), a detachment of American regulars and 'Canadian Volunteers' looted and torched the hamlet of St. David's (18 July 1814) in retaliation. Fourteen houses, two shops, and a grist mill were burned to the ground.

Seven days later, at the Battle of Lundy's Lane (25 July 1814), the military situation was retrieved. British troops -- with critical support from the Incorporated Militia of Upper Canada, the Glengarry Light Infantry Fencibles, the York Militia, the Lincoln Militia, and Indian allies from the Six Nations -- fought a fierce, and costly five-hour battle to stop the American advance. At its conclusion, the American invasion army withdrew to Fort Erie – in the southern part of the Niagara peninsula – and the fort was placed under siege by British troops. After a failed attempt to storm the fort (15 August 1814), the British forces withdrew to Chippawa where they prepared a strong defensive position.

Earlier, in June 1814, the Upper Canadian Tories had received news that the British armies in Europe and their European allies, had defeated and deposed Napoleon Bonaparte, and that heavy British troop reinforcements would be sent from Europe to Quebec. The Rev. John Strachan preached a sermon of General Thanksgiving in York for the allied victories in Europe, but in the Niagara peninsula and the western districts of Upper Canada, the situation remained desperate.

In the Niagara District, the American army of occupation was heavily reinforced in the fall of 1814 by the additional 5,000 troops under the command of Major-General George Izard, and the combined American force posed a critical threat to the greatly outnumbered British forces at Chippawa. However, the British forces were too well entrenched for Izard to risk a frontal assault, and the Americans were unable to exploit their great advantage in numbers. Moreover, the Niagara area had been stripped of its resources during almost three years of war and was unable to support an army of occupation.

When the Royal Navy managed to re-establish a naval supremacy on Lake Ontario in October 1814 and proceeded to interrupt the American supply line, a provisioning crisis ensured for the American army of occupation in the Niagara Peninsula. In early November, the American army blew up Fort Erie, and withdrew back across the Niagara River into winter quarters at Buffalo. The withdrawal of American troops, and the renegade 'Canadian Volunteers', ended the suffering which was being inflicted by military foragers and marauders upon the devastated Niagara frontier of Upper Canada.

On the Lake Erie Front, marauders from Detroit and American-occupied Amherstburg had launched a series of raids on the isolated settlements of the Western and London districts earlier in the year, and the raids had continued during the summer and fall of 1814. With the U.S. Navy in control of Lake Erie, and the earlier defeat of Procter's Right Division and the disbanding of the district militias, the western settlements were left defenceless. The Loyalist settlements along the shore of Lake Erie had continued to suffer from plundering by marauders who were led by renegade American settlers from Upper Canada.

The most feared of the marauders was Andrew Westbrook, an American immigrant, land speculator/entrepreneur, who had settled at Delaware in the Grand River Valley in 1794. He had joined the American invasion force of Brigadier-General William Hull during the summer of 1812, and once British troops were withdrawn from the western districts, Westbrook led bands of marauders -- as numerous as 100 men -- on raids that kidnapped loyal militia officers, plundered the homes of the loyal settlers, and stole horses. Westbrook raided Delaware (January 1814) and Oxford (April 1814), and led a series of raids on Port Talbot (May, July, and August 1814). In a final raid of September 1814, several homes and barns and the grist mill and saw mill of the Port Talbot settlement were burned, flour bins destroyed, and cattle slaughtered. Westbrook had been indicted for High Treason in May 1814, prior to the Ancaster treason trials, but had managed to evade capture.

The Tories were anxious to apprehend and prosecute traitors who were leading or guiding bands of American marauders in raids that were plundering the loyal inhabitants of the Upper Canadian settlements. There was also a need to discourage American settlers from providing aid and information to American military units who were launching raids into the western districts of Upper Canada.

In the western districts of Upper Canada, the American military raids of 1814 were different than the plundering raids of the marauders which were despoiling the Loyalist settlements in the western districts the previous year. The military raids were on a far larger scale; Upper Canadian settlements were attacked indiscriminately; and the military raiders carried out a deliberate scorched-earth form of warfare. The immediate objective was to make it impossible for a British army to live off the land in any advance in force against Detroit from Burlington Heights; and the ultimate aim was to preclude a British army from linking up with the Indians of the Northwest to carry the war to the American settlements of the Ohio Valley. The American military incursions devastated wide areas of the Western and London districts, and were carried out in quick strikes which made it difficult to organize any defence against them.

In May 1814, an American raiding party of 700 Pennsylvanian volunteers, under the command of Colonel John B. Campbell of the U.S. Army, was transported by a fleet of ships from Presque Isle [Erie] on Lake Erie to attack Port Dover near Long Point. The farms and mills of the Long Point settlements, which had provisioned British troops in the western district prior to Procter's defeat, were targeted for destruction. The American military raiding party included members of the 'Canadian Volunteers' under the command of a renegade American settler, Abraham Markle, a former member of the opposition in the House of Assembly of Upper Canada.

Guided by Markle, the American raiders devastated the Loyalist settlements of Port Dover (14 May 1814) and Ryerse (15 May 1814), and the farms between Port Dover and Turkey Point farther west. Upwards of twenty homes were looted, and the houses, barns, and several grist mills, saw mills, and distilleries were burned to the ground. Gardens were uprooted, crops destroyed in the field, horses stolen, and livestock -- cattle and pigs -- shot or butchered on the spot. Colonel Campbell, a Kentucky Indian fighter, denounced the residents as "old revolutionary Tories", and turned the Long Point settlements into a waste land.

The devastating raid on Port Dover resulted in a court martial for Colonel Campbell, and his re-assignment to the Niagara frontier. The U.S. Army court martial board rebuked Campbell for destroying private homes, but commended his destruction of enemy flour mills.

Several additional military raids in strength were launched by the Americans during the fall of 1814 against the western districts of Upper Canada to render the settlements incapable of provisioning any British military force that might advance against Detroit. The most devastating raid was that of Brigadier-General Duncan McArthur, the commander of the American Northwestern Army. On the 22 October 1814, McArthur departed from Detroit with a mounted force of 650 Kentucky and Ohio volunteers, 50 U.S. Rangers, and 70 American Indian allies. His objective was to destroy grist mills in the farming settlements of the Thames River Valley which had been settled mostly by non-Loyalist Americans at the turn of the 19th Century. McArthur penetrated over 150 miles along the Thames River – overrunning Baldoon, a rebuilt Moraviantown, and Oxford -- before crossing to the Grand River Valley, occupying Burford, and proceeding to Brant's Ford.

Faced with a force of Canadian militia and Indians who were ready to oppose his crossing of the Grand River from the opposite bank at Brant's Ford, and informed of the approach of British troops from Burlington Heights, McArthur turned southward and routed a 400-man Canadian militia force at Malcolm's Mills (6 November 1814) – the last battle of the war in Upper Canada. McArthur torched the mills, and then swung westward past a burnt-over Port Dover. He overran settlements along the Lake Erie Front – Simcoe and St. Thomas, as well as Chatham on the lower Thames River – in leaving a path of destruction on his return to Detroit.

In a period of 24 days, with stolen horses providing fresh mounts, McArthur covered a circuit of several hundred miles, burned five major grist mills -- out of a total of seven mills in the entire western part of the province – plundered homes, and destroyed produce and livestock indiscriminately. As of 1814, the American marauders were no longer making any distinction between the private property of Loyalist families that had previously been the focus of the plundering raids, and the property of the American settlers, in devastating the western settlements of Upper Canada.

Hundreds of Upper Canadians were left destitute and homeless, and hundreds more faced a winter of deprivation with flour, beef and pork in scarce supply for the coming winter of 1814-1815. The raids of the American marauders and the several American military raids totally devastated the farming settlements of western Upper Canada. Moreover, it was well known that it was renegade Upper Canadians — almost all of whom were non-Loyalist American settlers – who played a leading role in the destruction visited on the Niagara, London and Western Districts. It was traitors from among the American settlers of Upper Canada who provided information and assistance to the American invading forces, and who guided or led the raiders who pillaged the isolated settlements of the province.

The pillaging and suffering which was inflicted on the Upper Canadian settlements by American marauders, and the indiscriminate destruction of mills, farm produce, and livestock by U.S. Army raiders in the Western and London districts of Upper Canada during 1814 campaign, did have one positive repercussion. It turned the American settlers of Upper Canada against the American invaders and accomplished what the Tories had been struggling to achieve hitherto without much success. It united Upper Canadians in support of the war effort.

During the 1814 campaign season, the militia of the Niagara District and the western districts turned out in force to support British troops in defending Upper Canada against the American invaders. However, in western Upper Canada, there were still disaffected American settlers who remained eager to aid the American invaders in identifying and betraying the loyal inhabitants of the province. During McArthur's raid, when told by an informant that two of the loyal settlers had left their farms to warn the British troops at Burlington Heights, McArthur had immediately burned the house and barn of both men.

The pre-war Tory fears concerning the danger of admitting American settlers into Upper Canada was confirmed by what they saw during the war. Men did not change their political principles and allegiance when entering Upper Canada in search of free land grants. The war years showed, beyond a doubt, the danger of having the province settled by large numbers of settlers of a foreign allegiance who, in having no feelings of loyalty to the existing order, would not fight for King and Country.

In December 1814, a peace treaty – the Treaty of Ghent - was signed between Great Britain and the United States of America which restored the status quo ante bellum. It ended the immediate military struggle for the survival of Upper Canada, the treasonous activities of renegade American settlers, and the plundering of wide areas of the province by traitors and enemy forces. However, the equally critical ideological struggle, for the survival of the British national character of Upper Canada, was far from resolved. The immediate threat of conquest by a revolutionary power had been rebuffed, but the democratic republicanism born of the American Revolution, and the infidelity spawned by the French Revolution, had left a dubious and dangerous legacy that would continue to threaten the national character and wellbeing of the Loyalist province of Upper Canada. (18)

The Impact of the War

In its immediate impact upon Upper Canada -- in the suffering it engendered and the loss of life and destruction of property -- the War of 1812 was deeply deplored. Yet, at the same time the Upper Canadian Tories realized that the war had done much to awaken and strengthen a British national feeling in the province. Had the war not intervened when it did, it was evident that Upper Canada would have continued to be assimilated and eventually annexed to the American Republic. However, the war had interrupted that evolution, and contributed greatly to the preservation of the Province of Upper Canada as part of the British Empire in North America.

For the Rev. John Strachan, the very timing of the war and its immediate consequences appeared to be but another example of God's superintending Providence guiding all things and bringing good out of evil. For not only had the impact of the war reversed, to a notable extent, the growing Americanization of Upper Canada, but the military strength of the new American Republic could only have become more formidable if the conflict had been postponed.

Prior to the war, several of the leading Tories of the province were acutely concerned about maintaining the British national character of the Loyalist asylum and were determined to resist American influences on the province, but the bulk of the population had not shared their fears and antipathies where Americans were concerned. With the exception of the old Loyalists settlers – such as Richard Cartwright, who objected to non-Loyalist American settlers being admitted to Upper Canada -- the Americans had not been regarded as foreigners. And no steps were taken by the provincial government to prevent a great influx of American settlers into Upper Canada. The result -- just prior to the War of 1812 -- was that the non-Loyalist American settlers were in the majority in the province.

It was evident to the Upper Canadian Tories that if the unrestricted immigration and open land- granting system of the 1794-1812 period had continued for much longer, the province would have become totally Americanized. It was a settlement process that, if not curtailed by the war, would have invariably obliterated the British national character of the province, would have silenced the old Loyalists -- if not have led to their dispossession and persecution -- and would have resulted in the British connection being severed preparatory to the annexation of the province to the United States.

It was the war, the Tories noted, that had completely altered the public mind of the province. It had produced in the descendants of the Loyalists, and in the British immigrant settlers, a national character and feeling, a consciousness of their British heritage and a desire to preserve it. The war gave rise to a noticeable strengthening of loyalty to the Crown. In the postwar years, as was the case during the War of 1812, loyalty was identified with the Loyalist tradition of the American Revolution, because it was based upon the defence of the same principles against 'an ancient foe'.

It was asserted by the Tory elite of the province that the sons of the Loyalists in defending their asylum had shown the same loyalty and affection for their Sovereign, reverence for the law and the British constitution, devotion to one's country, and dedication to the unity of the British Empire, as had their fathers in fighting to put down treason and rebellion – unfortunately unsuccessfully – in the American colonies. In sum, Upper Canadians had preserved to themselves "the most exalted principles of moral rectitude" embodied in their British heritage. They had proven themselves as worthy heirs of the Loyalist tradition.

The hope was held out that the War of 1812 -- in strengthening the British national character and feeling of Upper Canada and pointing out the failings of British policy in the past -- had taught both Upper Canadians and the British government to appreciate their common interests. The war had benefited Upper Canada a great deal economically – except in the devastated areas of the Niagara District, the Grand and Thames river settlements, and at Long Point -- and had awakened an interest in developing the great natural advantages of the country. There was a palpable new consciousness and feeling that Upper Canada was well "on the road to Prosperity, to Population, to National Importance and Political consequence"; although still very much dependent upon British power for her continued survival.

In being acutely conscious of how narrowly the Province of Upper Canada had escaped absorption into the American Republic, the Upper Canadian Tories were moved to redouble their efforts to convince the mother country of her past failings in administering her colonies, and of the need to make provisions for strengthening the British national character of the Loyalist province and curtailing American emigration into the Province of Upper Canada. (19)

In the postwar period, the young Upper Canadian Tories were prepared to continue to play an active public role, with their fellow second-generation Loyalists and like-minded British immigrants, in promoting policies which would sustain and deepen the loyalty of Upper Canadians and strengthen the provincial government. During the war, it was the Rev. John Strachan who was outspoken in rallying Upper Canadians to defend the province, and it was the young Tories whom he had educated who had played a leading role as officers in the militia and in marshalling public support for the British troops. The young Tories had fought alongside British troops, had served on the committees attempting to deal with the problem of disaffection, and were active in the arrest and prosecution of suspected traitors. As such, they were aware of the conduct and opinions of most Upper Canadians during the war years, and they were in contact with those who could supply reliable corroborating information on the character of individuals in each district of the province.

The Upper Canadian Tories were very conscious of their unique position at the close of the War of 1812. If Upper Canada were to remain true to its Loyalist values and beliefs, it was essential that the loyal maintain their ascendancy in the province. In that endeavour, the war had proved extremely advantageous in that it had not only purged the province of traitors and 'false friends', whom a short-sighted immigration policy had introduced into the province, but it had served to distinguish friend from foe. Henceforth, it would be possible to discriminate in favour of appointing the loyal to positions of authority in government and on the bench in a situation where:

> every man will *know*, his Neighbour. The *Test* will have been applied to all and it will be the duty of all to bear in recollection to a more tranquil Period *how each* has conducted himself under it.

It was no mere accident that the ruling elite of Upper Canada in the immediate postwar decades was to be composed of men who had been strong supporters of the war effort in defence of Upper Canada; men who had actively served in the war; and men who had been outspoken during the war in defence of the Loyalist tradition and its values. In postwar Upper Canada, it was 'the loyal' who would be appointed to various public offices and positions of power and influence. The ruling elite would encompass men who had served as officers, and subalterns in the militia, or in several cases with the Incorporated Militia, throughout the war, and who retained a strong consciousness of the values and principles for which they had fought. These "Veterans of 1812" comprised a significant component of the postwar governing class in York and in local communities across the province.

The sense of identity of the postwar Tory elite in Upper Canada was further strengthened by another factor which made them a viable governing class. A significant number of the Tory elite, and its leadership, comprised former pupils of the Rev. John Strachan, who had himself played a major role in strengthening and sustaining the provincial war effort. These young men were among the best educated in Upper Canada, and almost exclusively so in some areas of the province where illiteracy was not uncommon. As early as 1813, Strachan was already introducing several of his former pupils – "very promising young Gentlemen", who had served in the military campaigns of the previous year - to the local British authorities as "the future hopes of the Province". And within three years of the end of the war, he could report, with little exaggeration, that: "my pupils [are] now the leading Characters in many parts of the Province".

Through a common experience in war, in education and in shared cultural, political and religious values, the postwar provincial Tory elite were for the most part united in their concept of what type of society Upper Canada -- or any country for that matter -- ought to evolve to ensure its peace, order and good government, and the promotion of its economic development. Moreover, they were highly conscious of the role which they believed that they were destined to play in public life in defending the traditional order. As such, they were acutely aware of the forces – democratic republicanism, anarchy, and infidelity – that threatened to overwhelm the Loyalist asylum of Upper Canada. The Upper Canadian Tory mind was marked by definite beliefs, biases, and predilections, and a commitment to the Loyalist tradition. It remained to be seen whether the Upper Canadian Tory elite would be able to sustain and strengthen the British national character of the Loyalist asylum of Upper Canada. (20)

Notes

The War of 1812

Frontispiece quotations: Hull's Proclamation of July 12, 1812; reprint in Appendix I, Bowler, "Propaganda in Upper Canada", 144-145; and Jefferson Papers, National Archives, Founders Online, Jefferson to Kosciuszko, 28 June 1812.

1. Strachan, "Address of the House of Assembly", 5 August 1812; Strachan, *Sermon for General Thanksgiving*, 1814, 17; *Kingston Gazette*, "Falkland" [Richard Cartwright], 30 June 1812; Bethune, *Memoir*, 42, Strachan, "Sermon to the Legislature", 12 August 1812. The quotation is from "Address of the House of Assembly to the people of Upper Canada", 5 August 1812, reprinted in Bowler, "Propaganda in Upper Canada", 150.

2. Spragge, ed., *Strachan Letter Book*, Strachan to the Honourable Mr. Wilberforce, 1 November 1812, 21-22; MacDonald, "Honourable Richard Cartwright", 170, paraphrase of Cartwright's "Address to the Militia", 15 December 1807; PAC, Robinson Papers, 1862-1905, John Beverley Robinson, "Address to the Militia of the Home District", n.d. [1813?]; PAO, Strachan Sermons, Box B, 1812, Ecclesiastics 41:3, "Fear not the sentence of Death", 8; Strachan, *Discourse*, 1810, 37; "Address of the House of Assembly to the People of Upper Canada", 5 August 1812, reprinted in Bowler, "Propaganda in Upper Canada", 154; and *Kingston Gazette*, 4 February and 11 February 1812, "Falkland" [Richard Cartwright]. The quotation is from "Falkland", 11 February 1812.

3. MacDonald, "Honourable Richard Cartwright", 169-170, Cartwright, "Address to the Militia", 1 December 1807; *Kingston Gazette*, "Falkland", 11 February 1812; PAO, Strachan Sermons, Box B, 1812, Ecclesiastics 41:3, "Fear not the sentence of Death", 79; Strachan, *Discourse*, 1810, 39-44; PAO, Strachan Sermons, Box B, 16 March 1806, St. Paul's Epistle to the Hebrews 12:11, "Chastening yieldeth Righteousness", 12-13; and Spragge, ed., *Strachan Letter Book*, 11-12, Strachan, "A Speech on presenting a banner to the 3d Regiment of York Militia --Prayer of Consecration", 27 April 1813. The quotations are from Strachan, *Discourse*, 1810, 41, 42-43 & 143, respectively.

4. *Kingston Gazette*, [Cartwright] "Falkland"; 11 February 1812; Spragge, *Strachan Letter Book*, 11-12, Strachan, 'A Speech to the 3d Regiment of York Militia', 27 April 1813; PAO, Strachan Sermons, Box C, 16 March 1806, St. Paul's Epistle to the Hebrews 12:11, "Chastening yieldeth Righteousness", 12-

13, and Box B, 1812, Ecclesiastics 41:3, "Fear not the sentence of Death", 1-11; Bethune, *Memoir*, 142-143, Strachan, "Sermon to the Legislature", 12 August 1812. The quotation is from Strachan, "Sermon to the Legislature", 142-143.

5. PAO, Strachan Sermons, Box C, 16 March 1806, St. Paul's Epistle to the Hebrews 12:11, "Chastening yieldeth Righteousness", 13, and Box B, 1812, Ecclesiastics 41:3, "Fear not the sentence of Death", 8; Bethune, *Memoir*, 142, Strachan, "'Sermon to the Legislature", 12 August 1812; PAO, Robinson Papers, 1813-1817, Strachan, 'Reasons for not moving the seat of government', 1816, 9; Spragge, ed., *Strachan Letter Book*, 25, Strachan to Captain Cameron, November 1813, and Spragge,146, Strachan to His Excellency, September 1813; and PAO, Robinson Papers, 1862-1905, John Beverley Robinson, "Address to the Militia", n.d. [1813?], 14. The quotations are from the sermon of 16 March 1806, and the sermon to the Legislature, 12 August 1812, respectively.

6. Spragge, ed., *Strachan Letter Book*, 26, Strachan to Captain Cameron, November 1812.

7. Ernest A. Cruikshank, "A Study of Disaffection in Upper Canada in 1812-15", *Transactions of the Royal Society of Canada*, Series III, 1912, (reprinted in M. Zaslow, ed., *The Defended Border, Upper Canada and the War of 1812* (Toronto: Macmillan, 1964), 205-207 and 214; G.M Craig, *Upper Canada, The Formative Years, 1784-1841*, (Toronto: McClelland and Stewart, 1963), 70-72; Strachan, "Address to the House of Assembly" reprinted in Bowler, "Propaganda in Upper Canada", 155. The quotation is from an "Address to Lt. Governor Gore from the magistrates, clergy and principal inhabitants of the Eastern District", March 1811, as quoted by Cruikshank, "Disaffection", 207.

8. "A Proclamation by William Hull, Brigadier-General and Commander of the Northwestern Army of the United States", 12 July 1812, reprinted in Appendix I, of Bowler, "Propaganda in Upper Canada", 144-145; and Cruikshank, "Disaffection", 208. The quotation is from Hull's Proclamation.

9. Craig, *Upper Canada*, 70-72; Cruikshank, "Disaffection", 208-209; Bowler, "Propaganda in Upper Canada", 16 & 25, quoting Isaac Brock's assessments of the situation in which he found himself in July-August 1812; and William M. Weekes, "The War of 1812; Civil Authority and Martial Law in Upper Canada", *Ontario History*, XLVIII, 1956. The first quotation is from a communication of Isaac Brock to Prevost, 12 July 1812, as quoted by Bowler, "Propaganda in Upper Canada", 16, and two following quotations are from Brock's pronouncement of 29 July 1812, as quoted by Cruikshank, "Disaffection", 209.

10. "Address of the House of Assembly to the people of Upper Canada", 5

August 1812, reprinted in Bowler, "Propaganda in Upper Canada", 152 & 155. Bowler (37-38) shows quite conclusively how Brock sought to conceal the extent of disaffection in Upper Canada and exaggerated the loyalty of the militia. That is not to deny the fact, however, that the Militia of Upper Canada did play a prominent part in the prosecution of the War in support of British troops, if not a decisive part at Detroit. The quotation is from the "Address", 155.

11. PAO, Strachan Sermons, Box B, 1812, Ecclesiastics 41:3, "Fear not the sentence of Death", 12. The quotations are from "Address of the House of Assembly to the people of Upper Canada", in Bowler, 151 &152, respectively.

12. Craig, *Upper Canada*, 71 &73; Spragge, ed., *Strachan Letter Book*, numerous letters: Strachan to John Richardson, 30 September 1812, 15; Strachan to Sir George Prevost, October 1812, 13; Strachan to the Rev. Dr. Morice, 1 November 1812, 19; Strachan to Capt. Cameron, November 1812, 26; Strachan to Marquis Wellesley, 1 November 1812, 30; Strachan to His Excellency, September 1813, 46; Strachan to Dr. James Brown, 30 October 1813, 49; and Strachan to Lt. Governor Gore, 1 January 1814, 54; PAO, Strachan Sermons, Box B, 1812, Ecclesiastics 41:3, "Fear not the sentence of Death", 16; and PAO, Robinson Papers, 1862-1905, John Beverley Robinson, "Address to the Militia", n.d. [1813?], 14. The quotations are from Strachan's letters to the Rev. Dr. Morice, 1 November 1812, and to Lt. Governor Gore, 1 January 1814, respectively.

[To provide a more meaningful historical context for the Tory view of their situation during the summer and fall of 1812, additional historical material on the battles of the 1812 campaign has been inserted into the original dissertation chapter from: J. Mackay Hitsman, *The Incredible War of 1812, A Military History* (revised ed., Robin Brass Studio Inc., 1999), 65-124; Alan Taylor, *The Civil War of 1812, American Citizens, British Subjects, Irish Rebels & Indian Allies* (New York: Alfred A. Knopf, 2010), 147-190; and Jon Latimer, *1812, War with America* (Cambridge: Harvard University Press, 2007), 60-83. The composition of Brock's force at Detroit is taken from Hitsman and Latimer. In contrast, Taylor states that Brock had a force of 385 regulars, 133 lake sailors, 807 Upper Canadian militia, and 600 Indians at Detroit.]

13. PAO, Merritt Papers, reel 1, "Address by Bishop Strachan, copied from proceedings of the Loyal and Patriotic society by Col. John Clarke"; Bowler, "Propaganda in Upper Canada", 33 & 44-45; C.P. Stacey, "The War of 1812 in Canadian History", *Ontario History*, L, 1958; C.E. Cartwright, ed., *Life and Letters*, 140, Richard Cartwright to Chief Justice Alcock, 14 March 1807; PAO, Robinson Papers, 1862-1905, J.B. Robinson, "Address to the Militia",

n.d. [1813?]; Spragge, ed., *Strachan Letter Book*, 6-7, Strachan, "Life of Col. Bishoppe", December 1813. The quotations are from Strachan, *Report of the Loyal and Patriotic Society of Upper Canada* (Montreal: William Gray, 1817). On 8 March 1813, the Legislature passed a Militia bill providing for the establishment of an Incorporated Militia of Upper Canada. Each volunteer was to receive $8.00, later increased by the government to $18.00, plus a grant of land for enlisting.

14. Craig, *Upper Canada*, 76-77; Cruikshank, "John Beverley Robinson and the trials for treason in 1814", *Ontario Historical Society Papers and Records*, XXV, 1929, 202; Cruikshank, "Disaffection", 213; and Weekes, "War of 1812", 1971, 197-199.

[To provide a more meaningful historical context for the efforts of the Upper Canadian Tories to deal with disaffection and treason during the summer of 1813, additional historical material has been added to the dissertation chapter with respect to the military situation during the summer of 1813. A fuller treatment of the military situation during the summer of 1813 can be found in: Hitsman, *The Incredible War of 1812*, 156-176; Taylor, *The Civil War of 1812*, 214-246; and Latimer, *1812, War with America*, 128-149 & 174-193.]

15. Cruikshank, "Disaffection", 210-213; PAO, Robinson Papers, J.B. Robinson Letter Book, 1812-15, J.B. Robinson, "Memorial to Lt. General Sir G. Drummond", 16 March 1815, 176. The quotations are from the York Magistrates proclamation of April 1813, extracts quoted by Cruikshank, "Disaffection", 212.

16. Cruikshank, "Disaffection", 213-215; Weekes, " War of 1812", 199; Public Archives of Canada (PAC), Upper Canada Sundries, vol. 16, "Report of the Committee appointed at York for the Report of disloyal Characters in the Home District", 16 August 1813; Cruikshank, "John Beverley Robinson and the trials for treason in 1814", *Ontario Historical Society Papers and Records*, 1929, vol. 25, 199-201; PAC, Upper Canada Sundries, vol. 16, , J.B. Robinson (Acting/Attorney General) to Major General de Rottenburg, 20 August 1813. The quotation is from Strachan's comments upon the recommendations of the Executive Council Committee Report of 14 August 1813, as quoted by Cruikshank, "John Beverley Robinson and the trials for treason in 1814", 200.

17. Craig, *Upper Canada*, 78-80; PAO, Robinson Papers, 1862- 1905, J.B. Robinson, "Address to the Militia", n.d. [1813?], 6-7; Weekes, "War of 1812", 203; Cruikshank, "John Beverley Robinson and the trials for treason", 203-205. Richard Cartwright also introduced into the Legislative Council, 26 February

1814, "An Act for the more speedy and effectual punishment of Traitors and Conspirators within the Province", which failed to pass the House of Assembly after receiving passage through the Legislative Council. As indicated by the defeat of Cartwright's bill, the Assembly was still unwilling to give the government of Upper Canada the full extent of the powers desired to deal with traitors.

[Additional historical information on the military battles of the fall of 1813 that had an impact on the Upper Canadian Tory mind, has been inserted into the existing dissertation text. The secondary sources used were: Hitsman, *The Incredible War of 1812*, 177-196; Latimer, *1812, War with America*, 174-216 & 224-231; and Taylor, *The Civil War of 1812*, 246-262 & 279-290. The inserts on the pillaging and destruction of the Loyalist settlement in Upper Canada during the fall of 1813 have been worked up from: Taylor, *The Civil War of 1812*, 238-264 & 313-314; Latimer, *1812, War with America*, 223-231; and George Sheppard, *Plunder, Profit, and Paroles, A Social History of the War of 1812 in Upper Canada* (Montreal/Kingston: McGill-Queen's University Press, 1994), 92-93. See also entries in the *Dictionary of Canadian Biography*, V, Elwood H. Jones, "Joseph Willcocks" and VIII, Robert Lochiel Fraser, "Benajah Mallory. As a youth, Mallory had fought with the Vermont Militia against the British forces during the American Revolution, and in 1795 had emigrated to Upper Canada with a group of American Methodists who settled at Burford in the Grand River Valley. He became a prosperous and prominent member of that settlement, and in 1894 was elected to the House of Assembly where he became a strong supporter of the government opposition under Joseph Willcocks.]

18. PAC, Upper Canada Sundries, vol. 16, John Beverley Robinson to Captain Robert Loring, Secretary, 4 April and 12 May 1814; PAO, Robinson Papers, John Beverley Robinson Letter Book 1812-1815, Robinson to Captain Robert Loring, Aide-de-Camp to Lt. General Gordon Drummond, 25 March 1814, 59; Cruikshank, "Disaffection", 216-218; Cruikshank, "John Beverley Robinson and the treason trials", 20 & 214; William R. Riddell, "The Ancaster 'Bloody Assize' of 1814", *Ontario Historical Society Papers and Records*, XX, 1923, 107-127; PAO, Robinson Papers, Letters to J.B. Robinson: Strachan to Robinson, 30 May and 2 June 1814; and Craig, *Upper Canada*, 81-82. Both quotations are from PAC, Upper Canada Sundries, Robinson to Captain Robert Loring, 4 April 1814.

[Additional historical information on the military situation in 1814 had been inserted into the original dissertation chapter to provide a context for the Tory hopes and fears at that time. The new sources used were: Taylor, *The Civil*

War of 1812, 387-392, 394-400; Hitsman, *The Incredible War*, 213-235 & 266; and Sheppard, *Plunder, Profit and Paroles*, 98. On the critical role played by the Upper Canadian militia units in the Battle of Lundy's Lane, see Richard Feltoe, *Redcoated Ploughboys, The Volunteer Battalion of Incorporated Militia of Upper Canada, 1813-1815* (Toronto: Dundurn Press, 2012), 253-291. Information on the role played by traitors in the devastating raids on Upper Canada has been inserted to account for the strenuous efforts by the Tories to combat sedition and treason among the American settlers. The new sources used were: Latimer, *1812 War with America*, 269-270 & 366; Taylor, *The Civil War of 1812*, 263, 265-267, 383, 385-387 & 390; Sheppard, *Plunder, Profit and Paroles*, 104-107, and Hitsman, *The Incredible War*, 219. See also *DCB*, Vol. VI, "Andrew Westbrook", and "Abraham Markle". Markle, who had emigrated to Upper Canada from New York State in 1806, was a major land speculator in Upper Canada, and wanted the province to become a republic open to American settlement.]

19. Strachan, *Sermon for General Thanksgiving*, 1814, 34; Strachan, *A Visit to Upper Canada*, 1819, 35; Spragge, *Strachan Letter Book, 1812-1834*, 9; Strachan, "Life of Col. Bishoppe", December 1813; PAO, Robinson Papers, "Charges to the Grand Jury 1829-41", J.B. Robinson Charge (Toronto), 1 April 1834, 11; Robinson, *Canada Bill*, 1840, 1-16.

20. Strachan, *Sermon for General Thanksgiving*, 1814, 36; Spragge, *Strachan Letter Book*, XX, Col. Harvey to Strachan, 9 February 1815; Robinson, *Canada Bill*, 1840, 37; PAO, Robinson Papers 1862- 1905, "Autobiographical sketch of John Beverley Robinson" (transcript copy), 14 March 1862, 4; PAO, Robinson Papers 1843-61, "List of the Commissioned Officers and Men serving in the Militia of the Home District (August 1812)", 22 March 1849, and "Circular letter from Robert Stanton, Secretary, with Resolution passed by the Veterans of 1812", 10 July 1860; Cruikshank, "John Beverley Robinson and the trials for treason", 191-192; Spragge, *Strachan Letter Book*, 43, Strachan to General de Rottenburg, 16 August 1813, and 18, Strachan to Dr. Brown, 1 December 1818. The quotation is from Lt. Col. John Harvey to John Strachan, 9 February 1815.

One manifestation of the Tory desire to strengthen the loyalty of postwar Upper Canada, was an insistence that militia deserters who had fled to the United States during the war, should be prevented from returning to Upper Canada. To that end, it was recommended that the government ought to hold out the threat that any deserter caught returning to the province would be court marshaled. The intent was not to execute deserters – the penalty in law -- but merely to hold out the threat of a court martial to keep deserters from returning. (See PAO,

J.B. Robinson Papers, In Letters, John Strachan to John Beverley Robinson, Attorney General of Upper Canada, 29 February 1816.)

For a discussion of the qualifications required for entry into the ruling elite of Upper Canada – whom the political agitators sought to disparage through characterizing the Tories as being a "Family Compact"– see: R. E. Saunders, "What was the Family Compact", *Ontario History*, XLIX, 1957, 165-178.

Chapter Two

The American Threat

The American Ideological Threat

The Politics & Character of America

The American Military Threat

The Crucial British Connection

The Strategic Value of Colonies

[Upon returning home from Washington, the outgoing President, Thomas Jefferson, wrote to the incumbent President, James Madison, to expand on the Republican Party policy of expanding 'the empire of liberty' (the United States) over the entire North American continent and the offshore islands by diplomacy and, where necessary, by war. At the time, Great Britain was heavily engaged in fighting Napoleon Bonaparte, who had just conquered Spain.]

".... Napoleon would give us the Floridas ... ... they are ours in the first moment of the first war, & until a war they are of no particular necessity for us, but altho' with difficulty, he will consent to our receiving Cuba into our union ....we should have then only to include the North [Canada] in our confederacy, which would be of course in the first war and we should have such an empire of liberty as she has never surveyed since the creation: & I am persuaded that no constitution was ever before so well calculated as ours for extensive empire & self-government."

Thomas Jefferson, Monticello, to President James Madison,
27 April 1809

"The Honourable John Macaulay", by George Théodore Berthon, 1857, Agnes Etherington Art Centre, Queen's University. A prominent Anglican Tory and second-generation Loyalist, John Macaulay of Kingston was a former student of the Rev. John Strachan, a prosperous merchant, an erstwhile proprietor/editor of The Kingston Chronicle, and a staunch defender of the balanced British Constitution and advocate of 'national' economic development policies. To Macaulay, the United States was a mobocracy that was subject to the whims of public opinion in the absence of a subordination to God's moral law. He resolutely opposed the importation of American democratic republican political values into Upper Canada.

Chapter Two

The American Threat

In seeking to defend the traditional political, social and religious order of the Loyalist asylum of Upper Canada against agitators and innovators, the Upper Canadian Tories were plagued by the presence of the archetype of the new revolutionary state -- the democratic republic of the United States of America -- on their very border. Immediately following the War of 1812, the Tories were acutely aware of their critical situation where the survival of Upper Canada was concerned. They faced an ideological threat, which was conveyed in the influx of American publications and polemics into the province, and they continued to fear the military threat that an expansionist American democratic republic posed to Upper Canada. Above all, they were haunted by the fear that Great Britain might abandon the inland colony of Upper Canada as being too difficult and costly to defend against any future American invasion.

Hence, the Tories made every effort to combat the impact of American publications on the public mind of Upper Canada, and they sought to publicly unmask the true character of the American democratic republic for the benefit of Upper Canadians who were viewed as being vulnerable to the lure of democratic republican propaganda. At the same time, the Tories strove to convince Great Britain that her North American colonies were a valuable commercial asset of strategic importance to the British Empire and well worth defending.

The American Ideological Threat

For the Upper Canadian Tories, there was much to fear in the presence in the province of numerous "scurrilous papers" and "spurious histories" of the American Revolution that were emanating from the United States. All such publications were adjudged to be particularly dangerous as they invariably denigrated the British government and praised American democracy and the revolutionary experience. The influx of American publications had become a subject of serious concern just prior to the outbreak of the War of 1812. At the time, it was noted that American principles were "beginning rapidly to find their way into this country and to corrupt the Loyalty of some of the best of our Subjects". Moreover, that concern continued unabated after the war. The objectionable publications reflected the bias of the democratic faction in the United

States and were viewed as diatribes against the British Constitution and calumnies on the character of King George III.

The chief difficulty, as viewed by the Tories, was that there was a lack of sufficient means to educate the population of the province in the virtues of the British Constitution, "which requires only to be known to be beloved". It was a lamentable situation where "thousands have never heard the name of our good king coupled with anything but tyranny and oppression", and there was no opportunity for Upper Canadians to acquire the information which was necessary to form a more correct view. In effect, the historical interpretation, which was put forward by American books in glorifying the American Revolution and the principles for which it stood, was a complete denial of the whole raison d'être of the Loyalist province of Upper Canada and the motives of its Loyalist founders.

The influence of American principles and interpretations of the American Revolution had to be counteracted. To that end, John Strachan was moved to publish a *Discourse on the Character of George III* (1810), and to enter upon the writing of a history of the American Revolution. Such publications were felt to be necessary to disabuse the people of Upper Canada of their mistaken notions, and to expose the many falsehoods which were being fostered by American authors. Yet so Americanized was Upper Canada in the immediate pre-war years, that Strachan felt the need to emphasize -- in the publication -- that his "harsh comments" on the American government were aimed principally at the dominant democratic faction in that country, and not at the American people. Nonetheless, Strachan was openly criticized for his supposedly anti-American comments by American residents of the province, such as Barnabas Bidwell in his pamphlet, *A Friend to Peace*. Yet, this was at a time when several of the leading members of the American Congress were openly calling for an invasion of Upper Canada to annex the province to the United States. (1)

Much to the chagrin of the Tories, even in the aftermath of the War of 1812, Upper Canada continued to be plagued by pre-war American immigrants, such as Barnabas Bidwell and his son Marshall Spring Bidwell, who constantly looked to American institutions as "the *ne plus ultra* of perfection", and who held up the American government as an object of envy. Moreover, in 1820 the Tories were deeply concerned to discover that an Upper Canadian newspaper had published several articles on the American Revolution which were marked by the same abuse of Great Britain as was found in American newspapers: viz.

> the same spirit of relentless malignity against Great Britain, the same diligence in mistaking and colouring fact, in mixing truth with falsehood, in sometimes omitting important circumstances, and at other times in amplifying them.

Such arguments demanded a refutation. The Tories sought to publish their views in letters to the editors, and in editorials in newspapers that supported the government. In doing so, they put forth what they regarded as being "statements of *facts – incontrovertible facts*" about the revolution and the American colonial experience, which were intended to counteract the 'boasting' of Americans and their deluded Upper Canadian sympathizers.

John Macaulay, the editor of the *Kingston Chronicle*, expressed the complaint that the political radicals in Upper Canada were continually proselytizing Upper Canadians in praising American institutions to which they attributed the superior prosperity of the United States, its freedom of the press, its energetic government, and even the eloquence of their Presidents. All of which, it appeared to the Tories were being constantly raised "to be cast in our teeth". (2)

In consciously acting to counteract the influence of American ideas and values upon the population of Upper Canada, the Tories were not merely arguing against a set of values which they viewed as being incompatible with their own; they were rejecting the very values themselves. They shared a general revulsion at the type of society which the United States was evolving, and the American experiment served for them as a plain and potent example of the workings and failures of popular government in a democratic republic.

The Politics and Character of America

Whether "in philosophically viewing the structure of their polity" or merely passing events, the Tories continually professed to see "nothing to envy in the United States". In seeking to preserve Upper Canada from the miseries of anarchy and revolutionary bloodshed, they subjected the United States to scrutiny throughout the whole period of their lives and were continually drawing lessons from a comparison of the British society and government with that of the United States to the detriment of the latter.

The recent history of the two nations, and their divergent conduct during the convulsions in Europe, was regarded as ample proof of the difference between the British national character and the national character of the Americans. While Britons had made great sacrifices and fought alone in defence of the civilized world for the security, independence, and peace of all nations, the Americans by their actions had proven themselves to be "traitors to the peace and happiness of the world" and "the betrayer of the liberty and independence of mankind". When Britain was in dire straits, seemingly in imminent danger of succumbing to the overwhelming power of Napoleon Bonaparte, the United States -- "lost to every feeling of honor and glory", "blinded with ambition", and "tempted by views of immediate aggrandizement" -- had not hesitated to ally herself with that tyrant in seeking to partake of the spoils of victory by attacking Canada.

The American invasion of Upper Canada and the several years of fighting and suffering which it inflicted upon the province, and American attempts "to poison [Upper Canadians] with their crude and debasing principles", had resulted in the Tories thoroughly detesting the United States. The plundering of Upper Canada by the American invaders reinforced the Tory admiration for the British polity and the British national character, which was strengthen further by the workings of the American political system as the Tories perceived it.

In commenting upon the American system of government, the Tories were always careful to draw a distinction between American theories and professions and the political and social reality which they witnessed. The Rev. John Strachan for one, at a very early date, professed to one of his Scottish academic confrères:

> that the praises bestowed upon the United States ... are very much misplaced. A few months' residence in America would greatly chastise a man's political notions. I have profited by my neighbourhood to Democracy. In point of real happiness,

the British are far superior to the inhabitants of this celebrated republic.

The Upper Canadian Tories were quick to point out that several of the leading British radicals who had visited America– including William Cobbett -- for all their praise of America and the American system of government, had returned to Britain thoroughly disappointed and chastened after having viewed the actual workings of the American government and the American national character.

Everywhere the Upper Canadian Tories looked as of the early 1820s, they saw what they regarded as proof of the degeneracy of the United States. They were appalled by the American government excusing the unprovoked invasion and occupation of Spanish Florida by General Andrew Jackson, by the aggressiveness of the American Government in expropriating Spanish territory, and by the acquiescence of the American people in the Missouri Compromise of 1820 which failed to outlaw slavery in the new states being admitted into the American Union.

In March 1818, General Andrew Jackson -- at the head of a 4,000-man U.S. army (including militia and Indian allies) – had invaded Spanish Florida to put an end to Seminole Indian raids against settlers in Georgia. General Jackson destroyed Indian villages and several settlements of runaway slaves, seized the Spanish forts at St. Marks and Pensacola, and occupied Spanish Florida. Two British subjects, who were engaged in trade with the Indians – Robert Ambrister and Alexander Arbuthnot – were seized and executed on orders from General Jackson. Although Jackson was publicly denounced by several leading members of Congress for his unauthorized attack on Spanish Florida and the execution of the two British subjects, a motion of censure failed to pass the House of Representatives. The American government took no action against the popular military officer, General Jackson.

With Spain distracted by unrest and uprisings in New Spain (Mexico) and its South American colonies, and too weak to resist the American forces, a Transcontinental Treaty (February 1819) was signed between the United States and Spain. All Spanish lands east of the Mississippi River – inclusive of Florida -- were ceded to the United States, and the southern boundary of the American Louisiana Purchase of 1803 was delineated from the Gulf of Mexico northwestward to the continental divide. West of the Rockies, Spain ceded its claim to the Oregon Country to the United States and agreed to recognize the 42 parallel of latitude as the southern boundary of the Oregon Country with New Spain from the Rockies to the Pacific Ocean.

In return, Spain received nothing. However, the delineation of the border between American lands and New Spain from the Mississippi River to the Pacific Ocean did imply that the United States recognized – or so it seemed -- the sovereignty of Spain over the Texas Territory and the territories of the South-West. The United States also agreed to pay U.S. citizens who were settled in Florida – primarily in West Florida (the Florida Panhandle) -- a sum of $5,000,000 to settle liability claims against Spain for damages supposedly suffered by the American settlers under Spanish rule before the American invasion.

As of 1819, the United States -- following the expansion of the American settlement frontier into the Ohio and Mississippi valleys -- had a balance of eleven slave-holding and eleven free states. A political crisis erupted when Missouri sought to enter the Union as a slave state. If admitted to the Union, Missouri would shift the balance of power in Congress in favour of the Southern slave states. The Missouri Compromise of 1820 avoided that situation. It enabled Missouri to enter the Union as a slave state, and the new state of Maine to enter as a free state, after the separation of the Maine territory from Massachusetts. The Compromise also prohibited slavery north of the 36 degrees/thirty minutes, parallel of latitude in the Louisiana Purchase territory west of the Mississippi River. However, there was an exception. Slavery was to be allowed within the borders of the projected state of Missouri, which was just north of that latitude. In sum, under the Missouri Compromise the balance between slave states and free states was maintained in the American Union, but an additional slave state was admitted to the American Union. However, there was a further problem.

The proposed Missouri State constitution banned free blacks and mulattoes from entering Missouri and prohibited the state legislature from freeing slaves without the consent of their owners. The American Congress baulked at admitting Missouri into the Union with such a constitution. A second compromise was worked out which bound the new state legislature – in a rather ambiguous fashion -- to recognize the rights of the citizens of other states who entered Missouri. Ultimately, Maine was accepted into the Union in March 1821 and Missouri in August 1821 upon Congress accepting the second compromise.

For the Upper Canadian Tories, the lack of any condemnation of General Jackson by the American government for his unprovoked invasion of Spanish Florida, and the failure of the United States to prevent the extension of slavery into new states joining the American Union, constituted a "melancholy instance of the triumph of sordid interest over just principle" and "a satire upon true liberty and equal rights". The invasion of Spanish Florida and the extension of slavery in the American Union were regarded as mark of eternal disgrace and black blots on the entire American Republic. The United States, when viewed from Canada, offered nothing that the Upper Canadian Tories preferred to their own polity, or to the British institutions and the British national character which sustained it. (3)

In the immediate postwar period, and thereafter, both observation and experience had convinced the Upper Canadian Tories that in all essential points of good government the United States was a complete failure. It was a land of 'disjointed democracy' where supreme power was in the hands of "the many-voiced and unmanageable multitude". The people were virtually sovereign, and the government was seemingly deprived even of the power of enforcing its own decrees.

Despite American boasts about enjoying freedom and liberty, the Tories observed that the United States was a country "subject to the slavery of *popular opinion*". It was a slavery that the Tories characterized – in engaging in hyperbole -- as "more intolerable than the chains of corporeal slavery" which that 'heartless republic' also tolerated within its polity. For the Tories, government by the "incontrollable will of the rabble" was the worst form of tyranny, as John Macaulay asserted:

> I look on the tyranny of one man ... to be an intolerable evil, and *on the tyranny of a hundred men to be a hundred times worse.*

Under such a system, the executive government of the United States was powerless to maintain its authority and preserve order in the body politic. In times of public ferment, the most horrible public outrages were committed in defiance of the law. It was a country where:

> summary justice is not unfrequently [sic] inflicted by a lawless mob on a person suspected of crime, *even after he had been acquitted by a jury of his peers.* (4)

In the United States, liberty had degenerated into license, and the whole of their society was characterized by a complete moral disorganization. In the American Republic, as in Israel of old in the absence of her king, "every man did that which was right in his own eyes". The American people in having rejected the authority of their legitimate monarch -- God's representative -- through violent revolution, were even refusing to publicly recognize the authority of Almighty God.

As viewed by the Tories, the United States existed in the worst of all possible situations:

> While we have there the anarchy of a pure democracy, we have no acknowledgment, in a national religion, of Him who ruleth in the kingdoms of men -- no admission, but too positive a rejection, of the principle, that the State should be built upon the foundation of the Gospel.

Not only was the United States suffering from an enfeebled government, but it was plagued by a large and restless population which was uncontrollable because of the lack of any grounding in high moral principles. Moreover, the proper order of society was completely inverted in a country:

> where ignorance and incapacity are invested with the functions of wisdom, and where, worse than all, the passion and depravity of the untutored and irresponsible million are bowed to by the enlightened and the virtuous.

It was a country where all distinctions of society had been leveled, with the result that there was no social subordination. The popular nature of American institutions, supported by their 'atheistic constitution', had produced a population which believed that all men were equal, with the result that those in authority failed to receive their due deference and respect. Children were seldom taught to have "that profound reverence for, and strict obedience to their parents", which not only sustained the family, but the whole social organism. In the absence of parental authority, discipline had broken down in all areas of life. Farmers could not control their labourers, and teachers were unable to command their pupils, in a situation where everyone did as he pleased.

Devoid of any higher standard of conduct than that of the will of the majority and holding learning in low esteem, the population of the United States was regarded as being totally "lost to right feeling and blind to all considerations of honour". The great prosperity of the war years, in acting upon such a population, had produced an ambitious and arrogant people. More than any other nation, the Americans were characterized by a rapacious materialistic outlook on life in that "they are hurried on to any action provided they gain money by it".

Moreover, the Americans were marked by a conspicuous national vanity that was unequalled anywhere else. It was reflected in their publications which overflowed with claims of their superiority "in virtue, wisdom, valour, liberty, government and every other excellence" to European nations and to their colonies which were regarded as peopled with "ignorant paupers and dastardly slaves". Despite the loud protestations of the Americans to the contrary, the Tories were convinced that "the Character of the Americans is generally speaking bad"; and it was a character that was reflected in the kind of government which prevailed in the United States. (5)

From what they observed, the Tories concluded that the American system of government was totally unprincipled and marred by much corruption not only in its administration, but also in its very laws and policy. In Britain, government was conducted by men of high principles and education, who were moved by feelings of honour and a concern to maintain their public reputation through the principled nature and propriety of their actions in responding to an educated public opinion. In contrast, in the United States, ignorance and incapacity held sway, and the people suffered under a government of uneducated and unprincipled men who were unrestrained by any such considerations because they lacked any sense of a public character.

This was not to say that America lacked men of respectability and moral worth, but they were not to be found at the head of government in that country. Even the highest offices, such as the Presidency and Vice-Presidency, were filled with men who were elected through the machinations of the dominant faction, and who were bound to serve the partisan interests of that faction.

American government left much to be desired. Congress was often the scene of shameless jobbing, and American administrations and public measures were too often marked by a meanness of spirit and/or by craft and duplicity. In the United States, the intrigues and interests of faction permeated all aspects of American public life, and even the judiciary was not sacrosanct where the clamour of office seekers for the spoils of electoral victory was concerned.

Although the Upper Canadian Tories readily admitted that in Britain offices were filled too much by favouritism, rather than by merit, and that less corruption was desirable, yet in any comparison of the British and American governments, the British system was held to be far superior. Under their new republican system of government, the Americans had declined a good deal from the colonial period in all the tests of good government. That decline had reached its nadir under the rule of the democratic faction where true liberty was not to be found. It was a situation where:

> the dominion of the party, which now regulates everything, renders all pretensions to liberty ridiculous. It is a faction that has always been turbulent, cruel, and vindictive, discovering oppressions where none existed, supporting insolence, and trampling upon virtue. (6)

As the decade of the 1820s unfolded, democratic anarchy was seen to be increasing its sway in the United States. And the elements of a sound Christianity, which had been conveyed to America within the 'scattered principles' of the various Protestant sects, were fast becoming lost in the absence of an established church. In the United States, innovators and 'seekers after change' were having their effect as the religious community of the nation was marked by a wild disorganization. In the battle to gain adherents to this or that sect, "religious fanaticism and religious knavery" were coming to the fore with the continual promotion of new religions amidst "the excitements of changing creeds and every varying forms and modes of faith". Not only was religion in the United States in a continual ferment, but the religious sects in their struggle for supremacy did not have any scruples about organizing themselves to gain political power and political influence for their own ends.

In viewing the United States, the Upper Canadian Tories never varied in their preference for the orderly and stable government of British institutions over the democratic republican principles and government of the United States. In the view of the Upper Canadian Tories, the United States was a politically and religiously distracted country – a country "born in bitterness and nurtured in convulsion" – wherein the people lived in a constant state of agitation and momentary excitement. The Americans were totally devoid of that love of order and stability which characterized the British people; whereas in Britain,

> authority, and those gradations of rank which are necessary to its stability, are steadily looked at, and are approved of as good and beneficial. [In contrast, in the United States] from the domestic circle outward to the political, natural sentiments of deference are faint, and authority means very little beyond the limits of actual force. (7)

The American experiment with the democratic form of government had proven a failure in providing good government. Unable to protect and promote virtue or to restrain vice, or to honour and maintain its engagements, the American system of government was thoroughly repudiated by the thinking and disinterested elements of its own population. More generally, the American system of government was repudiated by all men who were astute enough to perceive behind the facade of loud and frequent appeals to the declaration of 'the inalienable rights of man', its many corruptions, its toleration of slavery, and its efforts to exterminate the Indian nations with whom it came in contact.

In viewing the innovations which Americans had made in church and state, and their denial or destruction of the traditional supports of good government and social order, the Tories were thoroughly convinced that the American experiment could not last. To the Tory mind, the repercussions of popular sovereignty in both politics and religion, and the democratic anarchy that it spawned, were such that they believed the collapse of the United States to be imminent. From what the Tories observed of the development of American democracy, it had inverted the natural social hierarchy and invested the people with a dangerous unrestrained power over the whole of society.

From the assertion of Richard Cartwright in 1812 that the collision of factions would soon result in the subjugation of America to some ambitious leader, to the assertion of John Macaulay in 1819 -- upon taking account of General Jackson's military exploits in Spanish Florida -- that the American experiment would terminate in the despotism of a military ruler, to the prediction by the Rev. John Bethune – much later in 1838 -- that the American democracy was top heavy and would ultimately collapse of its own unwieldiness, the Tories consistently maintained that the American experiment with democracy would not end well.

In rebuttal of those Upper Canadians who professed to admire the United States, and the American system of government, the Tories countered:

> it only lives by the absence of powerful neighbours -- and because its vast territory gives ample room for rebellious spirits to scatter and do as they please without much regard to law or order.

Of the two models of governments at hand for their perusal, there was no doubt in the mind of the Tories as to which form of government was best suited for promoting the wellbeing of the Province of Upper Canada. Yet, paradoxically, it was the very presence of the United States on the border of Upper Canada which, while it exposed to view the workings of democracy and reinforced the Tory antipathy to democratic leveling and the separation of church and state, also gave sustenance and encouragement to the opponents of the Tories in Upper Canada who were bent on importing American political principles and ideals into the province and overturning the existing order.

For the Upper Canadian Tories, the United States posed an ideological threat to the Loyalist asylum of Upper Canada as well as a continuing military threat. It was the external relations of Upper Canada with Britain and the United States which would ultimately determine whether the Province would survive as a political entity independent of the United States in North America. In sum, the Tories were acutely aware that the maintenance of the unity of the British Empire and a continued strengthening of the British connection was critical to all their hopes and aspirations. (8)

The American Military Threat

Although the War of 1812 had ended with the defeat of American invasion attempts, it had not resolved the ultimate question of the fate of the Province of Upper Canada. Time had been gained which could be turned to good purpose, and more time was available as the province was no longer viewed as being in any immediate danger of another attack from the United States. Nonetheless, the spectre of a future attack by the Americans, at a time of their own choosing, troubled the Tory mind. The United States continued to pose a real military threat to the very survival of Upper Canada; and it was the fear of that perceived military threat which conditioned to a very great extent the Tory response to the American Republic.

On the one hand, the Tory elite were filled with a feeling of pride in their war service, of admiration for British principles and institutions, and of gratitude for the role which Britain had played in defending Upper Canada during the war. They detested the American democrats, and thoroughly rejected the American experience. On the other hand, the Tories were acutely conscious of their perilous situation in postwar Upper Canada, and of a critical need to maintain a peacefully co-existence with the American behemoth.

The Province of Upper Canada had a population of just under 100,000 at the close of the War of 1812, and the two Canadian provinces – Upper Canada and Lower Canada – had a combined population of 300,000 British subjects. In contrast, New York State alone had a rapidly growing population of almost 1,000,000, and the entire population of the United States, as of 1820, was slightly more than 9,500,000 of whom 1,500,000 were slaves.

Thus, in the immediate postwar period the leading Tories were anxious that the spirit of hostility, which existed between Britain and the United States, be dampened. They also admonished Upper Canadians, as good Christians, to respond to Americans "with kindness and hospitality" and to put aside "all turbulent and hostile passions". The survival of Upper Canada was at stake.

In viewing the desperate situation of Upper Canada, John Beverley Robinson conveyed to the Colonial Office a rather wistful wish that an alliance might be concluded between Britain and the United States. He maintained that an alliance -- based on friendship, common origins, a common language, and common interests between two enterprising nations -- would prevent the calamity of any future war between them, and would promote the security, peace and happiness of the world, as well as of Upper Canada in particular. He expressed the rather forlorn hope that:

> If, indeed, an alliance so natural could be firmly and lastingly cemented, it would be happy for the interests of mankind; --- it would create a power which, while it would be competent to repress the designs of destructive ambition, would itself threaten no ill to the repose or the freedom of the world; and which might secure a happy progress to the cause of civilization, science, and rational religion. (9)

Nevertheless, Robinson realized that there were many unresolved differences which would preclude such an alliance; and that they "must not turn a pleasing hope into a dangerous delusion". Even the existence of a mutually-beneficial commercial intercourse between the Britain and the United States could not be counted on to provide an interest sufficient to maintain a peaceful relationship between them. Trade could be equally a potential source of conflict, as Britain had experienced already during the Napoleonic Wars.

Differences and disputes would invariably occur between the two countries. Although Britain -- as the Tories interpreted her actions -- had laboured diligently to settle all outstanding disputes with the United States prior to the War of 1812, the intransigence and corruption of the character of the American government could not be overcome. It was evident that the Americans respected only superior force in the resolution of disputes and differences, and they could not be expected to change their ways. In dealing with the Americans, one had to keep in mind that:

> if they are conscious of their ability to remove any check they experience, there is not, either in their past history or in their general temper, any assurance that they will forbear the attempt. (10)

The American temper was marked by a "lust for war, and ambition for extended rule" which was evident both during the War of 1812 and in their conduct thereafter. In 1812, at a time when Britain had been sorely pressed and seemingly in danger of imminent defeat, the United States had disregarded the best interests of the civilized world, allied herself with a European despot, and attacked Canada in the hopes of conquering the Canadian provinces. However, the defeat, which the United States suffered in that endeavour, had not curbed the American appetite for conquest.

Far from being satisfied with lands more extensive than needed for its present population, the United States was clearly bent on extending its boundaries at the expense of its neighbours. The Indian lands to the West and the Northwest, and the Spanish territories to the South were continually being encroached upon by American settlers, and the Tories were convinced that the Americans were "looking wistfully towards Canada on the north".

Both Spain in Florida and the Indian nations of the South and the Northwest had suffered from an aggressive American expansionism. U.S. troops were seen to be establishing forts in Indian territory as a prelude to a calculated extermination of the Indian tribes and the annexation of their lands to the United States. While elsewhere, the incursion of American settlers and adventurers into the Texas territory of the newly-independent Republic of Mexico boded ill for its future. Everywhere, the Americans had shown a blatant disregard for the rights of other nations. It was noted that:

> These nations are not in the territories of the United States, but the Americans go to seek them, build houses, & clear lands

within their precincts & when such are destroyed, they raise a noise & make it a cause of war.

It appeared that such actions were condoned, if not initiated, by the American government. Even General Jackson's arbitrary invasion of Spanish Florida in 1818 -- which the Tories regarded, along with his execution of the Englishmen Arbuthnot and Ambrister, as "a gross outrage on humanity, a daring violation of the law of nations" -- had been excused by the American government. Indeed, the American government had taken advantage of the weakness of Spain to coerce that country into ceding Florida and other Spanish territories to the United States.

Such conduct and actions on the part of the Americans provided little assurance that they would respect the integrity of the Province of Upper Canada. Moreover, there was much evidence to the contrary. In the immediate postwar period, the Americans were busy in establishing and garrisoning military posts along the shores of the Great Lakes and on Lake Champlain, and in constructing military roads to their northern frontier, as well as in constructing defensive works along the Atlantic Coast which would counteract British sea power in any future war.

Faced by these military developments and the known character of the United States – as the Tories interpreted it -- John Macaulay was moved to express the forlorn hope that the future development of British-American trade might serve to abate American aggressiveness:

> that in short these benefits, while they serve to dispel the charm
> and false glare of conquest, may induce the people of those States
> to sit down contented with the vast territory they already possess,
> and allow their neighbours to enjoy similar privileges. (11)

In witnessing the ongoing efforts of the United States to erect new fortifications along the Canadian frontier, the Upper Canadian Tories were deeply concerned about the danger of a future American invasion. Not only was there nothing in the American character or experience to indicate a peaceful intent on their part, but it appeared that the Americans were "continually plotting, directly or indirectly, the expulsion of the British from North America". It was believed that behind American boastings about their military prowess and potential greatness, was a basic feeling of insecurity and uneasiness over the influence that Britain possessed over their country, particularly over the western territories through her friendship with the Indians.

Unfortunately, the insecurity of the Americans had given rise to an opinion amongst them – which the Tories found quite painful to contemplate – that so long as Britain continued to possess territory in North America, the American Union would never be secure. What was equally worrisome for the Tories was that the interests of the various States and territories of the Union, except for the South, were such as would lead them to favour the annexation of Upper Canada to the United States.

The Western territories, it was believed, wished to expel Britain to increase their control over the Indians whom they were engaged in exterminating; New York, Pennsylvania and Vermont desired to gain control over the St. Lawrence River communication; and the New England States wanted to gain a preponderance in Congress over the political alignment of the Western and Southern States by adding Upper Canada to the Union. Moreover, the conquest and annexation of the Canadian provinces – Upper Canada and Lower Canada -- would facilitate the effort of the United States to achieve its ultimate aim: the driving of Great Britain completely from the North American Continent. American hopes, fears, and interests all seemed to combine to one end: the fostering of a desire to conquer Upper Canada, as a prelude to expelling Great Britain from North America. (12)

The Crucial British Connection

In their concern for the survival of Upper Canada, the Tories were well aware that the province had almost succumbed to the American invasion of the summer of 1812 before British troops could be brought into the field, and that it was the British troops to whom they owed their preservation. Moreover, the war-like actions of the United States against Spanish Florida and the Indian nations showed clearly what Upper Canada could expect should she ever be deprived of the protection which was being furnished by Great Britain. It was only the knowledge of the cost and sacrifices which a war with England would bring that induced the Americans to introduce a little moderation into their relations with Upper Canada, and to refrain from launching yet another war of conquest. The only way that Upper Canada could find peace and security -- in the face of the threat of American expansionism -- was for Great Britain to undertake to fortify the province, and to make it clear to the Americans that she intended to use all her power to defend the borders and the commerce of the province.

The Tories realized that the construction of a proper defensive system for Upper Canada would entail a great expense; and, as early as 1820, they were fully conscious of the fact that "unfortunately Great Britain has too many embarrassments to attend to this matter as amply as our perfect security would seem to require". However, they continued to call for Britain to fortify and garrison the province because of their conviction that sooner or later, whenever British forces were preoccupied elsewhere in the world, the Americans would launch an attack upon Upper Canada.

Regardless of whether the American government coveted Upper Canada or not, there was a real danger that if the province were too weak to defend itself, it would encourage some American adventurer to plan another Texas expedition. The American people were subject to ungovernable impulses. They were fierce and warlike when Britain was entangled in a multiplicity of foreign conflicts; yet moderate when British naval and military forces were uncommitted elsewhere. There was also a danger that "the temporary ascendancy of a particular party" over the government of the United States, might result in the United States starting a war that would be fatal to the continued existence of Upper Canada.

In sum, the Tory mind was besieged with fear and anxiety concerning the survival of the Loyalist asylum of Upper Canada. In assessing their plight, John Beverley Robinson was moved to voice the lament that Upper Canada:

> has unhappily for itself & its few inhabitants, to look forward to a constant struggle for independence agt [sic] a powerful & unprincipled neighbour who will obviously seize upon the moment when G. Britain is most embarrassed & most occupied

in other quarters, no matter in how good or glorious a cause she may be engaged, to attempt to rob her of her colonies. (13)

In viewing the United States, the Tories readily perceived its developing power and opulence. They were convinced that it was only a matter of time -- given the phenomenally rapid growth of the American population and its seemingly unlimited resources -- until the United States would be more powerful than any single state in Europe. That awesome potential power boded ill for the future security of Upper Canada.

For the immediate future, the danger was that "the Americans were always at home and ready to attack"; whereas Upper Canada was militarily weak, and its primary defender was 3,000 miles away. Thus, an absolute security was unattainable anywhere in the province, and there was no prospect of any immediate improvement in the military situation. The Tories realized that:

> it must continue to be so until years of rapidly increasing prosperity may give to Canada a population whose united efforts can suffice to withstand the first shock of invasion & maintain the contest till assistance can come.

The Province of Upper Canada could never hope to match American military resources, but with British support the Upper Canadian Tories were prepared to dedicate themselves to the struggle for the preservation of their Loyalist asylum. Nonetheless, they remained acutely conscious that:

> the unfortunate Inhabitants of Canada ... are doomed to a constant anxious speculation about the probable loss or preservation of everything they possess, of their very country. (14)

The anxiety felt by the Tories over the probability of a future American attack and their uneasiness over the relative weakness of Upper Canada, was in turn further aggravated by a parallel fear that Britain might abandon the province altogether.

Not only were the liberal-Whigs in Britain -- in following the lead of the *Edinburgh Review* -- showing a decided aversion to the maintenance of colonies, but several of the leading members of the Whig Party in parliament were openly advocating that Canada be *"given up"* to the Americans. Moreover, British public opinion was clearly opposed to spending monies for the benefit of the colonies; and that public attitude could not but have an influence on the British Parliament, even on a Tory government committed to the defence of the British Empire.

For the Upper Canadian Tories, it was readily understandable that the British public was opposed to heavy expenditures in the colonies. In the previous century, except for the French Revolutionary Wars, it was colonial disputes that had led to wars and the imposition of heavy tax levies on the people of Britain. Moreover, the Tories realized that the defence of Canada, given its inland location, proximity to the United States, and its exposed borders, would demand an expenditure of treasure and blood on a scale comparable to what had been expended by Britain in times past in defending its interests in wars upon the European continent.

In being aware of the heavy cost of defending Canada, the Tories were at great pains to convince successive British governments that the fate of Upper Canada was not a matter which should be decided purely upon pecuniary considerations. In their estimate, Britain was bound by national honour, and her past pledges of protection, to come to the defence of the province. The people of Upper Canada were British subjects, and were part of the national family as much as residents of the British Isles. Hence, the Canadian provinces were entitled to the same protection as British subjects at Home, regardless of any additional cost involved.

If she were to continue to receive the respect of other nations, Britain must defend her possessions against aggression, "just as an individual protects his property, even at the peril of his life". Moreover, Upper Canada was considered to have a binding claim upon British support in that a goodly portion of the population of the province consisted of Loyalists. Britain had encouraged the Loyalists to settle in Canada and had granted them lands in recognition of their loyalty and the numerous sacrifices which they had made on her behalf at the time of the American rebellion.

To the Tories, there was no question, but that Great Britain was committed by honour and duty to the defence of the Loyalist Asylum of Upper Canada, and by a debt of gratitude to the Loyalists.

> In declaring for the unity of the Empire, they hazarded their lives & lost their property. They are therefore connected with England by the nearest dearest ties, & it is not easy to name any sum of money when their claims for protection are considered that can justify their desertion by Great Britain. Indeed, she is pledged to protect the Inhabitants of Upper Canada in their lives & properties & in all the rights & privileges of Englishmen.

The Loyalists and their descendants had given proof of their continued loyalty and devotion during the War of 1812, and the postwar growth in population through an extensive British emigration was strengthening the province and its attachment to Britain. However, should the mother country choose to ignore the suffering and sacrifices of Loyalists and abandon them, it would be to her own great disgrace and would leave Upper Canadians feeling "exceedingly bitter". (15)

In maintaining that Britain had irrevocably committed herself to the preservation of Upper Canada, and ought to continue to live up to that commitment, the Tories did not see themselves as indulging in any special pleading. They sincerely believed that colonies were a definite asset to the Empire. Moreover, they thought that the North American colonies were destined to play an important role in the future prosperity of the Empire. Admittedly, that value was prospective rather than actual but, to the Tories, it was real nonetheless. In British North America, Upper Canada alone was envisaged as being capable of eventually supporting a population of seven or eight million people, who would eventually contribute appreciably to the strength of the British Empire.

Despite the financial burden which the retention of Canada imposed on Britain, that country was judged -- as early as 1822 -- to be well compensated for its financial outlays. The Canadian provinces were providing employment for British shipping, a market for British manufactures, and a home for Britain's surplus population. Moreover, greater benefits would accrue to Britain over time through the growth of population and the economic development of Canada.

Indeed, a decade later, John Beverley Robinson was to have the satisfaction of quoting statistics from the Board of Trade returns for 1836 which vindicated the Tory contention that the true national interest of Great Britain lay in the development of her colonial trade and the preservation of her colonies. The Board of Trade returns indicated that although the British government had sought -- as a deliberate matter of policy since 1823 -- to increase the market for British manufactures in Europe, the value of the trade with the British North American colonies was far greater. The North American colonial trade in the export of British manufactured goods was nearly £500,000 sterling greater than the total value of the exports to France, Spain, Prussia, Sweden and Denmark taken altogether, and was almost double Britain's exports to Russia.

A similar situation existed with respect to British shipping. The trade of Britain with her colonies had more than doubled over the previous twenty-five years. The tonnage of British shipping which was engaged in the Canadian trade alone exceeded that of the British trade with six foreign nations: France, Prussia, Sweden, Denmark, Norway and the United States of America.

For the Tories, the trade figures proved conclusively their long-held contention that the colonial trade was essential to the commercial wealth and national greatness of Great Britain. As for Upper Canadians, the Tories maintained that only the blind could fail to recognize the critical value of the British tie and not see:

> our true national interests, and the quarter from which we must look for our wealth, our security and independence in future times.

The Strategic Value of Colonies

What perplexed and dismayed the Upper Canadian Tories, as expressed by the Rev. John Strachan, was:

> that British Statesmen of all parties are totally unaware, I might say altogether ignorant, of the vast importance of our North American Provinces to the future strength and grandeur of the British Empire.

Britain should realize that she needed her colonies as much as they needed her. The naval supremacy of Great Britain, the very basis of her power and security, depended on the retention of her colonies. It was obvious that "without colonies, Great Britain would not command the seas. Her greatness & her colonies will go together."

Whether Britain was aware of it or not, the Upper Canadian Tories were convinced that the North American colonies were vital to her future security vis-à-vis the United States. It was a rising power, which, in the Tory view, was hostile to all the best interests of Great Britain. The United States was "a jealous and ambitious rival" of a formidable strength, which "must in time become *the most formidable* of all her opponents". (16)

The retention of the British North American colonies was essential to the security of Great Britain for several reasons. Strategically, the very position of the North American colonies, when combined with British control of the West Indies, gave Britain a complete command of the Atlantic Ocean, which would enable the Royal Navy to control the American seacoast in any future war.

Britain could only be threatened by a naval power, and the United States, despite its potential military power, was lacking in a solid basis for the development of a large navy. Unlike the British North American colonies on the Atlantic seaboard, with their commodious harbours, and their large fisheries which served as a very important nursery of seamen, the United States was lacking in such a potential accession to their naval strength. Only the coastal region from New York to Maine produced seamen in any numbers, and the length of the American coast was not half as extensive as that of the British North American colonies.

As viewed by the Tories, the mere retention of the North American colonies by Britain was of a great strategic value. It served to limit the potential growth of American naval power by denying them access to a large body of trained seamen who were capable of manning warships. Moreover, it was equally critical that the British North American colonies not be added to that "already overgrown confederation of republics" because the loss of the British North American colonies would certainly be followed by the loss of the colonies in the British West Indies. In turn, the loss of the British West Indies together with the loss of the British North American colonies, would greatly detract from the military capabilities of Great Britain in any future war with the United States, and would seriously erode the supremacy of the Royal Navy on the Atlantic seaboard of North America. (17)

The strategic value of the British North American colonies was also increasing in importance with their economic development. With their growing export trade, the North American colonies were becoming capable of supplying the needs of the West Indies and other parts of the British Empire, which would render them independent of the trade of the United States and the countries of northern Europe. The British North American colonies – and the Province of Upper Canada, in particular -- were fast approaching the time when their exports to the West Indies would be sufficient to free the British islands from their dependence upon the United States for lumber, fish and flour. Such a development would render the British West Indies independent of any American power to coerce them should that country, as a matter of policy, decide to withhold supplies to force them "to solicit the protection of the United States".

The late war had shown how vulnerable Britain was to a trade embargo. When the Baltic countries denied Britain access to their naval stores and lumber during the war, she had turned to her British North America colonies for her critical supplies. Yet had the British North American colonies become part of the United States, and were the United States allied with the Northern Powers, Britain would have found it difficult, if not impossible, to secure the supplies required for the Royal Navy on which her independence depended.

On all counts, it was obvious to the Upper Canadian Tories that Britain ought to preserve and strengthen her North American colonies. Their abandonment would not only constitute a betrayal of the Loyalists, but was extremely short-sighted in that such an action:

> though of apparently small moment, strikes at the root of all our Colonial Policy & blasts forever that union of interests & independence of the whole Empire within itself, which the true Statesman desires to establish. (18)

Leaving aside all sentiment and obligation, for strategic reasons if nothing else, it was essential that Britain take advantage of the buttress which a protecting Providence – "the Almighty hand [which] rules the destinies of nations" – had provided to protect the British monarchy against future shocks.

Although the colonies of British North America were incapable of standing on their own against the power of the United States, it was evident that given the fertility of the soil, their rapidly growing population, and their increasing wealth and expanding trade, the North American colonies were advancing in all that constituted power. The ultimate question to be resolved, and the one which the Tories continually posed to the Colonial Office, was: would Britain sustain the colonies as a home for Englishmen, Irishmen and Scotchmen on a continent that might someday control the fate of nations, or would the colonies be abandoned to provide an even further accretion of strength to the American Union?

The Tories never sought to deny that that the fate of Upper Canada was in British hands. It was for Britain to decide whether the Province of Upper Canada was worth the expense which its defence would entail, and to weigh whether the advantages of its retention were exceeded by its liabilities. The Upper Canadian Tories called upon Britain to decide once and for all, and to let her intentions be known. No other course was consistent with honour and good faith. In short:

> If it be said however & truly said that Great Britain laments, but has not the power of defending Upper Canada, that the expence [sic] of giving us effectual assistance is too much for her finances, & that imperious necessity & not inclination decrees our abandonment, we bow in silence. We wish not to remain a burden, but let all this be fairly & candidly stated that we may provide as well as we can for our future security.

Despite such proud utterances, the Upper Canadian Tories were acutely aware that their security, and very survival, depended upon British military aid in time of war, and equally important on the maintaining of a conviction in the minds of both the American alien settlers and disaffected Upper Canadians that British support would invariably be forthcoming should the province be attacked.

The Tories were convinced that the Americans would not hesitate to attack Upper Canada, if it were left defenceless through Britain being unable or unwilling to come to its aid. In such a situation, it was evident that if the people of Upper Canada were not confident of receiving the support of Great Britain in any future war with the United States, they would succumb to discouragement and a want of confidence in their ability to preserve their country.

Hence, where the defence of the province was concerned, it was very important that the people receive an assurance from the British Government that Upper Canada would not be abandoned in wartime, or left open to invasion through a temporary strategic retreat of the British forces to Quebec. Otherwise, such fears would prove destructive of their affection and allegiance to the government. It was axiomatic that: "Protection and obedience are reciprocal".

For the Tories, it was imperative that Britain take every step possible to strengthen the defences of Upper Canada in keeping with some "deliberately settled plan" to provide evidence that Upper Canada would be defended in any future war. Hence, they called upon the British government to erect permanent defences in Upper Canada that would "speak plainly that they mean to keep the Country". The aim was not only to discourage an American attack, but to "quiet restless spirits, to animate the loyal and contented, and to restore the confidence of the province", which was periodically torn by doubts as to whether Upper Canada would, or could, survive as a province of the British Empire in the face of an aggressive American expansionism. (19)

The postwar Tory fears concerning the difficult of defending Upper Canada, and their doubts about the willingness of the British government to undertake the heavy cost of defending the province, were soon relieved to some extent by the Duke of Wellington, the Master General of the Board of Ordnance (1819-1827). In drawing on earlier reports on the state of the defences of Canada by the Duke of Richmond (Governor-in-Chief of British North America, 1818-1819) and Lt. Col. John Harvey

(Aide-de-Camp to Richmond), Wellington developed a strategic plan for engineering a system of defence for Upper Canada.

The Wellington defence plan covered both Canadian provinces. It called for the erection of permanent fortification on the frontiers of Upper and Lower Canada and the construction of an interior network of waterways and canals to interconnect with the defensive works and to link the frontier forts with the ocean port of Montreal. The forts were to be able to withstand a siege by American troops until the garrison troops and militia could be relieved by British troop reinforcement proceeding inland on the interior water communications network. The construction of the interior water communication was intended to enable British troops, munitions, and supplies to continue to be forwarded into the interior in wartime in the event of an American invasion force succeeding in cutting the upper St. Lawrence River communication and/or the Americans succeeding in gaining a naval supremacy on the lower Great Lakes. (20)

Earlier, in November 1818, the Duke of Richmond, when faced with the seemingly overwhelmingly difficult task of defending Upper Canada, had recommended that the province be abandoned on the outbreak of war; and that British troops should be withdrawn to Kingston. It was his intention that the Province of Upper Canada would be recovered during the eventual peace negotiations in exchange for whatever gains the British forces might make elsewhere. (21) However, for the Upper Canadian Tories such a plan portended the destruction of the British national character of Upper Canada and the loyalty of the province. It would entail the dispossession and expulsion of the old Loyalists and the leading young Tories during any prolonged American occupation.

It was Lt. Col. Harvey, an English Anglican Tory -- and close friend and correspondent of the Rev. John Strachan -- who maintained that Upper Canada had to be defended in any future war with the United States, and who, in the immediate postwar period, prepared a plan of defence for doing so. (22). Subsequently, the Duke of Wellington, in working out his strategic plan for the defence of the Canadian provinces, took account of the arguments articulated by Lt. Col. Harvey against abandoning Upper

Canada in wartime to be overrun by American invasion forces. (23) Thereafter, it was the Upper Canadian Tories who were the strongest supporters of the efforts of the Board of Ordnance in London to construct the fortifications and interior canals that were required to implement Wellington's grand defence strategy.

For the Tories, the implementation of the defence strategy of the Duke of Wellington was an integral component of their broader national policy by which they sought to strengthen and preserve the Province of Upper Canada against the threat posed by the democratic republicanism and expansionism of the new American Republic. It was a struggle for survival that had not only military implications, but political, religious and social ramifications as well.

Notes

The American Threat

Frontispiece quotation: Jefferson Papers, National Archives, Founders Online, Jefferson to Madison, 27 April 1809.

1. Strachan, *Discourse*, 1810, iii-iv; and PAO, Macaulay Papers, reel 1, John Bethune to John Macaulay, 21 December 1810. [See also, Scott McLean, "Before the *Christian Guardian*: American Methodist Periodicals in the Upper Canadian Backwoods, 1818-1829", *Papers of the Bibliographical Society of Canada*, vol. 49, No. 2, Fall 2014, 143-165. This article makes clear that there was an organized system of importing 'American Methodist' religious tracts and American books into Upper Canada which was based on their distribution and sale by Methodist circuit preachers from the United States. The article provides an overview of the origins of the practice in the 1790 to 1818 period and, more specifically, the impact on Upper Canada of the monthly *Methodist Magazine* (January 1818 -) and the weekly *Christian Advocate and Journal* (September 1826 -). These publications lost their influence with the founding of a Canadian Methodist newspaper, the weekly *Christian Guardian* (November 1829 -) under the editorship of Egerton Ryerson. The article comments as well on the cultural linkage between the 'American Methodists' of Upper Canada and Methodism in the United States which persisted long after the split of the 'American Methodists' in Upper Canada from the Genesee Conference of New York in 1828 upon the establishment of a separate Methodist Episcopal Church in Canada.]

2. Strachan, *Sermon on the death of Cartwright*, 3 September 1815, 37; *Kingston Chronicle*, (Macaulay editorials), 14 and 11 June 1819; and *Kingston Chronicle*, [Strachan] "Letters to Robert Walsh Esq.", No. 8, 24 March and No. 10, 21 April 1820. The quotation is from Letter No. 8, 24 March 1820.

3. *The Church*, (Bethune editorial), 1 June 1839; Strachan, *Sermon on the death of Cartwright*, 3 September 1815, 38-39; Strachan, *Sermon for General Thanksgiving*, 3 June 1814, 33 & 37; PAO, Robinson Papers John Beverley Robinson Diaries, 1815-17, October 31, [1815], 62; *The Church*, (Bethune editorial), 17 November 1838; *Kingston Chronicle* (Macaulay editorials), 4 & 11 June 1819 and 31 March 1820; and Spragge, *Strachan Letter Book*, vii-viii, Strachan to Dr. Brown, 20 October 1807 and 21 October 1809. The Quotation is from Strachan to Brown, 21 October 1809, vii.

[On the American invasion of Spanish Florida, see Anderson, *The Dominion of War*, 237-238 & 240-246; and Internet: "Transcontinental Treaty" (Adams-Onis Treaty). Surprisingly, the Tories did not mention an earlier atrocity committed by Andrew Jackson in Spanish Florida during the War of 1812. In response to skirmishes between the 'Red Sticks' of the Creek nation and American settlers, Jackson led a militia force into West Florida that attacked and slaughtered the 'Red Sticks', and forced the Creeks, by the Treaty of Fort Jackson (9 August 1814), to cede over half of their territory – 23 million acres in present day Georgia and Alabama – to the United States. (Anderson, *The Dominion of War*, 231- 233. See also, A.J. Langguth, *Driven West, Andrew Jackson and the Trail of Tears to the Civil War* (New York: Simon & Schuster, 2010), 5-6, and Internet: "Missouri Compromise".]

4. Spragge, *Strachan Letter Book*, viii, Strachan to Dr. Brown, 21 October 1809; Strachan, Sermon on the death of Cartwright, 3 September 1815, 28 & 38; *The Church*, (Bethune editorials), 31 March & 3 November 1838 and 13 February 1841; *The Church*, Speech by Christopher Hagerman, 21 November 1840; PAO, Macaulay Papers, reel 2, Reverend Robert D, Cartwright to John Macaulay, 4 July 1835; *Kingston Chronicle*, (Macaulay editorials), 4 & 11 June 1819; and PAC, Merritt Papers, vol. 13, John Beverley Robinson to W.H. Merritt, 27 December 1837. The quotations are from Macaulay's editorials of 14 & 11 June 1819, respectively.

[Christopher Hagerman (1792-1847) was a lawyer and second-generation Loyalist from Kingston. Although he was not a former pupil of John Strachan, he was a member of the provincial Tory elite, and an ardent supporter of the 'Established Church', the monarchy, and the British tie – a strong "Churchman and King's Man". He was an outspoken supporter of the government in the House of Assembly during the 1830s and served as Solicitor General (1829-1837) and Attorney General (1837-1840). See Robert L. Fraser, "Hagerman, Christopher Alexander", *Dictionary of Canadian Biography*, VII.]

5. *The Church*, (Bethune editorials), 31 March & 17 November 1838, and 13 February 1841; *Kingston Chronicle*, [Strachan], Letter to Robert Walsh No. 13, 14 July 1820, Strachan, *Sermon for General Thanksgiving*, 3 June 1814, 33; and Spragge, *Strachan Letter Book*, viii, Strachan to Dr. Brown, 20 October 1807 and 9 October 1808. The quotations are from the Bethune editorials of 13 February 1841 and 31 March 1838, respectively.

[The Constitution of the United States of 1787 is a totally secular document that makes no mention of God in any capacity. The Preamble reads: "We, the people of the United States, in order to form a more perfect Union, establish justice, insure domestic tranquility, provide for the common defence, provide for the general welfare, and secure the blessings of liberty to ourselves and our posterity, do ordain and establish this Constitution for the United States of America."

Religion was mentioned only subsequently in the First Amendment of December 1791, which established the separation of Church and State and freedom of religion. It reads: "Congress shall make no law respecting an establishment of religion, or prohibiting the free exercise thereof, or abridging the freedom of speech, or of the press, or the right of the people peacefully to assembly, and to petition the government for a redress of grievances."]

6. Strachan, *Discourse*, 1810, iii-iv; Strachan, *Sermon on the death of Cartwright*, 3 September 1815, 27-28, 37-38 & 40; *Kingston Chronicle*, (Macaulay editorial), 11 June 1819; *The Church*, (Bethune editorial), 13 February 1841; Spragge, *Strachan Letter Book*, viii, Strachan to Dr. Brown, 9 October 1808 and 21 October 1809. The quotation is from the Strachan, *Sermon*, 3 September 1815.

7. *The Church*, (Bethune editorials) 31 March and 3 & 17 November 1838; and *The Church*, "England and America", 1 December 1838. The quotation is from the "England and America" article of 1 December 1838. The Tory view of the involvement of religious sects in American politics is in keeping with their earlier view that the American evangelical sectarians in their belief in political activism and "ecclesiastical democracy" were a real threat to the traditional church-state monarchical polity of Upper Canada. It was a view which the Tories held from a very early date and accounts for their striving to combat the spread of American religious sects into Upper Canada.

8. *The Church*, (Bethune editorials), 3 and 17 November 1838; *The Church*, "Christian Loyalty", 22 December 1838; *York Gazette*, "Falkland" (Richard Cartwright), 26 February 1812; *Kingston Chronicle*, (Macaulay editorial), 11 June 1819; PAC, Merritt Papers, vol. 26, John Strachan to W.H. Merritt, 16 May 1856; and *The Church*, "England and America", 1 December 1838. The quotation is from Strachan to Merritt, 1 December 1838.

9. Robinson, *Canada Bill*, 1840, 15; Strachan, *Sermon for General Thanksgiving*, 3 June 1814, 34; *Kingston Chronicle*, (Macaulay editorial), 26 November 1819 and 8 December 1820; Strachan, *Sermon on the death of Cartwright*, 3 September 1815, 41; John Strachan and John Beverley Robinson, *Observations on the Policy of a General Union of all the British Provinces of North America* (London: W. Cloves, 1824), 5; John Beverly Robinson, *A Letter to the Right Hon. Earl Bathurst, K.G. on the Policy of Uniting the British North-American Colonies* (26 December 1824), 47- 49. The quotation is from Robinson pamphlet *Letter to Earl Bathurst*, 26 December 1824, 48.

[Census data has been inserted into the original dissertation text from Taylor, *The Civil War of 1812*, 140, and the Internet: U.S. Census Data for 1820.]

10. Spragge, Strachan Letter Book, 185, Strachan to Dr. Brown, 1 December 1818; *Kingston Chronicle*, (Macaulay editorial), 26 November 1819; Robinson, *Letter to Earl Bathurst*, 26 December 1824, 47- 49. The quotation is from Robinson, *Letter to Earl Bathurst*, 26 December 1824, 48.

11. *Kingston Chronicle*, (Macaulay editorials), 9 July, 26 November & 24 December 1819, and 8 December 1820, and 12 July & 30 August 1822, and 26 December 1824; Spragge, ed., *Strachan Letter Book*, 23, Strachan to Hon. Mr. Wilberforce, 1 November 1812. The quotations are from Strachan to Wilberforce, 1 November 1812, and *Kingston Chronicle*, 26 November 1819, respectively. As late as 29 March 1839, Robinson also expressed the hope that a growing intercourse between Britain and the United States would tend to restrain the Americans from a rupture with England; although earlier he had expressed a different opinion that trade relations would sooner or later provide some occasion for serious differences between the two powers because of the American temper. (PAO, Robinson Papers, 1839-1842, 19, Robinson to Marquess of Normanby, Secretary of State for War and the Colonies, on measures necessary for restoring security and confidence in Canada; and Robinson, *Letter to Earl Bathurst*, 26 December 1824, 48).

[On American expansionism, and its impact on Spanish Florida, the Indian tribes of the South and the North-West, and on Mexico, see Anderson & Cayton, *The Dominion of War, Empire and Liberty in North America, 1500-2000* (London: Penguin Books, 2005), 229-273. This study supports the far older Tory interpretation of American expansionism. See also Reginald C. Stuart, *United States Expansionism and British North America, 1775- 1871* (Chapel Hill, North Carolina: University of North Carolina Press, 1988). For Stuart, American expansionism, which grew out of the American Revolution, was a 'defensive expansionism' motivated primarily by a desire to attain security for the new Republic by removing Great Britain from North America by negotiation or by force. From an Upper Canadian Tory perspective, the adherence to such a policy by the United States raised the spectre of a war for survival and the ultimate threat of a forced annexation to the American Republic.]

12. *Kingston Chronicle*, (Macaulay editorial), 26 November 1819 and 30 August 1822; Strachan and Robinson, *Observations on the Policy of a General Union*, 1824, 5; PAO, Robinson Papers 1813- 1817, 6-7, Strachan, "Reasons against removing the Seat of government of Upper Canada from York to Kingston", 1816; Spragge, *Strachan Letter Book*, 23, Strachan to Hon. Mr. Wilberforce, 1 November 1812, and 9, Strachan, "Remarks on the Subject of the removing the seat of Government to Kingston", October 1815.

[Immediately after the War of 1812, the British government proposed that the capital of the province be moved from York (Toronto) to Kingston, which was far more secure against attack in wartime. However, the Upper Canadian Tory elite in York opposed the move as they feared it would facilitate the abandonment of Upper Canada -- west of Kingston -- by the British Army in wartime. They also had vested interests in York. In opposing the British government proposal, the Tories elaborated on their view of the American military threat.]

13. *Kingston Chronicle*, (Macaulay editorials), 26 November & 24 December 1819, and 8 December 1820; Strachan and Robinson, *Observations on the Policy*

of a General Union, 1824, 5; Robinson Paper, 18-19, Robinson to Marquess of Normanby on restoring security and confidence, 29 March 1839; PAO, Merritt Papers, vol. 13, J.B. Robinson to W.H. Merritt, 27 December 1837; *The Church*, (Bethune editorial), 13 February 1841; Robinson, *Canada Bill*, 1840, 49; and PAO, Robinson Papers, 1813-17, 14, John Beverley Robinson, "Draft argument against the Removal of the Seat of Government", 1816. The quote is from the Robinson, "Draft argument", 1816, 14.

14. Robinson, *Letter to Earl Bathurst*, 26 December 1824, 4 - 9; and Robinson, "Removal of the Seat of Government", 1816, 8-12. The quotations are from Robinson, "Removal", 1816, 8 & 10, respectively.

15. Robinson to Marquess Normanby, on restoring security and confidence, 29 March 1839, 20-24; PAO, Robinson Papers, J.B. Robinson Letterbook, 1814 - 1862, 11, Robinson to Strachan, 29 June 1822, and 241, Strachan to Robinson, 1 September 1822; PAO, Robinson Papers, 1813-17, 3 & 8, Strachan, " Reasons against removing the seat of Government of Upper Canada from York to Kingston", 1816; and Robinson, *Letter to Earl Bathurst*, 26 December 1824, 6; and Spragge, *Strachan Letter Book*, 84, Strachan to Col. Harvey, February 1815. The quotation is from Strachan, "Reasons against removing the Seat of Government", 1816, 3.

16. Robinson, *Letter to Earl Bathurst*, 26 December,1824, 2 & 4; PAO, Strachan Papers, reel 3, Strachan to My Dear Sir, 18 January 1836; Robinson, "'Plan for General Legislative Union", 1822, 32; Strachan and Robinson, *Observations on the Policy of a General Union*, 1824, 5; PAO, Robinson Papers, J.B. Robinson Letterbook, 1814-1862, 241, Strachan to Robinson, 1 September 1822; and Robinson, *Canada Bill*, 1840, 75-79. The quotations are from Robinson, *Canada Bill*, 1840, 78, and the Strachan letters of 18 January 1836 and 1 September 1822, respectively.

17. Robinson, *Letter to Earl Bathurst*, 26 December 1824, 4; Strachan, *Remarks on Emigration from the United Kingdom, Addressed to Robert Wilmot Horton, Esq., m.p., Chairman of the Select Committee of Emigration in the last Parliament* (London: John Murray, 1827), 142; Strachan and Robinson, *Observations on the Policy of a General Union*, 1824, 5 & 7; and *Kingston Chronicle*, (Macaulay editorial), 30 August 1822.

18. Robinson Papers, 1813-1817, Strachan, "Reasons against removing the Seat of Government", 1816, 7 & 8; Spragge, *Strachan Letter Book*, 97, Strachan, "Remarks on the subject of removing the seat of Government to Kingston", October 1815; Robinson, "Plan for a General Legislative Union", 1822, 33; and Robinson, *Canada Bill*, 1840, 40- 41. The quotation is from Strachan, "Reasons against removing the Seat of Government", 1816, 7.

19. Robinson, *Canada Bill*, 1840, 40-41; Strachan, "Reasons against removing the Seat of Government", 1816, 2-3 & 8-9; Robinson, "Draft argument against

the Removal of the seat of Government", 1816, 9-10; Charles R. Sanderson, ed., *The Arthur Papers*, vol. I, 417, J.B. Robinson to Lt. Governor Arthur, 5 December 1838; Spragge, *Strachan Letter Book*, 9, "Remarks on the subject of removing the seat of Government to Kingston", October 1815; *Kingston Chronicle*, (Macaulay editorial) 2 December 1819; Robinson, Plan for a General Legislative Union", 1822, 32; PAC, Merritt Papers, vol. 13, J.B. Robinson to William Merritt, 27 December 1837; and Robinson, "Letter to Marquess Normanby on restoring security and confidence", 29 March 1839, 20 & 29. The quotation is from Strachan, "Reasons against removing the Seat of Government", 1816, 3.

[The final section of this chapter has been added to the dissertation text with the new references cited below.]

20. Wellington to My Dear Lord [Bathurst], "Memorandum on the Defence of Canada", London, 1 March 1819, in *Despatches, Correspondence, and Memoranda of Field Marshal Arthur, Duke of Wellington, K.G.*, vol. I (London: John Murray, 1867), 36-44.

21. Library and Archives Canada (LAC), MG11, CO42, vol. 179, reel B-141, 119-122, Duke of Richmond to Earl Bathurst, 10 November 1818.

22. LAC, MG11, CO42, vol. 358, reel B-297, 7-21, John Beverley Robinson to Lord Bathurst, 15 February 1816. The Tories concurred with Lt. Col Harvey who pointed out to the Colonial Office that a strategy of withdrawing British troops from Upper Canada upon the outbreak of war -- as advocated by the Duke of Richmond -- would do nothing to protect the persons and property of the loyal British subjects of Upper Canada. They would be left vulnerable to attack, harassment, and despoilment, at the hands of American marauders during any period of American occupation.

23. National Archives of Scotland, GD45/3/332, 1080- 1085, Lt. Col. Harvey, "Memorandum on the defence of the Canadas", 7 November 1818. The Library and Archives Canada has a microfilm copy of the Harvey Report (Dalhousie Muniments, MG24, A12, reel A533, Film 9, Section 3), but it is illegible in some parts. It was Lt. Col. Harvey who devised and led the surprise night attack by British troops -- at the Battle of Stoney Creek (6 June 1813) -- that stopped the American invasion army of Major-General Henry Dearborn in its advance against the Burlington Heights. See Phillip Buckner, "Harvey, Sir John", *Dictionary of Canadian Biography*, VIII.

Chapter Three

The Exclusion of Aliens

The Exclusion of Americans

The Alien Question: the Tory View

The Barnabas Bidwell Controversy

The Ruling of the Law Officers' of the Crown

The Tory Strategic Position

The Radicals & the Alien Question

The Provincial Naturalization Act of March 1827

A Betrayal in Great Britain

A Bittersweet Settlement

British Immigrant Radicals

"Shall we, who have sought out for ourselves, through wildernesses, with the greatest difficulties and exertion, a new home, after having lost all which we once considered our patrimony – yield up to interlopers an equal claim with ourselves to the highest offices in our Government?

"Communications"
Kingston Chronicle, 29 March 1822.

Breathes there the man with soul so dead,
Who never to himself hath said:
'This is my own, my native land!'

Sir Walter Scott
The Lay of the Last Minstrel
Canto Sixth, "Patriotism; Innominatus"

John Beverley Robinson, portrait by Francis Hoppner Meyer, 1842, Archives of Ontario. A second-generation Loyalist and former student and protégé of the Rev. John Strachan, Robinson was a lawyer by profession with a distinguished career of public service. He commanded a York militia company on active service during the War of 1812, served as the Attorney-General for Upper Canada during the 1820s, and was the leader of the Tories in the House of Assembly prior to his appointment as Chief Justice in 1829. Robinson was concerned to limit American immigration until the British national character of the Province could be well-established and capable of readily assimilating new arrivals.

Chapter Three

The Exclusion of Aliens

Although their view of England was somewhat idealized, the Upper Canadian Tories had a very definite conception of what type of society – an English society – that they wished to build in Upper Canada, and the proper relationship of their Loyalist asylum to the Crown and the Imperial Parliament in London. Moreover, they articulated the policies that they wanted to see implemented by the provincial and Imperial governments acting in a mutually supportive relationship. In total, their proposed policies were designated a "National Policy" which was aimed at the maintenance of the traditional church-state polity in Upper Canada, the strengthening of the British national character of the province, and the encouraging of British emigration to increase the population, economy and the military strength of the Loyalist Province.

In seeking to maintain and strengthen the 'British national character' of the Loyalist Asylum of Upper Canada, the Tories took steps to discourage Americans from settling in Upper Canada in a conscious effort to prevent the thinly-populated pioneer province from being inundated by an influx of American settlers as the American settlement frontier advanced westward.

The Exclusion of Americans

In seeking to implement their National Policy, the Upper Canadian realized that if the British national character and feeling of Upper Canada were to be strengthened, and the traditional order preserved, it was essential that the province should be settled exclusively with British subjects for an extended period. To that end, in the immediate postwar period the Upper Canadian Tories wanted American emigration to be stopped. Not only did the Tories want American citizens to be excluded from settling in Upper Canada as a matter of policy, but even British subjects who had lived for any length of time in the United States were to be discouraged from migrating into the province. It was a policy that the Tories wanted to be implemented, and maintained in force, until such a time as:

> a sort of foundation or neucleus [sic] was formed of Emigrants from Europe in the new settlements by which they might acquire

a British tone and character. After this, to slide gradually, but silently, into the System pursued before the war.

A restrictive immigration policy was held to be necessary until a British national character and feeling could become firmly established, and especially in the new settlements that had been founded prior to the War through an earlier influx of American settlers. The existing American settlers were to be assimilated through encouraging British emigration into Upper Canada, and the integration of large number of British immigrants into American-settled areas. Once the American settlers were assimilated, and a British tone and character firmly established, then Upper Canada could afford to return to the open immigration system pursued before the War of 1812.

The danger involved in permitting Americans to settle in great numbers in the province had been amply proven during the War of 1812 when there was a great deal of disaffection apparent among the American residents of the province. In areas where they were in a majority, several leaders of the American communities and a significant number of American settlers had joined the invaders and fought alongside the American forces, while others had provided information and assistance to the invaders. During the War, there were numerous instances where American settlers refused to turn out with the militia, deserted from the militia, or sought out the American forces and 'surrendered' to obtain their parole so that they could avoid having to serve in the militia of Upper Canada. More generally, where the Americans residents of Upper Canada were concerned, it appeared that their "disposition to rebel" had been restrained only by their fear of having insufficient numbers to engage British troops and overthrow the provincial government.

It was not a case of all of the American residents having engaged in sedition or treasonable activities during the war. John Beverley Robinson freely admitted that, despite the disloyal conduct of a significant number of American residents of Upper Canada,

> there were very many honourable exceptions, and in truth the majority deserved to be differently characterized. But, if even in those times there was, on-the-whole, more of strength than danger in this portion of the population of Upper Canada, the

predilection of Americans for American institutions posed a potential danger which could not with safety be disregarded.

The postwar Tory fears in that regard were clearly a continuation of the concerns which had been expressed in the prewar period by Richard Cartwright who had objected to the influx of American settlers at that time. Cartwright had observed that the mere act of emigration into Upper Canada would not alter the "political principles or prejudices" of the American settlers; nor would the Oath of Allegiance serve "at once to cheek the bias of the mind". Americans were imbued with democratic republican principles, and their "predilection for those maxims and modes of estimating and conducting the concerns of the public" would invariably influence their political conduct and would prove detrimental to all efforts to strengthen and maintain the British national character of Upper Canada and the British connection. (1)

The Upper Canadian Tories were pleased to see that the War of 1812 had made the British government aware of the danger inherent in permitting American emigration into the Province; and that a "more just and cautious policy" was required to ensure that the province would be settled by loyal immigrants from Great Britain. The Tories supported wholeheartedly a new policy which was embodied in the Instructions that the Colonial Secretary, Lord Bathurst, forwarded to Upper Canada in January 1815. The Lt. Governor, Francis Gore, was ordered to ensure that the provincial government would "use its best endeavours to prevent subjects of the United States from settling in the colony".

In response, after consulting with his Executive Council, the Lt. Governor issued a Proclamation (24 October 1815) in which the magistrates were ordered to refrain from administering the oath of allegiance "to persons coming from the United States", unless specifically licensed to do so by the Lt. Governor. Prior to the War of 1812, Americans had freely entered Upper Canada to settle. They had received Crown land grants or purchased land without hinder, and after a seven years' residence had exercised all the political rights of British subjects. However, under the Proclamation of October 1815 that ease of settlement for Americans came to an end. No one would be permitted to acquire land without taking the Oath of Allegiance, and the oath would not be administered to

Americans seeking to settle in Upper Canada. As such, the Proclamation effectively precluded Americans from securing a legal title to any land that they might acquire, and hence from settling in Upper Canada. (2)

The attempt to exclude American aliens from settling in Upper Canada gave rise to a political issue that caused the Tories a great deal of trouble and involved the government of Upper Canada in a prolonged legal wrangling. As early as 1817, the new alien policy met with a strong opposition in the House of Assembly.

Initially, the Tories dismissed the opposition to the alien exclusion policy as simply the "selfish views of some great land speculators". It was obvious that the leaders of the opposition in the House of Assembly, and several of their supporters in the Legislative Council, were men with large land holdings who wanted to encourage American emigration to Upper Canada to enhance the value of their wastelands. However, the matter became much more serious when opposition members began to marshal legal arguments against the alien exclusion policy. Indeed, the Assembly went so far as to pass a series of resolutions which denied the right of the provincial government to exclude Americans.

The resolutions were put forward by Lt. Col. Robert Nichol, the member for Norfolk. Nichol possessed a distinguished war record as Quarter Master General of the Militia and was a former strong supporter of the Crown. However, during the War of 1812, he had been ruined financially when his mills, commercial buildings, and farm holdings were destroyed in the American raid on Port Dover (14 May 1814). He needed to sell some of his large landholdings at a good price to re-establish his mills and various other enterprises, and a heavy influx of American immigrants into the province would raise land prices and increase land purchases.

The resolutions that Robert Nichol brought forward in the House of Assembly, declared that Acts of the British Parliament governing immigration took precedent over a provincial executive order: viz. the Proclamation issued by Lt. Governor Gore. The British Parliament by the 'Settlers in American Colonies Act' (30 George III, c. 27, 1790) -- had invited 'Late Loyalist' Americans to settle in Canada. Upon arrival, the prospective settlers were required to take the Oath of Allegiance to the King and to swear that they intended to become permanent residents.

The second act cited by Robert Nichol was an earlier British statute, the Naturalization Act (13 George II, c. 7, 1739). It provided a legal means for naturalizing aliens. The Naturalization Act – which became effective as of 1740 – enabled immigrants who were "born out of the allegiance of His Majesty" to become naturalized British subjects in the American colonies after a residence of seven years, with the proviso that they must swear the Oath of Allegiance to the King in open court, profess the Christian faith, swear to uphold the Protestant succession to the British Crown, and have taken the sacrament of communion in a Protestant church. Once the alien immigrants were naturalized, they had the legal right as British subjects to purchase and own property in the colony and to exercise the civil rights of a British subject. When enacted, the Naturalization Act was intended to apply to foreign Protestants – principally French Huguenots -- who were seeking to settle in the American and West Indian colonies of Great Britain.

In citing the two acts of the Imperial Parliament, the government opposition maintained that the provincial Proclamation of Lt. Governor Gore could be ignored by the magistrates. Americans had a right to settle in Upper Canada, and after a seven years' residence could apply to be naturalized as British subjects. What the Nichol resolutions ignored, however, was that under the terms of the Naturalization Act, if it were to be enforced, American aliens settling in Upper Canada had no right to own land. They would not be able to secure a legal title to their property until they became naturalized as a British subject through taking the Oath of Allegiance, and that could be done only after a seven years' residence. Moreover, under the Constitutional Act of 1791 only 'natural born Subjects of his Majesty's Dominions', or a naturalized British subject, or a subject acquired through conquest, had the right to vote and to stand for election to the Assembly.

The alien question posed a real conundrum where the property rights and political rights of American settlers were concerned. In response to the Assembly resolutions, Lt. Governor Gore prorogued the Legislature to put the question in abeyance until the provincial government could consult with the Colonial Office on the legal issues being raised in the Assembly.

In focusing on the legal problem posed by American citizens wanting to settle in Upper Canada, a related question was initially ignored: viz. whether the existing pre-War American settlers of over seven years' residence in Upper Canada, had ever fulfilled the terms of the Naturalization Act to become British subjects. (3)

With the Assembly of Upper Canada questioning the legality of the provincial government effort to exclude American settlers, Lord Bathurst, the Secretary of State for War and the Colonies, acted to clarify his Instructions. In doing so, he added a new dimension to the alien controversy. In a dispatch of 30 November 1817, Bathurst supported the Assembly's contention that the 'Settlers in American Colonies Act' of 1790 entitled American settlers to take the oath of allegiance and to reside in the province, but he pointed out that the taking of the oath of allegiance did not qualify citizens of the United States to hold property in the province. The applicable Imperial Statute was the Naturalization Act of 1740. Under that Act, a foreign national could become naturalized only after a seven years' residence, and it was upon becoming a naturalized British subject that the right was gained to legally acquire and possess property in a British province. Thus, Bathurst emphasized that it "requires a seven-year residence to hold lands".

Lord Bathurst directed that the Naturalization Act of 1740 was to be enforced by the provincial government; and that the Americans who had migrated into Canada following the War of 1812 -- and thus had not been in Upper Canada for a period of seven years -- were to be dispossessed of their property. As aliens, they were not entitled to own property in an English colony. Apparently, an assumption was made by Bathurst that the American aliens who were resident in Upper Canada for more than seven years, would have gone through the naturalization process which entitled them to own property in Upper Canada.

The Alien Question: the Tory View

Although the Upper Canadian Tories agreed with the legal interpretation of the Naturalization Act by the Colonial Office, they were alarmed at the potential political repercussions and legal confusion over property rights that an enforcement of the Naturalization Act would entail. The

Tories strongly supported the provincial government effort to exclude Americans from settling in Upper Canada by refusing to administer the oath of allegiance to them. Moreover, the Tories wanted political rights to be denied to American settlers who had neglected, or had refused, to swear the Oath of Allegiance to the King. In failing to comply with the terms of the Naturalization Act of 1740, they were aliens living in Upper Canada. Nonetheless, for the Tories, it was highly objectionable that the provincial government would even consider dispossessing the American settlers of their existing property. What the Tories wanted was simply to discourage American emigration to Upper Canada by precluding new arrivals from purchasing land and obtaining Crown land grants. Moreover, for the Tories, there was a more serious political problem.

The Tories were willing to admit that the Naturalization Act of 1740 -- which originally applied only to foreign Protestants who were seeking to settle in the American colonies and the British West Indies -- could be construed to permit American settlers to become a naturalized British subject with the right to hold land in the Province of Upper Canada. The problem was -- as the Tories explained to the Colonial Office -- that "not one" of the American settlers in Upper Canada had ever fulfilled the requirements of the Naturalization Act of 1740 to become a naturalized British subject. They had not taken the Oath of Allegiance to the King.

Nonetheless, it was recognized that if the provincial government refused to recognize the right of the postwar American settlers to own property in Upper Canada, because they had not been naturalized, it would call into question the property rights of all the American who were settled in the province. Where the American settlers were concerned:

> The truth is they have been admitted to hold lands by an indulgence not to be defended by law and as they have never conformed themselves to the conditions required, nothing could be more foolish, impolitic & dangerous as calling the matter up. It would call up several delicate questions about the oath of allegiance & who are or are not subjects which had better sleep. At the same time, no Person from the other side could consider his title to land secure or be able to bring a writ of ejectment against another who had got possession of his property.

The very question of who was, or was not, an alien by law was "not perfectly established". It was a question which was fraught with difficulties and which only the British parliament could resolve by enactments clarifying who was, and was not, a British subject.

To John Beverley Robinson, there were three basic questions at issue. In the first place, the question as to whether Americans, who were born in the American colonies before 1783 and who continued to reside in the United States following the recognition of its independence in that year, were to be regarded as aliens despite their British birth. If so, there was no process by which such people could be naturalized in Upper Canada because they were not "born out of the King's allegiance" and could not come under the terms of the Naturalization Act of 1740, which was the only existing naturalization law.

Secondly, there was a question as to whether the recognition by Great Britain of American independence had deprived the former British subjects – the newly-constituted American citizens -- of their British citizenship; and thirdly, a related question concerned the allegiance of their descendants who were born after 1783 in the new American Republic. If American independence did not deprive British subjects of their allegiance to the King, then their children would be British subjects. By law, the children of fathers who were British subjects, although born out of the King's allegiance in a foreign country, took the nationality of their father. Hence, if the American citizens, who were born in the British colonies before the Declaration of Independence, were to continue to be recognized as British subjects, their children who were born in the new United States of America would possess "a double allegiance".

If the former British subjects in the United States remained British subjects in law, and their children possessed a dual allegiance, most American citizens -- those born before 1783 and their children -- could enter Upper Canada with all the rights of British subjects. Yet that was a "monstrous absurdity" as the Americans who had invaded Upper Canada during the War of 1812 were treated as foreign subjects, and were not adjudged to be guilty of treason in rebellion against their Sovereign.

On the other hand, if American independence did absolve all British subjects who were residents of the American colonies in 1783 of their former allegiance, what did that imply for the Loyalists who had fought for the Crown, and who continued to reside in the newly-independent country of the United States of America for a time prior to migrating to Upper Canada. In sum, before the government of Upper Canada could take any action to deal with American aliens, it was essential that the British Parliament act to clearly define by statute who was and was not an alien. Such an act was needed to clarify the status of the Loyalists, and to protect the property titles of the Americans who had settled in Upper Canada prior to the late War. (4)

The Upper Canadian Tories had no desire to disturb the American residents of the province in their property rights, no matter on how questionable a legality they might rest. However, the Tories did not approve of the non-naturalized American aliens possessing the political rights of voting, standing for election to the Assembly, and being eligible for public appointments. As aliens, the non-naturalized American settlers were not entitled to such political rights in law, although they were being exercised by the Americans resident in Upper Canada.

The Rev. John Strachan took the position that the British Parliament ought to repeal the part of the Naturalization Act of 1740 that enabled an alien to become a naturalized British subject after a seven-years' residence. He favoured the passage of legislation by the Imperial Parliament to secure the land titles of the existing American settlers in Upper Canada, but he did not want them to be able to become naturalized and, by so doing, to have the full political rights of British subjects. Presumably, his experience during the war years in viewing the disaffection, sedition, and treason in evidence among the American settlers, and his knowledge of their democratic republican principles, motivated that stance. However, it was not politically feasible to deprive the long-established American alien residents of Upper Canada of the political rights that they were already exercising.

The key political issue was that the opposition members of the Assembly favoured the continuance of the pre-war free movement of Americans into Upper Canada, with the American settlers enjoying the same *de facto* property and political rights as British subjects, to which the provincial government and the leading Tories of the province were adamantly opposed. However, a compromise was reached on political rights. Legislation was enacted by the provincial parliament that provided a legal means for the American aliens settled in Upper Canada to exercise the political rights that were otherwise reserved in law for British subjects and naturalized British subjects. A provincial Act (58 Geo.III, c. 9, 1818), stipulated that any British subject who had been "a bona fide resident" of a foreign country, or who had "taken the oath of allegiance to any other State or Power", would be eligible for election to the House of Assembly if they had resided in the province for seven years prior to that election, and swore the Oath of Allegiance.

The leading Tories did not approve of the presence of American aliens in the House of Assembly. After the election of July 1820, they noted that the Assembly of the Eighth Parliament (1821-1824) presented "a very curious assemblage of foreign importation". What the Tories found to be particularly alarming was the large number of American settlers who had been elected. In the new Assembly, they greatly augmented the strength of the opposition to the 'ministerial side' which was led by the Attorney General, John Beverley Robinson, the member for the York riding.

Earlier, in February 1818, Robinson had been appointed to the position of Attorney General, and in the July 1820 provincial election he had won a seat in the Assembly where he subsequently distinguished himself in drafting, presenting, and carrying government measures. Despite the requirements of the provincial Act of 1818, there were American settlers elected to the House of Assembly who had not sworn the Oath of Allegiance to the King, although they were otherwise qualified by the length of their residency in Upper Canada. Nonetheless, the American aliens were permitted to take their seats, but the Tories were roused to action when an 1821 bye-election brought into the House of Assembly a former American public official of a questionable moral character, Barnabas Bidwell. (5)

The Barnabas Bidwell Election Controversy

The Tories demanded that the election of Bidwell be declared null and void in that he was an "immoral character" who had reputedly embezzled public funds in the United States, and that he was unquestionably an American alien. When freeholders in Lennox and Addington – Bidwell's riding – petitioned against his election on the same grounds, the Tories took their arguments to the floor of the Assembly.

They charged that Bidwell had been charged with misappropriating public funds while serving as a public officer in the State of Massachusetts before fleeing to Upper Canada in 1810; and that, upon taking public office in that state, he had pledged an oath of allegiance to the United States which specifically required him to abjure and *"renounce forever all allegiance to the King of Great Britain"*. Through remaining in the United States after the revolution, and taking an oath of public office, Bidwell had clearly become a citizen of the United States. Moreover, it was believed that since coming into Upper Canada Bidwell had made no attempt to avail himself of the provisions of the Naturalization Act of 1740 to become a naturalized British subject. Thus, he was, and remained, an American citizen – an alien – and, consequently, he was ineligible for election to the House of Assembly.

In seeking to remove Bidwell from the House of Assembly, the Tories cited the Constitutional Act of 1791 (31 Geo. III, c. 31) which stipulated that only natural-born British subjects, subjects acquired by cession or conquest, and subjects naturalized by an act of the British Parliament, could vote and stand for election to the House of Assembly. Whether the American residents of Upper Canada were aliens, or not, was a debatable point in law. However, in the case of Barnabas Bidwell, he was clearly an alien in having abjured his British allegiance, and in failing to renew his British allegiance through complying with the requirements of the Naturalization Act while resident for over a decade in Upper Canada. (6)

In the United States, Bidwell, a lawyer by training and a prominent democratic republican, had served as a Congressman and Senator from Massachusetts, as well as Attorney General of the State, before fleeing to Upper Canada over charges that there were shortcomings in his financial accounts. During his American political career, he was a well-known defender of the policies of President Jefferson, and a pamphleteer who defended the American Revolution, praised the American constitution, and espoused democratic republican values. In effect, he was exactly the type of American immigrant that the Tories wanted to exclude from the government of the Province of Upper Canada.

In his defence before the Assembly, Bidwell argued that he was not guilty of the charge of misappropriating public monies; and that he was a British subject. That he was born in Massachusetts before the American Revolution, took no part in the rebellion, and had continued to be "a natural born subject of England". In addition, he claimed that the oath of allegiance that he had taken in Massachusetts was purely local, and not to the United States of America. Moreover, he maintained that his continued residence in the United States could not absolve him of his natural allegiance as that was perpetual by common law; whereas acquired allegiance adhered to the individual only so long as he remained in that particular country.

Furthermore, Bidwell maintained that the provincial act, 58 Geo. III, c. 9, of 1818, which declared that natural-born British subjects who became residents of other states, and then came into the province, were eligible after seven years to sit in the Assembly, gave him the right to sit in the House of Assembly. In support of Bidwell, it was argued that since the time of Lt. Governor Simcoe, Americans had been permitted to come into the province and upon swearing the Oath of Allegiance to the King, were permitted to acquire property – by grant or purchase – and after seven years were enfranchised regardless of whether they had become naturalized British subjects in "open court' under the terms of the Naturalization Act.

It was maintained by the supporters of Barnabas Bidwell that all Americans born before 1783 in the American colonies were British subjects and, in subsequently migrating to Upper Canada, they were merely renewing their allegiance by returning to a British colony. Thus, they were competent to hold land and were entitled, after a seven-year residence, to stand for election and, if elected, to sit in the Assembly. In effect, they did not have to be naturalized through swearing allegiance to the King under the terms of the Naturalization Act of 1740. These arguments, of course, raised the whole question once again as to who were, and who were not aliens among the American residents of Upper

Canada -- a question which the Tories wanted to avoid pending a clarification by the British Parliament. However, they could not stand by and allow a man whom they were convinced was an alien, and a man guilty of moral turpitude, to sit in the House of Assembly. (7)

While the Bidwell case was being debated in the Assembly, evidence was produced to prove that there were indeed two indictments outstanding in the United States against Barnabas Bidwell. He was charged with misapplying public funds and forging accounts to convert money into his own hands while serving as treasurer of Berkshire County in Massachusetts. Furthermore, a copy was secured of the oath of allegiance which Bidwell had sworn upon accepting office as the Attorney General of the State of Massachusetts. It clearly included, as part of the oath, an abjuring of allegiance to Great Britain. To which a magistrate in Lennox and Addington added an affidavit that in 1812 Bidwell had refused to take the oath of allegiance to the King when first asked to do so and that, when pressed, he had acquiesced in commenting that "he did not consider such an oath binding, as it was compulsory". To the leading Upper Canadian Tories, the evidence was totally damning, but the Assembly members had other concerns.

What loomed over the Bidwell issue was a broader issue which concerned the Loyalist settlers and their representatives in the Assembly. If individuals who resided in the American colonies at the time of Britain's recognition of American independence in 1783 were no longer British subjects, what was the nationality of the Loyalists who did not leave the American colonies until after 1783, and their descendants who were born in the United States prior to the family emigrating to Upper Canada? Were the Loyalists, who arrived in Upper Canada during the period 1784-1794, not British subjects?

At the instigation of Lt. Col. Robert Nichol, a resolution was passed to the effect that immoral conduct or crimes committed outside of Upper Canada were not of themselves grounds for expelling a member. Such conduct could be taken into consideration by the House, but "felony and treason committed in the province" were the only disqualifications by law under the Constitutional Act (chapter XXIII). Then the Assembly declared by a large majority that Barnabas Bidwell was "at the time of his election, a natural born subject of G. Britain"; that by the common law doctrine of allegiance, Bidwell in being born a British subject "could by no act, or choice of his own, divest himself of his allegiance" or be deprived of his birthright by Britain's recognition of American independence. Nonetheless, after denying that there was any legal incapacity that barred Bidwell from sitting, the members proceeded, by a one vote majority, to expel Barnabas Bidwell because of his 'unacceptable moral character'.

In voting the original resolution the Assembly members were acting to reassure the post-1783 Loyalists and the American settlers that they were British subjects and entitled to all the political rights of British subjects. Nonetheless, many members remained convinced that Bidwell was not qualified to sit in the Assembly because of his lax character in having committed a felony, which accounts for the passing of the subsequent vote to expel Barnabas Bidwell on moral grounds. The Tory leaders regretted the narrow margin of decision in the expulsion of Barnabas Bidwell; yet they were elated by "this grand triumph of the cause of correct principle and sound morals".

After having engaged in such a convoluted political manoeuvring to protect the political and property rights of the Late Loyalists and the American settlers, Robert Nichol proceeded to introduce a bill which precluded only a small class of American settlers from sitting in the Assembly. The bill, which was enacted into law, barred from the Assembly all persons who had abjured their British allegiance, or assumed a public office in the United States, or were convicted of a felony in that country. (8)

Under the new law, Barnabas Bidwell was ineligible for election to the Assembly on two of the three of the grounds cited, but for the Tories the exclusion was too narrow. They did not believe that a proper decision had been reached as to the nationality of Bidwell and the other American residents of Upper Canada who were born in the United States prior to 1783 and had neglected to become naturalized British subjects after settling in Upper Canada.

Attorney General Robinson continued to hold that Bidwell, contrary to the expressed opinion of the Assembly, was an alien. He had been born a British subject prior to the American Revolution, but the act of the British parliament recognizing American independence had "absolved from their allegiance all such native Americans as became citizens and subjects of the new government". Robinson maintained that in law:

> Parliament, concurring with the consent of the individual, could dissolve the tie of allegiance with all its relative rights and duties ....

According to the Tories, not only Barnabas Bidwell, but all of the American residents of Upper Canada who had remained in the United States after the Revolution and who -- after emigrating to Canada -- had neglected to be naturalized under the terms of the Naturalization Act of 1740 were aliens. They were ineligible to sit in the Assembly. Hence, for the Tories, the new provincial act did not go far enough in restricting American aliens from sitting in the Assembly. (9)

The Upper Canadian Tories wanted to exclude all resident American aliens from being eligible for election to the House of Assembly. Given the democratic republican principles of the American aliens, and the past utterances and activities of their elected representatives during the war years, they were regarded as posing a real danger to the stability of the province. It was believed that once in control of the Assembly, they would seek to change the Constitution and principles of government to accord with their foreign political, religious, and social values. However, in their determination to exclude American aliens from the Assembly, the Tory leaders neglected to take steps to publicly reassure the Loyalist settlers who had resided for a time in the United States after 1783, that they remained British subjects by their actions in supporting the Crown and the unity of Empire in opposing American independence.

The Marshall Spring Bidwell Election Controversy

While the Upper Canadian Tories were awaiting clarification from the British Parliament as to who was, and was not, a British subject, the alien question took a new turn. Following the expulsion of Barnabas

Bidwell from the Assembly, his son presented himself as a candidate in the bye-election which was called in 1823 to fill the vacant seat. Although Marshall Spring Bidwell was not disqualified from standing for election by the terms of the new provincial act, the returning officer for the riding refused to accept the younger Bidwell as a candidate. His candidacy was refused because he had been born in the United States after 1783 and had not been naturalized during over a decade of residency in Upper Canada. Therefore, he was an alien, and incapable of sitting in the provincial Assembly.

The younger Bidwell admitted that he had not been naturalized since coming to Upper Canada, but maintained that although born in the United States, he was the son of a natural-born British subject. At the time of his birth, his father had not yet accepted any public office in Massachusetts and had not yet abjured his British allegiance. Thus, by common law, he assumed the nationality of his father, and was to all intents and purposes a natural-born British subject.

In response, the Assembly passed several resolutions, which were strongly supported by the members from the ridings where the American settlers were in a majority. The resolutions declared that in the view of the House Marshall Spring Bidwell was eligible for membership and embodied a request that the Imperial Parliament pass legislation to assure the American settlers of "the enjoyment of their rights and properties". The Lt. Governor, Major-General Sir Peregrine Maitland, with the support of the leading Tories, also appealed to the British government for enactments which would secure to the American residents of Upper Canada their property titles, while protecting the security of the province in strictly excluding all aliens from standing for election to the House of Assembly.

The Ruling of the Law Officers of the Crown

For the Tories, there were two distinct legal problems at issue in the Alien question: the property rights of the American aliens, which the Tories were anxious to confirm; and political rights, which the Tories maintained that the American aliens were not entitled to in law. However, the radical leadership in the Assembly continually maintained that property rights and political rights were inseparable. (10)

In November 1824, the law officers of the Crown handed down a decision on a court case in Britain that established a precedent for the Upper Canada situation. In keeping with that precedent, the Law Officers of the Crown advised the British government that the both Bidwells were indeed aliens. The decision of the Law Officers was that all British subjects in the American colonies who remained in that country following the conclusion of the Treaty of Paris (3 September 1783) -- which recognized American Independence -- and took office there, or in general exercised the rights of citizenship of that country, were aliens. Persons born in the United States after 1783, whose parents had ceased to be British subjects, were likewise aliens.

The Law Officers concluded with a general statement that all American colonists who continued to live in the new United States of American after the recognition of American independence, were aliens. Therefore, those who had emigrated later to Upper Canada could legally neither hold land or exercise the franchise, nor run for or be appointed to office, until they had been naturalized by an act of the British Parliament.

The decision of the Law Officers of the Crown settled "the great constitutional question". The Law Officers upheld the contention of the Upper Canadian Tories that American residents of Upper Canada who had neglected to be naturalized, or who had refused to swear allegiance to the King, were aliens, and had no legal claim to being British subjects. It was well known that few of the American settlers had ever sought to avail themselves of the naturalization statute (13 Geo. II, c.7, 1740) to become naturalized British subjects. The question that remained was: what political rights, if any, ought to be bestowed upon these alien residents of Upper Canada? (11)

The Tory Strategic Position

For the Tories, the desire to exclude resident American aliens from the Assembly was not just a constitutional dispute. It involved a whole complex of Tory beliefs and values. The alien question issue struck at the very heart of the Tory 'national policy'. For the broader aims of the national policy to be realized, it was essential that political power and all public offices be retained in the hands of 'the loyal'. If aliens, particularly American citizens, were to attain political power, or at least attain sufficient power to become a political force, then many of the policies necessary to the maintenance of the British national character of the Loyalist Asylum of Upper Canada could be effectively frustrated.

Following on the decision of the Law Officers of the Crown, the Tories continued to be committed to recognizing, in law, the property rights of the American aliens who were resident of Upper Canada, but were not prepared to extend to aliens the political right of standing for election to the House of Assembly. Moreover, the Upper Canadian Tories remained committed to inhibiting any further American emigration into Upper Canada by supporting the provincial government in its refusal to authorize grants of Crown lands to prospective American immigrants.

In the Tory mind, there was a definite distinction between the Loyalists who had emigrated from the United States immediately following the American Revolution, and the Americans settlers who had migrated into Upper Canada to secure cheap land in the period from 1794 – when the District Land Boards were abolished – through to the War of 1812.

The Attorney General, John Beverley Robinson, expressed his belief that the Loyalists who had fought for the Royal cause and the unity of the Empire -- and those who had remained in the United States "due to various circumstances" for several years after the 1783 Treaty before migrating to Upper Canada -- were, and remained, British subjects. In his mind the *bona fide* Loyalists were the persons who had migrated to Upper Canada before the year 1798 – the year laid down by the British Government by which all Loyalists were to present their claims for a land grant – and who had established a public record of the losses that they had sustained in opposing the revolution.

> They could not, upon any principle of law or reason, be considered as having forfeited their allegiance, and lost their consequent rights, by the establishment of American independence, which they had openly, and by all means in their power, resisted at the hazard of their lives.

The American who had settled in Upper Canada in large numbers after 1798 were not Loyalists. They were a different case entirely. In the Tory mind, they were regarded as people who had come into the province for "motives of self-interest". They had emigrated to Upper Canada from the United States to obtain cheap lands, to speculate in land, or because of family connections, rather than from any attachment that they might have felt for the British Crown. Indeed, many were adjudged to have been indifferent to the form of government of the province.

The Tories maintained that the non-Loyalist Americans had not been invited to settle in the province. The Proclamation (February 1792) of Lt. Governor Simcoe had expressly declared that Crown land grants would be given only to men who "could prove their loyalty and good conduct". Nevertheless, before the War of 1812 the provincial government had been lax in admitting non-Loyalist Americans. They were permitted to settle in the province and were given Crown land grants regardless of whether or not they swore the Oath of Allegiance to the King. Moreover, the non-Loyalist Americans, who had neglected or refused to swear the Oath of Allegiance to the King, had been permitted to exercise the political rights of British subjects in Upper Canada, subject only to the seven- year residency requirement. The leading Anglican Tories of the province remained convinced that the non-Loyalist Americans should never have been permitted to settle in Upper Canada and, even after seven year's residence in Upper Canada, those who had neglected or refused to take the Oath of Allegiance to the King, had no right to vote, to stand for election, or to be appointed to public office.

Where the postwar exclusion of prospective American settlers was concerned, Attorney General Robinson pointed out that the Proclamation of Lt. Governor Gore (October 1815) – that had refused the Oath of Allegiance to prospective American settlers and precluded their obtaining land in Upper Canada -- could not have been "legally given or enforced" had the provincial government not been convinced that Americans seeking to enter Upper Canada were aliens. Yet, the arguments which were raised in the Assembly in maintaining the legality of the election of Barnabas Bidwell, created an issue where there was none before. (12)

During the alien question crisis over the election of Barnabas Bidwell and subsequently over the election of his son, Marshall Spring Bidwell, the Tories appealed to the "U.E. Loyalist Spirit" in denying that American aliens should be permitted to sit in the House of Assembly. The Tories re-iterated their belief that Upper Canada was a Loyalist asylum, a secure and safehaven that had been set aside by the British government as a home for Loyalists, whose fathers had sacrificed all they possessed in fighting for the Unity of Empire in "resisting an unnatural and foul rebellion".

Men, "who had committed treason and destroyed the constitution" or had taken an oath to serve the new American government, could not be permitted to sit in the House of Assembly of Upper Canada. It was absurd that American aliens, who were sitting in the House of Assembly, should take it upon themselves to decide whom to admit to the Province of Upper Canada. Motives of loyalty and love of country, as well as common sense, dictated that American aliens must be excluded from the Assembly.

"There was nothing of greater importance" than this question. Aliens, who through treason and rebellion had once subverted the British constitution and had but recently attacked Upper Canada, should not be allowed to enter the country and, after a short period of residence, be permitted to exercise the political rights of British subjects. If so, they might very well indulge "the same treasonable practices" and seek to overthrow the constitution of Upper Canada. Such men as Barnabas Bidwell, regardless of the length of their residency in Upper Canada were not entitled:

> to stand at the helm of State, to hold the scales of justice, and to temper the edge of its sword.

On one level, the Tory response to the election of Barnabas Bidwell was strictly a legal concern which was based on their knowledge of Imperial Acts and the Constitutional Act of 1791, but their reaction also bespoke a deeper fear and broader concern:

> Shall we, who have sought out for ourselves, through wildernesses, with the greatest difficulties and exertion, a new home, after having lost all which we once considered our patrimony – yield up to interlopers an equal claim with

ourselves to the highest offices in our Government? Shall we put poison in the vitals that it may the more speedily spread through the system? (13)

If the British Constitution and the British connection were to be preserved, then Americans could not be permitted to come into the province and play prominent parts in the public life of the country. Their democratic republican principles had brought about the separation of the American colonies from the mother country, and, in time, these men would seek to overturn the constitution of Upper Canada to the same end:

> For how can we expect men born under a Republican government and of republican education and principles to be heartily attached to any monarchical government? How, then can we expect American republicans to make loyal British subjects? Can we with safety trust such men with political power? Their conduct and their language proves already that we cannot.

Not only the maintenance of the constitution and the British national character of Upper Canada was at stake, but the very security of the province. In the event of another war with the United States, men such as Barnabas Bidwell who had taken an oath of allegiance to the United States could not be compelled to bear arms against that country. If he chose not to fight when called upon to do so, the British Government could do nothing but order him to leave the province. To permit such persons to come into the province or, if a resident already, to permit them to occupy important public offices, was dangerous in the extreme.

In sum, the admittance of American aliens to Upper Canada and their enjoyment of the full political rights of British subjects, posed a threat to everything that the Tories hoped to achieve in Upper Canada. The presence of a strong American contingent in the House of Assembly in promoting democratic republicanism would undermine the very national character of the province and the loyalty of its sons. To those who might not understand their strong feelings in that matter, the Upper Canadian Tories could but exclaim:

Unless birthright be secured by some inherent privilege, some peculiar and invisible claim, how can we expect our children to feel with the poet [Sir Walter Scott], who asks:

> Breathes there the man with soul so dead
> Who never to himself hath said,
> 'This is my own, my native land!'

The desire to exclude prospective American immigrants from the province, and to deny full political rights to American aliens who were already residents of the province, was simply aimed at keeping the provincial government in the hands of 'the Loyal'. It was not a matter of Tory self-seeking or of Tory economic self-interest.

Where economic self-interest was concerned, the Upper Canadian Tories and their supporters would have benefitted greatly by aligning themselves with Lt. Col. Robert Nichol in opposition to the effort by the provincial government to preclude Americans from settling in the province. The sale of land to Americans would have spurred economic development, would have greatly increased land prices, and would have enhanced the prosperity of Upper Canada. More directly, it would have directly benefitted the financial wellbeing of the leading Tories, most of whom were large landowners with uncultivated lands to sell. However, the free admission of Americans to Upper Canada would have constituted a travesty, a veritable apostasy, involving the rejection of the cherished principles and beliefs of the Tories.

For the Upper Canadian Tories, it was unacceptable to admit American aliens into Upper Canada in large numbers, and to allow American aliens to attain public office. Their democratic republican beliefs were a threat to the traditional social, religious and political order of the Loyalist asylum of Upper Canada. However, despite memories of the past disaffection and disloyal conduct of American settlers during the War of 1812, the leading Tories were conscious of political realities of the province which necessitated the working out of a compromise with respect to the political rights of the American settlers in Upper Canada. (14)

The Tory Naturalization Bill of 1825

Once the Law Officers of the Crown established that the American residents of Upper Canada, who had neglected to become naturalized in compliance with the terms of Naturalization Act of 1740, were aliens, it was apparent that legislation was needed on the alien question. While in London, John Beverley Robinson tried to convince the Colonial Office that an Imperial Act was required to confirm the property rights and bestow civil rights on the existing American alien residents of Upper Canada, while precluding any further American emigration into the province.

Rather than securing an act of the British parliament, Lord Bathurst communicated Instructions (22 July 1825) to the Lt. Governor of Upper Canada to secure a provincial act to recognize the "civil rights" of the American aliens already settled in Upper Canada. The Legislative Council responded by passing a bill which declared that former residents of the United States who were settled in the province, would be deemed "natural born subjects" to all intents and purposes, within the Province of Upper Canada.

The bill confirmed the American settlers in their property titles and admitted them to the full "Civil Rights of subjects", but it included a proviso to the effect that the act would not supersede any provincial acts which governed the admission of formers residents of the United States to the House of Assembly. Thus, the American residents of Upper Canada were to be naturalized as a group, but individuals among them who were felons, or who had adjured their British allegiance in holding public office in the United States, would still be excluded from the Assembly by the earlier provincial Act of 1823.

The Legislative Council bill reflected the change in policy of the Colonial Office with respect to the granting of political rights to Americans settlers in Upper Canada. However, the Attorney General, John Beverley Robinson, differed from his fellow Tories in objecting to the Legislative Council bill. He did so on strictly constitutional grounds. The Constitutional Act of 1791 (31 Geo. III, c.31) stipulated that only a *"subject naturalized by act of the British Parliament"* could vote or sit in the Assembly, and consequently, a provincial act of naturalization could not confer such political rights on American aliens. A provincial act could not contravene an act of the Imperial Parliament. Hence, Robinson argued that the provincial government would have to request that the Imperial Parliament pass an act to naturalize the American alien residents of Upper Canada.

In sum, as of 1825, the Tories in the Legislative Council and in the House of Assembly were united in holding that the American residents of Upper Canada were "not legally entitled" to political rights unless they were naturalized. However, as expressed by Attorney General Robinson, the Tories were prepared to accept an Imperial naturalization act that would entitle the existing American settlers to "every civil right of British subjects", but with the proviso that any naturalization act passed by the British parliament must not include Americans who might enter the province in the future.

One reason for the willingness of Robinson to acquiesce in the new Colonial Office policy was that he had become convinced that the postwar policy of Lord Bathurst, which excluded prospective American settlers from obtaining land grants in the province, was having the desired effect. The treating of Americans as aliens, and the refusal to let American immigrants take the oath of allegiance, had stopped the flow of American settlers into Upper Canada. Moreover, in the postwar period thousands of disbanded British soldiers and "British subjects of all classes" were now emigrating and settling in Upper Canada each year.

After a decade under the alien exclusion policy, John Beverley Robinson was convinced that there was little "to be apprehended on the score of a predilection for American institutions" on the part of the American settlers who were resident in Upper Canada. The bulk of the population would soon be composed of British immigrants and the Loyalists and their descendants. Moreover, Robinson was convinced that the strong feelings generated by the war among all classes of Upper Canadians, were sufficient to prevent any leaning towards the American form of government, or to the United States itself.

What Robinson failed to consider was that the many of the recent British immigrants were too busy clearing their land, and establishing their farms in a pioneer country, to become immediately involved in politics. In contrast, the bulk of the American settlers who had been settled for upwards of two decades in Upper Canada, had the time and the inclination to become involved in politics. It was their elected representatives who sought, through political machinations in the Assembly, to further their interest in maintaining an open immigration policy that would permit an unlimited American emigration into Upper Canada. Much to the surprise and chagrin of Attorney General Robinson, the naturalization bill of the Legislative Council was denounced in the House of Assembly. (15)

The Radicals and the Alien Question

The opposition to the naturalization bill of the Legislative Council was led by Dr. John Rolph and Marshall Spring Bidwell in the House of Assembly. The election of the younger Bidwell in the 1824 election was of a questionable legality, but the returning officer of the Lennox and Addington riding had allowed the votes cast for Bidwell to be counted. In the Assembly, Rolph charged that the Legislative Council bill was an 'insidious attempt' to disenfranchise the American settlers of Upper Canada – which was a specious claim! To the contrary, the naturalization bill confirmed their right to hold land and enfranchised American aliens – with the sole exception of convicted felons -- who were residents of Upper Canada for seven years. The rhetoric of Rolph was simply an effort to inflame the American aliens in Upper Canada and to strengthen their support for the radicals in the Assembly.

John Rolph (1793-1870) was a man whose political actions belied his origins. He was born in England, and while a youth had begun to study law before emigrating to Upper Canada in 1812 to join his family, who had emigrated just before the war. The Rolph family were staunch Anglican Tories. Upon arrival in Upper Canada, the family became closely associated with Colonel Thomas Talbot, an Anglican Tory of the Anglo-Irish Aristocracy, who held large land holdings on the Lake Erie Front and promoted the settlement of British immigrants in his Talbot Settlement. Two of the Rolph brothers became Anglican priests -- including one of whom studied for the priesthood under the Rev.

John Strachan – and, during the war, young John Rolph had served as a paymaster for the London District militia. However, during a sojourn in England (1818-1821) to study medicine and complete his law studies, John Rolph became imbued with Lockean-liberal political principles and the politics of the British radicals, Cobbett and Hunt.

After returning to Upper Canada, Rolph entered the bar and practiced medicine. In 1824, he was elected to the House of Assembly for Middlesex County, an American-settled area of the London District. Once in the Assembly, he had proceeded to join with Marshall Spring Bidwell in leading opposition members in attacks against government measures which were sponsored by John Beverley Robinson, the Attorney General and member for the Town of York.

Under the leadership of Rolph and the younger Bidwell, the Assembly passed a resolution (30 December 1825) calling for the enacting of a declaratory act by the provincial government to declare that all persons whose fathers or paternal grandfathers were born prior to 1783 in the American colonies were entitled to the full rights of British subjects upon settling in Upper Canada. In effect, Americans immigrants in Upper Canada, and any future American emigrants entering Upper Canada, who were born in the American colonies before 1783 or whose father or grandfather were born in the United States before 1783, were *ipso facto* British subjects. The Assembly resolution was supplemented by the passing of two addresses to the King. One called on the Imperial Parliament to confer the full rights of British subjects upon all residents of the province; and the second address called for an enactment to admit American settlers into the province without conditions.

The Tory supporters in the Assembly might disagree amongst themselves as to whether the existing American residents of Upper Canada ought to be admitted immediately to the full rights of British subjects. However, they could never accept the principle of the proposed declaratory act. Such an act, if passed, would have established the principle that any American who settled in Upper Canada was a British subject because the parents or grandparents had been born British subjects in the American colonies before the Revolution. Moreover, if the King were to grant the appeal conveyed in the second Assembly address to the Crown, it would have permitted a free migration of American settlers into Upper Canada regardless of whether their parents or grandparents were born in the American colonies prior to the Revolution. In effect, all American citizens would be eligible to settle in Upper Canada, to obtain Crown land grants, and to exercise the political rights of British subjects immediately upon their arrival. It was a recipe for the swamping of the Loyalist Asylum of Upper Canada with American democratic republicans.

Despite the best efforts of the Tories of the provincial government to resolve the alien question, and their ultimate willingness to grant the full rights of British subjects to all American aliens who were current residents of Upper Canada, all such efforts were totally rebuffed. It appeared to the Tories that the political radicals in the Assembly were working to keep the contentious issue alive by making demands that the neither the provincial government nor the Imperial Government could accept. (16)

To the further disappointment of the Upper Canadian Tories, the British government declined to pass a naturalization bill for Upper Canada. Instead the Colonial Office confined itself to removing the legal difficulties that, as Attorney General Robinson had pointed out, precluded the local legislature from passing a naturalization bill. A new act of the British Parliament (7 Geo IV, c. 68) amended the Constitutional Act of 1791 to permit persons who were naturalized by the Upper Canadian Legislature to vote, to sit in the assembly, and to be appointed to the Legislative Council.

The Provincial Naturalization Act of March 1827

Before detailed instructions were received from Lord Bathurst -- setting forth the nature of the naturalization bill which the British government was prepared to accept -- John Rolph took advantage of the enabling act of the Imperial Parliament. He introduced into the Assembly a naturalization bill, the "Civil Rights Bill", which declared that all residents of the province were British subjects who did not within six months register their desire to be exempted.

Once the Instructions of Lord Bathurst were received, the Tories in the Assembly proceeded to amend the Rolph bill to bring it into keeping with the wishes of the Colonial Office. Bathurst insisted that the Americans were aliens in law, and that the provincial naturalization act was not to naturalize Americans who might enter the province in future. The provisions of the proposed naturalization act must be confined to the American aliens currently settled in the province.

Where the terms of the provincial naturalization act were concerned, Lord Bathurst was equally explicit. American settlers who had resided in the province for seven years were to be immediately naturalized. More recent American settlers, after a seven years' residence in Upper Canada, were to be eligible to apply to be naturalized, and upon applying would be required to register and to subscribe to an oath abjuring their American citizenship.

The provincial Naturalization Act, which was enacted in March 1827, strictly followed the Instructions provided by the Colonial Office. It naturalized, without conditions, all persons who had resided in the province for seven years as of 26 May 1826, and provided that later arrivals, who were not already British subjects, could apply to become naturalized British subjects after a seven years' residence. (17)

The naturalization bill of March 1827 faced a strong opposition. In the Assembly, the opposition was led by John Rolph who was opposed to any amendment to his 'Civil Rights Bill'. Initially, the naturalization bill, which complied with the Instructions of Lord Bathurst, was defeated by the opposition members in the House of Assembly. Then the same naturalization bill that the radicals had managed to defeat was re-introduced by Rolph and passed by a small majority. It was one thing for the radicals of the Ninth Parliament (1824-1828) to oppose and obstruct any and all government measures in the House of Assembly, but still another to see a bill that would serve the best interests of their constituents go down to defeat by their own hand. Hence, the political machinations of John Rolph.

Once the Naturalization Act of 1827 was in force, John Rolph and his radical supporters proceeded to denounce it out of doors. A 'Central Committee' was established to organize meetings to denounce the provincial naturalization Act, and to gather signatures on a petition calling on the Imperial Parliament to exercise its power of disallowance.

To the Tories, the political manoeuvring of the radical opposition members in the Assembly, under the direction of Dr. John Rolph, was nothing more than "a farce" and an "electioneering clamour" which was aimed at "keeping the agitation open" by playing on the fears of the resident American aliens. Rolph knew that the American residents of Upper Canada were aliens; and that such an act was necessary to secure their property titles and civil rights. Indeed, the Tories concluded that it was the reason that Rolph had rescued the bill from defeat in the House of Assembly. Moreover, Rolph also knew that the British government -- after providing instructions on what the provincial Act was to include – would not turn around and disallow a provincial act that conformed to the Instructions received from Lord Bathurst, the Colonial Secretary.

It was particularly galling to the Tories that the opposition leaders in the Assembly were seeking to mislead the public as to the purpose of the government in passing the Act; and that they were making the "absurd charge" that the provincial Act threatened the settlers of American birth or descent with "the annihilation of their most valued and long enjoyed civil rights". The Tories could only express the hope that the people would see the "glaring inconsistencies' in the conduct of such men and, in doing so, that the American residents of Upper Canada would recognize "their own true interests."

For the Upper Canadian Tories, it was deplorable that the leaders of the opposition would seek "to work upon the passions of the public" in such a manner. Moreover, it was totally reprehensible that irresponsible radical newspapers were supporting the deception which was being practiced by the opposition. The anti-government newspapers were soon seeking to outdo each other in the abuse and invective that they heaped upon the provincial government, with one radical newspaper calling for a total resistance even if it entailed the "shedding of blood". (18)

It appeared that the leaders of the opposition in the Assembly, and the radical newspapers that supported them, would stop at nothing to discredit the provincial government in the eyes of the public. With respect to the terms of the Act, the opposition members claimed that it was "humiliating" and "degrading" for Americans to have to register their names; and that Americans should not be required to adjure their allegiance to the Government of the United States. Such claims received little sympathy from the Upper Canadian Tories. They pointed out that the terms of the provincial Naturalization Act (1827) were much more equitable than in other countries. The American government, by a law passed in 1820, required persons who were seeking to be naturalized to go into open court, to register their names, and to renounce all allegiance to any other government a minimum of two years before being admitted to citizenship.

As viewed by the Tories, the American Government clearly felt that such a procedure was "indispensable to the security, of her adopted children's loyalty", so why, they argued was a similar requirement opposed by the American residents of Upper Canada and their spokesmen? Why was the provincial Act being denounced as "uncalled for or oppressive"? It was true that in English law, the British-born could acquire, through naturalization in another country, a double allegiance, and could not renounce their British allegiance. However, American law recognized such a right to abjure one's allegiance with respect to its own citizens. Indeed, the American naturalization law required the abjuration of allegiance to any other country. Moreover, it implied that anyone who became an American citizen and later withdrew to another country could legally shed his American allegiance.

Since the American law admitted "expatriation", American citizens in Upper Canada could not properly object to taking an oath to abjure their American allegiance and to make them solely British subjects. Moreover, American residents of the province were to be given the full rights of natural-born British subjects. In return, they were only being asked to give their loyalty to the King – "that loyalty which acknowledges one object of attachment." (19)

The vehemence with which the American settlers in the province, and their elected representatives in the House of Assembly, attacked the provincial Naturalization Act, and the arguments that they raise in defence of their own position confirmed the worst fears of the Upper Canadian Tories. Not only did the opponents of the Naturalization Act want the province to be fully open to settlers from the United States, which the Tories believed would result in the province being "inundated with democrats", but the American aliens continued to exhibit a "partiality to a foreign government". If the American settlers truly supported the Constitution of their adopted country, how could they object to an act which bestowed the full rights of citizenship on them?

In such circumstances, the Upper Canadian Tories could not but conclude that those who could not bring themselves to abjure their allegiance to the United States were in truth "wedded to the United States", although residents of Upper Canada. It was believed that in the event of a war with the United States, the American aliens who were resident in Upper Canada would return to that country and proceed to march against "the country in which they had lined their purses". If they would not take such an oath of allegiance, it was best that they be singled out from the loyal before it was too late and, by their own choice, be denied the right to vote and stand for election to the Assembly. The very opinions of these people, as expressed by their representatives in the Assembly, smacked "rather much of an anti-monarchical spirit", and their efforts out of doors were clearly motivated "by Gourlay's principles" – a reference to the agrarian radical, Robert Gourlay, the Scottish immigrant who had generated a public agitation in 1818-1819 by organizing township meetings and calling for a provincial convention 'to radically change the government of Upper Canada'.

Dr. John Rolph, and the other *"promagators of faction"*, were viewed as seeking, by means of their resolutions, their public meetings, and a public petition, to manufacture discontent and discord in the province, and ultimately disaffection. For the Tories, it was a serious political crisis. A "strong excitation" was being aroused in the mind of the public by the prolonging of the alien question, and the misrepresentations which had been practiced by the opponents of the government throughout the whole period of the alien controversy. In the view of one anonymous government supporter, something had to be done to settle the issue quickly:

> to appease those feelings, which already enkindled by the fire of an enthusiasm ardent beyond all precedent, will, I fear, if not speedily extinguished, remit a flame which may consume the very altar of our Country's loyalty. – The golden opportunity for

shaking your attachment to our happy Constitution has arrived; the Demon of political discord is abroad; the demagogue and his emissaries are awake; I witness their exertions – lend an attentive ear to their argument; they are indefatigable; they are omnipresent; 'they go about like roaring lions seeking whom they may devour': and while I can despise the flimsy shallowness of their reasonings, I cannot help dreading the consequences, which may result from *their industry and their influence*.

In such a frame of mind, the Upper Canadian Tories did not welcome what transpired in the Imperial Parliament. (20)

A betrayal in Great Britain

In Britain, the resignation of the Prime Minister, Lord Liverpool, in February 1827 -- for health reasons -- brought the fall of his Tory government. It was succeeded by a coalition 'Canningnite' government which was composed of moderate Tories and several leading Whigs under Prime Minister George Canning. The leading Tories of the Liverpool government, including Lord Bathurst, refused to serve under Canning.

Lord Bathurst was replaced as Secretary of State for War and the Colonies by Lord Goderich, who lacked first-hand knowledge that Lord Bathurst had possessed with respect to the disaffection and disloyal conduct of many of the American settlers in Upper Canada during the War of 1812. Lord Goderich was blithely unaware of the threat that the permitting of an open emigration of Americans into Upper Canada posed to the British national character of the province and the British connection. In sum, Lord Goderich was open to conciliation and anxious to please.

After circulating a petition calling for the disallowance of the provincial Naturalization Act of 1827, the Central Committee of the Upper Canadian radicals chose Robert Randal, a member of the House of Assembly, to carry a petition to the Colonial Office in England.

Randal was a land speculator and entrepreneur from the United States. Prior to arriving in Upper Canada, he was cited for contempt by the

American Congress for attempting to bribe members of Congress to support and participate in a scheme to acquire and open for settlement a vast area of Indian lands in southern Michigan. With the failure of that enterprise, Randal had emigrated to Upper Canada. In 1798, he had obtained from the provincial government the lease of a water power site on the Niagara River where he established an ironworks and -- with the support of several financial backers/silent partners -- purchased a large adjacent property for commercial development. Subsequently, he had established additional enterprises in eastern Upper Canada at Cornwall on the St. Lawrence River and on the American side of the border in New York State. His eastern enterprises comprised a tannery and potash works in New York State, a ferry, and a mercantile house in Cornwall, and Randal became involved as well in the grain export business with partners in Montreal. He also secured a Crown land grant from the provincial government of Upper Canada that comprised a large waterpower site at the Chaudière Falls on the Ottawa River for a proposed second ironworks.

Overly extended and heavily in debt to his Montreal creditors, Randal had been imprisoned for debt in 1809 at Montreal in the Province of Lower Canada, and when released six years later had found that his original partners had secured control of his Niagara properties. Randal then entered upon a long series of court actions in Upper Canada in an unsuccessful effort to recover his share of the properties. For a time, Randal was represented by the acting Solicitor-General Henry John Boulton, the son of a prominent judge of the Court of King's Bench, and by D'Arcy Boulton, an English immigrant Tory. When Randal was unable to pay his substantial legal fees, young Boulton secured a judgement at law against him, and sold the Chaudière property to secure payment, without the consent of Randal.

Frustrated at every turn with the administration of justice, Randal became politicized, and in 1824 stood for election to the Assembly. On the hustings, Randal attacked the administration of justice, denounced government patronage, and became popular among the radicals as 'a martyr who had suffered at the hands of the Tory establishment'. He was elected to the House of Assembly from the 4th riding, Lincoln County, in the Niagara Peninsula.

During the summer of 1827, while in England to present the petition of the radicals, Randal was given a sympathetic hearing by the newly-appointed Colonial Secretary, Lord Goderich, who accepted the radical petition as an expression of the views of the people of Upper Canada. The provincial Naturalization Act of 1827 was disallowed. The Colonial Office took the stand that although it was drafted to meet the Instructions of Lord Bathurst, the former Colonial Secretary, it had not proven acceptable to Upper Canadians.

In yet another respect, the Upper Canadian radicals were fortunate in that the British government did not want to recognize the right to abjure allegiance. That clause of the provincial Naturalization Act of 1827 was directly in conflict with the position that the British government was maintaining in its international relations: viz. that a British subject could not abjure his allegiance. Hence, the Colonial Office did not want the Upper Canadian alien issue to be publicly debated in Parliament by the British radicals who had befriended, and were supporting, Robert Randal during his mission in England.

The disallowance of the provincial Naturalization Act of 1827 was a severe blow to the Upper Canadian Tories. Had the act been allowed to stand, they believed that it would have put an end to the agitation which was being carried on in Upper Canada. The radicals would have had to turn around and to have encouraged the American alien settlers of the province to comply with the act to enable their supporters to be naturalized and enfranchised for the upcoming 1828 provincial election. And, in so doing, the radicals would have undermined their own public denunciations of the Act. However, following the disallowance of the provincial Naturalization Act, Lord Goderich provided Instructions to Lt. Governor, Sir Peregrine Maitland, that set forth what was required in a new provincial naturalization act. The new act was to be in keeping with the supposed views of the people of Upper Canada, as conveyed by Robert Randal.

Subsequently the Lt. Governor and the Legislative Council acquiesced when Marshall Spring Bidwell introduced a bill in the Assembly which carried into effect the Instructions from Lord Goderich. The Tories had little choice but to support the provincial administration in the passing of the bill and its enactment into law. The new Naturalization Act of May 1828 declared that all persons who held Crown land grants, or public office, or had taken the oath of allegiance, or were residents of the province before 1820, were to be admitted to "all the privileges of British birth" with the full enjoyment of all property and civil rights. Those who were domiciled in Upper Canada as of March 1, 1828, but did not qualify otherwise for citizenship, were to receive such rights after a seven years' residence. (21) It was a complete victory for the political radicals and their supporters among the American aliens settled in Upper Canada, and it was a settlement of the alien question that was imposed upon Upper Canada by the Colonial Office.

A Bittersweet Settlement

The Upper Canadian Tories were deeply chagrined at the conduct of the Colonial Office in disallowing an act of the provincial legislature, and in giving credence to the special pleadings of the Upper Canadian radicals. However, there was also a sense of relief that "after infinite pains & perseverance", the issue appeared to be settled at last. Nonetheless, the Tories did not approve of the method of settlement – a simple declaratory act that bestowed citizenship rights upon American aliens who were resident in the province without their having to declare an allegiance to the Crown or to express any commitment to upholding the constitution and laws of the Province of Upper Canada. Moreover, the American settlers would be able to retain their American citizenship. Nonetheless, and most importantly, the Tories were pleased that the laws remained in force that were designed to restrict the future emigration of Americans into Upper Canada through denying grants of Crown lands to aliens.

All in all, the agitation over the alien question had extracted a heavy price in terms of the tranquility of the province. Following the expulsion of agrarian radical, Robert Gourlay, in 1819, the province had reverted to a peaceful and contented state. It was observed that the House of Assembly of the Eighth Parliament (1821-1824), despite having a very large number of 'foreigners' – American alien members -- had been cooperative initially in supporting government measures. However, the subsequent years of fierce debate and public agitation over the alien controversy had completely transformed the political character of the province. Many members of the Assembly had become alienated from the government, and on some issues the opposition in the Assembly had managed to secure a majority to block government initiatives.

A situation had developed which was in keeping with what the Tories had always feared. In sum, the fear that men would emerge to take advantage of any differences which existed between the different branches of the Legislature and, for their own ends, would not scruple to misrepresent the intent and actions of the government to foment discontent among the public against those in authority. In an immature colony, such as Upper Canada, the efforts of demagogues presented a constant danger to the wellbeing of the province, and the efforts of such men were a real threat to the peace and contentment of the province.

From the viewpoint of the Tories, the controversy which had developed over the alien question was most unfortunate. They had not wanted to raise the issue in being convinced that "nothing could be more foolish, impolitic & dangerous as calling the matter up". Once the issue was raised over the election of Barnabas Bidwell to the Assembly, the Tory elite struggled to reach an accommodation with an increasingly hostile radical element in the House of Assembly. The controversy had strained the relations between the different branches of Legislature and provided a means by which the political radicals in the Assembly were enabled to marshal public support in attacking the provincial government of Upper Canada.

With the radicals publicly claiming the credit for protecting the rights of the American settlers, and for resolving the Alien Question, the July 1828 election returned an overwhelming majority of opposition members to the Assembly. It was a situation which boded ill for the Tory effort to implement the National Policy programme, and that promised even more political strife for the future. The ultimate irony was that the Upper Canadian Tories, through their efforts to limit the political influence of the American alien residents in the province and to curtail any future American emigration to Upper Canada, had aroused a powerful antagonistic political force against them. It was a radical political force that rested on a strong support from among the American residents of Upper Canada. Moreover, it was led by British immigrant radicals and non-Loyalist American immigrants who espoused Lockean-liberal principles of government, who employed extra-parliamentary political tactics to foster public discontent, and who looked to the political radicals in Britain and the democratic republicans in the United States for inspiration.

Moreover, the effort of the provincial government to discourage Americans from settling in Upper Canada, by denying them Crown land grants, was soon circumvented. By the late 1820s, Americans were coming into the province and purchasing land in private sales in such numbers as to thoroughly alarm the provincial executive. In purchasing land by private sale, the Americans avoided the need to take the Oath of Allegiance which was required to attain a government land grant. The Colonial Office in Britain came to recognize the political danger and "impolicy" of the immigration situation but declined to take any action. (22)

British Immigrant Radicals

In their desire to preserve the British national character of Upper Canada, the Upper Canadian Tories were concerned not only to prevent the emigration of Americans into the province -- because of their objectionable democratic republican political principles -- but also were concerned about the character of many of the British immigrants settling in the Province.

The Tories were very conscious that they were living in an age of political upheaval and convulsions; and that the traditional order was under attack from the forces of 'anarchy and infidelity'. Hence, they believed that it was essential for the British national character, which sustained the traditional order of things in the Loyalist asylum of Upper Canada, to be maintained against the leveling spirit of the times. The "revolutionary spirit", which was permeating and disordering the mind of man, had to be combated from whatever quarter it threatened the traditional order.

The provincial government was sorely in need of measures to protect itself against foreign agitators because Upper Canada was not immune to 'the spirit of the times'. The Tories observed that:

never was sedition more barefaced -- never was there such a deluge of treason and blasphemy abroad in the world -- ... never was such vigour and skill displayed in the dissemination of licentiousness.

The actions of William Cobbett and Henry Hunt in England, and the Robert Gourlay agitation in Upper Canada, had shown the potential danger that the Province would face from one type of British immigrant – the political radical -- if the provincial government were unable to deal effectively with them.

In viewing the British immigrants arriving in Upper Canada during the first postwar decade, the Tories found little to reassure them that the "torrent of licentiousness, which threatens to destroy all the blessings of good government" in Great Britain, would leave the Province of Upper Canada unscathed:

> The truth is the vast emigration which hath of late years passed into the Province will not contribute much to our tranquility. Many of them have no religion, and more are inimical to regular government. Flying from the ranks of the radicals at home, they come here with increased assurance & think that in a colony they may go [to] greater lengths than they durst at home. (23)

To protect the province against the political intrigues and agitations of British immigrant radicals, the leading Tories wanted to keep in force the Sedition Act of 1804 (44 Geo III, c. 1), which had been enacted to protect the peace of the province against an earlier threat.

In Ireland, the Society of United Irishmen from its founding in 1791, had declared its adherence to the principles of the American and French revolutions, and secretly sought to secure the aid of troops from revolutionary France to spearhead a rebellion against Great Britain. The aim of the United Irishmen was to unite the Protestants and Catholics of Ireland in fighting for the establishment of an independent Irish republic, but that effort had failed when British troops crushed the United Irishmen Rebellion of 1798.

In the aftermath of the Irish rebellion, the provincial government of Upper Canada had become concerned that persons guilty of "treason and sedition" in Ireland might emigrate to Canada to continue their revolutionary political activities within the province. More particularly, it was feared that United Irishmen, who had been involved in the Irish uprising of 1798, were entering the Canadian provinces by way of the United States to stir up disaffection against the British government.

Faced with that earlier perceived threat to the peace of the province, the provincial government had secured the passage of the Sedition Act of 1804 (44 Geo. III, c. 1), and, in retrospect, the Upper Canadian Tories were strong supporters of the Sedition Act. They argued:

> that every political society ought to possess the power of excluding from its limits all strangers who evinced a disposition to excite dissensions and inflame discontents among its respective orders; or, in other words, to disturb the established government thereof.

Governments had a right to protect themselves again usurpers who were bent upon fostering discontent and disorder to facilitate their seizure of political power.

The Sedition Act of 1804 stipulated that upon a complaint being registered, anyone who had not resided in the province for six months, or had failed to take the oath of allegiance, could be called before the Lt. Governor, the Legislative Council, the Executive Council, or a Judge of the Court of King's Bench, "to give an account of himself". If the individual were found guilty of seeking "to alienate the minds of His Majesty's subjects" or of "a seditious intent to disturb the tranquility thereof", a warrant could be issued ordering the individual to leave the province, or the individual could be allowed to remain in the province upon providing a surety for good behaviour.

John Beverley Robinson took the lead in arguing in favour of keeping the Sedition Act of 1804 in force, but the Tories were faced -- after the July 1828 provincial election -- with an Assembly that was dominated by opposition members who supported the radical leaders in demanding that the Act be repealed. In such a situation, the provincial government executive acquiesced, and in 1829 repealed the Sedition Act. In sum,

British radicals and American democrats were henceforth to be free -- upon entering the province -- to preach sedition and foment public unrest through engaging in extra-parliamentary agitations and forming voluntary organizations to influence public opinion against the government and/or its policies. (24)

The Naturalization Act of May 1828 and the repeal of the Sedition Act in 1829, were severe blows to the dual effort of the Upper Canadian Tories to strengthen the British national character of the province, and to maintain peace, order and social harmony within the province. Yet in the settlement of the alien question controversy, the Colonial Office under Lord Goderich had totally undermined the Upper Canadian Tories through opting for a naturalization act in keeping with what the political radicals and their supporters among the American settlers and the land speculators of Upper Canada, wanted. It became evident that the Upper Canadian Tories could not count on the Colonial Office being supportive of efforts to maintain the British national character of the Province of Upper Canada.

Secondly, the implementation of the National Policy was dependent on 'the Loyal' of the province -- the descendants of the Loyalists, the British Tory immigrants, the native-born Tories, and the loyal of the War of 1812 -- retaining control of the provincial government, with a strong representation in the Executive Council. To that end, the leading Upper Canadian Tories were united in wanting to exclude American emigration into Upper Canada until the British national character of Upper Canadians could become firmly established. There was no intention to deprive the existing American settlers of their property. Indeed, the Tories had been anxious that an act of the British parliament be obtained to confirm the property rights of the American aliens who were residents of the province. However, the Tories were opposed on both principle and legal grounds to the resident American aliens exercising the same political rights as British subjects in Upper Canada.

Ultimately, the Upper Canadian Tories realized that some compromise was necessary. They strove to find a moderate position on naturalization that would do justice to the American aliens who were residents of Upper Canada. As of 1827, the Tories were willing to enact legislation to provide for the naturalization of the American aliens who were resident in Upper

Canada and for the security of their property titles, as well as to grant full political rights to resident American aliens after the legal requirement of seven years' residence was attained. However, the Tories continued to seek to prevent a further influx of Americans into the province through supporting the provincial government in its refusal to grant Crown lands to prospective American immigrants.

Despite their best efforts to arrive at a reasonable and judicious settlement of the alien controversy, the Upper Canadian Tories were defeated by the misrepresentations and political machinations of the leading radicals in the House of Assembly and on the hustings. Henceforth, the Tories would have to depend on British immigration to swamp the American settlers who were resident in Upper Canada, and on a hope that the wave of British immigrants entering Upper Canada would include but few radicals.

In Upper Canada, it was the American settlers -- who were imbued with democratic republican ideals -- who provided the strongest electoral support for the radical opposition to the provincial government in the Assembly. Initially, the opposition was spearheaded by Dr. John Rolph, a British immigrant, who employed the extra-parliamentary political tactics of British radicals – political meetings, petitions, and House of Assembly committees -- to foment discontent and disrupt the provincial government during the decade of the 1820s. When the opposition democratic radicals coalesced into a political party – the Reform Party – as of the end of the decade, it was under the leadership of an American immigrant, Marshall Spring Bidwell, who was a Jeffersonian democrat.

As the decade evolved, the support of the American settlers for the democratic radicals was strengthened in the Assembly, and in the press, by the accession of radicals and liberal-whigs from amongst the postwar British immigration into the Province of Upper Canada. However, it was the alien question, and the fears raised by that issue among the non-Loyalist American settlers, and even among some Loyalists, that was responsible for the initial arousing of public support for the political radicals at the hustings and in the House of Assembly where they constituted a vocal opposition to the provincial government and the Tory establishment.

Notes

The Exclusion of Aliens

1. Spragge, *Strachan Letter Book*, 166, Strachan to Col. Harvey 22 June 1818, and 92, Strachan, 'Remarks sent to Sir George Murray', 1815; Robinson, *Letter to Earl Bathurst*, 26 December 1824, 6-7; C.E. Cartwright, ed., *Life and Letters of Richard Cartwright*, 96, Richard Cartwright to General Hunter, 23 August 1799. The quotations are from Strachan to Col. Harvey, 22 June 1818, 166; and Robinson, *Letter to Earl Bathurst*, 26 December 1824, 6, respectively.

2. Doughty, A.G. and Norah Story, *Documents relating to the Constitutional History of Canada 1819-28* (Ottawa: King's Printer, 1935), 1, Gore to Bathurst, 7 April 1817; MTCL, J.B. Robinson, *Speech in Committee on the Bill for Conferring Civil Rights*, 1825, 15; Robinson, *Letter to Earl Bathurst*, 26 December 1824, 6; and Dunham, *Political Unrest*, 73-74. During the war, Lord Bathurst had instructed the Commander-in-Chief, Sir George Prevost, as early as 8 September 1814, to make every effort to prevent Americans from settling in Upper Canada. However, Lt. Governor Gore was clearly acting in response to Instructions received from Lord Bathurst on 10 January 1815. (See Doughty and Story, *Documents*, 1-2, Gore to Bathurst, 7 April 1817.

3. Spragge, *Strachan Letter Book*, 166, Strachan to Col. Harvey, 22 June 1818; J. B. Robinson, *Speech in Committee*, 1825, 16-17; *Kingston Chronicle*, 12 February 1819, [Strachan], "For the Kingston Chronicle"; Doughty and Story, *Documents,* 2, Gore to Bathurst, 7 April 1817; Craig, *Upper Canada*, 114; Aileen Dunham, *Political Unrest in Upper Canada, 1815-1836* (Carleton Library, 1965), 48 & 74; and A. G. Doughty and Duncan A. MacArthur, eds., *Documents relating to the Constitutional History of Canada, 1791-1818* (Ottawa: King's Printer, 1914), 537,"Act respecting the Eligibility of Persons to be returned to the Legislative Assembly", 1 April 1818. The Naturalization Act of 1740 included a separate provision for Jews and Quakers to be naturalized. They were excused from the communion requirement and were administered a modified oath. 'Papists' -- Roman Catholics -- were excluded from becoming naturalized British subjects in the American colonies.

4. Spragge, ed., *Strachan Letter Book*, 166, Strachan to Col. Harvey, 22 June 1818; Doughty and Story, *Documents*, 6-8, "Opinion of the Attorney General [Robinson}, April 1818, and 5, Bathurst to Samuel Smith, 30 November 1817; Craig, *Upper Canada*, 114-115; Dunham, *Political Unrest*, 73-74. The quotation is from Strachan to Col. Harvey, 22 June 1818.

[Samuel Smith (1756-1826) was a member of the Executive Council of Upper Canada, who served as President of the province, from June 1817 to August 1818, during the interregnum between the departure of Lt. Governor Francis Gore and the arrival of the new Lt. Governor, Sir Peregrine Maitland. See DCB, vol. VI, S.R. Mealing, "Smith, Samuel".]

5. Dunham, *Political Unrest*, 74; Spragge, ed., *Strachan Letter Book*, 92, Strachan, "Remarks to Sir George Murray", 1815; Craig, *Upper Canada*, 115, and *Kingston Chronicle*, 29 March 1822, "Communications". See also, PAO, Macaulay Papers, reel 1, Strachan to John Macaulay, 26 June 1820, 15 March 1821 & 18 November 1821, and J.B. Robinson to John Macaulay, 18 November 1821; and PAC, [Francis Collins], *An Abridged View of the Alien Question Unmasked, by the Editor of the Canadian Freeman* (York: Freeman Office, 1826), 3. Strachan in his "Remarks to Sir George Murray', 1815, called for "So much of the 31 repealed as makes a man a citizen in seven years". However, Spragge (*Strachan Letter Book*, 242, footnote 205), points out that Strachan must have meant the 13 Geo. II, c. 7, because the 31 Geo. III, c.31 – the Constitutional Act of 1791 -- does not refer to any length of residence. Hence, the Strachan comment has been corrected in the text.

6. PAO, Macaulay Papers, Reel 1, J.B. Robinson to John Macaulay, 18 November 1821, and Strachan to John Macaulay, 18 November 1821; J.B. Robinson, *Speech in Committee*, 1825, 22-23 & 25; *Kingston Chronicle*, 14 December 1821, "Provincial Parliament of Upper Canada", Speeches by Jonas Jones and the Attorney General [J.B. Robinson], and 22 February 1822, "Provincial Parliament", Speech by Christopher Hagerman.

[Jonas Jones (1791-1848), was a Brockville lawyer, and an independent member of the Assembly. He was a second-generation Loyalist, from a prominent Anglican family in Augusta Township, and a former pupil of the Rev. John Strachan at the Cornwall District Grammar School. Jones had served with the 1St Leeds Militia during the War of 1812. In the Legislature, he was a strong defender of the balanced constitution and the rights of the Assembly, and a proponent of public works. He played a leading role in the prosecution of Robert Gourlay, and the ouster of Barnabas Bidwell from the Assembly. See also, *Dictionary of Canadian Biography Online*, Vol. VII, Robert L. Fraser, "Jones, Jonas".]

7. *Kingston Chronicle*, 14 December 1821, "Provincial Parliament", Speeches by Barnabas Bidwell, John Willson, and the Attorney General [J.B. Robinson], and 22 February 1822, speeches by William W. Baldwin and Christopher Hagerman. See also, Doughty and MacArthur, eds., *Documents*, "Act respecting

Eligibility of Persons to be Returned to the Legislative Assembly" (58 Geo. III, c.9, 1818), 537. [See also, *DCB*, Vol. VI, G.H. Patterson, "Bidwell, Barnabas".]

8. *Kingston Chronicle*, 1 February 1822, "Provincial Parliament", Testimony of Mr. William O'Driscol and of Mr. Williams, the magistrate for Lennox and Addington, and 22 February 1822, Speech by Francis Baby, and 8 February & 22 February 1822, Speeches by Col. Robert Nichol. See also, J.B. Robinson, *Speech in Committee*, 1825, 23; *Kingston Chronicle* (Macaulay editorial), 11 January 1822; and Craig, *Upper Canada*, 116.

9. J.B. Robinson, *Speech in Committee*, 1825, 12 & 24-25; and *Kingston Chronicle*, 22 February 1822, "Provisional Parliament", Speech of Christopher Hagerman. The quotation is from Robinson, *Speech in Committee*, 24.

10. Doughty and Story, eds., *Documents*, 155, "Case of Marshall Spring Bidwell", and 157-159, "Trial of Lennox and Addington Election", 13 February 1823; Robinson, *Speech in Committee*, 1825, 26; *Kingston Chronicle* (Macaulay editorial), 22 February 1822; *U.E. Loyalist* (Robert Stanton editorial), 22 September 1823; and Craig, *Upper Canada*, 117-118.

[One presumes that the insistence by the radicals that property rights and political rights were inseparable was based on their knowledge that it was the property rights issue – fear of losing their farms – that roused the American residents of Upper Canada to political action. Hence, the supposed inseparable linkage of political rights and property rights was used as an excuse by the radicals in the Assembly to thwart Tory efforts to achieve an expeditious settlement of the property issue by itself. In keeping the property issue alive, it enabled the radicals -- on the hustings – to gain support by making the specious claim that the Tories wanted to deprive American residents of their property and political rights. Other than taxes, which were non-existent in Upper Canada, there were few issues that would inflame pioneer settlers sufficiently to overcome their disinterest in government, and their aversion to seeking election to travel to York to sit in the Assembly. However, the fear conjured up by the radicals that the American settlers were going to lose their farms, was one such issue.]

11. Doughty and Story, eds., *Documents*, 234-235, "Opinion of British Law Officers in Bidwell's Case, 13 November 1824; Dunham, *Political Unrest*, 76-77; Robinson, *Speech in Committee*, 1825, 29 & 31-32; *U.E. Loyalist*, "Vindex", 17 March 1827 and "Britannicus" 28 April 1827. A second legal decision was handed down by the Law Officers of the Crown in 1826 to clarify the nationality of the sons of the Loyalists. By this ruling, the children of Loyalists -- who had served with the British forces during the American Revolution -- continued to retain their British citizenship even though they resided in the United States for a time after the recognition of the independence of the United States in 1783.

[It is a rather curious phenomenon that Canadian historians deprecate the Upper Canadian Tories for seeking to deny political rights to the American aliens who were resident in the province without making it clear that in doing so the Tories sought, at the same time, to protect the property rights and the civil liberties of the American settlers who continued to have access to the courts under the rule of law. In viewing the Alien Question, historians ought to put the question in a proper context by mentioning the disaffection and traitorous activities of American settlers during the War of 1812, the refusal of American settlers to become naturalized through taking the Oath of Allegiance to the King, and the treatment meted out earlier by the American revolutionaries in confiscating the property of the Loyalists, in denying the Loyalists their political and civil rights, and in driving them out of the new republic of the United States simply because of their political beliefs in loyalty to the Crown, the balanced British constitution, and the Unity of Empire. Moreover, the Tory argument that Upper Canada was established as a Loyalist Asylum was not something that was "dusted off and appropriated by the Tories" as claimed by some Canadian historians. (See, for example, the interpretation set forth by David Mills, *The Idea of Loyalty in Upper Canada, 1784-1850* (Montreal-Kington: McGill-Queen's University Press, 1988), 34-51, & especially 41-42.]

12. J.B. Robinson, *Speech in Committee*, 1825, 4-7, 11-13 & 53-54; *U.E. Loyalist*, "Vindex", 17 March 1827 and "Britannicus", 28 April 1827; Cartwright, ed., *Life and Letters of Richard Cartwright*, 97, Richard Cartwright to General Hunter, 23 August 1799; Doughty and MacArthur, eds., *Documents*, 194, "35 Geo. III, c.2 (1795)". The quotation is from Robinson, *Speech in Committee*, 1825, 5.

13. *Kingston Chronicle*, "Provincial Parliament", 22 February 1822, Speech of Hagerman, and 14 December 1821, Speech of the Attorney General [J.B. Robinson]; *Kingston Chronicle*, "Communications, 29 March 1822. Both quotes are from "Communications" piece, 29 March 1822. For the terms of the Constitutional Act of 1791 (31 Geo. III, c. 31), which governed eligibility for election to the Assembly, see Adam Shortt and Arthur G. Doughty, *Documents relating to the constitutional history of Canada, 1759-91*, (Ottawa: King's Printer, 1918), 699.

14. *Kingston Chronicle*, "Provincial Parliament", 22 February 1822, Speech of Hagerman; [Collins], *Alien Question*, 1826, 12-13, quoting "Catharus" (from the Kingston Chronicle); and *Kingston Chronicle*, "Communications", 29 March 1822. The quotations are from "Catharus", 13, and "Communications", 29 March 1822, respectively. The verse of Sir Walter Scott quoted in the *Kingston Chronicle* "Communications" column of 29 March is from *The Lay of the Last Minstrel*, Canto Sixth, "Patriotism, Innominatus".

15. *U.E. Loyalist* (Robert Stanton editorial), 22 September 1827; [Collins], *Alien Question*, 1826, 4-8 & 12-14; Robinson, *Speech in Committee*, 1825, 8-14, 42-51 & 55-56; Craig, *Upper Canada*, 116-117; PAO, Robinson Papers, 1823-37, "Draft of letter, J.B. Robinson to Mr. Horton, Under-Secretary, concerning the Naturalization Bill, 6 March 1827, 2-3, and Robinson, *Letter to Earl Bathurst*, 26 December 1824, 6-7. The Legislative Council bill of 1825 is reproduced in the *U.E. Loyalist*, 22 September 1827. Judging by the content of the speeches quoted in the contemporary press, the main protagonists in the alien question debates in the Assembly were the Attorney General (John Beverley Robinson), Jonas Jones, and Christopher Hagerman, who spoke for the provincial government position, and William Warren Baldwin, Col. Robert Nichol, George Hamilton, and John Willson who spoke in support of the Bidwells and the political rights claimed by the American aliens resident in Upper Canada. The Rev. John Strachan took a leading part in forming the views of the Legislative Council.

As of 1824, Robinson felt that the American residents of Upper Canada were "now so insignificant a class" that they no longer threatened to Americanize the country in either its character or its political predilections. However, Francis Collins, who was the editor of the *Canadian Freeman*, a radical newspaper, and an outspoken champion of the American residents, observed that: "the Speaker [John Willson], nearly half the Assembly, and it is thought at least two-thirds of the people are American immigrants" (Collins, *Alien Question*, 1826, 12). The difference in estimates of the population may well be the result of a deliberate effort by the radicals to blur the distinction between Loyalists and the non-Loyalist American settlers. In their arguments, the radicals maintained that if the property and civil rights of the American residents of Upper Canada were to be placed in question, it would affect every settler who came from the United States, including the Loyalists. The confusion engendered by the arguments of the radicals, in linking property and civil rights, as well as the self-interest of several Loyalist land speculators, accounts for the fact that some Loyalists supported the radicals in opposition to the provincial government during the Alien Controversy.

16. *U.E. Loyalist* (Robert Stanton editorial), 22 September 1827; Dunham, *Political Unrest*, 77-78; [Collins], *Alien Question*, 1826, 6-8 & 12-14; Doughty and Story, eds., *Documents*, "Address of the Assembly, Upper Canada", 13 January 1826. [See also, *DCB*, IX, G. M. Craig, "Rolph, John" & VI, H.P. Gundy, "Collins, Francis".]

17. PAO, Macaulay Papers, reel 1, J. B. Robinson to John Macaulay, 25 July 1826; Dunham, *Political Unrest*, 78-79; *U.E. Loyalist*, "Proceedings in Parliament", 9 December 1826. See also *U.E. Loyalist*, speeches of John

Rolph, the Attorney General [J.B. Robinson], Jonas Jones, and M.S. Bidwell, 16 December 1816, "The Naturalization bill as Reported by the Committee", 6 January 1827, the speech of the Attorney General, 27 January 1827, and the division on the naturalization bill vote in the House of Assembly, 10 February 1827. The provincial Naturalization bill of 1827 was based strictly on the Instructions received from Lord Bathurst, which embodied precisely what J.B. Robinson, the Attorney General for Upper Canada had recommended to the Colonial Office. The only exception was the clause, inserted at the insistence of Lord Bathurst, that Americans had to abjure their allegiance to the United States upon taking the Oath of Allegiance to the King.

18. Dunham, *Political Unrest*, 79; *U.E. Loyalist* [Robert Stanton editorials], 27 January 1827, 3 & 10 March 1827, 28 April 1827, 7 July 1827 & 12 January 1828; and *U.E. Loyalist*, "Proceedings in Parliament", speeches by Robert Randall and the Attorney General [J.B. Robinson], 3 February 1827, and by John Johnson Lefferty, 27 January 1827. See also *U.E. Loyalist*: "Stepsure", 5 May 1827, "Vindex", 17 March 1827 & "Britannicus", 28 April 1827.

[John Johnson Lefferty (1777 -1842) was born in the American colonies during the American Revolution and subsequently brought to Upper Canada by his Loyalist family. During the War of 1812, he served as an assistant surgeon of militia, and suffered the loss of his home on Lundy's Lane when it was burnt by the Americans. After the war, he became established as a doctor and apothecary in St. Catharine's, and was elected to the Assembly in 1825. Once in the Assembly, he opposed the provincial government on the alien question. (*DCB*, VII, Peter A. Russell, "Lefferty (Lafferty), John Johnston"). The confusion that the radicals managed to sow in the public mind over the alien question, is well illustrated by Lefferty, who feared that he would be designated an 'alien' for having been born in the United States. Hence, in the Assembly Lefferty supported the radicals on the alien question but was an independent on most other issues.]

19. *U.E. Loyalist*, "Vindex", 17 March 1827 & "To the Anglo Americans", 28 April 1827.

20. *U.E. Loyalist* [Robert Stanton editorial], 13 January 1827, reprint "From the Kingston Chronicle", 21 April 1827 & "Britannicus", 28 April 1827 & "Vindex", 17 March 1827 & "Stepsure", 6 January 1827. The quotation is from "Vindex", 17 March 1827. [On Gourlay, see: S.F. Wise, "Gourlay, Robert Fleming", *DCB*, IX.]

21. Craig, *Upper Canada*, 121-122; Dunham, *Political Unrest*, 79-80; *U.E. Loyalist* (Robert Stanton editorial), 8 September 1827, "Stepsure", 5 May

1827 & "From the York Observer, 15 September 1827; and Doughty and Story, *Documents, 1819-1828,* "Upper Canada Naturalization Act, 1828", 422- 425. [See *DCB,* VI, Paul Romney, "Randal, Robert".]

22. PAO, Robinson Papers, Letterbook 1814-1862, J.B. Robinson to Peter Robinson, 30 April 1828; PAO, Macaulay Papers, reel 1, J.B. Robinson to John Macaulay, 25 July 1826; Dunham, *Political Unrest,* 115 & 82.

In retrospect, nothing was resolved where the Alien Question was concerned. In 1841, the revived Reform Party, in the new House of Assembly under the Union of the Canadas, sought to secure the passage of a new naturalization act. The Reformers wanted an act to declare all aliens who had entered the province before 1828 and neglected to seek naturalization, and those who entered between 1828 and 1841, who were not covered by the previous act, to be entitled to all the rights of British subjects. Once again, the Tories found such a proposal to be totally objectionable. John Macaulay, for one, objected that: "the privilege of being a British subject was held too cheap when it was offered to persons before they said they desire it." See, Charles R. Sanderson, ed., *The Arthur Papers; being the Canadian papers, mainly confidential, private, and demi-official of Sir George Arthur* (Toronto: Toronto Public Library and University of Toronto), vol. III, 442-443, John Macaulay to Sir George Arthur, 9 August 1841.) No doubt, it was similar actions of this nature by the Reformers that contributed to an earlier conclusion by Sir George Arthur, the Lt. Governor of Upper Canada (1838-1839), that the Reformers were "the American party". See Craig, *Upper Canada,* 270.

23. PAO, Macaulay Papers, reel 1, Strachan to John Macaulay, 18 November 1821.

24. Strachan speech, *Kingston Chronicle,* 30 March 1821; Riddell, *The Life of William Dummer Powell,* 114-115; Craig, *Upper Canada,* 98-99; and Richard Cartwright to John Strachan, 17 March 1804, in C. E. Cartwright, *Life and Letters of the late Hon. Richard Cartwright,* 128-130. The quotation is from Cartwright to Strachan, 129. For the Sedition Act, see: Doughty & Story, eds., *Documents, 1819-1828,* 15-18, "An Act for the better securing of the Province against all Sedition attempts or Designs to disturb the tranquility thereof" (44 Geo. IV, c 1, 1804). Strachan stated that the Sedition Act of 1804 had only been invoked once, which was in the expulsion of Robert Gourlay from the province. However, Dunham (*Political Unrest,* 58), states: "So far as we know, it had been applied only twice [before Gourlay], in both cases against Americans during the war"

Chapter Four

A Spiritually-independent Clergy

Support for the National Church Clergy

Procuring Clergymen

Educating a native-born Clergy

Seeking British Government Support

The Religious Duty of the State

Tithes, Government Grants & Endowments

An Independent National Clergy

The Clergy Reserves Strategy

Managing the Clergy Reserves

The Church of Scotland & the Clergy Reserves

Defending the Clergy Reserves

A new Clergy Reserves Corporate Charter

"[The] basis of the church of Christ is not secular but spiritual; it is not to be considered merely a civil institution – an erection or portion of the State; -- nor does it depend upon the breath of Government or upon the enactments of human law. On the contrary, it is an ordnance of God, the place where his honor dwelleth, the appointed instrument for preserving the faith in purity, and dispensing the truths of the Gospel for the instruction and salvation of mankind."

Archdeacon John Strachan, "Address"
The Church, 25 November 1837.

"View of King St., looking E. from Toronto St.", lithography by Thomas Young, 1834, showing the St. James' Anglican Church of the Venerable John Strachan, D.D., Archdeacon of York. The newly-constructed, stone masonry, Neoclassical structure was consecrated in 1833. Subsequently, Anglican churches in Canada were built in what became a characteristic Anglican Gothic Revival style.

Chapter Four

A Spiritually-independent Clergy

To the Upper Canadian Anglican Tories, the best means of evangelizing the province, of maintaining the integrity of the British constitution, and of strengthening the British national character of Upper Canada, was through the ministrations of an effective Established Church. While calling for the extension of the ministrations of the Church of England as part of their National Policy, the Tories strove to retain the clergy reserves endowment solely for the benefit of the Established Church. It was a land endowment that had been bestowed by the Crown with the enacting of the Constitutional Act of 1791 which contained a clause stipulating that $1/7^{th}$ of the land surveyed in each township was to be reserved for the support of "a Protestant Clergy".

Through the leasing of clergy reserve lots, the Anglican Tories hoped to secure a substantial permanent revenue for the National Church – the Church of England – that could be used to finance three objectives: the training of parish priests; the erection of churches and rectories with a priest in each parish; and the provision of a secure income for the clergy to enable the priests to provide spiritual and moral guidance for their parish independent of both the dictates of the state and the whims of the people.

Initially, until the clergy reserves lands could be rendered fully productive, it was held that government ought to provide direct financial assistance to the Anglican clergy because of the very exigencies of the situation. The vast extent of the Province of Upper Canada, and a rapidly expanding pioneer population, placed demands upon the Established Church in ministering to the religious needs of the province that could not be met, in the short term, without government financial aid.

Support for the National Church Clergy

With respect to the clergy reserves endowment, the major problem prior to 1826 was the availability of free grants of Crown land for immigrants which made it difficult to lease the lands set aside for the support of the "a Protestant Clergy". Thus, in the immediate postwar period, a situation existed where an alternative source of financial support needed to be secured to extend the ministrations of the established Church of England. Previously, in the older settled areas of the province, churches had been built by means of voluntary subscriptions, but in the newer areas of settlement, which now required the services of a parish priest, the congregations were yet "to be made" amongst a population of new arrivals that was "in general too indifferent to give much and in many cases ... too poor."

Immediately after the War, the British government had provided £800 for constructing churches, but that sum had proved to be totally inadequate for constructing even a single large church. The construction of "a decent church" and a parsonage could cost as much as £1500 and £800, respectively. Not only was substantially more support required for building purposes, but salaries needed to be increased. The existing government allowance of £100 per annum for a Church of England clergyman, even when supplemented by the £50 which was provided by the Society for the Propagation of the Gospel in Foreign Parts was held to be too small a salary. It did not provide an income sufficient "to enable a Clergyman to maintain that respectable situation in society which is essential to his usefulness". In Upper Canada, a common servant received "more than half that sum".

The Colonial Office was advised that the British government ought to double the salary that it provided for clergymen of the Established Church, as should the Society for the Propagation of the Gospel, to provide clergymen with a total income of £300 per annum. It was pointed out that the value of money had depreciated three or four time since the S.P.G. began providing salaries for colonial clergy in 1701. However, the securing of adequate salaries for the Church of England clergy was not the only objective where the National Church was concerned.

Procuring Clergymen

If the Church of England were going to exercise a proper influence upon the moral, religious and political character of the Province of Upper Canada, it was essential that "effective men" be procured to preach 'the Word'. As the Rev. John Strachan explained:

> Everything ... will depend on the patronage, and the pure and right exercise of it; for unless they get ministers who will attract and influence the great mass of the people, the object of these Churches will be altogether frustrated. (1)

Prior to the war, it had been extremely difficult to secure clergymen. England was the only source of supply, and clergymen were loath to venture to Upper Canada in view of "the character it had obtained from exaggerated descriptions of the cold, sterility of the soil, and general wretchedness of the inhabitants". For years, the Church of England had laboured to increase the number of clergymen in the diocese, but progress had been disappointedly slow in view of the magnitude of the task at hand. From a single clergyman, the Rev. Dr. John Stuart of Kingston in the early days of Loyalist settlement, the number of Anglican clergymen had grown to three in 1800, six in 1812, seven by 1815, and finally ten in 1819, with a further increase of two ministers being realized during that same year. In such circumstances, Upper Canada did not, and could not, experience "the advantage of an established church", and the province was left open to the inroads by "sectaries of all descriptions". It was a lamentable situation that had long been a subject of complaint on the part of the Upper Canadian Anglican Tories.

Educating a native-born Clergy

Even before the creation of the Province of Upper Canada in 1791, there were Anglican Loyalists who had appealed to the British government to establish clergymen and schools in the various areas of new settlement. The appeal was based on a fear that "if decent, orderly Men were not soon sent, Methodists and other Enthusiasts", who were imbued with principles and sentiments formed in "the Republican States of America", would soon overrun the Province. Of necessity, the Anglican clergy in Upper Canada had taken on the responsibility for educating young men who were candidates for entry into the priesthood. Over time, that necessity would develop into a decided preference for educating young Upper Canadian candidates for the clergy, in preference to clergymen emigrating from England.

After the War, with the state of the province improving and the negative misconceptions about the province being exposed through travelogues published by visitors to the province, more clergymen were expected to emigrate from Britain than in the past. The Anglican Tories welcomed the aid of clergymen who were willing to emigrate from Britain, but nonetheless were committed to educating a native clergy from among the sons of the Loyalists and the British immigrants. It was the District Grammar Schools that were counted on to provide candidates for the priesthood. Prior to the War, the Cornwall District Grammar School of the Rev. John Strachan, had succeeded in producing educated young men who were capable of undertaking divinity studies for entry into that "respectable Profession". Moreover, as of 1815, there were already three young men, graduates of the Cornwall school, who were preparing for Holy Orders through studying divinity under his tutelage.

In the view of the Upper Canadian Tories, a native-born clergy was preferable to a clergy imported from England. As Richard Cartwright explained just prior to the War:

> the State of Society & the Habits & Manners of the people there are so different from what they are here that English Clergymen are not likely to assimilate very happily with those whom they come to instruct; and this Point is the more worthy of Attention as the Congregation is to be formed chiefly from those who are not professed Members of the Church; and the Success of the Clergyman in the Object of his mission will depend very much on his personal Influence & Conciliatory Manners; ....

and furthermore,

> if brought up and educated in this Province, the clergy will be more useful among the people, and [will be] more happy themselves; and care may be taken that they be equally Loyal, and attached to the Mother Country.

The situation in Upper Canada demanded a missionary effort on the part of the Church clergy and would put demands upon them that were best met by natives of the province. If the people were to be "gradually [brought] into Order", it would have to be through ministers preaching 'the Word' throughout the province to awaken "a religious spirit". Moreover, the clergy would have to avoid giving offense to "even ... unreasonable prejudices" in all things where the essentials of religion were not concerned. For that task, native Upper Canadians were held to be far better suited than English clergymen and, particularly so, as even under the best of circumstances "few men of ability" would likely choose to emigrate to the colony from the Mother Country. (2)

In seeking to educate a native clergy, the Church of England in Upper Canada was faced with the problem of securing financial support for the maintenance of divinity students. Richard Cartwright, for one, was confident that if sufficient funding could be secured for the support of clerical candidates, "there [was] little Doubt but the required number of useful Clergymen would, in a few years be provided in the Province itself".

As early as 1812, Cartwright noted that "some very promising [young] men" were graduating from the District Grammar Schools who were intent upon entering the clerical profession, but they were being deterred by the expense that was involved in pursuing such a career. Clerical candidates could not be ordained until they reached the age of twenty-three; whereas other professions could be commenced at the age of twenty-one. That situation placed an extra financial burden upon the families of clerical candidates which, in most cases, their families could not afford to bear.

Although the Rev. John Strachan was willing to undertake the education of clerical candidates free of charge, it was estimated that the mere maintenance of a boarding student would cost £50 each year over a four-year course of study. In the absence of college foundations, such as existed in England for the education of Anglican clergy, it was hoped that revenues from the lease of clergy reserve lots might be applied in part for the support of theology students. However, the clergy reserves land endowment was largely unproductive during the pre-war years, which forced the Rev. Strachan to adopt several different approaches to acquire financial support for the education of divinity students.

An approach to wealthy individuals of his acquaintance in England gained some monies, and an appeal to the Society for the Propagation of the Gospel was successful when in 1815 the Society agreed to grant £200 per annum for the education of four divinity students. However, the money received was not sufficient to meet the religious needs of the province, and the grant did not involve any long-term funding commitment. The S.P.G. grant was limited to four years on the assumption that the provincial legislature -- "in a short time" -- would provide support for the education of clerical students of the Established Church.

An appeal was made also to the provincial Legislature for a government grant for the support of the education of clerical candidates. The grant was solicited in presenting the argument that the province was suffering from a dearth of clergymen; and that if the young men of the province were not enabled to come forward to that "honourable profession", it would be "given to Strangers". During the 1816 and 1817 sessions of the Legislature, an effort was made to secure an appropriation of £500 per year, for a period of ten years, in support of the education of divinity students. In both years, the bill passed the Assembly, which was comprised of representatives of the Loyalist settlers, but was rejected by the Legislative Council, which was dominated by Scots immigrant merchants and land speculators. That rejection forced the established Church of England to depend upon the efforts of individual ministers to educate candidates for the ministry.

In responding to what he regarded as a neglect of their duty on the part of the members of the Legislative Council, the Rev. Strachan sought to convince the Lt. Governor to alter its composition by appointing Churchmen to that body. That objective was accomplished in 1820 when the new Lt. Governor, Sir Peregrine Maitland, appointed four Churchmen, inclusive of the Rev. John Strachan, to the Legislative Council to better protect and promote the interests of the Established Church. (3)

Seeking British Government Support

Where the ordained clergy of the Church of England were concerned, the Rev. Strachan called upon the British government as a matter of "national policy" to increase their allotted stipend from £100 to £200 per annum. However, that appeal was but part of a much more extensive plan, which was to secure additional financial grants to support a major increase in the number of the Church of England clergy in Upper Canada.

Given that the Imperial government was already expending £700,000 per annum to maintain the civil and military establishments in Canada, the Rev. Strachan maintained that the Colonial Office should not begrudge granting a sum of some £40,000 per year – "scarcely the expense of a single regiment" – to promote the extension of the Established Church. In his view:

> Were two or three hundred Clergymen ... living in the Canadas amidst their Congregations and paid through the munificent arrangements of the British Government, they would infuse into the population a tone and feeling entirely English and acquiring by degrees the direction of Education, which the Clergy at home have always possessed, the very first feelings and opinions of the youth would be British.

The active support of the British government was essential to the success of the religious plans of the Upper Canadian Tories, and, for that matter, to the implementation of their entire National Policy of the postwar years. In appealing to the British government for financial support for the Anglican clergy, the Rev. John Strachan sought to convince the Colonial Office of his belief that "the attachment of the Colonies to the Metropolis depends infinitely more upon moral and religious feelings, than political arrangement, or even commercial advantage". Nonetheless, underlying his arguments as to the benefits which financial aid to the Upper Canadian clergy would yield for the Imperial Government was a deeper concern for the welfare of the people of the province and a strong consciousness of the Christian duty of the State. (4)

Since the Upper Canadian Tories believed that all government was ordained by God, and subject to His moral law, to their minds "the sovereign Power of the state" could not be indifferent to "religious truth". Nor could the state be indifferent to the securing of religious instruction for its subjects any more than it could choose to neglect their education by denying public support for the establishment of a provincial school system.

The Religious Duty of the State

In any well-ordered state, the government had a duty to support the Christian Church, which in Great Britain and the colonies was the established Church of England. Indeed, the Rev. Strachan was adamant in asserting that:

> it is the bounden duty of Rulers to support the true Religion, and bring the benefits and ministrations within the reach of all their population.

Not only were the best interests of religion to be realized by bringing religious truth, and hence salvation, to a greater number of souls than would otherwise be possible, but the best interests of society itself required that the state fulfill its duty toward the National Church. The provision of "an adequate and permanent maintenance" for the establishment of religion was the best means of fostering and sustaining a proper moral character among the people, and of securing thereby "the peace, and happiness of society". Indeed, it was held that the balance between liberty and authority depended ultimately upon religion.

In the absence of religious values and beliefs, and the restraint which they placed upon the individual both in government and society, neither life nor property would be secure. It was argued that the "due administration of public justice" and social peace "depend upon the religious obligation which the mind attaches to an oath". For the Tories, the Christian religion was responsible for such social order as man possessed, and for the freedom that grew out of that order as:

> it is clear, that whatever degree of rational and substantial freedom we at this moment enjoy, is to be traced to the influence of pure and undefiled Religion – we are free only in proportion as we are holy. The Church of Christ is therefore the parent of civil and religious liberty.

The Established Church was an integral part of the British Constitution as it had evolved under God's permissive providence; and the British government was admonished not to compromise the integrity of the constitution and the welfare of the colonists by denying the National Church support for her ministrations in Upper Canada. (5)

Tithes, Government Grants & Endowments

In the pre-war period, efforts had been made to secure effective aid from the British government for the support of the Church of England in Upper Canada, but with indifferent results. There were three traditional means of support for a national Church – the legal enforcement of tithes, direct government grants, and the bestowal of land endowments – and they had been found to be impracticable, unreliable, and unproductive, respectively.

In Britain, the right of the state to enforce the payment of tithes upon all British subjects -- for the support of the Established Church -- was well established, whether the residents of a parish were members of the national church or not, but that was not the case in Upper Canada.

In the Canadas, the British government had accepted the legality of tithes which the Church of England was receiving from two parishes in Lower Canada, and the Quebec Act of 1774 had recognized the right of the Roman Catholic Church to collect tithes from its adherents in the former Province of Quebec. Nonetheless, efforts by Bishop Mountain of the Diocese of Quebec to enforce the right of tithe in Upper Canada, following the founding of that province, had been discouraged by Lt. Governor Simcoe. He had maintained that as American settlers were unaccustomed to such levies, the enforcing of tithes would be neither "useful to the Clergy or palatable to the People". It would be a "most dangerous" resort. However, in the postwar period the Upper Canadian Tories had no intention of attempting to enforce a right of tithe. They were convinced that the clergy reserves land endowment – one-seventh of the land in each township survey -- was "evidently given as a full equivalent". (6)

With respect to direct government aid, the government of the former Province of Quebec had contributed financial support to the Anglican clergy. In 1789, the Rev. John Stuart of Kingston was granted a salary of £100 per annum and, as of 1813, the provincial revenues of Upper Canada were providing financial support for six clergymen of the Church of England. Yet, that source of financial support had proved unreliable after the War.

During the postwar depression, when the Crown revenues were insufficient to meet the cost of the civil establishment, the Legislature was called upon to vote monies to supplement the Crown revenues. The House of Assembly of 1820 -- which for the first time included a large contingent of representatives from among the pre-war, non-Loyalist American settlers -- had responded by cutting specific items from the civil list and had refused to vote monies for clerical salaries. In doing so, the Assembly maintained that the clergymen should be supported by the Clergy Reserves. Indeed, a year earlier, Robert Gourlay – the political agitator -- had criticized the payment of clerical salaries as an abuse of public money. However, the problem for the Tories was that the clergy reserves lands that were under lease were yielding little income for the benefit of the clergy.

In the changed postwar political environment, it became clear that the Established Church, if it were to be placed upon "a more respectable footing" in Upper Canada, could not rely upon the provincial government for support. It was evident that little aid would be forthcoming from the Legislature wherein the House of Assembly was coming under the domination of the pre-war, non-Loyalist American settlers.

Fortunately, the British government had taken it upon itself to pay, through grants to the Society for the Propagation of the Gospel in Foreign Parts, the salaries of clergymen of the Church of England in the colonies. On his part, the Rev. Strachan called on the British government to augment considerably the salaries paid to the clergy through the SPG and had requested that the British government increase its support to provide salary grants sufficient to support at least 200 clergy in the Province. However, government grants were not regarded as the best means of ensuring the welfare of the Established Church. Even if the requested increase were granted, which it was not, reliance could not be placed upon the British government as a long-term source of income for the Anglican clergy of Upper Canada. (7)

An Independent National Clergy

The Upper Canadian Tories were concerned about the danger of the Established Church of Upper Canada becoming dependent upon the provincial government for financial grants which might be curtailed at any time, and upon British government grants to the SPG for colonial clerical salaries which were dependent on an annual vote in Parliament in Britain. However, there was also a much deeper concern for the spiritual independence of the Church, which was based on the Anglican concept of the Church: viz.

> the basis of the church of Christ is not secular but spiritual; it is not to be considered merely a civil institution -- an erection or portion of the State; -- nor does it depend upon the breath

of Government or upon the enactments of human law. On the contrary, it is an ordinance of God, the place where his honor dwelleth, -- the appointed instrument for preserving the faith in purity and dispensing the truths of the Gospel for the instruction and salvation of mankind.

Although the Established Church enjoyed state support in one form or another, it was deemed essential that the Church maintain its independence of the state in all matters spiritual. In the Tory view, the critical problem was the need to maintain a balance between the political and the religious establishments in a situation wherein state and church were mutually supportive, while avoiding either an Erastian system (in which the state would dominate the National Church) or a theocracy (in which the National Church would dominate the state). To the Anglican Tory mind, the best means of securing the spiritual independence of the Church, free from dictation by the state and from a dependence upon the whims of the people, was through the establishment of a vested corporate right of the Established Church in landed property. Land grants which were made by the Crown, such as the Clergy Reserves, once safely vested in the Church as a corporation, were held to be a secure source of income as inviolable as private property.

While the clergy reserves land endowment remained unproductive, a reliance upon voluntary offerings from the people was adjudged to be "too precarious". Even under the best of circumstances, it was likely to cultivate a dependence totally "inconsistent with the respectability and independence of the Clergy". Hence, the Tories were forced -- despite misgivings -- to call upon the British government for financial support. (8)

The Upper Canadian Tories realized that they would have to rely upon the British government, almost exclusively "at the beginning", if the religious component of their National Policy were to be realized. Moreover, the ultimate success of a strategy of religious comprehension, as well as the circumstances which prevailed in the Province of Upper Canada, precluded a turning to the people for support, even if there had been a desire to do so. In seeking to extend the ministrations of the Established Church, the Anglican Tories were convinced that:

> Not much Aid or Co-operation is to be expected on the Part of the people, a large majority of whom are of persuasions different from the established Church: and they will become Members of it only in the Event of its growing up without their being called upon for any pecuniary Assistance.

The fear was that if the people were in any way required to provide support for a minister, they would insist that it be one of their own denomination which would defeat the whole scheme of religious comprehension. On the other hand, if financial support were to be provided for the Anglican clergy by the British government, the Tories were confident that:

> When a sufficient Number of respectable Clergymen shall be established through the Country much will undoubtedly be done by their means. Many will resort to them rather than be at the Expense of supporting other religious Teachers; and the rising Generation may, for the most Part, become gradually to be Members of the Church. (7)

Despite an initial dependence on financial support from the British government, the ultimate aim was to make use of the revenues from the leasing of clergy reserves lots to erect and endow parsonages and rectories, and to pay clerical salaries, while maintaining the spiritual independence of the clergy. The hope was that the leasing of the clergy reserve lots in the new areas of settlement would provide a secure source of revenue, independent of both the state and the people, which would increase continually to keep pace with the growing needs of the Church.

The Clergy Reserves Strategy

Before parishes could be formed, and ministers presented to endowed parsonages and rectories, two difficulties had to be surmounted. On the one hand, to avoid 'embarrassment and alarm', political action was needed to assure the population that the induction of clergymen into parishes would not be followed by any attempt to enforce tithes upon the residents of the parishes; and, on the other hand, there was a management problem that needed to be addressed if the clergy reserves land endowment was to be rendered productive.

Until the clergy reserve lots could be leased profitably, they would not yield a sufficient income to support the endowment of a parsonage or rectory. Thus, it was essential that the reserve lots, which were already leased, be rendered productive through better management. Otherwise, the endowment of parsonages and rectories would have to be delayed until the price of land increased to the point where the clergy reserve lots could be readily leased for revenue purposes.

While the Crown continued to grant land "for nothing" in fee simple – which was the situation prior to 1826 -- there was, and would be, little demand for clergy reserves leases outside of the older settled areas; however, it was expected that:

> as the settlements extend, they will be more sought after, and become productive; so that, in a few years, there is every reason to believe, that they will yield enough to maintain a considerable number of clergymen.

Such was the clerical support strategy that the Upper Canadian Tories evolved, under the leadership of the Rev. John Strachan, to meet the peculiar circumstances of the Established Church in Upper Canada. It was a strategy which they would struggle to implement in defending the clergy reserves land endowment in the decades after the War of 1812. (10)

To remove any apprehension felt by Upper Canadians that the establishment of rectories might be followed by efforts to enforce the tithe, the Rev. John Strachan was instrumental in having the provincial Legislature pass a declaratory act to the effect that the right of tithes would have no standing in law in Upper Canada. As explained by the Rev. Strachan:

> This is giving up nothing and sets the question at rest for ever, and it became the more expedient for 'till it was settled we could not proceed a single step.

The first bill passed the provincial Legislature and was reserved by the Lt. Governor for the decision of the Crown. However, it languished in Britain. Another bill to the same effect was passed in 1821 and, after receiving the royal assent, became law in February 1823. The Tithe Declaratory Act stated that:

> Whereas, notwithstanding, his majesty had been graciously pleased to reserve, for the support of a Protestant Clergy in this province, one-seventh of all lands granted therein, doubts have been suggested that the Tithe of the produce of the land might still be legally demanded ...by the Rector of any parish ....; Be it enacted ... that no Tithes shall be claimed demanded, or received, by any Ecclesiastical Parson, Rector or Vicar, of the Protestant Church within this province, any law, custom, or usage, to the contrary notwithstanding.

To the Tories, this act was very important. It cleared the way for the institution of parsonages and rectories by allaying any possible grounds for concern or fear, and hence opposition, on the part of non-Anglicans that they would be forced to pay the tithe. It had also the additional merit of being yet another public recognition on the part of the provincial legislature of the exclusive right of the Church of England to the Clergy Reserves. The very wording of the act, in the Tory view, made it perfectly clear that the provincial government recognized that the clergy reserves lands had been set aside for the support of the Church of England in lieu of its traditional right of tithes. The whole question regarding the legality of tithes in Upper Canada appeared to be thus resolved. However, maintaining the exclusive claim of the Church of England to the clergy reserves endowment would prove to be much more difficult. (11)

The Upper Canadian Tories were aware that the principal potential difficulty that they faced was inherent in the phrase "for the support and maintenance of a Protestant clergy" which was used in the Constitutional Act (clause xxxvi) in referencing the purpose of the clergy reserves land endowment. Nevertheless, they felt confident that there was no validity to the argument – which had been put forward in the House of Assembly -- that in appropriating the Clergy Reserves for the support of 'a Protestant Clergy', the framers of the Constitutional Act had intended the phrase to comprehend 'all the denominations tolerated in Great Britain'. To the Tories, it was perfectly clear that the term 'Protestant Clergy' was used in contradistinction to the Roman Catholic Clergy, and that the phrase referred exclusively to the ministers of the Church of England. (12)

Managing the Clergy Reserves

Initially, what troubled the Upper Canadian Anglican Tories -- and the Rev. John Strachan in particular -- was the fact that under the management of the Executive Council, few of the clergy reserve lots were leased during the immediate postwar years. Moreover, the arrears of rent, which were owed on the existing leased properties, had grown quite large. In the two-year period ending in 1814, only six leases were taken out; whereas there were 450 leases granted two years earlier. Moreover, the rents that were received totaled only £570 over that two-year period, and the amount of the arrears on the rents rose from £1406 to £2465. In 1818, the Rev. Strachan calculated that the clergy reserve leases should have been yielding £730 annually, "if strictly enforced", for the support of the Church of England clergy. He also discovered that there were applications on hand for more leases which, if taken out, would have yielded an additional £450 per annum. However, the Executive Council was failing to address the problem.

Although the Executive Council was aware of the problem of rent arrears and had realized the need to call defaulters to account, its efforts to do so had been only half-hearted in the face of several problems. There was a difficulty in securing the payment of rents because of a scarcity of money in frontier communities, and the great distances that the sheriffs had to go to collect rents which in individual cases amounted to very little. Moreover, potential applicants for new leases were discouraged by the great expense and loss of time which was involved in having to go to York to petition the Executive Council for a lease, and the delays involved in waiting for leases to be granted. To the Tories, the solution to the problem was to vest the administration of the clergy reserve lands in the hands of a corporation to be tasked with leasing the reserve lots and collecting the rents. (13)

In response, a plan was developed by the Rev. John Strachan. The administration of the Clergy Reserves was to be improved by appointing local agents to process applications for leases under the direction of a corporation which was to be located at York, and better communications were to be developed to facilitate the co-operation of the local agents and the sheriffs in carrying out the directives of the corporation.

The corporation itself was to be placed under the direction of the Lt. Governor and Executive Council. It was felt that the corporation should be composed of both clergy and laity to bring their different qualities to bear. On the one hand, the clergy was vitally interested in the management of the clergy reserves endowment, but they were "too much separated" to attend effectively of themselves to the business of the running the corporation. On the other hand, a lay body, in receiving no remuneration and no ultimate benefit from the income of the leased reserve lots, would not attend to their administration as diligently as the clergy.

Hence, the legislation, as drawn up by John Beverley Robinson, provided for a corporation to be established at York to superintend the Clergy Reserves. The members were to comprise the Lord Bishop of Quebec, the Church of England clergy resident in the province, and the Inspector General and the Surveyor General of the province. The corporation was to be empowered to enact bye laws to manage the Clergy Reserves, to collect rents from the leased lots, and to appoint local agents in each district who were to receive applications for leasing the reserves lots. Furthermore, the corporation was to deliver -- after deducting operating expenses -- all revenues to the Receiver General of the province, and to open its accounts for an annual inspection by the Lt. Governor. The clergy corporation itself, in its superintendence of the reserves endowment, was to be subject to whatever instructions the Lt. Governor "with the advice of the Executive Council", should lay down for its direction. In effect, a system of administration was to be established which was closely tied to the provincial government executive, but which had a large clerical input, and combined a high degree of centralized authority and direction with the benefit of a local administration in close contact with the people. (14)

Once the requested Clergy Reserves Corporation Charter was granted by the Crown in 1819, the members of the board were duly appointed. One of the members of the board was the Rev. John Strachan, who served as the Chairman and spokesman for the corporation in the Executive Council. In the beginning, the principal concern was to improve the administration of the Clergy Reserves. Delays were to be eliminated through processing lease applications in each district rather than at York, and leases that had been granted for lots that remained unoccupied were to be revoked, "after giving reasonable notice". Other objectives were to increase the rents to a more reasonable level, and to fix the leases for a period of twenty-one years with lessees to be assured that they would be given the right of first refusal upon the renewal of their lease.

At the first two meetings of the Clergy Reserves Corporation (March & April 1820), steps were taken to implement that policy. Records were examined, and the clergymen of the Established Church were appointed as the local agents of the Board. They were to handle the local applications for leases, to make sure that the applicants took the Oath of Allegiance, and to collect the fee which the provincial government demanded for completing the transaction. The sheriffs were instructed to advise defaulters that if arrears of rent were not paid up within six months, "steps would be taken to compel payment".

With the establishment of the Clergy Reserves Corporation, it seemed that the clergy reserves land endowment would finally realize its purpose. The Rev. Strachan was confident that initially the lease payments, which were now to be regularly collected, would enable at least four clergymen to be supported, as well as an additional £200 or £300 to be appropriated towards the erection of churches and parsonages. The expected increase in income thereafter, even on the grounds of "the most sober calculations", was expected to furnish sufficient funds in total to provide the salary for an additional clergyman every one or two years in Upper Canada. Moreover, Strachan calculated that eventually, once all the clergy reserve lots were leased in each township, it would bring in £1225 per annum which, after the expenses of administration were deducted, "would yield a decent provision for several clergymen" in each township.

In sum, with better management, the Clergy Reserves would yield enough monies to permit the gradual erection of parsonages and rectories with a sufficient income for the support of additional clergymen to look after the religious needs of a growing population. It was a process by which the Established Church could extend its ministrations throughout the Province of Upper Canada, while retaining its spiritual independence from both the whims of the people and the dictates of the state. (15)

Despite such high hopes on the part of the Anglican Tories that a better system of management would render the Clergy Reserves productive, the first year of administration by the Clergy Reserves Corporation brought only disappointments and frustrations. The Corporation realized only £150 from the rent of existing leases in 1821, and the new leases of that year yielded only an additional £14 in revenue, while adding an additional £134 to the total of rents in arrears. The lessees proved unable or unwilling to pay, and the sheriffs declined to pursue the collection of rents in arrears. Threats by the Corporation to evict defaulters, who were over twelve months in arrears with their rent, faltered on the legal question of whether sheriffs were competent to carry out such an order.

During the following year, while John Beverley Robinson, the provincial Attorney General, sought a legal decision from the Law Officers of the Crown in England, rent arrears continued to mount. A total of £333 in arrears was reached by the end of 1822 on the new leases alone. Moreover, there were members of the House of Assembly who continued to criticize the Clergy Reserves and the Crown Reserves, as obstacles to the building of roads and a hindrance to the economic development of the province.

Such public criticism was a matter of some concern to the Anglican Tories. In response, Strachan and Robinson advocated that "a fraction" of the Crown reserve lots – which, like the Clergy Reserves, also accounted for one-seventh of the surveyed lots of each township -- be sold "in the troubled districts" to allay discontent. Although it was not "an auspicious time for selling reserves'; nonetheless, it was deemed a politic thing to do. At the same time, both Strachan and Robinson maintained that "a *temporary inconvenience*" did not justify any tampering with the Clergy Reserves. Further developments during the year 1823, however, forced them to modify that determination. In that year, rent arrears continued to climb, and two-thirds of what income the reserves did yield was "swallowed up" by the costs of administration and, to a lesser extent, in paying the sheriffs who received a fee of five percent of the arrears of any rent that they collected. (16)

To the Clergy Reserves Corporation, it was obvious where the source of their difficulties lay. On the one hand, Upper Canadians and immigrants clearly preferred land in fee simple to leasing. And as long as the Crown continued to grant good lands gratis to the sons of Loyalists, and to sell it for "a mere trifle" to immigrants, the demand for clergy reserve leases would remain small, even where the lots were very advantageously situated. On the other hand, the prevalence of cheap land necessitated that lease rents had to be kept to an "almost nominal amount", which discouraged the sheriffs from making a determined effort to collect the rents "from persons scattered over a surface of nearly 40,000 square miles". It was apparent that only time could resolve such difficulties. In the meantime, however, the Anglican clergy were receiving very little income from the Clergy Reserves, while they were becoming a source of religious discontent, which was a matter of some concern. (17)

The Church of Scotland & the Clergy Reserves

As the Rev. Strachan had predicted earlier, the grant by the British government in 1817 of a salary of £100 per annum for each of four Roman Catholic priests in Upper Canada, had encouraged the Presbyterian congregations of Upper Canada to make similar demands. They had organized themselves into a presbytery and secured recognition from the Church of Scotland as 'an associate synod' which enabled the Presbyterian congregations to speak with one voice in claiming financial support from the government for their ministers. When viewed in retrospect, it was a doubly ironic situation for the Tories. During a postwar depression, when the Crown revenues of Upper Canada were insufficient to cover the civil list and provide financial support for the established Church of England clergy, the British government had granted salaries for the Roman Catholic priests in Upper Canada. Moreover, three years later a newly-elected Assembly – which was dominated by the members from the non-Loyalist American areas of settlement -- would refuse to vote provincial government clerical salaries, which left the Lt. Governor with no alternative but to pay the clerical salaries out of the 'military chest'. However, in the immediate postwar period, the attention of the Tories was focused on the Presbyterian request that the government provide financial support for their ministers.

Faced with a postwar depression in the provincial economy, in 1819 the congregation of Niagara Presbyterians had initially petitioned the Lt.

Governor for the grant of £100 per annum "out of funds arising from the Clergy Reserves, or any other fund at your Excellency's disposal", for the support of 'a respectable minister' whom they hoped to obtain from the Church of Scotland. The petition was forwarded, in turn by Lt. Governor Maitland, to the Colonial Office with a recommendation that some financial aid be furnished to the Presbyterians, but not from the clergy reserves endowment.

In response, the Colonial Office sought an opinion from the Law Officers of the Crown. The Law Officers ruled that the clergy of the Church of Scotland, but not dissenting ministers, might be included under the meaning of the term 'a Protestant clergy'; and that the Governor would be justified in making a provision from 'the rents and profits' of the clergy reserves land endowment to the Church of Scotland. Only the Church of England, however, was entitled by the Constitutional Act to be invested with endowed rectories, which might include "all or any part" of the Clergy Reserves in any township.

On the basis of that legal decision, the Colonial Secretary -- Lord Bathurst -- instructed Lt. Governor Maitland that the first priority of the local executive should be to provide a competent provision for the Church of England clergy, but that in parishes where the adherents of the Church of Scotland might "greatly predominate", it was "both advisable and proper that a proportionate allotment should be reserved for the provision for a minister of that Church". Lt. Governor Maitland, however, chose to keep his instructions confidential, and informed the Presbyterians that their request would have to be refused as funds were not immediately available, which was true. Undeterred, the newly-constituted Presbyterian synod had continued to agitate for financial support from the provincial government. It was an agitation which was spurred by the knowledge that the Church of England had realized £150 from the clergy reserves endowment in 1821, which was viewed as a harbinger of substantial revenues to come. (18)

In their initial petitions, the Presbyterians had appealed to the beneficence of government on the grounds of their needs. They pointed out that the Roman Catholic clergy enjoyed the right of tithes in Upper Canada; and that the "Established Church of England" in Upper Canada received financial support from the Society for the Propagation of the Gospel. In contrast, the Church of Scotland lacked any general provision for its clergy. What was requested was a government grant that would enable its adherents -- the Scots and Scotch Irish, whom it was maintained comprised the bulk of the immigrants settling in Upper Canada – to obtain "regular and respectable" clergymen from the Church of Scotland. Their ministrations, it was declared, would promote "the religious and moral improvement" of Upper Canadians, and served to "attach them to the parent country by the strongest bonds".

The petitioners claimed also that government support for the Church of Scotland was particularly necessary in a political point of view to counteract sectarian preachers who "disseminate political disaffection with religious fanaticism" and "destroy every principle of real Religion or Morality". The Presbyterians saw their adherents as particularly vulnerable to such a threat because they lacked any provision to enable them to support their own clergy, and "derived no benefit from the Established Church of England" which controlled the Clergy Reserves. Their adherents, it was claimed, were faced with the prospect of either remaining destitute of religion or attaching themselves to the American religious sects. (19) There was no mention of a third alternative: that their adherents might join the established Church of England.

Thereafter, the Presbyterians introduced a new argument in claiming that the Church of Scotland was entitled to share in the clergy reserves endowment on constitutional grounds. The new claim was put forward in December 1823 in several resolutions which were submitted to the House of Assembly by a leading lay member of the Church of Scotland, William Morris of the Perth settlement.

The Morris resolutions declared that since the Act of Union of 1707 had united the kingdoms of England and Scotland upon an equal footing and had recognized the establishment of two national churches – the Church of England and the Church of Scotland – "within their respective Kingdoms", that consequently both churches were entitled to share in all subsequent benefits. It was also declared that the conquest of Canada had been a British achievement, and not a purely English achievement, and that therefore the Church of Scotland had "an equal claim to enjoy advantages which might be derived from the said conquest".

What was implied by the Morris resolutions was that the Church of Scotland enjoyed a co-establishment in Upper Canada with the Church of England, and that consequently the Church of Scotland was entitled to an equitable share in the revenues of the clergy reserve lands under the 'Protestant clergy' provision in the Constitutional Act.

The Morris resolutions, which passed the House of Assembly, were defeated in the Legislative Council by a close vote of 6 to 5. A subsequent Address of the Assembly to the King (5 January 1824), however, adopted a more moderate tone. It submitted that if the clergy reserves land endowment set aside for "a Protestant Clergy' had not been intended to include the Church of Scotland that His Majesty might see fit to consider making a proper provision for the clergy of the Scottish church. (20)

Defending the Clergy Reserves

The Upper Canadian Anglican Tories totally rejected any claim of the Church of Scotland to a share in the clergy reserves endowment. They continued to maintain that the phrase 'a Protestant clergy', as used in the Constitutional Act, meant solely the clergy of the Church of England as distinct from the Roman Catholic clergy. In the view of the Anglican Tories, the Presbyterians were putting "a forced construction" on the phrase and were completely ignoring the terminology of the rest of the Act which referred specifically, and solely, to the Church of England. There was no doubt that the clergy reserve lands belonged exclusively to the Church of England by law.

When informed of the earlier opinion of the Law Officer of the Crown, the Tories considered that judgement to be "unsound" and:

> an opinion which contradicts the spirit of all the clauses of the 31 Geo. 3d, chap. 31 regarding the Reserves and their appropriation, and in truth contradicts itself.

Various acts of the provincial government -- such as the Marriage Acts of 1793 and 1798, and Clergy Reserves Corporation charter of 1819, respectively -- had given legal recognition to the Church of England as the established church of Upper Canada and the Clergy Reserves Corporation charter had recognized its exclusive right to the clergy reserves endowment. Moreover, none of these acts, at the time of their enactment, had evoked any claim that the Church of England was not the established church of Upper Canada, or that the Church of Scotland was co-established. In the opinion of the Anglican Tories, the claims put forth in the Morris resolutions was "too feeble" to be taken seriously.

By the terms of the actual Act of Union of 1707, the rights of the Church of Scotland were recognized, but its establishment was specifically "restricted to the Kingdom of Scotland". Moreover, Upper Canada was an English colony, rather than British, and it was English law, not the law of Scotland, which prevailed there. To the Tories, the Church of Scotland was not in any way entitled to either a share of the clergy reserves endowment, or to co-establishment in Upper Canada. In both cases:

> [their] claim was considered idle, and supposed to proceed from a disappointment, which they had met with in an application to Government for salaries for their ministers. (21)

In contrast, according to the Anglican Tories, the Church of England was the "lawfully established Church" in the colonies, and it had been so established by the Crown. In acting in accordance with his coronation oath to maintain the established religion in his realm, the King had earlier appointed a bishop to the Diocese of Quebec -- which included what would become the Province of Upper Canada -- and the Diocese of Quebec was within the Episcopal Province of Canterbury which, in effect, established the Church of England in Upper Canada. (22).

Although convinced that the rights and property of the Church of England were "clearly and explicitly recognized by the Law", the Anglican Tories still experienced "a most serious alarm" that the claims of the Presbyterians were finding supporters in the House of Assembly. Nonetheless, in resisting such unwarranted demands, the Tories believed that they were merely defending the rights of the Church of England as established in law. They were confident:

that the plain statement of facts, elucidating the religious situation of this Province, ... will not only invalidate the allegations of their opponents, but preserve to the Church of England those rights and privileges unimpaired which she has so long enjoyed in this colony. (23)

In defending the rights of the Church of England to the clergy reserves endowment, the Upper Canadian Tories -- and the Rev. John Strachan in particular -- were convinced that any compromise in the direction of acceding to the fallacious claims of the Church of Scotland was both undesirable and impolitic. It was feared that such an action would undermine the prerogatives of the Church of England as the Established Church of Upper Canada and would imply "that there is no such thing, here, as a Constitution in Church & State". If the meaning of the phrase "Protestant Clergy" were extended to include the Church of Scotland, 'where would its meaning terminate?'

Hitherto, the other religious denominations had "expressed no jealousy" against the Clergy Reserves. It was expected, however, that once the endowment began to yield substantial revenues, the other Protestant churches and the sects would attempt to secure a portion for themselves; and:

> unless some remedy be found, the legislature will interfere, and what they may not obtain from reason, they may carry from persevering obstinacy.

For the Tories, it was particularly disconcerting that the 'evangelical sectarians' in the Assembly had supported the Morris resolutions and the Address to the Crown requesting financial support from the British government for the Church of Scotland. There were also parties outside of the province who were declaring support for the claim of the Presbyterian synod to an equal share of the clergy reserve revenues. At Quebec, Lord Dalhousie, the newly-appointed Governor-in-Chief/Commander-in-Chief -- who was an Elder in the Church of Scotland -- objected to the exclusion of the Presbyterian clergy of Upper Canada from sharing in the clergy reserves endowment. Lord Dalhousie favoured the outright sale of the Clergy Reserve lots for the benefit of the two national churches. Moreover, in March 1823, the House of Assembly of Lower Canada passed an Address to the King which called upon the British government to support the claims of the Church of Scotland to a share of the clergy reserves in both provinces and included a plea that the dissenting churches share also in the revenue from the Clergy Reserves on the grounds of their substantial numbers in Upper Canada. It was this last plea wherein the Tories saw a real danger.

The Anglican Tories feared that the sectarians were beginning to feel free "to plunder the Church". Initially, the Tories had believed -- following the passing of the Tithe Declaratory Act of February 1823 – that the sectarians, who believed in the separation of church and state, would be content. With the passage of the Tithe Declaratory Act, the sectarians no longer had to fear the imposition of tithes in Upper Canada, and the denial of the right to tithe on the part of the Established Church was in keeping with the religious beliefs of the sectarians. However, the effect of the Tithe Act was the contrary to what the Tories had expected. In the Assembly, it was the members of the Methodist Episcopal Church and the Baptists -- both denominations of which believed in voluntaryism and were opposed to government aid to churches -- who supported the political radicals and the Presbyterian members in passing the Morris resolutions.

The Tories claimed that the sectarians admitted in private, if not in public, that should the demands of the Church of Scotland to a share of the Clergy Reserves be once admitted, it would result in "the opening of the door for all persuasions". In effect, as the Tories viewed the situation, the sectarians;

> believed that the ministers of the Kirk of Scotland had no better right than any other Protestant denomination, but that they supported their claim because, should the Scotch, under the name of a national Church, succeed, the legal meaning of ... [Protestant] Clergy would be extended; and then their claim, as they were far more numerous than the Scotch, would become irresistible.

In sum, the Anglican Tories feared that should the phrase 'a Protestant clergy' of the Constitutional Act be extended to encompass the Church of Scotland, its meaning would be challenged and further extended to include the dissenting Protestant sects. (24)

The Upper Canadian Anglican Tories were aware that the Church of Scotland shared their fears for the moral and religious condition of the province, and that the Church of Scotland was equally conscious of the threat which the American religious sects posed the political character of the province. Hence, they deeply deplored the attacks by the Kirkites on the established Church of England, and its rights and prerogatives. In the past, it had been a common experience, as Lt. Governor Maitland informed the Colonial Office, for Presbyterian immigrants to attend services in the Church of England where a minister of the Kirk was unavailable; and that:

> those, indeed, who in Scotland were zealous Presbyterians, are found everywhere in Canada among the most exemplary and active supporters of the English Church; and until these claims had begun to be agitated, any idea of the distinction between them appeared to be scarcely regarded among themselves, and had little observable influence of any kind upon their conduct.

Nonetheless, the Anglican Tories remained adamant that whatever financial aid government might grant to the Presbyterians should go to ministers of the individual congregations and not to "the Church, as a Church"; that the extension of the Scottish Church should not be funded by government; and that any support which might be provided by government should not be from the clergy reserves endowment. (25)

A new Clergy Reserves Corporate Charter

A more immediate problem was how to make the Clergy Reserves productive. As of February 1824, if not earlier, it was evident that the leasing system, under the direction of the Clergy Reserves Corporation, was not working effectively. Changes needed to be made. In that month, the Rev. Strachan petitioned the Colonial Office to secure from the British parliament a new charter which would permit the Clergy Reserves Corporation to sell up to one-half of the clergy reserve lots, while retaining sufficient lands in each township to endow three or four parsonages when needed. He further recommended that the proposed act provide for the monies so raised to be placed in 'British funds' with the interest only going to the support of the Church of England clergy;

that the corporation be given the right to re-lease or sell the lots of defaulters, subject to the payment of compensation for any buildings that had been erected on the land; and that the local legislature be forbidden to interfere in the disposition of the clergy reserves lands.

The Colonial Office was informed that once the exclusive right of the Church of England to the Clergy Reserves was confirmed and "placed beyond the hope of envy and the reach of malice", numerous benefits would accrue. It was expected that the lessees in default would promptly pay their rent rather than risk being denied a renewal of their lease or would take advantage of the opportunity for "an advantageous purchase" of their leased lot; the sale of numerous lots would put an end to most complaints; and it would remove any temptation in wartime for lessees to support an invading army that might offer them ownership of their leased lands. And most importantly, the monies so raised and invested would enable the Established Church to multiply her clergy "to any number that might be required", while at the same time relieving the Society for the Propagation of the Gospel and the Imperial government of a worrisome and unwanted financial burden. Moreover, it was pointed out that the investment of the monies in British funds would constitute "a new link of attachment" to the mother country, while the confirmation of the rights of the Church of England would put an end to the agitation of the Scottish Kirk in Upper Canada. (26)

In May 1824 and again in November 1826, the Rev. Strachan submitted petitions to the Colonial Office in support of the request for a new Clergy Reserves Corporation charter. For the most part, the petitions differed little in detail, but the 1826 petition did recommend that the parliamentary act provide for the potential sale of all the Clergy Reserves, rather than one-half of the lots as previously requested; and that the Lt. Governor – Sir Peregrine Maitland -- rather than the Clergy Reserves Corporation, should decide what would be sold.

In support of the November 1826 petition, Strachan attached a draft of a proposed new charter for the Clergy Reserves Corporation which further strengthened the connection between Church and State. In addition, to the Inspector General and Surveyor General sitting on the board, he proposed that the Attorney General and Solicitor General be added; and that the clerical representation be reduced. Rather than all the Anglican clergy being members of the Corporation, he recommended that it comprise only the Bishop of Quebec, the two Archdeacons of the Church in Upper Canada, and twelve of the most senior clergymen in the province, with the Bishop serving as President, and the archdeacons as vice-presidents.

More explicit recommendations were made as well with respect to the terms that should govern the investment and distribution of the Clergy Reserves revenues. The monies, which were raised by selling or mortgaging the reserve lots, were to be invested in public stocks, English government securities, or the funds of Great Britain, in keeping with the distribution decided upon by the Clergy Reserve Corporation. The dividends were to be distributed -- once the administrative costs were deducted -- in two ways: one-third for the payment of salaries for the Church of England clergy; and two-thirds to maintain and improve the reserves and glebe lands and to erect and keep in repair churches and parsonages.

At that time, the Inspector General, James (Jacques) Baby, was a Roman Catholic, and the Surveyor General, Thomas Ridout, was a member of the Church of England. The proposed new additions to the Clergy Reserves Corporation -- the Attorney General, John Beverley Robinson, and the Solicitor General, Henry John Boulton -- were both High Church Anglicans and former pupils at the Cornwall District Grammar School of the Rev. John Strachan. (27)

While the Rev. Strachan petitioned the British government to secure a new charter that would permit the sale of the clergy reserves lots, adherents of the Church of Scotland continued to agitate for recognition of their proffered claim to an equal share in the proceeds of the Clergy Reserves. However, a new political development further complicated the clergy reserves situation. The effort of the Anglican Tories to attain their ideal of a financially and spiritually-independent national church clergy to disseminate Christianity and serve as the moral leader and conscience of each parish, provoked a hostile opposition.

The initial claims of the Church of Scotland to a co-establishment with the Church of England and to a half-share of the Clergy Reserves, was superseded by vehement attacks launched against the Clergy Reserves, and ultimately the entire concept of an established church, by the evangelical sectarians of Upper Canada. The arguments and claims put forth by the sectarians were quickly taken up by the political radicals in commencing an agitation that would result in the Clergy Reserves, the establishment of the Church of England, and the prerogatives of the National Church, becoming major political issues within the Province of Upper Canada.

Notes

A Spiritually-independent Clergy

1. Spragge, ed., *Strachan Letter Book* (SLB), 73-74, Strachan, 'Report on Religion', 1 March 1815; Bethune, *Memoir of John Strachan*, 58, extract of a letter to Dr. Chalmers, n.d. [c.1815]. The quotation is from Strachan to Chalmers.

2. *Christian Recorder*, I, 5 & 10-12, March 1819, "History and Present State of Religion"; Spragge, *SLB*, 72-74, Strachan, "Report on Religion", 1 March 1815, and 187, Strachan to Rev. Charles Stewart, 11 January 1819; Douglas Library, Queen's University, Cartwright Letterbook, II, Letter of the Magistrates to Sir John Johnson, 22 December 1787; Preston, ed., *Kingston before the War*, 176, Rev. Stuart to Bishop Inglis, 5 July 1791; Hodgins, ed., *Documentary History of Education in Upper Canada* (DHE), I, 213, Strachan, Memorandum to Lt. Governor Maitland, March 1826; PAO, Cartwright Letterbook, IV, 344-345, R. Cartwright, "Memoir respecting the present State of the Episcopal Church in U.C. & the means of its Amelioration", 26 February 1812. The quotations are from Cartwright "Memoir", 344- 345, and Strachan "Report on Religion", 74, respectively.

3. PAO, Cartwright Letterbook, IV, 345, Cartwright, 'Memoir respecting the present State of the Episcopal Church', 26 February 1812; PAO, Strachan Papers, "To the Honourable, the Commons of Upper Canada in Provincial Parliament assembled, The Petition of John Strachan, D.D.", 1818; Spragge, ed., *SLB*, 14-15, Strachan to Isaac Todd, 1 October 1812, and 126, Strachan to the Lord Bishop of Quebec, 30 September 1816; and MTCL, Strachan Papers, Strachan to the Lord Bishop, 12 May 1817. For a discussion of the continuing effort of John Strachan to educate clerical candidates in Upper Canada, see J.D. Purdy, "John Strachan and the Diocesan Theological Institute at Cobourg, 1842-52", *Ontario History*, LXV, June 1973, 113-123.

4. Strachan, *Sermon preached at York, U.C., July 3rd 1825, on the death of the late Lord Bishop of Quebec by John Strachan, D.D.* (Kingston: James Macfarlane, 1826), 26-27; and Spragge, ed., *SLB*, Strachan to the Colonial Office, 5 June 1824. The quotation is from the letter.

5. Strachan, *The Church of the Redeemed, A Sermon preached 5th October 1836* (Toronto: R. Stanton, 1836), 49-50 & 55; and *Kingston Chronicle*, 30

April 1831, "Address of the Legislative Council". The quotations are from *The Church of the Redeemed*, 49 & 50, respectively.

6. *Kingston Chronicle*, [Rev. A.H. Burwell], "One of the People", 31 December 1831; John S. Moir, ed., *Church and State*, 149-152, "Instructions to Governor Carleton", 177; and Provincial Archives of Ontario (PAO), Robinson Papers, 1806-1812, 27-28, "Royal Instructions to Prevost", 22 October 1811; Spragge, ed., *SLB*, 75, 'Report on Religion',1March 1815, and 104, Strachan to the Lord Bishop of Quebec, 18 March 1816.

John Moir (*Church and State*, 149) has pointed out that the whole question of whether the Church of England possessed the legal right to enforce the collection of tithes in Upper Canada was clouded with uncertainty. The Constitutional Act clauses passed by the House of Commons specifically stated that the clergy reserves endowment was being bestowed "in lieu of tithes" -- yet another indication that the Clergy Reserves were intended for the support of the Church of England -- but that phrase had been deleted in its passage through the House of Lords. (See also, *The Church*, 21 November 1840, Hagerman Speech).

7. Preston, ed., *Kingston before the War of 1812*, lxi-lxii; Cruikshank, *Correspondence of Simcoe*, I, 236, Cartwright to Simcoe, 12 October 1792, and V, 257, Bishop Mountain to J.G. Simcoe, 25 June 1795; Spragge, ed., *SLB*, 43-44, Strachan to Your Honor, 6 September 1813; MTCL, Strachan Papers, Strachan to the Lord Bishop, 13 December 1820; *Kingston Chronicle*, 12 February 1819, [Strachan], "For the Kingston Chronicle"; PAO, Strachan Papers, Strachan to His Excellency Lt. Governor Maitland, 1818; and PAO, Strachan Papers, reel 2, 2, Strachan, "Canada Church Establishment", 16 May 1827.

The Tory fears about relying on financial grants from the British government to support the clergy of the Established Church in Upper Canada, were not exaggerated. In 1831, the new liberal-Whig government of Lord Grey announced that British government grants to the Society for the Propagation of the Gospel in Foreign Parts would be gradually reduced in 1832 and terminated in 1834, which they were.

8. Cruikshank, *Correspondence of Simcoe*, V, 257, Bishop Mountain to J.G. Simcoe, 25 June 1795; *The Church*, 7 June 1844, "The Monarch's Headship in the Relations of Church and State, Part II (From "Episcopacy and Presbytery' by the Rev. A. Boyd)"; *The Church*, 25 November 1837, Strachan 'Address';

PAO, Strachan Papers, reel 8, package 2, 6, "Religious Instruction", n.d.; Strachan, *A Charge Delivered to the Clergy of the Diocese of Toronto at the Primary Visitation, 9 September 1841* (Toronto: H.&W. Rowsell,1841),17; *Kingston Chronicle*, 28 January 1832, "One of the People", quoting at length from Edmund Burke, *Reflections on the Revolution in France* (1790); and Strachan, *Letter to Frankland Lewis*, 1830, 81. The quotation is from the Strachan 'Address', 25 November 1837.

9. PAO, Cartwright Letterbook, IV, 346-347, Richard Cartwright, 'Memoir respecting the resent State of the Episcopal Church', 26 February 1812. The quotations are from 346 and 347, respectively.

10. PAO, Strachan Papers, Strachan to Maitland, 1818; Moir, ed., *Church and State*, 109-110, "The Constitutional Act, 1791"; Wilson, *Clergy Reserves*, 64, Strachan, "Report to the Executive Council", 20 October 1818; MTCL, Strachan, *The Church of the Redeemed*, 48; Moir, ed., *Church and State*, 205-206. "Report of Archdeacon John Strachan on the Establishment of the Upper Canadian Rectories", 12 October 1837; and James [John] Strachan, *A Visit to Upper Canada*, 1820, 124-125. The quotation is from *A Visit to Upper Canada*, 124-125.

11. PAO, Strachan Papers, Strachan to Maitland, 1818; *U.E. Loyalist*, 23 December 1826, "Proceedings in Parliament", speech of Attorney General J.B. Robinson; Strachan, *Letters to the Honorable William Morris, being Strictures on the Correspondence of that Gentleman with the Colonial Office as a Delegate from the Presbyterian Body in Canada* (Cobourg, U.C.: R.D. Chatterton, 1838), 47; Wilson, *Clergy Reserves*, 63, Strachan to the Lord Bishop, 18 March 1818; Moir, ed., Church and State, 206, 'Report of Archdeacon Strachan', 12 October 1837; Strachan, *Observations on the Provision for the Maintenance of a Protestant Clergy in the Province of Upper and Lower Canada* (London: R. Gilbert, 1827), Appendix II, 42, "An Act relative to the right of Tithes within this Province, promulgated 20 February 1823"; *The Church*, (Bethune editorial), 3 March 1838. The quotations are from Strachan to the Lord Bishop, 18 March 1818, and "An Act relative to the right of Tithe', respectively.

12. PAO, Strachan Papers, Strachan to Maitland, 1818.

13. PAO, Strachan Papers, Strachan to Maitland, 1818; and Alan Wilson, *The Clergy Reserves of Upper Canada, a Canadian Mortmain* (Toronto: University of Toronto Press, 1968), 37- 44 & 63. This paragraph draws

heavily upon the work of Alan Wilson as cited. For an account of the earlier efforts of the Executive Council to augment the revenues generated by the clergy and crown reserves land endowments, see Wilson, 27-38.

14. PAO, Strachan Papers, Strachan to Maitland, 1818; and Wilson, *Clergy Reserves*, 4I-45, and 64-65. The Anglican Tory belief in the necessity of keeping the clergy of the Church of England independent of any control by either the laity or the state is exemplified in a comment by Bishop Mountain. He had misgivings about the proposal by the Rev. John Strachan in 1818 that the Inspector General and the Surveyor General of Upper Canada be appointed members of the proposed clergy corporation for administering the clergy reserves lands. Bishop Mountain approved of the plan (20 August 1819), but believed that the best principle was to have the lands exclusively in the hands of the clergy who were the most interested in making them productive. His fear was that the lay members, at some future date, might achieve a paramount interest in the corporation. (Wilson, *The Clergy Reserves*, 64).

15. PAO, Strachan Papers, Strachan to Maitland, 1818; and Wilson, *The Clergy Reserves*, 45.

16. Wilson, *Clergy Reserves*, 44-45, 68 & 72-73; and Strachan, *Observations on the Provision for the Maintenance of a Protestant Clergy*, 13.

17. Wilson, *Clergy Reserves*, 44; PAO, Strachan Papers, reel 2, 3, Strachan, 'Canada Church Establishment', 16 May 1827.

18. Spragge, ed., *SLB*, 208-209, Strachan to the Lord Bishop, 19 February 1821; Moir, ed., *Church and State*, 161, "Petition of the Presbyterian Inhabitants of the Town of Niagara and vicinity to Lieutenant-Governor Sir P. Maitland", 30 March 1819, and 161-162, "Opinion of the Law Officers of the Crown, to Earl Bathurst", 15 November 1819; Wilson, *Clergy Reserves*, 67-68. See also, Strachan, *Letter to Frankland Lewis*, 1830, 18-34.

19. Moir, ed., *Church and State*, 162-163, "Memorial to Earl Bathurst from Members in Canada of the Church of Scotland", 12 November 1820, and 164, Lord Dalhousie to Lord Bathurst, 18 January 1821.

20. *U.E. Loyalist*, (Robert Stanton editorial), 12 January 1828; *The Church*, (A.N. Bethune editorials), 3 March 1838 and 1 February 1840; Strachan, *Observations on the Provision for the Maintenance of a Protestant Clergy*, 1827, 13; Doughty and Story, eds., *Documents relating to the Constitutional History of Canada, 1819-28* (Ottawa: King's Printer, 1935), 205, "Resolutions

of Assembly, Upper Canada", and 31, Strachan, "Speech in the Legislative Council", 1828. [See also, H.J. Bridgman, "Morris, William", DCB, VIII.]

21. Moir, ed. *Church and State*, 166, "Petition of the Corporation for Superintending, Managing and Conducting the Clergy Reserves in Upper Canada to the House of Lords", 22 April 1823; *The Church*, 18 November 1837, Strachan, "Address to the Clergy of the Archdeaconry of York, By the Hon. and Rev. The Archdeacon of York – Delivered at Toronto, on Wednesday, the 13th September 1837"; *U.E. Loyalist*, (Stanton editorial), 12 January 1828; Wilson, *Clergy Reserves*, 68; Strachan, *Observations on the Provision for the Maintenance of a Protestant Clergy*, 13-14, & 16, and Appendix, 33, 'Religious State of Upper Canada'; *U.E. Loyalist* (Stanton Editorial), 23 December 1826, "Proceedings in Parliament", speech of the Attorney General, J.B. Robinson. The quotations are from Strachan, 'Address to the Clergy', 13 September 1837, and Strachan, *Observations*, 13, respectively. [See online, The Solon Law Archives, "The Constitutional Act, 1791"].

A.H. Young in an article "The Church of England in Upper Canada" (Queen's Quarterly, 1931, 147 & 150), supports the Anglican Tory argument that the Church of Scotland was not an established church in Upper Canada. Young argues that in the 18th Century the phrases 'Protestant Religion' and 'Protestant Clergy' meant "the religion and clergy of the Church of England, and none other". Moreover, Young attests that the Act of Union (1707) provided for the continuation of the status of the Church of England as the established Church, "guaranteed the rights and the status of the Church in the colonies" and recognized the Church of Scotland as the established church in Scotland. Hence, Professor Young concluded: "By implication, if not direct statement, therefore, the latter Church was established in Scotland only, and not in the colonies".

Aileen Dunham, *Political Unrest in Upper Canada, 1815-1836* (Ottawa: Carleton Library, 1963, 86-87, 1st ed. 1927), appears to accept without question the argument of the adherents of the Church of Scotland that Upper Canada was a British colony with two Protestant religious establishments. To the contrary, Upper Canada was an English colony, and the British government held that the Church of England was the only Protestant established church in the Province of Upper Canada. The Roman Catholic Church was established earlier under the Quebec Act of 1774.

22. Strachan, "Religious State of Upper Canada", 33, in *Observations on the Provisions for the Maintenance of a Protestant Clergy*, 1827. Dunham

(*Political Unrest*, 86), summaries some of the arguments employed by the Anglican Tories to refute the claim that Upper Canada was a British colony in which the Church of Scotland enjoyed a joint establishment with the Church of England. One Act that the Tories cited in support of their argument was the Act of Uniformity (1 Elizabeth, c.2, 1559), which provided that the Church of England was to be the established church in England, as well as "within any other [of] your majesty's dominions or countries that now or hereafter shall be".

23. *U.E. Loyalist* (Stanton editorial), 12 January 1828; Moir, ed., *Church and State*, 165-166, "Petition of the Corporation for Superintending the Clergy Reserves", 22 April 1823. The quotation is from the 'Petition of the Corporation', 165-166.

24. Moir, ed., *Church and State*, 166, 'Petition of the Corporation', 22 April 1823; Wilson, *Clergy Reserves*, 68 (quoting Bishop Mountain); Strachan, *Observations on the Provision for the Maintenance of a Protestant Clergy*, 14 & 18-20; Strachan, *Observations on a Bill for Uniting the Provinces*, 1824, 35-36; and Doughty and Story, *Documents*, 205, footnote. The quotations are from Strachan, *Bill for Uniting*, 36, and Strachan, *Observations on the Provision*, 20, respectively. [See also Peter Burroughs, "Ramsay, George, 9th Earl of Dalhousie, DCB, VII.]

25. Moir, ed., *Church and State*, 166-167, Lt. Governor Maitland to Earl Bathurst, 27 December 1823; Strachan, 'Speech in Legislative Council', 1828, 32; and PAO, Macaulay Papers, reel 1, Robert Stanton to John Macaulay, 3 September 1827. The quotation is from Maitland to Bathurst, 166.

26. Moir, ed., *Church and State*, 167, "Memorandum of J. Strachan and Sir P. Maitland, enclosed in a dispatch to Earl Bathurst", 4 February 1824; PAO, Strachan Papers, reel 2, Strachan, "Canada Church Establishment", 16 May 1827, 3; Doughty and Story, *Documents*, 275-276, "Opinion of the Executive Council", 21 November 1825; Wilson, *The Clergy Reserves*, 70-71, 74-75, 88-89; and Strachan, *Observations on the Provision*, 1827, 12-13.

The fact that the Tories readily admitted that "there was some foundation for the complaint" that the clergy reserves lots were obstacles to road building, does not mean that they agreed with their opponents that the reserves should be sold off immediately. To the contrary, the Tories did everything in their power to address the problem. However, they observed that it was the large landholders – land speculators -- who were stirring up criticisms against the Clergy Reserves to take attention away from the obstacle posed by their own undeveloped lands. Alan Wilson tends to support that contention of the Anglican Tories. See Wilson, *The Clergy Reserves*, 47-51.

27. This paragraph is based upon the clauses proposed for the amended Clergy Reserves Corporation charter that Strachan submitted to the Colonial Office in his petitions of May 1824 and November 1826. See Wilson, *The Clergy Reserves*, 89-90.

Chapter Five

The Politics of Religion

A Growing Agitation

Appeals to the British Government

The Strachan Letter & Ecclesiastical Chart of 1827

Partisan attacks on the Established Church

The Methodist-Radical Appeal to the House of Commons

The Sectarian Attack on the Church of England

The 'Saddlebags Assembly of 1829-1830

The Marriage Law Controversy

The Clergy Reserves Sales & Improvement Act

An Extra-parliamentary Association

"It would be unjust and impolitic to exalt [the Church of England] by exclusive and peculiar rights, above all others of His Majesty's Subjects who are equally loyal, conscientious and deserving. ... ... If the church is incorporated with the state, [the dissenters] are compelled by the obligation of conscience to oppose one of the civil institutions of the country, a part of the government itself. It is in fact their duty to do so."

Report of the Select Committee [Bidwell Report],
House of Assembly, March 1828.

"The Reverend Egerton Ryerson", portrait by William Gush; Engraved by Thomas A Dean, 1838, Toronto Reference Library. The son of an Anglican-Tory Loyalist, Egerton Ryerson was converted to 'American Methodism' as a young man and became a zealous Methodist circuit-riding preacher. He published attacks on the prerogatives of the established Church of England and played a leading role in the political agitations calling for the separation of church and state in Upper Canada.

Chapter Five

The Politics of Religion

By the mid-1820s, with the prospect that the Clergy Reserves would soon produce substantial revenues for the established Church of England, adherents of the Church of Scotland and the religious sectarians of Upper Canada launched increasingly vehement political attacks against Anglican control of the clergy reserves land endowment. It was an assault in which the democratic radicals of the House of Assembly allied themselves even more closely with the religious sects in making a common cause against the Church of England establishment in Upper Canada. Initially the attack took the form of a demand that every Protestant denomination share in the Clergy Reserves, but in 1826 the nature of the attack changed dramatically. The Rev. Egerton Ryerson, a convert to the Methodist Episcopal Church, began to attack the establish Church and the church-state polity in drawing on evangelical religious principles – 'voluntaryism', 'religious equality', and the 'separation of church and state' – that the Tories recognized as embodying the rhetoric and language of American evangelical Protestantism.

The relentless attacks by the evangelical sectarians soon took the form of a religious crusade in which the Tories -- who believed in a reasoned argument and rational debate on public issues -- were at a great disadvantage. They had to defend the Clergy Reserves in the public realm against attacks generated and sustained by religious zealots, and amidst a continual political agitation kept up by the democratic radicals in the House of Assembly. The Rev. Egerton Ryerson worked closely with the radical political leaders – Dr. John Rolph, Marshall Spring Bidwell, Jesse Ketchum, and even the volatile William Lyon Mackenzie – in the drafting of Assembly resolutions and addresses, and petitions, for circulation among their Reform supporters. In doing so, the evangelical sects and their radical political allies not only denounced the exclusive claim of the Church of England to the Clergy Reserves but attacked the very legitimacy of the concept of an established church and the existing church-state polity. Faced with unrelenting attacks on the Clergy Reserves and the National Church, the Anglican Tories struggled to render the Clergy Reserves productive, to place the reserve revenues beyond the reach of a hostile Assembly, and to combat the machinations of the sectarian-radical alliance in the political sphere.

A Growing Agitation

What was worrisome for the Anglican Tory elite -- almost a decade after the War of 1812 -- was that the democratic radicals in the House of Assembly, with the encouragement of their sectarian supporters, appeared to be making a concerted effort to foment public hostility towards the established Church of England and its possession of the clergy reserves land endowment. When the radicals achieved a majority in the House of Assembly, following the July 1824 provincial election, an Address to the King was issued which 'prayed' that his Majesty would apply the revenues from the clergy reserve leases towards the support of 'the Protestant Clergy of every denomination' throughout the Province. It was an Address that shocked the adherents of the Church of Scotland, as well as the Anglican Tory elite.

Thereafter, in January 1826, by a vote of 31 to 2, the Assembly passed another Address to the King that called for the clergy reserves revenues to be divided among the Protestant religious denomination of Upper Canada, and which, for the first time, raised the possibility – as an alternative – that the revenues from the clergy reserves might be devoted to a non-religious purpose. The Address called for an end to any further appropriations of land for religious purposes as new townships were surveyed, denounced the vast extent of the existing Clergy Reserves, and declared:

> that the lands set apart in this Province for the maintenance and support of a Protestant Clergy, ought not to be employed by any one denomination of Protestants, to the exclusion, of their Christian brethren of other denominations, equally conscientious in their respective modes of worshipping God, and equally entitled, as dutiful and loyal Subjects, to the protection of your Majesty's benign and liberal government.

The Address concluded that it was both "expedient and just" that the clergy reserves land endowment and "any funds arising from the sales thereof" should be used for the benefit of the various Christian denominations of the province, or if such a division proved impracticable, that the monies should be devoted to education and for the general improvement of the Province of Upper Canada.

In effect, the Address of the Assembly called upon the King George IV to violate the constitution of the province. Under the Constitutional Act of 1791, the Provincial Legislature had the right to pass acts pertaining to the clergy reserves endowment, but only within a proscribed constitutional process, and with the consent of the Provincial Legislature and the Lt. Governor, and all such acts were to be reserved for 'the pleasure of the Crown'. The King had no right to intervene in the distribution of the clergy reserves funds, without the consent of the Imperial Parliament. Under clause 42 of the Constitutional Act, any provincial act "to vary or repeal" the provisions of the Act respecting the Clergy Reserves, or to introduce changes that "in any manner relate to or effect the Establishment or Discipline of the Church of England", was to be laid before both Houses of Parliament in Great Britain for thirty days before receiving the assent of the King, and such an act was not to be assented to by "his Majesty, his Heirs, or Successors" if either House objected within that thirty-day period. Not only was the request of the House of Assembly unconstitutional, it ignored the charter rights of the Clergy Reserves Corporation of Upper Canada and its existence as a corporation under the law. (1)

William Morris, the leading Elder of the Church of Scotland, was indignant that the professed claim of his church for a half share of the clergy reserves endowment was being treated by the Assembly as no better than that of "the most obscure sect". For the Anglican Tory elite, the Address to the King constituted "a final proof" of their own argument that any giving way to the claim of the Kirk for a half share of the Clergy Reserves endowment would merely serve to provoke the religious sects to agitate for a share. It was now evident to all why the sectarians in the Assembly had supported the claims of the Church of Scotland in a previous session of the Legislature. It was simply a means of opening a debate on the distribution of the revenues from the Clergy Reserves whereby the other churches and the sects would be able to present arguments in favour of their sharing in the revenues. (2)

In Britain, the Colonial Office continued to adhere to its earlier position that some support would be provided for the Church of Scotland 'as soon as funds were available'. To that end, when the Canada Company – a British land development company -- was granted a Royal charter in

August 1826 to purchase and develop uncultivated Crown lands in the Canadian provinces, a provision was made for the support of religion from the Casual and Territorial Revenues of the Crown. The monies were to be taken from revenues that accrued to the Province from the purchase of Crown lands by the Canada Company.

The Church of Scotland was granted an annual allowance of £750 and some glebe lots, and a similar annual grant and some glebe lots were provided for the support the Roman Catholic clergy in Upper Canada. Where the Clergy Reserves were concerned, Lord Bathurst, the Colonial Secretary, maintained that the financial grant was sufficient to support the Kirk, and that the Clergy Reserves endowment was solely for the support of the Church of England clergy. Any surplus in the revenues from the Clergy Reserves, beyond the needs of the Anglican clergy, would be disposed of by the British government.

The Anglican Tories were pleased with this turn of events in the confirmation of the exclusive Church of England claim to the Clergy Reserves. Moreover, they expected that the adherents of the Church of Scotland would be satisfied with the financial grant and would cease their agitation. Such, however, was not the case. The £750 annual allowance to the Church of Scotland was a much greater income than the clergy reserves endowment was currently yielding the Church of England; yet a veritable pamphlet war erupted between the Kirkites and the defenders of the Church of England. (3)

The pamphlet war was instigated several months earlier when a recent Scots immigrant, the Rev. John Barclay -- the newly-appointed Church of Scotland minister at Kingston -- published a tract that re-iterated the claims of the Morris resolutions, and added a denunciation of episcopacy as being opposed to 'the genius of the people". The Tories deplored the abuse and invective which the pamphlet contained, and rushed replies into print to expose the ill-founded assertions propounded by the Rev. Barclay. Nonetheless, as of the summer of 1826, there was still a hope that the agitation over the Clergy Reserves would soon dissipate. As one Anglican Tory, Robert Stanton, exclaimed:

> I am not positive but I rather think the claims of the Kirk are set completely at rest, in Canada, & the appearance of the

pamphlet strengthens the belief -- bearing as it does all the marks of disappointed rage.

Such a hope was misplaced. It soon gave way to astonishment at the efforts which the Presbyterians were making "to keep discord alive", and to a feeling of exasperation and apprehension over the ill-effects which such a public controversy was having on the peace and social harmony of the province. Stanton commented further:

> After all, what is [it] they want! What is their object: is it to destroy the best feelings of Society, and to disturb the harmony which has for many years so happily reigned among the various Sects in the Country. Before the Scotch parson came among us, we had peace. (4)

Nevertheless, the Anglican Tories were encouraged in their struggle to maintain the right of the Church of England to the Clergy Reserves by their observation that not all the members of the Church of Scotland supported the claims being made by William Morris and the Rev. Barclay; and that some Methodists were openly dismissive of the claim that the Church of Scotland was co-established in Upper Canada.

A pamphlet that was published by "a Methodist minister" – presumably the Wesleyan Methodist minister at Kingston – provided encouragement to the Tories. The pamphlet asserted that although the other denominations would gladly accept a share of the clergy reserves revenues, they did not expect to receive anything. They would rather side with the Church of England than see the Kirk receive monies on a claim that was founded not in law, but simply on the basis of their particular needs. Judged on such grounds, it was asserted that whether in terms of usefulness, numbers, good moral conduct, or loyalty, the claims of the Kirk were no better than, or in many ways not as good as, that of other religious denominations in Upper Canada. In effect, the 'Methodist minister' called upon all the churches and sects to accept, with a good grace, the existing state of things – that Upper Canada had an established Church of England supported by a clergy reserves land endowment -- which was long established in the constitution and the law. However, the pamphlet contained a warning that if another religious denomination were exalted in "a new order of things", even the most moderate would consider themselves aggrieved and would strongly express their discontent. To the Anglican Tories, such an argument, which closely paralleled their own views, reinforced their determination to deny any share of the Clergy Reserves endowment to the Church of Scotland. (5)

In December 1826, William Morris took the Anglican Tories completely by surprise when he submitted "a flaming set of resolutions" to the House of Assembly. The resolutions attacked the clergy of the Church of England, re-asserted the claims of the Kirk to a share of the Clergy Reserves, and stated that the Clergy Reserves should be sold, and the monies applied for the benefit of all the Protestant churches and sects, and for the general purposes of education.

To the Tories, the conduct of Morris was ungracious and contradictory. It was held to be motivated by disappointment at the Kirk being denied its demand for 'half of the clergy reserves' on the specious claim that the Church of Scotland was an established church within the British Empire, and not just in Scotland. In the Tory view, Morris was "doing his Church a great deal of harm" in that, although his resolutions were adopted by the majority in the Assembly,

> that majority is composed of persons who would involve anything like an established Church in ruin – he will have cause by & bye to cry out: preserve me from my friends.

Subsequently, William Morris was appointed to an Assembly committee to draft a bill to provide for the sale of the Clergy Reserves. However, the Anglican Tories were not unduly alarmed. The Assembly had no authority to authorize the sale of the Clergy Reserves, and the Tories were in control of the twelve-member Legislative Council, of which the Rev. John Strachan was a member. The bill for the sale of the Clergy Reserves was rejected by the Legislative Council when it was brought forward from the Assembly.

What struck Robert Stanton as "the unkindest state of all" was that it was a [former] Anglican, Dr. John Rolph who led the democratic radicals in supporting the Morris resolutions in the Assembly. Rolph was a son of a staunch Anglican Tory family. He had been educated for the Church and had once intended to take clerical orders. For Stanton, it was evident that the Clergy Reserves were to be made "the cat's paw for another party struggle" at a time when the alien question controversy, which had previously fostered discontent, was approaching a settlement. (6)

The Tories were greatly encouraged by the statement of the Colonial Secretary, Lord Bathurst, in support of the right of the Church of England to the Clergy Reserves endowment, and the prospect of securing the right to sell the Clergy Reserves and invest the monies for the support of the Anglican clergy. However, it was these very same developments that had motivated William Morris of the Church of Scotland, and evangelical sectarians, to support the democratic radicals in the launching of an assault against the clergy reserves endowment.

The strategy of the radical leadership in the Assembly, as reported by the Tories, was to discourage the Imperial Government from passing any act that would permit the sale of the clergy reserves lots and the investment of the monies solely for the benefit of the Anglican Church in Upper Canada. In the Assembly debates, a wide variety of arguments were voiced against the exclusive claims of the Church of England to the Clergy Reserves. The radicals asserted that although the Colonial Office seemed to uphold the exclusive claims of the Church of England, it was "only an opinion of Lord Bathurst", and was totally unacceptable. From that point, arguments diverged.

William Morris continued to reiterate the right of the Kirk to a half share in the Clergy Reserves revenues, while expressing his willingness to acquiesce in all the dissenting churches and religious sects sharing in the endowment. John Rolph called for a division of the endowment among all the Protestant churches and sects. He declared that the phrase 'a Protestant clergy' of the Constitutional Act meant all Protestant denominations, and he exclaimed that any recognition of the Church of England claim to an exclusive possession was 'repugnant to the Constitutional Act'. Moreover, the clergy reserves lots were declared to be 'nuisances' which inhibited the building of highways, "yielded nothing", and if left in the possession of the Church of England would "run to waste by bad farming and mismanagement".

On the other hand, there were some opposition members in the Assembly who recognized the legal and constitutional rights of the Church of

England to the Clergy Reserves endowment in Upper Canada. They expressed their belief that there was "no doubt the law gave it to them", and that neither the Kirk nor the evangelical sects had any right to a share of the Clergy Reserves revenues. Nonetheless, a division of the Clergy Reserves was called for in arguing that the amount of land reserved was "too much for any one sect" [sic]. Still other members pointed out that the Church of England would benefit by an equal division of the clergy reserve revenues to the same extend as the other Protestant churches and the sects.

Further arguments were propounded to the effect that the "voice of the country" should determine the issue; that the Church of England adherents were not the most numerous religious denomination in the province; and that the Anglican clergy were already in receipt of monies from the Society for the Propagation of the Gospel in Foreign Parts. Moreover, it was asserted that the possession of the total revenues from the Clergy Reserves would be "the worst thing that could be done" to the Anglican clergy. They "would become idle and neglect their flocks, while the good and faithful Clergyman was starving". Most of the arguments that were presented in the Assembly were old and familiar, and constituted -- from the viewpoint of the Tory elite -- merely self-serving justifications for despoiling the Church of England of its clergy reserves land endowment. During the Assembly debates, however, a totally new argument was introduced. (7)

In one of his speeches, John Rolph denounced the principle of an established church. He held up the United States as a proper example to follow where there was a separation of church and state and declared that "a young country" like Upper Canada should not imitate England. He then launched into strident appeals to the members of the Assembly to free the province from "Ecclesiastical domination" and "Ecclesiastical chains", and to save Upper Canada from succumbing to the "horrors of religious persecution" that would invariably issue from a Church establishment. To forewarn members of "what had taken place, and what might happen again", several selections were read from a book that described the martyrdom of the Protestant Archbishop Cranmer – in 1556 at the hands of the Roman Catholic Church establishment under Queen Mary -- amidst assurances from Dr. Rolph that:

many more such instances might be found and that too when a Protestant Established Church had the domination, and wherever power was given, its abuse was to be apprehended.

At the same time, ringing declarations were made that "Conscience should be free", and that "freedom could not be obtained if it was loaded with restrictions", all of which were accompanied by an assertion that the sale and equal division of the proceeds of the Clergy Reserves would represent "a great extension of Religious liberty". (8)

The Tories replied, in the main, that any proposal that the proceeds of the Clergy Reserves be divided among all the Protestant churches and sects was particularly "unjust". The provincial legislature in passing the Tithe Declaratory Act in 1823 had rescinded any legal right of tithe that the Church of England might have possessed, as an established church in Upper Canada, on the basis that the Church of England already enjoyed the support of the clergy reserves endowment. Now, three years later, the Assembly was prepared to deprive the Church of England of the land endowment that had been granted by the Crown, in the Constitutional Act, to the established Church of England in lieu of tithes.

Although most of the arguments that were raised in the Assembly to justify a division of the proceeds of the Clergy Reserves endowment had been answered long before, they were addressed again by the Tory members. John Beverley Robinson, the Attorney General, member for York, and the leading spokesman for the Anglican Tories in the Assembly, made a point of responding to the denunciations of church establishments by John Rolph.

Robinson asserted that it was "absurd and inconsistent" to make references to the religious persecutions of "a barbarous age". Several centuries had passed since then without any such occurrences, and there were no grounds at all for any apprehension in the present age. As to the arguments concerning freedom of conscience, Robinson pointed out that it was merely a debating tactic to tie the question of the Clergy Reserves to the broader principle of religious liberty. Robinson asserted that:

> he was not aware that in this Country there was anything to prevent any man worshipping according to the dictates of his

conscience -- the allusions made on this subject was in his opinion uncalled for, and in no manner connected with the question – he had never heard of any complaints on this subject, and the measure now before the House, whether adopted or not, would in no wise interfere with that Religious toleration which had always existed in the Country.

To the Tories, neither a church establishment nor the possession of the Clergy Reserves by the Established Church, were inconsistent with religious liberty. In Upper Canada, there was a complete freedom of religion and freedom of conscience. No one was under any obligation to support or to attend the Established Church. (9)

Appeals to the British Government

With the commencement of the year 1827, the Upper Canadian Anglican Tories were still confident that the right of the Church of England to the Clergy Reserves would be vindicated by the Imperial Parliament. It was expected that Parliament would grant the proposed new charter requested for the Clergy Reserve Corporation; and yet, the Tories were prepared "to submit as becomes us" if the decision of the Imperial government should go against them. Despite the "harangues" and the "unmerited and vulgar abuse" which their attackers continued to pour upon the Church of England and her clergy in the House of Assembly, and in the radical press, and a deep concern about the ill-effects of the resultant "unchristian feeling" upon society, the Tories were still reasonably confident of the ultimate success of their plans for the sale of clergy reserves lots and the investment of the monies for the benefit of the clergy of the Established Church.

The Tory view of the agitation in the House of Assembly over the Clergy Reserves was perhaps best expressed by Robert Stanton who wrote in a private communication:

> The controversy carried on in the papers, assuming, as it does a religious cast, is truly a painful one. I am sick of reading the papers of the day. The plot thickens, and the intentions of our Presbyterian brethren are coming to a head. ... The *right* to a share in the Clergy Reserves is strongly insisted upon & I am rather pleased that the question is joined on this issue -- if reason

& argument & a fair construction of law are allowed to have any weight in the decision of such a question, I feel satisfied that we must be successful -- they have raised a violent clamor, and have not spared even threats to accomplish their purposes.

To secure the support of a majority of the members in the House of Assembly, the Morris resolutions of December 1826 had called for a division of the proceeds of the Clergy Reserves amongst all the Protestant churches and sects of Upper Canada. However, with the defeat of the Assembly bill in the Legislative Council, the Presbyterians resorted to an appeal to the Imperial parliament in seeking to secure recognition of their earlier claim to a half-share in the Clergy Reserves endowment.

Despite much provocation, the Anglican clergy and leading laymen of the Church purposely refrained from engaging in an exchange of abuse with the supporters of the Kirk. The Anglican Tories were confident that "a formal and open discussion" of the merits of the case in the Imperial parliament would uphold the position of the Church of England on the Clergy Reserves. As expressed by Robert Stanton:

> The faith of an Act of the British Parliament stands pledged to us for these reserves, and ... I should hope we have little to fear. On this account, I am pleased that they have determined on a reference to the Imperial Parliament.

As to the demands of the evangelical religious sects for an equal division of the Clergy Reserves revenues, as expressed by their representatives in the Assembly, the Tories were equally opposed. They held to their long-stated opinion that if the British government gave way to 'the pretensions' of the Kirk that, ultimately, the Church of England would have to accept an equal division of the proceeds of the Clergy Reserves to put an end to the controversy. It was observed that already the various dissenting sects were putting forth claims for a share. Robert Stanton remarked privately, and rather facetiously, that he expected the "Ranters, Jumpers, Menonists [sic], Tinkers, Davidites, &c &c", and even the Unitarians, would demand a share:

> Our Parliament will be converted into a Theological Seminary. We shall have a fine time of it, depend upon it. (10)

During the late summer of 1827, the Anglican Tories were pleased to learn that the personal efforts of the Rev. John Strachan -- during an extended visit in England -- had resulted in the enactment of a Sales and Improvement Act (Clergy Reserves, Canada Act, 7 & 8 Geo. IV, c.62, July 1827) by the Imperial Parliament. The Sales and Improvement Act did not include a new charter for the Clergy Reserves Corporation, as the Tories had wanted, but it did authorize the Governor-in-Chief (in effect, the Lt. Governor), with the advice of his Executive Council, to sell up to one-quarter of the reserves to a maximum of 100,000 acres in any given year. The Sales Act specified that the monies raised from the sales were to be used to cover the cost of administering and improving the Clergy Reserves and for the support of the 'Protestant Clergy' as cited in the Constitutional Act of 1791, which encompassed the erection of parsonages and rectories for the benefit of the Church of England. The claim of the Church of Scotland to a half-share in the clergy reserves was not recognized. Nonetheless, the Anglican Tories adhered to their position that some "distinct *provision*" might be made by government for the support of the Kirk, so long as funds were not diverted from the clergy reserves revenues.

At last, it seemed that the efforts to defend the clergy reserves endowment were successful, and that the Established Church would be in possession of an independent source of income. The monies raised through the projected sale of the clergy reserves lands would render the Anglican clergy spiritually independent of both the state and the whims of the people and able to speak out on religious and moral issues. It was expected that the sale would yield a significant income which, once invested, would enable the ministrations of the national church to be rapidly extended to eventually comprehend the bulk of the population of Upper Canada. Earlier, in November 1825, the Lt. Governor – Major General Sir Peregrine Maitland -- was in receipt of Instructions from the Colonial Office (dated 22 July 1824), to proceed with the endowment and erection of parsonages and rectories in the province, and he was anxious to do so. With the commencement of sales of the Clergy Reserves pending, it appeared that sufficient funds would soon be available for that purpose. (11)

During more than a year in England – from the spring 1826 through the early summer of 1827 – while seeking to secure a new charter for the Clergy Reserves Corporation and the right to sell the reserves lots -- the Rev. John Strachan had been successful in promoting the interests of the Established Church of Upper Canada on several fronts. While in England, he had managed to secure from Parliament the passage of the Clergy Reserves Sale and Improvement Act that authorized the sale of a large portion of the Clergy Reserves. He had secured also the grant of a royal charter for the establishment of a "University of King's College" at York in Upper Canada, with a land endowment of 225,944 acres of Crown Reserve lands, and an annual grant of £1,000 from the Canada Land Company payments for a period of years.

The Act provided for an official Visitor (the Anglican Bishop of the Diocese), a Chancellor (the Lt. Governor), and a President (the Archdeacon of York – Dr. John Strachan), and a governing council which was to comprise the Chancellor and the President, as well as seven professors who had to be members of the Church of England and subscribers to the Thirty-Nine Articles of the Anglican faith. The university was to be open to students of all faiths with no religious tests for entry or graduation, except for the students in the Divinity School of the projected university. The King's College Charter was remarkably liberal, and more so than any contemporary university in Britain or the United States in having no religious tests for entry or graduation; yet it was to be a decidedly Anglican institution in its governance and teaching staff.

The Rev. Strachan had managed as well to divert the Colonial Office from its plan to sell the Clergy Reserves to the Canada Company at an unreasonably low price per acre, and while in England was appointed Archdeacon of York upon the former incumbent, the Rev. George Okill Stuart, being appointed Archdeacon of Kingston.

The Strachan Letter and Ecclesiastical Chart of 1827

While Strachan was in England, the Scottish members of the British Parliament had opposed the Clergy Reserves bill for its exclusion of the Church of Scotland from a share in the proceeds of the endowment.

During the debates, a Scots radical, Joseph Hume, made two bald assertions: viz. that the Church of Scotland had thirty congregations in Upper Canada, while the Clergy of the Church of England, although numerous, had no congregations of any significance; and that only two of the forty-four members of the House of Assembly were adherents of the Church of England. The Under-Secretary of State for War and the Colonies, Robert Wilmot Horton, had immediately requested that Archdeacon Strachan prepare a reply. It comprised a letter, dated 16 May 1827, to Wilmot Horton with an attached "Ecclesiastical Chart for the Diocese of Upper Canada, for 1827". The letter and the ecclesiastical chart, which named and listed the clergy of the various denominations in Upper Canada, were subsequently printed by the House of Commons. (12)

In the letter, Archdeacon Strachan responded initially to the two assertions which had been made by Joseph Hume. To the contrary, Strachan pointed out that there were thirty clergymen of the Established Church in Upper Canada who were serving 58 large and respectable congregations, either with a regular or occasional church service. Moreover, of the 44 members of the House of Assembly, eighteen were adherents of the Church of England, twenty-three were of various other denominations, and only three or four members were 'Scotch Presbyterians'.

The purpose and extent of the Clergy Reserves was explained, as well as the difficulties which were being experienced in trying to render them productive, the benefits which would be gained by securing the power to sell the reserves, and the fact that the existing leases were currently yielding no more than a total of £400 per annum to the Church of England.

Strachan maintained that only the dearth of money had prevented a greater extension of the Established Church; and that the interests of the Church had suffered in consequence. In the absence of the influence of the National Church clergy, the "sectaries", whose ministers were "almost invariably from the United States where they gather their knowledge and form their sentiments", were gaining an undue influence in the province. Moreover, the Methodist preachers were under the orders of an American conference of the Methodist Episcopal Church, and their influence and instruction was "hostile to our institutions, both civil and religious." Nevertheless, the situation was not regarded as irretrievable. Earlier, Strachan had expressed his conviction to the Colonial Office -- with respect to the Clergy Reserves -- that:

> An authority to sell [will] I am persuaded enable us to get in a few years so much a head on the Sectaries that they must never again become formidable.

In his May 1827 letter, Strachan maintained that the estrangement which existed between the Church of England and the adherents of the Kirk over Clergy Reserves differences, was purely temporary. There were signs already – an opinion that Strachan had formed prior to his departure from Upper Canada in the spring of 1826 -- that the 'hard feelings' were dissipating, which gave rise to the hope that "the times of bickering & bitterness will be forgotten".

Once again, Strachan expressed his view that if the financial means were to be available for the maintenance of two or three hundred clergymen of the Established Church in Upper Canada, that they would draw "the respectable part of the inhabitants" into the Church in the new settlement areas. Through their teachings and influence, the national clergy would impart "an entirely English tone and feeling" to the entire population. Moreover, if the extension of the National Church were to be coupled with a gradual increase of control over the direction of education by the clergy of the Church of England, "the very first feelings, sentiments and opinions of the youth must become British". He further maintained that:

> the tendency of the population is towards the Church of England, and nothing but the want of moderate support prevents her from spreading over the whole province.

Among the thirty clergymen of the Church of England in Upper Canada, Strachan counted a Lutheran minister who had converted to the Church of England and a Presbyterian minister who had approached Strachan about joining the Church. Moreover, the Church of England had forty-five churches in the province, ten of which were in the process of erection. Five vacant churches and the ten new churches would require the provision of a salary for a minister. It was calculated that, when fully populated, the province would require the services of some 2,000 clergymen – "a very small number for a country nearly as large as England".

The potential income from the leases and sales of Clergy Reserves lots was not considered exorbitant for the establishment and maintenance of a spiritually-independent clergyman in a comfortable and respectable position in each parish of the province. Once parsonages and rectories were endowed throughout the province, it would facilitate the comprehension of the bulk of the population within the National Church, would provide for the religious needs of the province, and would enable the clergy to strengthen the British national character of the province through teaching its youth. (13)

In the Ecclesiastical Chart, Strachan provided the names of the 28 Anglican ministers who were appointed to a parish, and of the Lutheran minister convert, as well as the names and locations of six Presbyterian ministers of independent congregations that had no formal connection with the Kirk in Scotland, and the names and locations of two congregations that did have a Church of Scotland clergyman in residence. Two additional Church of Scotland congregations were noted as currently lacking a minister. The Ecclesiastical Chart concluded with a general comment on the number of Methodist ministers in Upper Canada, and the general lack of a formal education in theology on the part of the sectarian preachers in the province:

> As the Methodists have no settled Clergymen, it has been found difficult to ascertain the number of Itinerants employed, but it is presumed to be considerable, perhaps twenty to thirty in the whole province; one from England [a Wesleyan Methodist minister], settled at Kingston, appears to be a very superior person. The other denominations have very few teachers, and those seemingly very ignorant; .... (14)

When the Ecclesiastical Chart and the May 1827 letter of Archdeacon Strachan were published in Upper Canada in September 1827, it raised a storm of indignation among the religious sects, and the publication gave rise to denunciations of the views of Archdeacon Strachan in the opposition newspapers. It also served to strengthen the support of the 'American Methodists' for the democratic radicals in the assembly.

Partisan Attacks on the Established Church

Two years earlier, the 'American Methodists' had taken offence when the Rev. Strachan -- in a sermon preached on the death of Bishop Mountain (3 July 1825) -- had publicly deplored the "ignorance" (viz. lack of education) of the sectarian preachers in Upper Canada. He had claimed that they came "almost universally from the Republican States of America" where they were imbued with principles that were not supportive of "the political institutions of England". Moreover, Strachan had praised the concept of a church establishment in exclaiming that:

> No country can be called Christian, which does not give public support to Christianity. (15)

The publication of the Ecclesiastical Chart in September 1827 brought to the fore, once again, the arguments that the Methodists had raised a year earlier in opposition to similar assertions made by the Rev. Strachan in the funeral sermon. At that time, the Rev. Egerton Ryerson published a letter that had expressed the views of the 'American Methodists' in denouncing the union of church and state, and the prerogatives enjoyed by the Church of England in Upper Canada.

In the public letter of May 1826, Ryerson had denied that the preachers of the Episcopal Methodist Church were mostly Americans or were infected with American republican principles. In addition, Ryerson had confirmed the worst fears of the Anglican Tories in attacking the episcopal system of church government for not being found in Scripture (which the Tories had never claimed was the case), and in claiming that the Church of England was not a part of the British constitution (while the Tories held that it was). Moreover, he had upheld 'voluntaryism' as the proper Christian means of supporting a church (while the Tories believed in state support under the union of church and state).

Ryerson had advocated also the principle of 'religious equality'. On the one hand, religious equality involved a demand that the evangelical sects ought to have the same rights as the traditional churches -- Anglican,

Roman Catholic, Church of Scotland, Lutheran and Congregationalist – with respect to the solemnizing of marriages and the ownership of property as a church corporation. On the other hand, 'religious equality' was an aggressive battle cry. As interpreted by the evangelical sectarians, 'religious equality' demanded that the Church of England be stripped of the Clergy Reserves endowment and deprived of its establishment prerogatives; that the clergy of the Church of England be removed from the Legislature and their public positions and functions in Upper Canada; and that the status of the Church of England as the Established Church of Upper Canada be terminated through the 'separation of church and state'.

For the Tories, the professed beliefs of the Rev. Egerton Ryerson in 'the separation of church and state', 'religious equality', and 'voluntaryism', comprised political, religious, and cultural values that were particularly American, and contrary to the principles and values of the British Constitution and the Loyalist cultural heritage of the province. It was deplored that members of the Methodist Episcopal Church – and the evangelical sects more generally – were becoming increasingly politically active. The 'American Methodists' were making common cause with the democratic radicals in the Assembly who were espousing the religious principles and beliefs of the evangelicals. Moreover, both the sectarians and their radical allies were adopting the aggressive extra-parliamentary protest tactics of the political radicals in Britain.

In response to the September 1827 publication of Strachan's letter and Ecclesiastical Chart in Upper Canada, the Assembly received a series of petitions during the following winter. They included one great petition with 6,000 names that denounced the Ecclesiastical Chart comments of Archdeacon Strachan. (16) In response, the Assembly appointed a select committee to investigate the claims of the petitioners, including the claim set forth in several of the petitions that the signers and their children were in danger of suffering "from ecclesiastical domination".

The Select Committee was chaired by Marshall Spring Bidwell (an American immigrant, and a staunch Jeffersonian democrat), and was composed of the leading radicals in the Assembly. Members of the

Executive Council were summoned to appear for questioning, as well as members of the Legislative Council, and members of the Assembly itself. In addition, prominent citizens and ministers of the various religious denominations were summoned to testify before the Select Committee. Archdeacon Strachan, in a speech to the Legislative Council, defended his Ecclesiastical Chart. He professed that it was 'drawn up quickly from memory, without access to any reliable sources of information', and that although it contained "some errors, it was basically sound".

Select Committee Report, House of Assembly (March 1828)

The Select Committee of the Assembly completed its report in March 1828. The report denied that the tendency of the people was towards the Church of England, attributed the success of the Church of England to the support which it received from England, and maintained that its clergymen could readily be supported by their own congregations. It was further asserted that the Church of England ought not to receive any support from Great Britain to proselytize the members of the other denominations. The Select Committee expressed its regret with respect to the insinuations that had been made against the Methodist clergy, and proclaimed them to be "pious men", who had not failed in "their Christian duty" to promote an attachment to the Sovereign and obedience to the law. Moreover, the Committee claimed that in Upper Canada, there were several denominations with more members than the Church of England, and "probably many more persons" who did not belong to any church.

One clause of the Assembly report conveyed an attack on the entire concept of an established church:

> It would be unjust and impolitic to exalt this church, by exclusive and peculiar rights, above all others of His Majesty's Subjects who are equally loyal, conscientious and deserving. A country in where there is an established Church from which a vast majority of the subjects are dissenters, must be in a lamentable state. ... ... If the church is incorporated with the state, they are compelled by the obligation of conscience to oppose one of the civil institutions of the country, a part of the government itself. It is in fact their duty to do so.

> ... It is well known that there is in the minds of the people generally a strong and settled aversion to anything like an established Church. ... There is besides no necessity for such an establishment.

The report of the Select Committee of the Assembly – the Bidwell Report -- concluded that there was no reason to suppose that a church establishment "will promote and strengthen loyalty, and all other virtues" any better than the other denominations; and it was pointed out that in New York State, "where all denominations have by law equal rights", the [Anglican] Episcopal Church was in "a respectable and flourishing state". (17)

The Methodist-Radical Appeal to the House of Commons, 1828

In the spring of 1828, while on business in London, the Rev. George Ryerson – a Methodist preacher and the eldest of the Ryerson brothers – was delegated to place several Upper Canadian petitions before a Select Committee of the House of Commons on the Civil Government of Canada. He informed the Committee that the petitioners wanted the Clergy Reserves to be sold and the proceeds used to support public schools and to promote public improvements, and he read into the record the resolutions that had been passed by the House of Assembly in December 1826. One of the resolutions declared that to interpret the phrase "a Protestant Clergy" to apply solely to the Church of England, was "contrary to the spirit and meaning" of the Constitutional Act; and another resolution called for the sale of the Clergy Reserves lands with the proceeds to provide funding:

> for district and common schools, and the endowment of a provincial seminary for learning, and in aid of erecting places of public worship for all denominations of Christians.

In testifying before the Committee, the Rev. George Ryerson defended the Methodists as being 'loyal British subjects' and questioned the accuracy and completeness of the Ecclesiastical Chart. He maintained that the Methodists were by far the largest religious denomination in Upper Canada; that the Independent Presbyterians and Church of Scotland Presbyterians together had the next largest denomination; and that the Anglican and Baptist denominations were about equal in numbers and close to the Presbyterians. One-fifth of Upper Canadians were not affiliated with any denomination; and the Roman Catholics were only a few in number and comprised mostly some French Canadians in the west of the province and some Highland Scots in the eastern part of the province. There was also a significant number of Quakers and Menonists [sic] in several large German settlements.

Ryerson attested that religion had never been a political issue before in Upper Canada, but:

> the ecclesiastical chart and the charter of the college have tended to unite all the different denominations of Christians together in a party opposed to the Church of England, and to those who uphold its exclusive claims. They have not opposed the Church before, but they feel themselves called upon to do it in defence of their civil rights and religious liberties now.

He gave his opinion that if the Clergy Reserves were to be sold and the proceeds used for the benefit of the people of the province, that if the projected 'Anglican university' were to be made completely non-denominational, and that if the Legislative Council could be made more responsive to the wishes of the people, it would put an end to all "jealousy, contention and dissatisfaction" and would "restore harmony and confidence in the colony". On a more general note, he commented that Upper Canadians were universally opposed to any proposed union of Upper Canada with the Province of Lower Canada, but favoured the annexation of the Island of Montreal to Upper Canada to provide the inland province with a seaport. It would put an end to interprovincial disputes over the division of the revenues which were derived from import duties.

The Rev. George Ryerson concluded his testimony by reassuring the members of the parliamentary committee that:

> The inhabitants of Upper Canada do not wish for or want a *democracy*. They prefer British government to that of the United States. ... Liberal institutions will bring many valuable immigrants from the United States, men who would prefer

liberty under a regular government to the anarchy and strife of democracy. (18)

The testimony of the Rev. George Ryerson was such as would appeal to the radicals on the Select Committee, to members of the House of Commons of a radical or liberal-Whig persuasion, and perhaps even to moderate Tory members, although the argument based on the so-called 'spirit' of the Constitutional Act was rather weak and highly questionable. However, the new Tory Government of the Duke of Wellington continued to adhere to the Clergy Reserves Sale and Improvement Act that the Colonial Secretary, William Huskisson, had guided through Parliament the previous year.

The Sectarian Attack on the Church of England

In the lead-up to the July 1828 provincial election, the sectarian attacks on the Established Church, the Clergy Reserves, and the newly-bestowed Charter for the University of King's College increased in animosity. The Rev. Egerton Ryerson of the Methodist Episcopal Church published a series of eight letters -- during May 1828 -- in which he attacked the assertions that had been made by Archdeacon Strachan in his now public Letter and Ecclesiastical Chart. Ryerson reasserted the arguments that were presented earlier by the democratic radicals and their sectarian allies in attacking the Church of England establishment and the Clergy Reserves. He also introduced a new argument.

The claims of Archdeacon Strachan -- that the teachings of the Established Church provided a strong support for political stability and good government, would render 'the feelings of the people entirely English', and would strengthen the connection of the colony to the mother country -- were denounced by Ryerson as being "disgraceful in the eyes of Christ". In serving a political purpose, it made the Church:

> an engine of the state, or even an ally of the state, ... a support of the royal as opposed to the popular form of government.

Furthermore, Ryerson questioned the legitimacy of the Church of England as an established church in Upper Canada. He confronted Anglicans with the claim that:

according to your own principles, the Church of England, ought not to be established in Upper Canada with peculiar legal privileges and endowments.

In support of that contention, the published *Works* of the English Anglican Whig, the Rev. William Paley, were cited by Ryerson to the effect that a church establishment ought to be based on "the general opinion and wishes of the people – the *voix populi*." The Rev. Paley – a renowned Christian apologist, philosopher, and utilitarian – asserted that the 'chief magistrate' in seeking to establish a national church for any country ought to select whichever Christian denomination was supported by the majority of the nation. On that basis, Ryerson argued that in Upper Canada -- where the Anglicans were but one of several religious denominations, and not the most numerous -- the establishment of the Church of England was lacking in legitimacy.

The arguments of the Rev. Paley in favour of the public benefits of a church establishment were ignored by Ryerson. He simply asserted – his own personal opinion -- that "the majority of the people" of Upper Canada were opposed to the entire principle of a church establishment. Moreover, Ryerson questioned whether a church establishment could promote "peace and happiness" among the people.

Among the criticisms that were leveled at the maintenance of an established church in Upper Canada was the oft-repeated claim that any union of church and state would prove fatal to the spiritually of the established church, would lead to abuses and corruption of the purity of her doctrine, and would undermine the religious zeal of her clergy. More particularly, it was asserted that a church establishment in Upper Canada -- in control of the Clergy Reserves, the establishment of schools, colleges, and universities through Archdeacon Strachan, the President of the General Board of Education – would have a strong influence on the provincial government. It threatened to "extinguish the light of liberty" and posed a danger to "the rights and liberties of all men".

Furthermore, it was stated that, historically, church establishments had fostered religious intolerance and the persecution of religious dissenters. Attention was called to the 'blood of the martyrs' who were persecuted in Germany in the conflict over church establishments during the Religious

Wars, the persecutions by the Roman Catholic Church establishment of the Huguenots in France at the time of Louis XIV and the persecutions of the Dutch Protestants in Holland under the Roman Catholic Church of the Spanish Hapsburgs.

More particularly, in England, the persecution and expulsion of the Calvinist 'Puritan' clergy from the Established Church of England under Charles II was cited, and a bald statement made to the effect that "the Bishops of the House of Lords are always the enemies of religious freedom". Moreover, it was asserted that in the American colonies:

> the clergy of England in America, with few exceptions, supported those enslaving enactments which were saddled upon the Americans by the Imperial Administration.

After attacking the entire concept of an established church, condemning the Anglican clergy for their loyalty to the Crown during the American Revolution, and declaring that the Church of England ought not to be the established church of Upper Canada, Ryerson then made a novel assertion. In a public letter of 18 May 1828 (Letter Six), he asserted that the Church of England was not established by law in Upper Canada. He argued that there was no one parliamentary enactment that declared the Church of England to be the established church of Upper Canada, and hence it was not legally established. Then Ryerson drew attention to the clause in the Constitution Act that gave the Legislature the right to alter or amend the prerogatives and endowments that the Church of England enjoyed in Upper Canada. He neglected to mention that any such provincial act would require the assent of both Houses of Parliament, but his intention was quite clear with respect to the Clergy Reserves. There was an accompanying assertion that financial provisions were needed for churches and schools in keeping with "the wants and wishes of the majority of the population" of the Province.

Furthermore, with respect to the Clergy Reserves, Ryerson revived a claim, made earlier by Dr. John Rolph in the Assembly debate, that the phrase "a Protestant Clergy" in the Constitutional Act did not refer specifically to the clergy of the Church of England. In ignoring the accepted historical meaning and common usage of the phrase "Protestant Clergy" as a synonym for the established Church of England clergy, Ryerson reiterated an earlier claim of the democratic radicals that the phrase referred to 'all of the Protestant Clergy' of the province, in contradistinction to the Roman Catholic clergy. Moreover, Ryerson claimed that the sectarian ministers were included in the phrase 'a Protestant Clergy' because the great English barrister, Sir William Blackstone in his *Commentaries on the Laws of England* (1765) had asserted that the ministers of the dissenting sects were 'clergy' in so far as the law was concerned'. Hence, a conclusion was drawn that "all clergy [of the Protestant churches and sects] are without distinction Protestant Clergy".

In sum, the Rev. Egerton Ryerson maintained that the religious sects of Upper Canada had a right to a share of the clergy reserve revenues, and that right was being denied by the Anglican Tories who were supposedly placing a selfishly-narrow interpretation upon the phrase 'a Protestant Clergy'. The earlier Address of the Assembly to the King in 1824, that had 'prayed' for a distribution of the revenues from the Clergy Reserves 'among all of the Protestant clergy', was now converted into an argument that all 'Protestant clergy' of Upper Canada – inclusive of the ministers of the dissenting churches and the preachers of the religious sects -- were entitled to an equal share of the revenues. A new 'grievance' was born in that the sectarian 'clergy' were supposedly being denied their legitimate share of the revenues yielded by the Clergy Reserves. How a minister of a religious sect that believed in voluntaryism could demand financial support from a land endowment that was established by the Crown, remained unexplained.

Having set forth arguments which were aimed at undermining the Church of England establishment and its claim to an exclusive possession of the Clergy Reserves revenues, Ryerson then sounded an alarm to rouse the sectarians to support the radicals of the Reform Party in the July 1828 provincial election. The sectarians were called upon to unite to oppose "every infringement of our religious liberties". They were warned, in the common rhetoric of evangelical preachers, that:

> an ecclesiastical establishment begins to show itself here, and the iron claws of the beast are about grappling the civil and religious interests and liberties of the people; .... We

see more than half a million people exposed to the imminent danger, and feel it is our duty to give the alarm, before we ourselves and our posterity are forever bound in chains, ... Of all scourges, with which mankind is cursed, Ecclesiastical tyranny is the worst.

...we are now brought to the conclusion that every judicious friend of government ought to be laboring to separate religion from the state. (19)

The 'Saddlebag Assembly', Tenth Parliament, January 1829- March 1830

In the subsequent provincial election of July 1828, the Reform Party attained a majority in the Assembly. In time, the Assembly came to be known as the 'Saddlebags Assembly' because of the large number of 'American Methodist' members. They had stood for election and benefitted from a heavy turnout of the evangelical sectarians during the election in responding to the furor that the May 1828 letters of the Rev. Egerton Ryerson had generated.

In each session of the Tenth Parliament, a bill was passed -- in early1829 and again in early 1830 – that called for the Clergy Reserves lands to be sold, and the proceeds devoted to education and internal improvements. It was a new tactic to secure the support of all the Reform members of the Assembly, inclusive of the evangelical sectarian members who remained strict voluntaryists. In both sessions, the bill to that effect was defeated in the Legislative Council where the Anglican Tories commanded a majority. (20) However, the new Lt. Governor, Major-General Sir John Colborne – who had assumed office in November 1828 – quickly analyzed the situation. He realized that the democratic radicals and their sectarian allies -- principally the 'American Methodists' -- posed a grave threat not only to the Clergy Reserves, but to the established Church of England and the 'peace, order and good government' of the province.

To counteract the political influence and strength of the democratic radicals and their sectarian allies, Colborne and his Anglican Tory supporters began to look for support to the British immigrants who were emigrating to Upper Canada in increasingly great numbers during the early 1830s. It was believed that the British immigrants would not only strengthen the British national character of the province, but would be supporters of the British Constitution, the church-state union, and the unity of the British Empire. Hence, every effort was made by the provincial government to encourage British emigration, to provide the British immigrants with settlement information and advice upon their arrival, to guide new immigrants to the new areas of settlement, and to provide support for the Emigrant Societies in Upper Canada that were providing the new immigrants with aid and assistance where and when needed. Moreover, an effort was made by the provincial government to encourage British immigrants to settle in the London and Western districts where the non-Loyalist American settlers and their descendants were the most numerous.

Once the new British immigrants completed their settlement duties and were in possession of their land title and the right to vote, it was expected that -- regardless of whether they were Tories, Whigs, or radicals in Britain -- they would support the Tories in Upper Canada. The rationale for that assumption was explained somewhat later – in 1833 -- by a conservative newspaper editor. In Britain, there were political differences and divisions over the powers of the House of Commons and the reform of the constitution, but all members – except for some prominent radicals – were loyal to the British constitution and the Crown. The political situation was different in Upper Canada, where the political contest was evolving into a struggle between monarchical government and democratic republicanism. In such a contest, the British immigrant Whigs and British political radicals would support the Tories in upholding monarchical government.

In sum, given the nature of politics in Upper Canada, Lt. Governor Colborne and the Tories were confident of receiving the future support of the new British immigrant settlers -- regardless of their home political affiliations -- to bolster the defence of monarchical government, the balanced constitution, the church-state polity, and the Imperial connection. (21)

During the Tenth Parliament (1829-1830), an effort was made to resolve the long-festering marriage law issue through the provincial government sponsoring legislation to extend the right to solemnize marriage to 'the clergy' of the religious sects. It was the one issue, more than any other, that had brought the religious sects into politics initially; that had forged their alliance with the democratic radicals of Upper Canada; and that had fostered discontent among the religious sects since the very founding of the province.

The provincial government initiative to resolve the marriage issue was in keeping with the desire of Lt. Governor Colborne, and his Executive Council, to undermine public support for the Reform Party. Where the marriage law was concerned, it was a situation where there was a willingness, and a compelling rationale, for a broadening of the marriage law to authorize preachers of the religious sects to perform marriages. Despite a concern as to whether proper records would be maintained, and the solemnity of the holy sacrament of marriage respected, a long-held Tory political position was sacrificed for the achievement of a greater good: social peace and, hopefully, the lessening of sectarian support for the Reform Party in its attacks on the Established Church and the Clergy Reserves.

The Marriage Law Political Controversy

From the beginning of settlement, marriages among the Loyalist refugees were performed by justices of the peace, by the Anglican chaplain of a military regiment, or by the commanding officer of a fort, in the absence of a parish priest of the Church of England. There was no uniform system for maintaining marriage records, and at that time, only the Church of England clergy -- and the Roman Catholic clergy -- were authorized in law to perform marriages. Soon after the 1791 founding of the Province of Upper Canada, the Legislature under Lt. Governor, Lt. Col. John Graves Simcoe, had passed a marriage act.

The Marriage Act of 1793 had legitimized all marriages contracted previously. The Act stipulated that all marriages would be legally recognized for couples who, within three years of the passing of the act, secured an affidavit confirming their marriage and entered their marriage, and the names of their children, on a register which was to be kept by the local Justice of the Peace. Secondly, the act decreed that if a couple who were planning to be married, lived more than eighteen miles from an Anglican clergyman in a district with fewer than five Anglican clergy, then the local Justice of the Peace could conduct the marriage ceremony in accordance with the rites of the established Church of England. Where there were more than five Anglican clergy in a district – at a time when Upper Canada was divided into four districts -- the Justices of the Peace of that district were not authorized to conduct marriages. In effect, the Marriage Act of 1793 was a compromise that was intended to meet an immediate practical need, while maintaining the legal status of the established Church of England as the sole Protestant church authorized to solemnize marriages in Upper Canada.

Following the return to England of Lt. Governor Simcoe -- who was a staunch defender of the rights and prerogatives of the established Church of England – a new marriage act was enacted. The Marriage Act of 1798 authorized the clergy of the Church of Scotland, the Lutheran Church, and the 'Calvinists' [the Congregational Church], to solemnize marriages in situations where one of the individuals to be married had been a member of that particular religious denomination for a period of at least six months. To perform the marriage ceremony, a dissenting minister had to be regularly ordained -- as confirmed by a certificate issued by a magistrate in Quarter Sessions -- and had to have taken the Oath of Allegiance to the King. Prior to the marriage ceremony, the traditional banns had to be read for three Sundays in a row, and after the wedding, the marriage certificate was to be registered with the Clerk of the Peace.

The rationale that was given for extending the right to perform marriages to the clergy of the dissenting churches was political as well as religious. Despite their dissenting status in Upper Canada, it was noted that each of the dissenting churches was established in another country, had a learned and regularly-ordained clergy, and an established ritual, and the dissenting churches were supporters of the traditional order in its political, social and religious aspects. Indeed, the dissenting churches were regarded as allies of the established Church of England in resisting the spread of infidelity, anarchy, and fanaticism, which promoted 'sedition'. Another factor was that in Upper Canada, as of 1798, many of the adherents of the dissenting churches were Loyalists. On the other hand, the exclusion of the preachers of the various evangelical religious sects from the marriage law was quite deliberate. They were self-proclaimed preachers who espoused a wide variety of different religious beliefs and principles. To the Tories, the sectarian preachers appeared to be united only in "their refusal to conform to the Established Religion of the Province".

Attempts to enforce the marriage law had been made under an earlier act of the British Parliament: 'An Act for the better prevention of Clandestine Marriages' (1753). It had made the performance of a marriage ceremony by an unauthorized clergyman, or other person, a felony punishable by transportation for fourteen years to the American colonies. (Only Jews and Quakers were exempt from prosecution under the Act.) However, in Upper Canada only a few sectarian preachers were ever prosecuted under the Clandestine Marriages Act for illegally performing a marriage ceremony and, given the severity of the punishment, juries either had acquitted the accused or, if convicted, the felon had been readily pardoned by the Lt. Governor.

Nonetheless, the Upper Canadian Marriage Act of 1798 had divided Upper Canadians along religious lines, and it became a major political issue following the influx of a massive wave of non-Loyalist Americans who settled in Upper Canada -- to secure free Crown land grants -- in the two decades prior to the War of 1812. At that time, the Upper Canadian Tories were alarmed that the province was being populated by American settlers who had no preference for, or attachment to, the civil and religious institutions of the Province. What had been equally alarming to the Anglican Tories was that many of the American immigrants, who were settling in Upper Canada, were either dissenters or adherents of American evangelical religious sects. Among the non-Loyalist American settlers, the Methodist Episcopal Church enjoyed the most adherents and proved to be the most successful in converting the frontier settlers. American Methodism had expanded quickly through the efforts of itinerant preachers who were sent into the Province from the United States.

As early as 1800, the Assembly had passed a bill to authorize Methodist preachers to conduct marriage ceremonies and to legalize the marriages that had been performed previously by the itinerant preachers. The bill was rejected by the Legislative Council, as was similarly the case over succeeding years when, at each session of the provincial parliament, the democratic radicals brought forward a bill to amend the marriage law. Within the provincial government, and particularly among the Upper Canadian Anglican Tories, there was a strong objection to extending the marriage law to include the self-ordained 'American Methodist' preachers as well as the preachers of the other sects.

In the pre-war period, the Methodist preachers were not viewed as being true members of the Christian clergy. They were characterized as uneducated and rustic part-time preachers, who were untrained in theology and given to an irrational religious zeal and highly-emotional preaching. Moreover, they were itinerants with no permanent ties to the community and were mostly Americans who were regarded as imbued with the 'spirit of democracy' and religious principles that were 'highly prejudicial to the peace of Society'.

Where enforcement of the marriage law was concerned, a new act was passed in 1821 that had reduced the offense for the performance of a marriage ceremony – 'by an unauthorized minister of religion, justice of the peace, or any other person' -- to a mere misdemeanour. However, the very next year, an attempt to prosecute a sectarian preacher, for conducting a marriage ceremony, was thwarted when the grand jury returned a verdict of 'no bill'. Thereafter, the marriage law had become a dead letter in terms of enforcement. Nonetheless, it had continued to serve as a potent symbol of a perceived injustice and was viewed as a major 'grievance' by the sectarian opponents of the provincial government.

For the evangelical sectarians, the marriage law constituted a denial of 'religious equality' and it drove them to support the democratic radicals of the Assembly. On their part, the radicals responded to their sectarian supporters by submitting a bill to amend the marriage law at each session of the provincial parliament. For the radicals, the rejection of their marriage law bills, by the Legislative Council, was a major 'grievance'. On the hustings, it provided fodder for the radical claim that the Legislative Council was denying 'the voice of the people'.

In the first session of the 'Saddlebags Assembly' of January 1829, the radicals once again introduced their customary resolution to amend the marriage law. A marriage law amendment bill was passed that provided an expanded list of the clergy who were to be authorized to perform the marriage ceremony in the Province of Upper Canada. In addition to the Church of England clergy, and the dissenting clergies of the Church of Scotland, the Lutheran Church, and the Congregational Church who were legally entitled to perform marriages under the earlier Act, the list also included the sectarian preachers: "the Baptists, Methodists, Quakers, Menonists [sic], and the Tinkers or Moravians". The resultant marriage bill was strongly supported in the House of Assembly, which was dominated by a radical majority. For the first time, the Legislative Council, rather than rejecting the bill, cooperated with the Assembly in the passing of the marriage bill. Following its passage through the Legislature, the revised marriage bill was reserved by Lt. Governor Colborne for 'His Majesty's pleasure'.

In the absence of any response from the Crown, the same marriage law amendment bill was introduced in the Assembly again, during the first session of parliament following the October 1830 provincial election. However, this time the marriage bill was introduced by the Attorney General, Henry John Boulton, as a provincial government measure. The bill was passed by a large majority of 44 to 8 in the Assembly of the new Eleventh Parliament (January 1831-March 1834) in which the conservatives enjoyed a large majority. The marriage bill was under discussion in the Legislative Council when the Lt. Governor learned – through the receipt of a dispatch from London – that the marriage amendment act of the previous provincial parliament had received the royal assent.

For the provincial government, the intention of the new Marriage Law of 1831 was to put an end to the contentious marriage law political issue. To do so necessitated an acknowledgement, and a legal recognition, that the part-time preachers of the religious sects were Christian ministers and equally worthy of administering the sacrament of holy matrimony as the professional clergy of the Established Church of England and the clergy of the dissenting churches. Many of the sectarian preachers were regarded – by the Tories and liberal-Whigs -- as ill-educated enthusiasts who were lacked any sustained training in theology and were not properly ordained in the tradition of the Christian Church. It was a painful concession for the professional clergy who were well-educated men of culture, who were thoroughly trained in theology and were regularly ordained. Moreover, the professional clergy of the traditional churches were highly conscious of a need to sustain the social status of the clergy in an age which was becoming increasingly infested with the levelling 'spirit of democracy' and with self-proclaimed ministers who had supposedly received 'the call' to preach the Word of God.

Nonetheless, the Tory establishment had reached a conclusion that the marriage law needed to be amended to encompass the sectarian preachers. It was a political issue that had evolved to the point where it was pitting a large majority of the Assembly – the laity of all religions -- against the provincial government and its Legislative Council bulwark. (22) However, the new Marriage Act of 1831 did not end the involvement of the religious sects in politics, or their demand for 'religious equality' more generally. Nonetheless, it constituted a major step by Lt. Governor Colborne to address public 'grievances' and weaken support for the Reform Party.

The marriage law initiative of the provincial government, under Lt. Governor Colborne, was yet another example of the willingness of Archdeacon John Strachan -- and his Anglican Tory supporters who dominated the Executive and Legislative councils -- to make concessions on some issues to better protect and promote a greater good. Where religion was concerned, the greater good consisted of the evangelizing of the Province of Upper Canada by means of a spiritually-independent Anglican clergy fully supported by the revenues yielded by the clergy reserves endowment. The preservation of the clergy reserves endowment, under the control of the established Church of England, was the *sine qua non* for achieving that Christian objective.

Less than a decade earlier, the Rev. Strachan had followed a similar political strategy to undermine opposition to the Clergy Reserves. He was instrumental in the promoting of the Tithe Act legislation of 1823 which denied the traditional right of the Established Church to levy tithes within a parish on the stated grounds that the clergy reserves endowment was provided for the support of the National Church of Upper Canada. The intention had been to weaken the opposition to the established National Church, and to secure yet another legislative recognition of the property rights of the Church of England in the Clergy Reserves. The Tithe Act had surrendered nothing of substance. Upper Canadians were not paying tithes to the established Church of England, and no effort had ever been made to claim a right to tithes, or to enforce a collection of tithes in the province, nor was there ever any intention to do so.

In 1829-1831, the strong support of the Executive Council for the provincial government reversal of its long-standing opposition to an extension of the marriage law was yet another instance where a concession was deemed necessary. It was an effort to undermine public support for a political party – the Reform Party – which was attacking the Clergy Reserves. At that time, the Executive Council comprised six High Church Anglican Tories -- Archdeacon John Strachan, two of his former pupils, John Beverley Robinson (the Chief Justice) and George Herchmer Markland, as well as Peter Robinson (the Commissioner of Crown Lands, and elder brother of John Beverley Robinson), Joseph Wells and John Elmsley Jr. -- and one Roman Catholic, James Baby. All the members of the Executive Council were close friends and associates of Archdeacon Strachan and were members of the provincial Tory establishment. (23)

While working towards a settlement of the marriage law issue, the provincial government also had sought to resolve the contentious clergy reserves issue while protecting the interests of the established Church of England. That effort was based on the earlier initiative, on the part of Archdeacon John Strachan, that had culminated in the securing of a Clergy Reserves Sales and Improvement Act of 1827 from the British Parliament. The Act, which proceeded the arrival of Lt. Governor Colborne in Upper Canada, was intended to quiet the public agitation over the Clergy Reserves through selling off the Clergy Reserves lots, while using the monies raised to provide a long-term financial security for the Anglican clergy.

The Clergy Reserves Sales and Improvement Act

In 1828, preparations had proceeded to inaugurate the sale of clergy reserves lots as authorized by the Sales and Improvement Act – an act that was based on the scheme that the Rev. John Strachan had submitted to the Colonial Office during his visit to England. The basic intention was, as always, to achieve a secure and permanent investment income for the clergy of the established Church of England. Once such an income was secured, it would render the National Church clergy spiritually independent, and capable of serving as the authoritative voice of the Christian religion and morality in the parishes of Upper Canada. In sum, the Anglican clergy would be free of any dependence on government or subjection to coercion at the whim of the people.

William Huskisson, the Colonial Secretary, made it clear that the object, in authorizing the sales, was to provide a financial support for the Church of England clergy and to remove any impediment that the Clergy Reserves posed to the expansion of future settlement. He added the proviso that no township was to be totally deprived of clergy reserves lots in the sales process, and that "a tract of 300 to 400 acres should be reserved as a Glebe for the Protestant Clergyman who may in future times be settled in the township".

In Upper Canada, an Anglican Tory, Peter Robinson, the Commissioner of Crown Lands, was appointed to administer the authorized sale per annum of upwards of a quarter of the Clergy Reserves lots – as many as 100,000 acres annually. Upon assuming the office, Robinson posted a performance bond of £5,000 and two sureties each posted £2,500 bonds. His duties were to select and evaluate the 200-acre reserve lots that were to be sold in each district, to fix the price for the lots to be sold, to carry out the sale, and to collect the purchase monies. After deducting administrative expenses, the revenues were to be forwarded, semi-annually, to be invested in the public funds of Great Britain. In keeping with the terms of the Sales and Improvement Act, the interest that accrued from that investment – at a return of three-percent interest -- was to be employed to cover the administrative expenses, to provide support for 'the Protestant Clergy', and provide funding for the improvement of the remaining Clergy Reserves lots – such as road clearing -- to preclude them becoming an impediment to the expansion of settlement.

The lots were to be sold for a down payment of ten percent, with the purchase price to be paid off in nine equal annual payments, with interest. Purchasers were given the option of making earlier payments, if they so desired. In addition to new lot sales, existing lessees were given the option of a conversion of their lease into freehold, if they wished to purchase their lot at an agreed price. To preclude speculators from purchasing the clergy reserves lots, the granting of the land title was withheld until a lot was settled. Moreover, to facilitate the spread of new settlement, there was a provision that Clergy Reserves in the front ranges of new township surveys could be exchanged for lots in the back range of a township.

When sales of the clergy reserves lots commenced in January 1829, the program proved to be highly popular. Public complaints against the Clergy Reserves all but ceased, and farmers were reported to be purchasing the reserves lots for their sons to farm. (24) Nonetheless, the radicals in the Assembly, and the sectarians out of doors, continued their agitation against Anglican control of the Clergy Reserves, the prerogatives of the Church of England establishment, and the Charter of the projected University of King's College.

An Extra-parliamentary Association

Following the death of King George IV in June 1830, the provincial parliament was disolved and a provincial election held in October. At that time, with the province prospering through land sales during a period of heavy British immigration, and the sale of the clergy reserves lots proving highly popular, the political situation looked promising for the Anglican Tories in defending the established order. The long-festering alien question had been settled in May 1828, the marriage law amendment act was awaiting the royal assent, and the new Lt. Governor, Sir John Colborne -- an English Anglican-Tory – was enjoying an initial popularity with his willingness to address public grievances. In the provincial election of October 1830, the conservatives secured a strong majority in the House of Assembly. Several prominent Reform Party members of the Assembly – inclusive of William Warren Baldwin, Robert Baldwin, and Dr. John Rolph – were defeated at the hustings, as well as many of the Methodist members of the former 'Saddlebags Assembly'. The conservatives captured 37 of the 54 seats in an expanded House of Assembly.

When the provincial Parliament opened in January 1831, a staunch tory, Archibald McLean, was elected Speaker of the House by twelve votes over Marshall Spring Bidwell, the radical leader of the Reform Party. McLean was a member of the Church of Scotland, and former pupil of the Rev. John Strachan at the Cornwall District Grammar School. The conservatives enjoyed a large majority in the House of Assembly and were characterized by their loyalty to the Crown and the balanced British Constitution, and a belief in the traditional hierarchical social order. However, they were not united in support of any party program, and decidedly not in defence of the exclusive claim of the Church of England to the clergy reserves endowment. Indeed, Archibald McLean adhered to the view that the Church of Scotland was entitled to a one-half share of the Clergy Reserves endowment.

In contrast, under the leadership of Marshall Spring Bidwell, the Reformers were a disciplined party that was united under the banner of 'responsible government' in the Eleventh Parliament (January 1831-March 1834). As a self-styled "glorious minority', the Reform party continued to bring forward resolutions each session that called for all clergy reserves lots to be immediately sold and the proceeds devoted to education and internal improvements. The Reform Party resolutions were voted down in the Assembly, or rejected by the Legislative Council, but they served to keep the radicals united in the Assembly and their partisan political issues and 'grievances' before the public. (25)

Faced with a conservative Assembly in Upper Canada, the leaders of the agitation against the Church of England establishment and its control over the Clergy Reserves and the University of King's College Charter, shifted their focus to the Imperial Parliament. When the Tory government of the Duke of Wellington fell in November 1830 and was succeeded by the liberal-Whig reform government of Earl Grey, the Upper Canadian agitators – a coterie of liberal-Whigs, democratic radicals, and sectarian preachers -- saw an opportunity to renew their assault on the Clergy Reserves through an appeal to the new Reform Government in Britain. It was a time when the leaders of the Reform Party in Upper Canada, and their supporters, were euphoric over the coming to power of a liberal-Whig reform government in Britain. For the Reformers, it appeared to be the dawning of a whole new liberal era in which reform would triumph in Upper Canada, with the support of a liberal-Whig government in Britain.

In December 1830, a meeting was held in York under the chairmanship of Dr. William Warren Baldwin. At the meeting, a new extra-parliamentary association, the 'Friends of Religious Liberty', was formed with his son, Robert Baldwin, a prominent lawyer, elected as the President. At the suggestion of Dr. Thomas David Morrison, it was decided to forward a petition to the House of Commons, rather than to the Crown. Among the prominent members of the 'Friends of Religious Liberty' were three Anglicans (the two Baldwins who were liberal-whig constitutional Reformers, and Joseph Cawthra, a wealthy merchant/Reformer), a prosperous Methodist doctor (Dr. Morrison), and three evangelical preachers (the Rev. Egerton Ryerson and the Rev. William Smith who were 'American Methodists', and an Independent Presbyterian, the Rev. William Jenkins). In addition, there were two radical members of the Assembly present: Jesse Ketchum (a prominent Methodist philanthropist/tannery owner); and the radical newspaper editor, William Lyon Mackenzie, who was raised a Secessionist Presbyterian in Scotland. The petition was drafted by the Rev. Egerton Ryerson and Jesse Ketchum.

Thereafter, the Friends of Religious Liberty formed a Committee of 23 members, inclusive of the original nine members, to circulate the petition for signatures. The full Committee comprised: the three Anglicans, ten Presbyterians, eight 'American Methodists', one Baptist, and one Quaker. During the winter of 1830-1831, when travel was relatively easy over snow roads and frozen rivers, 10,000 signatures were gathered by the evangelical preachers on their circuits. In the spring, the Rev. George Ryerson was appointed to carry the petition to Britain where he met with the Colonial Secretary, Lord Goderich. The petition was also presented to the fall session of the House of Commons

-- in October 1831 -- by the British radical, Joseph Hume. The extent to which the Friends of Religious Liberty petition represented the views of a provincial population of over 260,000 persons, remained a moot point.

In their petition, the Friends of Religious Liberty prayed for Parliament to leave ministers of religion to be supported by their own congregations by ending all grants for the support of religion, to end all political distinctions based on religious faith by removing ministers of religion "from seats and places of political power" in the Provincial Government, and to grant "equal rights and privileges" to the clergy of all denominations of Christians, in particular with respect to the right to solemnize marriages. (In the interim, since the petition was drafted, the new provincial Marriage Act of 1831 had been enacted, which put an end to the marriage law issue.) In addition, the petition included a request that Parliament modify the King's College Charter "to exclude all sectarian tests and preferences", and that Parliament take steps:

> to appropriate the proceeds of the sale of lands heretofore set apart for the support of a Protestant Clergy, to the purposes of general education and various internal improvements.

Without specifically saying so, the Friends of Religious Liberty were requesting that the British Parliament, under the new liberal-Whig reform government, revolutionize the Provincial Government of Upper Canada through the legislating of a complete separation of church and state. It was a revolution that was to be accomplished by removing the Anglican clergy from all legislative, executive, and administrative bodies in the province, by the introduction of the sectarian 'voluntaryist' principle through the ending of British parliamentary grants to the Society for the Propagation of the Gospel (SPG) for the support of the Church of England clergy in Upper Canada, by the stripping the proposed University of King's College -- which already had a more liberal charter than any existing British or American university – of any religious affiliation, and by the secularization of the Clergy Reserves through diverting the revenue from land sales to the provincial Legislature for the support of education and internal improvements. It was a direct attack on the constitution of Upper Canada, the church-state union, and the established Church of England in Upper Canada, in the guise of a plea for an 'extension of civil and religious liberty'. (26)

In making such demands, the Upper Canadian agitators totally misunderstood the nature of the liberal-Whig Party which was governed by the great aristocratic families of Britain. The Whig party believed in parliamentary sovereignty, and under the Prime Minister, Earl Grey, was committed to parliamentary reform through an extension of the franchise to encompass the middle class and to the eliminate of rotten boroughs. Moreover, the Whigs had long advocated the repeal of The Corporation Act (1661) and The Test Act (1673) to end the religious tests that barred dissenters and Roman Catholics from a full participation in public life. Nonetheless, in Britain the religious toleration cause had but recently achieved its goal with the passage by parliament of the Sacramental Test Act (1828) and the Catholic Emancipation Act (1829) that relieved the political disabilities of the dissenters and Roman Catholics, respectively. Ironically, both acts were enacted under the Tory government of the Duke of Wellington, which had previously opposed the repeal of the so-called 'test acts'.

Despite their liberal-reform reputation, the Whigs in Britain were social conservatives who believed in a natural social hierarchy and only a limited parliamentary reform. Some of the parliamentary Radicals, who supported the Whig Party, were in favour of the disestablishment of the Church of England, but most Whigs were advocates of a reform of the Established Church, not the abolition of the church-state polity. Many shared the view of the Anglican whig, utilitarian philosopher, the Rev. William Paley, in valuing the established Church of England for its social utility in inculcating religious beliefs that sustained the social order.

The Colonial Secretary, Lord Goderich (Fredrick John Robinson), was a moderate Tory from a landed family. He had been elevated to the peerage as Viscount Goderich during the mid-1820s when he served as Chancellor of the Exchequer in the Tory administration of Lord Liverpool. Subsequently, he had served as Colonial Secretary and Leader of the House of Lords in a short-lived, moderate Tory-Whig coalition government in 1827 under Prime Minister George Canning. When Canning died, Goderich had succeeded him as Prime Minister at the head of the coalition government until it disintegrated in January 1828. Thereafter, Goderich had spoken in favour of parliamentary reform and the abolition of slavery throughout the British Empire, and in 1830 joined the new liberal-Whig reform government of Earl Grey as Secretary of State for War and the Colonies. Lord Goderich was a staunch supporter of the established Church of England. In sum, neither Lord Goderich, nor the Whig Government of Earl Grey, was about to overthrow the church-state polity of Upper Canada; although an effort was made to appease the political and religious agitators in Upper Canada to reduce their hostility towards the established Church of England. (27)

In response to the 'Friends of Religious Liberty' petition, Goderich prepared new Instructions for Lt. Governor Colborne. He was instructed to obtain the passage of a provincial act that would do two things. It was to vest the existing Clergy Reserves in the hands of the Crown, as Crown lands, and to remove the clause of the Constitutional Act of 1791 requiring the setting aside of one-seventh of the land in new township surveys for a clergy reserve. Moreover, Colborne was instructed to request that the Clergy Reserves Corporation surrender its charter.

The intention was to reduce discontent by stopping the setting aside of any further clergy reserves lots in new township surveys, and to place the interest from the investment of the revenue from the existing reserves lots (both leased and sold) in the Casual and Territorial Revenues of the Crown in Upper Canada, which was under the control of the Lt. Governor. Subsequently, Lord Goderich instructed the Lt. Governor, Sir John Colborne, that once the Anglican clergy were adequately supported, he was to provide financial grants to the Church of Scotland, to the 'Roman Catholic missions', and to the Methodists "in communication with the Wesleyan Methodists of Britain". The Church of Scotland and the 'Roman Catholic missions' in Upper Canada were already in receipt of an annual government grant. Nonetheless, the willingness of the Colonial Office to increase the government grants for the two traditional churches was intended to dissipate any feelings of 'jealousy' that the might be felt over the monies received by the Church of England from the Clergy Reserves Fund as that source of revenue increased through land sales.

The Goderich policy of providing increased financial support for the two traditional churches of Scotland and of Rome, and of undertaking to provide support for clergy of the Wesleyan Methodist Connexion, was what the Upper Canadian Anglican Tories had long advocated.

The Tories had expressed their support for the government providing financial grants to the dissenting churches and the Wesleyan Methodists with the proviso that the grants be paid from the Casual and Territorial Revenues of the Crown, and not from the Clergy Reserves Fund. However, there was one totally surprising development. The Colonial Secretary, Lord Goderich, informed Sir John Colborne that the Colonial Office was willing to see financial aid provided for the religious sects but had concluded -- given the limited Crown revenues -- that it was not feasible at present. It remained undetermined whether the voluntaryist religious sects would accept financial aid from government, if it were to be offered.

For the moderate Tory, Lord Goderich, the great objective was 'the diffusion of a religious feeling' among the people of Upper Canada, and the achievement of "a state of religious peace". In seeking to resolve the clergy reserves issue, Goderich also had a deeper motive. He wanted to protect the interests of the National Church and to expand its ministrations throughout the entire province. Hence, in a private communication, Lt. Governor Colborne was instructed to make sure that the proposed provincial clergy reserves act did not remove the clauses of the Constitution Act pertaining to the establishment of Church of England rectories and parsonages. Colborne was also instructed to take steps -- before the projected resumption of the Clergy Reserves by the Crown -- to divide each township into two parishes, to erect a rectory (residence) for each parish priest, and to attach a glebe of from 100 to 300 acres, depending on the local circumstances, to provide an additional revenue for the clergy of the National Church, the established Church of England.

In believing that the carrying out of his Instructions would provide a secure financial support for the future of the Established Church of Upper Canada, Lord Goderich announced that the British government would greatly reduce its grants to the Society for the Propagation of the Gospel in Foreign Parts as of 1832, and would end the financial grants in 1834. That was a particularly bitter blow to the Anglican Tories as the SPG was contributing substantially to the salaries of most of the Church of England clergy of Upper Canada in utilizing the British government grant money, while the clergy reserves revenues were being invested in

British funds to provide a secure future income for the Anglican clergy. Where the King's College political issue was concerned, Lord Goderich sent instructions to the Lt. Governor to request that the King's College Charter be surrendered to enable the land endowment to be managed by the provincial government for education purposes.

When the Instructions from the Colonial Office – minus the private communication – were presented to the House of Assembly in November 1832, the Goderich plan received little interest or support. A stalemate ensued. The Assembly, which had a conservative majority, continued to insist that the clergy reserve revenues ought to be controlled by the Legislature and devoted to education and internal improvements; whereas, the Legislative Council, which was dominated by High Church Anglican Tories, was opposed to any interference by the Assembly in the management of the clergy reserves endowment. On its part, the Colonial Office insisted that the clergy reserves issue had to be settled by an act of the provincial parliament which, under the Constitution of Upper Canada, would need to be approved by both the House of Commons and the House of Lords of the Imperial Parliament. Moreover, the situation was further complicated in that the High Church Anglican Tories, who were in control of the Clergy Reserves Corporation and the King's College Corporation, refused to surrender their respective charters.

Despite the lack of a settlement of the Clergy Reserves issue, the liberal-Whig government in Britain proceeded to phase out financial grants to the Society for the Propagation of the Gospel in Foreign Parts. However, the Colonial Office allowed the sale of the Clergy Reserves lots to proceed unhindered and removed the 100,000-acre annual limit on sales that had been imposed earlier. For the Upper Canadian Tories, the planned termination of parliamentary grants to the SPG made it imperative that they continue the struggle to retain the revenues, from the sales of the Clergy Reserves, solely for the benefit of the Church of England clergy. (28)

For Archdeacon Strachan, the attacks on the Clergy Reserves and the Church of England establishment were totally uncalled for and reprehensible. For a period of almost thirty years, from the founding of the 'Loyalist Asylum' of Upper Canada in 1791, there had been no public criticism of the Clergy Reserves as an obstacle to settlement. No one had denied that the Church of England was the established religion of the province, and no other religious denomination had made any claim for a share of the Clergy Reserves land endowment. That had changed only when the Clergy Reserves began to yield a revenue.

The original Loyalist settlers were loyal to the British Constitution and the Unity of Empire, as were most of the British immigrants. It was recognized that not all of the American immigrants, upon entering Upper Canada, were attached to the traditional British 'civil and religious institutions' of the Province. Nonetheless, they had received free land grants from the Crown, and had come to an English colony in which one-seventh of the land in each township was reserved for the support of the clergy of the established Church of England, and one-seventh as a Crown reserve. Such land reserves were common in many of the American states for the support of education and were by no means unusual in frontier areas. Moreover, Archdeacon Strachan expressed his view that the American immigrants, upon entering Upper Canada, must have been fully aware that:

> we are living under a British Constitution, and that our Establishments, Civil and Religious, are modeled upon that admirable fabric; [and] it is reasonable to assume that they were prepared to acquiesce in those institutions, and entertained no design of overturning them.

In Upper Canada, American immigrants had benefitted greatly in living under the British Constitution and the rule of law and in enjoying a security of property. Once the Oath of Allegiance to the King was sworn, and the settlement duties performed, the Americans who were settled in Upper Canada had a legal right to vote and to stand for election to the House of Assembly. Moreover, under the provincial Naturalization Act of May 1828, American settlers who declined to take the Oath of Allegiance to the King, but who were domiciled in Upper Canada prior to March 1, 1828, would enjoy the full civil rights of a British subject after a seven years' residence. What was more, Upper Canadians paid no direct taxes, and during the early years of settlement, the British Government had paid the entire cost of the civil government and the judiciary, as well as the costs incurred in road building and in defending the colony. Yet the hostility of the American evangelical sectarians towards the established Church of England was palpable, as was their hostility to the Clergy Reserves.

It was galling to the Upper Canadian Tories, that a Select Committee of the House of Commons in Britain would give credence to the claims of a comparatively small, "exceedingly clamorous, minority" of Upper Canadians – the so-called "Friends of Religious Liberty" -- who were attacking the civil and religious establishment of the Loyalist Province and the clergy reserves endowment. And it was particularly so when, at the same time, the liberal-Whig government in Britain was insistent that the legal rights and prerogatives of the Roman Catholic Church, and the far larger land endowments of the Roman Catholic clergy and of the Roman Catholic religious orders in Lower Canada, were sacrosanct. (29)

If the Clergy Reserves in the Province of Upper Canada were to be preserved from despoliation by the democratic radicals and their sectarian allies, it would have to be through the efforts of the provincial government with the support of the Anglican Tories. (30)

Notes

The Politics of Religion

Frontispiece quotation: *Report of the Select Committee to which was referred the petition of Bulkley Waters and others, entitled, The Petition of Christians of all denominations in Upper Canada, and other petitions on the same subject of E.W. Armstrong & others* (York: House of Assembly, March 1828). The aggressive language and threatening political stance expressed in the paragraph quoted from the House of Assembly report, is typical of the mindset of the sectarian adherents of American evangelical Protestantism within the Reform Party.

Much of this chapter was written originally as part of an exceptionally-long chapter, "A Spiritually-independent Clergy', in the original draft of the dissertation, but has been moved to the beginning of this new chapter, "The Politics of Religion". Additional historical material has been inserted, and added, to set forth the principles and arguments of the sectarians, and to capture their inveterate hostility to a church establishment and the union of church and state.

1. Strachan, 'Speech in Legislative Council', 1828, 32; and Doughty and Story, *Documents*, "Address of Assembly, Upper Canada", 27 January 1826, 282-283. The quotation is from the *Documents*, 283. For the social, religious and political principles of the American evangelical sects of the Great Awakening of the 1740s and the subsequent American revolutionary period, see: Alan Heimert, *Religion and the American Mind, From the Great Awakening to the Revolution* (Cambridge, Massachusetts: Harvard University Press, 1966).

2. Strachan, *Observations on the Provision*, 1827, 20-21; and Craig, *Upper Canada*, 172.

3. Moir, ed., *Church and State*, 168, R.W. Horton, Under Secretary of State for War and the Colonies, to Rev. Dr. Mearns, 9 June 1825, and 168, Earl Bathurst to Lord Dalhousie, 6 June 1826, and 169-170, Earl Bathurst to Maitland, 6 October 1826; Strachan, "Speech in Legislative Council', 1828, 33; Doughty and Story, *Documents*, 203-204, "Opinion of James Stephen, 9 January 1824"; Wilson, *Clergy Reserves*, 89, Strachan to Maitland, 16 July 1826; PAO,

Macaulay Papers, reel 1, R. Stanton to John Macaulay, 29 June 1826 and 3 September 1827; and *The Church*, (Bethune editorial), 3 March 1838.

4. Provincial Archives of Ontario (PAO), Macaulay Papers, reel 1, John B. Robinson to John Macaulay, 11 April 1826, and Robert Stanton to J. Macaulay, 29 June, and series of letters 8, 15, 22 and 25 July and 5 August 1826. The quotations are from Stanton to Macaulay, 29 June and 15 July 1826, respectively. [Robert Stanton was the Canadian-born son of a former Royal Navy Officer, William Stanton, the Sergeant-at-Arms of the House of Assembly at York. Young Stanton was a former pupil of John Strachan, and a staunch Anglican Tory, who as of 1826 was the King's Printer responsible for publishing the *Upper Canada Gazette*, as well as the editor of the *UE Loyalist*. (Hilary Bates Neary, "Stanton, Robert", *Dictionary of Canadian Biography*, IX.) See also, Robert Lochiel Fraser, "Barclay, John", *DCB*, VI.]

5. PAO, Macaulay Papers, reel 1, Robert Stanton to John Macauley, 22 July 1826; *The Church*, (Bethune editorial), 3 March 1838; and Strachan, "Religious State of Upper Canada", 29-31 in *Observations on the Provision for the Maintenance of a Protestant Clergy*, 1827. Much of this paragraph is derived from Strachan "Religious State of Upper Canada", 31, in which he quotes at length from an 1826 pamphlet addressed to Lord Liverpool from a "dissenting (Methodist) clergyman".

It is presumed that the pamphlet was written by the English Wesleyan Methodist minister at Kingston, because of an analysis of the content, and the subsequent reference by Strachan, in the Ecclesiastical Chart, to the Wesleyan minister at Kingston as being "a very superior person". It was the sectarians, principally the preachers of the Methodist Episcopal Church -- whom the Tories referred to as "American Methodists" or "Yankee Methodists", who were in the forefront in denouncing the union of church and state, the Church of England establishment, and the Biblical legitimacy of the Anglican episcopal system of church government.

6. *U.E. Loyalist*, 23 December 1826, "Proceedings in Parliament"; PAO, Macaulay Papers, Robert Stanton to John Macaulay, 17 & 24 December 1826; *The Church*, (Bethune editorial), 3 March 1838; and *U.E. Loyalist*, (Stanton editorial), 12 January 1828. The quotations are from Stanton to Macaulay, 24 December 1826.

7. *U. E. Loyalist*, 23 & 30 December 1826, "Proceedings in Parliament, speeches of John Rolph, William Morris, James Wilson, and Mr. Coleman on December

15 and Rolph on December 21. With respect to the strategy of the radicals in the Assembly, see the Rolph speech of December 21st.

8. *U.E. Loyalist*, 23 & 30 December 1826 and 13 January 1827, "Proceedings in Parliament", speeches of John Rolph of 15 and 21 December 1826 and 3 January 1827. The quotation is from the speech of Rolph, 3 January 1827.

9. *U.E. Loyalist*, 16 & 23 December 1826 and 13 January 1827, "Proceedings in Parliament", speeches of Attorney General Robinson, 11 and 15 December 1626, and 3 January 1827. The quotation is from the speech of Robinson of 11 December 1826.

10. PAO, Strachan Papers, Strachan Letter Book, 1327-39, 6-7, Strachan to the Bishop of Quebec, 5 November 1827; PAO, Macaulay Papers, reel 1, Strachan to John Macaulay 7 December 1827, and Robert Stanton to Macaulay, 20 January, 31 July and 27 August 1827. The first two quotations are from Stanton to Macaulay, 20 January 1827, and the third from the Stanton to Macaulay, 28 August 1827, respectively.

11. Wilson, *Clergy Reserves*, 93-94; PAO, Macaulay Papers, reel 1, Robert Stanton to John Macaulay, 8 July 1826, and 13 & 20 September 1827; MTCL, Strachan Papers, Strachan to Wilmot Horton, 15 May 1826; Doughty and Story, *Documents*, 274-275, "Opinion of Executive Council, Upper Canada, 21 November 1825"; Hodgins, ed., *DHE*, 1, 213, Strachan, Memorandum to Maitland, March 1826.

12. Craig, *Upper Canada*, 173-174 & 184; and Dunham, *Political Unrest*, 91.

13. PAO, Strachan Papers, reel 2, *Canada Church Establishment: Copy of a Letter addressed to R.J. Wilmot Horton, Esq. by the Rev. Dr. Strachan, Archdeacon of York, Upper Canada, dated 16 May 1827, respecting the State of the Church in that Province* (printed by the House of Commons, 22 May 1827). See also MTCL, Strachan Papers, Strachan to Wilmot Horton, 15 May 1826; and PAO, Strachan Papers, Strachan Letter Book, 1827-34, Strachan to Archdeacon George Mountain, 31 December 1827, point 10th. The quotations are from Strachan to Wilmot Horton, 15 May 1826, and Strachan, *Canada Church Establishment*, 16 May 1827, respectively.

One problem that plagued the Tory elite was that there were many Anglicans in Upper Canada – moderate Tories and Anglican Whigs, inclusive of members of the House of Assembly -- who were willing to sacrifice the clergy reserves endowment for the sake of achieving social peace and religious harmony through appeasing the evangelical sectarians and their democratic radical allies.

14. PAO, Strachan Papers, reel 2, Strachan, *Canada Church Establishment*, "Ecclesiastical Chart for the Diocese of Upper Canada, for 1827", 16 May 1827. In the newly-independent Methodist Episcopal Church in Upper Canada as of 1828, there were 48 itinerant preachers of whom a good many were part-time preachers with a secondary occupation. Three years earlier, while under the direction of the Genesee Conference of New York State, the Methodist elders had lamented the general lack of education among the young Methodist preachers. (Goldwin French, *Parsons & Politics,* 103 & 77.) The claim by the Rev. John Strachan in 1827 that the 'American Methodists' preachers were poorly educated and were mostly from the United States where they absorbed their political principles, appears to have been completely accurate, despite the vehement protestations of the Rev. Ryerson and the radical members of the Assembly to the contrary.

15. Strachan, *Sermon preached at York, U.C., July 3rd, 1825*; Dunham, *Political Unrest*, 91; and Craig, *Upper Canada*, 172-173. As early as 1824, the "American Methodist' ministers in Upper Canada had requested authorization to set up a separate Canadian conference. However, the circuit preachers of the Methodist Episcopal Church in the province remained under the superintendence of the Genesee Conference of the Methodist Episcopal Church of America until October 1828 when a separate 'Methodist Episcopal Church in Canada' was formed. During the pre-war and immediate post-war years, most of the Methodist preachers were from the United States or were trained in the United States and assigned to the circuits in Upper Canada by the American conference. As of the early 1820s, the Methodist ministers underwent only a brief trial period of study before being assigned to a circuit. Some of itinerant preachers were noted "more for their piety and exhortations in preaching than their learning and knowledge of theology". Only in 1824 did the Genesee conference establish a seminary -- at Cozenovia in upper New York State -- for the education of Methodist ministers. (Nathan Bangs, D.D., *A History of the Methodist Episcopal Church, Vol. III, From the years 1817 to the Year 1828* (New York, T. Mason & G. Lane, 1840), 45, 48, 288, 388 & 390-394; and Goldwin French, *Parsons & Politics,* 42, 45 & 69. Thereafter, the new Methodist preachers studied at the Cozenovia seminary in the absence of an Upper Canadian Methodist seminary.

16. *Colonial Advocate*, 11 May 1826, by "A Methodist Preacher" [Egerton Ryerson]. The Ryerson family experience, from the Tory viewpoint, was a potent example of the ill-effects of itinerant 'American Methodist' preachers holding camp meetings in the province in the absence of clergymen of the Established Church. The patriarch of the Ryerson family, Col. Joseph Ryerson, was an Anglican Tory Loyalist from New Jersey. He saw active service as an officer of a Loyalist regiment during the American revolutionary war, and

eventually settled in Norfolk County, Upper Canada, where he served as a magistrate and commanded a Norfolk Militia regiment during War of 1812. To his chagrin, after the War, his wife and five of his six sons – inclusive of Egerton -- were converted to Methodism by itinerant 'American Methodist' evangelical preachers. The five Ryerson brother who were converted, all became Methodist preachers and proceeded, with all the zeal of converts, to attack and foster hostility towards the established Church of England. See Sissons, *Egerton Ryerson*, I, 23-28; Wilson, *Clergy Reserves*, 70; and R.C. Good, "Strachan Letter Book", 27, Strachan to Dr. Hamilton, 14 August 1828, and 33, Strachan to Hargreaves, 15 August 1828. In the two letters cited, Strachan refers to the 'hostility' of the Ryerson brothers towards the Church of England. In 1827, there were 8,594 Methodists in Upper Canada (Bangs, III, 432); and the Province had a population of 177,174 (Statistics Canada online, Censuses of Canada, 1665-1871).

17. Craig, *Upper Canada*, 174-175; Dunham, *Political Unrest*, 91-92; and Select Committee Report, by Marshall Spring Bidwell, Peter Perry Esquire, John Matthews Esquire, Hugh Christopher Thomson, and George Hamilton Esquire (York: Ordered by the House of Assembly to be printed, March 1828). The quotation is from the Select Committee Report.

The Select Committee Report of the House of Assembly was reprinted in its entirety years later in an article by the Rev. Dr. Ryerson, "Canadian Methodism; Its Epochs and Characteristics" in the *Canadian Methodist Magazine*, vol. XII, July-December 1880, 29-36. The quotation cited in the chapter text can be found as well on page 32 of the magazine reprint. The strident language, the nature of the argument, and the threatening tone, of the Select Committee Report of the House of Assembly is typical of the writings of Egerton Ryerson. It appears that Ryerson wrote the Select Committee report for the Bidwell Committee.

18. Great Britain, House of Commons, *Report from the Select Committee on the Civil Government of Canada* (Ordered printed by the House of Commons, 22 July 1828), 216- 223, Testimony of Mr. George Ryerson, 19 June 1828. The quotations are from pages 220, 218-219 & 223, respectively, of the Ryerson testimony.

19. *Letters from the Reverend Egerton Ryerson to the Hon. and Reverend Doctor Strachan, published originally in the Upper Canada Herald* (Kingston, U.C.: Herald Office, 1828). The quotations are from: Letter 4, 11 May 1828, 13; Letter 7, 28 May 1828, 26; and Letter 4, 11 May 1828, 14 & 16, respectively. For the views of William Paley on church establishment, see: *The Works of William Paley, D.D., in Five Volumes, Volume III, containing the Principles*

of Moral and Political Philosophy (Newport, Rhode Island: Rousmaniere and Barber, 1811), 461-462. The Church of England in Upper Canada was far from enjoying the traditional character, rights, and local parish administration function of the established Church in England and actually possessed a very limited establishment. See, William Westfall, *Two Worlds, The Protestant Culture of Nineteenth-Century Ontario* (Montreal & Kingston: McGill-Queen's University Press, 93-97.

The religion of the preachers of the Methodist Episcopal Church in Upper Canada -- whom the Tories referred to as 'American Methodists' -- was a product of the evolution of American evangelical Protestantism. The religious principles of the 'American Methodists' were derived from the evangelical Calvinist sectarians of the Great Awakening (1730s-1740s) in the Thirteen Colonies; and the political activism of the 'American Methodists' was spurred by a confounding of the religious principles of the evangelical Calvinists with the political principles of the revolutionaries during the American Revolution (1776-1783). See, Heimet, *Religion and the American Mind*, 454-524. The democratic egalitarian character and levelling spirit of the 'American Methodists' was formed subsequently during the Second Great Awakening (1790-1820) in the northern United States. See, Nathan O. Hatch, *The Democratization of American Christianity* (New Haven: Yale University Press, 1989).

20. Dunham, *Political Unrest*, 115-116; and Craig, *Upper Canada*, 175-176. On the extremely partisan character of the House of Assembly under a radical majority – which was composed to a large extent of 'American Methodists' -- during the Tenth Parliament (1829-1830), and the erratic political activities and charged political rhetoric of William Lyon Mackenzie, see Le Sueur, *William Lyon Mackenzie*, 120-140.

21. This section is based on Craig, *Upper Canada*, 228-229.

22. Craig, *Upper Canada*, 28, 30-31 & 55-56; William Renwick Riddell, "The Law of Marriage in Upper Canada", *Canadian Historical Review*, II, no. 3, September 1921, 226-248; and William Renwick Riddell, "The Criminal Law in Reference to Marriage in Upper Canada", *Ontario Historical Society, Papers & Records*, XXI, 1924, 233-235. On the Tory view of the American settlers, see: Chapter One. On the character of the early Methodist preachers, see: French, *Parsons & Politics*, 21-23. For a further elaboration, by the Rev. John Strachan, on the nature of the threat posed by the poorly educated, part-time, sectarian preachers to the social standing of the professional clergy, see Fahey, *The Anglican Experience in Upper Canada*, 95-96.

23. On the members of the Executive Council, see: Armstrong, *Handbook of Upper Canadian Chronology*, 13-14, and their respective online biographical entries in the *Dictionary of Canadian Biography*. For the three lesser-known members, see: *DCB*, VI, John Clarke, "Baby, James"; VIII, G. M. Craig, "Wells, Joseph"; and IX, Henri Pilon, "Elmsley, John".

24. Alan Wilson, *The Clergy Reserves of Upper Canada, A Canadian Mortmain* (Toronto: University of Toronto Press, 1968), 93-94, 98-99, 103-104,106-108 & 113, and page 127 on the popularity of the clergy reserves sales. After the passage of the Clergy Reserves Sales and Improvement Act of July 1827, the Clergy Reserves Corporation continued its independent existence in leasing clergy reserve lots and administering the leased lots, with the attendant problems associated with collecting the rents. As of June 1830, no new leases were let in keeping with Instructions received from the Whig government in Britain. The Corporation continued in existence to administer the existing leases, but little revenue was raised from lease payments, once the administrative costs were paid. (Wilson, 99-103 & 116).

25. Craig, *Upper Canada*, 195-197; Dunham, *Political Unrest*, 117-120; Sissons, *Egerton Ryerson*, I, 119 & 126; and LeSueur, *Mackenzie*, 141-142 & 147. See also, *DCB*, IX, Bruce W. Hodgins, "McLean, Archibald".

26. Sissons, *Egerton Ryerson*, I, 129-130; Wilson, The *Clergy Reserves of Upper Canadas*, 113-114; and French, *Parsons & Politics*, 118-119. The quotations are from a reprint of the petition in Sissons, I, 130. See also, *DCB*, VII, Paul Romney, "Cawthra, Joseph" and John S. Moir, "Jenkins, William", and VIII, Victor Loring Russell, "Morrison, Thomas David", as well as DRC IX, Lillian F. Gates, "Ketchum, Jesse". On the euphoria felt by the Reformers in learning of the coming to power of a liberal-Whig reform government in Britain, see Craig, *Upper Canada*, 197-198.

In calling for 'the exclusion of all sectarian tests and preferences' in relation to the existing Charter of King's College University, what The Friends of Religious Liberty were demanding, in effect, was that the professors to be engaged would not have to subscribe to the Thirty-Nine Articles of the Church of England. The aim was to removed Anglican control over the administration and teaching at the projected university, but there was no intention, at this date, to transform the projected King's College into a secular university. As of the early 1830s, there were no secular universities in existence in Britain or the United States. In Britain, there was an effort to establish a secular university, 'London University', as early as 1826. However, the proponents of the secular university were unable to secure a Royal Charter and the right to award degrees until 1836 when the University of London was established.

27. *Oxford Dictionary of National Biography*, 811-819, E.A. Smith, "Grey, Charles, second Earl Grey (1764-1845)", & 324-329, P.J. Jupp, "Robinson, Frederick John, first Viscount Goderich and first earl of Ripon (1782-1859)". On Whig politics, see Samuel H. Beer, *British Politics in the Collectivist Age* (New York: Vintage Books, 1960), 9-32. For a summary of the influence of the works of the Venerable William Paley, see: Wikipedia, "William Paley".

28. Wilson, *Clergy Reserves*, 114-122; Dunham, *Political Unrest*, 96-98; and Charles Lindsey, *The Clergy Reserves, their History and Present Position* (Toronto: North American Press, 1851), 19-23.

29. John Strachan, "A Letter to the Right Honourable Thomas Frankland Lewis, M.P.", 1 February 1830 in J.L. H. Henderson, ed., *John Strachan, Documents and Opinions* (Toronto: McClelland & Stewart,1969, 101-112, The quotation is from 102-103. Lewis was the chairman of the Select Committee of the House of Commons of 1828 on the Civil Government of Canada.

In their "Friends of Religious Liberty" petition to the British Parliament, the evangelical sectarians and democratic radicals of the Reform Party claimed that they were loyal to the Crown and the British Constitution; that they were the true representatives of the people; and that they were conveying the public opinion of the province. However, Archdeacon Strachan held a different view of the politics of Upper Canada, which he conveyed to the British parliament.

In responding to the Select Committee Report of the House of Commons (1828), Archdeacon Strachan maintained that the 'political dissenters', who were attacking the Clergy Reserves and the church-state polity of the Province of Upper Canada, were generally from among the non-Loyalist American settlers of Upper Canada, and that they were receiving some support from among the more recent British immigrant settlers. He observed further that what the 'political dissenters' sought was to overthrow the civil and religious establishments of the Loyalist Province of Upper Canada and to annex the Province to the United States. However, over the succeeding two decades, the nature and objective of the attacks on the Clergy Reserves and the Church-State polity, changed dramatically.

Two decades later, Bishop Strachan characterized the 'political dissenters' in more general terms, which reflected the changing nature, composition, and outlook of the electorate in Canada West (Upper Canada) following the influx of a heavy British immigration. Strachan remained convinced that the 'political dissenters' comprised only a small minority of the population but recognized that they were of widely different political and religious persuasions, and that they were receiving support from a public imbued with the growing secularism of the age. He observed that:

They are intrinsically few in number, but they are sure, in the present age of innovation and irreligion, to obtain the countenance of all those who agree on no other subjects but in their aversion to the public support of the Christian faith.

The Unitarian, who hates our Holy Church for the purity of her Creeds; the infidel, who regards her as a powerful instrument to disseminate Christianity among the people; the innovator, who would sacrifice the best interests of his country for the sake of carrying out a favourite theory; the Reformer, who sees abuses in everything, and is only at ease amid changes and revolutions; and the mere sectarian, who hopes to reduce the National Churches to an equality with himself. To these, we may add a few ignorant, though sincere Christians, who, from some extraordinary obtuseness of intellect, persuade themselves that true religion will be most effectually extended by destroying its support, ….; and to these we may perhaps add, some men of talent and piety, whose general character as members of society we may respect, though their opinions on this subject we regard with equal wonder and regret.

For Strachan at the mid-19th Century, the defence of Christianity and the preservation of social peace and order, required that "all conscientious denominations of Christians" unite against the political threat posed by 'infidelity and radical licentiousness'. (Bishop John Strachan, "A Charge Delivered to the Clergy of the Diocese of Toronto in May 1851", as quoted in Henderson, ed., John Strachan, Documents and Opinions, 257-258.)

30. For a history of the political struggle over the Clergy Reserves, which culminated in the secularization of the reserves under the United Province of Canada in 1854, see Wilson, *The Clergy Reserves of Upper Canada* (Toronto, 1968).

Chapter Six

Defending the Constitution

Extra-parliamentary Associations

The Loyalty election of June 1836

Conventions

Discontent, Disaffection & Disloyalty

The Principle of Loyalty

"To be governed by Laws, and not by the arbitrary will of any man or number of men, & to have the privilege of choosing those who are to have a voice in making the laws, are the distinctions of a free people".

Chief Justice John Beverley Robinson
"Charge delivered to the Grand Jury"
Toronto, 25 May 1841.

"Front St. W. looking n.w. from Front & Simcoe Sts., Toronto, Ont.", 1834, watercolour by John George Howard, Toronto Reference Library. The two-storey parliament buildings were constructed on Front Street in 1829-1832, and were designed by James G. Chewett, John G. Howard, and John Ewart. The centre structure held the chambers of the Legislative Assembly and the Legislative Council, with government offices housed in the east and west buildings.

Chapter Six

Defending the Constitution

During the 1820s, the democratic radicals of Reform Party of Upper Canada sought to gain public support by championing complaints that were being made by various opposition groups against the provincial government. In almost every case, the complaints were raised in the House of Assembly as supposed rights, and hence 'grievances': viz. a supposed right of non-naturalized American settlers to vote and to sit in the Assembly; a right of Americans to acquire land grants in Upper Canada; a right of the religious sects to share in the revenues of the clergy reserves endowment of the Established Church of England; a right of itinerant sectarian preachers to conduct marriage ceremonies; and a right of 'religious equality' which was held to be contravened by the prerogatives and endowments enjoyed by the Established Church of England in the province. In each case, the radicals called upon the Colonial Office in Britain to intervene, and to rectify the specific grievance. However, the one constant demand of the Reform Party was that the provincial government revenues and Crown patronage should be placed 'in the hands of the representatives of the people'. To that end, the radicals of the Reform Party continually sent petitions and deputations to the Colonial Office in England and consulted with the British radicals of the House of Commons for their support in championing the 'grievances' of the people of Upper Canada in the Imperial Parliament.

As of the year 1828, the Reform Party began to advocate a novel principle. It was the so-called principle of 'responsible government' which was regarded as a means by which the 'representatives of the people' in the House of Assembly could attain control over the provincial government revenues and patronage appointments and oust the Tories from their public positions. To arouse public support for the principle of 'responsible government', the Reformers turned to organizing extra-parliamentary associations. In doing so, they had a two-fold aim: to influence the provincial Legislature to call for the establishment of responsible government, and to convince the Colonial Office in London that 'public opinion' in Upper Canada favoured its implementation.

For the Tories, extra-parliamentary organizations, and politically-motivated attacks aimed at overthrowing the balance of the British constitution, had no place in a representative system of government under a limited monarchy and the rule of law. Moreover, it was feared that extra-parliamentary organizations might well evolve into a real threat to the very existence of the monarchical government of the province.

Extra-parliamentary Associations

For the Tories, extra-parliamentary voluntary associations were regarded as no better than parliamentary parties in that both engendered ill-will and hostile feelings towards other members of the state to the detriment of the welfare of the whole. Such political associations fostered and deepened divisions in society by turning differences of opinion into political issues. Through presenting only one side of every question, extra-parliamentary associations encouraged their adherents to resign their liberty of judgment and reason into the hands of the men who directed the associations. The members were committed to specific policies and, when elected to the Assembly, they were bound to support partisan policies with their votes. In effect, the members of the Assembly were reduced to being simply delegates of an outside association. In being committed to its partisan policies, they were not amenable to thinking for themselves through participating in rational debates.

All such extra-parliamentary organizations, vote-organizing activities, and partisan appeals to the electorate outside of the Legislature were distasteful to the Tories. The Tory attitude was perhaps best expressed by John Beverley Robinson, when serving as the member of the Assembly for York:

> It is not in my nature to smooth the way by management out of doors. This I feel & shall never attempt it. I never can court ignorance, prejudice & obstinacy.

A natural aversion to courting the electorate was further reinforced by the Tory belief that every man was accountable to God for his use of the franchise, and therefore it was essential that elections be conducted peaceably in the absence of organized efforts to influence the electorate. In sum, the voter ought to be "left to act individually, upon his own estimate of what is right". Little good could be expected to come from extra-parliamentary associations and societies. Although it was recognized that there might be some situations where a resort to an extra-parliamentary voluntary association might well be justified, on a temporary basis. That was particularly so when the constitution appeared to be in danger of being overthrown and needed to be defended. (1)

One such instance, when the Upper Canadian Tories were moved to welcome a resort to an extra-parliamentary political activism, was during the political crisis that followed the 1834 election. In February 1834 -- prior to the election -- the provincial Reformers held a Grand Convention. A reform candidate was selected to run in each riding, rather than having multiple reform candidates running against multiple tory candidates in a riding, and a platform of policies was framed to which the reform candidates had to pledge themselves. In addition, a "Vigilance Committee" was established in many ridings to organize the riding for election purposes, to provide speakers to address political meetings and rallies, and to ensure the presentation of a united Reform Party front on policy issues during the election. Through such organizing efforts and the avoidance of vote-splitting among their supporters, the newly-organized 'Reform Party' won a clear majority in the October 1834 election and gained a complete party control over the House of Assembly.

In viewing the results of the 1834 election, the Tories became concerned about 'the ill-effects' of the vigilance committees of the Reformers and their influence on the public mind. It was a concern which deepened greatly in December 1834 when the Reformers founded a major extra-parliamentary voluntary association, the "Canadian Alliance Society". It was organized by the Anglican-whig, Dr. William Warren Baldwin, and a leading democratic radical, Jesse Ketchum of Toronto, a Methodist convert from the Church of England.

The Canadian Alliance Society was modeled on the extra-parliamentary political associations that had been formed in Britain several years earlier. In Britain, extra-parliamentary voluntary associations had mobilized public opinion in favour of parliamentary reform through organizing large public meetings, publishing tracts, and gathering signatures on massive petitions for submission to parliament. In doing so, the British voluntary associations had succeeded in pressuring parliament to extend the franchise through the passage of the Great Reform Act of 1832. In Upper Canada, the general purpose of the Canadian Alliance Society was to mobilize public opinion to pressure the provincial legislature, and the Colonial Office, to acquiesce in the reforms demanded by the newly-constituted Reform party.

The Society was organized in Toronto (formerly York), and William Lyon Mackenzie was appointed the Corresponding Secretary with the responsibility to organize branch societies across the province. The immediate aim was to disseminate "political information" among the public by means of political tracts and pamphlets, to organize public meetings, circulate petitions, and secure the nomination of a candidate in each riding who would agree, once elected, to support the Reform Party programme in the House of Assembly. The society was open to everyone to join, with no fees, and no social distinctions.

The reform programme of the Canadian Alliance Society consisted of a commitment to the principle of 'responsible government', the abolition of the Legislative Council, the separation of church and state, a division of the revenues from the clergy reserves land endowment of the Established Church of England among the various Protestant religious denominations, the vote by secret ballot, the abolition of primogeniture, control of all provincial government revenue by 'the representatives of the people', amendments to the jury laws to make jury selection more democratic, a Canadian-controlled post office, elected justices of the peace, and the elimination of land company monopolies. More generally, the platform expressed an opposition to "all undue influence" in colonial affairs by the British Imperial government and for Upper Canada to have a written constitution "embodying and proclaiming the original principles of government".

Such a political programme constituted an unequivocal rejection of the balanced British constitution. It evinced a complete commitment to democratic government -- based on the unspoken principle of popular sovereignty -- and to a unicameral legislature that would control all government revenues and patronage appointments in the province. No mention was made of party government, but the majority party in the Assembly would determine the policies of the government, when and if the principle of 'responsible government' were implemented. Under such a principle, the Assembly would possess the power to replace the Executive Council if the members refused to carry out 'the will of the majority' of the Assembly in providing particular advice to the Lt. Governor, and, the corollary was that the Lt. Governor must acquiesce in the 'will of the people' as expressed by the majority of the elected members of the Assembly.

It remained unclear as to whether the Canadian Alliance Society was bent on seeking independence from Britain for the Province of Upper Canada. However, it was evident that the proposed written constitution would be based on Lockean-liberal principles of popular sovereignty and the separation of church and state, rather than the sovereignty of the Crown and the existing union of church and state. (2)

It was the efforts of the Canadian Alliance Society, to disseminate what the Tories regarded as principles which would be destructive of the British constitution and the British connection, that moved the Tories to join and provide active support for an extra-parliamentary society. That society was the British Constitutional Society which was organized by several of the leading conservatives in Toronto to defend the British tie by employing the same tactics as the Reformers in making a direct appeal to the people.

Although the Tories believed that the people -- if they were permitted to decide political issues in a rationale manner -- would act "in accordance with right" and would support the provincial government, such a situation did not exist in Upper Canada by the mid-1830s. Passions were aroused. It appeared that it would no longer suffice for 'a gentleman' to simply stand for office by declaring his intention, by issuing an election address, and by letting the people chose their representative on rational grounds. Now, the conservatives perceived that there was a need to organize, and to become directly involved in campaigning for votes within the ridings. The tireless efforts of the radicals of the Reform Party to propagate "insubordination and disaffection" among the people, demanded an antidote. As the Tories interpreted it:

> native good sense, like a sound physical constitution, is susceptible of perversion, and injury, and destruction from the application, unresisted and uncorrected, of unwholesome and deleterious nostrums: if not moved and directed by a salutary impulse, it may soon become the tool of an agency whose object is public disorder and political devastation. (3)

Thus, the Anglican Tories became strong supporters of, and active participants in the British Constitutional Society -- a conservative extra-parliamentary association. It was a voluntary association that was initially established, in July 1834, by the leading conservatives of Toronto in response to an unsettling publication by William Lyon Mackenzie. What had riled the conservatives of all stripes was the publication of a private letter to Mackenzie from a British parliamentary radical, Joseph Hume, in which it was advocated that the Upper Canadian radicals follow the example of the American revolutionaries in seeking "independence and freedom from the Baneful Domination of the Mother Country".

The British Constitutional Society required that its members in Toronto -- and the affiliated society members in the townships, counties and districts of Upper Canada -- pledge themselves to oppose, "by all lawful means", anyone who advocated independence from Britain, or the introduction of policies that would weaken the British connection. Loyalty to the Crown was the motivating factor, buttressed by the knowledge that the Imperial trade system was responsible for the wealth, population and prosperity of the Province. Initially, the British Constitutional Society was not directly involved in organizing ridings for electoral purposes, and the Reform Party managed to win the October 1834 provincial election.

The British Constitutional Society took on a more partisan political purpose in response to the political activities of the Canadian Alliance Society. The British Constitutional Society was dedicated anew to the preservation of the 'British constitution' and the British connection from destruction at the hands of the Reformers and began in April 1835 to take on an active political role in opposition to the Reform Party. More immediately, the Constitutionalists were motivated by a desire to counteract, in the public mind, a notorious publication, the 'Seventh Report of Grievances', which was produced by a Select Committee of the House of Assembly under the chairmanship of William Lyon Mackenzie (January 1835). It had set forth a seemingly endless list of 'grievances' under which Upper Canadians were supposedly suffering.

In response, the British Constitutional Society was organized province-wide along the lines of voluntary political associations in Britain and was open to all males of good character who were over twenty-one years of age, regardless of their social rank or religion. The aim of the British Constitutional Society was to inform the public of the true state of affairs in the Province, to point out how the Reformers in the Assembly were constantly encroaching upon the prerogatives of the Crown, and to appeal to the public to judge for themselves the validity of the supposed 'grievances' enunciated by Mackenzie.

The constitutional issue became critical in March 1836 when all six members of the Executive Council resigned over the refusal of the Lt. Governor to consult with them on public issues. Several weeks early, the new Lt. Governor, Sir Francis Bond Head, in seeking a more broadly representative body of advisers, had appointed two leading Reformers – Robert Baldwin and Dr. John Rolph – to his Executive Council, along with a career public servant, John Henry Dunn, the Receiver General. They had joined three Anglican Tories on the existing Executive Council: George Herchmer Markland, the Inspector General; Peter Robinson, the Crown Land Commissioner; and Joseph Wells, a landed member of the Legislative Council. However, Sir Francis soon became convinced that the two Reformers were republicans in their sympathies and policies, and he had ceased to consult with his Executive Council on public matters. In protest, the Executive Council had resigned in a body.

Initially, the entire Assembly – with but two exceptions -- sided with the Executive Council members, who stood on their constitutional right to be consulted for advice on provincial matters. There was unanimity among all 'parties' in defending the constitutional right of the Executive Council. However, when the Reformers began to interpret the issue as one of a denial of 'responsible government' on the part of the Lt. Governor, the Tories demurred. For conservatives, more generally, the issue was simply a matter of upholding the constitution against a Lt. Governor who was violating a constitutional practice in failing to consult his Executive Council for advice on public matters that affected the province.

The Executive Council had an established right in the British parliamentary tradition to be consulted for advice on public matters. However, for the High Church Tories, the existence of such a right – which they were defending -- did not imply that the Lt. Governor had to follow the advice of his Executive Council in all matters. The Tories called on the Colonial Office to instruct the Lt. Governor to follow the advice of his Executive Council on strictly local matters, while following the Instructions of the Crown on matters of an Imperial import.

Despite such differences, the conservatives of the Assembly -- inclusive of the Anglican Tories -- were united in holding that the Executive Council crisis was not a dispute over the principle of 'responsible government'. In supporting the Executive Council members, the conservatives were not advocating the principle that the provincial government must be made responsible to the representatives of the people by having the Executive Council composed of men who enjoyed the support of the majority party in the Assembly, or the corollary that the Lt. Governor must always act on the advice of his Executive Council in local matters.

When the Reform Party majority passed a resolution that called for the implementation of the principle of 'responsible government', the conservatives moved an amendment. It was proposed by a leading tory of the Assembly, Archibald McLean -- a Church of Scotland adherent and a former pupil of the Rev. John Strachan. The motion to amend stated that:

> any attempt on the part of the executive council to assume control over the affairs of the province, or to interfere with the administration of the government thereof, without the sanction of his Majesty or his representative, would be justly regarded by the people of this province as an illegal assumption of power, and in direct violation of the declared object for which such a Council had been appointed.

The conservative motion was defeated by a vote of 31 to 20 in the Assembly, and when the Reform-dominated Assembly voted to stop supplies to incapacitate the provincial government administration, Sir Francis retaliated. He refused his assent to the money bills already passed by the two houses and prorogued the Legislature. A month later, the Legislature was dissolved by the Lt. Governor, and the writs were issued for a new election. (4)

The Loyalty Election of June 1836

During the June 1836 election campaign in Upper Canada, the leading members of the British Constitutional Society spent a great deal of time and effort in distributing political tracts, holding public meetings and making speeches, all of which were calculated to counteract the electoral campaign of the Reform party, and its Canadian Alliance Society affiliate.

For the first time, conservatives of various persuasions were united in a political campaign in appealing directly to the people on a province-wide basis. What the Constitutionalists referred to as the "treasonable effusions of the Revolutionists" were collected and diffused throughout the countryside to enable the people to judge for themselves what the Reformers were saying, and what they were seeking to achieve with their political programme of 'responsible government'. A single Constitutionalist candidate was nominated to run in each single riding, and two Constitutionalist candidates in the two-member ridings. Moreover, the British Constitutional Society affiliates in each township or county organized public meetings and conducted an active canvass to get out the vote among their conservative supporters during the election.

The Constitutionalists were aided in their election strategy by the new Lt. Governor Sir Francis Bond Head. Sir Francis was convinced that the Reformers -- by means of their principle of 'responsible government – aimed to gain control over the provincial government and the distribution of Crown patronage; and that the implementation of 'responsible government' would bring about a severance of the British connection. Given the seriousness of the election issue, he decided to make a direct appeal to the people, whom he called upon "to think for themselves". During the election, Loyalty Addresses were received by the Lt. Governor from the various districts of Upper Canada, and the Lt. Governor issued a series of public replies.

In his replies to the Loyalty Addresses, and in an Address to the electors, Sir Francis set forth a simple clear message: that the Reformers were republicans in their political principles, and that their principle of 'responsible government' would lead to a separation of Upper Canada from the mother country. He appealed to public feelings of loyalty to the British Constitution and the King, and of attachment to the mother country, and declared that he would defend the balanced constitution and Crown patronage from usurpation by "irresponsible individuals". The electorate were called upon to reject the deceitful pronouncements of demagogues, and the demands of a "factious opposition", and to join "the side of religion, order and true liberty". Moreover, Sir Francis promised to promote "the peace and prosperity of the province" through Upper Canada continuing to receive the numerous benefits of belonging to the British Empire. (5)

The Lt. Governor deliberately aimed his message at the conservative elements of the province, and particularly to the British immigrant settlers. Since 1829, a massive influx of British immigrants had almost doubled the population of Upper Canada – from 197,815 to 374,359 as of 1836 -- and a good many of the British immigrants of that period had completed their settlement duties and acquired title to their lands. Thus, they were eligible to vote in the June 1836 election.

During the electoral campaign, a Declaration of the principles of the British Constitutional Society was distributed province wide, and in Toronto a 'door-to-door' canvass was conducted in each ward and an Address to the Electors of the City of Toronto was disseminated. Under the direction of the Secretary of the British Constitutional Society, John Kent -- an English-immigrant, Anglican Tory – over 100,000 broadsides, inclusive of the Lt. Governor's pronouncements and the Address to the electors of Toronto, were printed on the presses of Robert Stanton, the proprietor of the *Upper Canada Gazette*. To reach all the conservative elements in Upper Canada, the broadsides were published not only in English, but also in German (for the Lutheran Germans) and in Gaelic (for the Scottish Roman Catholic Highlanders). Robert Stanton, who held the appointment of King's Printer, was an Anglican Tory, a founder of the British American Assurance Company, and a former pupil of the Rev. John Strachan.

During the June 1836 election, the Constitutionalists drew their support from a remarkable coalition of Irish Protestant Orangemen, Scottish and English Roman Catholics, and recent British immigrants (tories, whigs, and even former British radicals), as well as from the Anglican Tories of

Upper Canada and the descendants of the Loyalists of various political persuasions. More generally, the Constitutionalists received support as well from the English Wesleyan Methodists, adherents of the Church of Scotland, and the Blacks of Upper Canada, who were strong supporters of the conservatives in their effort to maintain the balanced British constitution and the Imperial connection.

Within the conservative electoral coalition were former political opponents of the Anglican Tories who supported Constitutionalist candidates on the loyalty issue; although they remained opposed to the exclusive prerogatives and privileges that were enjoyed by the Established Church of England in Upper Canada, and to the Anglican control of the education system in the province. However, all conservatives were united in defence of the balanced British constitution, in loyalty to the Crown, and in defence of the British connection. For the first time, the conservative elements presented a united front in an election and campaigned on clearly-defined loyalties.

Earlier, the conservatives had won a majority in the provincial election of October 1830, but they were not in control of the Assembly during the following Legislative sessions of 1830-1834. At that time, a tory newspaper, *The Patriot*, had lamented that "the administration party" was unable to dominate the Assembly as the conservative members:

> have no acknowledged leader – no mutual understanding – and no common or uniform system of action ... while the party of which Mr. [Marshall Spring] Bidwell is the head – is a well-drilled and compact little body – always at their post, and always ready to follow their leader.

The Reformers -- who won the following election of October 1834 -- were united in support of a party electoral platform and, consequently, they controlled the Assembly sessions of 1834-1836, in addition to having been the dominate element in the previous parliament. The fundamental problem for the conservatives -- who were supporters of the government administration -- was their rejection of the entire concept of party government. They believed that members were elected as representatives of the people to decide issues through rational debate in parliament, based on their view of the common good and well-being of 'the nation'. The conservatives rejected the Reform Party position that the members of the House of Assembly were elected as delegates to serve the particular interests of their constituents, and were required to vote according to their party affiliation in support of a party platform.

In supporting the British Constitutional Society, the Tories in no way violated their belief in the proper role of a member of parliament. In the election of June 1836, the British Constitutional Society provided a principle – loyalty – under which conservatives of all stripes could unite in defence of the balanced British Constitution, the prerogatives of the Crown, and the maintenance of the British connection. Under the banner of the Constitutional Society, conservatives could seek election to the Assembly without compromising their independence by being forced to subscribe to a party platform. Once elected, they were free to vote on various public issues according to their own judgement and conscience. (6)

Even the Rev. Egerton Ryerson of the Methodist Episcopal Church – who was an ardent supporter of the political radicals of the Reform Party in their attacks upon the established Church of England, the Clergy Reserves land endowment, and Anglican control over education – opposed the Reformers during the June 1836 election. Ryerson had become disillusioned with his radical allies. During a trip to England in 1833, he had discovered, to his surprise, that the leading British radicals -- from whom the Upper Canadian radicals drew their inspiration -- were irreligious men of a republican persuasion, and that several of the leading British radicals were lacking in moral character. Moreover, that disillusionment had deepened further the following year when William Lyon Mackenzie published the so-called 'baneful domination letter' in which the British radical, Joseph Hume, advocated that the Upper Canadian radicals emulate the American revolutionaries in seeking their independence from the Mother Country.

When the radicals and liberal-whigs of the Reform Party adopted 'responsible government' as their common main policy plank, Ryerson published his view that such a principle of government would destroy the balance of the constitution. In having the executive drawn from the leaders of the majority in the Assembly, it would annihilate the royal prerogative. The executive power would no longer represent the sovereignty of the Crown, and the province would become a *de facto* independent republic. For Egerton Ryerson, the question was whether Upper Canada would remain a province of the British Empire or become an American state. For Upper Canadians, it was a choice between either the maintenance of a limited constitutional monarchy and the British connection, or republicanism, independence, and absorption by the United States.

Ryerson agreed with the Reformers that the existing constitution was "corrupt", or corrupted, in the sense that the Tories -- through their domination of the government administration in the Executive Council and the Legislative Council – were blocking reforms advocated by 'the representatives of the people' in the House of Assembly. Thus, Ryerson considered the constitution to be unbalanced in practice. However, he believed in reforming the existing system from within through petitions to the Crown and addresses to the Colonial Office for redress.

Ryerson was opposed to untried constitutional innovations, such as the responsible government principle. Indeed, the stand taken by the Rev. Egerton Ryerson – in giving his support to the Constitutionalists during the loyalty election of 1836 -- appears to have been representative of many erstwhile supporters of the reform movement. More particularly, it accounts for the broad coalition of diverse groups and rival religious denominations in Upper Canada that supported the Constitutionalist candidates at the polls, in addition to descendants of the Loyalists, British immigrants, and the veterans of the War of 1812, in an election that focused solely on loyalty to the Crown and the maintenance of the 'British Constitution' and the British connection. (7)

During the election, and earlier in their public pronouncements, the Reformers tried to defuse the' loyalty to the constitution' issue by presenting 'responsible government' as simply a reform of the constitution. They reiterated the argument that the constitution had become corrupted and unbalanced in Upper Canada through the Executive Council and the Legislative Council being dominated by the Anglican Tories. The Reformers maintained that the best means of restoring the balanced constitution to its true form -- in "the image and transcript of the British Constitution" -- was through the introduction of 'responsible government'. It would make the government more responsive to public opinion, and would provide greater self-government for Upper Canadians. One of the reform leaders, Dr. John Rolph, was more forthright. He declared that "the full blessings of the constitution" would be received only when the representatives of the people secured "control over the public purse and general expenditure".

As of the June 1836 election, the Reformers had a very clear understanding of what their principle of 'responsible government' implied. As Robert Baldwin explained, in a letter to the Colonial Secretary, Lord Glenelg (18 July 1836), the principle of 'responsible government':

> consists of nothing more than having the Provincial Government, as far as regards the internal Affairs of the province, conducted by the Lieutenant Governor (as Representative of the paramount Authority of the Mother Country), with the Advice and Assistance of the Executive Council acting as a Provincial Cabinet, and composed of Men possessed of the public Confidence, whose Opinions and Policy would be in harmony with the Opinions and Policy of the Representatives of the People.

If the members of 'the cabinet' lost the confidence of the representatives of the people in the House of Assembly, they were to be dismissed and replaced by new councilors from the Assembly who could command the support of the majority in the Assembly.

Robert Baldwin called on the Colonial Secretary to send out a new Lt. Governor with Royal Instructions to implement the principle of responsible government, and assured Lord Glenelg that responsible government was not inconsistent with "the paramount Authority of the Mother Country" – the sovereignty of the Crown. The provincial cabinet would only serve as advisors, with the Lt. Governor continuing to hold the power of consent to legislation. Moreover, the granting of responsible government would not deprive the Lt. Governor of all control over government patronage but, even if it did so, Robert Baldwin asked:

> is the Patronage in the Hands of the Lieutenant Governor the great Object for which England desires to retain Upper Canada?

What remained unanswered by Robert Baldwin was: how could a Lt. Governor reject the advice of his Cabinet on any provincial matter, if he were under instructions to act in accordance with the principle of responsible government?

For William Warren Baldwin and his son Robert Baldwin -- who were well-educated Anglican whigs -- responsible government was viewed as strictly a constitutional principle. It was a means by which the Legislature could exercise control over the executive power of the Crown and promote local self-government under the leadership of moderate liberal-Whig Reformers; whereas for the more radical members of the Reform Party responsible government was viewed as a panacea for all the ills of society. One Reform newspaper, the *Brockville Recorder*, effused that responsible government, once implemented, would put an end to 'all our grievances', and would bring 'peace and contentment' and a 'spirit of enterprise' to Upper Canada. It was a heady stuff! However, in the loyalty election of June 1836, both Robert Baldwin and William Warren Baldwin had declined to stand as candidates for the Reform Party in opposition to the British Constitutional Society whose supporters were defending the British Constitution, monarchical government, and the British tie. The Baldwins looked to the liberal-Whig government in Britain for the achievement of their novel system of 'responsible government'. (8)

With the loyalty issue predominating on the hustings, the Reformers were routed during the June 1836 election. Half of the reform leaders – inclusive of Marshall Spring Bidwell, Peter Perry, and William Lyon Mackenzie – were defeated. Province-wide only seventeen Reform Party candidates were elected, inclusive of three Reform leaders: Dr. John Rolph; Dr. Charles Duncombe; and Dr. Thomas David Morrison. In contrast, a total of forty-five Constitutionalists were elected to the 62-seat House of Assembly.

In the new House of Assembly, the conservatives enjoyed a decided majority, and among the Constitutionalist members were prominent Anglican Tories: Henry Sherwood, Christopher Alexander Hagerman, Jonas Jones, John Solomon Cartwright (son of Richard Cartwright), and Allan Napier MacNab, who was elected the Speaker of the House.

In the previous sessions of the Twelfth Parliament – following the 1834 election -- the Reform Party had held an eleven-seat majority in the Assembly; whereas, in the new Thirteenth Parliament, it was the conservatives who enjoyed a majority of twenty-eight members. In sum, the Loyalty Election of June 1836 was a devastating blow to the Reform Party. When placed to a vote, the electorate of Upper Canada had thoroughly rejected 'the principle of responsible government'.

In the election, the Reformers managed to maintain their traditional core support from the non-Loyalist, American-settled areas of the province – principally north of Toronto along Yonge Street in the Home District, west of Brantford in the London District, and in Hastings County in the Bay of Quinte area of the Midland District -- as well as, more generally, among the religious sectarians, inclusive of members of the Methodist Episcopal Church who had refused to follow their former spokesperson, the Rev. Egerton Ryerson, in supporting the Constitutionalists. In contrast to the Methodists of American descent, Ryerson, who was raised and educated within an Anglican-Tory Loyalist family -- before his conversion to Methodism -- remained loyal to the Crown, the Constitution, and the British Empire, as did most of the Loyalist families. Among the Loyalists who supported the Constitutionalists were members of the Wesleyan Methodist Church in British North America. In contrast, the Reform Party received the support of the Methodists of American origin, as well as – it appears – the support of Irish Catholic immigrants, Quakers (Hicksites), Baptists, and the Separate Congregationalists during the 1836 loyalty election. (9)

The extra-parliamentary electoral activity of the Upper Canadian Anglican Tories, in actively supporting the British Constitutional Society during the June1836 election, was a complete departure from their belief as to how elections ought to be conducted. However, in their own eyes, it was excusable in that the electoral appeal of the British Constitutional Society was based on principle and called upon the people to give their suffrage to men who were loyal supporters of the constitution and the British connection. Once elected, the Constitutionalists retained their independence in the House to vote in favour of policies which -- in their individual judgement -- would best promote the public good and well-being of the province. In contrast, the candidates of the Reform Party were delegates who were bound to support the party platform, including the call for the implementation of the so-called 'responsible government' principle.

Although the Anglican Tories were strong adherents of the British Constitutional Society, they had had reservations about the Lt. Governor, the Sovereign's representative, becoming personally involved in local politics during the 1836 loyalty election. For the Tories, the King's representative had a duty to maintain the constitution unimpaired and to remain above the interests of party. Whether Sir Francis Bond Head went too far in publicly setting forth the position of the Crown on the constitutional issue, and in denouncing the republican views of the Reformers, was a moot point. John Beverley Robinson, the Chief Justice, was opposed to arguing constitutional principles in public, but other Anglican Tories, such as Christopher Hagerman, the Solicitor General, were strong advocates of appealing directly to "the reasoning faculties" of the people, with clear statements of Tory principles and achievements. (10)

Following their devastating defeat at the polls, and the discrediting of their principle of responsible government, the Reformers regrouped. As of October 1836, they formed yet another political organization, the Toronto Political Union, under the presidency of William Warren Baldwin. This time, the tactic was to encourage a fuller public participation in reform politics, to hold debates on public issues, and to seek to influence the liberal-Whig government in Britain to implement responsible government in the two Canadian provinces. However, with the onset of an economic depression, the contraction of credit, and bank foreclosures on farmers, mechanics and shopkeepers, the radicals among the Reformers were roused to action. They took over the Toronto Political Union organization from the liberal-Whig Reformers.

In March 1837, William Warren Baldwin resigned as president of the Toronto Political Union, and the radicals of the Union forwarded a petition to the King in which the legitimacy of the elected Assembly was denied, and a claim made that the Assembly was not a truly representative body. That assertion was based on a claim made by William Lyon Mackenzie, and several of the leading radicals, that the Tories had 'stolen the election' of June 1836 by a coercion of the voters at the poles, and a fanciful belief that if a new 'fair election' election were held, the Reform Party would emerge victorious. Hence, a claim was made that the members of the Assembly were not representative of 'the will of the people'. In keeping with that assumption, the petition contained a declaration that the Reformers no longer held the acts of the Legislature to be legitimate and legally-binding.

The petition was followed, in May 1837, by a declaration of the Toronto Political Union – which was published in Mackenzie's newspaper, the *Constitution* -- that in such a time of economic crisis, the people possessed an 'indefeasible right' to send delegates to a general convention 'to discuss changes in the provincial constitution of the sort that would lead to a resolution of their long-held grievances'. (11)

Conventions

The Upper Canadian Tories disliked the very aims and methods of political parties and extra-parliamentary associations, but their real fear was focused on the concept of a 'convention'. It was an extra-parliamentary political organization that the agrarian democratic radical, Robert Gourlay, had sought to introduce into the province during the immediate postwar period, and which the radical Reformers were seeking to revive. For the Tories, conventions were not only unconstitutional, but were a real threat to the political stability of Upper Canada. They represented an effort to establish "a fourth power in the government". As viewed by the Tories, conventions were objectionable because they usurped the legitimate role of the House of Assembly as the branch of government representing the people.

The danger which was inherent in conventions -- such as the convention proposed by the radical Reformers of the Toronto Political Union -- was that despite the attendees being elected by no one in particular, and regardless of their paucity of numbers and lack of any appreciable public support, the convention supporters would invariably claim that resolutions passed by the convention represented 'the will of the people'. Moreover, the Tories feared that a convention would attempt "to influence the public mind against the constituted authorities" and would seek to coerce the government to adopt whatever resolutions were passed by the convention delegates. Such was the purpose and pretensions of the organizers of conventions, which degraded the independence of parliament.

The Upper Canadian Tories had been strong supporters of an earlier provincial government effort to ban conventions with the passage of "An Act to prevent Certain Meetings within this province" (October 1818) which declared conventions to be illegal. In support of the bill, the government supporters had argued that conventions were "repugnant to the spirit of the Constitution"; and that the delegates to a convention were not "the constitutional representatives of the people". Convention delegates did not represent anyone but themselves as individuals. However, at that time, it was made clear that the new law did not infringe upon the existing constitutional right of the people to petition the Crown for a redress of grievances.

In opposing the efforts of Robert Gourlay to organize a convention, the Tories had denounced the concept as being a democratic radical ideal, with overtones of direct democracy. They maintained that the existing constitution provided a means by which public grievances could be expressed and redressed – through petitions to the Crown, motions submitted by the representatives of the people in the Assembly, and Assembly addresses to the Crown -- without any need to resort to extra-parliamentary conventions. Two years later, in 1820, when the public life of the province was no longer disturbed by political unrest, the Act which had prohibited conventions was repealed by the Legislature at the instigation of the Lt. Governor, Sir Peregrine Maitland. The legislation was no longer considered necessary for the protection of the peace and order of society.

Nonetheless, the Upper Canadian Tories were strong supporters of the right of parliament to act to protect the prerogative of the Assembly as the representative body constituted to make known the views and interests of the people. What the Tories opposed was the usurpation of the constitutional role of the Assembly by the radical Reformers who -- through organizing a political convention -- were seeking to further their partisan political interests. However, in May 1837 when the Toronto Political Union called for a convention "to discuss changes to the constitution", there was no longer any law in force to prevent the holding of what the Tories regarded as a potentially revolutionary gathering of the discontented. (12)

Faced with the demand of the Reformers for responsible government, the provincial government responded -- with the support of the Legislative Council and the strong conservative majority in the House of Assembly – by enacting new provincial legislation. An act was passed that was intended to preserve the independence of the Crown in its executive function from encroachment by the Assembly, to maintain the separation of powers in the balanced British constitution, and to strengthen the independence of the popular branch of the legislature by precluding the Assembly from being dominated by the ministers of the Crown.

The new Act – which was based on a bill introduced by Allan Napier MacNab -- received Royal assent in April 1837. It barred members of the Assembly from sitting in the Executive Council, which effectively precluded Reformers, who might be appointed to the Executive Council, from continuing to sit as leaders of a political party in the Assembly. As such, the Act precluded the introduction of the so-called 'responsible government' principle by ensuring that members of the House of Assembly, upon receiving an appointment to the Executive Council, would have to resign their seat in the lower House. Thus, the Executive Council would retain its independence of the Assembly, and the Assembly would remain free from being dominated by the ministers of the Crown. In keeping with the new principle – even before the new Act was passed -- a moderate Tory, William Henry Draper, resigned his seat in the House of Assembly -- in December 1836 -- upon being appointed to the Executive Council by the Lt. Governor, Sir Francis Bond Head. (13)

Discontent, Disaffection & Disloyalty

The fears of the Tories regarding the potential revolutionary nature of conventions were heightened during the summer of 1837 as Upper Canada continued to suffer under the impact of an increasingly severe economic depression. The discontent of the radical Reformers was fueled not only by the economic dislocations and bank foreclosures, but also by an unexpected rebuff from the Whig government in Britain. The liberal-Whig government of Lord Melbourne had become convinced that the policy of appeasement, that had been followed by Lord Gleneg, the Secretary of State for War and the Colonies, in dealing with the parti Patriote radicals in Lower Canada, was a complete failure. Hence, a change in policy was introduced.

Faced with a continuing political crisis in the Province of Lower Canada, Lord John Russell, the Secretary of State for the Home Department, secured the enactment by parliament of Ten Resolutions which pertained to both Canadian provinces. The Russell Resolutions of March 1837, as adopted by the Imperial Parliament, specifically addressed the demands of the Assembly of Lower Canada and its refusal to vote supply. Parliament resolved that it was "unadvisable" to grant the demand for an elective Legislative Council, or to render the Executive Council subject "to the responsibility demanded by the House of Assembly". To the chagrin of the Upper Canadian Reformers, parliament -- under the direction of a leading parliamentary reformer and the leader of the liberal-Whigs in the House of Commons, Lord John Russell -- publicly rejected the key demands of the Reformers of Upper and Lower Canada, and, more particularly, denied the principle of 'responsible government'.

The Russell resolutions enraged William Lyon Mackenzie, who denounced the parliamentary enactment as an act of "colonial despotism". In his newspaper, *The Constitution*, he called for a boycott of British manufactured goods, and encouraged Lower Canadians to assert their independence. In doing so, he claimed that:

> There are thousands, aye tens of thousands of Englishmen, Scotchmen, and above all, of Irishmen, now in the United States, who only wait till the standard be planted in Lower Canada, to throw their strength and numbers on the side of democracy. (14)

By the end of July, Mackenzie was busy in attempting to organize branches of the Toronto Political Union province-wide in preparation for the projected convention, and he began to serialize a notorious revolutionary pamphlet: *Common Sense*, by Thomas Paine. At the time of its original publication in 1776 -- during the American Revolution -- the pamphlet had convinced many American colonists to support the cause of independence from Britain.

Paine had argued that all men were created equal, with equal natural rights; that all hereditary distinctions of rank between monarchs, aristocrats and the people were false; and that such distinctions invariable led – even under a balanced constitution -- to monarchical or aristocratic tyranny, the exploitation of the people, and the destruction of their rights. According to Paine – as articulated in his 1776 pamphlet -- the American colonies had no need of such distinctions of rank. America was a different country than Britain. America was composed of men from the various countries of Europe and had different interests than the Imperial power. Britain ruled the colonies for her own economic benefit, and under British rule the colonies were drawn needlessly into European wars. For Paine, the answer was for the colonists to assert themselves in declaring their independence from Britain, which he argued meant "no more than that we should make our own laws".

To that end, he had proposed that the American colonies hold a Continental Conference to draft a 'Charter of the United Colonies', and to establish a written constitution for the government of the united colonies. The proposed Charter was viewed as being similar to the Magna Carta of England, in securing "the freedom and property of all men" and "the free exercise of religion, according to the dictates of conscience". Once a constitution was drafted, the conference would disband, and each of the colonies would elect delegates to a Congress to form the "new national government" under the constitution. It was proposed further that the Congress would meet annually to elect a President, and to establish laws which would require a 3/5s majority to enact. The objective of the projected continental government -- in the words of Thomas Paine -- was declared to be: "the greatest sum of individual happiness, with the least national expense." (15)

Several weeks after the re-printing of Paine's *Common Sense*, the Reformers of the Toronto Political Union made the purpose of their projected convention even more explicit. On the 2 August 1837, Mackenzie published "The Declaration of the Reformers of the City of Toronto to their Fellow-Reformers in Upper Canada". It was a document that was based directly on the 'Declaration of Independence' (4 July 1776) of the American revolutionaries and was influenced in part by the earlier arguments of Thomas Paine for colonial independence.

The 'Declaration of the Reformers' drew on several principles and beliefs articulated in the political philosophy of John Locke, but they were principles and beliefs that were embedded in the United States Declaration of Independence. The Lockean-liberal principles and beliefs expressed in the American Declaration of Independence were adopted simply to support, and provide a justification for, the Reform Party demand for 'responsible government'.

The 'Declaration of the Reformers' was drafted by two leading Reformers: Dr. John Rolph, and William John O'Grady, a defrocked Irish Catholic Priest and radical newspaper editor. It had been approved at a Reform meeting, two days earlier at the brewery of John Doel in Toronto. The opening statement asserted that:

> Government is founded on the authority and is installed for the benefit of the people; when, therefore, any government long and systematically ceases to answer the great ends of its foundation, the people have a natural right given then by their Creator to seek after and establish such institutions as will yield the greatest quality of happiness to the greatest number.

The Declaration listed the supposed 'grievances' that the provincial government had refused to address, charged that the British government had been inattentive to the rights of the people in neglecting to act on their petitions, and declared that the people:

> now have to choose, on the one hand, between submission to the same blighting policy as hath desolated Ireland, and, on the other hand, the patriotic achievement of cheap, honest and responsible government such as the United States had achieved through a successful revolution.

Upper Canadians were assured that they were entitled to the same liberty as the Americans enjoyed; and that it could be achieved, "without the shedding of blood", by organizing political associations, and by selecting delegates to attend a convention to be held in Toronto. Once assembled, the delegates would be "armed with suitable powers, as a Congress, to seek an effectual remedy for the grievances of the colonies".

Furthermore, Upper Canadians were called upon "to make common cause" with the Reformers of Lower Canada in their efforts to defend "civil and religious liberty" against what was declared to be the unconstitutional acts of the British government. By this time, Mackenzie was in private contact with Dr. Wolfred Nelson -- one of the most radical English-Canadian members of the French-Canadian parti Patriote in the Lower Canadian Assembly.

The key 'grievance' of the Declaration of the Reformers was that the government of Upper Canada was "irresponsible". Except for the House of Assembly, government institutions, public offices, and the judiciary were appointive rather than elective, the representatives of the people did not fully control government revenues, and it was maintained that the British government in far-off London did not understand the interests of Upper Canadians. The Declaration was signed by Dr. Thomas David Morrison, Chairman of the Toronto Committee of the Toronto Political Union, and eighteen committee members, inclusive of William Lyon Mackenzie. (16)

Meanwhile, efforts continued by the Reformers to organize branches of the Toronto Political Union province-wide, and to secure the selection of delegates to attend the projected convention. Mackenzie had prepared an elaborate plan for a multi-tiered democratic selection process. According to his organizational scheme, the local branch unions of the Toronto Political Union were to elect representatives to township committees, which would elect representatives to county committees, and, in turn, the country committees would elect representative to a district meeting that would select delegates for the convention. The number of district delegates was to be based on the relative size of the population of the districts. In reality, the seven Toronto delegates were simply selected from among the leaders of the nineteen Reformers who attended the July 31st meeting that approved the 'Declaration of the Reformers'. At that meeting, a Committee of Vigilance was formed, and Mackenzie was appointed as the "agent and corresponding secretary" with the duty to organize and speak at Reform meetings across the province.

A second Reform meeting, to select convention delegates, was held at Newmarket, 30 miles north of Toronto, on 3rd August 1837. It was hosted by the leaders of the Children of Peace – a Quaker sect that believed in an egalitarian democracy in both religion and politics. The meeting formed a branch of the Toronto Political Union, selected six delegates for the convention, and established a Vigilance Committee. The convention delegates who were selected at the Toronto and Newmarket meetings were the Reform leaders of the Toronto Political Union. Out of a provincial population of upwards of 400,000 persons, a coterie of zealous radical Reformers – who could not accept the rejection of their principle of 'responsible' government both at the polls and by the British government – were organizing meetings to select delegates to attend a convention. They were securing the selection of themselves as delegates, and they were setting the agenda for a convention that was supposedly to speak for 'the people' of Upper Canada in demanding a reform of the constitution through the institution of the principle of 'responsible government' and the drafting of a new constitution. (17)

By the fall of 1837, the moderate liberal-whig Reform leaders – such as the Baldwins -- had withdrawn from politics. They believed in seeking reform from within the existing political system and were unwilling to support the radical convention proposal of Mackenzie. When invited, even Marshall Spring Bidwell – a Jeffersonian democratic, and leader of the Reform Party -- had refused to serve as a delegate to the projected convention. However, as the moderate Reformers withdrew into private life, the radical Reformers openly looked to the United States for their model of government. Years earlier, in 1829, Mackenzie had toured the United States, and was impressed with its economic prosperity and rapid development. He had become an ardent admirer of the egalitarian democratic republicanism of General Andrew Jackson, the two-term President of the United States (March 1829-March 1837).

Mackenzie praised Jackson for his opposition to banks as exploiters of farmers, his hard currency policy with its rejection of paper money, his opposition to imprisonment for debt, and the 'spoils' system which struck Mackenzie as a convenient way to remove tory office holders after an election. More generally, Mackenzie came to admire what he saw as 'the virtuous simplicity' of the state governments in the United States and their 'republican frugality'. His republican ideal was a 'government of farmers', such as he believed was realized in the newly-constituted State of Michigan. (18)

In contrast, the Upper Canadian Tories were admirers of the existing balanced British Constitution, the union of church and state, and an appointed judiciary, and were strongly opposed to any effort to change the constitution of the province by extra-parliamentary means. It was regarded as an extremely dangerous initiative as there were no limits in place to control where extra-parliamentary partisan activities might lead. The Tories were also strong supporters of the banking system, trade and commerce, government economic development policies, and the establishment of industries. They favoured transportation improvements and were focused on the construction of arterial roads and bridges, canals, and harbour facilities, and the introduction of steamboats.

In early November 1837, following an outbreak of acts of violence in Lower Canada, and signs of a growing political unrest within that province in response to the Russell Resolutions, the Lt. Governor of Upper Canada, Sir Francis Bond Head, transferred the British garrison troops of Upper Canada to the lower province as a precaution against an uprising there. With the Province of Upper Canada devoid of troops, Mackenzie called a private meeting of fifteen Reform leaders in Toronto and proposed that they immediately seize control of the provincial government in a coup d'état. What Mackenzie advocated was that the Reformers engage the workers of two large Toronto manufacturing works -- Dutcher's foundrymen and Armstrong's axemen-- to aid them in seizing the Lt. Governor and occupying the City Hall, where a stand of 4,000 arms and ammunition were stored. The City was defenseless, and its citizens unarmed. Once the Reformers were armed with the muskets, and in possession of the provincial capital, they would be able to quickly establish a provisional government.

Mackenzie's idea was to force the Lt. Governor to grant the principle of 'responsible government' and to call an election for what he referred to as "a new and fairly chosen" Assembly. If the Lt. Governor refused, the option was "to go at once for independence". Apparently, Mackenzie had come to believe his own rhetoric: that the election of June 1836 had been stolen by 'corruption and intimidation' at the polls; and that a new election would lead to a Reform Party triumph. In reality, whatever intimidation that might have been felt by the Reformers -- during open voting in the 1836 loyalty election -- was more likely to have been due to the large numbers of Constitutionalist supporters who turned out to vote in that single-issue campaign.

At the Toronto meeting, one of the Reform leaders, Dr. Thomas David Morrison, strongly opposed Mackenzie's proposal in maintaining that the proposed coup constituted 'an act of treason'. The meeting broke up with no decision having been made. However, subsequently, Mackenzie managed to convince Rolph and Morrison that the provincial government might well be taken by surprise and overthrown in a bloodless coup d'état. In response, Mackenzie was delegated to investigate the views of the farmers of the Home District, north of Toronto, who were the core supporters of the Reform Party, while another Reform Party stalwart, Jesse Lloyd, was sent to Lower Canada to determine the situation there. In the interim, the attention of the radical Reformers continued to be focused on the projected convention as they prepared a draft constitution for establishing a democratic government, if not an independent democratic republic. (19)

On the 13th November 1837, the Reformers approved a draft constitution for Upper Canada at a Toronto meeting that was attended by farmers, labourers and mechanics, as well as the radical Reform Party leaders. The constitution was intended for potential adoption by the convention should the British government continue to refuse to grant 'responsible government' to the province. The preamble claimed that the British government had violated the Constitution of 1791, and usurped the people's rights, through denying them the full blessings of the British constitution. What the Reformers meant was that the British Government had supposedly done so by refusing to implement their principle of 'responsible government'.

The draft constitution consisted of an enumeration, in a list of eighty-one clauses, most of which were the traditional 'rights of Englishmen' already enjoyed by Upper Canadians, but inclusive of specific rights set forth in the amendments to the American Constitution, such as freedom of speech, of the press, and of peaceful assembly, and the right to bear arms.

More particularly, the draft constitution had clauses that gave effect to policies long-advocated by the Reformers, as well as several clauses that were clearly attributable to Mackenzie. The preamble contained a bald statement of popular sovereignty and independence:

> We, the people of the State of Upper Canada, acknowledging with gratitude the grace and beneficence of God, in permitting us to make choice of our form of Government, and in order to establish justice, ensure domestic tranquility, provide for a common defence, promote the general welfare, and secure the blessing of civil and religious liberty, to ourselves and our posterity, do establish this Constitution.

Among the specific Reform Party clauses were: the separation of church and state, 'religious equality', and a clause that all Canada Company lands, Crown and Clergy Reserve lands, and the land endowment bestowed by the Crown under the King's College Charter for the creation of a provincial university, were to be taken up by the Legislature for the support of the Common Schools. Clerics were not to hold any seat in government, or in any civil or military office of the state, and there was to be no religious test to qualify for any public office or position of trust. Moreover, the state was to be prohibited from granting "heredity emoluments, privileges or honours", and there were to be no sinecure offices. Pensions were to be granted only by the Legislature. Intestate real estate was to be divided equally, and the laws of entail were to be repealed.

All public revenues were to be paid to the provincial Treasury, and monies were to be appropriated only by the Legislature. To encourage [American] immigration, aliens were to be allowed "to hold and convey real estate." In the new republican State of Canada, there were to be no chartered banks, and no bank note currency. It was specified that: "Labour is the only means of creating wealth". Moreover, slavery and involuntary servitude were to be outlawed and "people of colour", who were new immigrants, were to have the same rights as their fellow Canadians upon taking an oath to support the constitution of the new republic. (20)

As slavery no longer existed in Upper Canada, the clause of the draft Reform Constitution which sought to outlaw slavery and involuntary servitude had no relevance within the province. As early as 1793, the Lt. Governor of Upper Canada, John Graves Simcoe – an English Tory -- had secured the passage of an "Act to prevent the further introduction of slaves and to limit the term of contract for servitude within the province". That act had made it illegal to import slaves into Upper Canada, and provided that the children of female slaves (domestics) would be free when they reached twenty-five years of age. Although existing slaves continued in bondage, the intention of the act was to eventually put an end to slavery in Upper Canada. Lt. Governor Simcoe had wanted to abolish slavery immediately and completely but had had to settle for a gradual abolition of slavery to secure the support of the provincial Legislature.

Prior to the passage of the 1793 anti-slavery act, there were perhaps as many as three hundred slaves in Upper Canada, mostly domestics, brought into the Province by the Loyalists refugees. The slaves were held by the leading Loyalist families and the major merchants of the province. However, by the War of 1812, the number of slaves in Upper Canada had dramatically declined under the impact of the provisions of the 1793 Act, a growing public opposition to slavery, the selling of slaves into the United States to avoid having to free them, and the practice of manumission with slaves being freed upon the death of 'their master' in accordance with the will of the deceased.

In 1819, a legal issue had been raised as to whether American slave owners had the right to enter Upper Canada to retrieve 'their property' – a fugitive slave – and whether the provincial government and courts were required in law to act in support of the slave owner in recovering 'his property'. In response, the Attorney-General – John Beverley Robinson – issued a legal decision declaring that since Upper Canada was an English colony in which the Law of England was "the rule of decision" in questions related to property and civil rights, it followed that fugitive slaves, resident in Upper Canada, were free men. (Within England, slavery had been outlawed by a court order as early as June 1772.) Had Robinson decided otherwise the Underground Railroad in the United States would have lost its purpose, and American slaves would have lost their hope of following the North Star to freedom in Canada. The Robinson legal decision had the effect as well in outlawing slavery within Upper Canada at a time when there was but a very small number of slaves remaining in bondage -- mostly in menial domestic positions -- who had not been freed under the workings of the 1793 Provincial Act.

More generally, even before the draft Constitution of the radical Reformers was promulgated in November 1837, slavery no longer existed in the British Empire. In 1833, the British parliament passed an Act to Abolish Slavery which took effect on 1 August 1834. The colonies in which slavery was specifically outlawed within the British Empire, did not include the British North American provinces. In the British North American provinces, slavery had long since been abolished through the court decisions of judges -- judicial legislation -- or by the issuing of an obiter dictum by the provincial Chief Justice as was the case, as early as 1798, in Lower Canada. (21)

In sum, as of November 1837, when the draft constitution of the radical Reformers called for the outlawing of slavery, there were no slaves in Upper Canada. The small black population of Upper Canada was comprised of the freed descendants of the slaves who had been brought into the new province by Loyalist refugees prior to 1793, and free black immigrants from the United States, as well as a small, but growing, number of fugitive slaves from the United States who sought freedom in Upper Canada. (22)

In contrast, in the United States slavery was imbedded in the Constitution with a slave counting as three-fifths of a person for proportioning the number of each state's representatives in the House of Representatives. By the 1830s, slavery had been curtailed in most northern states of the American Union, with statutes providing for the freeing of young slaves on the attainment of their 25th birthday, but slavery and a domestic slave trade continued to flourish in the American southern states. There were over two million slaves in the United States, which accounted for almost one-sixth of the American population. Moreover, slave states were being admitted to the American Union – Alabama in 1819, Missouri in 1821, and Arkansas in 1836. In their draft constitution, what the radical Reformers appear to have been seeking was to establish that once the projected independent republican State of Upper Canada entered the American Union, it would do so as a free state. (23)

Under the November 1837 draft constitution of the Reformers, the State of Upper Canada was to be an independent democratic republic with a Governor, who was to be elected for a three-year term, a Senate of 24 members who would be elected for a four-year term, and a House of Assembly of 72 members who would be elected for a two-year term. All power belonged to the people, and the Governor was to exercise his executive function in all matters as decided upon by the Legislature (the Senate and House of Assembly). Elections were to be confined to a two-day period.

All government ministers, civil administrators and the judiciary, except for the Justices of the Peace, were to be appointed by the Governor, with the consent of the Senate, and all government and civil officers were to be liable to impeachment by the Legislature. Supreme Court judges were to serve during good behavior, but Justices of the Peace were to be elected for a three-year term, and sheriffs, coroners and registrars elected for a four-year term. Sheriffs were to be ineligible to stand for re-election. The ridings of the House of Assembly were to be apportioned strictly according to the population of the counties, with a census to be taken every four years. (24)

Such was the draft constitution that the Reformers of the Toronto Political Union were prepared to submit to their convention for adoption as a means of resolving their 'grievances' with the monarchical government of the Province of Upper Canada. It was a constitution that was anathema to the Anglican Tories – and conservatives, more generally -- as it provided for the establishment of a secular democratic republic. On the one hand, the political rights and freedoms that were enunciated in the draft constitution were such as were enjoyed already by Upper Canadians -- as British subjects living under a constitutional monarchy and the rule of law – except for the specified right to bear arms. However, on the other hand, the Lockean-liberal political philosophy – in particular, the concept of popular sovereignty -- which underlay the draft constitution of the Reformers, as well as the several clauses of the draft constitution that pertained directly to political issues in Upper Canada, were contrary to almost everything in which the Tories believed.

A month earlier, Mackenzie had made the future of the independent republican State of Upper Canada quite clear. He had published a piece in which Upper Canadians were assured that they would be better off if the province were to become a state of the American union. Not only would Upper Canadians gain local self-government, but they would enjoy universal manhood suffrage and the vote by secret ballot. (25)

As of the third week of November, Mackenzie proceeded north to attend a secret Reform meeting which was held on November 18th near Hope (Sharon) on Yonge Street. It was attended by the six Reform Party leaders of that region who had been selected earlier as convention delegates. At the meeting, Mackenzie spoke of the draft constitution, and the benefits of independence, and presented a new proposal for seizing control of the provincial government in a coup d'état.

At the meeting, it was reported -- by Jesse Lloyd -- that the Lower Canadians were planning a revolt. In response, Mackenzie declared that Upper Canadians needed to take advantage of the situation. He assured the Reform meeting that if the farmers of the Home District were to march in force on Toronto, it could be taken without a shot being fired. He emphasized that the British garrison troops had been dispatched to Lower Canada, that the City was almost totally defenceless, and that 'the tories' would be cowed into submission by a massive show of armed force. Once the Lt. Governor and his advisors were arrested, and the arms at City Hall seized, a provisional government could be established, and a republic declared.

Mackenzie maintained further that British troops would not be able to intervene in Upper Canada, once the insurrection was underway in Lower Canada. The troops would be tied down in the fighting in that province and, once a provisional government was established in Upper Canada, thousands of Americans would come to the defence of the new republic. Moreover, he claimed that half of Toronto would turn out in support of the marchers; that the tories of the province – most of whom were farmers -- would not take up arms against "their friends and neighbours"; and that, once a democratic republican government was established, the British government would not undertake to wage a costly war against it.

At the Hope meeting, Mackenzie engaged in an act of duplicity. He assured the Reform Party leaders in attendance that the Toronto reformers concurred in the immediate undertaking of a coup, which was not the case. However, with that assurance, an agreement was reached. A 23-man Vigilance Committee – which had been established earlier to gain public support for the projected convention – was charged with gathering arms and organizing the farmers of the Home District to undertake the coup. A date was set -- Thursday, December 7, 1837 – for the Reformers to rendezvous at Montgomery's Tavern, four miles north of Toronto, to march into the City in an armed show of force to take the provincial authorities by surprise and seize the government.

To encourage farmers to support the planned coup, Mackenzie promised that each participant in the march would receive 300 acres of land for their family from the Clergy or Crown reserves, and that those who were leasing Clergy Reserve lots, or farming lands being purchased from the Canada Land Company, would receive a free title to their land to enable them to become members of the 'independent yeomanry'. Those who refused to join were warned that their lands might be confiscated, as had happened to the tories during the American Revolution. It was expected by Mackenzie that 4,000 to 5,000 men would join in the march on Toronto.

When Mackenzie returned to the City, the Reform Party leaders in Toronto were informed of a *fait accompli* -- that an uprising was set for the 7th of December. However, the Toronto Reformers were soon encouraged by the news from Lower Canada. On November 23, 1837, at the Battle of Saint-Denis, a detachment of British troops was driven from the field by a large force of French-Canadian rebels that had gathered in the Richelieu Valley under the leadership of Dr. Wolfred Nelson. (26)

As of the end of November 1837, with the Reformers of the Toronto Political Union holding meetings in the countryside north of Toronto, and preparing to stage a coup d'état, the moderate Reform Party leaders who might have restrained Mackenzie were no longer active in the Toronto Political Union. On the other hand, there were several prominent Reform Party leaders, such as Dr. John Rolph and Dr. Thomas David Morrison, who continued to conspire in secret with Mackenzie in furtherance of the planned march on Toronto.

As the planning for the coup d'état proceeded, Dr. Rolph was selected to serve as President of the new republic. It was agreed that he and Dr. Morrison would join with the rebels upon their entry into the City, and that they would do so with as many men as they could muster from among the Reformers in Toronto. To explain away the organizing activities and meetings of the vigilance committees of the Toronto Political Union, Mackenzie announced that the projected convention would be held in Toronto on the 31st December 1837.

None of the moderate Reform leaders acted to inform the provincial government that Mackenzie was planning a seizure of power to establish an independent democratic republic. The Tories were unaware that the Reformers of the Toronto Political Union were planning a coup. Nonetheless, the principles which were being espoused by Mackenzie in his newspaper, the *Constitution* – supposedly in preparation for the proposed convention -- reconfirmed the Tory conviction that the Reformers were lacking in loyalty to the Crown, the constitution, and the British connection. (27)

The Principle of Loyalty

In essence, the support of the Tories for the maintenance of the prerogatives, privileges, and rights of all three branches of the provincial government – the Crown (represented by the Lt. Governor), the appointed Legislative Council, and the elective House of Assembly -- was based on their loyalty to the established constitution: the Constitutional Act of 1791, which they viewed as "*the image and transcript of the British Constitution*". For the Tories, Upper Canada was a 'Loyalist Asylum', and many of the leading Tories were second-generation Loyalists who were very conscious of the sacrifice that their fathers had made in "the Royal cause". They knew that their families had received Crown land grants for their loyalty to the Crown and Empire and believed that the Province of Upper Canada was established in 1791 as a Loyalist sanctuary for their benefit. As the sons of Loyalists, they could do no less than their fathers in providing an "open and steady support of principles and institutions which they knew to be justly entitled to their obedience and respect".

Among the leading Tories also were found British immigrants who supported the established monarchical form of government, identified themselves with the Loyalist heritage of the province, and supported the maintenance of the Imperial connection. Not all sons of the Loyalists and British immigrants were loyal to the Crown and Empire. When the Tories spoke of 'the loyal', they were referring primarily to the men who were known to have defended Upper Canada during the War of 1812, and who, in doing so, fought for the principles of the British Constitution and the institutions which embodied it, and the Imperial connection, out of loyalty to the Crown, and a desire to preserve the Loyalist heritage of the province. Indeed, many of the leading Tories were veterans of the War of 1812 who had been on active service with the militia during the war.

The Tories prided themselves on their loyalty to the Crown. They felt ties of "affection and respect" for the Sovereign of their country and believed that they were bound by their "duty to God, to their Sovereign, and to their country", to obey legitimate authority, and to defend the monarchical form of government in all its integrity. They were quick to assert that their support of government, and efforts to keep the constitution unimpaired, were not attributable to any "innate subservience to power, for sordid purposes" as their opponents charged. On the contrary, they maintained that their loyalty was attributable to:

> the existence of that principle which is plainly and solemnly enjoined by the Christian religion, and of that feeling the most-manly and honourable in our nature, which teaches us to stand by the right, through good report and evil report, and to cling the closer to what is just and good, in proportion as we see it to be ungenerously assailed.

To be a supporter of government and a defender of duly-constituted authority, in seeking to confine "each branch of the Legislature resolutely within certain well-defined limits", was regarded as being in no way incompatible with respect and support for the liberty and privileges which the subject enjoyed. Loyalty and patriotism were perfectly in keeping with the maintenance of the rights of the subject, because it was the balanced constitution which, when kept inviolate, guaranteed them. (28)

Notes

Defending the Constitution

Frontispiece quotation: PAO, Robinson Papers, Charges to the Grand Juries, 1829-41, Chief Justice J.B. Robinson, "Charge delivered at Toronto", 25 May 1841.

Three sections of this chapter – specifically, the sections on "Extra-parliamentary Associations", "Conventions", and "The Principle of Loyalty" – were originally part of a chapter on "The Constitution of Upper Canada" in the abortive Ph.D. dissertation on 'The Upper Canadian Tory Mind'. The three sections have been removed and incorporated into this new chapter, which was prepared to provide an historical context for the Tory efforts to defend the balanced constitution. As such, this chapter conveys the nature of the threat posed by extra-parliamentary associations and political conventions, and it provides insights into the political demands and the character of the democratic radicals and liberal-Whigs of the Reform Party who were attacking the provincial government, the balanced British constitution, and the established order.

1. *The Church*, 17 May 1844, "Political Associations" (From the *Niagara Chronicle*), and 24 May 1844, (Bethune editorial); PAO, Macaulay Papers, reel 1, 19 February 1821, J.B. Robinson to John Macaulay, & reel 2, 20 May, 6 June & 16 July 1836, Robert Stanton to John Macaulay; and PAO, Robinson Papers, Charges to the Grand Juries, 1829-41, J.B. Robinson, "Charge at Toronto", 25 May 1841, 13. The quotation is from Robinson to Macaulay, 19 February 1821.

2. Craig, *Upper Canada*, 222. [See also, Jeffrey L. McNairn, *The Capacity to Judge, Public Opinion and Deliberative Democracy in Upper Canada, 1791-1854* (Toronto: University of Toronto Press, 2000), 107 &112. The Canadian Alliance Society was a successor to an even earlier extra-parliamentary radical electoral organization: the Upper Canada Central Political Union, which was formed in York in November 1832. Subsequently the Central Political Union branches sent delegates to a Grand Convention of Delegates, which was held in York, on 27 February 1834, to establish a 'party' platform and to nominate an 'official' radical candidate for each riding, or two candidates for dual-member ridings, in the coming election. See, Albert Schrauwers, *'Union is Strength', W.L. Mackenzie, The Children of Peace, and the Emergence of Joint Stock Democracy*

in Upper Canada (Toronto: University of Toronto Press, 2009), 129-141.]

3. *The Church*, 17 May 1844, "Political Associations" (From the *Niagara Chronicle*), and 24 May 1844, (Bethune editorial). The quotation is from *The Church*, 24 May 1844.

4. Craig, *Upper Canada*, 234-236; and William Dawson LeSueur, *William Lyon Mackenzie: A Reinterpretation*, A.B. McKillop, ed., (Toronto: Macmillan/Carleton Library, 1979), 256-260 & 262-265. [See also, McNairn, *The Capacity to Judge*, 107-108, 191-193 & 197-200.] The quotation is from the defeated conservative motion of 5 April 1836, as quoted by LeSeuer, 262. See also a pamphlet: "British Constitutional Society, Upper Canada: at a meeting of a number of members of the original Constitutional Society of York, and other friends of the British connexion, in the City of Toronto, held at Morrison's Tavern, on Tuesday, the 1st day of July 1834", Circular, signed by George Gurnett, Secretary, 19 July 1834. [See also Read and Stagg, eds. *The Rebellion of 1837 in Upper Canada*, 13-14, Doc. A8, "Declaration of the British Constitutional Society, Toronto", 10 May 1836, W.B Jarvis, President. Initially, the society had ninety-two members. Its avowed purpose, and fundamental principle, was to maintain the British connection.]

In his memoir (*A Narrative*, 1839, 68-69), Sir Francis Bond Head commented on the resignation of his Executive Council and claimed that the Executive Council had demanded that he implement the principle of 'responsible government' and permit the Councilors to consult the public whenever the Lt. Governor refused their advice, which was a violation of their oath of secrecy as councilors. These may have been the initial demands of Robert Baldwin, when he was first approached by Head with an offer of an appointment to the Executive Council, but the resignations of 12 March 1836 were over Head's refusal to seek the advice of his Executive Council on provincial matters. Hence, the resignation of the Tory members, as well as the Reform members.

5. Aileen Dunham, *Political Unrest in Upper Canada, 1815-1836* (Toronto: McClelland & Stewart Ltd, 1963/Carleton Library reprint, 1969), 172-173; LeSueur, 266-267; and McNairn, *The Capacity to Judge*, 198-199, and David Mills, *The Idea of Loyalty in Upper Canada, 1784-1850* (Kingston & Montreal: McGill-Queen's University Press, 1988), 79-80; and *DCB*, X, S.F. Wise, "Head, Sir Francis Bond".

6. Craig, 236-238; LeSueur, 266-268; McNairn, 198-202; Mills, 79-90; and Robin W. Winks, *The Blacks in Canada, A History*, 2nd ed. (Montreal & Kingston: McGill-Queen's University Press, 1997), 149. See also, *DCB*, IX,

Hilary Bates Neary, "Stanton, Robert". The quotation from *The Patriot* is taken from the *DCB*, X, G.M. Craig, "Bidwell, Marshall Spring", and is also quoted in part by Mills, 82. See also, "Declaration of the British Constitutional Society, Toronto, 10 May 1836", Document A8, in Colin Read & Ronald J. Stagg, *The Rebellion of 1837 in Upper Canada, A Collection of Documents* (Toronto: The Champlain Society, 1985), 13-14.

7. Mills, 57-70, 81-82 & 84. See also Craig, 229, and LeSueur, 276-278. Later, during the Metcalfe crisis of 1843-1844, the Rev. Egerton Ryerson would declare that 'responsible government' was in essence, 'party government', which he viewed as being "a system of political and moral corruption". (Mills, 192/n54.) It was a view that was shared by the Upper Canadian Tories.

8. Mills, *The Idea of Loyalty*, 97-99. This description of the views of the Reformers draws heavily on the historical research material presented by Mills -- a former student of S.F. Wise -- in a chapter on "The Controversy over Legitimate Opposition: Reform Loyalty before the Rebellion". The quotations are from a letter, Robert Baldwin to Lord Glenelg, the Colonial Secretary, 18 July 1836, as reprinted in Gerald M. Craig, ed. *Discontent in Upper Canada* (Toronto: Copp Clark, 1974), 74-75, "The Baldwin Concept of Responsible Government". On the Whig values of the Baldwins, see Michael S. Cross, *A Biography of Robert Baldwin, The Morning Star of Memory* (Don Mills, Ontario: Oxford University Press, 2012), 313-320.

9. LeSueur, 267-269, Craig, 235-236; Mills, 67-68, and Armstrong, *Handbook of Upper Canadian Chronology*, 75- 78, "Thirteen Parliament, 1836-1841". On the Irish Catholics, see: DCB, VII, Curtis Fahey, "O'Grady, William John".

10. PAO, Macaulay Papers, reel 2, 20 May, 6 June & 16 July 1836, Robert Stanton to John Macaulay. See also, McNairn, *The Capacity to Judge*, 197 & 200.

11. Albert Schrauwers, *'Union is Strength'*, 192-193. On Mackenzie's claims concerning the June 1836 election, see: LeSueur, *William Lyon Mackenzie*, 269-271. The Children of Peace were staunch political and financial supporters of Mackenzie in the Fourth Riding of York. They were members of a Quaker sect of the Hope (Sharon) settlement on Yonge Street which was under the leadership of an American immigrant, David Willson, who believed in the separation of church and state, and an egalitarian democracy in both religion and the politics. The conceit of the Reform Party leaders in viewing themselves as the sole defenders of the rights and liberties of the people, and the true representatives

of 'the people', is clearly in evidence in the resolutions establishing the Toronto Political Union. See Read & Stagg, eds., *The Rebellion of 1873*, 49-63, Documents A46, A47, A48 & A50.

12. *Kingston Chronicle*, 8 January 1819, (Macaulay editorial), and 12 February 1819, Strachan, "For the Kingston Chronicle"; Spragge, ed., *Strachan Letterbook*, 171, Strachan to Lt. Col. Harvey, 27 July 1818, & 169, Strachan to the Administrator, 3 July 1818, & 182, Strachan to the Hon. Francis Gore, 8 December 1818; *U.E. Loyalist*, (Robert Stanton editorial), 29 December 1827. The "Act to prevent certain meeting within this province" (59 Geo. III c.11), was repealed by the 60 Geo. III, c. 4 of March 7, 1820. The Tories defended the constitutional right of the people to petition the Crown for redress of grievances against attempts by the Assembly to deny such a right. The Assembly asserted a claim that petitions should be addressed solely to itself as the sole legitimate representatives of 'the people'. See *U.E. Loyalist*, 6 January 1827, "Stepsure" (From the *Kingston Chronicle*).

13. Schrauwers, *'Union is Strength'*, 188-189.

14. Craig, *Upper Canada*, 244. [See also Wikipedia.org: "Resolutions intended to be proposed by Lord John Russell, in a committee of the whole, relative to the affairs of Canada", March 1837.] Mackenzie was also angered by a decision of the Lt. Governor to keep the Legislature of Upper Canada in session following the death of King William IV on 20 June 1837, rather than dissolving the Legislature, and calling for a new election in keeping with parliamentary tradition. The quotation is from *The Constitution*, 5 July 1837, as quoted by Craig, 244.

15. Craig, *Upper Canada*, 244. See also: Google Books, online reprint: *Common Sense by Thomas Paine* (Rockville, Maryland: Arc Manor Classic Reprints, 2008).

16. Online reprint: "The Declaration of the Reformers of the City of Toronto to their Fellow-Reformers in Upper Canada", as published by William Lyon Mackenzie, *The Constitution*, 2 August 1837. See also: LeSueur, *Mackenzie,* 284, Craig, *Upper Canada*, 244, and *DCB*, IX, John Beswarick Thompson, "Nelson, Wolfred" & VIII, Victor Loring Russell, "Morrison, Thomas David" & VII, Curtis Fahey, "O'Grady, William John". The quotations are from the Declaration.

17. Schrauwers, *'Union is Strength'*, 194-196; and Charles Lindsey, *The Life and Times of William Lyon Mackenzie, with an Account of the Canadian Rebellion*

of 1837, and the subsequent Frontier Disturbances, Chiefly from Unpublished Documents, II (Toronto, Canada West: P.R. Randall, 1862), 15-19.

18. Craig, *Upper Canada*, 211 & 243-244; and Schrauwers, *'Union is Strength'*, 151.

19. Le Sueur, *Mackenzie*, 290-291; Schrauwers, 197; and Craig, 247. See also, *DCB*, VII, Ronald J. Stagg, "Lloyd, Jesse".

20. Colin Read & Ronald J. Stagg, eds., *The Rebellion of 1837 in Upper Canada, A Collection of Documents* (Toronto: The Champlain Society, 1985), 95- 102, "W. L. Mackenzie's Constitution".

21. William Renwick Riddell, "Method of Abolition of Slavery in England, Scotland and Upper Canada Compared", *Ontario Historical Society, Papers and Records*, XXVII, 1931, 511-513; and British Statutes (online), 3-4 William IV, C. 73, 1833, "Act to Abolish Slavery". By the Slave Trade Act of 1807, the British parliament had outlawed the Atlantic slave trade, and thereafter a Royal Navy Squadron was stationed on the West African coast to suppress the slave trade. In Upper Canada in the post-War of 1812 period, the leading Anglicans, Wesleyan Methodists, Methodists, Quakers and Baptists clerics and religious leaders were noted for their outspoken opposition to slavery, but slavery was not a major domestic political issue. On the slavery situation, see: *The Journal of Negro History*, vol. 5, no. 3, July 1920, William Renwick Riddell, "Upper Canada – Early Period," 316-339 & "The Fugitive Slave in Upper Canada", 340-358. For a more comprehensive study of the Blacks in Canada, see: Robin W. Winks, *The Blacks in Canada: A History* (Montreal: McGill-Queen's University Press, 1997, 1st ed. 1971), and especially pp. 96 -101 & 110-112 on the outlawing of slavery. In his work, Winks fails to mention, and hence to realize, the significance of the 1819 legal decision of Attorney-General Robinson in outlawing slavery in the Province of Upper Canada.

22. The composition of the black community in Upper Canada varied over time. For an excellent analysis of its composition at mid-century, see: Michael Wayne, "The Black Population of Canada West on the Eve of the American Civil War: A Reassessment Based on the Manuscript Census of 1861", *Histoire Social/Social History*, 1995, 472-481.

23. Wikipedia, "Slavery in the United States". Slavery was not outlawed throughout the entire United States until the enacting, in December 1865, of the Thirteen Amendment to the United States Constitution. Earlier, when drafting the American Constitution, and even earlier during the Revolutionary period, the

American political elite was acutely aware of the hypocrisy and inconsistency of their pronouncements on 'freedom and liberty' while chattel slavery was tolerated. However, there was a concern that the abolition of slavery would ruin the economy of many states and the colonial trade with the West Indies. See Bernard Bailyn, *The Ideological Origins of the American Revolution* (Cambridge, Mass.: Harvard University Press, 1967/1992, 232-246.)

24. Read & Stagg, eds., *The Rebellion of 1837*, 95- 102, "W. L. Mackenzie's Constitution". The clause calling for the Supreme Court judges to be appointed by the Governor to serve 'during good behaviour' was not innovative. The only difference was that the appointment would be made by an elected Governor in the new republic instead of the Crown's representative, the Lt. Governor. Judges already served 'during good behaviour' in Upper Canada. In England, the appointed judges of the superior courts served 'during good behaviour' and could only be removed by an address of parliament assented to by the Crown. In Upper Canada, the appointed judges had served 'at the pleasure of the Crown' until 1831 when their tenure was converted to 'during good behaviour'.

25. [William Lyon Mackenzie], *The Constitution*, 4 October 1837, as cited by Craig, *Upper Canada*, 245.

26. Schrauwers, *'Union is Strength'*, 197-199; and Lindsey, *The Life and Times*, II, 15 & 56-57. See also, *DCB*, IX, Fred H. Armstrong & Ronald J. Stagg, "Mackenzie, William Lyon" & VII, Ronald J. Stagg, "Lount, Samuel".

27. Craig, *Upper Canada*, 246; and *DCB*, IX, "Mackenzie".

28. Robinson, *Canada and the Canada Bill*, 1840, 24-26; Strachan, *Sermon on the Death of Cartwright*, 3 September 1815, 36-37; and [John Macaulay et al] *Report of the Select Committee of the Legislative Council*, 13 February 1838. The quotation is from Robinson, *Canada Bill*, 26. The Tory principles of loyalty were consistent over time.

[For a more recent study of the concept of loyalty, see: David Mills, *The Idea of Loyalty in Upper Canada, 1784-1850* (Kingston & Montreal: McGill-Queen's Press, 1988). Mills sees the moderate Reformers – as distinct from the Mackenzie radicals -- as loyal oppositionists who were trying to restore the balanced British constitution, which he maintains – in agreeing with the Reformers -- was corrupted through being dominated by 'exclusionist tories' who were ensconced in the Legislative Council and Executive Council. Mills fails to see the revolutionary nature of the principle of 'responsible government'. Moreover, the Tories were not 'exclusionist' in any sense other than merit and proven loyalty to the Crown and Empire. Competent individuals of good education, social standing, and moral character, regardless of their religion affiliation or ethnic origin, were appointed by the Lt. Governor to public office at all levels, with the advice of Tories in his Executive Council. Indeed, one problem that the Upper Canadian Tories faced, in the immediate post-War of 1812 period, was the finding of enough literate and well-educated individuals to serve in public positions.]

Chapter Seven

The Revolt of the Radicals

The Rebellion Travesty of December 1837

The Duncombe Uprising of December 1837

Preparing to Indict the Rebels

The Character of the Rebels

The 'Rebellion' of 1837: a Tory View

Maintaining Civil Government & the Rule of Law

The Treason Trials

Sentencing the Rebels

Tory Reflections

"But when disloyalty so rears its crest, as to attack even majesty itself, it is called by way of eminent distinction, high treason, alta proditio;
....

... by statute 54 Geo. III, c. 146 [1814], the judgement in all cases of high treason is, that the offender shall be drawn on a hurdle to the place of execution, and be there hanged by the neck until he be dead, and that afterwards his head shall be severed from his body, and his body, divided into four quarters, shall be disposed of as the king shall think fit; with power to the king, by special warrant, to dispense with the drawing, and to direct beheading instead."

William Blackstone
Commentaries on the Laws of England,
Vol. IV, Of Public Wrongs.

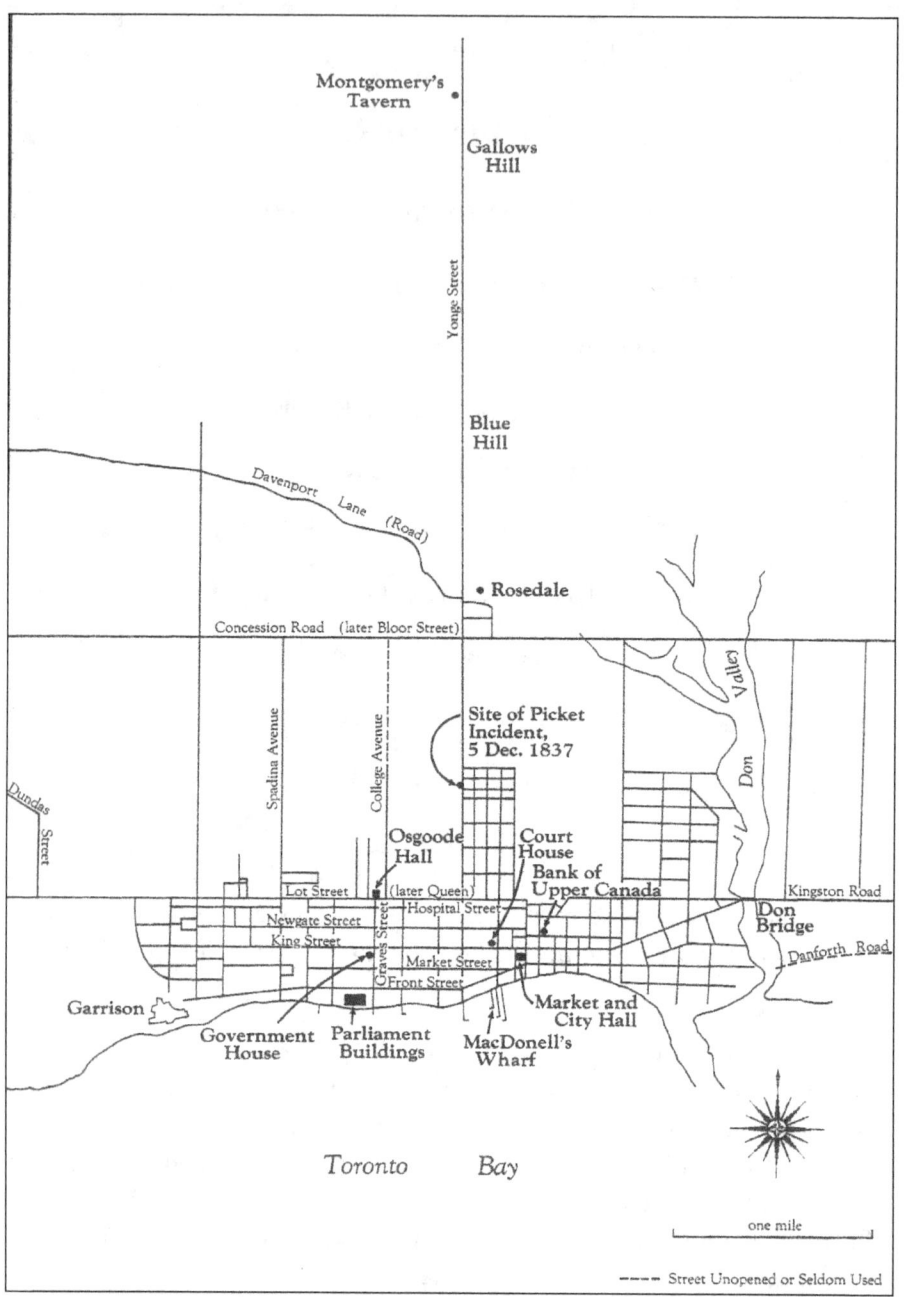

Map of "Toronto & Environs, 1837" in Read & Stagg, eds., The Rebellion of 1837 in *Upper Canada, A Collection of Documents* (Toronto: The Champlain Society/Ontario Heritage Foundation, 1985). Shown are the wharf where the loyal militia regiments were landed by steamboat during the December 1837 rebellion, the location of the City Hall arms depot, the site of the Don River Bridge on the Kingston Road; and the sites along Yonge Street associated with the rebellion: viz. the picket site; Rosedale; Gallows Hill; and Montgomery's Tavern.

Chapter Seven

The Revolt of the Radicals

For the Upper Canadian Tories, the outbreak of a rebellion in December 1837 came as a complete shock. They were alarmed earlier at the activities of the Reformers in seeking to organize a provincial convention but did not expect an armed uprising would evolve from that effort. It was inconceivable to the Tories -- even as a rebel force was massing north of Toronto -- that anyone in Upper Canada would rebel against Her Majesty's Provincial Government. Upper Canadians were living in a constitutional monarchy under the rule of law, enjoyed a complete freedom of conscience and religious liberty, and possessed an almost universal manhood suffrage. They paid no direct taxes; many of the settlers had received a free land grant from the Crown; and the province benefited greatly – economically -- from Imperial trade preferences within the British Empire, and from British military expenditures in defence of Upper Canada. Nonetheless, uprisings did take place in the Home District north of Toronto and in the London District under the leadership of egalitarian democratic republicans: William Lyon Mackenzie and Dr. Charles Duncombe, respectively.

The Anglican Tories of Upper Canada played a leading role, both militarily and politically, during the rebellion of December 1837 in preventing the constitution from being subverted and Her Majesty's Provincial Government overthrown by the rebels; and it was the Anglican Tories who played the leading role in the subsequent prosecution of the captured rebels. More generally, the rebellion served to confirm several Tory preconceptions and beliefs about the character of the radical Reformers and their ultimate objective.

The Rebellion Travesty of December 1837

When William Lyon Mackenzie returned to Toronto -- from the secret meeting of November 18th, with the Reform leaders in the village of Hope (Sharon) north of the City -- he informed the leading Reformers of the Toronto Political Union that December 7th had been set for a 'march on Toronto'; and that the Vigilance Committee of the Home District was organizing the farmers for the march and collecting arms for the volunteers. Faced with a *fait accompli*, the Toronto Reform Party leaders concurred in sending Mackenzie back north to address Reform meetings to raise additional volunteers for the planned descent on the City.

The arguments presented, which pertained to the ease with which the provincial government could be seized in a coup d'état by simply marching in force against Toronto, remained the same as Mackenzie had set forth earlier in addressing the Reform Party leaders earlier in Hope, as did the inducements held out to farmers to join in the march.

At the same time, the goal of the planned coup d'état was set forth. On November 27th, Mackenzie prepared a broadside containing a declaration of Independence which was to be distributed to the rebels when they gathered at Montgomery's Tavern for the march on Toronto. In the broadside, there was no statement of any grievance that would justify a rebellion in Upper Canada, or any mention of 'responsible government'. The declaration contained simply exhortations to rebel, bombastic rhetoric, and an ominous threat where the loyal supporters of the provincial government were concerned. The opening statement expressed a belief that the rebel Reformers were partaking of the revolutionary 'spirit of the age':

INDEPENDENCE!

There have been Nineteen strikes for Independence from European Tyranny on the Continent of the Americas. [North and South America]. They were all successful. ... .

CANADIANS! Do you love Freedom? Who dare deny it! Do you hate oppression? Who dare deny it! Do you wish perpetual peace ... [and] a government bound to enforce the law to do to each other as you wish to be done by? Then buckle on your armor, and put down the villains who oppress and enslave our country. ... One short hour will deliver our country from the oppressor; and freedom in religion, peace, and tranquility, equal laws, and an improved country will be the prize. ... ... If we move now as one man to crush the tyrant's power, to establish free institutions founded on God's law, we will prosper. ....

Mark all those who join our enemies, act as spies for them, fight for them, or aid them; these men's properties shall pay the expense of the struggle; they are traitors to Canadian freedom, and as such we will deal with them. .... The promised land is now before us – up then and take it -- ....

MARK MY WORDS, CANADIANS! The struggle is begun .... We cannot be reconciled to Britain ...; we are determined never to rest until independence is ours – the prize is a splendid one. ....

The Independence broadside repeated earlier promises of "several hundred acres to every volunteer', and the grant of a free land title to settlers who were purchasing Canada Company lots or leasing Clergy Reserve lots. Moreover, in a new departure, there was a declaration that public lands would be used for "education, internal improvements and the public good", and a prediction that an influx of men of property and wealth "from other lands" (the American states), would increase four-fold the value of farm properties following the overthrow of the colonial government.

Two days later, on November 29th, Mackenzie published an even more explicit threat to supporters of the provincial government administration. In his newspaper, *The Constitution*, the 'tories' were admonished that:

> if found in the act of fighting against the people to uphold a despotism, they would lose their lands, be banished [from] the country as traitors, and their wealth used to defray the expense of the unnatural and cruel contest their covetousness had given rise to. (1)

In sum, if the 'tories' offered any resistance to the rebel seizure of power, they would be held personally responsible for any suffering and destruction of property that might ensue. Their property would be expropriated; they would be driven into exile; and their confiscated lands and supposed 'wealth' would be used to pay for the cost of the rebellion. The 'tories' were to receive no mercy. Those who resisted the second coming of the American Revolution would suffer the same fate that the Loyalists had experienced earlier at the hands of the American revolutionaries.

On Sunday, December 3rd, when Mackenzie arrived at Montgomery's Tavern – 4½ miles north of Toronto, on Yonge Street -- he found several hundred supporters variously armed with pikes, cudgels, pitchforks, fowling pieces and rifles. They had arrived at Montgomery's Tavern four days earlier than planned in response to a communication from Dr. Rolph of the Toronto executive committee. In fearing that the provincial government might discover their plot and arrest the leaders of the Toronto Political Union, Rolph had directed the Home District rebels to assemble at Montgomery's Tavern that Sunday, rather than wait for Thursday, December 7th. With the change of plan, the timing of the planned coup d'état was disrupted. When the marchers arrived at Montgomery's Tavern, after a long trudge down Yonge Street in the snows of a Canadian winter, they found that no arrangements had been made to provide them with food or shelter. Provisions had to be requisitioned from sympathizers on the neighbouring farms, while the men found whatever shelter they could on site.

Two Reform Party stalwarts, Samuel Lount and Anthony Anderson, were placed in command to direct the projected march on Toronto, and a guard was posted to block Yonge Street – opposite Montgomery's Tavern -- to keep government supporters from entering the city from the north. At that point, Dr. Rolph contacted Mackenzie to inform him that British troops had inflicted a severe defeat on the French-Canadian rebels in Lower Canada, at St. Charles on November 25th. It raised the spectre that British troops might soon be freed to return to Upper Canada from suppressing the rebellion in Lower Canada. Mackenzie faced a dilemma. Should he abandon the attempted coup, or should he march on Toronto immediately while the city remained defenceless? He did neither.

The next morning -- Monday, December 4th -- Mackenzie rode south down Yonge Street with Anderson, and two other horsemen, on a reconnaissance mission. Half way to Toronto they encountered William Powell – an Anglican Tory, and the grandson of the former Chief Justice, William Dummer Powell – who was riding out with a friend to investigate rumours of rebel activity north of the city. In an ensuing exchange, Powell shot and killed Anderson, and escaped to Toronto to raise the alarm. Any hope that Mackenzie had of seizing the City by surprise was lost.

A day earlier, rumours of a planned uprising had reached Toronto, and Colonel James Fitzgibbon, the Acting-Adjutant General of Militia, had tried to convince Sir Francis Bond Head to call out the militia and prepare defences for the City. However, neither the Lt. Governor, nor the Tory establishment in the City had given any credence to the rumours, but once

William Powell rode back into the City on the morning of December 4th, the church bells were rung to raise the alarm that an insurrection was underway. The City Hall was immediately fortified, and volunteers were issued muskets and ammunition for the defence of the City. Messages were sent by men on horseback westward to Hamilton and Niagara, and eastward to Cobourg and Kingston, to call out the loyal militias to come to the defence of Her Majesty's Provincial Government. Otherwise, the City remained almost defenceless, with the British Army garrison troops having been dispatched to Lower Canada.

In the late afternoon of Monday, December 4th, Colonel Robert Moodie, a retired half-pay British Army officer, was fired upon and mortally wounded when he attempted to gallop past the rebel guard post on Yonge Street. In being unaware that an alarm had been raised already that morning in Toronto, Colonel Moodie was attempting to warn the Lt. Governor of the uprising. With two men having been killed, and his plan for a surprise seizure of the provincial government unraveling, Mackenzie's actions became quite erratic the next day.

As of Tuesday, December 5th, there were 700 to 800 rebels gathered at Montgomery's Tavern, and a decision was made to move immediately on Toronto. On the march, Mackenzie stopped at the hamlet of Rosedale, where several prominent Torontonians had their homes. He entered, and personally torched the house of Dr. Robert Horne, a well-known Tory, and had to be restrained -- by Samuel Lount and another leading rebel, David Gibson -- from burning down the house of a second well-known Tory, the Sheriff of the Home District, William Botsford Jarvis.

In the City, word had spread quickly that a rebel force – reportedly of 'several thousand men' -- was descending on Toronto, and there was a great deal of anxiety and confusion as the smoke from the firing of Dr. Horne's house was clearly visible on the horizon several miles away. There were frightening rumours -- apparently circulated by Dr. John Rolph -- that Mackenzie would seize and execute the Lt. Governor and the leading officials of the government and would burn much of the city, if any resistance was offered to its occupation by the rebels. In response, Lady Head and the wives and children of the leading Tories, were placed on a steamer in the harbor. A full head of steam was built up, with the vessel held ready to cross the lake to the United States if the City should fall to the rebels. Among the armed defenders of the provincial government in the City were the Chief Justice, John Beverley Robinson, three Puisne Judges, James Buchanan Macaulay, Jonas Jones and Archibald McLean, and 'most of the respectable inhabitants'.

To gain time while the loyal militias rallied to the defence of the provincial government, and hopefully to avoid a great deal of bloodshed, the Lt. Governor Head, Sir Francis Bond Head, sent two Reformers, Robert Baldwin and Dr. John Rolph, out under a flag of truce to negotiate with their former Reform Party associate, Mackenzie. The rebels were offered a complete amnesty, if they would return to their homes, and Mackenzie was asked what they were seeking. He replied: "independence". His more specific demands were that the Lt. Governor, Sir Francis Bond Head, should be recalled to Britain; that responsible government should be immediately granted; and that the rebels should receive a written declaration of amnesty. It was impossible for the Lt. Governor to grant Mackenzie's demands, and negotiations were broken off. The Lt. Governor could have granted amnesty to the rebels – excluding the men who had killed Col. Moodie – and could have resigned his position, but he did not have the authority to grant the principle of 'responsible government' had he been so inclined, which he was not.

In a private conversation, Rolph -- who was playing a double game -- informed Mackenzie that the City was still virtually defenceless and advised him to march on Toronto that night.

In the late afternoon, the rebel column advanced down Yonge Street towards Toronto. On the outskirts of the City, the rebels encountered a 24-man picket that Sheriff William Botsford Jarvis had concealed in the bush along the roadside. At his command, the picket fired a musket volley at the advancing rebels that killed one man and mortally wounded two others, whereupon Jarvis withdrew his men back to Toronto to sound the alarm and warn the City of the approach of the rebels. In the enveloping shadows of a bush road lined with a thick forest, the rebels became confused in thinking that they were under fire from a large force of militia. They panicked and fled in disorder back to their encampment on Gallows Hill -- near Montgomery's Tavern -- where they regrouped under the harangues of Mackenzie and the efforts of several other rebel leaders.

During the night, and the next morning, over half of the rebel force departed to return home. The men had come to overthrow the provincial government by a show of force, and to receive a grant of 300-acres of free land for participating in the march on Toronto. They had not turned out to fight against armed defenders in a frontal assault on the City. Indeed, among the rebel force that had advanced towards Toronto, there were twenty-seven pacifists of the Children of Peace. (2)

In the City, the defensive position of the provincial government had improved as the day progressed. Once word spread of the uprising, loyal militia companies were called out across the province to descend on Toronto to defend the provincial government. As of Tuesday morning, December 5th, the Lt. Governor had had only 300 men under arms, but that evening Allan Napier MacNab – a veteran of the War of 1812, and the Speaker of the House of Assembly -- arrived by steamboat from Hamilton with sixty-five militiamen – 'the men of Gore'. It was a mild winter to that date, and the lake had not yet frozen over. Almost simultaneously, 70 men of the Scarborough militia marched into the City, under the command of Colonel Allan Maclean, a half-pay officer, formerly of the 91st Regiment of the British Army. During the evening, and into the night, volunteers continued to flow into the City. By Tuesday night, there were over 500 fully-armed men deployed to defend the provincial capital.

As news of the uprising spread along the shores of Lake Ontario, steamboats -- that had been docked for the winter -- were fired up to transport militia units to the defence of Her Majesty's Provincial Government. The next day, Wednesday, December 6th, militia companies began arriving, in relays of steamboats, from the towns and villages of the eastern districts, and from the Niagara District in the west. As the militiamen disembarked from each steamboat docking in the harbor at Toronto, they received "loud hurraes" from the militia companies that had arrived previously and were forming up and receiving their orders as to where to deploy for the defence of the City. Some militiamen brought rifles with them, but most were unarmed. Upon arrival, they were armed with muskets and ammunition from the City Hall depot. It was similarly the case with the volunteers who marched into the City, by road, from the surrounding villages of Peel County. With the influx of militia companies and volunteers who were determined to defend the provincial government against the insurgents, the confidence of the defenders of the City soared.

In contrast, in the rebel encampment, by Wednesday the men were becoming totally dispirited. Mackenzie's force was reduced to only 350 to 400 men as the number of rebels departing for home exceeded the number of new arrivals at Montgomery's Tavern. Moreover, the rebel force had received reports that militiamen were massing in the city and were well armed. Nonetheless, the rebel leaders persisted in their purpose.

During the day, Mackenzie sent out a hasty message for publication in the *Buffalo Whig and Journal* in New York State. It was a desperate appeal to secure the support of the thousands of American volunteers whom he had expected would cross the border to defend the democratic republican State of Canada, once it was declared. Now, he called for an immediate American incursion in force to support and save his attempted coup d'état. He wrote:

> The reformers of this part of Upper Canada have taken up arms in defence of the principle of independence of European domination – in plain words they wish this province to be a free, sovereign and independent state. They request all the assistance which the free citizens of your republic may choose to afford.

A message was also sent to the Reform Party leaders of the London District to inform them of the uprising and to request that they send support. To learn more about the forces that were being raised against him in the eastern districts, Mackenzie took a party of rebels and stopped the Montreal-Toronto stagecoach on Dundas Street. He rifled through the baggage of the passengers, opened the letters and packages in the Royal Mail, and relieved the mail packages and the passengers of money in a blatant act of highway robbery.

The next morning, Thursday, December 7th, Mackenzie sent a 60-man rebel force under the command of Peter Matthews -- an activist in the Pickering Township branch of the Toronto Political Union -- to destroy the bridge over the Don River, on the Kingston Road, at the eastern outskirts of Toronto. The intent was to cut off loyal militia forces who might seek to reach Toronto by road from the eastern districts. In the ensuing action, the bridge was set afire, several nearby homes were torched, and one defender was killed, before the rebel force was driven off by a militia force from Toronto. The Toronto militia force included volunteer firefighters who managed to save the bridge, with the aid of a fire company pump-engine that was raced to the site from Toronto.

As a diversion, the rebel operation was also a total failure. Mackenzie had hoped that an assault on the Don River Bridge would draw the militia forces away from attacking his encampment on Gallows Hill. He planned to hold out nearby, at his headquarters in Montgomery's Tavern, in the expectation that more Reform Party supporters -- from the Home District, and from the London District farther west -- would arrive to join the rebellion, as well as the 'thousands of American volunteers' whom he expected would cross the border to help him to 'liberate' Upper Canada. It was a forlorn hope. (3)

By the morning of Thursday, December 7th, there were 1500 loyal militiamen under arms in Toronto, and the City was bustling with military activity associated with the provisioning, arming, organizing, and forming up of a large militia force to march northward to engage the rebels. The main column, of about 600-700 men, was placed under the immediate command of militia Colonel Allan Napier MacNab, the flank company on the right (east wing, comprising some 200 men), was under the command of militia Colonel Samuel Peters Jarvis, and the flank company on the left (west wing, comprising some 120 men), was under the command of militia Colonel William Chisholm. The militia companies that remained deployed in Toronto, to man the defences of the City, were under the command of militia Colonel James Buchanan Macaulay, a Justice of the Court of Queen's Bench.

The four militia officers were born and educated in British North America – in Upper Canada or Nova Scotia (Chisholm);

and all had seen active service in the defence of Upper Canada during the fighting of the War of 1812. Three of the officers in command were Anglicans, and Col. William Chisholm was a Scots Presbyterian. MacNab and Chisholm were moderate tories of a pragmatic bent; whereas Samuel Peters Jarvis and James Buchanan Macaulay were philosophical Tories, who were former pupils of the Rev. John Strachan at the Cornwall District Grammar School. All four of the commanding militia officers were second-generation Loyalists.

The militiamen were fully armed, and many were furnished from the City Hall Depot with muskets that were equipped with bayonets. The main column was accompanied by a detachment of militia cavalry (York Dragoons) under the command of George Taylor Denison, and by a militia artillery unit, with two field guns (6 pounders), under the command of a city magistrate/militia Major Thomas Carfrae of the 1st East York Artillery. The militia force was under the overall command of the Acting Adjutant-General of Militia, Colonel James Fitzgibbon, a former British Army Officer of the 49th Regiment, who had fought with distinction in the defence of Upper Canada during the War of 1812.

With the church bells ringing across the city, flags waving, crowds cheering, and two bands playing martial tunes, the militia force marched northward at noon from Toronto to engage the rebels at Montgomery's Tavern. The main column marched straight up Yonge Street, with the left flank company to the west marching up College Avenue and penetrating beyond into the bush along the west side of Yonge Street. The right flank company, which had departed Toronto earlier in the morning, was scouring the woods to the east of Yonge Street as the main column advanced. The flank companies were deployed to protect the main column from any surprise attack that might be launched against its flank from the dense bush along Yonge Street north of the City.

After an hour's march, the main column of militia was fired upon by a force of about 100 riflemen that the rebels had hurriedly assembled across the road at Gallows Hill, and from rebels situated in the bush along the road. When Major Carfrae moved up the two artillery pieces and commenced canister fire, the rebel riflemen began to withdraw back into the woods. Upon receiving several volleys of musket fire, and additional canister shot from the two artillery pieces, the rebels – who may have numbered as few as 200 men in total – turned and ran for their lives through the underbrush. When the militia force reached Montgomery's Tavern, where a guard of rebels was holding a small number of prisoners, the two artillery pieces were moved up. Each fired a round through the Tavern, which panicked the rebels who fled into the bush without putting up a fight. Subsequently, Montgomery's Tavern was searched and set ablaze by order of the Lt. Governor, Sir Francis Bond Head, who was with the militia force, but not in a military command role.

Thereafter, the militia force advanced in strength a further four miles up Yonge Street to Hog's Hollow where the rebels were reported to be regrouping, but none were found. The cavalry was engaged in pursuing the fleeing rebels, but the Dragoons were unable to do so effectively in the thick underbrush of the surrounding forest. Only a small number of the rebels were captured. In one last action, the Lt. Governor sent a detachment to burn the nearby farm house of David Gibson -- one of the rebel leaders -- in retaliation for the burning of the house of Dr. Horne.

The defeat of the rebels was sudden and complete. The rebels were initially engaged at 1:00pm on Gallows Hill and by 5:00pm the militia force was back in Toronto, with the rebels having been thoroughly routed and forced to flee for their lives. MacKenzie and his fellow rebel leaders were in hiding. It was expected that they would try to pass incognito into the Niagara Peninsula to attempt a crossing of the Niagara River into the United States.

In the afternoon's brief action, seven rebels were killed, four were mortally wounded, and fourteen suffered less serious wounds. The attacking militia force did not suffer any serious casualties, either killed or severely wounded, but three militiamen were slightly wounded. Mackenzie was seen fleeing from the skirmish by horse -- up Yonge Street -- with four or five others, but he left behind a carpet bag that was retrieved from Montgomery's Tavern. It contained a list of the names of the rebels who had participated in the planned coup d'état. Presumably, the list was compiled to record those who were to receive their promised 300 acres of land. (4)

Once the rebels were dispersed, Lt. Governor Head immediately set the captured rebels free. Moreover, with the sole exception of the militia detachment that took livestock and produce from the farm of David Gibson, there was to be no plundering or destruction of the properties of the rebels in the Home District. On the same day that the rebels were routed, the Lt. Governor published a proclamation of clemency in Toronto.

The Proclamation of Clemency chastised the rebels for taking up arms at the instigation of "a few malignant and disloyal men", for seeking to murder the Queen's Subjects, and for the burning and destruction of private property, and it praised the loyal militias for their rapid turnout in defence of Her Majesty's Provincial Government. In addition, the Proclamation offered a reward for the apprehension and bringing to trial of the rebel leaders: £1,000 for William Lyon Mackenzie, and £500 for each of David Gibson, Samuel Lount, Jesse Lloyd, and Silas Fletcher. The only exceptions to the grant of clemency were the rebel leaders so-named, and anyone who was personally involved in the commitment of a murder, a robbery, or an act of arson, during the rebellion. Otherwise, the grant of clemency extended to all the rebels. In the words of the Proclamation, they were:

> called [upon] to return to their duty to their Sovereign – to obey the Laws – and to live henceforward as good and faithful Subjects – and they will find the Government of their Queen as indulgent as it is just. (5)

The Duncombe Uprising of December 1837

When word arrived in Toronto of an uprising in the London District, Col. MacNab was given command of a 500-man detachment of militia and dispatched from Toronto to restore order. MacNab proceeded immediately by steamboat to Hamilton where he raised more men and marched to Brant's Ford (Brantford) with a force of 800 militia. It was a strategic centre on the Dundas Street military road that connected York, in the Home District, with the London District to the west. The reported western uprising was situated in an American-settled area of the Province, around the villages of Burford, Oakland, Scotland and

Sodom (Norwichville), on the Lake Erie Front, some ten miles west of the Brant's Ford crossing of the Grand River.

Earlier, on either the 6th or 7th of December, when it had become known in the London District that Mackenzie had gathered a large rebel force at Montgomery's Tavern for a march on Toronto, two of the leading Reformers of the London District branch of the Toronto Political Union, Eliakim Malcolm of Scotland and Dr. Charles Duncombe of Burford, had established a vigilance committee to rally support for the Mackenzie rebels. Meetings were held in the surrounding villages to raise volunteers, and arms and ammunition were collected with the intention of marching on Brantford, and then Hamilton. It was expected that Reform Party supporters in both areas would rise in support of Mackenzie.

Participants in the western uprising were promised 200 acres of land, as well as a payment of $12 a month for their period of service, and were informed that Toronto was about to fall, or had already fallen, to Mackenzie's men. Moreover, the western rebels were assured that they would receive public support throughout the province during their march on Toronto; and that the 'tories' would be too intimidated to offer any resistance. Duncombe proclaimed also that the rebels would receive American aid in defending the independent democratic republic that Mackenzie was going to establish.

By December 13th the rebel force, under the command of Dr. Duncombe, numbered about 400 men. However, the rebels were poorly armed with but a small number of rifles and pikes and were in receipt of disheartening news. The evening before the rebels learned that Mackenzie's uprising had been crushed; that Col. MacNab was at Brantford with an 800-man militia force that was well armed; and that John B. Askin -- a Justice of the Peace and veteran of the War of 1812 -- was marching eastward from London to join up with MacNab. Askin had a force of 150 militiamen and was approaching the rebels from the rear.

At Brantford, on the morning of December 14th, MacNab learned that a large rebel force was encamped at Oakland, just eight miles to the southwest. He secured information on the local road system and the terrain at the rebel encampment and worked out a plan of attack. The rebels were to be engaged in a simultaneous assault by two columns of militia issuing from separate access roads with the intention of driving the rebels back towards the woods where a force of Indians was to be positioned. In leaving a large militia force to defend Brantford, MacNab planned to advance on Oakland that evening with 300 of his Hamilton militia, 150 volunteers from Brantford, and 100 Indian warriors from the Six Nations Reserve.

The MacNab militia force experienced a major disappointment when news was received that the rebels had retreated westward, rather than stand and fight. However, the day was not lost. At the hastily abandoned rebel camp the buried papers of Eliakim Malcolm were discovered which contained a muster roll of the rebels, and the military situation of MacNab continued to improve. That afternoon he was joined by hundreds of militiamen in four companies that had been raised -- by militia colonels -- from the settlements around Brantford. Moreover, during the evening, additional volunteers arrived to join the government force.

With his rapidly growing numbers, MacNab planned to march early the next morning on the rebel headquarters at the Village of Sodom (Norwichville/Norwich) in the Township of Norwich. With 1600 men at his command, Colonel MacNab informed his superiors that his force was "six times" larger than needed to confront the rebels, but that he did not want to turn away the loyal militia companies. They had marched through the night to join his force and were anxious to participate in a crushing of the rebels. MacNab faced two problems: how to provision his large militia force; and how to secure enough arms to fully equip the large number of volunteers who had joined his pacification campaign. (6)

At Toronto, militia companies had continued to pour into the City following the dispersal of the rebels at Gallows Hill and Montgomery's Tavern on Thursday, December 7th. On Friday, the steamer *Traveller* had arrived from Fort Henry at Kingston carrying 1,000 arms and boxes of ammunition and two artillery pieces under escort by fifteen well-armed men, and on Saturday a further 500 militia marched into the City. And on Sunday, December 9th, several militia regiments arrived from Cobourg and Port Hope under the command of militia Colonel George Strange Boulton, an Anglican Tory. With the City of Toronto well defended, Sir Francis issued a proclamation that declared the provincial capital secure; and stated that there was no longer any need for the loyal militias to come to the aid of the Her Majesty's Provincial Government. On the other hand, the militia dragoons continued to be employed in scouring the countryside to hunt down and apprehend the rebel leaders. (7)

In the London District, memories remained strong among the Loyalist population with respect to the harsh treatment that their forbearers had suffered at the hands of the American revolutionaries during the American Revolution. There were also fresh memories of the disaffection that had been shown by the American settlers during the War of 1812, and of the terrible suffering and loses of property that had been experienced by the loyal population in the Western, London, and Niagara districts through the treasonable activities of a significant number of the American settlers during the War.

More generally, Upper Canadians were aware that the Reformers had been thoroughly defeated -- and their principle of 'responsible government' rejected -- during the Loyalty Election of June 1836, and now the radicals of the Reform Party were seen to be trying to force their American democratic republicanism upon Upper Canadians by a resort to arms. In response, the loyal militiamen had turned out in large numbers across the province with a determination to crush the rebels.

On the 15th December, the 150-man London militia company, under John B. Askin, joined up with MacNab's division, which was moving westward from Brantford towards the Village of Sodom to pacify Norwich Township. Upon receiving word that the rebels intended to make a stand at the Village of Scotland -- on the road to Sodom -- MacNab immediately contacted the Yarmouth [County] Volunteers, who were marching to join him from the south-west with a 200-man force, and the Simcoe militia which was approaching from the south with 284 men. His plan was to launch a coordinated attack on the rebels from three different directions.

The Yarmouth and Simcoe militia columns were ordered to take up positions near the Village of Scotland upon their arrival. As soon as

MacNab's division launched an attack on the rebel position at Scotland from the east, the two militia columns were to march immediately towards the sound of rifle and musket fire. The plan was to cut off the retreat of the rebels, and to capture them *en masse*. However, when the Yarmouth Volunteers approached the Village of Scotland, they learned that it was already in the hands of MacNab. His cavalry (militia dragoons) had found the site deserted. The rebels had melted away rather than suffer a devastating defeat at the hands of a vastly superior force, which was determined to put an end to the uprising. Duncombe and Malcolm, and the other rebel leaders, had long since fled westward in seeking to escape across the Detroit River into the United States.

The next day, deputations were received from the Duncombe rebels who had heard of the clemency granted to the Mackenzie rebels, and wanted to surrender. One petition, which was signed by 103 rebels of Norwich Township, appealed for mercy and asked for the granting of "a pardon for our offences" against Her Majesty's Government. The signees promised that, if pardoned, they would surrender their arms, and henceforth remain "peaceable and loyal subjects" of Queen Victoria. The petition also conveyed an offer of help in apprehending the ringleaders of the insurrection. The rebels accused their leaders of having misled and induced them into rebelling, and of having abandoned them "to answer with our lives and property" for their actions.

During the day, almost two hundred rebels marched into camp and gave up such arms as they had. MacNab told the rebels that by their act of treason they had "forfeited their lives and properties". Nonetheless, he let them return to their homes -- on their own recognizance -- upon the understanding that they would surrender themselves for trial, to be tried for treason, should the Lt. Governor decline to offer them clemency. Subsequently, MacNab reported:

> from all I have seen and heard, many of these unfortunate men have been grossly deceived by the traitor Duncombe & his colleagues, & I firmly believe that many of them will return to their allegiance, and yet be numbered among Her Majesty's faithful and loyal subjects.

Thereafter, patrols were organized to apprehend the rebel leaders and the unregenerate rebels who had not come forward to surrender. To facilitate the arrest of the known rebel leaders, the Lt. Governor posted a reward of £500 for the apprehension of Charles Duncombe, £250 for each of Eliakim Malcolm, Finlay Malcolm (brother), and Robert Alway, as well as £100 for each of [David] Anderson and Joshua Doan. (8)

Under the common law, it was 'high treason' to take part in an insurrection with the aim of overthrowing the government by force. The penalty in law for high treason was to be hanged until dead, and then to be drawn and quartered. Moreover, high treason was a felony which was punishable by "the forfeiture of either lands or goods, or both at the common law". (9)

Preparing to Indict the Rebels

Although the Lt. Governor had issued a General Proclamation of Clemency to the rebels under Mackenzie who would abandon the insurrection, surrender their arms, and submit themselves to the laws of the province, many rebels had not done so. Moreover, no grant of clemency was made to the rebels of the London District, who had risen in revolt after the grant of clemency to the participants in the Mackenzie uprising. To ensure the public peace, and protect the loyal inhabitants of the province, Sir Francis Bond Head directed that the character and conduct of every rebel-at-large, upon being apprehended and imprisoned, was to be investigated by a Committee of Magistrates to determine whether the individual ought to be set free, or arraigned before a grand jury for potential indictment and trial on a charge of high treason. In the interim, no public official or magistrate was to free any rebel prisoner until his conduct could be investigated.

To commence the prosecution of the captured rebels, five men were empowered to serve as special magistrates. They were empowered "to inquire into the origin and design of the conspiracy", to examine the imprisoned rebels, and "to take evidence upon such charges of Treason, Felony, or Sedition", as might be brought against an accused before a grand jury. To that end, the Justices of the Peace, Sheriffs, Constables, and "all other Peace Officers", and the loyal subjects of the Queen, were ordered to provide support for the commissioners in the execution of their warrants. The appointed special magistrates were: the Vice-chancellor of the newly-established Court of Chancery, Robert Sympson Jameson; two members of the Executive Council, Robert Baldwin Sullivan and William Allan; a Surrogate Judge of the Home District and newly-appointed Chancery Court Judge, John Godfrey Spragge; and a Toronto magistrate, Alexander Wood. (10)

Jameson, Sullivan, and Spragge were well-educated individuals and prominent provincial lawyers. Jameson, was a distinguished English lawyer who had emigrated to Upper Canada as recently as 1833, and had served briefly as the Attorney General of the province before his appointment to the Bench. Sullivan was the Commissioner of Crown Lands, as well as a member of the Executive Council. Both William Allan and Alexander Wood were eminent Toronto businessmen. Wood was a former Commissioner of the Court of Requests, as well as a Toronto magistrate; and Allan was a member of the Legislative Council, as well as a member of the Executive Council and a Director of the Bank of Upper Canada. In all respects, the Special Commissioners were staunch supporters of the rule of law and the balanced British Constitution.

Three of the five Special Commissioners were adherents of the Church of England, and two William Allan and Alexander Wood were either members of the Church of Scotland or were Anglican converts. The Commissioners were staunch tories, except for Robert Baldwin Sullivan who was a self-professed 'Colonial Whig'. Sullivan observed that there were two conservative elements in Upper Canada: those who adhered to the conservative cause "from principle, or attachment and sentiment to the British constitution" and those who did so out of self-interest with the conservatives promising "prosperity, public credit, and public improvement."

Sullivan was a cousin of Robert Baldwin, and a former Reformer who broke with the Reform Party -- and with his cousin Robert, who was his law firm partner -- upon accepting an appointment to the Executive Council from the Lt. Governor, Sir Francis Bond Head, in March 1836. Given his checkered political career, Sullivan appears to have belonged to the second category of Upper Canadian conservatives. All five men were quite competent to examine the rebel prisoners and collect evidence of "Treason, Felony or Sedition" for presentation to a grand jury. (11)

In Upper Canada, a grand jury comprised 24 freeholders, selected by the Sheriff of the district, and was charged with determining whether there was sufficient evidence for an accused to be indicted for trial. The presiding judge would explain the charge against an accused to the grand jury, as well as any points of law at issue, and the prosecutor would present the evidence against the accused. Upon deliberation, if the grand jury decided that there was sufficient evidence to warrant the laying of a charge against the accused, it would return a 'true bill' to have the accused held over for trial. If there was insufficient evidence, the grand jury would return a 'nolle prosequi', and the accused would be set free. Once a 'true bill' was returned, the public prosecutor – the Attorney General of Upper Canada – would issue an indictment setting forth the charges laid against the accused, who would be held and tried before the customary twelve-man jury in a court trial under a presiding Judge of the Court of Queen's Bench. (12)

In the aftermath of the Mackenzie uprising over 400 rebels were apprehended and disarmed by the loyal militias, and, after the Duncombe uprising, another 500 suspected rebels were imprisoned by the Volunteer Militia Companies that were organized by Colonel MacNab in the London and Western districts. The Volunteer Militia Companies were charged with keeping the peace, maintaining order, and apprehending the leaders of the uprising and any rebels who had committed an act of arson, murder, destruction of property, and/or robbery. In the aftermath of the uprisings, there were many witnesses in the local communities who could identify the leaders of the rebellion, as well as the rank and file participants, and the authorities had the names of most of the rebels from the muster rolls that had been compiled by MacKenzie and Eliakim Malcolm, respectively.

The apprehended rebels were retained in custody and imprisoned in the public buildings and the district gaol in Toronto, Hamilton, and London. Most of the rebel leaders – including William Lyon Mackenzie, David Gibson, Jesse Lloyd and Silas Fletcher, as well as Eliakim Malcolm, Dr. Charles Duncombe, David Anderson, and Joshua Doan -- managed to escape across the border into the United States following the collapse of the uprisings. However, some of the secondary rebel leaders -- inclusive of Samuel Lount, Peter Matthews, Anthony Van Egmont, Robert Alway, and Finlay Malcolm -- were captured. Dr. Thomas David Morrison was arrested in Toronto for his suspected complicity in the uprising, but Dr. John Rolph – the projected President of the Republic of Upper Canada – escaped to the United States. Rolph had fled on December 5th, upon becoming aware of the failure of Mackenzie's attempted descent on Toronto.

Marshall Spring Bidwell, the widely-recognized leader of the Reform Party, had departed for the United States on December 9th after being advised to do so by the Lt. Governor, Sir Francis Bond Head. At Montgomery's Tavern, a rebel flag had been found that bore the inscription "Bidwell and the glorious minority, 1837", which raised the prospect that Bidwell, the former leader of the Reform Party, might be charged with complicity in the uprising.

Marshall Spring Bidwell did not have any known active involvement with the uprisings, which was not the case with many prominent Reform Party members in Upper Canada. Several leaders of the Reform Party had broken with Mackenzie prior to the 1836 loyalty election: viz. the Anglican whigs, Dr. William Warren Baldwin and Robert Baldwin, and the democratic radicals Jesse Ketchum and Peter Perry. Bidwell had distanced himself – at least publicly -- from Mackenzie after the devastating defeat of the Reform Party in the June 1836 loyalty election. Otherwise, it was the leaders of the Reform Party who took an active and leading role in the December 1837 uprisings.

The rebel leaders were the same men who were the leading organizers and spokesmen for the various branches of the Toronto Political Union in the Home and London districts, and, in most cases, they were also the delegates who had been selected to attend the projected Reform Party convention in Toronto. Moreover, five of the rebel conspirators were Reform Party members of the House of Assembly who had managed to withstand the electoral sweep of the Constitutionalists in the Loyalty Election of June 1836: David Gibson, 1st York Riding; Dr. John Rolph, Norfolk County; Dr. Charles Duncombe and Robert Alway, Oxford County; and Dr. Thomas David Morrison, 3rd York Riding. (13)

The Character of the Rebels

What was evident, from the examinations held of the captured rebel prisoners, was that most of the rebels were from farming areas, and that they comprised a broad cross-section of occupations: farmers, labourers, artisans, innkeepers, millers and shopkeepers, as well as merchants, medical doctors/lawyers, and several teachers. Moreover, the farming communities from which the rebels were drawn -- from the Home District north of Toronto and the London District -- were comparatively prosperous, and were known for having well-maintained farms on good agricultural land. However, what characterized the rebels, and set them apart, was that they were from American-settled areas of the province, and that a very large majority of the rebels were American immigrants, or the first-generation sons of American immigrants.

Among the rebels were found some British immigrants from the American-settled areas, Protestant Irishmen and Englishmen, who had marched with the rebels, but later claimed that they were coerced into joining the uprisings by their American neighbours. In contrast, the British immigrants from the Loyalist and British-immigrant settlements areas were uniformly loyal in turning out with the local militia companies to suppress the uprisings. More particularly, the Scots – both Protestant and Roman Catholic – were staunchly and uniformly loyal to the Crown, except for some evangelical Presbyterian Scots immigrants among whom the most glaring example was William Lyon Mackenzie. The Indians of Upper Canada, and the Irish Protestants, inclusive of the ultra-Protestant Orangemen, were strong supporters of Her Majesty's Provincial Government and the British connection, as were the families of the Loyalist communities. Members of these communities had turned out in large numbers to serve with their county militia companies, or as volunteers, to fight the rebels, as had the Indians of the Six Nations Reserve. The Black communities, which were comprised of Loyalist Blacks and/or free Black immigrants and fugitive slaves from the United States, were equally united against the rebels.

Another characteristic of the rebels was that they were either non-religious or adherents of the dissenting sects: Universalists (Unitarians), Quakers (Hicksites), Free-will Baptists, and 'American Methodists' (Methodist Episcopal Church adherents). However, the members of the dissenting sects were not uniformly found on the side of the rebels. In the Loyalist communities, there were many supporters of the Crown among the members of the Baptist and 'American Methodist' congregations; and the Baptists and 'American Methodists' of the Black communities were uniformly loyal to the Her Majesty's Provincial Government. Although the Blacks were largely adherents of the evangelical sects, they did not join the rebels. Regardless of their democratic religious principles, they had even stronger motives for loyalty to the Crown and for actively resisting any attempt by the rebels to terminate the British connection. If the rebels were to succeed in establishing an independent democratic republic in Upper Canada, there was a fear among the Blacks that the new republic might well proceed to join the American Union. There was a similar fear among the Loyalist communities. For the descendants of the Loyalists, the rebel uprising was viewed as a second coming of the American rebellion. Once again, they responded to a call to defend the Crown and the Unity of Empire, in fear of being dispossessed of their property and driven into exile should the rebels succeed in overthrowing the Provincial Government.

Few Irish Catholics were found among the rebels, although the Irish Catholics were strong supporters of William Lyon Mackenzie and his egalitarian democratic republicanism. In the case of the Irish Roman Catholic immigrants, bitter memories of the anti-Irish Catholic penal laws in Ireland – under the Anglo-Irish Ascendancy of the 18th Century – and of the failed Rebellion of the United Irishmen in 1798, determined their political sympathies.

In Upper Canada, members of the Church of England, the Church of Scotland, the Roman Catholic Church (Scots and English), and the Wesleyan Methodists, were staunch supporters of the Crown and the British connection. That was likewise the case with the half-pay Army and Royal Navy officers, and most of the discharged British Army veterans who had settled in Upper Canada since the War of 1812. Where religion was concerned, it was the Anglican Tories – among both the native-born Upper Canadians and British immigrants – who provided the leadership in defending Her Majesty's Provincial Government. Anglicans were in the forefront in commanding and serving in the companies of the loyal militia regiments that turned out to fight against the rebels during the uprisings of December 1837. During that time of crisis, it was the Anglican Tories who provided the critical leadership in defending the government, and who, within the government administration, provided a steady support and advice to the Lt. Governor, Sir Francis Bond Head. It was a point of satisfaction, with the Anglican Tories, that only a few Anglicans were found among the rank and file of the Mackenzie rebels, and none among the Duncombe rebels. (14)

The 'Rebellion' of 1837: A Tory View

For the Tories, the uprisings in the Home and London districts of Upper Canada were the product of the democratic republican political ideas of the American settlers. American immigrants were believers in the republican government system of the United States of America, which had been established through a political revolution; they were admirers of Jacksonian democracy in its populist emphasis on democratic egalitarianism and agrarianism; and they were adherents of the political philosophy of John Locke in being steeped in beliefs in popular sovereignty, the right of rebellion by the people in response to government abuses, laissez-faire government, and the separation of church and state. Moreover, among the American settlers there was a belief – which later came to be referred to as 'manifest destiny' -- that the American republic was destined to spread 'republican freedom' and 'democracy' over the entire North American continent. (15)

Another factor seen in the uprisings was religious sectarianism, which the Upper Canadian Tories had long viewed as a danger to the state. The sectarians rejected the traditional social, political and religious order. They believed in personal salvation, spiritual rebirth, the spirit of the Holy Ghost within regenerated man, and Biblical literalism. They believed as well in the 'will of the people'. which were superior to any political authority and the teachings of the traditional Christian churches in providing moral guidance and determining the good of the individual. Moreover, the congregations of the religious sects were 'voluntary societies' with a democratic system of organization of their congregations, and their preaching was based on emotional appeals rather than reason. Sectarian preachers did not preach loyalty to the Crown, or the duty of obedience to a legitimately-established government. Their spiritual concerns were personal and focused on 'the inner light'. Where politics was concerned, the sectarians were believers in an absolute separation of church and state, 'voluntaryism', 'religious equality', and an egalitarian democracy. (16)

For the Tories, there was no justification at all for the rebellion. Upper Canadians were living under a limited constitutional monarchy which embodied a balanced constitution and the rule of law, and under which everyone enjoyed peace and 'the protection of life, liberty and property'. Moreover, all property owners held the right to vote for the members of the popular branch of the government. Indeed, Upper Canadians enjoyed a broad property franchise which, in practice, was almost a system of universal manhood suffrage. They were inhabitants of a country which, "under God's bountiful Providence", was visibly increasing in wealth, power and prosperity, and in which men "of a middle station in life" could readily attain "a comfortable and secure living". Moreover, there was no direct taxation, a complete freedom of conscience and freedom of religion, and the established Church of England had no right – either in law or by custom in Upper Canada -- to impose any payment of tithes on dissenters.

In seeking to establish a republican system of government through subverting the constitution and overthrowing Her Majesty's Provincial Government, the rebels had committed what was viewed by the Tories as "the terrible crime" of high treason. From a moral point of view, as expressed by the Anglican clergy, it was evident that the rebels had descended into 'wickedness' in engaging in murder, arson, and robbery in seeking to attain their own political ends. They had been forgetful of their sworn allegiance to the Queen and their duty to obey the lawful authority of the Sovereign.

The rebels were viewed as a 'revolutionary faction' that had adopted 'traitorous designs', and that had sought – under the suasion of "the chief agitator, Mr. Mackenzie and a few score deluded men" -- to subvert the constitution and overthrow the established government. It was regarded as obvious that the rebels had intended to take advantage of the rebellion in Lower Canada, and the absence of British troops from Upper Canada, to seize power. It was also obvious that they had counted on 'foreign aid'

– by way of military support from supposedly 'thousands' of American sympathizers -- to defend the independent democratic 'Republic of Upper Canada' that they intended to establish. From the Tory viewpoint, there was no actual grievance, or complaint, or supposed arbitrary act of government, that could be cited to justify such a revolt. The Province of Upper Canada was by no means ill-governed, and the people were not oppressed in any manner. (17)

In reports of February 1838 on the state of the province, the Tories of the Legislative Council and the conservatives of the House of Assembly waxed enthusiastic concerning the way in which Upper Canadians had turned out to defend Her Majesty's Government, the constitution, and the rule of law. As expressed by a Select Committee of the Legislative Council:

> But there is nothing connected with this remarkable crisis upon which it is so satisfactory and pleasing to reflect, as the very striking proof it has afforded of the loyal and patriotic feelings of the great body of the people of Upper Canada. The instant it was known that the Government was threatened with violence, all distinctions of religion and country were laid aside, and with a noble ardour, which can never be forgotten by those who witnessed it, the people rushed forward by the thousands to put down the rebellion, and to preserve the supremacy of the laws.

The Tories were particularly struck by the evidence of the 'Hand of Providence' in the 'favourable circumstance' of the mildness of the winter weather of December 1837. At a time of year when the Lake Ontario would normally have been frozen over and the navigation closed for the winter, the mildness of the weather had enabled steamboats to be employed to reach the farthest ports on the lake. On the open water, relays of steamboats had been able to rush militia companies, arms and munitions, to the defence of the capital, which enabled the rebellion to be put down quickly, with but the loss of only one life – Col. Moodie -- on the part of Her Majesty's loyal subjects. The alternative mode of transport on primitive roads, over such great distances, would have involved many difficulties and delays in marshalling militia companies and marching on York to defend the capital of the province, and such delays might well have enabled the rebels to capture the City. Once in possession of Toronto, and well-armed from the City Hall depot, the rebels would have been readier to fight, and the suppression of the rebellion might well have entailed a great deal of bloodshed.

For the Tories, such circumstances were viewed as being too favourable, for the duly-constituted government, to be ascribed simply to chance. Thus, in the New Year, a day of Public Thanksgiving was proclaimed by the Lt. Governor, Sir Francis Bond Head. Tuesday, February 6th, was designated as the day for the offering of "Prayers, Praises and Thanksgivings" to Almighty God for the intervention of Divine Providence in delivering Upper Canada from "the dangers and calamities of the unnatural Insurrection and Rebellion" that had afflicted the province. (18)

The Tories learned several lessons from the rebellion. On the one hand, it was evident that the object of most of the Reform Party leaders was the establishment of an independent democratic republic in Upper Canada, and not constitutional reform. Hence, the policy of appeasement and conciliation that the liberal-Whig government in Britain had followed, in responding to the 'clamour' and demands of the Upper Canadian Reformers was viewed as 'sheer folly'. If persisted in, it would have led Upper Canada "into anarchy and ruin". On the other hand, the Tories began to realize the power of the press.

Prior to the rebellion, the radical press had been unopposed in the outlying farming communities of Upper Canada in spreading what the Tories deemed to be 'falsehoods' and 'venom' against the government. In the aftermath of the rebellion, a conclusion was reached that what was needed was not censorship, but the promotion of public education through the establishment of a government newspaper to defend the balanced constitution of the province against attacks, to disseminate sound information, and to enlighten the public on political issues. The new Tory outlook was reflected initially in the actions of the British Constitutional Society during the loyalty election of June 1836. At that time, direct appeals were made to the people in defence of the British Constitution and loyalty to the Empire, and pamphlets were published to expose the demands and utterances of the radicals to public scrutiny.

As expressed in one newly-established newspaper, *The Church,* edited by an Anglican Tory, the Rev. A.N. Bethune:

> It may not be dignified, it may be attended with some inconvenience, for a government to descend into the area of daily discussion, and to defend its actions, as it were on trial before a jury of the country, -- it may be all this, and more – but it is nevertheless necessary for the preservation of the state.

The objective was to strengthen the social order, to preserve the constitution and the rule of law, and to allay discontent through enabling the public to be well-informed on public issues. If that were done, it was assumed that the public would see through falsehoods and would challenge the diatribes of demagogues, who would continually seek to mislead, seduce, and flatter the uninformed. (19)

Maintaining Civil Government & the Rule of Law

In the immediate aftermath of the uprisings in the Home and London districts, there was an initial problem in accommodating the large number of rebels who were incarcerated in Toronto, Hamilton and London. No sooner had the judges of the Special Commission commenced their examination of the prisoners than it became apparent that the loyal militias were being overzealous in rounding up not only the known participants in the uprisings for whom arrest warrants had been issued, but also outspoken individuals who were known to be disaffected and/ or simply Mackenzie sympathizers. Hence, over half of the prisoners were discharged by the Commissioners -- within several days, or at most within two weeks of their imprisonment -- for want of evidence of their having actively participated in the uprisings. Upon release, the prisoners were required to swear an oath to be 'a loyal and faithful subject of Her Majesty, the Queen'. If a prisoner refused to take the oath, he was retained in custody to be arraigned before a grand jury with the other prisoners.

Only the known leaders and fomenters of the uprisings, individuals found to have engaged in criminal behavior during the uprisings, and individuals who were clearly guilty of high treason based on the sworn testimony of two or more credible witnesses, were retained in custody to await arraignment before a grand jury. However, the district jails and the public buildings, where the prisoners were being detained, were still severely overcrowded. On the 28th December 1837, a Militia General Order was issued to address the problem. The officers of Militia were ordered to make no further arrests, except for "notorious offenders", while continuing to seize arms from 'the disaffected'. (20)

In the aftermath of the failed December uprisings in Upper Canada, the Tory establishment remained determined to maintain the constitution unimpaired in safeguarding the rule of law, the integrity of the court system, and the constitutional function of the Legislature which remained in session. There would be no suspension of the constitution in a resort to the imposition of martial law. Nor would there be any suspension of civil liberties beyond a temporary suspension of habeas corpus solely applicable to the incarcerated rebel prisoners. A limited suspension of habeas corpus was needed to enable the imprisoned rebels to be held in custody while their conduct was being investigated by the Special Commissioners, who would decide whether a prisoner should be released or held to appear before a Grand Jury for potential indictment.

The Chief Justice, John Beverley Robinson, was determined to try the captured rebels in state trials rather than have martial law declared and the rebel prisoners prosecuted by courts martial. In state trials, offenders would be prosecuted by the Crown with a judge of the Court of Queen's Bench presiding, and the Attorney General of the Province, Christopher Hagerman, acting as the prosecutor. The treason trials would proceed under the rule of law. In keeping with the common law, and the legal precedents established in earlier British treason trials, an accused would be entitled to a trial by a jury of his peers, to representation by legal counsel, and was to receive a copy of the indictment, a list of the empanelled jurors, and the names of witnesses, at least ten days before arraignment for trial. Moreover, the accused held the right to challenge the jury selection, and for cases to proceed to trial there had to be at least two creditable witnesses testifying for the prosecution against the accused. (21)

To facilitate the detention and trial of the rebels, Chief Justice Robinson drafted two pieces of legislation which were enacted by the provincial Legislature on the 12th of January 1838: a 'Detention Act' and an

'Effectual and Impartial Trial Act'. Both acts were based on British treason law precedents, and were of a temporary duration requiring renewal by the Legislature after one year. The 'Detention Act' effectively suspended habeas corpus in authorizing the authorities to apprehend and detain persons who were known, on the testimony of at least two reliable witnesses, to have engaged in acts of high treason, misprision (the concealment of knowledge of treasonable activities), and/or treasonable practices. It denied bail to such persons unless authorized by a warrant of the Lt. Governor.

The 'Effectual and Impartial Trial Act' was a precautionary act. It allowed for juries to be selected and trials to be held outside of a district – in cases where there might be a strong local sympathy for the rebels – and it limited the number of challenges that an accused could make in rejecting prospective jurors. The two provincial acts were drafted to facilitate the detention and prosecution of the prisoners who were charged with having committed acts of high treason, or of involvement in treasonable practices.

The Treason Trials

The Chief Justice, John Beverley Robinson and the puisne judges who were to preside at the treason trials, were determined to uphold the rule of law in seeking justice for Upper Canadians; yet were prepared to exercise mercy and leniency in the sentencing of the 'deluded rebels'. However, the holding of treason trials posed a serious problem for the judiciary. The judges were faced with daunting task in a situation where perhaps as many as four hundred prisoners might well be indicted on a charge of high treason. The prosecution of such a large number of defendants would entail a series of trials that would be time-consuming and expensive, and invariably would involve long delays during which some of the prisoners might succumb to disease or illness while imprisoned. To expedite the legal process, the Chief Justice, John Beverley Robinson, drafted and secured the passage – through the conservative Legislature – of a 'Conditional Pardoning Act' (6 March 1838).

Under the Conditional Pardoning Act, an individual indicted on a charge of high treason could plead guilty before the arraignment for trial, and petition the Lt. Governor for a conditional pardon. In response, the

Governor, "with the advice of the Executive Council", might grant a pardon on whatever terms and conditions were thought proper. In effect, if the petition was accepted, the petitioner would not stand trial for high treason, and would not face the death penalty. However, the successful petitioner, in having confessed his guilt, might receive a sentence of transportation to a penal colony (Australia) for life or for a term of years, a sentence of imprisonment in the new Kingston penitentiary, a sentence of banishment, or a full pardon, at the discretion of the Lt. Governor in representing Her Majesty. Moreover, the estate and property – real and personal—of the successful petitioner was to remain subject to forfeiture in the same manner as that of an offender convicted in court of the felony of high treason. Fugitives, who were under a charge of high treason *in absentia*, were excluded from petitioning for a conditional pardon. (22)

The legal strategy for the conduct of the treason trials was worked out by Chief Justice Robinson and the appointed Special Commission under Robert Sympson Jameson, with the support of the Executive Council. Traditionally, in Upper Canada under the Constitution of 1791, the Chief Justice was a member of the Executive Council with the responsibility to advise the government on legal matters and to oversee the drafting of government legislation. However, as of January 1831, the Whig government in Britain had informed the Lt. Governor that the Chief Justice was no longer to sit in the Executive Council, and that judges would be appointed to serve 'during good behaviour' and not 'during pleasure'. It was an effort by the liberal-Whig government in Britain to separate the judiciary from the government; whereas for the Tories the rule of law was an integral part of government as embodied in the traditional presence of the Chief Justice in the Executive Council and his involvement in the legislative process. Nonetheless, Chief Justice Robinson had resigned immediately from the Executive Council upon the receipt of the January 1831 instructions from the Colonial Office.

When the new Lt. Governor, Major-General Sir George Arthur, arrived in Upper Canada in late-March 1838, he not only supported the legal strategy in place for the prosecution of the incarcerated rebels, and the legislation enacted, but defended the leading role played by the Chief

Justice in securing the passage of the legislation. In a dispatch to the Colonial Office, Arthur maintained that Chief Justice Robinson was a man of 'high character and great experience' who was providing a needed service to the government, which also would benefit the rebels who were incarcerated while awaiting their day in court. (23)

At Toronto, the grand jury assizes opened on 8 March 1838 with the Chief Justice, John Beverley Robinson presiding. Of the 149 prisoners listed on the calendar, 113 were indicted on a charge of high treason, 30 prisoners had absconded (when out on bail), and six were discharged by the grand jury. Of the men indicted to stand trial, 104 pleaded guilty and petitioned for a conditional pardon, of whom three – Samuel Lount, Peter Matthews, and John Anderson -- were denied a conditional pardon. Lount was in command of the Mackenzie rebels when Col. Moodie was killed and the home of Dr. Horne burned; Matthews was in command of the rebels who killed a defender of the Don River Bridge, burned a house, and set fire to the bridge; and Anderson was the second in command to Matthews and had played a leading part in the Don Bridge 'atrocities'. The successful petitioners were released on bail, pending the pleasure of the Lt. Governor, and twelve prisoners were committed for trial.

The first of the treason trials -- the trial of Lount and Matthews -- commenced on 26 March 1838. Chief Justice Robinson presided, and the Attorney General Christopher Hagerman represented the Crown. Subsequently, a second puisne judge, Jonas Jones of the Court of Queen's Bench, presided over several of the Toronto treason trials which ran on into April. Of the twelve men brought to trial in Toronto, seven were found guilty and sentenced to death (inclusive of Lount, Matthews, and Anderson) four were acquitted (inclusive of Dr. Thomas David Morrison), and one defendant was simply discharged.

At Hamilton, the grand jury assizes commenced on 8 March 1838 and was presided over by puisne judge, James Buchanan Macaulay, of the Court of Queen's Bench. Out of 51 men indicted by the grand jury on a charge of treason, 24 successfully petitioned for a conditional pardon, and four petitions were rejected. Twenty-seven prisoners were held over for trial. The Hamilton treason trials commenced on 27 March 1838 with Judge

James Buchanan Macaulay presiding and the Solicitor General, William H. Draper, representing the Crown. Seventeen men were acquitted. Ten of the defendants were found guilty and sentenced to death.

At London, the grand jury assizes commenced in April 1838, and was presided over by puisne judge, Levius Peters Sherwood of the Court of Queen's Bench. A total of 58 prisoners were examined of whom two were discharged and the rest indicted. Of the prisoners indicted to stand trial, forty pleaded guilty and successfully petitioned for a conditional pardon, and one petition was denied. Ultimately, fifteen prisoners were prosecuted. The treason trials commenced on April 30th, and were presided over by Judge Sherwood with the Solicitor General, William H. Draper, representing the Crown. Of the men arraigned for trial on a charge of high treason, six were found guilty and received a death sentence. Nine were acquitted by the juries.

The treason trials were carried out in a strictly legal manner in adhering to the court procedures and legal precedents that had been established in earlier treason trials in England, and the trials were conducted fairly and impartially under the law. The indicted prisoners had the right to a trial by jury -- if they wished to stand trial rather than plead guilty in petitioning for a conditional pardon – and the prisoners had the right to legal representation and a right to challenge the jury selection. (23)

The four judges of the Court of Queen's Bench who presided over the treason trials – the Chief Justice, John Beverley Robinson, and three puisne judges, Levius Peters Sherwood, James Buchanan Macaulay, and Jonas Jones – were the Canadian-born sons of Loyalists. All were Anglican Tories who had thrived in private law practice before their elevation to the bench. They were members of the provincial social elite, were well-educated, and three of the judges (Robinson, Macaulay and Jones) were former pupils of the Rev. John Strachan at the Cornwall District Grammar School. All but Sherwood had been on active service, as young militia officers, in defending Upper Canada during the War of 1812 and had served as volunteers in defending Toronto against the Mackenzie rebels in December 1837. More particularly, Judge Macaulay had commanded the militia companies that were deployed to defend the City, while the main body of militia moved northward under Col. MacNab to engage the rebels at Montgomery's Tavern.

All four of the judges had been active in the public life, and had served as a member of the Provincial Legislature, before their respective appointments to the Bench. Levius Peters Sherwood was in the House of Assembly for two parliaments through securing election in 1812 and again in 1820 as the member for Leeds, and was a former Speaker of the House; Jonas Jones had served in three successive parliaments (1816, 1820, 1824) as the member for Grenville; and John Beverley Robinson had served for three parliaments (1820, 1824, 1828) as the member for the Town of York. James Buchanan Macaulay had received an appointment to the Executive Council where he had served for four years (1825-July 1829) prior to his appointment to the Bench, and Chief Justice Robinson had served as acting Attorney General (November 1812), as Solicitor General (1815-1818), as Attorney General (1818- July 1829), and as a member of the Executive Council (April 1829-January 1831). (25)

Sentencing the Rebels

A total of twenty-three rebels were found guilty of high treason in the treason trials at Toronto, Hamilton and London, and were sentenced to death. They were also guilty of having committed a felony which rendered their respective estates -- property and personal effects -- subject to confiscation. A further total of 165 prisoners successfully petitioned for a conditional pardon through pleading guilty to high treason. The guilty pleas enabled the rebel prisoners to escape the death penalty, but placed the decision on their punishment or full pardon in the hands of the Lt. Governor. In the Home District, most of the petitioners who received a conditional pardon were released on bail; whereas earlier, in Hamilton and London, many of the prisoners indicted for trial were released on bail by the Special Commissioners before the petitions for a conditional pardon were approved. (26)

Prior to the treason trials, the Tory Executive Council had informed the new Lt. Governor, Sir George Arthur, that the people of Upper Canada wanted the leaders of the rebellion to receive 'the severest penalty of the law' to discourage the disaffected from 'ever again' attempting to overthrow the government by force of arms. However, at the same time, the Executive Council was concerned to ensure that there would be fairness and consistency, across the province, in the sentencing of the prisoners granted a conditional pardon under the Pardoning Act, and in any commutation of death sentences that might be granted to the prisoners who were convicted of high treason and sentenced to death. To that end, while the treason trials were underway, Lt. Governor Arthur instructed the Special Commission -- under Robert Sympson Jameson, the chancellor of the Court of Chancery -- to prepare sentencing and commutation guidelines.

In the interim, on 12 April 1838, the first of the death sentences was carried out with the hanging of Samuel Lount and Peter Matthews in Toronto, and four more executions were scheduled for the 24th of April. Lt. Governor Arthur had approved the first two executions. However, prior to the second round of executions, Arthur informed the Colonial Secretary, Lord Glenlg, that there would be a respite in the carrying out of the death sentences until "Her Majesty's pleasure" became known. Lord Glenlg was also informed that a decision had been reached to grant 'a free and unconditional pardon' to the prisoners who had been released on bail. The decision to appeal to the Crown for a direction on whether to commute the death sentences, was in keeping with the view of judges of the Court of Queen's Bench. The Tory judges believed that an example had to be set through capital punishment to discourage the disaffected from taking up arms, but held that only the 'ringleaders' of the rebellion ought to be hanged with executions to be kept a minimum. (27)

In preparing their report -- the Jameson Report -- the special commissioners examined the evidence pertaining to each rebel who were convicted of high treason and sentenced to death during the treason trials, and each rebel who had pleaded guilty to high treason in petitioning under the Conditional Pardoning Act. The report recommended that the offenders who were found guilty of high treason, and of having committed a felony, should be divided into three distinct classes where the recommendations for a commutation of death sentence and the sentencing of a prisoner were concerned.

Class I comprised the leaders of the rebellion who had taken up arms, recruited others, played an active role in the conduct of the rebellion, and were viewed as dangerous opponents of the government. This class comprised twenty-two men who had been sentenced to death. The recommendation was that their death sentences be commuted to transportation to a penal colony for life.

Class II comprised thirty-two rebels who had pleaded guilty to high treason, petitioned under the Pardoning Act, and were granted a conditional pardon, but were known to be extremely hostile to the British government. It was recommended that these individuals – most of whom were American settlers or their descendants -- be sentenced to transportation for 'a short period', or, in some instances, that they simply be banished from the province.

Class III comprised two-subgroups: a group of 55 Upper Canadians who it was held had been 'deluded' into joining the rebellion; and ten American citizens who had joined Mackenzie at Montgomery's Tavern. It was recommended that the ten Americans -- who held no property in Upper Canada, and had joined the rebellion simply to engage in 'plunder' -- be treated as 'ordinary felons' and sentenced to the Kingston penitentiary for the specific crimes that they had committed. The deluded Upper Canadian rebels – if they were innocent of any crimes against person or property – were recommended for a grant of a full pardon (the Queen's pardon), with no confiscation of their property.

In separating the rebels, who had been granted a conditional pardon, into Class II or Class III, the commissioners took account of the moral character of the individual, as well as whether the individual was known to be virulently hostile to the British government, and whether the individual was deemed to pose a continuing threat to the peace and social harmony of the province. (28)

After examining the individual assessments of the convicted and confessed traitors, as prepared by the special commissioners, the two Court of Queen's Bench judges who were present in Toronto, Chief Justice Robinson and Judge Jones, reported on the legality of what was proposed. They found "no legal difficulty" and expressed their agreement with the Jameson Report recommendations. However, the two judges recommended further that, if the death sentences of the Class I convicts were to be commuted by Her Majesty, 'the worst' of the convicted traitors might be transported for fourteen years rather than for life, with the remainder of the convicted traitors transported for only seven years. For the two Queen's Bench judges, transportation was 'an appalling punishment' which was justified only in situations where it was necessary for public safety and security. It was regarded as 'a civil death' in separating the convict from his family and his country.

It was further suggested that the Class II confessed traitors under the Conditional Pardoning Act be further subdivided: that some offenders might be sentenced to transportation for seven years, and some to simply banishment. Still others of that class might merit being allowed to remain in the province in receipt of a full pardon. Moreover, there was a further recommendation that Her Majesty refrain from confiscating the property of the felons who received a full pardon for their treasonable activities.

Where the Class III convicts were concerned, it was recommended that the convicted American citizens, who were to be sentenced to serve time in the Kingston penitentiary, be given seven- year prison terms with the addition of a sentence of banishment to follow their imprisonment. There was little sympathy for American 'banditti' who came to Upper Canada to plunder British subjects. Where the 'deluded' Upper Canadian rebels were concerned, the judges were in accord with the recommendation of the special commissioners that these petitioners -- under the Conditional Pardoning Act -- receive a full pardon, and that Her Majesty abstain from confiscating their property.

More generally, the Tory judges recommended that a policy of mercy and forbearance be followed in granting pardons to the convicted and confessed traitors whenever it was judged to be 'just and safe for the public', and where the offender had not engaged in any previous 'open resistance to the Crown' or committed any 'atrocity' during the rebellion. In instances where several members of a single family were guilty of high treason, compassion was recommended through the granting of a full pardon to the lesser offenders, where no aggravated offence – murder, robbery or arson -- had been committed. Men were needed to work the family farms. Overall, the judges made it clear that they would have preferred that the convicted rebels – those who were not guilty of murder, robbery or arson -- be simply banished from the province, rather than sentenced to transportation. However, it was feared that, once banished, the zealous rebels would continue to agitate against the government from across the border in the United States. (29)

As of 30 May 1838, Lt. Governor Author informed the Colonial Office that thirty-two men in total (26 from the Home District) were to be transported. Subsequently, twelve of the convicts to be transported escaped from Fort Henry, one died at Kingston, and at least one sentence of transportation was commuted to banishment. Nine Upper Canadian convicts, who arrived in England on the first prison ship en route to Van Diem's Land (Tasmania), had their cases taken up by British radicals. Upon appeal to the English courts the sentences of transportation were commuted to banishment from Canada. Subsequently, the men sentenced to transportation were transported directly to Australia from port of Quebec along with the Lower Canadian rebels sentenced to transportation. However, only ten Upper Canadian rebels, among those who were sentenced to transportation or had their death sentence commuted to transportation, were ever transported to Van Diem's Land. Most of the rebel petitioners who had pleaded guilty to high treason under the Pardoning Act, and had received a conditional pardon, were subsequently granted a full pardon. The confiscation of the property of the rebel felons was left to the discretion of Her Majesty, and no property of a convicted, or confessed, rebel felon was ever confiscated. (30)

Tory Reflections

For the Upper Canadian Tories, the rebellion of December 1837 confirmed four long-held beliefs: that demagogues, if unopposed and unexposed, were capable of deluding men into destroying the peace, tranquility, and harmony of society; that political conventions were a threat to the public peace and to the proper functioning of the balanced British Constitution; that American immigrants did not change their democratic republican political principles upon crossing the border to settle in Upper Canada and were a disaffected element of the population;

and that the religious principles of the sectarians posed a serious threat to the traditional religious, social and political order of the Loyalist Asylum of Upper Canada.

The rebellion was regarded as a physical manifestation of an on-going 'battle of ideas' that pitted the traditional religious, social and political order, the balanced constitution under the sovereignty of the Crown, and the church-state union, against the forces of democratic levelling, popular sovereignty, and infidelity. For the Tories, the rebellion was the product of an ideological struggle as evidenced by the principles advocated by the Mackenzie rebels: egalitarianism, republicanism, voluntaryism in religion, popular sovereignty, and the separation of church and state. Moreover, it was clear that the Mackenzie rebels derived their political principles, ideas, and values from revolutionary sources: the American Declaration of Independence; the writings of Thomas Paine; the religious principles of the dissenting sects; and the political programme of the Jacksonian democrats in the United States.

The principle of 'responsible government', as espoused originally by the Anglican whig Dr. William Warren Baldwin, had united the democratic radicals, the egalitarian democratic republican radicals, the religious sectarians, and the liberal-whigs, within the Reform Party during the early 1830s. However, following the devastating defeat suffered by the Reformers in the June 1836 loyalty election, most of the Reform Party leadership, under the influence of Mackenzie, moved away from the demand for 'responsible government'. It was a political principle based on the Whig concept of parliamentary sovereignty, and was soon jettisoned by the Mackenzie rebels in favour of American republicanism, which was based on the principle of popular sovereignty and associated with the ideal of an agrarian egalitarian democracy.

Within their Christian world view, the basic cause of the rebellion was quite evident to the Anglican Tories of Upper Canada. As expressed by the Rev. A. N. Bethune -- an Anglican clergyman and former student of the Rev. John Strachan – the rebellion was attributable directly to the absence, or deficiency, of 'true religious principles' in the men who rebelled. Moreover, that deficiency was held to be due, in large part, to shortcomings in the education of those who were 'deluded' into taking part in "that wicked conspiracy". (31)

For the liberal-whig Reformers of British descent -- who turned out alongside the tories to fight against the rebels in defence of Her Majesty's Provincial Government, the British connection, and the British Constitution and the rule of law – the post-rebellion political situation was not one of total gloom and despair. It was recognized that the Reform Party was totally prostrate; and that if a general election were called "not one solitary opponent of the [conservative] government" would be returned. However, as expressed by a leading liberal-Whig, Adam Hope of St. Thomas:

> I hope that we are done with a base anti-British faction who have carried this noble Province by snarling agitation for these some years & we have now the prospect of a party of "juste milieu" reformers arising in the province.

With the American-immigrant Reform Party leaders, such as Dr. Charles Duncombe, and the rebel 'captains' -- who were mostly American immigrants and their sons -- having fled to the United States together with the Scottish immigrant agitator, William Lyon Mackenzie, the way was viewed as open for new leaders to establish a liberal-Whig reform party in Upper Canada.

The moderate Reformers of a liberal-Whig persuasion were opposed to the American republicanism and egalitarian democratic ideal of the radical wing of the Reform Party, and denounced the attempt at rebellion, which was associated with 'mob rule' and 'anarchy'. Although committed to political and social stability, the moderate Reformers still favoured political reforms. Moreover, they sympathized with 'the deluded rebels' who had been deceived by Mackenzie and Duncombe.

Both the Tories and liberal-Whigs stood for the rule of law, and for the punishment of the rebels in the civil court system (rather than by courts martial), and both Tories and the liberal-Whigs were against any declaration of martial law in Upper Canada as a means of dealing with the rebellion crisis and its aftermath. However, although the Tories and liberal-Whigs agreed on the necessity of prosecuting the rebels under the law, they differed in the extent to which they deemed it necessary to prosecute them. The liberal-Whigs were opposed to the sweeping arrests of the 'deluded' followers of Mackenzie and the large number of captured rebels who were being charged with treason. (32)

From the Anglican Tory standpoint, there was much for which to be thankful. It was evident in retrospect that the Upper Canadian rebels constituted a very small minority of the population; and that their support had been confined, for the most part, to several areas of concentrated American settlement. Moreover, the rebels had been totally overwhelmed, and thoroughly defeated, by the loyal population of the Province which had turned out *en masse* to put down the attempted coup d'état.

For the Tories, the uprisings of December 1837 reconfirmed their belief in the dangers posed to the constitution by political conventions. In their view, conventions were unconstitutional, and constituted an effort to establish a fourth power in government by-passing the House of Assembly, the Legislative Council, and the Executive Council. Invariably, the holding of political conventions was viewed as an attempt by a minority political interest to pressure the government to grant their partisan political demands through convention delegates claiming to represent public opinion. In Upper Canada, the convention movement of the Reform Party – which was organized through the branches of the Toronto Political Union – had set out to foment public discontent and to organize a convention to address a perceived need for political reforms and changes in the constitution. It had evolved into an organization dedicated to carrying out a coup d'état to subvert the constitution and overthrow Her Majesty's Provincial Government.

Nonetheless, the Anglican Tories were shocked that the democratic radicals would seek --through attempting a coup d'état -- to impose an egalitarian democratic republican form of government upon Upper Canadians. However, when the rebellion did take place, for the Tories it was no mere coincidence that leaders of the Reform Party -- with but a few notable exceptions – turned out to be the leaders of the rebellion, or that most of the rebel leaders and their followers were American immigrants or their sons. The Reform Party leaders had spent over a decade in attacking the traditional social, political and religious order in the Province of Upper Canada, and its most avid members, with but few exceptions, were from the American-settled areas of the Province.

As early as 1799, the Anglican Tory Loyalist, Richard Cartwright, had argued -- in opposing an unfettered non-Loyalist American migration into Upper Canada -- that 'men do not change their political principles' and 'bias of mind' in crossing a border. Indeed, from the earliest years of settlement, the American settlers, in their adherence to democratic republican beliefs and principles, were viewed as a serious potential threat to the future peace, order and good government of the Loyalist Asylum of Upper Canada. (33)

For the American immigrant settlers in Upper Canada -- who were strong believers in the American democratic republican form of government -- the appeal of Mackenzie's arguments was quite strong. When he maintained that an independent democratic republic could be established, 'without bloodshed', by simply marching in force upon a defenceless provincial capital, it was a convincing argument because the American settlers wanted to believe it. Indeed, it was evident that the American immigrant settlers and their sons welcomed the promise of the establishment of a democratic republican form of government and the promised 300 acres of free land. Moreover, there was the pleasing prospect that once an independent Republic of Upper Canada were established, it would join the American Union.

For the Anglican Tories of Upper Canada, the December 1837 uprisings – in the Home District north of Toronto and in the London District -- reconfirmed their apprehensions about the extent of disaffection among the non-Loyalist American immigrant settlers and among the members of the American religious sects who were in many cases one and the same. Once again, the Loyalist Asylum of Upper Canada had faced a threat to its constitution, the Unity of Empire, and to its very survival, as was the case during the War of 1812, but this time the immediate threat was from within. The Tory response was to confront the rebels in the field, to let the law take its course in dealing with the captured rebels, and to exercise mercy, forbearance, and compassion in the sentencing of the convicted rebels under the treason laws.

In rallying to the defence of the Her Majesty's Provincial Government during the December 1837 rebellion, and its aftermath, a great majority of Upper Canadians firmly rejected American 'republican freedom', 'democracy', and union with the United States, in favour of maintaining the balanced British constitution and the British Imperial connection. The egalitarian democratic republicans were completely shattered as a political force. One major threat against the Anglican Tory elite, in its efforts to defend the traditional social, religious and political order in the Loyalist Asylum of Upper Canada, had been crushed.

As of 1837, an English Tory officer of the Corps of Royal Engineers, Lt. Col. Richard Bonnycastle, observed that there were adherents of three different political persuasions in Upper Canada. There was a tory grouping which comprised descendants of the Loyalists and the original British settlers who were strongly attached to the British Constitution and loyalty to the Empire – and, one might add, to the traditional social, religious and political order. They were well represented among the provincial office holders at all levels, were well-connected through family interrelationships, and were large land holders. However, the Tory leaders were functionaries, rather than a moneyed interest, as much of their land was of little value under current market conditions. The Tory elite -- whom Bonnycastle denoted as the "High Tory Party" – had dominated the provincial government during the 1820s, but were described as struggling to maintain their 'own personal sway' in the Province as the decade of the 1830s unfolded.

The second political grouping, which Bonnycastle described as "Whig" – actually liberal-Whigs -- was believed to be the largest party. It was composed of recent British immigrants of all sorts: small farmers, gentlemen of means, men of the liberal professions and self-made men. It included many Upper Canadian farmers who were descendants of the Loyalists. The 'Whigs' were committed "to upholding the British constitution unimpaired, and the connection with the mother country unbroken". They favoured the reform of government abuses, and especially wanted to see an end to the 'Tory family' influence in appointments to public office. They wanted public office appointments to be open to "all men of talent and honour".

What Bonnycastle failed to acknowledge was that the Upper Canadian Tories shared his belief in a meritocracy, and 'careers open to talent', where government appointments were concerned. However, although adhering to the merit principle, the Tories favoured the appointments of native-born Upper Canadians of education, moral character, and achievement with a proven record of loyalty and service to Upper Canada, over newly-arrived British immigrants of similar educational and professional attainments and good moral character. It was a feeling of nativism on the part of the Upper Canadian Tories that played a decided part in the public appointments process in the Province of Upper Canada.

More generally, Bonnycastle noted that the Whigs were united in favouring the annexation of the Island of Montreal to Upper Canada to provide the province with a seaport, which was a political position shared by the Tories. Bonnycastle noted, as well, that "all of the people of colour" were of the whig persuasion.

The third political group, identified by Bonnycastle, consisted of the 'Radicals', whom he thought were almost as numerous as the Whigs. The radical wing of the Reform Party comprised both political democrats and egalitarian democratic republicans. It encompassed "all the American settlers and speculators in land", and some of "the simple and ignorant" among the earliest settlers, as well as "the lawless rabble and adventurers" who entered Upper Canada every year from the United States and Britain. The American settlers were viewed as being very shrewd, but only a few of the leaders of the Radicals were men of 'any real talent'. In the view of Bonnycastle, the Radicals had one overriding aim: "the accession to power and place of their leaders" through Upper Canada becoming an integral part of the American Union -- the State of Upper Canada. (34)

The egalitarian democratic republicans and the democratic radicals of the Reform Party were widely despised following the Rebellion of 1837. They were branded as 'traitors' for their association with Mackenzie, either as known supporters or as participants in his disastrous attempt at a coup d'état. With the arrests and prosecutions of the rebel Reformers and the fleeing of the radical leaders of the Reform Party to the United States, the egalitarian democratic republican and democratic radical elements of the Party lost their public voice and faded as a political force in Upper Canada.

There remained but one potential threat to the Tory political establishment: that the liberal-Whigs -- amongst the Loyalists and British immigrant communities in Upper Canada -- might become advocates of 'responsible government' in embracing its promise of opening political offices and government patronage to control by the elected members of the Assembly. However, such a development would require 'the principle of responsible government' to become disassociated in the public mind from the perception that it would lead to the overthrow of the British Constitution and the severing of the British Imperial connection.

Notes

The Revolt of the Radicals

Frontispiece quotations: William Blackstone, *Commentaries on the Laws of England, Volume IV, Of Public Wrongs, As adopted by Robert Malcom Kerr* (Boston: Beacon Press, 1962), 72 & 89.

1. Craig, *Upper Canada*, 247; LeSueur, *Mackenzie*, 291-292; and *DCB*, IX, Frederick H. Armstrong & Ronald J. Stagg, "Mackenzie, William Lyon". The quotation is from LeSueur, 292. For the outright lies, deceptions, and misleading statements employed by Mackenzie to dupe Reformers into supporting his proposed coup d'état, see: Read and Stagg, eds., *The Rebellion of 1837*, 113-114, Doc. B4, "Petition of Samuel Lount", 10 March 1838; 114-115, Doc. B5, "Statement of Charles Doan", 15 December 1837; 116-118, "Petition of Joseph Gould to Sir George Arthur", 4 May 1838; and 118-120, "Petition of Randal Wixon", 10 April 1838.

2. Colin Read & Ronald J. Stagg, eds., *The Rebellion of 1837 in Upper Canada, a Collection of Documents* (Toronto: The Champlain Society, 1985), Introduction xlii-l and Documents, 127- 160 & map, 129, "Toronto and Environs, 1837"; Schrauwers, *'Union is Strength'*, 200; LeSueur, 294-301; and Craig, *Upper Canada*, 247-248. For the texts of the Constitution published on the 15th November, and the broadside declaration of Independence of November 27, 1837, see Appendix E, 344-358 and Appendix F, 358-362, respectively, in Charles Lindsey, *The Life and Times of Wm. Lyon Mackenzie, with an account of the Canadian rebellion of 1837, and the subsequent Frontier disturbances, Chiefly from Unpublished Documents*, Vol. 1 (Toronto: P.R. Randall, 1862).

See also *DCB*, IX, Armstrong & Stagg, "Mackenzie, William Lyon" & *DCB*, VI, Ronald J. Stagg, "Lount, Samuel" & VII, Charles G. Roland, "Horne, Robert". Later, Samuel Lount explained that the firing of the picket on the advancing rebels caused them to retreat in confusion because they had been led to believe that the citizens of Toronto would welcome them. The rebels on the march were totally surprised to find themselves -- in his words -- "surrounded by a Country determined to resist our approaches to the City, and a Change of Government". (Read and Stagg, eds. *The Rebellion of 1837*, 151-152, Doc. B34, "Petition of Samuel Lount to Sir F.B. Head" 10 March 1838. See also, 157-158, Doc. P 39, "Statement of James Latimer" , a rebel, who confirms that the rebels turned and fled which fired upon by the picket.)

3. LeSueur, 301-306; Read & Stagg, eds., *The Rebellion of 1837*, Introduction, l-liii & documents,159-172 & 177; Lindsey, *Life & Times*, II, 80 & 89-93; Craig, *Upper Canada*, 248; and *DCB*, VI, Ronald J. Stagg, "Matthews, Peter". The quotation is from LeSueur, 306.

4. LeSueur, 302-303; Craig, 248-249; Read & Stagg, *The Rebellion*, liii-lv & documents, 175-182; and *DCB*, IX, "Mackenzie". See also *DCB*: IX, Peter Baskerville, "MacNab, Allan Napier"; VIII, Gordon Dodds, "Macaulay, Sir James Buchanan"; VIII, Douglas Leighton & Robert J. Burns, "Jarvis, Samuel Peters"; and VII, Walter Lewis, "Chisholm, William". In his self-serving account of the Dec. 7th skirmish, Mackenzie claimed later that his men fought "courageously" and "killed and wounded a large number of the enemy". (Read & Stagg, eds., *The Rebellion of 1837*, 179-180, Doc. B61, 12 May 1838.) Sir Francis Bond Head (*A Narrative*, 328) wrote on 28 December 1837 that there was a loss "of only one man killed on the side of the Constitutionalists". Presumably, Head was referring to the death of Col. Moodie. It appears that the rebel casualties were due to artillery fire, and that the exchange of musket and rifle fire was not at close range. Elsewhere, one government supporter was reported as killed in defending the Don River Bridge during the Mackenzie uprising.

5. Read & Stagg, eds., *The Rebellion of 1837*, liv-lv & 188-189, Doc. B67, "Proclamation", 7 December 1837. For the identity of the ring-leaders, and the instigators of the rebellion, as well as information on their motive for participating in an uprising, and their personal character, background, education, and occupations, see: John Barnett, "Silas Fletcher, Instigator of the Upper Canadian Rebellion", *Ontario History*, XLI, 1975, 7-35. All the rebel ringleaders, except for Mackenzie, had prospered in Upper Canada, owned extensive properties, and in several instances enjoyed lucrative government appointments. Their motive for rebelling was not economic or based on any real grievance; it was ideological. For example, David Gibson, a Scots immigrant, was a government land surveyor, a prosperous farmer, and a staunch Reformer. He fled to the United States following the rebellion. After receiving a pardon, Gibson returned to Upper Canada in 1848 and settled again on his farm, which had been maintained by relatives while he was in the United States. See *DCB*, IX, Ronald J. Stagg, "Gibson, David".

6. Read & Stagg, eds., *The Rebellion of 1837*, lviii-lix, lxii-lxiii, & 239-240, Doc. C62, "A Despatch from Allan MacNab", 14 December 1837, & 191-239, Docs. C1- C61, Examinations of the rebel prisoners; and *DCB*: IX, "MacNab"; X, C.M. Johnston, "Malcolm, Eliakim"; and IX, J.J. Talman, "Askin, Jean Baptist". See also, Colin Read, *The Rising in Western Upper Canada, 1837-*

1838: The Duncombe Revolt and After (Toronto: University of Toronto Press, 1982). (From Brantford, there was a bush road leading southwest eight miles to the village of Oakland and beyond to Burford, and a road from Burford south to Scotland, and a road connection from the Village of Scotland directly west to Village of Sodom, a total distance of 25 miles from Brantford. The Village of Sodom is now Norwich.)

7. Read & Stagg, eds., *The Rebellion of 1837*, 187-188, Doc. B66, 15 December 1837 & 190, Doc. B69, 20 December 1837. Peter Perry, who was a former leader of the radical reformers, and the son of a Loyalist, was among the Cobourg militia arriving in Toronto to fight the rebels. He shared Mackenzie's dream of an egalitarian community of independent yeoman farmers in Upper Canada, but, as the son of a Loyalist, Perry was a staunch defender of the British Constitution, including its appointed Legislative Council, and the British Imperial connection. He was also a proponent of 'responsible government' in believing – the Baldwin argument – that its implementation was necessary to achieve the full workings of the British Constitution in Upper Canada, and to make the Lt. Governor responsible to 'the people'. Such was the complexity of the political culture of Upper Canada. (Read & Stagg, 301-302, Doc. D55, 9 December 1837; and *DCB*, VIII, H.E. Turner, "Perry, Peter".)

8. Read and Stagg, eds., *The Rebellion of 1837*, lxii-lxv, & 240-241, Doc. C63, 24 December, 244-245, Doc. C68, 12 January 1838, 245-246, Doc. C69, 28 December 1837, 247-248, Doc. C72, 19 December 1837, 249-250, Doc. C75, 25 December 1837, and 341, Doc. E8, "Petition of Various Norwich Inhabitants", 22 December 1837. The quotation is from 245, Allan MacNab to Jonas Jones, 18 December 1837. See also *DCB*, IX, "MacNab, Allan Napier".

9. William Blackstone, *Commentaries on the Laws of England, Volume IV, Of Public Wrongs*, (Boston: Beacon Press 1962, revised. 1st. English ed. 1769, 1st American ed. 1770), 72, 75-78, 89 & 94.

10. Read and Stagg, eds., *The Rebellion of 1837*, 337-338, Doc. E3, "John Joseph, Government House, to E.G. O'Brien, 11 December 1837 & 338-340, Doc. E5, "Special Commission Established at Toronto, Government House", 11 December 1837. The Joseph communication provides the government rationale for arresting the rebels at large.

The response of American settlers in December in 1837 to Mackenzie's appeal to establish a democratic republic in Upper Canada is symptomatic of American expansionism in North America. Americans believed in 'manifest destiny' (even before the term was coined in 1846), and whether settling on Indian lands (the

Northwest and South), on Spanish lands (Florida), or on Mexican lands (Texas, and subsequently California), American settlers followed the same pattern. As soon as they had sufficient numbers, they would rebel and call on American sympathizers to provide armed assistance to overthrow the local authorities, would declare the establishment of an independent territory or a republic, and would subsequently join or be annexed by the United States. These uprisings often received the support of the militias of the neighbouring American states, and sometimes even the intervention of the Army of the United States. The American government surreptitiously supported American settlers in their efforts to annex foreign territories to the United States. In Upper Canada, the Loyalist settlers and British immigrant settlers, with the support of the British Army, proved strong enough – in contrast to the Indians and Mexicans -- to defend their homeland and put down the December 1837 uprisings in repelling the march northward of American manifest destiny.

11. See *Dictionary of Canadian Biography*: VII, "Wood, Alexander"; VIII, "Sullivan, Robert Baldwin", "Allan, William", and "Jameson, Robert Sympson"; and XI, "Spragge, John Godfrey". On the checkered political career of Robert Baldwin Sullivan, see: Michael S. Cross, *A Biography of Robert Baldwin, the Morning Star of Memory* (Oxford: University of Oxford Press, 2012), 214-215.

12. On the grand jury system in English law, see: Blackstone, *Commentaries on the Laws of England*, IV, "Indictment", 358-359.

13. Read and Stagg, eds. *The Rebellion of 1837*, lxiv, 242-244, Doc. C66, 15 December 1837, & 245-246, Doc. C72, 22 December 1837, & 187-188, Doc. B66, 15 December 1837, & 340-341, Doc. E7, 26 May 1840 & 283, Doc. D35, 16 December 1837 & 398, Doc. E74, 28 May 1838; Schrauwers, *'Union is Strength'*, 194-195; and F. Murray Greenwood and Barry Wright, eds. *Canadian State Trials, Volume II, Rebellion and Invasion in the Canadas, 1837-1839* (Toronto: University of Toronto Press, 2002), 19, 21, 43 & 63. See also the *Dictionary of Canadian Biography*, which has entries on the Reform leaders who split with Mackenzie prior to the Rebellion.

David Gibson, Dr. John Rolph, Dr. Chares Duncombe and Robert Alway were expelled in absentia from the House of Assembly during its first session in January 1838 for their role in the uprisings. Surprisingly, Dr. Thomas David Morrison appears to have retained his seat, as did Elias Moore, a Reform member for Middlesex County, who was arrested for actively supporting the Duncombe uprising. See: F.H. Armstrong, *Handbook of Upper Canadian Chronology and Territorial Legislation* (London, Ontario: University of Western Ontario, 1967), 75-78, "Thirteenth Parliament, 1836-1841".

In Upper Canada, medical doctors played a prominent role in the rebellion of 1837, as did the Dr. Wolfred Nelson and his brother Dr. Robert Nelson in Lower Canada. Medical doctors were also in the forefront in the United States in providing support and even leadership for the 'Patriot armies', and the Hunters' Lodges, in their attacks upon Upper Canada in 1838. Many medical doctors, whether educated in the United States or Britain, were imbued with the Lockean-liberal values of the Enlightenment and Thomas Paine's 'Rights of Man'. Eugene Perry Link, *The Social Ideas of American Physicians (1776-1976), Studies of the Humanitarian Tradition in Medicine* (Selinsgrove, PA: Susquehanna University Press, 1992), Preface & 100-110. Most of the medical doctors in Upper Canada were educated in the United States where they imbibed American political principles. To rectify that situation, the Tories were committed to the establishment of a university in Upper Canada -- King's College -- which was to have a medical faculty.

14. Read & Stagg, eds., *The Rebellion of 1837*, Introduction, lvi, lviii, lxv, lxvi & lxxxvii, and 246-247, Doc. C71, 24 December 1837 & 364-365, Doc. E39, 19 February 1838 & 254, Doc. D1, 20 November 1837 & 265, Doc. 14, "The Catholics' Declaration of Loyalty", 22 December 1837; and Mills, *The Idea of Loyalty*, 91; and Craig, *Upper Canada*, 246. On the role of American settlers in instigating the rebellion, see: John Barnett, "Silas Fletcher, Instigator of the Upper Canadian Rebellion", *Ontario History*, XLI, 1949, 7-35. On 11 December 1837, Lt. Governor Head authorized the raising of a "Corps of Negroes" and, in February 1838, "the coloured population" was publicly thanked by a Select Committee of the Legislative Council for their loyalty and service in arms in defending Upper Canada during the border incursions that followed the defeat of the 1837 Rebellion.

It appears that the American-immigrant Quakers who took an active part in the uprisings were adherents of a splinter group, the Hicksites, who rejected Christian beliefs and the quietism and pacifism of the orthodox Friends in favour of a belief in Unitarianism and evangelical Calvinist religious principles. Most of the rebel leaders, except for Mackenzie and Gibson, were 'American Methodists' or non-religious. Dr. John Rolph was from a staunch Anglican Tory family of British immigrants, but by the time of the rebellion he was attending the Methodist Episcopal Church in Toronto.

One historian, Curtis Fehey, maintains that 19 Anglicans were involved in Mackenzie's uprising, which is at odds with what contemporaries observed. See, Curtis Fehey, *The Anglican Experience in Upper Canada, 1791-1854* (Ottawa; Carleton University Press, 1991), 150, note 90. One presumes that the Anglican rebels were from among British immigrants who had settled among American settlers in the Home District and were coerced by the Vigilance

Committee to join the rebellion, or they were converts to a religious sect. There were no Anglicans among the Duncombe rebels.

15. Read and Stagg, eds., *The Rebellion of 1837*, Introduction, lxv; Craig, *Upper Canada*, 246; Schrauwers, *'Union Is Strength'*, 199-200; and Mills, *The Idea of Loyalty*, 91. In seeking to restore social harmony after the Rebellion, the reports prepared by a Select Committee of the Legislative Council (13 February 1838) and by a Select Committee of the House of Assembly (8 February 1838) on the state of the province, do not mention the leading role of the American immigrants and their first-generation descendants in the Rebellion of December 1837. The rebels were referred to simply as 'deluded men' and 'traitors'. However, Robert Baldwin Sullivan, the President of the Executive Council, did comment -- in a "Report on the State of the Province" (1 June 1838), that it was "not surprising" that the American settlers and their descendants would tend to support a movement favouring republican institutions. (See: Mills, 91).

Read and Stagg, eds., *The Rebellion of 1837*, Introduction, lvi, point out that many of the rebels were linked by family connections and personal loyalties; and that the rebels who were at Montgomery's Tavern – at one time or another in the period December 3rd - 7th -- numbered less than one thousand men in total. In sum, at their greatest strength, the rebels represented only about five percent of the population of but one district, the Home District. At that time, the Province of Upper Canada had a population of 450,000 and there were uprisings only in the American-settled areas of the Home and London districts. The belief that America 'republican freedom' and 'democracy' was destined to triumph over the entire North American continent was widespread among Americans in the early 19th Century. Earlier, it was strongly expressed in the writings of Thomas Jefferson at the time of the American Revolution.

16. Read and Stagg, eds., *The Rebellion of 1837*, Introduction, lvi-lvii, & 364-365, Doc. E39, "Extract of a Letter from Rev. Thomas Green". The Rev. Green, an Anglican cleric, investigated the religious affiliations of the rebel prisoners. More generally, the Upper Canadian Tories were very conscious of the role dissenting ministers, and even more so the religious sects, had played in encouraging and supporting the American revolutionaries during the American Revolution. In Upper Canada, the disaffection of the American religious sects is evident in a private letter of an American preacher, the Rev. James Marr of the Niagara Presbyterian Church. (*Ibid*, 308, Doc. E66, Rev. James Marr, Beamsville, to the Rev. Absalom Peters, 8 December 1837.)

The economic depression of 1837 was not a significant cause of the December 1837 uprisings in Upper Canada. To the contrary, it was an ideological conflict in which a traditional political order, which was based on Anglican Tory principles and values, was under attack by the non-Loyalist American settlers who were imbued with democratic republican political values, and who were largely religious sectarians. American immigrant settlers and the first-generation sons of American immigrants comprised the vast majority of the participants in the rebellion; and the rebels enjoyed a broad support within the American immigrant communities.

17. *Report of a Select Committee of the House of Assembly on the Political State of the Provinces of Upper and Lower Canada* (R. Stanton, Queen's Printer, 1838), 31-32 &37, 8 February 1838; and *Report from the Select Committee of the Legislative Council of Upper Canada on the State of the Province* (R. Stanton, Queen's Printer, 1838), 3-6, 13 February 1838; and Read and Stagg, 381-384, Doc. E 59, "Chief Justice's Address to Samuel Lount and Peter Matthews", 29 March 1838. The select committee reports were drafted by Henry Sherwood and John Macaulay, respectively, both of whom were Anglican Tories and former pupils of the Cornwall District Grammar School of the Rev. John Strachan. See also, Mills, *The Idea of Loyalty*, 90. Earlier, during the June 1836 election, the Methodist preacher, the Rev. Egerton Ryerson -- in reverting to the loyalties of his Anglican-Loyalist upbringing -- had similarly argued that the province was 'well and fairly governed'. (See: LeSueur, *Mackenzie*, 276-278.)

18. *Report of the Select Committee of the Legislative Council*, 4, 7- 14; *Report of the Select Committee of the House of Assembly*, 31 & 35; and Read and Stagg, 362-363, Doc. E36, "Day of Public Thanksgiving Ordered – Proclamation, Upper Canada", 22 July 1838. The quotation is from the Legislative Council report, 10-11. See also, Mills, *The Idea of Liberty*, 90-91.

19. *Report of the Select Committee of the Legislative Council*, 9-10, 13 February 1828; *Report of the Select Committee of the House of Assembly*, 35, 8 February 1838; and McNairn, *The Capacity to Judge*, 204-209. The quotation is from *The Church*, 2 February 1839, as quoted by McNairn, 208.

20. Read and Stagg, eds., *The Rebellion of 1837*, 353, Doc. E21, 26 December 1837 & 344-345, Doc. E13, 29 December 1837 & 340, Doc. E6, "Militia General Order", 28 December 1837.

21. F. Murray Greenwood and Barry Wright, eds., *Canadian State Trials, Volume II, Rebellion and Invasion in the Canadas, 1837-1839* (Toronto: University of Toronto Press, 2002), Introduction, 4-5, 9 & 25 and 64-67, Paul Romney and Barry Wright, "The Toronto Treason Trials, March-May 1838".

22. *Canadian State Trials*, II: 46, Rainer Baehre, "Trying the Rebels: Emergency Legislation and the Colonial Executive's Overall Legal Strategy in

the Upper Canadian Rebellion", and 461-462, Appendix D, "An Act to enable the Government of the Province to extend a Conditional Pardon in certain cases to Persons who have been concerned in the late insurrection" (1Vic. c.10, 6 March 1838). Another Act, drafted by Robinson, provided an expedited process for convicting fugitive rebels *in absentia* and enabling their estates to be confiscated: viz. 'Act to Provide for the More Speedy Attainder of Persons Indicted for High Treason, Who Have Fled from the Province, or Remained Concealed Therein, to Escape from Justice" (1 Vic. c.9, 6 March 1838). On the series of emergency acts drafted by Chief Justice Robinson to deal with the rebellion aftermath, see Baehre, 43-48. Some of the property of Mackenzie was seized at law by his creditors through the civil courts. However, no properties of the rebels were seized by the Crown; although the Tory provincial government, on behalf of the Crown, had every legal right to seize the property of convicted felons.

23. Baehre, "Trying the Rebels', 42-43 & 48. On the earlier efforts of the libral-Whig government in Britain to establish a judiciary independent of the government administration in Upper Canada, and the nature of the connection between Chief Justice Robinson and the Lt. Governor during the aftermath of the rebellion, see Brode, *Sir John Beverley Robinson*, 185 & 203-204.

24. *Canadian State Trials*, II: 62-99, Romney and Wright, "The Toronto Treason Trials", and II: 100-109, Read "The Treason Trials of 1838 in Western Upper Canada". There is some minor disagreement concerning the numbers cited for the men indicted, granted pardons, and acquitted in the Hamilton treason trials. See Romney and Wright, 91/fn. 16 and Read, 103-104 & 120/fn. 1. On the composition of the Toronto juries, see: Romney and Wright, 84-87. The treason trials summary presented herein draws heavily on historical information extracted from the two treason trail chapters in *Canadian State Trials*, II, as cited herein. On the conduct and impartiality of the Crown law officers during the treason trials, see *Canadian State Trials*, II, 471, private letter, William H. Draper to John Macaulay, Toronto, 10 August 1838.

25. *Dictionary of Canadian Biography*: VII: "Jones, Jonas" and "Sherwood, Levius Peters", *DCB*, VIII: "Macaulay, Sir James Buchanan", and *DCB*. IX: "Robinson, John Beverley". Following the June 1837 accession of Queen Victoria, the Court of Queen's Bench (the superior court) consisted of the Chief Justice and four puisne (associate) judges. Judge Sherwood had been appointed in October 1825, Judge Macaulay in July 1829, and Judge Jones and the fourth judge, Judge Archibald McLean, in March 1837. Robinson was appointed Chief Justice in July 1829. See Frederick H. Armstrong, *Handbook of Upper Canadian Chronology* (1967).

Judge McLean, a prominent Church of Scotland tory, would preside over the grand jury assizes and the treason trials held in Kingston, May- July 1838. Earlier, in February 1838, American 'patriots' had made an incursion into Upper Canada at Hickory Island, on the Upper St. Lawrence River, as part of a planned assault on Kingston. Upper Canadian rebel sympathizers -- from an American-settled area of the Midland District -- were arrested when they turned out in arms to support the 'patriot' invasion attempt and were put on trial for treason. See *DCB*, IX, Bruce W. Hodgins, "McLean, Archibald", and *Canadian State Trials*, II, Barry Wright, "The Kingston and London Courts Martial", 135-136. On the rebels of Hastings County, Midland District, and their abortive assault on Kingston, see: Betsy Dewar Boyce, *The Rebels of Hastings* (Toronto: University of Toronto Press, 1992); and Sir Richard Henry Bonnycastle, Lt. Col., Royal Engineers, *Canada, As It Was, Is, and May Be*, Vol. II (London: Colburn & Co., 1852), 69-99.

26. Romney & Wright, "The Toronto Treason Trials", 65 & 91/fn. 17; and Read, 'The Treason Trials in Western Upper Canada', 104-105.

27. Romney & Wright, 49, 68 & 81, Read, 104-105; and LAC, Upper Canada Sundries, RG5, A1, Civil Secretary Correspondence, vol. 192, reel C-6898, 106746, Allan Macdonell, Sheriff's Office, Hamilton, to John Joseph, Secretary to His Excellency, 21 April 1838. On the reluctance of the Tory judges of the Court of Queen's Bench to sanction capital punishment, see: *DCB*, IX, "Robinson, John Beverley", and *DCB*, VII "Jones, Jonas" and "Sherwood, Levius Peters".

28. Baehre, "Trying the Rebels", 49-53; and LAC, RG5 A1, vol. 251, reel C-6915, 136543-136587, 'Report of Commissioners Appointed to Inquire into Charges of Treason and Felony', n.d. [April 1838]. The report was prepared by Judge Jameson, and two members of the Special Commission: Alexander Wood and John Spragge. The figures provided in the special commissioners' report on the number of death sentences and number of petitioners, differ somewhat from the totals derived from the treason trial summaries. The special commission totals are probably the more accurate as they name the individuals and provide a comment on the past actions and political attitudes of each offender.

29. Baehre, "Trying the Rebels", 53-55; and LAC, RG5 A1, vol. 193, reel C-6899, 107301-107322, Jon. B. Robinson & J. Jones, to John Joseph, Secretary to His Excellency, Toronto, 2 May 1838.

30. Read, 'Treason Trails in Western Upper Canada', 105, Romney and Wright, "The Toronto Treason Trials, 88- 89, 91/fn17 & 92/ fn19; and Cassandra Pybus, "Patriot Exiles in Van Diemen's Land", 188, 190 & 200/fn.1. Compassion and

leniency were shown by the Tory judges in the sentencing of the rebels of the attempted coup d'état of December 1837. However, the sentences imposed subsequently on the American 'patriots' and fugitive Upper Canadian rebels who were captured during raids and military invasions into Upper Canada in 1838, and tried under the Lawless Aggressions Act, were much harsher. The men captured during the Short Hills Raid (21-23 June 1838) at Niagara, and during the invasions at Prescott (Battle of the Windmill, 12-16 November 1838) and at Windsor (Battle of Windsor, 4 December 1838) faced treason trials at Niagara or courts martial at Kingston and London, respectively. A total of eighteen men were sentenced to death and executed, and ninety-two were transported to Australia. See *Canadian State Trials*, II: 109-117, Read, 'Treason Trials in Western Upper Canada' -- The Niagara Trials; 130-159, Barry Wright, "The Kingston and London Courts Martial"; and 188-204, Cassandra Pybus, "Patriot Exiles in Van Diemen's Land". On the Lawless Aggressions Act, see Introduction, 27, and 160-187, of F. Murray Greenwood, "The Prince Affair: 'Gallant Colonel' or 'The Windsor Butcher'?"

31. *The Church* (Bethune editorial), 5 May 1838.

32. The summary of the liberal-Whig reform outlook is based on Read and Stagg, eds., *The Rebellion of 1837*, 252-253, Doc. C79, Adam Hope to Robert Hope, 24 December 1837. Adam Hope, a prominent merchant, reformer and Unitarian, served with the St. Thomas Volunteers [cavalry], during the rebellion. It appears that his British nationalist feelings and loyalty took precedence over the more general tendency of Unitarians to support the democratic radicals. See also: *DCB*, XI, Douglas McCall, "Hope, Adam".
33. The quotation is from C.E. Cartwright, ed., *Life and Letters of Richard Cartwright* (Toronto: Belford Bros., 1876), 96, Richard Cartwright to General Peter Hunter, Lt. Governor of Upper Canada, 23 August 1799.

34. Bonnycastle, *Canada As It Was, Is, and May Be*, vol. II, 133-135. For a contemporary account of the alienation of the English liberal-Whig immigrants from the Americanized Reform Party, see G.M Craig, ed., "Comments on Upper Canada in 1836 by Thomas Carr", *Ontario History*, xlviii, no. 4, 1955, 171-179.

Conclusion

Politics in Upper Canada

The High Tory Church Establishment

The Reform Party

The Principle of 'Responsible Government'

The Whigs & liberal-Whigs

The Democratic Radicals

The Evangelical Sectarians

The Egalitarian Democratic Republicans

Political Alignments in Upper Canada

American Evangelical Protestantism

Church Establishment & the Clergy Reserves Endowment

The Age of Delusion

The Tory Outlook

The American Ideological Threat

The American Imperialism Threat

The Demise of the Tories

The Return of the Rebels

A Lost Saturnia regna

The Tory Legacy

Conclusion

Politics in Upper Canada

In Upper Canada, it was the Tories who were dedicated to the maintenance of public order, the existing church-state polity, and the balanced British Constitution, and who were staunchly loyal to the Crown and the unity of the British Empire. Moreover, it was the Tories who had a national vision for the future of the Province, and who were committed to defending the Loyalist asylum in keeping with their Anglican Tory values, principles and beliefs. They strove to ensure the survival of Upper Canada as a separate 'nation' in North America in the face of the spectre of assimilation, annexation, or conquest by an expansionist democratic republic, the United States of America.

In contrast, three of the four politicized outgroups, who were aligned under the banner of the 'Reform Party', simply imported American political and/or religious principles and social values into Upper Canada and lacked any distinct national vision. The fourth outgroup -- the liberal-Whig Reformers -- was narrowly focused on a constitutional reform. Its members sought political power to gain control over government revenues and Crown patronage appointments, and to secularize government institutions. All four outgroups were opposed to the union of church and state, to the endowments and prerogatives of the established Church of England, and to the governing Anglican Tory gentry. Moreover, none of the outgroups were concerned with public order and social harmony, which was a hallmark of the Tory outlook.

The High Church Tory Establishment

In post-War of 1812 Upper Canada, the High Church Anglican Tories were the leading upholders of the conservative cause in the House of Assembly, the Legislative Council, and in the Executive Council. They defended the church-state polity, the rule of law, and the balanced constitution against encroachments by the House of Assembly, as well as upheld the sovereignty of the Crown, the rights of the people (the 'rights of Englishmen'), and the corporate endowments and prerogatives of the established Church of England. The High Church Anglican Tories were strong supporters as well of the 'national' education system that the Tory establishment was striving to establish under the direction of the established Church of England. However, what weakened and divided the conservative forces in Upper Canada was the conduct of the adherents of the Church of Scotland who supported the Reform Party when a claim that their church held a co-establishment status in Upper Canada was rejected by the Tories and, secondly, the conduct of the moderate Tories who for the sake of political peace and social harmony were willing to acquiesce in the demands of the dissenting churches and the religious sects for a share of the clergy reserves revenues.

The conservative cause was further weakened by the political tactics of the Reform Party in fomenting discontent through manipulating public opinion on several major public issues. The Reformers falsely claimed on the hustings that the Tory attempt to exclude American aliens from the vote and appointments to public office was an effort to revoke the land titles of all settlers from the United States, including the Loyalists and the naturalized American settlers, and to deny them their legal rights under the law. However, that was decidedly not the case. Secondly, the Reformers put forth the specious claim that the phrase 'a Protestant clergy' in the Constitutional Act of 1791 was meant to include all Protestant denominations, and that the dissenting churches and sects were being denied their just share of the clergy reserves revenues. In that manner, the Reform Party manufactured major grievances that divided the conservative forces of the Province of Upper Canada and drew the members of the various outgroups into supporting the Reform Party in opposition to the Tory establishment.

The King's College Charter of 1827 was another issue exploited by the Reform Party to divide the traditional churches. It was opposed by the Reformers despite the fact that it was the most liberal university charter in existence anywhere in Europe or the United States at that time. The university was to be open to all students to pursue a BA, MA, and Doctor of Arts, and "no religious tests or qualifications" were to be required for admittance or graduation. The only exception was for students graduating with the degree of Doctor of Divinity, who were to subscribe to the same oaths as taken by students graduating with a Doctor of Divinity degree at the University of Oxford. The university was to be funded by the sale of Crown lands obtained in exchange for more remote reserve lands that were set aside for educational purposes during the earlier administration of the English Tory, Lt. Governor John Graves Simcoe. A building fund was attained through a Crown grant of £1,000 per annum for sixteen years which the British government provided from the monies received from the Canada Company for Crown land purchases in Upper Canada. In addition, Archdeacon Strachan raised funds through a public appeal while in England. No taxes were to be imposed on Upper Canadians to support the university.

Nevertheless, despite the unprecedented openness of the projected King's College university, the Reformers agitated against the administration provided for the new university. Under the Charter, the Anglican Bishop of Quebec was to be a Visitor, the President of the College was to be the Archdeacon of York -- the Rt. Rev. Dr. John Strachan -- and the members of the College Council (seven staff professors) were required to be members of the Church of England and to subscribe to the Thirty-Nine Articles set forth in the Book of Common Prayer. In response, the sectarian supporters of the Reform Party complained that the university would be a missionary college for the conversion of their youth to the Church of England. And, in 1830, an extra-parliamentary Reform Party organization, the 'Friends of Religious Liberty', held a large public rally in Toronto. It was chaired by its President, Robert Baldwin, and managed to gain a reputed 10,000 signatures on a massive petition to the King that called for the King's College Charter to be modified 'to exclude all sectarian tests and preferences' -- a demand that focused on the religious requirements in force for teaching staff and the Church of England affiliation of the Visitor and President.

The agitation over the administration proposed for the projected university dragged on for years, with the Reform Party eventually calling for the establishment of a state-supported, secular university. Following the Loyalty Election of June 1836, an effort was made by the Tory establishment to achieve a compromise with a bill that was debated in both houses of the conservative dominated Legislature, and in March 1837 an Act was passed to amend the King's College Charter. The College Council members were no longer required to subscribe to the Thirty-Nine Articles, but they were required to acknowledge a belief in 'the authenticity and divine inspiration of the Old and New Testaments and in the Doctrine of the Holy Trinity' – a clause which excluded, for the most part, only deists, unitarians, atheists, and the irreligious from teaching at the university. Non-Anglican students were not required to attend the Church of England chapel services at the College.

The Council was increased to twelve members, inclusive of the Solicitor General, the Attorney General, and both speakers of the Legislature, which linked the provincial government directly to the administration of the projected university. (At the time, the Attorney General, Robert Sympson Jameson was an English-immigrant Anglican Tory; the Solicitor General was Christopher Alexander Hagerman, a second-generation Loyalist Anglican Tory; the Speaker of the Legislative Council was John Beverley Robinson, the Chief Justice of Upper Canada, a second-generation Loyalist, and an Anglican Tory; and the Speaker of the House of Assembly was Archibald McLean, a Scots Presbyterian tory, a defender of the interests of the Church of Scotland, and a former student of the Rev. John Strachan at the Cornwall District Grammar School.)

Despite the compromise effort, the onset of the rebellion of December 1837 and the appointment of a radical Whig, Lord Durham, as Governor-General and High Commissioner -- to administer the provinces of Upper Canada and Lower Canada, to investigate the causes of political unrest, and to recommend 'the form and future government' of the provinces -- entailed further delays, as did the political repercussions of the recommendations of the Durham Report on the Affairs of British North America (February 1839). King's College finally opened in 1843 after a sixteen-year struggle. (1)

The alien controversy, the dispute over the clergy reserves revenues, and the differences over the King's College Charter, were three major issues that the Reform Party exploited to arouse public opinion in the Province and did so through a series of public campaigns of agitation that were part of its pursuit of 'a politics of grievances'. It was a political tactic that divided the conservative religious denominations of Upper Canada on the several issues cited, and even divided the Anglicans themselves.

Among the conservatives were Loyalists, the native-born sons of Loyalists, British immigrants and their native-born sons, and more recent British immigrants, who wanted to preserve the British national culture in Upper Canada, the church-state polity, the rule of law, the balanced British constitution, and the Unity of the Empire. However, the conservatives of the province were not united in a political party, or on several major political issues.

Among the conservatives were philosophical Tories – the High Church Anglican Tories, who were the committed defenders of the balanced British constitution, the rule of law, the royal prerogatives, the church-state union and the prerogatives and endowments of the established Church of England -- and moderate Anglican Tories, who shared the same religious, constitutional, educational, and cultural values, but were willing to share the clergy reserves revenues with the other religious denominations in the interests of political peace and social harmony.

In Upper Canada, political behavior was largely determined by religious beliefs, values, and principles, which were commonly related in turn to the place of origin of immigrants and their respective social status. For some groups, notably the Irish Roman Catholics and the Black Upper Canadians, their historical experience and shared memories as a people, were a deciding factor in their political behavior.

The members of the traditional churches – the Church of Scotland, the Roman Catholic Church (Scots and English), and the Lutheran Church – were supporters of the traditional order, but they wavered in their support of the Tory establishment over the prerogatives and endowments enjoyed by the Church of England, and over Anglican control of the projected university. Indeed, the Church of Scotland adherents, following the rejection of their claim to a 'co-establishment', even aligned themselves for a time with the democratic radicals and evangelical sectarians with whom the Church of Scotland had little in common in its religious beliefs, social values, educational standards, and constitutional views. (Although not treated in this study, there were also 'situational conservatives' – primarily the merchants – who supported the established order because it was in their financial interest to support social and political stability, and a provincial government that – under the Tories – was committed to public order, the rule of law, trade and commerce, and a public financing of transport facilities. However, in the House of Assembly, the 'situational conservatives' were not prepared to defend the prerogatives and endowments of the Established Church.)

The conservative cause was further weakened by the Tory antipathy to political parties, and the Tory concept of the independent 'gentlemen' offering to serve the public in standing for election. During provincial elections, several conservatives might stand in the same riding, which had the effect of splitting the conservative vote; whereas their opponents – at a very early date -- organized a political party, the Reform Party, and held nomination meetings to select Reform candidates to stand at elections. The Reform Party established election committees – Vigilance Committees – to carry on an election campaign, and the Reformers focused on a single issue at each provincial election which was whatever political issue was being agitated at that time. Hence, only one official Reform Party candidate ran in a one-member riding, or two official Reform candidates in a two-member riding.

Where the Tories managed to secure election to the House of Assembly, their political influence was weakened by their concept of representation. The elected members were viewed as representatives of the people at large, who were to engage in a rational debate on public issues in the House of Assembly, and who, while making known the interests of his constituents on a public issue under discussion, were expected to vote according to their independent judgement of 'the national interest' on political issues. In contrast, the Reform Party members of the House of Assembly were regarded as elected delegates of the Party who were required to vote in unison for Reform motions, resolutions, and bills in the Assembly.

The Anglican Tories and their conservative supporters were united in their support of the balanced British Constitution, and by a fervent belief in the rule of law, equality before the law, and 'the historic rights of Englishmen' as set forth in the statutes of the British Constitution. Following the Rebellion of December 1837, the prisoners were prosecuted under the law in a judicial process in which the defendants who were indicted by a Grand Jury were placed on trial before a jury of their peers with legal representation by a defence lawyer. There was no resort to martial law, and only one law, the Habeas Corpus, was suspended – and only temporarily, and only for the rebel prisoners – to enable the imprisoned rebels to be held over for trial. Their retention of the rebel prisoners in jail without bail, was deemed necessary to preclude them from fleeing to the United States.

Although the penalty for high treason was to be hanged, drawn and quartered, with a right of the Crown to seize the property of a convicted felon, the Tories believed not only in justice under the rule of the law, but also in the virtue of mercy. Only two of the convicted rebels were hanged – Samuel Lount and Peter Matthews -- to set an example that treason would not be tolerated, and neither of the executed men was drawn and quartered. No property of the convicted or fugitive rebels was ever confiscated by the Crown. In the case of William Lyon Mackenzie, some of his property was seized, at law, by individuals seeking payment of his many outstanding debts. Otherwise the property of the convicted rebel felons, and of the fugitive rebels convicted in absentia, remained in the hands of their respective families. The adherence of the governing Tories to the rule of law during a rebellion contrasts greatly with the Loyalist experience during the American Revolution. In that earlier conflict, subjects loyal to the Crown had their property confiscated (both fixed and personal) without compensation, were driven out of the new country by rebel mobs, and did not receive any protection, under the law, from the public authorities or the courts.

It was the sons of the leading Loyalist and British-immigrant families of Upper Canada who were educated in the decade before the War of 1812 by the Rev. John Strachan, who comprised the backbone of the Tory political and social establishment of the Province in the postwar period. They were the young men whom the Rev. Strachan had inculcated with the principles, values, and beliefs of Anglican Toryism and the Anglican faith, who identified with the Anglican Loyalist tradition, and who rejected Lockean-liberalism and democratic republican values. The leading Tories were noteworthy for being well-educated 'gentlemen' within a frontier society that was largely lacking in any formal education in the pre-war period and within which – prior to the large postwar influx of British immigrants -- there were many who were functionally illiterate.

In the postwar period, the young Tories were well-represented in the professions – medicine, the law, and the National Church – and dominated the appointed Executive Council and Legislative Council of the provincial government, as well as served in the elective House of Assembly. They were notable for their loyalty to the Crown and the British Empire and, as young men, most of the leading young Tories had fought during the War of 1812 in the militia companies that aided the British troops in defending Upper Canada. It was the young Upper Canadian Tories who, in their postwar careers, were largely responsible for the governing of Upper Canada, for the drafting of government policies, and for administering the law.

In religion, the Upper Canadian Tories were in the tradition of the 18th Century Broad Church movement among Anglicans. They believed that an inclusive and comprehensive national church would attract adherents by preaching the Word and serving as a moral beacon and force for education in a frontier society. However, the Tories of Upper Canada, as distinct from the Latitudinarian Whig clergy of the late 17th Century Church of England, did not see the Christian religion as simply a rational form of belief and a source of morality that was supportive of the social order. For the Tories, human reason had its limits beyond which man had to rely on Revelation to understand the 'mysteries' of religion, man in his 'fallen nature' was prone to evil, and his reasoning power was corrupted. Fallen man could be redeemed only through hearing the Word, having faith in Christ as his Saviour, and partaking of the Christian sacraments – especially the receiving of God's grace through baptism, and the joining with Christ in righteousness through Holy Communion – which transformed the fallen character of man and made it possible to subordinate himself to God's moral law and to do good works in 'going unto perfection'.

For the Tories, the Church of England was the 'via media' between the Roman Catholic Church and the Protestant churches and sects. The Anglican Tories admired the Roman Catholic Church for its support of the traditional order against the revolutionary forces of irreligion and democratic anarchy, and its maintenance of Church traditions. However, the Tories could not accept the claim of the Bishop of Rome to supremacy over the national church of England, or the claim to Papal Infallibility in expounding Christian doctrine (which would become a Catholic doctrine itself in 1870), or the Roman Catholic belief in transubstantiation –

that during the sacrament of Communion the bread and the wine were transformed into the body and blood of Christ while retaining only its original appearance.

The Tories did not expect to comprehend Roman Catholics --primarily the French Catholics in the Western District and the Highland-Scots Catholics of Glengarry – within the Church of England. However, the Tories did believe that members of the traditional Protestant churches could be won over to the Church of England and that the Protestant sectarians could be assimilated back into the National Church, which was a Protestant Church in adhering to a belief in 'justification by faith alone'. What was required was for the Church of England to place a parish priest in each frontier community to preach the Word, to provide church services and religious and moral instruction, and to serve as a school teacher. Moreover, the parish priest was to serve as the voice of moral authority in the community which required that he be spiritually-independent, and not beholden to government or his parishioners for his sustenance. To implement such a plan required extensive financial investments, which was why the High Church Tories fought to retain the revenues from the clergy reserves land endowment for the Church of England. Since the Tories believed in religious toleration on both religious grounds (faith could not be coerced) and in terms of political realities (a coercion policy would destroy the peace and harmony of society and upset the social order), there was no thought of coercing Dissenters to adhere to the National Church.

The unhappy fate of the Upper Canadian Tories – in seeking to defend and strengthen the Loyalist Asylum of Upper Canada – was to find themselves in a position where their loyalty, dedication and sacrifice in support of the Crown and the British Empire was unappreciated and unreciprocated by a liberal-Whig government in Britain. Rather than providing support for the Tory establishment in resisting the demands of the House of Assembly, the British government continually sought to conciliate the Reformers who were attacking not only the balance of the British Constitution, but the very fabric of the church-state polity of Upper Canada, the prerogatives and property of the National Church, and the established social order.

It was an era when the liberal-Whigs in Britain were questioning the value of colonies and were opposed to large financial expenditures for the maintenance and defence of colonies. They were convinced that colonies would eventually separate from the Mother Country. Moreover, among the radicals of the Whig Party in Britain, there was an admiration for the American form of government, a belief in popular sovereignty, and a view that Canada would be better off – as a North American country – in adopting an American democratic republican system of government and in implementing a separation of church and state.

Despite the lack of support from the liberal-Whig governments in Britain, the Upper Canadian Tories strove to maintain and strengthen the traditional Christian church-state polity of the Loyalist Asylum of Upper Canada, to strengthen its 'British national character', and to defend Her Majesty's Provincial Government against its attackers, both foreign and domestic.

The Reform Party

The Reform Party of Upper Canada -- prior to the Rebellion of 1837 – was comprised of four distinct outgroups who were in opposition to the Tory establishment: viz. democratic radicals, evangelical sectarians, liberal-whig secularists, and egalitarian democratic republicans. Despite espousing different values and beliefs, the four groups were united in their opposition to the Tory establishment, to the union of church and state, and to the control of government patronage appointments by the Crown. After 1828, the four opposition groups were even more closely allied under the Reform Party banner in a common demand for the implementation of the principle of 'responsible government'.

With their system of party discipline, the Reform Party coalition managed to dominate the House of Assembly for several parliaments during the 1820s, and even during the sessions of the Eleventh Parliament (1830-1834), when the Reform party held only a minority of the seats. It was a situation that finally changed -- following the Loyalty Election of June 1836 -- when the conservatives coalesced under the banner of the British Constitutional Society to select a single Constitutional candidate to run on the loyalty issue in each riding, and two candidates for the two-member ridings.

Over the previous decade, the political activities of the Reformers were based on the example of the British radicals and focused on organizing extra-parliamentary political associations to carry on a campaign of public agitation. The overarching aim of the campaigns of agitation, the printing of pamphlets, and the circulation of public petitions, was to convince the Colonial Office in London that 'the people' wanted the British government to intervene in the provincial politics of Upper Canada to rectify whatever so-called 'grievance' was being complained of by one or other of the various opposition groups who were aligned under the Reform banner. It was a situation wherein the Tories were faced with a veritable 'politics of grievances' in which many of the grievances enunciated by the various opposition groups were simply complaints that some provincial government act or policy – which was supportive of the existing constitution and church-state polity of the Province of Upper Canada -- was not in keeping with their own particular religious principles and/or political beliefs.

In Upper Canada, the political situation was complicated by the fact that the four opposition groups had divergent aims and interests, and embodied differing ideologies. What they had in common was primarily a pervading resentment of the Tory establishment of the province. Whether opposed to the church-state polity of the province, the endowments and prerogatives possessed by the National Church, the political and social status of the Upper Canadian Tory elite, and/or the control of the Crown over patronage appointments, the four opposition groups were united under the umbrella of the Reform Party. They were united in seeking to supplant the Tory establishment and attain political power and control over government revenues and patronage. The Tory establishment was constantly attacked through the speeches of the Reform leaders on the hustings and in public meetings, through motions moved by the Reform Party members in the House of Assembly, newspaper articles in the radical press, the publication of political tracts, and the circulation of petitions. All such efforts were aimed at fostering political unrest and disaffection through the raising of a succession of 'popular grievances' as part of a continual campaign of agitation.

The public petitions were not forwarded to the Lt. Governor of Upper Canada for redress. To the contrary, the petitions were forwarded directly to the King and, after the accession of a Reform Government to power in Britain (in November 1830), to the Colonial Office and to the radical allies of the Reformers in Britain for submission directly to the House of Commons. In addition, in Upper Canada the Reformers organized extra-parliamentary societies and political conventions that set forth Reform Party policies and passed resolutions that, when forwarded to the British government, were presented as representing the views of 'the people' of Upper Canada.

Although the opposition groups -- who were aligned in the Reform Party in attacking the Tories -- adhered to decidedly different worldviews, as well as different views of religion and differing social values, they shared a common belief in individualism, popular sovereignty, and a common hostility towards the Tory establishment. They were aligned in continually attacking what they perceived as 'the enemy': the Tory establishment, which embodied, and upheld, the traditional order, the monarchical form of government, and its mainstay the established Church of England, and which was composed of 'educated gentlemen' of a superior social status.

Although the Reform Party encompassed liberal-Whig secularists from among the pre-war British immigrants and from among the Loyalists and their descendants – and at least one prominent Old Whig, William Warren Baldwin – the Reform Party of the late 1820s - early 1830s was not a British liberal-Whig party, nor was it animated by Lockean-liberal principles *per se*. The Reform Party leaders looked to the United States for their model of a system of democratic government with secular institutions. Moreover, in attacking the church-state alliance in Upper Canada, the Reformers based their arguments on the religious principles of American evangelical Protestantism -- 'religious equality', 'voluntaryism', and the 'separation of church and state' – and, oddly enough, even expressed an old fear of the American evangelical sects that a church establishment would lead invariably to 'ecclesiastical domination' and 'religious persecutions'.

The Reformers argued that Upper Canada was a new country, similar to the United States, to which secular democratic institutions were considered to be better suited than the British Constitution which was based on a social hierarchy and the union of Church and State. However, in demanding democratic institutions, the separation of church and state, and – after 1828 -- the implementation of the principle of 'responsible government', the Reformers refrained from any open attack on the British Constitution itself. Indeed, responsible government was presented to the public as a principle that would bestow 'the full workings' of the British Constitution upon Upper Canada, which was an argument that masked its revolutionary implications where the balance of the constitution was concerned.

From its inception during the early 1820s, the Reform Party was dominated by the democratic radicals and evangelical sectarians and imbued with American political ideas and evangelical religious principles, as was evident in the speeches of the Reform leaders in the House of Assembly. That political bias was evident as well in the party programme, which was set forth in the petitions that the extra-parliamentary societies of the Reform Party forwarded to Britain: viz. The Friends of Religious Liberty petition (December 1830), and the Canadian Alliance Society petition (December 1834). It was the growing recognition of the American democratic character of the Reform Party, and the threat that it was perceived to pose to the British Constitution and to the Unity of the Empire, that brought about the founding of the British Constitutional Society in Toronto. It was a society that was dedicated to maintaining the balanced British Constitution against political assaults emanating from the Reformers in the House of Assembly, and to the preservation of the British Imperial tie and its commercial benefits. It was a conservative organization; and, although not based on any deeper Tory values, the British Constitutional Society and its aims were strongly supported by the Upper Canadian Anglican Tories.

Through publications and loyalty appeals to the public, the British Constitutional Society succeeded in turning the liberal-Whigs – among the Loyalist descendants and the British settlers -- against the Reform Party. The Constitutionalists were highly successful in convincing the electorate that the June 1836 provincial election was a test of loyalty in pitting the upholders of monarchical government and the preservation of the Unity of the Empire against those who believed in American democratic republicanism and independence from the Empire. The result was a devastating defeat of the Reform Party at the polls, and the election of a large conservative majority in the House of Assembly.

Moreover, it was a conservative majority that was prepared to work with the Tory establishment in the Legislative Council and the Executive Council, in promoting the 'peace, order and good government' of Upper Canada.

Following the crushing defeat of the Reform Party in the June1836 Loyalty Election, the more moderate leaders of the Reform Party withdrew from active politics – inclusive of Marshall Spring Bidwell, and eventually William Warren Baldwin and his son, Robert Baldwin. As a result, the Reform Party came under the influence of the egalitarian democratic republicans of whom the most high-profile leader was the volatile William Lyon Mackenzie. During the early 1830s, the proponents of an egalitarian democratic republicanism had been a growing element in the Reform Party. They were a faction that was heavily influenced by egalitarian democratic ideas drawn from American Jacksonian democracy, Jeffersonian agrarianism, and the American revolutionary experience. The political ideas of the egalitarian democratic republicans were far more radical than anything that had been advocated earlier by the democratic radical element of the Reform Party of Upper Canada, or by the liberal-Whig Reformers and radicals in the British Parliament.

When the liberal-Whig Government in Britain -- in the spring of 1837 -- enacted the Ten Russell Resolution that rejected the principle of 'responsible government' as constituting a denial of the sovereignty of the Crown, Mackenzie and the egalitarian democratic republicans of the Reform Party entered upon an increasingly radical course. In July 1837, Mackenzie published a revolutionary document – Tom Paine's *Common Sense* (1776) -- that extolled the equality of all men, and that had called upon the American colonists to organize a Congress to seek their independence from Britain; and, in August 1837, the Toronto Reformers issued a "Declaration of the Reformers of the City of Toronto and their Fellow-Reformers in Upper Canada", that was based directly on the American Declaration of Independence. The Declaration called upon Upper Canadians to follow the American example and to hold a political convention to establish 'a cheap, honest and responsible government' such as the American people had achieved through a successful revolution. Nonetheless, Upper Canadians were assured that a revolution could be achieved 'without bloodshed'. It was argued that the British government would acquiesce in recognizing the political rights of Upper Canadians, and their political demands, once they were set forth by the people in a political convention. It was scheduled to be held in Toronto on the 31st of December 1837.

In preparation for the supposed peaceful political revolution, the Toronto Reformers prepared a draft Constitution (November 1837) to be considered for adoption by the proposed convention. The list of rights comprised the Lockean-liberal natural rights of the American Declaration of Independence, and the rights articulated subsequently by the various amendments to the American Constitution. Most of the civil rights were the same as 'the historic rights of Englishmen' already enjoyed by Upper Canadians under the British Constitution. The revolutionary element of the draft Constitution was the declaration of the complete separation of church and state, the principle of popular sovereignty, the right of rebellion, the right to bear arms, and the right to choose independence from Britain. Several specific Reform policies were included, such as a commitment to 'religious equality' which involved stripping the National Church of its prerogatives and the clergy reserves endowment, and the appropriation by the Legislature of all government revenues and Crown land endowments – the Crown Reserves of land, and the King's College land endowment – as well as the rejection of titles and honorary emoluments. It was a constitution that, if implemented, would have transformed Upper Canada into an independent egalitarian democratic republic, a sister republic to the United States of America.

In basing their 'Declaration of the Reformers of the City of Toronto' on the American Declaration of Independence, the Reformers adopted the basic principles of the political philosophy of John Locke However, the Toronto Reformers took the Lockean concepts of the inalienable natural rights of the individual to life, liberty and property, and of government originating in a compact based on the consent of the people, to their logical conclusion in declaring their belief in the natural equality of man and in a majoritarian democracy based on universal manhood suffrage. Hence, the demand of the Reformers for a unicameral legislature, and an elected Governor bound to carry out his executive responsibilities at the direction of the legislature. One oddity was the inclusion in the 'Declaration of the Reformers of Toronto' of a clause derived from the utilitarian philosophy of the British philosophical radicals (the Benthamites) to the effect that the purpose of government was to achieve 'the greatest happiness for the greatest number'.

It was but a short step from organizing a political convention to set forth the supposed political demands of 'the people' with the intent of bringing about a peaceful revolution in government, to the taking up of arms to achieve a revolution by force. Through the machinations of William Lyon Mackenzie, the egalitarian democratic republicans of the Reform Party were led into a hopeless rebellion in December 1837 that destroyed the Reform Party as a political force in Upper Canada.

In contrast to the Anglican Tories, the Reform Party was not philosophically oriented or possessed of a unified body of political thought. The political principles enunciated by the Reform Party were simply borrowed from the contemporary politics in the United States, and from the religious principles of the evangelical sectarians. Except for William Warren Baldwin, who thought about the Imperial relationship and introduced the novel concept of 'responsible government', the Upper Canadian Reformers simply borrowed whatever contemporary political ideas in the United States or Britain that were suited to advancing their political aims.

Only a very few educated 'gentlemen' adhered to the Reform Party. The most prominent were: Dr. John Rolph, who had been raised and educated as an Anglican before converting to the Methodist Episcopal Church; Marshall Spring Bidwell, a Congregationalist; Dr. William Warren Baldwin, an Anglo-Irish, Anglican-Whig immigrant, and his eldest son, Robert Baldwin, a tormented soul. Young Baldwin was inculcated with Anglican Tory values, beliefs and principles, by the Rev. John Strachan, as a youth at the Home District Grammar School, but he had liberal-Whig principles, and an alliance with the democratic radicals, imposed on him by his father who pressured his son to champion the Reform cause. In aligning himself with the Reform Party, young Baldwin alienated himself from his peers -- his former fellow students among the young Tory 'gentlemen' who were coming into power and prominence in the postwar period -- and from the distinguished Tory branch of the Baldwin family.

The Principle of 'Responsible Government'

It was in March 1828 that William Warren Baldwin introduced the novel principle of 'responsible government' into the politics of Upper Canada. It was initially expressed as a demand that the Lt. Governor 'govern the internal affairs of the province in keeping with the advice of his Executive Council', which was to be composed of members of the House of Assembly who could command the support of a majority in that House. In effect, under the principle of 'responsible government' -- if granted -- the provincial government would be under the control of the House of Assembly with the Lt. Governor required to follow the advice of his Executive Council on local matters.

Although the Whigs (Old Whigs and liberal-Whigs) were, at that time, a minor element in the Reform Party, the principle of 'responsible government' was seized upon by the Reform Party as a single-issue political demand that would provide a means of attaining political power, of gaining control over government patronage appointments, and of ousting the provincial Tory establishment from public office. Moreover, the principle of responsible government provided the various opposition groups in Upper Canada with an overriding unity, and some coherence, within the Reform Party. The Reformers sought to legitimize their grasp for power by claiming that they, and they alone, represented 'the wishes of the people', and that the principle of 'responsible government' was a legitimate reform that was needed to bring the constitution of Upper Canada into accordance with the British Constitution as it functioned in Britain.

What the Reformers were demanding with their principle of 'responsible government' was not actually in keeping with how the British Constitution functioned. In Britain, ministers, with but few exceptions, were appointed from the House of Lords (the landed estates); and the electorate was based on a very limited property franchise. The 'common people' --and before 1832 even the middle class -- lacked the vote. According to an Old Whig, Edmund Burke, the various interests of the realm enjoyed a 'virtual representation' in the House of Commons through the members of parliament representing the various interests of the realm, but that claim ignored the fact the many members owed their election to the influence of a noble patron or to being nominated to stand for a proprietorial borough under the control of a noble family, and were not free to vote according to their own wishes.

In contrast in Upper Canada -- under the 40-shilling property franchise with the ready availability of land grants -- almost every British subject resident in the province held the vote. Hence, the implementation of the principle of 'responsible government' -- in making the provincial administration dependent on the support of a majority in the House of Assembly to hold office -- would have transformed the Province of Upper Canada into a majoritarian democracy. The government would be subject to the will of the majority as expressed at provincial elections. In effect, what the Reformers were seeking was a revolutionary change in government through the introduction of the principle of a local popular sovereignty within the British Empire.

More generally, the Tories were opposed to the principle of 'responsible government' because it was a principle that was destructive of the legislative balance of the British constitution and a denial of the sovereignty of the Crown. If the principle of 'responsible government' were implemented, the Lt. Governor would have to take the advice of the Executive Council on local matters and would have to appoint his advisors from among the members of the House of Assembly who were able to command a majority in that legislative body. In effect, the Constitution of 1791 – the constitution of Upper Canada – would be totally overthrown. Under the principle of 'responsible government', the House of Assembly would become the sovereign power in local matters, and the participation in government of the landed or property interest in the form of the appointed 'gentlemen' in the Legislative Council would be rendered nugatory. It would result in a partisan party government with the leaders of the majority party in the House of Assembly governing the province.

For the Tories, sovereignty resided in the Crown, and not with the populace. The concept of 'responsible government' was a denial of the Tory concept of the Crown exercising the sovereign power for the promotion of the common good and the well-being of 'the nation'. It also ran counter to the Tory belief in government by an educated elite—

Christian 'gentlemen' -- of sound moral values that would serve the common good of the nation in the Legislature through election to the House of Assembly and through appointment to the Legislative Council. Moreover, it was Christian 'gentlemen' who, upon appointment to the Executive Council, would provide sound advice to the Lt. Governor in support of the common good and the 'national interest' in rising above partisan politics and the sectional interests.

The Whigs & liberal-Whigs

There were liberal-Whigs among the Loyalists and their descendants and among the British immigrants, who were supporters of the Reform Party during the 1820s, as well as some Old Whigs such as the Anglo-Irish immigrant, Dr. William Warren Baldwin, who aligned themselves with the Reform Party.

William Warren Baldwin (1775-1844) was a 'gentleman', a well-educated lawyer, a doctor (University of Edinburgh, 1797), a judge, and a major land speculator of substantial wealth in Upper Canada. He was born in County Cork, Ireland, and was a member of an Anglican family of the Anglo-Irish gentry that had emigrated from Ireland in 1798 to escape a growing political unrest that culminated in the rebellion of the United Irishmen latter in that year. Baldwin, a resident of York (Toronto), was elected to the House of Assembly in 1820, as a declared supporter of 'the British Constitution' and 'British liberty' (as distinct from a belief in Lockean inalienable natural rights). During the Eighth Parliament (1821-1824), he spoke in favour of the retention of primogeniture and of a landed aristocracy as the strongest supports of the freedoms guaranteed by the British Constitution. He denounced democracy, called for retrenchment in government expenditures, and made clear his belief in local self-government for Upper Canada, the separation of church and state, and a natural hierarchical society. Moreover, he called for a repeal of the Sedition Act of 1804, which had been used to banish the Scots-immigrant agitator, Robert Gourlay, from Upper Canada. In all respects, William Warren Baldwin was a classic Old Whig parliamentarian. (2)

It was in keeping with his belief in local self-government that Baldwin developed his concept of the principle of responsible government that was adopted by the Reform Party and brought him into a close association with that Party and its radical politics. Elected again to the Assembly during the 1828 provincial election as a Reformer, Baldwin came to be viewed as the senior statesman of the party who added an aura of respectability to the Reform alliance which was lacking in support from respectable gentlemen. Baldwin lost his seat in the October 1830 election, and after the coming to power of a liberal-Whig Reform government in Britain in November 1830, he shifted his attention to the Imperial Parliament. In following the tactics of British political radicals, he began to organize and finance a series of extra-parliamentary societies with the aim of rousing public opinion in favour of Reform Party policies. The ultimate aim was to forward massive petitions to the House of Commons to convince the Reform Government in Britain to implement the principle of responsible government in Upper Canada, and to institute a complete separation of church and state in the province.

William Warren Baldwin was instrumental in organizing and financing several extra-parliamentary associations: the Friends of Religious Liberty (December 1830); the Canadian Alliance Society (December 1834); and subsequently, the Toronto Political Union (October 1836). In each of these endeavours, he worked closely with the leading democratic radicals of the Reform Party, and their allies among the evangelical sectarians, in promoting Reform Party policies. His close association with the democratic radicals of the Reform Party, and his willingness to promote their democratic political principles and evangelical religious principles, marks a curious evolution for an Old Whig. However, not all Whigs were able to bring themselves to support the Reform Party of Upper Canada as it became more and more radical in its political program.

During the early 1830s, the number of liberal-Whigs in Upper Canada increased rapidly with a large influx of British immigrant dissenters from the urban areas of Britain. Initially, the liberal-Whigs were not a strong political factor in Upper Canada. The new settlers concentrated on clearing and farming their land and could not vote until they completed their settlement duties and gained full title to their land. The British immigrant liberal-Whigs were arguably the largest political group in Upper Canada as of the mid-1830s.

The British immigrant liberal-Whigs tended to support the Reform Party, but they could not support the Reformers after the December 1834 publication of the Canadian Alliance Society platform which associated the Reform Party with American democratic republicanism and the overthrow of the British Constitution and the social order. Moreover, that was similarly the case with the liberal-Whigs among the Loyalists and their descendants who had supported the Reform Party as recently as the October 1834 provincial election that had resulted in a solid Reform majority in the House of Assembly. (A contributing electoral factor was the Reform Party declaring its support for tariffs on imports of American farm produce which the Tories opposed in wanting to attract American grain shipments for export through the newly-constructed Welland Canal and the St. Lawrence River commercial transport system.)

It was the Loyalty Election of June 1836 that brought the defection of the Loyalist liberal-Whigs of Upper Canada from the Reform Party, and the entry of the British immigrant liberal-Whigs into politics in large numbers. In that election, the liberal-Whigs combined with conservatives of all stripes – under the banner of the British Constitutional Society -- to defend the British Constitution and Imperial Unity. Moreover, the Reform Party principle of responsible government was rejected as it had come to be viewed by the liberal-Whigs – through the efforts of the British Constitutional Society -- as a denial of the sovereignty of the King in Parliament and as being destructive of the union of the British Empire.

The Democratic Radicals

The democratic radicals were a major element in the Reform Party of Upper Canada who wanted democratic elective institutions to make government more responsive to 'the people'. Among the democratic radicals were some descendants of the Loyalists as well as American settlers, but they differed in their ultimate objectives. The Loyalist supporters among the democratic radicals wanted a more democratic form of government within the existing limited constitutional monarchy of Upper Canada, but they remained loyal to the Crown and the Unity of the British Empire. In contrast, the American settlers among the democratic radicals looked to the United States for their ideal form of government and were a disaffected element within the Province. In the

House of Assembly, the leader of the democratic radicals was Marshall Spring Bidwell, an American immigrant, a lawyer, and a Jeffersonian agrarian democrat. Bidwell emerged as one of the leaders of the Reform Party during the Alien Question agitation of the early 1820s, and as the undisputed leader of the Reform Party thereafter.

The democratic radicals were united in their demand for democratic elective institutions, and – after 1828 – in their support for the principle of 'responsible government', until the period of the Loyalty Election of June 1836. At that time, the democratic radicals of Loyalist descent voted in large numbers in support of the British Constitution and the Unity of Empire, and in December 1837 turned out again in large numbers under the local Tory political leaders to defend Her Majesty's Provincial Government against the rebel uprising led by William Lyon Mackenzie. In contrast, it was the democratic radicals among the non-Loyalist American settlers who continued to support the Reform Party in the June 1836 Loyalty Election, and who sympathized with the Mackenzie rebels of the December 1837 Rebellion.

The democratic radicals of the Reform Party were focused on local and sectional issues, and the redress of particular 'grievances' – real or imagined – and lacked any overriding concept of a national interest or of a common good that transcended their immediate concerns. Moreover, in contrast to the Tories, the democratic radicals lacked any concern for the maintenance of public order or for social harmony as evidenced by their deliberate efforts to foster political unrest and to foment public agitations that disturbed the peace of society. Through their political machinations, they placed the different 'interests' within society in conflict, and deliberately fostered ill-will, discontent and disaffection among the populace.

The democratic radicals were bereft of a national vision for the future of Upper Canada. They had no policies for developing a national character for the province, or for encouraging its economic development. They borrowed their political ideas from American politics and were oblivious to the threat posed to the future survival of Upper Canada -- as a separate political entity in North America -- by the growing power and aggressive expansionism of the new democratic republic, the United States of

America. The democratic radicals believed in laissez-faire government, were averse to government levying direct taxes for public purposes – such as for the support of schools -- and their ideal society was agrarian and composed of independent yeomen farmers.

The Evangelical Sectarians

The evangelical sectarians were another major group supporting the Reform Party; although there was an overlap with the democratic radicals of whom many were evangelical sectarians. Among the evangelical sectarian Reformers, the most outspoken were the 'American Methodists'. They sought, in the name of their religious principles of 'religious equality', 'voluntaryism', and the 'separation of church and state', to strip the Church of England of its endowments and prerogatives and even of its establishment status. The itinerant preachers of the 'American Methodists' were not only strong supporters of the Reform Party but were political activists who fostered -- among their adherents -- a belief in political activism which was based on their religious principles.

The leading spokesperson for the evangelical sectarians was the Rev. Egerton Ryerson who, although raised and educated in a staunch Anglican Tory-Loyalist family, was converted as a young adult to the Methodist Episcopal Church under the influence of 'American Methodist' circuit-riding preachers. Ryerson was a zealous convert who became a Methodist circuit-riding preacher, a Methodist newspaper editor (*Christian Guardian*), and a highly-skilled polemicist who articulated the religious principles and beliefs of the evangelical sectarians. Ryerson not only sought to undermine the Church of England establishment in his religious writings, but he colluded with the democratic radicals of the Reform Party in preparing Assembly bills that attacked the legitimacy of the Church of England establishment, the claim of the Church of England to the clergy reserves revenues, and the unity of church and state in Upper Canada.

Ryerson worked closely also with the democratic radicals in the drafting of petitions for circulation and submission to the House of Assembly, the Crown, and the House of Commons in Britain, on religious issues. However, at the time of the June 1836 Loyalty Election, and subsequently during the December 1837 coup d'état attempt by the Reformers – principally by the egalitarian democratic republican element of the Reform Party -- Ryerson emerged as a strong public supporter of Her Majesty's Provincial Government in keeping with his Loyalist heritage. The position of Ryerson at that time was in direct contrast to his 'American Methodist' co-religionists among the American settlers, who were strong supporters of Mackenzie, as distinct from the English Wesleyan Methodists who were staunch supporters of Her Majesty's Provincial Government.

In the postwar politics of Upper Canada, the 'American Methodists' wielded a political influence, and an electoral clout, that was far greater than their numbers would suggest. In the decades prior to the War of 1812, the 'American Methodists' were the largest religious denomination in the province, and probably accounted for a slight majority of the population. However, with the heavy postwar influx of British immigrants, the 'American Methodists' were soon reduced to a minority group in the provincial population. However, in a pioneer farming community, where families were living on isolated clearing in the bush and struggling to clear the land, there was little incentive to get involved in politics, or to trudge miles through the bush to vote in a provincial election. In contrast, the 'American Methodists' were highly motivated by their religious zeal, their religious principles, and their religious duty of political activism, to make the effort to vote to defeat 'the enemy': the Church-State establishment of the Province of Upper Canada. Moreover, with their system of itinerant preachers and camp meetings, the 'American Methodists' could be readily energized to vote by the circuit-riding preachers who stirred up a religious fervor through emotional appeals to deeply-held religious principles and feelings of resentment at the social status of the members of the Tory establishment.

It was the support of the evangelical sectarians that enabled the democratic radicals to make the distribution of the clergy reserves revenues a major political issue with the sectarian preachers rallying their adherents to turn out the vote. That effort resulted in the so-called "Saddlebags parliament" – the Tenth Parliament of 1829-1830 – which was dominated by 'American Methodist' members. In contrast, the conservative forces failed to realize the importance of appealing directly the electorate. It was a period in which -- by the early 1830s -- public opinion was becoming a significant factor in the politics of the province, concomitant with the growth of literacy among the populace. Prior to the War of 1812, the Tories of Upper Canada had published numerous missives appealing to the patriotism of Upper Canadians to resist a threatening American invasion. They had done so to combat a defeatist mentality that was gaining ground in the province, and that was based on a belief in the futility of any resistance to an American invasion. However, in the postwar years, the Tories were slow to revive that earlier approach of appealing directly to the people on public issues.

Political campaigning and catering to the electorate was anathema to the Tories. Ultimately, many Tories did support the British Constitutional Society during the critical June 1836 Loyalty Election, and Anglican Tories did play a leading role in that campaign. However, other leading Tories, such as John Beverley Robinson, continued to feel an unease about 'gentlemen' engaging in political electioneering. Under the umbrella of the British Constitutional Society, the conservative forces of the province held public meetings, circulated political tracts, published election addresses, and canvassed conservatives to get out the vote in support of the maintenance of the British Constitution, loyalty to the King, and the Unity of Empire, and, in doing so, to reject the Reform Party concept of 'responsible government'. As a result, the Reform Party suffered a devastating defeat at the polls, despite the electoral support of their 'American Methodist' allies.

The Egalitarian Democratic Republicans

The egalitarian democratic republicans emerged as a recognizable element within the Reform Party during the early-1830s in articulating their distinctive political ideas. They were admirers of Jeffersonian agrarian republicanism and Jacksonian Democracy in the United States and wanted to foment a social revolution in Upper Canada through establishing an egalitarian democratic republic of small independent farmers. It was the egalitarian democratic republicans, under the volatile leadership of William Lyon Mackenzie, who rebelled in December 1837 in a futile attempt to establish -- by force of arms -- an independent democratic republic on the American model: the projected 'State of Upper Canada'. Mackenzie, a Secessionist-Presbyterian, Scots immigrant, was regarded by the Tories – and by many non-Tories – as 'a grievance monger, and an outright demagogue'.

The political principles and social values of the egalitarian democratic republicans were taken directly from American politics of the era, and from American constitutional history. William Lyon Mackenzie was an ardent admirer of the self-evident natural rights, and popular sovereignty of the American Constitution, as well as of Jeffersonian agrarianism, and the political and social egalitarianism of Jacksonian Democracy. Mackenzie admired what he perceived to be the simplicity and frugality of 'the governments of farmers' in the American frontier states, American universal manhood suffrage (which, in the United States, excluded Blacks and Indians), American elective institutions at all levels of government, and what he regarded as 'American civil and religious liberty' in the separation of church and state. He called for the independence of Upper Canada from the British Empire, and the establishment of a government on the American model. Moreover, Mackenzie called for the adoption of the policies of the administration of President Andrew Jackson (March 1829-March 1837) which included an opposition to banks, to paper money, to government involvement in economic development projects, and an end to imprisonment for debt. Indeed, Mackenzie was prepared to adopt even the Jacksonian 'spoils system' as a way of removing the Tories from their public positions after an election.

As a political movement, egalitarian democratic republicanism represented the extrapolation of the Lockean-liberal belief in the compact theory of the origin of government and society, and the belief in the inalienable natural rights pertaining to man as an individual, to their logical conclusion: a belief in popular sovereignty – universal male suffrage -- an egalitarian society, and a democratic government of the common man with a government following the general will as expressed by the vote of the majority. As such, those who adhered to the beliefs and principles of egalitarian democratic republicanism were a direct threat to the Tory political establishment, to the Tory concept of government by an educated elite of cultured Christian gentlemen, to the balanced British Constitution, and to the 'natural' social hierarchy of the Province of Upper Canada.

Egalitarian democratic republicanism was a totally foreign import into Upper Canada. It enjoyed little adherence among the public at large as indicated by the lack of support for, and rapid collapse of, the attempted coup d'état by William Lyon Mackenzie in December 1837.

It was only through misleading his sympathizers as to the extent to which the Reformers of Upper Canada would support a rebellion, and as to the supposed ease with which a coup d'état could be carried out 'without bloodshed', that Mackenzie was able to marshal what little support he did receive for the rebel march on Toronto. In contrast, the Anglican Tories received the support of almost the entire province in taking the lead to defend Her Majesty's Provincial Government, and they were highly successful in rallying Upper Canadians to resist the rebels. In doing so, it was the Anglican Tories who played a critical role – as they had during the War of 1812 -- in preserving Upper Canada as a province of the British Empire, and who prevented the establishment of an independent democratic republic – the State of Upper Canada – which, more than likely, would have joined the American Union soon after becoming independent.

With the collapse of the attempted coup d'état, the egalitarian democratic republicans were thoroughly discredited, and destroyed as a political force in Upper Canada. With the leaders of that faction having fled to the United States, their followers were left disillusioned and disheartened. It was a political movement that no longer posed a threat to the Tory establishment in Upper Canada. Egalitarian democratic republicanism was a body of political thought derived from contemporary American politics. It embodied the very antithesis of the constitutional principles and the political, social and religious values, on which the Loyalist Province of Upper Canada was founded.

Political Alignments in Upper Canada

None of the opposition groups were mutually exclusive or drew their members exclusively from but one social or religious segment of society, or any one class or occupation. Generally-speaking, Loyalist families and British immigrants were well-represented among the supporters of the Tory establishment as well as among the liberal-Whig Reformers, and Loyalist descendants were found among the democratic radicals. The egalitarian democratic republicans, under the leadership of

William Lyon Mackenzie, drew their active support mainly from among the American settlers in Upper Canada who were mostly 'American Methodists' or 'infidels' (men of no religious affiliation), but included Free-will Baptists, Independent Congregationalists, Unitarians, Hicksite-Quakers, and members of a Children of Peace sect. The egalitarian democratic republicans were supported as well by the Irish Roman Catholic immigrants.

In contrast, the core of the Tory establishment was composed, for the most part, of the native-born sons of Loyalists and the native-born sons of the early pre-War British immigrants. The Tory establishment received support from among the more recent heavy influx of rural British immigrants, as well as from the retired half-pay officers of the British Army and the Royal Navy, and the post-War of 1812 soldier-settlers. When defending the British Constitution and the unity of the British Empire, the Tories also received the support of the British immigrant liberal-Whigs who came from urban areas of Britain where the dissenting churches and manufacturing interests were strong.

Among the supporters of Mackenzie were tradesmen, adherents of the evangelical sects, radical newspaper editors, land speculators and some merchants, workers in manufacturing enterprises, as well as farmers, who were heavily represented, but not exclusively so. Most of the Tory supporters were also farmers, given the composition of Upper Canadian society at that time. Most of the rebel leaders were from the American-settled areas of the province, and were doctors and lawyers or both, except for Mackenzie who was a radical newspaper owner/editor.

The Tory leaders were men of a superior education and held the social status of a 'gentlemen'. They predominated in public positions within the institutions of the traditional church-state polity: in the provincial government, in the judiciary, in the legal profession, and in the established National Church, as well as in mercantile pursuits. The Tories were upholders of the church-state alliance and the prerogatives and endowments of the Church of England, the balanced British Constitution, and the sovereignty of the Crown, and were supported by the more 'respectable element' of the population in the towns, villages and settlements of the province.

Conclusion

Except for several liberal-Whig leaders of the Reform Party -- who were lawyers and doctors or both -- the various opposition groups were composed mostly of men of a lower social status, and of a general lack of education, who resented the social status of the Tory 'gentlemen', their learning, and the political power and patronage that the Tories enjoyed. The disaffected aligned themselves under the umbrella of the Reform Party, and its principle of 'responsible government' which was viewed as a means of wresting political power, and control over government revenues and patronage appointments, from the hands of the Tory establishment. In Upper Canada, social status was a factor in determining political behavior, but the main determinants of political behavior were the political principles and beliefs of the various groups which were largely derived from their religious beliefs and, for the irreligious, from the political ideas that they had been acquired in their country of origin.

Where religion was concerned, members of the evangelical sects – generally speaking, the 'American Methodists', Free-Will Baptists, and Independent or Separate Congregationalists -- supported the democratic radicals, and the egalitarian democratic republicans similarly drew most of their support primarily from among the evangelical Protestant sects in the American-settled areas. The sectarians who rejected egalitarian democratic republicanism were from the Loyalist families who remained loyal to the British constitution and the Unity of Empire, as illustrated by the results of the June 1836 Loyalty Election and the massive turnout of 'the loyal' in the suppression of the attempted rebel coup d'état of December 1837. That was similarly the case with the Black communities of Upper Canada who rallied to the support of the government during the Loyalty Election and the rebellion period.

Although the Upper Canadian Blacks were adherents generally of either the Free-will Baptist or 'American Methodist' sects, they were adamantly opposed to Mackenzie's egalitarian democratic republicanism. They feared that if an independent democratic republic were established in Upper Canada, the new republic might well join the American Union. The Black communities saw themselves as being dependent on the British government and the Unity of the Empire for their freedom and security. They were staunchly loyal to the Crown and were opposed to the attempted coup d'état of William Lyon Mackenzie.

The traditional churches were supporters of the provincial government and the established traditional order. The political establishment was largely composed of native-born Anglicans, but it included Church of Scotland adherents and prominent Scots and French-Canadian Roman Catholics from their respective areas of concentrated settlement. Generally-speaking, the Anglican Tory establishment enjoyed the support of the members of the established Church of England, the Scots and English members of the established Roman Catholic Church, and the adherents of the Church of Scotland, the Lutheran Church, and the English Wesleyan Methodists; although divisions appeared over two public issues: the distribution of the clergy reserves revenues, and the establishment of 44 Church of England rectories by the Lt. Governor, Sir John Colborne, in January 1836.

Appointments to the Legislative Council, to government offices, the bench and the magistracy, were distributed among the members of the traditional churches. Candidates for appointment to public positions were assessed on their moral character and education, with attention being paid to the individual's social standing – his status as a 'gentleman' – his professional standing, and leadership role in the local community. In evaluating candidates for appointment to government positions, a decided preference was given to 'the loyal' who had proven their loyalty in the fighting of the War of 1812, and there was also a nativist factor. Under the Tory regime, a preference was given to appointing native-born Upper Canadians over British immigrants of equal character, stature, education and qualifications. In sum, the Tory establishment was composed for the most part of the 'respectable' subjects of the Crown in Upper Canada who were well-educated, who tended to be native born, and many of whom were adherents of the established Church of England.

There were some Anglicans among the democratic radicals, but very few, if any, among the egalitarian democratic republicans with but one glaring exception: Dr. John Rolph, an English immigrant. He was raised and educated in a staunch Anglican-Tory family, but became a democratic radical following a sojourn (1809-1812) in studying law at the Inner Temple in London, England. Following his entry into politics in Upper Canada as a democratic radical, Rolph attended the Methodist Episcopal Church. Rolph was recognized as a leading democratic radical within the Reform Party, which was under the leadership of Marshal Spring Bidwell, an American immigrant. They were close associates during the political agitations of the 1820s but took a different path with the emergence of the egalitarian democratic republican movement of the early 1830s. Rolph embraced egalitarian democratic republicanism. He surreptitiously supported Mackenzie in his plans for a coup d'état but kept aloof publicly. In contrast, Bidwell left politics following the devastating defeat of the Reform Party in the Loyalty Election of June 1836, and broke with Mackenzie when the latter began to call upon Upper Canadians to rebel and establish an independent democratic republic in Upper Canada.

Most of the rebel supporters of the failed coup d'état of December 1837 were from the American-settled areas of Upper Canada and were staunch members of the Reform Party. With several notable exceptions -- the Baldwins (father and son), Marshall Spring Bidwell, and Peter Perry -- the leaders of the Reform Party were well represented among the leaders of the attempted coup d'état, inclusive of Reform Party members of the House of Assembly. Moreover, adherents of the evangelical religious sects were heavily represented among the rebels from the American-settled areas.

The character of politics in Upper Canada conforms closely to what an American cultural historian, Robert Kelley (*The Transatlantic Persuasion: The Liberal-Democratic Mind in the Age of Gladstone*, 1969) has identified as being typical of the political behavior of various 'outgroups' -- in Britain, the United States and Canada, during the later course of the 19th Century. It was a period when outgroups aligned themselves together, under the "Liberal and Democratic banners", to attack the governing establishment of their country. The various outgroups, according to Kelley, had a very narrow outlook, often held mutually antagonistic views, and commonly engaged in single-issue politics, but were united in "their image of the enemy": the traditional 'authoritarian political establishment', and a social order that effectively excluded members of the outgroups from political power and influence. Moreover, the political elite provoked a resentment on the part of members of the various outgroups for its social status, education, occupation of public offices, and its influence over government programmes and patronage. (3) Such aggressive behavior was typical of the various outgroups in Upper Canada during the early 19th Century, who united under the umbrella of the Reform Party to espouse seemingly 'liberal and democratic' ideas in uniting to attack the Tory establishment. Among the supporters of the Reform Party of Upper Canada, there were few men of a social standing and education approaching that of the 'gentlemen' of the Tory establishment.

In the Reform Party, the few patrician leaders – such as the Baldwins, father and son -- had little in common in terms of education, literacy, culture or social status with the democratic radical Reformers, and practically nothing in common with the egalitarian democratic republican Reformers, such as William Lyon Mackenzie. Similarly, the British immigrant liberal-Whigs had little in common with the American settlers of the evangelical Protestant sects, and their self-proclaimed and generally poorly-educated preachers. However, the various outgroups were aligned together in attacking the Tory establishment and the church-state union, and in seeking to strip the established Church of England of its endowments and prerogatives. They were united in their view of a common 'enemy': the Tory establishment, that stood between them and their desired attainment of political power and control over government revenues and patronage, as well as over the clergy reserves endowment and revenues.

American Evangelical Protestantism

In Upper Canada, the Tories were totally opposed to the evangelical religious sects ever attaining a predominance of power in the province because of their adverse cultural values: religious, social, and political. In seeking to exclude American settlers from Upper Canada in the immediate postwar period – the politics of the Alien Question -- the Tories were concerned not only with the Lockean-liberal political principles of prospective American settlers, but equally important – and perhaps more so – with the evangelical religious principles, beliefs, and values of the American frontier population.

The Upper Canadian Tories were acutely conscious of the revolutionary nature of the social, political, and religious values and beliefs of evangelical sectarians, and the past fervent participation of the religious sectarians in the American Revolution. The evangelical religious threat, that the Upper Canadian Tories faced in the post-War of 1812 period, was a product of the evolution of American evangelical Protestantism from the Great Awakening (1730s-1740s) in the American colonies, through the politicization of the evangelical sects during the American Revolution (1776-1783), and their social transformation during the Second Great Awakening (1790s-1820s) in the northern United States.

The Upper Canadian Tory view of the role of religious dissenters and the evangelical sectarians in facilitating and supporting the American Revolution was by no means exaggerated, as more recent studies have confirmed. In a groundbreaking work, an American historian and Professor of American Literature, the late Alan Heimert (*Religion and the American Mind,* 1969), has argued that the evangelical sectarians played a major role in the success of the American Revolution. In that conflict, the orthodox clergy of the Congregational churches of New England were rather reluctant to support the American revolutionaries, but they had done so in citing Lockean-liberal principles; whereas the American Revolution, as a popular movement, drew its inspiration from the religious values of the evangelical Calvinist religious sects which were founded in the American colonies during the Great Awakening, prior to the Revolution.

As argued by Heimert, the religious revivals of the Great Awakening that spread throughout the American colonies, had fostered "independence and rebellion" in their wake. Not only did the evangelical Calvinist preachers of the Great Awakening harbour an ingrained aversion to monarchy (which was derived from their Puritan origins), but, according to Heimert, they "provided pre-Revolutionary America with a radical, even democratic, social and political ideology". Moreover, it was a political ideology, which was rooted in their religious beliefs and worldview, and which the evangelical Calvinists felt compelled -- by their concept of political activism -- to impose 'on the minds and wills' of their fellow American colonists. It was their religious principles and commitment to political activism that accounts for the strong support of the evangelical Calvinists for the revolutionary cause during the American Revolution.

The Great Awakening (1730s-1740s)

The major instigator of the Great Awakening, and the theologian who defined the religious beliefs of the evangelical Calvinists, was the Rev. Jonathan Edwards (1703-1758), a Yale University graduate (MA, 1723) and an ordained minister of the established Congregational Church of the Massachusetts Bay Colony. As a young minister, Edwards was appalled at a growing materialism, rationalism, and deism in 18th Century New England, and the spread of a rationalist natural religion in the Congregational Church. In response, the Rev. Edwards focused his preaching on the traditional covenant theology of the earlier Puritan tradition, divine Revelation, and the Christian faith. He sought to spread 'the Word' to the people in preaching at religious revivals where he engaged in an emotional style of preaching that was aimed at awakening a hunger for redemption in the hearts of his hearers. Through his emotive preaching at religious revivals, and his writings on theology, it was Edwards who shaped the evolution of a new religious movement: evangelical Calvinism.

Edwards rejected the Calvinist doctrine that God had eternally predestined some men to salvation through a free grant of His saving grace, and that others were predestined for eternal damnation. To the contrary, Edwards held that 'fallen man', although totally depraved, still possessed a rational element and could be redeemed if he had a faith in Christ and hungered in his heart after God's mercy and saving Grace.

For Edwards, conversion was an instantaneous experience, instigated by hearing the Word of God preached, in which the entire character of man became totally transformed upon the Holy Spirit entering the heart in conveying God's saving grace. It was a New Birth in which the regenerated felt a joyful and rapturous feeling of spiritual rebirth, and godliness in being cleansed of sin and embraced by God in a covenant of grace that promised eternal life (salvation) and an escape from the fires of hell. Rebirth brought the regenerated into a communion with their fellow 'saints' who had been called into the faith, who had received God's grace, and who were living a godly life in obedience to God's Will as revealed in Scripture. During the Great Awakening, instantaneous conversion and rebirth became the key doctrines of the evangelical

Calvinist sects, together with a belief in the central role of emotion in the religious conversion experience (rather than rational thought), and a belief in a coming millennium as conceptualized by Jonathan Edwards.

Edwards continued to believe in predestination, but not with respect to an eternally predestined salvation of individuals, but rather with respect to the future salvation of mankind. He rejected the cataclysmic concept of a Battle of Armageddon bringing about the defeat of evil by God immediately preceding the Second Coming of Christ. He substituted a view of redeemed man as progressing towards an earthy millennium that, once established with the coming of Christ, would bring a thousand years of felicity for 'the reborn' -- in living with Christ, in obedience to the Will of God, before the Day of Judgement. It was a belief that in God's grand design, the work of Creation, the actions of Providence, and the bestowals of God's grace, were moving mankind towards a predestined good – the happiness of God's people in His Earthly Kingdom: "the Kingdom of Light". It was a gradual process which man could not alter, but the work of redemption could be facilitated and accelerated through the evangelical clergy preaching the Word, holding religious revivals, and propagating the Gospels. The purpose was to awaken in the heart of all hearers, a hunger for God's mercy and saving Grace, and a faith in Christ, that would further the work of the Holy Spirit in regenerating humanity worldwide.

For Edwards, it was the collective will of the people that would bring about the Lord's Kingdom, and in his optimism -- born of the widespread success of Great Awakening in the American colonies -- he preached that the millennial society was approaching and would fulfill God's grand design. What was envisaged was not a society of material wealth, but a millennial society that embodied a union of the redeemed – the saints – in a 'kingdom of light and love' wherein holiness, purity of morals, peace and happiness would reign. Public virtue was defined as 'love to being in general'-- a love of mankind. The evangelical Calvinists looked not to Nature for God's Moral Law, or to the institutions and laws of man to guide their conduct, but rather to Biblical revelation and the Holy Spirit 'within the hearts and minds' of the saints who had been redeemed and transformed by God's saving grace.

Alarmed by the emotional preaching of the Rev. Edwards, and his insistence on the necessity of 'natural man' (depraved fallen man) undergoing a rebirth (New Birth) to live a godly life of faith and to participate in the sacrament of communion, the Congregational Church expelled Edwards from his pulpit. In a further effort to stem the spread of evangelical Calvinism among the people – which was expanding rapidly amongst the lower orders -- the established Congregational Church in the Massachusetts Bay Colony and Connecticut sought to enforce church attendance and the collection of tithes – through the colonial governments levying fines—and refused to recognize any right of members of a congregation to 'break the covenant' and withdraw from the established Congregational Church.

In response, the evangelical Calvinist preachers proclaimed a 'right of private judgement' (the right to decide on one's personal religious beliefs), a right to 'religious liberty' (the right to preach their own religious beliefs and to leave the local congregation of the established Congregational Church), and a right of 'religious equality' (an equal right to establish new evangelical congregations in keeping with the right that the orthodox Congregational Church enjoyed to establish new congregations, without suffering any religious or political impediments). The exercise of the latter right led to the founding of several different independent evangelical sects among which were the Separate Congregationalist (or New Light Congregationalist) congregations.

With their strong stress on action by 'the will of the people' in all religious affairs, and a parallel preference for a democratic form of government within their congregations, the evangelical Calvinist preachers and their congregations embodied a radical challenge to the existing religious order in Colonial America, as well as to the social and political order. Once they had committed themselves to militant action to achieve the millennial society -- the Kingdom of God on Earth – evangelical Calvinism became a potent revolutionary force in America. This was particularly so when the evangelical Calvinist preachers came to preach that the millennium would be attained when political power was in the hands of God's people – the saints -- and began to view the traditional political establishment, the hierarchical social order, and the established churches, as an impediment to the achievement of the Kingdom of God on Earth and a threat to the civil and religious liberties of God's people. Moreover, during the 1760s when the British government proposed to establish a Church of England bishopric in the American colonies, the evangelical Calvinists had reacted aggressively in opposing that initiative. They declared their fear that an episcopacy would lead to 'ecclesiastical tyranny' and 'ecclesiastical domination', and that fear in turn had become part of the evangelical mentality.

The American Revolution

With the onset of the American Revolution, the 'religious liberty' principle of the evangelical Calvinists became identified with the 'political liberty' slogan of the American revolutionaries. In the process, King George III came to be branded as a 'tyrant' who was conceived of as being a diabolical opponent of liberty and the law of love, and as an 'anti-Christ' who had to be overthrown 'by God's people' to free America from European corruption. For the evangelical Calvinists, the American revolutionary struggle was transformed into a religious and moral crusade to bring about the 'state of perfect freedom and happiness' which, they believed, would usher in the millennium – God's Earthly Kingdom of Light – following the revolution.

During the American Revolution, the evangelical Calvinist preachers and the members of their congregations were among the most ardent supporters of the revolutionaries, and evangelical Calvinists were well-represented in the ranks of the Continental Army. Moreover, at the conclusion of the revolutionary war, it was the evangelical sectarians who were in the forefront in persecuting and driving out the Loyalists in keeping with a new religious doctrine of 'retributive justice' that called upon 'the saints' to punish the unredeemed and to oust them from the new republic preparatory to attaining the millenarian union of love in God's Earthly Kingdom. The evangelical Calvinists were characterized by a tendency to view anyone whom they perceived as presenting an impediment to the attainment of the rule of the saints, as being an 'enemy' or a 'tyrant'. (4)

The Second Great Awakening

During the Second Great Awakening (1790-1820), American evangelical Protestantism was led by the 'American Methodists' and Free-Will Baptists and differed in its political and social character from the earlier evangelical Calvinism, as well as in the nature of the instantaneous conversion experience. The evangelical sectarians of the new wave of religious revivals retained the religious principles of the earlier evangelical Calvinism – a belief in 'religious equality', 'religious liberty', and 'the right of private judgement' – as well as a hostility to church establishments which were associated with 'ecclesiastical domination' and 'ecclesiastical tyranny'. To these earlier religious principles and attitudes were added an ardent belief in the religious principles of 'voluntaryism' and 'the separation of church and state', a strong antipathy to monarchical government, and a novel 'democratic levelling spirit' that was hostile to the political culture of the 'gentleman', to social hierarchies, to traditional authority, and to church hierarchies.

In their political views, the evangelical sectarians of the Second Great Awakening were a product of a popular culture movement that grew out of the rhetoric of the American Revolution. The new movement was marked by a belief in popular sovereignty, in government based on the consent of the people, and a belief that 'all men were born equal'. As such, the evangelical sectarians of the Second Great Awakening were strong believers in democracy and government by the people (the saints). They were egalitarian democratic republicans, and American patriots who gloried in the American Revolution and associated their religious principles and beliefs with the political and social values of the new democratic republic, the United States of America.

Where theology was concerned, the evangelical sectarians of the Second Great Awakening retained the belief in instantaneous conversion and the millenarian worldview of the earlier evangelical Calvinists, but the cultural values of the evangelicals were transformed. The revivalism of the late 18th Century was a radical religious movement characterized by an individualistic outlook, Biblical literalism, a disdain for theology and ecclesiastical authority, and a rejection of clerical learning. The evangelicals believed that anyone who was moved by the Holy Spirit and 'felt the call' to preach, could do so. They rejected natural religion, denied that human reason had any role in the redemption of man, and were marked by a strong anti-clericalism. The evangelicals of the Second Great Awakening – particularly the 'American Methodists' -- were noted for holding camp meetings characterized by highly-emotional preaching and instantaneous conversions that were accompanied by emotional outbursts of unrestrained enthusiasm. Moreover, the evangelical sectarians not only viewed themselves as an elect, God's people, who were destined for salvation, but believed that they possessed an inner light – the Holy Spirit residing within their hearts and minds – that provided them with a moral guidance superior to any political or religious authority. (5)

A gnostic revolutionary mentality

Leaving aside the religious beliefs and principles, and the highly-emotional conversion experience of the evangelical sectarians -- which the Anglican Tory clerics found highly-questionable in terms of orthodox Christian theology -- what the Tories found very unsettling was the psychology of the so-called 'elect' and the aggressive millenarian behavior of the evangelical sectarians of Upper Canada. They were characterized as possessing a self-righteous and presumptuous attitude, and an irrational hostility to the established Church of England. They viewed themselves as 'saints' who were possessed of an 'inner light' in being filled with the Holy Spirit, and they regarded "all the rest of mankind as corrupt, hardened, perverse, and the children of Satan". As such, evangelical sectarianism was seen by the Tories as constituting a serious threat to the social order, religious peace, and 'the harmony of society'. The evangelical sectarians quoted Scripture out of context, had no settled doctrine or system of beliefs, relied heavily on preaching by uneducated, self-proclaimed preachers, and lacked a Christian priesthood to administer the sacraments.

It was further noted by the Tories that the evangelical sectarians of Upper Canada had no national vision, national spirit, or a social conscience. They were inward looking and focused on the union of the 'saints' in their religious community and were indifferent to public concerns unless a particular issue, or an existing situation, contradicted their religious principles and beliefs.

The conduct and political behaviour of the evangelical sectarians in attacking the Tory establishment was based not only on their religious principles and their financial interest in seeking a share of the clergy reserves revenues, but also on a deeper psychological motivation. In seeking to understand the hostility of the evangelical sects towards the established Church of England, the Tories had only to read an analysis – which was provided several centuries earlier by Richard Hooker -- of the behavior and worldview of the Puritan rebels at the time of the English Reformation. The hostility of the sectarians to the Tory establishment in Upper Canada, and the traditional order, was a product of a deeper gnostic (self-divinization) movement within evangelical sectarianism that closely paralleled the nature of the earlier Puritan assault on the Church of England during the late 16th and 17th centuries.

In their religious zeal and commitment to social and political activism in the pursuit of their cause – 'religious equality', the 'separation of church and state', and 'voluntaryism' – the evangelical sectarians of Upper Canada conformed in large part to the portrait that Richard Hooker drew of the Puritan revolutionaries of his day. According to Hooker -- as summarized by an American political scientist, Eric Voegelin (*The New Science of Politics*, 1952) -- the Puritans in England sought, through agitation, to foster a popular enmity towards the established order by attributing every fault or ill of society to the upper social ranks and to government action or inaction, while focusing their assaults on the particular institutions that they wished to reform or destroy. The Puritans saw themselves as an 'elect' who would bring in a new world order and a new form of government under the rule of 'the saints', and they justified their attacks on the existing order as being aimed at removing 'evil' from the world, or simply the 'enemies' of the saints. In promoting their cause, the Puritans were prone to cite Scripture out of context, to ignore Scripture that was incompatible with their doctrine, and to portray themselves as 'victims' of the establishment. Moreover, in being religious zealots committed to a revolutionary course of action, the Puritans shunned all rational discussion and public debate on their views. (6)

Evangelical Sectarianism in Upper Canada

In Upper Canada, the evangelical sectarians exhibited the same character and gnostic revolutionary mentality as the earlier English Puritans.

Moreover, it is evident that their religious principles and millenarian worldview were derived from the American evangelical Calvinism of the Great Awakening of the 1730s-1740s, their political activism from a confounding of their religious principles with the political principles of the revolutionaries during the American Revolution (1776-1783), and their social values from American evangelical Protestantism as it had evolved during the Second Great Awakening (1790s-1820s) under the leadership of the 'American Methodists' and Free-Will Baptists. In the northern United States, as well as in Upper Canada, it was the 'American Methodists' who predominated in the evangelical Protestant movement of the late 18th and early 19th centuries.

In comparing the rhetoric in the published polemics of the Rev. Egerton Ryerson – an 'American Methodist' convert -- with the religious principles and political behavior of the American evangelical Protestants, it is evident that the 'American Methodists' of Upper Canada were an integral part of that religious movement. The 'American Methodists' of Upper Canada held the same religious principles – 'religious equality', 'voluntaryism', and 'the separation of church and state' -- and shared an inveterate hostility to episcopacy and church establishments which they associated with 'ecclesiastical domination' and 'ecclesiastical tyranny'. They saw themselves as an elect – 'the saints of the world' – and were driven by a common millenarian gnostic mentality to an aggressive social and political activism to realize 'the rule of the saints'. There was the same identification of religious liberty with the political 'liberties of the people', and the same inclination to see anyone who opposed the evangelical concept of religious equality, social equality, and the separation of church and state, as being an 'enemy' and a 'tyrant' who had to be overthrown. That inclination can be seen in the outright hostility of the 'American Methodists' towards the established Church of England in Upper Canada, and the personal animosity that they exhibited towards the Rev. John Strachan – the personification of the Tory establishment -- as evidenced in the published writings of the Rev. Egerton Ryerson.

In his political writings and private communications, Ryerson often referred to his Tory opponents as 'the enemy' and, in attacking the established Church of England, he portrayed the church episcopacy as 'the great beast' that needed to be overthrown to achieve 'Christian liberty'. Moreover, the National Church was denounced for supposedly posing a threat to impose an 'ecclesiastical tyranny'. In the rhetoric and political behavior of the evangelical sectarians of Upper Canada, there is the same mentality and conviction as found among the earlier evangelical Calvinist sectarians in the American colonies. There is also the same concept of the religious duty of 'the saints' to act to redress public grievances, and to oppose and overthrow any ruler or institution that precluded the realization of the community of 'the saints' – the 'reborn' of this world -- and the spread of 'Christian liberty' through personal freedom. For the evangelicals, the natural state of man was to be in possession of 'Christian liberty', which they defined as the moral capacity and personal freedom possessed by regenerated man in choosing to obey God's Will in doing what is just, good and honest, without being inhibited or 'enslaved' by an established church, secular authorities, or traditional church dogmas.

What the Tories faced in Upper Canada was a revolutionary religious movement – American evangelical Protestantism – that was conveyed into Upper Canada by the American settlers who belonged to the various American religious sects. Among the immigrant religious sects, the most influential was the Methodist Episcopal Church which sent its preachers on circuits into Upper Canada to preach and hold camp meetings to convert sinners and establish new congregations of 'the elect'. It was an evangelical Protestant religious movement that was characterized by an aggressive millenarian mentality and demands for 'religious equality' and 'the separation of church and state' that, if implemented, would have destroyed the church-state polity of the Loyalist Asylum of Upper Canada.

The principle of 'religious equality' was used to justify a demand that the clergy reserves land endowment revenues be shared equally among the Protestant religious denominations, and it was buttressed by the specious argument that the phrase 'a Protestant Clergy' -- in the clauses of the Constitutional Act pertaining to the Clergy Reserves – meant all Protestant denominations. It was an argument that was simply fabricated as a means of providing a seemingly plausible claim for the religious sects, and the dissenting churches, to a share of the clergy reserves revenues. The fact that the evangelical sectarians were voluntaryists, who were opposed in principle to the acceptance of what was regarded as corrupting monies from the state, only added to their hypocrisy.

Where politics was concerned, it was the religious principles of the evangelical sectarians and their millenarian psychology that propelled them into an active involvement in the campaigns of agitation launched by the democratic radicals. Under their combined influence, the Reform Party pursued a 'politics of grievances' which involved the evangelical preachers engaging in direct attacks on the legitimacy of the established Church of England, on the endowments and prerogatives of the National Church, and against the church-state union, as well as against the Tory political establishment. There was little that was reasoned or rational in the attacks that the evangelical sectarians launched against the traditional order and its established institutions.

Given the religious zeal of the evangelical sectarians to weaken and destroy the church-state union and the church establishment in Upper Canada – which were viewed as impediments to the establishment of the community of 'saints' in God's Earthly Kingdom, the Kingdom of Light -- there was no room for compromise. The Tories found that out in passing the Tithe Act of 1823 which renounced the traditional right of the established Church of England to collect the tithe in a parish. The Tories had done so voluntarily in the hope that the evangelical sectarians would cease their agitation over the minor financial support that was being received -- at that date -- by the Church from the leasing of clergy reserve lots. In response, the evangelical sectarians and their radical democrat allies redoubled their attacks on the clergy reserves endowment.

There was also a discernably strong egalitarian democratic strain within the mindset of the evangelical sectarians of Upper Canada – particularly among the 'American Methodists' -- that was derived from the character of the religious movement of the Second Great Awakening in the United States. It was no accident, that the evangelical sectarians of Upper Canada actively supported the democratic radicals during the 1820s, and that the egalitarian democratic republicans who joined the rebels in the attempted coup d'état in December 1837 were commonly one and the same as the evangelical sectarians from the American-settled areas of the Province. Moreover, the assertion by the Rev. Dr. Strachan in 1827 that the Methodist itinerant preachers were poorly educated, and that they had 'formed their ideas' in the United States, was indubitably true.

The evangelical sectarians lacked any national political vision for the future of the Province of Upper Canada. They were focused on their millenarian vision wherein Upper Canadians needed to be reborn through hearing the preaching of 'the Word', having faith in Christ, and undergoing an emotional instantaneous conversion in receiving God's saving grace. Once reborn, it was the duty of community of 'the elect' to act to overcome all impediments to the realization of God's Earthly Kingdom of Light. The vision of the evangelical Protestant sectarians was focused upon bringing into being the thousand-year rule of the 'reborn' in God's Earthly Kingdom wherein 'the saints' would be united in a community of love with Jesus Christ prior to the Day of Judgement. The millennium was envisaged as a period of perfect happiness for man on earth in living in accordance with God's Will, as revealed in Scripture. The evangelical Protestants did not possess any vision of a common good, or of a national political purpose, that embraced all Upper Canadians. They were focused on the well-being, salvation, and religious interests of their own community: 'the saints'.

More recently, a Canadian historian, William Westfall *('Two Worlds', The Protestant Culture of Nineteenth Century Ontario*, 1989), has argued that the major evangelical sects in Upper Canada transformed themselves by mid-century into mainstream Protestant churches. That assertion in turn casts a new light on the Tory belief that the Church of England was well positioned to evangelize the province and, in doing so to succeed in their policy of religious comprehension.

The Anglican Tory clerics of Upper Canada had believed that with the development of the amenities of civilization in the frontier communities and the spread of education, the adherents of the religious sects would come to reject the emotional exhortations of uneducated, self-proclaimed preachers in favour of a rational religion of moderation and decorum preached by educated and regularly-ordained ministers of the

Church of England. The belief that the sectarians would return to the National Church was the basic assumption underlying the Tory concept of religious comprehension in Upper Canada. However, although the Tories proved to be highly prescient in anticipating a social phenomenon that would favour the growth of the National Church, what transpired did not benefit the Church of England other than in contributing to a dramatic decrease in sectarian attacks.

According to Westfall, the transformation of Methodism was typical of the process by which the evangelical sects transformed themselves into mainstream Protestant churches. Methodism in Upper Canada faced a crisis during the 1840s as religious revivals and camp meetings, highly-emotive preaching, and the emotional outbursts of the sudden conversion experience --that had characterized the evangelical 'American Methodists' -- began to fall out of favour within the increasingly affluent and educated Methodist community and with the young Methodist ministers who were graduates in theology of the Methodist seminary, the Upper Canada Academy (1836-1892) in Cobourg. In response, the Methodist religious leadership abandoned religious revivals, downplayed the significance of camp meetings and emotive hell-fire preaching, and moved away from the evangelical concept of a sudden, emotional, conversion experience. They began to emphasize the need for an educated clergy to preach 'the Word' with a sense of moderation and decorum, and a programme of church building was instituted to serve the Methodists congregations. There was a new emphasis on reason and gradualism in religion, conventional prayer, and a focus on regular church services, the ministration of the sacraments, and the establishing of regular Sunday schools to inculcate religious beliefs and moral values in the young.

In that process, the concept of the church was transformed from simply a place of worship to the House of God, wherein the spirit of God resided; and the former American evangelical Protestant emphasis on a sudden 'new birth' accompanied by an 'otherworldliness' in withdrawing from the cares of the world, was superseded by a new emphasis on living a good (moral) life, attending church, and doing good works in the larger community. An indication of the nature of the new Methodist religious culture is evident in the *Christian Guardian* (7 August 1844) recommending to Methodists a sermon by Bishop Strachan on the Christian duty to do good works in imitation of Christ. Within the new religious culture, the religious zeal of the Methodists was channeled into combatting secularism and improving the moral character of society. (7)

In viewing the transformation of the former Methodist Episcopal Church in Upper Canada as of the mid-19th Century – a process in which the Rev. Egerton Ryerson played a surprising role -- an impartial observer might well wonder whether he was focused on creating a second Anglican Church in Upper Canada, minus the church establishment status. One wonders as well, if not for the constant attacks launched against the established Church of England by the sectarian preachers, whether the members of the religious sects would have gravitated to the National Church as the society of Upper Canada matured and became better educated and respectable. However, that movement did not occur as the religious leaders of the evangelical sects transformed their sects into traditional Christian churches of order, reason, and respectability, and rejected the irrational emotionalism of the evangelical revivalism of their origins.

In the Methodist transformation, it was the British Wesleyan Methodists who took the lead. (8) Westfall sees a unified Protestant religious culture emerging in Canada West by the mid-19th Century – or, more specifically, by the time of the 1867 Confederation of the provinces. (9) Yet, it was the Church of England that clearly provided the church model and the requisite Christian knowledge for the transformation of the evangelical sects into orthodox Christian churches. In that transformation the sectarians drew on the works of the Anglican divines, the King James' Bible, the Book of Common Prayer, the traditional Christian church service and ministration of the sacraments of the Church of England, and the Gothic Revival architecture of the Anglican churches.

Church Establishment and the Clergy Reserves Endowment

In defending the clergy reserves endowment of the Church of England, the Tories of Upper Canada maintained that the Church of England was an established church in the Province of Upper Canada, and that the phrase "a Protestant Clergy" in the Constitutional Act of 1791 referred exclusively to the Church of England. Hence, the Tories maintained that the revenues yielded by the lease and sale of clergy reserves lots were intended to support the established Church of England; that the Church of Scotland was not a co-established church in Upper Canada; and that the sectarians possessed no legitimate constitutional or legal claim to a share of the clergy reserves revenues.

What is irrefutable is that the Church of England was the *de facto* established church of the Province of Upper Canada; although the Reform Party questioned its legal status as an established church in law. Neither the Quebec Act (1774) nor the Constitutional Act (1791) specifically stated that the Church of England was established in Canada, despite the provisions made in the Constitutional Act for the support of 'a Protestant Clergy'. However, the Loyalists who settled in Upper Canada had accepted that the Church of England was a lawfully established church in the Province, as had the democratic radicals during the 1820s when they objected to having an Established Church. It was the Rev. Egerton Ryerson, in his May 1828 public letters, who first openly denied that the Church of England was legally established in Upper Canada in arguing that there was no Imperial statute that specifically proclaimed its establishment. Thereafter, the prerogatives of the Church of England, the church-state alliance, and the clergy reserve endowment were attacked by the 'American Methodist' preachers, and their democratic radical allies of the Reform Party, as being a violation of 'religious equality' and an unwarranted imposition on the people of Upper Canada.

Despite the arguments made by the Reformers and their evangelical allies, it is obvious that the British government in establishing the clergy reserves land endowment to provide support for 'a Protestant clergy' in Upper Canada was referencing the Church of England. The only qualification was that the Governor was empowered to divert any excess revenues, beyond the needs of the Established Church, to other government priorities which, at best, left the door open for the Governor to extend some financial aid to the Church of Scotland from the clergy reserves revenues, if he chose to do so. It could not be construed to deny the claim of the Anglican Tories that the endowment was intended for the support of the Church of England, or to call into question their contention that the clergy reserves revenues ought to be directed – given the great extent of the needs of the National Church in Upper Canada – to that specified purpose.

In the 18th Century in England, the phrase 'Protestant clergy' meant the Church of England and no other religion. Moreover, from a strictly legal position -- as the Tories themselves pointed out -- the Act of Uniformity (1 Eliz. C.2, 1559) had specifically enacted that the Church of England was to be the established Church of the existing English colonies and any English colonies to be established thereafter within Her Majesty's Dominions. Although that statute had long lay in abeyance where the former American colonies were concerned, it had not been repealed, and the Province of Upper Canada was an English colony.

There was never any intention on the part of the British government -- in drafting the Constitutional Act -- to provide financial support for the dissenting churches and evangelical sects who, with the support of the Reform Party, subsequently advanced a self-serving claim that the phrase "a Protestant Clergy", in the Constitutional Act, referred to all the Protestant religious denominations of the province, and entitled them to a share in the clergy reserves endowment revenues.

Similarly, the argument that the Church of Scotland was co-established in Upper Canada was totally fallacious. As the Tories pointed out, the Province of Upper Canada was an English colony in law, and not a British colony. Moreover, the Act of Union (1707) -- that united the kingdoms of England and Scotland under the name of the United Kingdom of Great Britain – had provided that the Church of England was to remain the established church in England, and that the established national Church of England was "guaranteed the rights and the status of the Church in the colonies". The Church of Scotland was recognized as established only in Scotland.

The persistent attacks on the Church of England and its possession of the clergy reserves endowment, by the Church of Scotland adherents and by the evangelical sectarians, were motivated largely by self-interest in a financial sense, and by a religious concern that a strong National Church might well attract their adherents. The claim of the Church of Scotland to a share of the clergy reserves revenues on the grounds of being co-established in Upper Canada was totally without any foundation in statute law.

For the evangelical sectarians there was an additional motivation provided by their ardent belief in the religious principles of 'religious equality' and 'the separation of church and state', and their strong animosity towards the concept of an established church. It was their religious principles and their bias of mind that motivated them to want to weaken, if not destroy, the established Church of England in Upper Canada. In sum, neither the Church of Scotland nor the evangelical sectarian congregations had any legitimate claim to participate in a distribution of the clergy reserves revenues.

In supporting such claims, the Reform Party evinced a willful ignorance in their interpretation of the constitution that ignored the constitutional arguments set forth by the Tories, the conventional and accepted meaning of the term 'Protestant Clergy' in England, and the customary practice of the British government to provide support for the clergy of the national church, the Church of England, within a church-state polity. It appears that the Reform Party engaged in a deliberate effort to foment discontent and anger against the governing Tory establishment through promoting the specious claim that all dissenting churches and religious sects were entitled to a share of the clergy reserves revenues under the terms of the Constitution of 1791. It was a deliberate effort to fabricate a grievance -- where none existed -- to gain adherents for the Reform Party.

The Age of Delusion

In the pre-War of 1812 period, the Upper Canadian Tories were acutely aware that they were living in a revolutionary age in both Europe and North America. In the American colonies, the legitimate colonial governments had been overthrown during the American Revolution (1776-1783). The traditional political order and the rule of law was destroyed by the revolutionists during the revolution. It was a revolution that was based – in theory – upon Lockean-liberal values: inalienable natural rights to the pursuit of life, liberty and happiness, an asserted right of the people to rebel against a government judged to have abused its trust, the principles of popular sovereignty and the separation of church and state. In France, the French Revolution (1789-1799) had witnessed the overthrow of the royal government dynasty, the installation of a democratic republican government, and a subsequent Reign of Terror.

Under the dictatorship of Maximilien Robespierre (September 1794-July 1794) opponents of the new regime were executed by executive fiat and the Roman Catholic Church was persecuted by the revolutionaries who were motivated by a rabid anti-clericalism. Moreover, in France a period of democratic anarchy had been succeeded by a ruthless military dictatorship, under Napoleon Bonaparte, that had plunged Europe into a series of unlimited wars that were unprecedented in the loss of life, the destruction of property, and dynastic upheavals. For the Tories, it was an 'Age of Delusion', for man to think that peace, order, and good government could be achieved by the rule of democrats and infidels who based their legitimacy on the support of the mob and their power to imprison and execute their opponents.

From the viewpoint of the Tories -- who believed in a rational cosmic order, original sin, faith in Christ as the Redeemer, and God's moral law as revealed in Nature and by Revelation -- those who advocated that man could live a good life of moral virtue simply by 'following reason' in the pursuit of one's enlightened self-interest (Locke), or his affections and the 'inner light' (the evangelical sectarians), or majority opinion (the democratic radicals), or his passions and 'the general will' (Rousseau), were highly irrational men. For the Upper Canadian Tories, the so-called 'Age of Reason' of the 18th Century was an irreligious and irrational age in which moral philosophy and political philosophy had degenerated from the philosophical works of the Ancients, and from the works of the medieval Scholastics -- such as Thomas Aquinas, who synthesized the philosophy of Artistotle on natural law and rational man with Christian theology -- and from the theology and political philosophy of Richard Hooker, the great Anglican theologian.

For the Tories, an age that believed in the pursuit of one's enlightened self-interest and individual happiness and well-being as the proper goal of man, that viewed government as established only to protect life, liberty, and property without an overriding moral and religious purpose and with no commitment to the promotion of the well-being of the people, that failed to acknowledge the concept of a 'common good' based on eternal moral verities, that rejected the Christian religion and Revelation, that embraced deism, or atheism and anti-clericalism, and that regarded fallible human reason as the sole guide to virtue, the good, and morality, was truly an Age of Delusion.

The view of the Upper Canadian Tories that the so-called 'Age of Reason' was, in fact, an 'Age of Delusion', is consistent with an argument made by an American political philosopher, Eric Voegelin (*The New Science of Politics*, 1952). Voegelin has argued that men who believed in a science of order -- "the classic and Christian science of man", wherein the given order of society and its representative institutions reflect a cosmic order that represents 'the truth' and that is inextricably bound up with the ultimate purpose of human existence -- must regard those who assail that order, and deny its validity, as being disloyal and dispensers of falsehood. According to Voegelin, the more that opponents of 'the Christian science of man' moved away from that order in attacking and denying its validity, the less rational they appeared to the upholders of the traditional order. Thus, for the believers in that order, the purported 'Age of Reason', in denying the Christian cosmic order, was a highly irrational age.

The Tory Outlook

In the decade prior to the War of 1812 years, the Anglican Tories of Upper Canada were pre-occupied with the forces of democratic republicanism, infidelity, and anti-clericalism, and the mob violence that were associated with the French Revolution. It was Europe that was regarded as the centre of the new revolutionary age, and the source of a serious ideological threat to the peace, order and social harmony of Upper Canada and to its Christian national character. However, that situation changed dramatically with the defeat of Napoleonic France, and the forming of the Holy Alliance (September 1815) of Prussia, Russia, and Austria, to defend Christian values and resist the spread of democratic republicanism and infidelity. Political stability and order were strengthened still further by the subsequent forming of the Quintuple Alliance (1818) whereby Austria, Russia, Prussia, the United Kingdom of Great Britain, and the restored French monarchy, pledged their support for the existing royal dynasties of Europe and their common determination to resist revolutionary movements. With order seemingly restored in Europe, the attention of the Tories of Upper Canada came to focus directly on the threat that the neighbouring democratic republic, the United States of America, posed to the Loyalist Asylum of Upper Canada.

In the pre-war period, several Tories had recognized that the large influx of non-Loyalist immigrants from the United States posed a threat to the survival of the Province of Upper Canada as a Loyalist asylum and colony of the British Empire, but it was the War of 1812 that awakened the Tories of Upper Canada more generally to the nature of an existential threat to the political culture of the province that was emanating from the American republic. The problem of disaffection among the American settlers during the War, and instances of outright treason, made it evident that Upper Canada was menaced not only by the aggressive expansionism of the new democratic republic, but by the spread into Upper Canada of its novel political ideology.

The immediate threat was ideological. It took the form of the infiltration of American cultural, political, and religious values among the residents of Upper Canada owing to their living next to a democratic republic, the United States of America. Moreover, in its exposed geographical position on the settlement frontier of North America, Upper Canada was directly threatened by an influx of American democratic-republican immigrants, by the evangelical religious principles being preached by 'American Methodist' preachers who had extended their circuits into Upper Canada, and by American publications that eulogized the American revolutionary experience and the supposedly superior virtues of the democratic republican form of government.

In seeking to defend Upper Canada against the ideological threat posed by the United States, the Upper Canadian Tories identified their struggle with the earlier Loyalist experience not only with respect to a shared loyalty to the Crown and the Unity of Empire, but also in keeping with the Anglican-Tory Loyalists rejection of the Lockean-liberal values of the American Revolution. The Anglican Tory-Loyalists were the one group among the Loyalists who espoused a political philosophy that rejected the basic tenets of Lockean liberalism, and it was the Anglican Tory element in the Loyalist expulsion with which the Upper Canadian Tories identified. An American historian, William Nelson has argued

(*The American Tory*, 1961) that it was the Anglican Tories in the American Colonies who alone presented a philosophical challenge to the thoroughgoing Lockean-liberal political culture that emerged out of the American revolutionary experience.

The American Threat: Ideology

What the Tories of Upper Canada faced on their very borders was a new republic – the United States of America -- that espoused a revolutionary democratic republicanism that had its origins in the American revolutionary experience. Indeed, in many ways the clash of ideologies in Upper Canada represented a second coming of the American Revolution for the families of the Tory Loyalists, on both political and philosophical grounds. As Bernard Bailyn (*The Intellectual Origins of the American Revolution*, 1967) has argued, the American Revolution was essentially "a conflict of ideas and political values" – an ideological battle.

For Bailyn, a distinguished American historian of the Colonial and Revolutionary eras, the American Revolution had its intellectual origins in a belief on the part of the colonists that they were defending the English tradition of liberty against encroachments by the King, and impositions by parliament, on 'the rights of Englishmen'. Gradually the colonial dispute took on greater implications as colonial pamphleteers and polemicists began to produce political tracts that set forth radical political ideas pertaining to inalienable natural rights, popular sovereignty, equal political rights, a right of resistance against tyranny, and various ideas pertaining to religious and political liberty.

The political tracts, which were widely circulated in the colonies, drew on the writings of the British radical Whigs of the 18th Century, the earlier writings of John Locke (*Two Treatises on Government*, 1689), and the 17th Century writings of the Puritan radicals of the English Civil War and Commonwealth period. Borrowings were made also from the major works of the 18th Century philosophes on natural rights and Natural Law, from William Blackstone (*Commentaries on the Laws of England*, 1765) on the English Common Law, and from Montesquieu (*De L'esprit des loix*, 1748, English ed., 1750) which traced the evolution of English liberty to the separation of powers in the balanced British Constitution. However, a new element was added by the colonial pamphleteers: viz.

expressions of a belief in the exceptionalism of the American people, that was derived from the New England Puritan covenant theology regarding 'God's chosen people'. To the mix of radical political ideas was added the call of Thomas Paine (*Common Sense*, 1776) for American independence and the establishment of a republican form of government by the people, in arguing that the monarchical and aristocratic forms of government, if either were adopted, would inevitably degenerate into a tyranny.

There were contradictions and inconsistencies within the body of radical ideas, concepts and beliefs espoused by the polemicists and pamphleteers in the American colonies, but gradually a new political paradigm was forged. Following a period of intense intellectual ferment, 1763-1776, the political culture and worldview of the American colonists was totally transformed, as well as their view of the place of America in the world. The American colonies came to be viewed as a beacon in the struggle to preserve liberty in contrast to what was perceived as the degeneracy of political liberty and the spread of corruption in the British Parliament under the earlier Whig administration (1721-1742) of Robert Walpole and the Whig Oligarchs (1742-1760). What emerged in the American colonies was a new worldview that united the revolutionaries of the Thirteen American colonies. (10)

The American Declaration of Independence of 1776 marked the culmination of that transformation in the political thought of the American colonists, or at least the transformation in the thought of the leading proponents of the Revolution. That sea change in the political beliefs and worldview of the American colonists was captured in the declaratory second paragraph:

> We hold these truths to be self-evident, that all men are created equal, that they are endowed with certain inalienable Rights, that among these are Life, Liberty, and the pursuit of Happiness – that to secure these rights, Governments are instituted among men, deriving their just powers from the consent of the governed – That whenever any Form of Government becomes destructive of these ends, it is the Right of the People to alter

or abolish it, and to institute a new Government, laying the foundation on such principles and organizing its powers in such form, as to them shall seem most likely to effect their Safety and Happiness ....

To justify a rebellion and the declaration of independence, the Declaration listed a 'long train of abuses' in which the King George III was held to have violated the traditional rights of the American colonists as British subjects.

The entire American Declaration of Independence was based on the tenets of the Lockean-liberal political philosophy in its emphasis on inalienable natural rights pertaining to the individual, its view of the role of government as limited to securing and protecting individual rights, the concept of government originating in a compact and based on the consent of the governed (popular sovereignty), and the right of rebellion in response to abuses of power, as well as its emphasis on the pursuit of personal freedom and happiness as the ultimate good and virtue in life. However, there was a difference in the concept of popular sovereignty. For Locke, the principle of popular sovereignty pertained to the original founding of government by the consent of the people; whereas for the American revolutionaries the principle of popular sovereignty implied the implementation of a universal manhood suffrage (excluding Blacks and Indians) and government by the people. The American revolutionaries rejected the Old Whig concept of a 'virtual representation' of the interests of the people by a political elite.

The Declaration of Independence was not a Christian document, nor was it strictly secular. It was a deist document, in which the independence of the new United States of America was declared to rest on a right of a people to dissolve their existing 'political bonds' in response to abuses of authority, and "to assume among the powers of the earth that separate and equal status to which the Laws of Nature and of Nature's God entitles them". It was a declaration of the existence of inalienable natural rights pertaining to man as an individual, inclusive of a right of rebellion to resist government abuses, and of a belief that such rights were established by God in Nature. However, God was relegated to the periphery as the inalienable natural rights of man were declared to be 'self-evident truths' established in Natural Law for once and for all time by God. As such, the declaration was an arbitrary statement of abstract rights that the revolutionaries adopted from the political theory of John Locke and used to justify their rebellion and the formation of a new government of their own devising. (11)

The American revolutionaries believed in the sovereignty of the people and universal manhood suffrage, but wanted a representative democracy, rather than a direct democracy. They had a negative view of human nature as susceptible to corruption and prone to a lust for power and saw the antidote in a novel constitutional balance based on a functional separation of powers among the executive power, a bicameral legislature, and an independent judiciary in keeping with the political theory of Montesquieu. It was a departure from the traditional English concept of a constitution in which the legislative institutions of government in parliament were based on a balance of the social orders: the monarch, the landed aristocracy, and the commons.

The founders of the new American Republic also rejected the traditional English concept of a dynamic unwritten constitution. The America founders believed in a written constitution and the enshrining of fundamental rights that would not be subject to change at the whim of any popular movement. The subsequent American Constitution of 1787, and the Bill of Rights of 1789, embodied these new American beliefs. However, ultimately, the founding fathers of the new republic looked to the American people for the defence of their liberties which -- they believed -- depended upon the vigilance and the moral character of 'a virtuous people'.

Bailyn argued further that the American Revolution was strictly a political revolution in which the leaders showed little concern for addressing social or economic inequalities. Nonetheless, he acknowledged that there was a revolutionary social and religious aspect to the American Revolution. The evangelical Calvinists sects – 'the New Light Presbyterians, the Separate Baptists, and the Strict Congregationalists, and, after 1770, the Methodists' – were ardent supporters of the Revolution who identified their principle of religious liberty with the political liberty of the revolutionaries. The evangelical sects -- and the Separate Baptists, in particular -- were 'fiercely belligerent' in denouncing church establishments, in demanding a separation of church and state, and in arguing for religious, political, and social equality. (12)

Ultimately, the First Amendment to the United States Constitution -- in the Bill of Rights of September 1789 – confirmed the separation of church and state and the freedom of religion in declaring that: "Congress shall make no law respecting an established religion or prohibiting the free exercise thereof ...." However, it was only a partial victory in the eyes of the evangelical Calvinist sectarians who were committed to social equality, as well as political and religious equality.

For the Upper Canadian Tories, it was quite apparent that the revolutionary nature of the new American political ideology posed a direct threat to the peace, order and stability of the traditional church-state Christian polity of Upper Canada. Moreover, Upper Canada was a Loyalist Asylum founded by men who had fought against the democratic republicanism of the American revolutionists during the American Revolution (1776-1783). The Loyalists had sacrificed everything that they possessed in defence of the traditional order and loyalty to the Crown and the Unity of Empire in the Thirteen Colonies. They had been forced to flee into a wilderness to escape from the persecution – personal abuse, despoliation and seizure of property -- that the triumphant American revolutionists inflicted on their former 'tory' neighbours.

For the Upper Canadian Tories, any government of Upper Canada that permitted large numbers of non-Loyalist Americans -- American democratic republicans -- to settle in the Loyalist Asylum of Upper Canada was not only undermining the traditional order and culture of the Loyalist Province, but denying everything that the Loyalists had fought for and believed in. In the pre-War of 1812 period, Upper Canadian Anglican Tories had tried to prevent non-Loyalist Americans from receiving land grants and settling in Upper Canada, but their efforts were thwarted when Lt. Governor John Graves Simcoe abolished the Land Boards (1794) that had screened prospective immigrants from the United States for their loyalty during the American Revolution. In the postwar period, it was the Tory effort to stem the flow of American settlers into Upper Canada, and to deny the vote to American settlers who refused to become naturalized by taking the Oath of Allegiance to the King, that gave rise to the Alien Question. It was a controversy that invigorated the Reform Party during the early 1820s by providing government opposition groups – primarily the democratic radicals and the evangelical sectarians -- with a political issue on which they could unite and use to secure the electoral support of the American settlers in attacking the Tory establishment.

Where immigration was concerned, the Upper Canadian Tories maintained that Her Majesty's Provincial Government had the right to exclude foreigners from settling in Upper Canada whose political and cultural values were seen to pose a threat to the peace and order of the Loyalist province. Moreover, it was feared that, in the event of a future war with the United States, American aliens settled in Canada would pose a potentially severe problem of disaffection as evidenced by the earlier conduct of American settlers during the War of 1812. Non-British subjects -- foreigners -- did not possess a right to emigrate to Upper Canada. To the contrary, it was a privilege that the Crown granted to foreigners, and it could be withdrawn if they were deemed to pose a threat to the peace, order, and stability of the state and the well-being of its people. Moreover, the Tories maintained that aliens who were settled in Upper Canada, but who refused or neglected to take the Oath of Allegiance to the King, were to be denied the exercise of political rights – the right to vote and to stand for election – and were not eligible for appointment to public office. Such political rights and privileges were reserved for British subjects by birth, naturalization or conquest, although the property rights and civil rights of alien settlers were protected under the law and the principle of equality before the law. For the Tories, the provincial government had a duty to protect and sustain the British national culture of the Province of Upper Canada.

The American Threat: Imperialism

An equally ominous threat to the very survival of the Province of Upper Canada was American imperialism, which was driven by an expansionist republicanism that was marked by a determination to remove the British government – and all European governments -- from the North American continent by an aggressive foreign policy or, failing that, by the force of arms. It was a Jeffersonian policy of the American Revolution period that was born of a determination to spread American democratic republicanism everywhere 'in the New World'. On their part, the American people had come to believe that it was the destiny of their new American Republic to rule over the entire North American continent and its off-shore islands – a belief that became known later as 'manifest destiny'.

It was an expansionist frame of mind that led the American Republic to make war on the adjacent Spanish colony in Florida, on the Indian tribes of the South and Northwest, on the British North American colonies (War of 1812), and on the new Mexican Republic (founded October 1824), with the aim of conquering and annexing the lands of the neighbouring nations to the United States of America. In the case of Upper Canada, the survival of the Province -- in the face of American aggression during the War of 1812 -- was attributable solely to the British Army, whom the Upper Canadian Tories did everything possible to support in seeking to overcome 'a defeatist attitude' among the loyal population of the province. The young Tories served as officers in the provincial militia companies that provided military and logistical support for the British regulars, and young Tories played a significant role in several of the early and decisive military actions of the war: at Detroit with Major-General Brock (August 1812) and in the driving of the Americans off the heights at Niagara during the Battle of Queenston Heights (October 1812). Nonetheless, in the absence of the British Army regiments, Upper Canada would have succumbed to conquest and annexation by the United States during the War of 1812.

Subsequently, the Tories feared that Upper Canada would either be conquered in yet another invasion by the American Army, or eventually annexed to the American Union through the people of Upper Canada becoming 'Americanized'. They realized that Upper Canada would manage to survive only if a concerted effort were made to strengthen the 'British national character' of the province. To that end, the Upper Canadian Tories counted upon the active support of the British government for Her Majesty's Provincial Government of Upper Canada, for the National Church and the retention of its prerogatives and supporting endowments, for the maintenance of the balanced British Constitution and the royal prerogatives, and the existing church-state polity of Upper Canada. The primary fear of the Tories was that the British government might abandon the Province of Upper Canada, which was particularly difficult and expensive to defend owing to its inland location where the might of the Royal Navy could not be brought to bear. To counteract any tendency on the part of the British government to abandon Upper Canada, the Tories were conspicuous in declaring, and showing, their loyalty to the Crown and the unity of the British Empire. Moreover, they continually called upon the British government to acknowledge its duty to defend British subjects who were resident in the Province of Upper Canada.

In defending the traditional order in the Loyalist asylum of Upper Canada, the Tories found themselves living a precarious existence in which the very survival of the Province and their own dispossession were at stake. It was this realization of the precariousness of their situation that gave rise to the Tory National Policy, which was formulated to strengthen the loyalty of the Province and its capacity to defend itself both ideologically and militarily. In return for their loyalty to the Crown, the British Constitution, and the unity of Empire, the Tories expected that they would receive the unstinted aid of the British government in support of the National Policy objectives and their Tory governing establishment, as well as an outright commitment of the military might of the British Empire to the defence of the Province of Upper Canada. It had proved to be a forlorn hope.

The Demise of the Tories

The unhappy fate of the Upper Canadian Tories, who continually strove to defend and strengthen the Loyalist Asylum of Upper Canada, was to find themselves in a position where their loyalty, dedication, and sacrifices in support of the Crown and the British Empire were unappreciated and unreciprocated by liberal-Whig reform governments in Britain. To the contrary, a succession of liberal-Whig governments continually sought to conciliate the Reformers of Upper Canada who were attacking not only the balanced British Constitution, but the very fabric of the church-state polity of the Province and the institutions that sustained it.

Following the defeat of the attempted coup d'état – the so-called rebellion of December 1837 by Reform Party members -- the Tories in Upper Canada controlled the Executive Council, dominated the appointed Legislative Council, and enjoyed the support of a large conservative majority in the elective House of Assembly. However, the Tories were to suffer three major blows in succession, at the hands of liberal-Whig governments in Britain, that intervened directly into the politics of Upper Canada, and brought about the destruction of the Tory governing establishment, its political influence, and the church-state polity of the Loyalist asylum of Upper Canada: viz. the recommendations of the Durham Report (March 1839); the imposed union of the two Canadian provinces (February 1841); and the commitment of a new free-trade British liberal-Whig government to the principle of colonial responsible government (November 1846), which brought into power a highly-partisan Reform Government in the new United Province of Canada.

The Durham Report (1839)

After two decades of defending the traditional church-state polity in the Loyalist Asylum of Upper Canada and shaping its development, the Tories were dismayed to learn that the liberal-Whig Government of Viscount Melbourne had appointed a leading British radical-Whig, John George Lambton, Earl of Durham, as both Governor-General of the British North American Provinces and as a High Commissioner charged with inquiring into the causes of the 1837 rebellions in Upper and Lower Canada, and with making recommendations regarding the future "Form and Administration of the Civil Government".

Lord Durham stayed in Lower Canada for five months – May-November 1838 – while the British radical-Whig members of the Durham Commission pursued their enquiries. The Tories of Upper Canada were ignored. Only one brief visit was made by Lord Durham and his Commissioners to Upper Canada -- in July 1838 -- by steamboat to Niagara Falls for a four-day visit. On the return trip, they stopped briefly in Toronto where a private meeting was held with Dr. William Warren Baldwin and Robert Baldwin of the Reform Party. The principle of responsible government was explained to Lord Durham, and he agreed to accept a further written submission from Robert Baldwin on the political situation in Upper Canada. The Durham Commission did not consult with the leading Tories of Upper Canada but, to the contrary, the Commission was well-informed on the Reform Party view of the politics of Upper Canada and the nature of that party. (13)

Upon returning to Britain, the Durham Commission produced a report for Parliament: viz. *Report on the Affairs of British North America from The Earl of Durham, Her Majesty's High Commissioner* (February 1839). When copies of the report arrived in Canada, the Upper Canadian Tories were shocked and appalled at the recommendations. The Durham Report advocated a union of the two Canadian provinces (to enable the English of both provinces to combine in a united legislature to gradually assimilate the French 'race' and promote economic development), the introduction of 'responsible government' (to enable the colonists to govern themselves in local affairs), and the secularization of the Clergy Reserves (to end religious strife and to free up additional land for settlement by British immigrants). The later claim was decidedly false and misleading at a time when the Clergy Reserve lots were already being sold at a rapid rate by the Clergy Reserves Corporation of the established Church of England.

Where the Reform Party of Upper Canada was concerned, Durham was quite candid in reporting that many Reformers wanted an American system of government, and that most Reform members of the Assembly were 'representatives of sectional interests with no concept of the general good'. He observed also that the Reform Party, which was united in attacking 'a common opponent' – the Tory establishment -- was composed of different factions that appeared to be "seeking utterly different or incompatible objects". However, in the Durham Report, the Reform Party caricature of the Upper Canadian Tories was taken up without question.

The Tory elite was denounced as being 'a selfish oligarchy' that maintained a monopoly of power, and whose control over patronage and 'alleged jobbery' – it was claimed – had produced a widespread dissatisfaction. The Tories were declared to be responsible for the Province of Upper Canada lagging far behind the neighbouring American states in its economic progress and wealth. Moreover, the Upper Canadian Tories were portrayed as reactionaries who were trying to impose an 'old world' religious system upon Upper Canada, 'contrary to the wishes of the people'. In contrast, the Reformers of Upper Canada were praised for their altruism in wanting simply to secure a provincial administration composed of men "possessing the confidence of the Assembly".

The charge that the Tories were responsible for a supposed economic backwardness of Upper Canada as compared to the United States, was absurd. It was the Tories who had invested government monies in public works – primarily the Burlington Bay Canal (1823-1832), the Welland Canal (1824-1833), and the commencement of work on the Cornwall Canal (1834-37/work suspended) which was part of a projected St. Lawrence River canals system; and it was the Tories who had founded the Upper Canadian banking system. To the contrary, it was the Reformers who had opposed provincial government expenditures on major public works, and the Mackenzie faction of the Reform Party that had opposed the introduction of a paper currency and the establishing of banks. Moreover, the United States was a long-settled, populous country with a large population and surplus capital; whereas Upper Canada was a sparsely-populated province, which was being settled by British immigrants who, for the most part, had little capital to invest. As of 1840, the United States had a population of 17 million; whereas the Province of Upper Canada had a population of just over 400,000 persons in an area of North America that had been a heavily-forested wilderness less than fifty-years earlier.

In Upper Canada, the widely-publicized recommendations of the Durham Report had the perverse effect – from a Tory perspective -- of reviving the disgraced Reform Party. Once again, the stalwarts of the Reform Party called for the implementation of 'responsible government', and for the Clergy Reserves to be secularized and the funds vested in the Legislature, to which was added a demand for a union of the two Canadian provinces.

Encouraged by the Durham Report recommendations, Robert Baldwin and Francis Hincks – a liberal-Whig, Anglo-Irish, Presbyterian immigrant from Cork -- began to rebuild the Reform Party in Upper Canada as a British liberal-Whig party. A newspaper, the *Examiner*, was established in Toronto with a masthead calling for "Responsible Government and the Voluntary Principle", and was used by Hincks, the owner-editor, to lead a campaign for 'parliamentary government on the British model'. Shorn of its former public image as a democratic republican party with American political leanings, the revitalized Reform Party began to hold public meetings – 'Durham Meetings' -- at which resolutions were passed in favour of the Durham recommendations, and at which the Tories were denounced as obstacles to the economic progress and freedom of Upper Canada. In doing so, the new liberal-Whig leaders of the Reform Party – which remained composed of democratic radicals and evangelical sectarians, and even former egalitarian democratic republicans -- began to attract the support of the British liberal-Whig immigrants, which weakened the existing conservative alliance that had been providing stability, order, and good government to Upper Canada since the June 1836 Loyalty Election.

In calling for the implementation of the principle of 'responsible government', Lord Durham gave a legitimacy to the concept. He provided an assurance to Upper Canadians that the implementation of 'responsible government' would not destroy the unity of the British Empire or violate the sovereignty of the Crown. In his report, he saw no conflict in the exercise of 'responsible government' on the local provincial level and the sovereignty of the Crown upon Imperial matters, with Imperial and foreign trade, diplomacy, defence, and Crown lands being reserved to the King in Parliament. (14)

Whether they realized it or not, what the Baldwins, Francis Hincks, and Lord Durham were advocating was the older medieval concept of a divisible sovereignty whereby a monarch could delegate specific sovereign (palatine) powers to a vassal, a trading company or a plantation (colony), over a territory within the King's realm, in return for the performance of specified duties, and fidelity and allegiance to the Crown. (15)

The Union of the Canadas (1841)

The second major blow to the Tory governing elite in Upper Canada came with the active intervention of the liberal-Whig Government of Britain in the politics of the Province in seeking to impose the policies advocated by the Durham Report. In September 1839, a leading member of the liberal-Whig Government in Britain, Charles Poulett Thomson, was appointed as Governor-in-Chief for the British North America provinces. His instructions were to secure the assent of the two Canadian colonies to a legislative union, and to settle the Clergy Reserves issue by securing an act to distribute the revenues among the various religious denominations of the Province of Upper Canada. However, the British liberal-Whig Government – which believed in the modern concept of indivisible sovereignty – refused to grant the principle of 'responsible government'. It was viewed as a violation of the sovereignty of Parliament: viz. the King in Parliament. Nonetheless, Thomson was instructed to work in harmony with the Legislature on public issues, and to make every effort to implement the various recommendations of the Durham Report. For the British government, the primary purpose of the projected union of the Canadas was to place the French-Canadians in a minority within the Legislature of an English colony to facilitate their gradual assimilation. A second failed rebellion in the Montreal District of Lower Canada in November 1838, had served only to strengthen the British government in its belief that the French-Canadians needed to be assimilated.

In October 1839, Thomson arrived at Quebec. He quickly secured approval for a union of the two Canadian provinces from the appointed Special Council that had been governing Lower Canada since the 1837 Rebellion. Almost immediately, he proceeded to Toronto, and immersed himself in provincial politics with the aim of undermining the power and influence of the Tory governing elite that was opposed to the proposed union of the provinces.

To gain legislative support for the proposed union, Thomson announced that he intended to govern "in accordance with the well understood wishes and interests of the people", and that the heavy debt of Upper Canada – incurred in canal building -- would be taken over by the proposed union government. Then he proceeded to form an Executive Council of moderates in promising to promote 'harmony and good government', to pursue a programme of moderate reform, and to foster economic development with the aid of a British government interest guarantee for a £1.5-million loan for public works and debt repayment. By such inducements and rhetoric -- at a time when Upper Canada was still feeling the ill-effects of the general economic depression of 1837 -- Thomson managed to secure the passage of a Union Bill through the conservative Legislature of Upper Canada. He intentionally isolated the members of the former Tory political establishment whom he referred to as "a miserable little oligarchy".

Following the passage of the Act of Union, Thomson received his reward from the liberal-Whig Government in Britain. In August 1840, he was raised to the peerage as Lord Sydenham. In February 1841, the new United Province of Canada was promulgated, and in the ensuring election the High Church Tories -- who had been the main proponents of public works while in power -- were severely disadvantaged in running against the declared 'Unionists' – Reformers, conservatives, and moderate Tories -- who supported Lord Sydenham on the basis of a campaign promise that his government would introduce a major programme of public works.

Within six months of the Union of the Canadas, Lord Sydenham established a Board of Works to undertake a five-year programme of public works construction which was to focus on waterways improvements: the construction of canals; lighthouses and navigation aids; harbor and river improvements; timbers slides and booms; as well as the upgrading of arterial roads connecting navigable waterways. The High Church Tories were shunted aside and lost their power and influence under the union of the provinces.

In the United Province of Canada, a succession of British liberal-Whig Governors – Lord Sydenham, Lord Bagot, Lord Metcalfe, and Earl Cathcart – managed to form government ministries composed of moderate English-speaking members -- moderate Tories, conservatives, and moderate Reformers -- from Canada West (Upper Canada) and Canada East (Lower Canada), with the occasional adherence of an individual French-Canadian member willing to accept an appointment to the Executive Council. In the Assembly, the large bloc of French-Canadian representatives -- who were strongly united under the leadership of Louis-Hippolyte Lafontaine -- remained opposed to the Union of the Canadas and to the new provincial government.

Under the Union, the Executive Council took a novel form; although its traditional role as strictly an advisory body to the Governor was retained. In the new system of government, each minister was the head of a department (a reform recommended in the Durham Report), each minister was responsible to the Governor for the administration of his department, and the ministers were appointed almost exclusively from among members of the Legislative Assembly. Moreover, the survival of a ministry depended upon the maintenance of the support of a majority in the Legislative Assembly.

The new ministerial system of government -- as established by Lord Sydenham -- depended on the Governor being able to attract, to a government ministry, prominent moderates of various political persuasions who were willing to serve under a Governor that governed above party and distributed Crown patronage in a non-partisan manner. The intention was to promote 'harmony' between the Executive Council, the Legislative Council, and the House of Assembly in a system of limited responsible government. It was a system of government in which the Governor strove to promote policies and measures that could command the support of a majority in the Legislature – the Assembly and the Legislative Council -- while the Crown retained control over Crown revenues and patronage, and the traditional constitutional right to reserve legislative acts for Her Majesties' Pleasure, if deemed requisite.

Under the ministerial government system of Sydenham and his successors as Governors of the United Province of Canada, the High Church Tories were largely excluded from a succession of government ministries and from appointments to the new Legislative Council of the United Province of Canada. (16)

In the field of education, the Upper Canadian Anglian Tories suffered yet another setback. In September 1844, it was announced that Egerton Ryerson had been appointed as the new Superintendent of Education for Canada West (Upper Canada). It was an appointment made by Governor Metcalfe to attract the support of the sectarians for his government, and as a reward to Ryerson for his public defence of the Governor's prerogatives during a November 1843 patronage dispute. Five years' earlier, Egerton Ryerson had expressed -- in a private communication to one of his brothers, the Rev. John Ryerson -- the need for the Methodists to seize whatever opportunity they could to stamp their "Constitutional & Scriptural, political & religious doctrines" upon the public mind and, in so doing, "to give the tone to the future government, and legislation in the province". Now Egerton Ryerson had the opportunity. After a leisurely ten-month tour of Britain and the Continent to study different systems of education, he was instrumental in securing the passage of new education acts that re-organized the existing school system of Canada West and its financial basis, that established a new curriculum for the schools with a list of authorized books for use in the schools. (17)

Seeing the 'national' education system that they had established falling under the control of Egerton Ryerson was an alarming and frustrating experience for the Upper Canadian Anglican Tories, but the very nadir of their existence came with the introduction of the principle of responsible government.

'Responsible Government' (1848)

The third major blow to the High Church Tories came when a new free-trade, liberal-Whig Government gained power in Britain under Lord John Russell, with Earl Grey as Colonial Secretary. In November 1846, Grey introduce a new policy of granting responsible government to 'the advanced colonies' of Nova Scotia and Canada, and appointed Lord Elgin -- the son-in-law of the late Lord Durham -- as Governor-General of the United Province of Canada. Lord Elgin was instructed that he was to refrain from attempting to form a government ministry; and that the government was to be "transferred to, and carried on by", an Executive Council supported by the party commanding a majority in the Assembly.

Earlier, the Tories had feared that under a union of the two Canadian provinces, a revived Reform Party of Canada West would form an alliance in the Legislative Assembly with a large bloc of anti-government French-Canadian representatives from Canada East, to oppose the provincial government and demand the implementation of the principle of 'responsible government'. Indeed, under the union, such an alliance did materialize. Through the efforts of Francis Hincks, the Reform Party of Canada West under Robert Baldwin formed an alliance with the French-Canadian bloc of representatives under Louis-Hippolyte Lafontaine to demand 'responsible government'.

Despite the earlier refusal of Lafontaine to join a government ministry, the Sydenham system of forming government ministries had proved workable in providing good government, in maintaining the support of a slim majority in the House of Assembly, and in promoting public works with financing obtained on the basis of the British government loan guarantee. Under the successors to Sydenham, the aim of assimilating the French was abandoned, and restrictions on the French language in government were removed as part of a continuing effort to win over the French-Canadian bloc to the support of a succession of government ministries. It was a futile gesture as the restrictions on the use of the French-language in the provincial parliament had never been enforced. However, the political situation changed dramatically when the Reform alliance gained a solid majority, in both Canada West and Canada East, in the provincial election of November 1847.

When the Assembly reconvened in March 1848, a weak government ministry composed of moderate Tories and conservatives, from Canada West and Canada East, was defeated on a non-confidence motion. Under the principle of 'responsible government', the Reform Party took power, and formed a Reform ministry that brought government policy and administration, and government patronage appointments, under the direct control of a partisan political party.

Under the Reform Party governments of Baldwin-Lafontaine (March 1848-October 1851) and Hincks-Morin (October 1851-September 1854), the Tories were continually denigrated and denounced and, with the introduction of an American 'spoils system' of government, the Tories were systematically purged from public offices by the vindictive, and highly-partisan, Reform Party governments. A secularization policy was introduced that destroyed almost all vestiges of the former church-state polity in Canada West, including the secularization of King's College university (1849), and the secularization of the Clergy Reserves (1854). A Rebellion Losses Bill (1849) was passed, principally to financially compensate the French-Canadian rebels for the damages that their properties had incurred during their rebellions of 1837 and 1838.

The Return of the Rebels

For the former Anglican Tory establishment, the partisan patronage system that the Reform Party introduced, once in power, was yet another shock. Under the Reform Party governments, well-known rebel sympathizers received government patronage appointments, as well as fugitive rebels who returned to Canada after receiving a pardon – either an individual pardon received earlier upon request from Governor Metcalfe, or under a general pardon under an 1849 Amnesty Act. (18) Even William Lyon Mackezie, the leader of the Upper Canadian rebels, and Louis-Joseph Papineau the leader of the Lower Canadian rebels, were pardoned and permitted to return to Canada. Following his election to the Assembly as a Reform candidate for Haldimand County in 1851, Mackenzie was offered a government position as general agent for the Crown Lands Department under Dr. John Rolph, the new Commissioner of Crown Lands. The offer was withdrawn subsequently, supposedly because Mackenzie insisted on retaining his independence from Reform Party discipline in the House of Assembly. (19) For the Upper Canadian Anglican Tories, the world was turned upside down.

A lost Saturnia regna

As viewed by the Anglican Tories, the introduction of 'responsible government' brought not only partisan party government, but a catering to public opinion wherever it might lead, and an acceptance of political expediency as the guide to political action. It ushered in a new political era, which the Tories characterized as marked by "extravagance, self-seeking, and corruption". However, the Tory rejection of the new order ran much deeper than their objection to partisan party politics and their exclusion from power.

For the Tories of Upper Canada, the new political system reflected a new social order that they characterized as one marked by "a spirit of democracy", "insubordination", "political expediency", "secularism", and "materialism", all of which were values that were totally the adverse of their own. (20) In rejecting the new order, the Tories lamented the passing of a "*Saturnia regna*" (a Golden Age) when Upper Canada was under the "government of *gentlemen*", when 'character', 'public virtue', 'integrity', and 'self-denial' were duly recognized, and government was conducted on 'sound principle and justice'. (21) Yet, the former Tory political elite were confident that in God's good time everything would be set right again. The explanation for this stance can be found in the governing beliefs of the Tory mind.

It was not possible for the true Tories to abandon the principles for which they stood to court popularity or government favour. Nor could they agree to any suggestion that their principles were no longer applicable for governing an increasingly secular society, nor accept that their day had passed. To the contrary, they believed that what they stood for were eternal and immutable principles of right in keeping with God's scheme of things and the needs of man's nature. Democratic egalitarianism and infidelity might triumph for a time, but it was expected that in one or two generations, perhaps less, the people would come to see "what is for their good". Society would be reconstituted on its proper foundations. (22) Thus, the Tory elite remained loyal to the traditional order in being confident in their belief that "the cause of loyalty is the cause of God, and that, if cast down for a period, it would re-assert its lost sway". As 'Christian patriots', they could do no less.

To the true Tories, all actions of man were to be judged in terms of religion, for the Christian faith provided the moral principles and rules of conduct by which all men ought to act, and for which they were accountable to a higher power. (23) The corollary was the belief that the conservative body of the nation was the true governing party because Toryism and conservatism – the latter of which by the mid-19th Century in Canada, was but "a diluted Toryism" – embraced Christian principles. (24) Nonetheless, those conservatives who in the political strife of the 1840s were willing to sacrifice the prerogatives and endowments of the Established Church to placate public opinion were admonished that in doing so, they not only "cut the chords of Conservative vitality" but were risking the chastisement of God's Providence. They were branded as being apostates. For the staunch Tories:

> The individual who would separate a deep religious influence from his political creed, may call himself a Conservative; but we are constrained to say that he is ignorant of the grand and leading principle by which the body of which he professes himself a member, are, or ought to be, guided.

Conservatism, it was insisted, must have "a religious basis". All true conservatives were bound by their beliefs to heed the Biblical injunction to 'Fear God and Honour the King'. The Christian religion was the mainstay of the traditional order, of the rights and duties of man as established in keeping with God's Moral Law, and of the British Constitution which had evolved under God's superintending Providence in keeping with Christian values. (25)

In viewing the United Province of Canada and the British Empire at mid-century, Bishop Strachan could not but lament what had transpired. He wrote:

> I am still the same Tory that you knew me to be forty years ago, and am of the opinion that till we had responsible government in the colony we knew nothing of the corruption of government. Now the ministry, as they call it, whether conservative or reform, seem to have no other object than to get good places. All is party and, I may say, all is corruption; and it matters not which faction is in power. Moreover, the Free Trade dogma seems to destroy the colonial system. The Navigation Laws have made Great Britain what she is. The repeal of these laws will complete the infatuation which reigns supreme in the mother country. In a few years, she will sink to an equality with Sweden and Danemark [sic]. There may be some sense in free trade reciprocity; but free trade on one side is contrary to common sense." (26)

The Tory Legacy

In Upper Canada, it was the Anglican Tories who sought to maintain the Province as a Loyalist asylum within the British Empire, and who did so by defending the traditional church-state polity and in espousing a Christian political philosophy that differed from the secular Lockean-liberalism of the United States of America. Moreover, it was the Tories who were instrumental in preserving the Province of Upper Canada from conquest and/or assimilation by the American Republic; it was the Tories who had a national vision for the future of Upper Canada and the British North American provinces more generally; and it was the Tories who struggled to implement a national policy to strength the province –

politically, culturally, economically, and militarily -- to ensure its survival and prosperity as a distinct political entity in North America. Without the sacrifices and achievements of the Upper Canadian Tories, there would have been no British North American provinces to unite in the Dominion of Canada at Confederation in 1867 or, at least, no Province of Canada West to lead the way.

It was the Tories who laid the foundations for the nation that was to come in the future establishment of the Dominion of Canada, in that they provided a national consciousness and national purpose for the building of an independent nation on the northern half of the North American Continent – a nation that was to be based on cultural, political, and religious values that were distinct from the democratic republicanism and secularism of the American Republic. The Anglican Tories were striving to establish a Christian 'nation' in the Loyalist asylum of Upper Canada that was to be based on a monarchical form of government under the balanced British Constitution, an inclusive National Church, and a national system of education under the direction of the established Church of England, a 'British national character', loyalty to the Crown, and an adherence to the unity of the British Empire. It was a nation that, in its political life, was to be fully inclusive of French-Canadians. They were to be gradually and peacefully assimilated into the national political culture through English language instruction in bilingual Roman Catholic schools – taught by bilingual Scots immigrants – while retaining their religion and French-language within their local community and the family. Above all it was a nation that was to have a strong Christian moral character, a steadfast Christian faith, and a belief in a Day of Judgement. They lived in keeping with the belief that "in all things there is a right and wrong, and it is not a matter of indifference which side we take".

Today, there is much academic debate concerning the 'philosophical rational', if any, for Confederation, the extent of the influence of the liberal political thought of John Locke on the British North America Act (1867), and the nature of the Canadian political identity. (27) Yet, no one – to the author's knowledge – has studied the extent to which the British North America Act encompasses Anglican Tory political thought – the beliefs, values and principles of the Anglican Tories of the British North American colonies. That is particularly surprising in that the Tory value system is readily evident in the fundamental clause that empowered Parliament, in the name of the Queen, "to make Laws for the Peace, Order and good Government" of the new Dominion of Canada. (28)

More generally, in focusing their histories of Upper Canada on political agitators and outgroups, and ignoring the Tory national vision, the substantial contributions of the Anglican Tories to the development of the Province of Upper Canada, and the Tory political philosophy that provided a rationale for striving to build a nation in North American independent of the United States, liberal-Whig historians have produced a history of Canada that is truly "hollow at the core".

Notes

Conclusion

Frontispiece quotation: Bishop John Strachan to Robert Gillespie, Strachan Letterbook 1844-49, 273, as quoted in Henderson, ed., *John Strachan, Documents and Opinions*, 178.

1. On the Tory contribution to education, see: Craig, *Upper Canada*, 181-187; J.D. Purdy, "John Strachan's Educational Policies, 1815-1841", *Ontario History*, LXIV, 1972, 45-64; and G.W. Spragge, "John Strachan's Contribution to Education, 1800-23", *Canadian Historical Review*, XXII, 1941, 147-158. See also online text: *The Charter of the University of King's College at York in Upper Canada* (London: R. Gilbert, 1827/ reprint: Kingston, Upper Canada: H.C. Thomson, 1828). See also "An Act to Amend the Charter of the University of King's College" (7th William IV, c. xvi, 4 March1837) in J. George Hodgins, *Documentary History of Education in Upper Canada*, Vol. III: 1836-1840, 88-89.

The Reformers categorized the Upper Canadian Tory elite as a self-serving, corrupt and unprogressive 'Family Compact', and despite that partisan epithet lacking any historical validity, Canadian historians have continued to employ it. For a refutation of that pejorative epithet, see: Robert E. Saunders, "What was the Family Compact", *Ontario History*, XLIX, 1957, No. 4, 165-178; and Denis McKim, "Upper Canadian Thermidor: The Family Compact & the counter-revolutionary Atlantic", *Ontario History*, CVI, 2014, No. 2, 235-262. Saunders views the Tory elite as being composed of educated men of culture: "a quasi-aristocracy of bureaucrats and professional men (principally lawyers)"; McKim argues that the Tories were advocates of "an alternative model of colonial development".

2. On the entry of William Warren Baldwin into politics, see: *Dictionary of Canadian Biography*, VII, Robert L. Fraser, "Baldwin, William Warren". The biographical entry has an excellent bibliography on the studies devoted to the concept of 'responsible government' and the attainment of responsible government in Canada. However, the present study is concerned solely with the view of the Tory elite on the principle of responsible government.

3. Robert Kelley, *The Transatlantic Persuasion: The Liberal-Democratic Mind in the Age of Gladstone* (New York: Alfred A. Knopf, 1969).

4. This summary of the religious principles, beliefs and values of the evangelical Calvinists and the role of the Rev. Jonathan Edwards in the evolution of that

religious movement in the period of the Great Awakening, is based on a close reading of Alan Heimert, *Religion and the American Mind, From the Great Awaking to the Revolution* (Cambridge, Massachusetts: Harvard University Press, 1966), 1-236. The section on the theology of Edwards, with respect to his view of 'natural man' (fallen man) and the concept of instantaneous conversion, has been further influenced by a reading of Conrad Cherry, *The Theology of Jonathan Edwards, A Reappraisal* (Bloomington: Indiana University Press, 1990, 1st ed., 1966), x-xii & 59-60. Any errors or misconceptions in summarizing the interpretations and arguments presented in these two studies is entirely the responsibility of the author. On the role of the evangelical Calvinists in the American Revolution, see Heimert, 294-461.

5. See Nathan O. Hatch, *The Democratization of American Christianity* (New Haven & London: Yale University Press, 1989), 3-77.

6. Eric Voegelin, *The New Science of Politics, An Introduction* (Chicago: University of Chicago Press, 1967), 135-138.

7. William Westfall, *Two Worlds, The Protestant Culture of Nineteenth Century Ontario* (Kingston & Montreal: McGill-Queen's University Press, 1989), 68-81. One might add to the Westfall treatment that the transformation of the religious culture of Methodism within the new Wesleyan Methodist Church in Canada (ca. 1840s-1860s), marked a rejection of the American evangelical Protestantism of 'American Methodism' in Upper Canada as it had evolved from the evangelical Calvinism of its original expounder in the American colonies, the Rev. George Whitefield (1714-1770). The radical social and political character of American evangelical Protestantism was gradual supplanted in Canada West by the conservative British Wesleyan evangelical Protestantism which was rooted in Anglicanism and the concept of Prevenient Grace of the founder of Methodism, the Rev. John Wesley (1703-1791). In England, camp meetings and religious revivals were banned by the Wesleyan Methodists prior to 1820.

The 1842 census of Canada West (Upper Canada) recorded the religious population as: Church of England (107,291), Church of Scotland and various Presbyterian sects (77,929), Roman Catholic Church (65,203), the several Methodist sects (55,667), Quakers (5,200), Lutherans (4,534), Congregationalists (4,253), Jews (1,105), and Other Denominations (19,422). In addition, there was a very large category of 'Not Given' (81,348).

8. Based on the union terms imposed on the Canada Methodist Conference in 1833 by the British Wesleyans, Goldwin French (*Parsons & Politics*, 142)

has commented that: "Perhaps without realizing it, the Canadian Societies committed themselves to a program of assimilation to the English form of Methodism led by the Wesleyan missionaries". Indeed, that was the case, but it must have been evident to one and all at the time. The Wesleyan missionaries took over the editorship of the *Christian Guardian* and turned it into a strictly religious newspaper, took over the teaching at the Upper Canadian Academy which was placed under a Tory Wesleyan missionary principal, and the Canadian Methodist Conference of 1834, while under a Wesleyan President, abandoned the traditional American Methodist religious principle of 'voluntaryism'. The Congress voted to seek funding from the British government for the Upper Canada Academy, and expressed a willingness to 'reluctantly submit", if offered funding from any future distribution of the clergy reserves revenues among the Protestant religious denominations of Upper Canada. (French, *Parsons & Politics*, 140-141, 152-160.)

The willingness of the leadership of the Upper Canadian Methodists to accept a union dominated by the British Wesleyan Methodists had a number of causes: a fear that the well-financed British Wesleyan Methodists were about to send missionaries into Upper Canada to compete with the preachers of the newly-independent Methodist Episcopal Church in Canada; a severe financial crisis within the new Upper Canadian Methodist Church; and a significant and growing loss of members. It appears that by the early 1830s, Upper Canadians were beginning to turn away from the emotional religion of camp meetings, revivals, sudden conversions, and the hell-fire preaching that was characteristic of the American evangelical Protestantism of Upper Canadian Methodism. The Methodist Episcopal Church was failing to attract British immigrants who were entering Upper Canada by the tens of thousands each year. On the Upper Canadian Methodist preaching, see: Westfall, 171-172.

9. On the new unified Protestant culture of mid-19th Century Canada West/Ontario, see Westfall, *Two Worlds*, 191-209, and especially 198-205 on the role of religion in society. The Westfall interpretation of a Protestant consensus at mid-Century has been questioned – or, more correctly, has been qualified -- recently. An argument has been made that the earlier evangelical voluntaryist culture of Upper Canadian Methodism --'American Methodism', as distinct from British Wesleyan Methodism -- continued to have a significant political impact in an unrelenting demand for the secularization of the Clergy Reserves and the complete separation of church and state. (See James Forbes, "Contesting the Protestant Consensus: Voluntarists, Methodists, and the Persistence of Evangelical Dissent in Upper Canada", *Ontario History*, vol. 108, no. 2, Fall 2016, 189-214.)

10. Bernard Bailyn, *The Ideological Origins of the American Revolution* (Cambridge, Mass.: Harvard University Press, 1967). On the British radical whig pamphleteers of the 18th Century whose ideas directly impacted the thought of the American revolutionaries, see Caroline Robbins, *The Eighteenth-Century Commonwealthman, Studies in the Transmission, Development and Circumstance of English Liberal Thought from the Restoration of Charles II until the War with the Thirteen Colonies* (Cambridge, Mass.: Harvard University Press, 1961, 1st ed. 1959). Robbins analyzes the political and social ideas of the leading radical whigs of the 18th Century, whom she calls the 'real whigs', and their borrowings from the earlier political tracts of the English Puritan revolutionaries of the 17th Century.

11. See online text "The Declaration of Independence: "In Congress, July 4, 1776. The Unanimous Declaration of the thirteen United States of America."

12. Bailyn, *The Ideological Origins*, 47, 144, 199-204, 252, 261-265, 282-284, 290 & 301. Although Bailyn does not provide any comparisons with the British system of a balanced constitution, one can add that the American separation of powers – Executive, Legislative and Judicial -- differed from the Old Tory concept of the legislative balance of the constitution. In the Tory concept, the balance was in the Legislature with the King, the House of Lords and the House of Commons each having a necessary role to play in the passing of legislation; and the King held the sovereign power – a separate executive function -- in executing and enforcing the laws enacted. The courts were an adjunct of the executive in administering the laws of the realm.

The liberal-Whigs held to the same concept of a legislative balance of the British constitution – with the King, the House of Lords and the House of Commons all having a necessary role in the enacting of laws – however, for the liberal-Whigs sovereignty resided in Parliament – the King in Parliament – with the executive as well as the legislative function of government under the control of Parliament. Moreover, the liberal-Whigs held that the judiciary ought to be independent of the executive, which was achieved by the tenure of judges in Britain being 'during good behaviour' rather than 'during pleasure' of the King which was an older constitutional concept. In Upper Canada, the tenure of judges was 'during pleasure' until 1831 when the liberal-Whig government in Britain decreed that henceforth judges would hold office 'during good behaviour', and were to be independent of government. The Chief Justice of the King's Bench was no longer permitted to hold his traditional seat in the Executive Council – where formerly he had advised the government on constitutional issues -- and was no longer permitted to serve as the Speaker of the Legislative Council – where formerly he had assisted the Legislative Council through reviewing the legal context and the phrasing of bills passed by the House of Assembly.

13. Craig, *Upper Canada*, 252-260; and *DCB*, VII, Fernand Ouellet, "Lambton, John George, 1st Earl of Durham" and IX, Jacques Monet, "LaFontaine, Sir Louis-Hippolyte. Craig provides an excellent overview of the political situation in Upper Canada following the Rebellion of December 1837.

14. Great Britain, House of Commons, *Report on the Affairs of British North America from The Earl of Durham, Her Majesty's High Commissioner* (Printed by Order of the House of Commons, 11 February 1839); and Craig, *Upper Canada*, 260-270. See also, *DCB*, XI, William G. Ormsby, "Hincks, Sir Francis". Craig sets forth the response of the Upper Canadian Tories to the Durham Report.

15. On the older medieval concept of divisible sovereignty, see Robert W. Passfield, *Phips' Amphibious Assault on Canada – 1690* (Amazon.com, 2011), 'Where Sovereignty Lay', especially 91-94.

16. *DCB*, VII. Phillip Buckner, "Thomson, Charles Edward Poulett, 1st Baron Sydenham": Craig, *Upper Canada*, 270- 275; and J. M. S. Careless, *The Union of the Canadas, The Growth of Canadian Institutions, 1841-1857* (Toronto: McClelland and Stewart Ltd., 1967), 3-5, 9-10, 12 & 38-39. On the Special Council see online: Steven Watt, "Authoritarianism, Constitutionalism, and the Special Council of Lower Canada, 1838-1841", McGill University MA Thesis, July 1997.

As of 1840, the outstanding public debt of the Province of Upper Canada was £1,179, 949, of which approximately 23% of the total debt was incurred in providing government financial support to the Welland Canal Company – a joint private -public enterprise -- for the construction of the Welland Canal. (Aitken, *The Welland Canal Company*, 148.) On the public works initiated by Sydenham, see Robert W. Passfield, "Waterways", in Norman R. Ball, ed., *Building Canada, a History of Public Works* (Toronto: University of Toronto Press, 1988), 118-120.

17. R.D. Gidney, "Ryerson, Egerton", *DCB*, XI; and Goldwin French, *Parsons & Politics*, 229-230, 234 -235. See also French (*Parsons & Politics*, 172) wherein a letter is partially quoted from Egerton Ryerson to the Rev. John Ryerson of 4 April 1838. Egerton Ryerson's statement of his aim to shape the

public mind of Upper Canada was in reference to his wanting to regain the editorship of the *Christian Guardian* newspaper to disseminated Methodist religious, political and constitutional views. In February 1841, Ryerson used similar words again about the opportunity to form public opinion when he advocated the founding of a government newspaper to support the ministerial government of Lord Sydenham. (See McNairn, *The Capacity to Judge*, 213.) His later appointment as Superintendent of Education for Canada West gave him an even greater opportunity to form public opinion to his own evangelical Protestant views in directing the education of the youth of the province.

18. Careless, *Union of the Canadas*, 37-41, 46-47, 109-126; and Curtis Fahey, *The Anglican Experience in Upper Canada, 1791-1854* (Ottawa: Carleton University Press, 1991), "Defeat", 163-196. The Fahey treatment is marred by his interpretation of the Anglican Tories as being situational conservatives whom he views as simply fighting an embittered rearguard action in defence of "ideals of the past". Augustin-Norbert Morin was an ardent Ultramontane Roman Catholic, and a French-Canadian nationalist who had drafted the 92 Resolutions of the parti Patriote in 1834. During the 1837 Rebellion, Morin tried to raise a rebel force at Quebec, but failed miserably. See *DCB*, IX, Jean-Marc Paradis, "Morin, Augustin-Norbert".

Under the Union, the effort of a succession of Governors to maintain the Sydenham system of ministerial government, headed by the Governor governing above party in harmony with a majority in the House of Assembly, was continually under siege by Robert Baldwin. With the support of the large French-Canadian bloc under Louis-Hippolyte LaFontaine, Baldwin continually indulged in a highly-partisan Reform Party politics. He demanded a full implementation of the principle of responsible government and was adamant that all government patronage be distribute for the benefit of the majority party in the House of Assembly. (See, Cross, *A Biography of Robert Baldwin*, 116-156, and especially 151-157.) For a study of the general elections under the Union of the Canadas, and the political machinations of the period 1841 through 1854, see: Paul G. Cornell, *The Alignment of Political Groups in Canada, 1841-1867* (Toronto: University of Toronto Press, 1962), 3-35.

The Reform Party demand for the implementation of 'responsible government' reached its climax in November 1843, when the Reform members of the Executive Council demanded – in citing the principle of responsible government -- that Lord Metcalfe not make any government appointments without their advice, and that no appointments be made 'prejudicial to their influence'. The subsequent resignation of the ministers over the patronage issue and appeals by Lord Metcalfe to the public to defend the balance of the British Constitution, gave rise to the 'Metcalfe crisis'. On the public debate that raged over the nature of the balanced British constitution, the sovereignty of the Crown, and the meaning of the principle of responsible government, see McNairn (*The Capacity to Judge*), 237-271. In the October 1844 provincial election, the Reformers of Canada West were reduced to twelve seats, versus 28 seats for the government supporters. However, in Canada East, the French bloc under Lafontaine returned 25 members, versus only fourteen government supporters, and apparently an independent. Hence, the Reform Party of Lafontaine-Baldwin remained a political force in the House of Assembly in demanding responsible government.

19. On the return of Mackenzie to Canada, see DCB, IX, Frederick Armstrong and Ronald J. Stagg, "Mackenzie, William Lyon"; and William Dawson LeSueur, *William Lyon Mackenzie: A Reinterpretation*, ed. A.B. McKillop (Toronto: Macmillan Co., 1979), 363-385.

[The following endnotes pertain to the chapter section on 'A lost Saturnia regna' which was originally researched and written up over forty years' ago as part of the Introduction to the abortive Ph.D. dissertation in which the author sought to frame the intellectual study. It was moved to this Conclusion to convey the Tory view of politics under the Union of the Provinces, and of party politics following the gaining of political power by Reform governments following the adoption of the principle of responsible government.]

20. *The Church* (Bethune editorials), 10 July 1841 & 19 April 1844; PAO, Macaulay Papers, reel 4, J.B. Robinson to John Macaulay, 31 December 1847; PAO, Strachan Letterbook 1844-49, reel 12, Strachan to Robert Gillespie, 2 February 1848; and PAO, Robinson Papers, Robinson Letterbook 1814-62, 160-161, J.B. Robinson to Strachan, 8 April 1851.

21. PAO, Strachan Papers, reel 6, 61, John Macaulay to J.B. Robinson, 22 February 1850. See also, PAO, Macaulay Papers, reel 4, William Macaulay to Ann Macaulay, 8 August 1845.

22. PAO, Robinson Letterbook 1814-62, 167-68, J.B. Robinson to Strachan, 8 April 1851. See also, PAO, Strachan Papers, reel 6, 61, John Macaulay to J.B. Robinson, 22 February 1850; and PAO, Macaulay Papers, reel 4, William Macaulay to Ann Macaulay, 27 January 1841.

23. *The Church* (Bethune editorials), 1 May 1841, 10 July 1841 & 29 July 1842.

24. PAO, Strachan Papers, reel 6, 61, John Macaulay to J.B. Robinson, 22 February 1850.

25. *The Church* (Bethune editorials), 1 May 1841, 19 April 1844 & 24 May 1844. The quotation is from the editorial of 1 May 1841.

26. Bishop John Strachan to Robert Gillespie, Strachan Letterbook 1844-49, 273, as quoted in Henderson, ed., *John Strachan, Documents and Opinions*, 178.

27. [See, for example, Janet Ajzenstat, *The Canadian Founding, John Locke and Parliament* (Montreal & Kingston: McGill-Queen's University Press, 2007), Preface and 1-21.]

28. The British North America Act (30 Victoria, Cap. 3, 1867), VI – Distribution of Legislative Powers, 91. Powers of the Parliament.

Bibliography

Primary Sources – Archival

Public Archives of Canada (PAC). (Now Library & Archives Canada.) Sources cited.

> MG11, Colonial Office, London, CO42, Canada, "Q" Series: Original Correspondence,
>
>> Secretary of State, reel B-141, vol. 179: July-December 1818; and
>>
>> Upper Canada Public Offices and Miscellaneous, reel B-297, vol. 358: 1818.
>
> Upper Canada Sundries, RG5, A1, Civil Secretary Correspondence:
>
> vol. 16, "Report on disloyal Characters in the Home District", 16 August 1813;
>
> vol. 192, 'Report Sherriff's Office, Hamilton, to His Excellency', 21 April 1838;
>
> vol. 193, 'J.B. Robinson and Jonas Jones to His Excellency', 2 May 1838; and
>
> vol. 251, "Report of Commissioners Appointed to the Inquire into Charges of Treason and Felony", n.d. [April 1838].

Public Archives of Ontario (PAO). (Now Archives of Ontario.)

> John Beverley Robinson family fonds, 1784, 1803-1905:
>
>> Charges to the Grand Juries, 1829-1841;
>>
>> John Beverley Robinson Letterbooks, 1812-1862.
>>
>> John Beverley Robinson Diaries, 1815-1817.
>
> John Strachan Fonds:
>
>> Strachan Papers 1799-1867.

Letterbooks, 1812-1867.

Sermons, 1799-1867.

Macaulay Family fonds, 1773-1874.

William Hamilton Merritt family fonds, 1774-1890.

Queen's University Archives

Richard Cartwright Jr. Family Papers

Letterbooks, 1786-1812.

National Archives of Scotland

GD45/3/332. 1080-1085, Lt. Col. John Harvey, "Memorandum on the defence of the Canadas", 7 November 1818.

Primary Sources – Published

"An Act to Amend the Charter of the University of King's College" (4 March1837) in J. George Hodgins, *Documentary History of Education in Upper Canada*, Vol. III: 1836-1840, 88-89.

Blackstone, William. *Commentaries on the Laws of England, Volume IV, Of Public Wrongs* (1st ed., 1770, reprint Boston: Beacon Press, 1962).

Bethune, A.N. M*emoir of the Right Reverend John Strachan, First Bishop of Toronto* (Toronto: Henry Rowsell, 1870).

Cartwright, C. E., ed. *Life and Letters of Richard Cartwright* (Toronto: Belford Bros., 1876).

Colonial Advocate (York), several issues and articles as cited.

The Charter of the University of King's College at York in Upper Canada (London: R. Gilbert, 1827; reprint: Kingston, Upper Canada: H.C. Thomson, 1828).

Christian Recorder, 1819-1821, issues and articles as cited.

The Church, 1838-1844, several issues and articles as cited.

Common Sense by Thomas Paine (Rockville, Maryland: Arc Manor Classic Reprints, 2008).

Craig, Gerald M., ed. *Discontent in Upper Canada* (Toronto: Copp Clark, 1974).

Cruikshank, Ernest A., Brigadier General, L.L.D., ed. *The Correspondence of Lieut. Governor John Graves Simcoe with Allied Documents relating to His Administration of the Government of Upper Canada*, Volume I: 1789-1793 and Supplementary Volume V: 1792-1796 (Toronto: Ontario Historical Society, 1923 & 1931).

Doughty, A.G. & Norah Story, eds., *Documents relating to the Constitutional History of Canada, 1819-28* (Ottawa: King's Printer, 1935).

Doughty, A.G. & Duncan A. MacArthur, eds., *Documents relating to the Constitutional History of Canada, 17691-1818* (Ottawa: Kings' Printer, 1914.

Great Britain, House of Commons. *Canada Church Establishment, Copy of a Letter addressed to R.J. Wilmot Horton, Esq. by the Rev. Dr. Strachan, Archdeacon of York, Upper Canada, dated 16 May 1827, respecting the State of the Church in that Province* (Printed by Order of House of Commons, 22 May 1827).

Great Britain, House of Commons. *Report from the Selected Committee on the Civil Government of Canada* (Ordered printed by the House of Commons, 22 July 1828).

Great Britain, House of Commons. *Report on the Affairs of British North America from the Earl of Durham, Her Majesty's High Commissioner* (Printed by Order of the House of Commons, 11 February 1839).

Henderson, J.L.H., ed., *John Strachan, Documents and Opinions* (Toronto: McClelland & Stewart, 1969).

Hodgins, John George, ed. *Documentary History of Education in Upper Canada from the passing of the Constitutional Act of 1791 to the Closure of Rev. Dr. Ryerson's Administration of the Education Department in 1876*, vol. I: 1790-1830; vol. II: 1831-1836, vol. III: 1836-1840; vol. IV: 1841-1843, and vol. V: 1843-1846 (Toronto: Warwick Bro's & Rutter, Printers, 1894 -1897).

Kingston Chronicle, 1819-1821, 1823-1825, & 1831-1832.

Kingston Gazette, 1812, several issues and articles as cited.

Letter from the Reverend Egerton Ryerson to the Hon. And Reverend Doctor Strachan, published originally in the Upper Canada Herald (Kingston, U.C.: Herald Office, 1828).

Library of Congress. The Thomas Jefferson Papers at the Library of Congress: Series I, General Correspondence, 1651-1827 (Online Manuscript Collection).

Moir, John S., ed. *Church and State in Canada, 1627-1867: basic documents* (Toronto: McClelland & Stewart, 1967).

Paley, William. *The Works of William Paley D.D. in Five Volumes, Volume III containing the Principles of Moral and Political Philosophy* (Newport, Rhode Island: Rousmaniere and Barber, 1811).

Preston, Richard A., ed. *Kingston before the War of 1812: a collection of documents* (Toronto: Champlain Society Publication, 1959).

Read, Colin & Ronald J. Stagg, eds. *The Rebellion of 1837 in Upper Canada, A Collection of Documents* (Toronto: The Champlain Society, 1985).

Report from the Select Committee of the Legislative Council of Upper Canada on the State of the Province (R. Stanton: Queen's Printer, 1838.

Report of a Select Committee of the House of Assembly on the Political State of the Provinces of Upper and Lower Canada (R. Stanton: Queen's Printer, 1838).

Sanderson, Charles R., ed. *The Arthur Papers – Being the papers mainly confidential, private and demi-official of Sir George Arthur, K.C.H., Last Lieutenant-Governor of Upper Canada* (Toronto: Toronto Public Libraries), vol. I: 1822-1838, vol. II: 1839-1840 & vol. III:1840-1850.

Shortt, Adam & Arthur G. Doughty, eds. *Documents relating to the constitutional history of Canada, 1759-91* (Ottawa: King's Printer, 1918).

Spragge, George W., ed. *The John Strachan Letter Book: 1812-1834* (Toronto: Ontario Historical Society, 1946).

Strachan, John. "Address of the House of Assembly to the People of Upper Canada", 5 August 1812, in R.A. Bowler, "Propaganda in Upper Canada, A study of Propaganda Directed at the People of Upper Canada during the War of 1812", M.A. Thesis, Queen's University, 1964, 150.

U.E. Loyalist (York), 1823-1828.

Wellington, Duke of [son], ed. *Despatches, Correspondence, and Memoranda of Field Marshal Arthur, Duke of Wellington, K.G.*, vol. I (London: John Murray, 1867).

York Gazette, 1812.

Metropolitan Toronto Central Library (Now Toronto Reference Library)

Report of the Select Committee to which was referred the petition of Bulkley Waters and others, entitled, The Petition of Christians of all denominations in Upper Canada, and other petitions on the same subject of E.W. Armstrong & others, by Marshall Spring Bidwell, Peter Perry Esquire, John Matthews Esquire, Hugh Christopher Thomson, and George Hamilton Esquire (York: Ordered by the House of Assembly to be Printed, March 1828).

Robinson, John Beverley. *Canada and the Canada Bill: Being an Examination of the Prosed Measure for the Future Government of Canada* (London: J. Hutchard & Son, 1840).

Robinson, John Beverley. *A Letter to the Right Hon. Earl Bathurst, K.G. on the Policy of Uniting the British North-American Colonies* (London: Printed by William Clowes, 1825).

Robinson, John Beverley, *Speech in Committee on the Bill for Conferring Civil Rights on certain Inhabitants of this Province* (York: King's Printer, 1825.

Strachan, John. *A Charge Delivered to the Clergy of the Diocese of Toronto at the Primary Visitation, 9 September 1841* (Toronto: H & W Rowsell, 1841).

Strachan, John. *The Church of the Redeemed, A Sermon preached 5th October 1836* (Toronto: R. Stanton, 1836).

Strachan, John. *A Discourse on the Character of King George the Third, Addressed to the Inhabitants of British America* (Montreal: Nahum Mower, 1810).

Strachan, John. *A Letter to the Right Honourable Thomas Frankland Lewis, M.P.* (York: R. Stanton, 1830).

Strachan, John. *Letters to the Honorable William Morris, being Strictures on the Correspondence of that Gentleman with the Colonial Office as a Delegate from the Presbyterian Body in Canada* (Cobourg, Upper Canada: R.D. Chatterton, 1838).

Strachan, John. *Observations on a Bill for Uniting the Legislative Councils and Assemblies of the Provinces of Lower Canada and Upper Canada in one Legislature* (London: W. Clowes, 1824).

Strachan, John & John Beverley Robinson, *Observations on the Policy of a General Union of all the British Provinces of North America* (London: W. Clowes, 1824).

Strachan, John. *Observations on the Provision for the Maintenance of a Protestant Clergy in the Provinces of Upper and Lower Canada* (London: R. Gilbert, 1827).

Strachan, John. *Remarks on Emigration from the United Kingdom, Addressed to Robert Wilmot Horton, Esq., M.P., Chairman of the Select Committee of Emigration in the last Parliament* (London: John Murray, 1827).

Strachan, John. *Report of the Loyal and Patriotic Society of Upper Canada* (Montreal: William Gray, 1817).

Strachan, John. A *Sermon on the death of the Honourable Richard Cartwright, Preached at Kingston, 3 September 1815* (Montreal: W. Gray, 1816).

Strachan, John. A *Sermon Preached at York, Upper Canada on Third June, Being the Day appointed for a General Thanksgiving* (Montreal: William Gray, 1814).

Strachan, John. *Sermon preached at York, U.C., July 3rd1825, on the death of the late Lord Bishop of Quebec* (Kingston: James Macfarlane, 1826).

Strachan, James [John]. *A visit to the Province of Upper Canada in 1819* (Aberdeen: D. Chalmers & Co. 1820).

Public Archives of Canada (now Library and Archives Canada)

[Collins, Francis] *An Abridged View of the Alien Question Unmasked by the Editor of the Canadian Freeman* (York: Freeman Office, 1826).

Secondary Sources – Books

Armstrong, Frederick H. *A Handbook of Upper Canadian Chronology and Territorial Legislation* (London, Ontario: The University of Western Ontario, 1967).

Anderson, Fred & Andrew Cayton. *The Dominion of War, Empire and Liberty in North America, 1500-2000* (New York: Penguin Books, 2005).

Bailyn, Bernard. *The Ideological Origins of the American Revolution* (Cambridge, Massachusetts: Harvard University Press, 1967/1992).

Bangs, Nathan, D.D. *A History of the Methodist Episcopal Church, vol. III, From the years 1817 to the Year 1828* (New York: T. Mason & G. Lane, 1840).

Beer, Samuel H. *British Politics in the Collectivist Age* (New York: Random House/Vintage Books, 1969).

Bonnycastle, Sir Richard Henry, Lt. Col., Corps of Royal Engineers, *Canada, As It Was, Is, and May Be*, Vol. II (London: Colburn & Co., 1852).

Boyce, Betsy Dewar, *The Rebels of Hastings* (Toronto: University of Toronto Press, 1992).

Brode, Patrick. *Sir John Beverley Robinson, Bone and Sinew of the Compact* (Toronto: University of Toronto Press for The Osgood Society, 1984).

Butterfield, Herbert. *The Whig Interpretation of History* (New York: W.W. Norton, 1965).

Careless, J.M.S. *The Union of the Canadas, The Growth of Canadian Institutions, 1841-1857* (Toronto: McClelland & Stewart Ltd., 1967).

Cherry, Conrad. *The Theology of Jonathan Edwards, A Reappraisal* (Bloomington: Indiana University Press, 1990).

Cornell, Paul G. *The Alignment of Political Groups in Canada, 1841-1867* (Toronto: University of Toronto Press, 1962).

Craig, G.M. *Upper Canada, The Formative Years, 1784-1841* (Toronto: McClelland and Steward, 1963).

Cross, Michael S. *A Biography of Robert Baldwin, The Morning Star of Memory* (Don Mills: Ontario: Oxford University Press, 2012).

Dent, John Charles. *The Story of the Upper Canadian Rebellion*, volume I (Toronto: C. Blackett Robinson, 1885).

Dunham, Aileen. *Political Unrest in Upper Canada, 1815-1836* (Toronto: McClelland & Stewart, 1969).

Fehey, Curtis. *The Anglican Experience in Upper Canada, 1791-1854* (Ottawa: Carleton University Press, 1991).

Feltoe, Richard. *Redcoated Ploughboys, The Volunteer Battalion of Incorporated Militia of Upper Canada, 1813-1815* (Toronto: Dundurn Press, 2012).

Figgis, J.N. *Studies of Political Thought from Gerson to Grotius, 1414-1625* (Cambridge: Cambridge University Press, 1956 (First ed., 1907).

French, Goldwin. *Parsons & Politics, The rôle of the Wesleyan Methodists in Upper Canada and the Maritimes from 1780 to 1855* (Toronto: The Ryerson Press, 1962).

Greenwood, F. Murray & Barry Wright, eds. *Canadian State Trials, Volume II, Rebellion and Invasion in the Canada, 1837-1839* (Toronto: University of Toronto Press, 2002), Part One: Upper Canada: 41-61, Rainer Baehre, "Trying the Rebels: Emergency Legislation and the Colonial Executive's Overall Legal Strategy in the Upper Canadian Rebellion"; 62-99, Paul Romney & Barry Wright, "The Toronto Treason Trials, March-May 1838"; 100-129, Colin Read, "The Treason Trials in Western Upper Canada"; 130-159, Barry Wright, "The Kingston and London Courts Martial, Treason in Eastern Upper Canada"; 160-187, F. Murray Greenwood, "The Prince Affair: 'Gallant Colonel' or 'The Windsor Butcher'?; and188-204, Cassandra Pybus, "Patriot Exiles in Van Diemen's Land".

Hatch, Nathan O. *The Democratization of American Christianity*. (New Haven & London: Yale University Press, 1989).

Head, Sir Francis B., Bart. *A Narrative* (London: John Murray, 1839).

Heimert, Alan. *Religion and the American mind, From the Great Awakening to the Revolution* (Cambridge, Mass.: Harvard University Press, 1966).

Hitsman, J. Mackay. *The Incredible War of 1812, A Military History* (revised ed., Robin Brass Studio Inc., 1999).

Jasanoff, Maya. *Liberty's Exiles, American Loyalists in the Revolutionary World* (New York: Alfred A. Knoff, 2011).

Kelly, Robert. *The Transatlantic Persuasion: The Liberal-Democratic Mind in the Age of Gladstone* (New York: Alfred A. Knopf, 1969).

Langguth, A.J. *Driven West, Andrew Jackson and the Trail of Tears to the Civil War* (New York: Simon & Schuster, 2010).

Latimer, Jon. *1812, War with America* (Cambridge: Harvard University Press, 2007).

LeSueur, William Dawson. *William Lyon Mackenzie: A Reinterpretation*, A.B. McKillop, ed. (Toronto: Macmillan/Carleton Library, 1979).

Lindsay, Charles. *The Life and Times of William Lyon Mackenzie with an Account of the Canadian Rebellion of 1837 and the subsequent Frontier Disturbances. Chiefly from Unpublished Documents*, II (Toronto, Canada West: P.R. Randall, 1862).

Link, Eugene Perry. *The Social Ideas of American Physicians (1776-1976), Studies in the Humanitarian Tradition in Medicine* (Selinsgrove, PA: Susquehanna University Press, 1992).

McNairn, Jeffrey L. *The Capacity to Judge: Public Opinion and Deliberative Democracy in Upper Canada, 1791-1854* (Toronto: University of Toronto Press, 2000).

Miller, Perry. *Errand into the Wilderness* (Cambridge, Mass.: Harvard University Press), 1956.

Mills, David. *The Idea of Loyalty in Upper Canada, 1784-1850* (Montreal-Kingston: McGill-Queen's University Press, 1988).

Moore, Christopher. *The Loyalists, Revolution, Exile, Settlement* (Toronto: Macmillan of Canada, 1984).

Read, Colin. *The Rising in Western Upper Canada, 1837-1838: The Duncombe Revolt and After* (Toronto: University of Toronto Press, 1982).

Riddell, William Renwick. *The Life of William Dummer Powell: First Judge at Detroit and Fifth Chief Justice of Upper Canada* (Lansing: Michigan Historical Commission, 1924).

Schrauwers, Albert. *"Union is Strength', W.L. Mackenzie, The Children of Peace, and The Emergence of Joint Stock Democracy in Upper Canada* (Toronto: University of Toronto Press, 2009).

Sheppard, George. *Plunder, Profit, and Paroles, A Social History of the War of 1812 in Upper Canada* (Montreal/Kingston: McGill-Queen's University Press, 1994).

Sissons, C.B. *Egerton Ryerson, His Life and Letters, vol. I* (Toronto: Clarke, Irwin, 1937).

Stromberg, R.N. *An Intellectual History of Modern Europe* (New York: Appleton-Century-Crofts, 1966).

Stuart, Reginald C. *United States Expansionism and British North America, 1775- 1871* (Chapel Hill, North Carolina: University of North Carolina Press, 1988).

Taylor, Alan. *The Civil War of 1812, American Citizens, British Subjects, Irish Rebels & Indian Allies* (New York: Alfred A. Knopf, 2010).

Voegelin, Eric. *The New Science of Politics, An Introduction* (Chicago: University of Chicago Press, 1989).

Westfall, William. *Two Worlds, The Protestant Culture of Nineteenth Century Ontario* (Kingston & Montreal: McGill-Queen's University Press, 1989).

Wilson, Alan. *The Clergy Reserves of Upper Canada, a Canadian Mortmain* (Toronto: University of Toronto Press, 1968).

Winks, Robin W. *The Blacks in Canada: A History* (Montreal: McGill-Queen's University Press, 1997, 1st. ed. 1972).

Secondary Sources – Articles & Chapters in Books

Barnett, John. "Silas Fletcher, Instigator of the Upper Canadian Rebellion", *Ontario History*, XLI, 1975, 7-35.

Cruikshank, Ernest A. "John Beverley Robinson and the trials for treason in 1814", *Ontario Historical Society Papers and Records*, XXV, 1929, 191-219.

Cruikshank, Ernest A. "A Study of Disaffection in Upper Canada in 1812-1815", *Transactions of the Royal Society of Canada,* Series III, 1912; reprinted in Morris Zaslow, ed., *The Defended Border, Upper Canada and the War of 1812* (Toronto: Macmillan, 1964).

Dictionary of Canadian Biography, numerous biographical entries as cited.

Fryer, Mary Beacock. "The War out of Niagara", 73-93 & "First Large-Scale Migration, 1784-1800", 97-127, in *Loyal She Remains, A Pictorial history of Ontario* (Toronto: United Empire Loyalists' Association of Canada, 1984).

Macdonald, Donald C. "Honourable Richard Cartwright, 1759-1815", *Three History Theses* (Ontario Department of Public Records and Archives, 1961), 69-170.

McKim, Denis. "Upper Canadian Thermidor: The Family Compact & the counter-revolutionary Atlantic", *Ontario History*, CVI, 2014, No. 2, 235-262.

Oxford Dictionary of National Biography: Jupp, P.J. "Robinson, Frederick John, first Viscount Goderich and first earl of Ripon (1782-839), 324-329; and Smith, E.A. "Grey, Charles, second Earl Grey (1764-1845), 811-819.

McLean, Scott. "Before the *Christian Guardian*: American Methodist Periodicals in the Upper Canadian Backwoods, 1818-1829", *Papers of the Bibliographical Society of Canada*, vol. 49, No. 2, Fall 2014, 143-165.

Passfield, Robert W. "Where Sovereignty Lay", 91-94 in Robert W. Passfield, *Phips' Amphibious Assault on Canada – 1690* (Published by Author, Amazon.com, 2011).

Purdy, J.D. "John Strachan and the Diocesan Theological Institute at Cobourg, 1842-52", *Ontario History*, LXV, June 1973, 113-123.

Purdy, J.D. "John Strachan's Educational Policies, 1815-1841", *Ontario History*, LXIV, 1972, 45-64.

Riddell, William R. "The Ancaster 'Bloody Assize' of 1814", *Ontario Historical Society Papers and Records*, XX, 1923, 107-127.

Riddell, William Renwick. "The Criminal Law in Reference to Marriage in Upper Canada", Ontario Historical Society Papers and Records, XXI, 1924, 233-235.

Riddell, William Renwick. "The Law of Marriage in Upper Canada", *Canadian Historical Review*, II, No. 3, September 1921, 226-248.

Riddell, William Renwick. "Method of Abolition of Slavery in England, Scotland and Upper Canada Compared", Ontario Historical Society Papers and Records, XXVII, 1931, 511-516.

Riddell, William Renwick. "Upper Canada – Early Period", 316-339 and "The Fugitive Slave in Upper Canada", 340-358, *The Journal of Negro History*, Vol. 5, No. 3, July 1920.

Saunders, R.E. "What was the Family Compact", *Ontario History*, XLIX, 1957, 165-178.

Spragge, G.W. "John Strachan's Contribution to Education, 1800-23", *Canadian Historical Review*, XXII, 1941, 147-158.

Stacey, C.P. "The War of 1812 in Canadian History", *Ontario History*, L, 1958, 153-159.

Wayne, Michael. "The Black Population of Canada West on the Eve of the American Civil War: A reassessment Based on the Manuscript Census of 1861", *Historie Social/Social History*, 1995, 472-481.

Wise, S.F. "The Annexation Movement and Its Effect on Canadian Opinion, 1837-67", in S.F. Wise & R.C. Brown, *Canada Views the United States, Nineteenth-century Political Attitudes* (Toronto: Macmillan, 1967).

Wise S. F. "Colonial Attitudes from the Era of the War of 1812 to the Rebellion of 1837" in S. F. Wise & Robert Craig Brown, *Canada Views the United States* (Toronto: Macmillan of Canada, 1967).

Wise, S.F. "Conservatism and Political Development: The Canadian Case", *The South Atlantic Quarterly*, LXIX, 1970, 226-243.

Wise, S.F. "Upper Canada and the Conservative Tradition" in Edith Firth, ed., *Profiles of a Province, Studies in the History of Ontario* (Toronto: The Ontario Historical Society, 1967), 20-33.

Young, A.H. "The Church of England in Upper Canada", *Queen's Quarterly*, 1930, 147-152.

Theses

Bowler, R.A. "Propaganda in Upper Canada, A Study of the Propaganda Directed at the People of Upper Canada during the War of 1812" (M.A. Thesis, Queen's University, September 1964).

Good, R. C. "Letter book of John Strachan, 1827-1834" (M.A. Thesis, University of Toronto, 1940).

Macdonald, Donald C. "Richard Cartwright, 1759-1815" in *Three History Theses: Published Under the Auspices of the Ontario Department of Public Records and Archives* (Toronto: Department of Public Records and Archives, 1961).

Watt, Steven. "Authoritarianism, Constitutionalism, and the Special Council of Lower Canada, 1838-1841" (MA Thesis, McGill University, July 1997).

Bibliographical Addendum

There are two collections of books in the John W. Graham Library of Trinity College, University of Toronto, that pertain to the Rev. John Strachan: the Strachan List Books, and the SPCK Special Collection.

The Strachan List comprises over 500 works that Strachan bequeathed to Trinity College from his private library. There are numerous religious volumes – inclusive of the works of Richard Hooker -- as well as British literary magazines and reviews, and Christian periodicals. The historical works are rather eclectic in embracing a history of the Church of Christ, histories of the Reformation, a history of the Council of Trent, ecclesiastical histories, a history of Scotland, a history of the reformation in Scotland, and a history of the Protestant episcopal church in the United States, Hebrew history, and a Histoire des Juifs. There are biographies of John Milton, John Knox, George Washington, Joseph Brant, Lorenzo de' Medici, and Bishop Hobart of New York, as well as classical works of Cicero, and a history of ancient Greece.

There are several works on moral philosophy, and a number of books on natural philosophy (science), as well as works on the state in relation to the church, the rights of war and peace, the English Constitution, feudal law, British state trials, civil government, the hereditary rights of the Crown, and Justinian's Institutes, as well as a book on political economy.

The SPCK Special Collection comprises the books that the Rev. Strachan selected for the Divinity College library of the projected University of King's College in 1827 and purchased with a financial grant from the Society for Promoting Christian Knowledge (SPCK). There are 104 works – 369 volumes – on a wide variety of religious subjects: theology, natural religion, moral philosophy, the history of the Reformation, the Gospels, and ecclesiastical history.

Appendices

Appendix A - Egerton Ryerson & the English moderate Tories

Appendix B - The young Tories of Upper Canada

Appendix C - Terminology

Rejection of Democracy

The belief of the Upper Canadian Anglican Tories that democracy was one of the worst systems of government known to man -- in being a threat to public order, true liberty under the law, and constitutional government -- was grounded in their familiarity with the Classics. Moreover, it was a belief that was strengthened by their historical knowledge that during the French Revolution egalitarian democratic republicanism had degenerated into democratic anarchy, the Reign of Terror (1793), and ultimately a military dictatorship under Napoleon Bonaparte. In the Socratic dialogue, *The Republic*, Plato provided a vivid description of the character of Athenian democracy in maintaining that democracies invariably breed an excess of freedom and license, and degenerate into tyrannies. (See, Plato, *The Republic* [ca. 380BC], 'Democracy and the Democratic Man', No. 555-561 and 'Despotism and the Despotic Man', No. 562-576).

Appendix A

Egerton Ryerson & the English Moderate Tories

An intriguing description of the political parties and the leading political personages of England was published in the Methodist *Christian Guardian* (October 30, 1833) by the editor, the Rev. Egerton Ryerson, from observations made during an extended stay in England over the previous summer. Prior to the publication of the article, which was entitled, "Impressions made by our late Visit to England", Ryerson had been a staunch supporter of the Reform Party of Upper Canada. He had colluded with the democratic radicals of the House of Assembly on the drafting of public petitions, was directly involved with the radicals in framing their attacks on the Clergy Reserves and the Church of England establishment, and was actively engaged in political attacks on the Tory church-state establishment. However, after closely observing English politics during his sojourn in England, the views of Ryerson on the respective character of the English Tories, Whigs, and Radicals was totally transformed.

Ryerson astounded Upper Canadians by his turnabout in praising the moderate English Tories for their religious moral principles, their piety, honour and liberality. Yet, he retained his inveterate hostility towards the Tories of Upper Canada, and his zeal for the evangelical Protestant religious principles of the American Methodists – viz. 'religious equality', 'voluntaryism', and 'the separation of church and state' -- which he interpreted as requiring that the Church of England be stripped of its establishment status, its historic prerogatives, and its clergy reserves land endowment. Historians have found it difficult to characterize the political outlook of Egerton Ryerson in examining his seemingly contradictory series of publications and political involvements, but oddly enough they have not sought an explanation for his behavior in the American evangelical Protestant religious beliefs, values and principles of his mind and the circumstance of his Loyalist upbringing.

Origin of the 'English Impressions' article

During the spring of 1833, the Rev. Egerton Ryerson went to England to promote a union of the newly-independent Methodist Episcopal Church in Canada – which in 1828 had separated from the Methodist Episcopal Church in the United States -- with the Wesleyan Methodist Connexion in Britain. While in England, Ryerson presented an "Address from Upper Canada to the King" to the Colonial Office. The petition denied that the Church of England was established in Upper Canada and called upon the British government to divert the proceeds from the sale and lease of lots of the clergy reserves endowment from the Clergy Reserves Corporation of the Church of England in Upper Canada to the general purposes of education in that Province.

In several subsequent meetings at the Colonial Office with Lord Stanley, the Colonial Secretary, Ryerson lobbied for the grant of a royal charter for a Methodist seminary -- the Upper Canadian Academy at Cobourg in Upper Canada -- as well as for financial support from the British Government to complete the construction of the new Academy building, and to cover the salaries of the teachers that were to be recruited to teach at the Academy. While lobbying the Reform Government of Lord Grey, Ryerson worked quite closely with the leading Radicals in the House of Commons – Joseph Hume, John Arthur Roebuck, and William Cobbett – as well as with the Upper Canadian radical, William Lyon Mackenzie, who was in England to present yet another of his list of 'grievances' to the Colonial Office.

While in England (April-August 1833), Ryerson had several occasions to attend the debates in the House of Commons. He listened to the speeches of the leading members of all parties and discovered that his political views -- which he admitted were based on hear-say and what he had read in Upper Canada -- did not correspond with the reality of what he saw of British politics at first hand. (1) Presumably Ryerson had formed his earlier views of English politics and society under the influence of the 'American Methodist' preachers of the Genesee Conference of New York on their circuits in Upper Canada, from his readings of American religious newspapers, books and tracts that were sold by the American preachers on their Canadian circuits, and from the radical press of Upper Canada which was in the hands of British immigrant radicals. (2)

Before departing from England, Ryerson managed to work out an agreement for a union of the Methodist Episcopal Church in Canada with the British Wesleyan Methodist Connexion to form a new Canadian church, the Wesleyan Methodist Church in Canada. When Egerton Ryerson returned to Upper Canada in September 1833, he reported on the terms of the union to the Canadian Methodist Conference, received a vote of approval, and was re-appointed to his former position as editor of the *Christian Guardian*. (3) Thereafter, he proceeded to publish an article on his 'English impressions' in the newspaper.

Impressions made by our late Visit to England

More times than we can tell have we been asked, since our return to Canada, 'What do you think of England?' ... . We will merely state the impressions made upon our own mind during four months' residence in England, in regard to public men, religious bodies, and the general state of the nation.

There are three great political parties in England – Tories, Whigs and Radicals, and two descriptions of characters constituting each party. Of the first, there is the *moderate* and *ultra* tory. An English ultra tory is what we believe has usually been meant and understood in Canada by the *unqualified* term *tory*; this is, a lordling in power, a tyrant in politics, and a bigot in religion. In religion, he is superstitious or skeptical, as it happens, in morals, he is profane or devout, sensual or abstemious, spendthrift or miser, as inclination and interest may prompt; in opinions, he is as intolerant as he is illiberal.

This description of partisans, we believe, is headed by the Duke of Cumberland, and is followed not "a-far off" by that powerful party, which presents such a formidable array of numbers, rank, wealth, talent, science, and literature, headed by the Hero of Waterloo [the Duke of Wellington, the Leader of the parliamentary Tories from his seat in the House of Lords]. This shade of the tory party appears to be headed in the House of Commons by Sir R. Inglis, member for Oxford University, and is supported, on most questions, by that most subtle and ingenious politician and fascinating speaker, Sir R. Peel, with his numerous train of followers and admirers. Among those who support the distinguishing measure of this party are men of the highest Christian virtue and piety; and our decided impression is, that it embraces the major party of the talent and wealth, and learning of the British nation. The acknowledged and leading organs of this party are *Blackwood's Magazine* and the *London Quarterly*.

The other branch of this great political party is what is called the *moderate* tory. In political *theory* he agrees with his high-toned neighbor; but he acts from *religious* principles, and this governs his private as well as public life – he contemplates the good of the nation and the welfare of mankind, without regard to party measures, and uninfluenced by political sectarianism. To this class belongs a considerable portion of the *evangelical clergy*, and, we think, a majority of the Wesleyan Methodists. This class, embracing for the most part, within the sphere of its religious exertions, the Bible Tracts, Church, and Wesleyan Missionary Societies, evidently includes the great body of the piety, Christian enterprise, and sterling virtue of the nation.

It repudiates connexion with any avowedly political party; -- its politics are those of justice – its charities are liberal – its measures are disinterested – its honour is inviolable – its supports established institutions from the authority of the Divine word instead of the caprice of expedience; moderate, but unbending and persevering in its purposes; and in time of party excitement, alike hated and denounced by the ultra tory, the crabbed whig, and the radical leveler.

Such was our impression of the true character of what, by the periodical press in *England*, is termed a moderate tory. From this theory (to which he seldom or never insists upon your subscribing) we in some respects dissent; but his integrity, his honesty, his consistency, his genuine liberality and religious beneficence, claim respect and imitation. Of this class, Lord Goderich (now Earl Ripon) is a fair specimen and bright ornament; as may be supposed by his despatches to the government of this and other British North American Colonies; and to this class, we understood in England, that His Excellency the Lieutenant Governor, Sir John Colborne, had always been attached and associated.

The second great political, and now ruling party in England, are the *whigs* – ... [which party] is now rather popular than otherwise in England. It is, however, not so popular as it was before the passing of the Reform Bill – as the Whig administration has not fulfilled the expectations of the public in its measures of retrenchment and reform. The whig appears to differ in *theory* from the tory in this, that he interprets the constitution, obedience to it, and all measures in regard to its administration, upon the *principles of expedience*, and is therefore always pliant in his professions, and is ever ready to suit his measures to *The Times*; an indefinite term, that also designates the most extensively circulated daily paper in England, or in the world, which is the leading organ of the Whig party, backed by the formidable power and lofty periods of the *Edinburgh Quarterly*: whereas the tory maintains the implied contract of existing institutions and established usages, and the authority of Revelation as the true foundation of obedience to the civil government. To us, the theory of the truth lies between the two; in practice there is but little difference.

The present Whig ministry have not retrenched a farthing of their own salaries (with one or two exceptions) any more than did their predecessors in office; and the present Premier [Earl Grey] had inducted more of his relatives into lucrative offices and livings, during the last two years, than did Lord Liverpool during the whole of his [Tory] administration. The leaders of this [Whig] party in the House of lords are Earl Grey and the Lord Chancellor [Henry Brougham]; at the head of the list in the House of Commons stand the names of Mr. Stanley, Lord Althorp, Lord John Russell, and Mr. McAuley [Thomas Babington Macaulay]. In this class are also included many of the most learned and popular ministers of dissenting congregations. There appears to be no peculiar tendency in the examples, influence, and measures of the great politicians of this school to improve the religious and moral condition of the nation.

The third political sect is called *Radicals*; apparently headed by Messrs. Hume and Attwood; the former of whom, though acute, indefatigable, persevering, popular on financial questions, and always to the point, and heard with respect and attention in the House of Commons, has no influence as a religious man; has never been known to promote any religious measure or object as such, and has opposed every measure or the better observance of the Sabbath, and even introduced a motion to defeat the bill for the abolition of colonial slavery; and Mr. Attwood, the head of the celebrated Birmingham political union, is (if we may judge from hearing him speak two or three times in the House of Commons) a conceited, boisterous, hollow-headed declaimer. Never did we hear any public man speak, of whom we formed so unfavourable an opinion, as of Thomas Attwood.

Radicalism in England appeared to us to be but another word for Republicanism, with the name of King instead of President. This school, however, includes all the Infidels, Unitarians and Socinians [sic] in the Kingdom; together with a majority of the population of the manufacturing districts. The notorious infidel character of the majority of the political leaders, and periodical publications of this party, deter the virtuous part of the nation from associating with them, though some of the brightest ornaments of the English pulpit and nation – [the Non-conformist ministers] --have leaned to their leading doctrines in theory.

And perhaps one of the most formidable obstacles to a wise, safe and effectual reform of the political, ecclesiastical and religious abuses in England, is the notorious want of religious virtue or integrity in many of the leading politicians who have lamentably succeeded in getting their names identified with *reform*; which keeps the truly religious portion of the nation aloof, and compels it, in practice, to occupy a neutral ground. And it is not a little remarkable that that very description of the public press which, in England, advocates the lowest radicalism, is the foremost in opposing and slandering the Methodists in this Province. Hence, the fact that some of these

Editors have been among the lowest of the English Radicals previous to their egress from the Mother Country.

Upon the whole, our impressions of the religious and moral character, patriotism, and influence of the several political parties into which the British nations is unhappily divided, were materially different in some respects, from personal observation, from what they had been by hear-say and reading.

The conclusions to which we came were,

That there is nothing in the peculiar tenets of the different political parties, that can reasonably debar their advocates from religious communion with each other, -- and, therefore would never be made a condition of it; since there are included in each [party], men of generous patriotism, inviolable integrity, solid learning, and scriptural orthodoxy, and piety.

That no Christian could safely and wisely identify himself with either of them, since they all alike – as parties – seek their own honour and gain, and care little or nothing for the interests of what he regards as the sum of human happiness.

That the most rational and effectual means for a true Christian to reform vice and correct abuses, is to know, enjoy, and always abound in the work of Him who went about doing good." (4)

The analysis of English politics, religion, and society prepared by Egerton Ryerson, in October 1833, reveals much about his political views and religious values, as well as his character and prejudices. Overall, it presents an intriguing analysis of English politics of the period but is marred by a flippant remark that the English Ultra-Tories were 'what in Canada was regarded as a tory': viz. 'lordlings in power', 'tyrants in politics', and 'bigots in religion', as well as 'intolerant' and 'illiberal'. In that respect, it presents a highly-bias characterization of the Ultra-Tories of England, and a totally false aspersion with respect to the High Church Anglican Tories of Upper Canada.

Such a denigrating remark had much to do with the political and religious animosities engendered in Upper Canada over the clergy reserves issue, and Tory resistance to sectarian and radical attacks on the prerogatives of the Established Church, than to any observations made in England.

The English Ultra-Tories whom Ryerson was denouncing, and denigrating, and indirectly comparing with the Upper Canadian Anglican Tories, were a group of Anglican Tories who were staunch defenders of the union of church and state, and the prerogatives of the established Church of England. They were adamantly opposed to the political emancipation of Roman Catholics, and in 1829 had withdrawn their support from the Tory Government of the Duke of Wellington upon the passage of the Catholic Emancipation Act. (5) As staunch defenders of the union of church and state, the Church of England establishment, and the historic rights and prerogatives of the Church of England, the Ultra-Tories were an anathema to Egerton Ryerson who believed fervently in the evangelical Protestant religious principles of 'religious equality', 'voluntaryism' and 'the separation of church and state'.

Where the institutions of government were concerned, Ryerson found little difference between the Tory and the Whig as each supported the continued union of the church and state in England. Whether he realized it or not, they did so for different reasons. The Tory because of a belief in the necessary union of church and state to provide moral government and the common good of the nation, in the integral role of the National Church in the British Constitution, and in the educational role of an established Church in forming the national character, as well as a belief in the religious function of a national church in the redemption of man; whereas for the Whigs, the established Church was valued primarily for fulfilling a useful social function in maintaining public order through reconciling the masses to their station in life. It should not have been a surprise to Egerton Ryerson that the liberal-Whigs were not interested in promoting religion. They were adherents of the political philosophy of John Locke (1632-1704) and, hence, did not believe that government had a religious or moral purpose.

Whatever the case, the published observations of Egerton Ryerson on the Christian character, piety, education, and talents of the members of the Tory Party, on the political expediency and lack of any religious commitment on the part of the Whig Party, and on the irreligion, secularism, and republicanism of the Radicals, constituted a radical departure from the general views held by the 'American Methodists' of Upper Canada and from that of their political associates, the democratic radicals of the Reform Party. For the opponents of the Upper Canadian Tories, it was a shock that was compounded by the revelation that the moderate tories in England were supported by "a considerable portion of the *evangelical clergy*", and possibly "a majority of the Wesleyan Methodists".

In the conclusion to his article, Ryerson did not advocate that Methodists ought to support the moderate Tories in politics. He identified with Reform and wanted to see what he regarded as "ecclesiastical and religious abuses in England" addressed, which for him meant the disestablishment of the Church of England and the confiscation of the religious endowments of the National Church. However, for Ryerson, it was not possible for Christians in England to wholehearted support the reform movement as the reform leaders were irreligious, were lacking in religious virtue, and did not adhere to evangelical religious principles. Rather than call on Methodists to support the moderate Tories, Ryerson drew on his otherworldly evangelical worldview in advocating that the true Christian ought to focus as an individual on pursuing Christ's work – the evangelizing of mankind through the Gospel message -- and the living of a good life.

What is odd about the 'English Impressions' article is that the analysis presented begs the conclusion that the Methodists of Upper Canada ought to support the moderate Tories in politics; yet, Ryerson did not enunciate such a view. What the article conveyed was a newly-gained appreciation for the religious and moral character of the English moderate Tories whom the English Wesleyan Methodists supported in politics. However, Egerton Ryerson was not a convert to English Wesleyan Methodism, nor was he a moderate Tory.

Theologically he was imbued with the religious beliefs, values and principles of 'American Methodism' which was a unique strain of Methodism that was Calvinist in its origins, was dedicated to the principles of 'religious equality', 'voluntaryism' and 'the separation of church and state, and, historically, had undergone an evolution away from the traditional conservative social values of British Wesleyan Methodism. The 'American Methodists' had developed a distinct egalitarian democratic frame of mind. (6)

Similarly, Ryerson was not a moderate Tory in theology, in his politics, or in his social values. The Anglican moderate Tories were believers in a rational religion as opposed to the emotional 'inner light' religion of the 'American Methodists', and the moderate Tories were accepting of the traditional hierarchical social order in contrast to the levelling character of the 'American Methodists'. Moreover, the moderate Tories believed in the union of church and state through an established national church; whereas the 'American Methodists' were hostile to the established Church of England in Upper Canada and campaigned to have it disestablished.

Simply put, what Egerton Ryerson admired about the English moderate Tories was that they conducted their lives -- both private and public -- in keeping with the Christian religious and moral values, that in politics they were devoted to the common good and well-being of the nation rather than partisan or local interests, and that they believed in religious toleration. In sum, Egerton Ryerson was not advocating that the Upper Canadian Methodists abandon their support for the democratic radicals and give their support to the moderate Tories. Yet, that was the conclusion reached by many Canadian Methodists, and the democratic radicals of the Reform Party, upon reading the 'English Impressions' article.

What was truly shocking to all and sundry was the total transformation – a complete reversal -- of Ryerson's earlier view of his former radical allies in Britain, and by implication his confreres among the democratic radicals in Upper Canada. While in England, Ryerson realized that his British radical allies were not truly religious men, had no interest in promoting religion – the evangelizing of society – and were not men of a strong Christian moral character. Indeed, the Rev. Ryerson was appalled that the British Radical leader, Joseph Hume – whom the Upper Canadian Reformers held in a particularly high esteem – had spoken in the House of Commons against a bill to outlaw slavery in the British Empire.

Impact of the 'English Impressions' article

The 'English Impressions' article created a sensation in Upper Canada. It resulted in Ryerson being immediately castigated by William Lyon Mackenzie -- that same day -- in a supplemental issue of the *Colonial Advocate* in which extreme language was used by Mackenzie to describe Ryerson and his supposed new Tory allies. It was language in keeping with the rhetoric commonly employed by the democratic radicals and, ironically, by the evangelical sectarians as well: viz.

> The Christian Guardian, under the management of Egerton Ryerson, has gone over to the enemy – press, type, and all – and hoisted the colours of a cruel, vindictive, Tory priesthood ....
>
> ... a deadly blow has been struck in England at the liberties of the people of Upper Canada, by as subtle and ungrateful an adversary, in the guise of an old and familiar friend, as ever crossed the Atlantic.

Ryerson was further accused of being "a Jesuit in the garb of a Methodist preacher", a "Deserter", and a new ally of "the church and state gentry".

On a personal note, there was good reason for Mackenzie to be angry and indignant. While in England, Ryerson had held meetings and discussions with Makenzie and the British radicals during the spring of 1833, and Mackenzie had accompanied Ryerson on his initial visit to the Colonial Office to present the 'Petition to the King'. Clearly, Mackenzie had no inclination that Ryerson had become disillusioned with the British radicals, and by extension with the Upper Canadian democratic radicals. Mackenzie attributed Ryerson's 'betrayal' to the conservative influence of the British Wesleyan Methodists.

The 'English Impressions' article resulted in a complete break between Egerton Ryerson and the democratic radicals of the Reform Party with whom he had been associated since the 1826 publication by Ryerson of an article, "A Methodist Preacher", in the *Colonial Advocate* (11 May 1826) of which William Lyon Mackenzie was the proprietor/editor. In that article, Ryerson had attacked the Church of England in claiming that its episcopal system of church government was not scriptural; and that the Church of England was not part of the British Constitution. He had demanded that the Church be stripped of its clergy reserves endowment, as well as its establishment prerogatives though the separation of church and state.

Over the succeeding half-dozen years, Ryerson had been closely identified with, and heavily involved with Mackenzie and the democratic radicals of the Reform Party in drafting public petitions and in framing and fomenting attacks against the Tory establishment, in calling for the ending all financial grants for the Church of England from the provincial and British governments and the SPG, and in demanding that the clergy reserves revenues be distributed among the Protestant denominations of Upper Canada or diverted to education. Their association was so close, that in the public mind, Ryerson and Mackenzie were regarded as the two leaders of the democratic radical wing of the Reform Party. (7)

After the public split between Ryerson and Mackenzie, most of the 'American Methodist' preachers and their congregations continued to support the democratic radicals of the Reform Party. The Methodist circuit-riding preachers reported to Egerton, in his capacity as editor, that they were encountering 'a torrent of opposition' against the *Christian Guardian* article. Five Methodist preachers, including a younger brother of Egerton, the Rev. Edwy Ryerson, signed a letter stating that they "had not changed their political views", and "still felt themselves to be connected with the Reformers". (8)

A decidedly minority Methodist view was enunciated in a private communication to Egerton from an older brother, the Rev. John Ryerson, the most conservative of the Ryerson brothers. He welcomed the split with the democratic radicals that the publication of the 'English Impressions' had brought about. John Ryerson wrote:

> Your article on the Political Parties of England has created much excitement throughout these parts. The only good that can result from it is the breaking up of the union which has hitherto existed between us and the radicals. Were it not for this, I should much regret its appearance. But we had got so closely linked with those extreme men, in one way or another,

> that we cannot expect to get rid of them without feeling the shock, and, perhaps, it may well come now as anytime.
>
> We have reason to respect Sir John Colborne [the Lt. Governor] & it is our duty and interest to support the *Government*. Although there may be some abuses which have crept in, yet, I believe that we enjoy as many political and religious advantages as any people. Our public affairs are as well managed as in any other country. As it respects the *Reformers*, so called, take Bidwell and Rolph from them & there is not scarcely one man of *character*, Honour or even decency among them, but with few exceptions (I mean the leaders), they are a banditti or compleat vagabonds... We have a host of Radicles in our Church – I am sorry to say it, but it is so. The best way for the present is for us to have nothing to say about Polliticks, but treat the Government with great respect. ... .
>
> Although you never were a Radicle; yet, have not we all leaned too much towards them, and will we not now smart for it a little! (9)

In his published defence, Egerton Ryerson insisted that he was not a traitor to the Reform cause. His association with the democratic radicals, he maintained, was not a political alliance but rather a case of an alignment of common interests in which he was religiously motivated by his deep belief in, and commitment to, the evangelical Protestant religious principles: 'religious equality', 'the separation of church and state', and 'voluntaryism'. He claimed that his political activity was strictly religious and aimed only at opposing "those who had shown an inveterate and unprincipled hostility to Methodism". (Apparently the Tories who refused to capitulate to his demands that evangelical religious principles be imposed on the church and state in Upper Canada, were *ipso facto* 'hostile to Methodism'.)

Nonetheless, despite the assertions of the Rev. Egerton Ryerson that he had never been a democratic radical, and that he had only engaged in politics on religious issues, the Reformers of Upper Canada did not distinguish between the religious radicalism of the Rev. Egerton Ryerson and the democratic radicalism of the Reform Party, in condemning Ryerson for a betrayal of the reform cause. (10)

C. B. Sissons, a Methodist historian, in his biography of Ryerson, *Egerton Ryerson, His Life and Letters* (1937), classified Ryerson as a 'liberal-conservative'. (11) However, such was not the case. Egerton Ryerson did hold a liberal-Whig view of the balance of the British Constitution, and a conservative Loyalist belief in loyalty to the Crown and the unity of the Empire, but he was not a conservative in his religious beliefs or social views. His American evangelical Protestant religious beliefs in 'religious equality', and the 'separation of church and state' were revolutionary in that, if implemented, the existing church-state polity of Upper Canada would have been overthrown and the existing social order undermined.

From the viewpoint of 'ideas influence actions', a study of the mind of Egerton Ryerson would be quite intriguing and would help explain his favourable view of the moderate English Tories and his rejection of the democratic radicals following his personal observations of English politics and society. It would contribute as well to a better understanding of the mentality of a significant component of the population of postwar Upper Canada, the young men and women of Anglican Loyalist families who were converted to Methodism by the 'American Methodist' circuit-riding preachers.

Ryerson was born into a staunch Anglican Tory Loyalist family, but under the influence of the preaching of Methodist circuit-riding preachers he had suffered a crisis of conscience, underwent a highly-emotional conversion to 'American Methodism', and imbibed the beliefs of American evangelical Protestantism and its inveterate hostility towards an established church and a church-state polity. Yet, he remained loyal to the Crown, to the balanced British Constitution, and to the unity of the British Empire. The moral philosophy and political philosophy of the Anglican liberal-Whig, the Rev. William Paley, had a significant influence on the thought of Egerton Ryerson; although he was quite selective in his borrowings from Paley. Ryerson ignored the arguments of Paley in favour of an established church, while using Paley's criteria for justifying a church establishment to attack the established Church of Upper Canada as illegitimate because it did not encompass the majority of the population of the province. (12)

The diverse responses of Egerton Ryerson to public issues, in both religion and politics in Upper Canada, were the product of the duality of a mind formed by Loyalism and American evangelical Protestantism in combination with a highly-assertive personality governed by a religious zeal that drove him to actions aimed at the attainment of 'what he thought was right'.

Notes

1. On Ryerson's time in England, see: J. [John] George Hodgins, ed., *'The Story of my Life' by the late Rev. Egerton Ryerson, D.D., L.L.D., Being Reminiscences of Sixty Years' of Public Service in Canada* (Toronto: William Briggs, 1883), 115-122; and C. B. [Charles Bruce] Sissons, *Egerton Ryerson, His Life and Letters*, vol. I (Toronto: Clarke, Irwin & Company, 1937), 171-193.

2. The 'American Methodist' preachers were highly active in distributing evangelical religious tracts and in selling American magazines and book to their adherents in Upper Canada. See Scott McLaren, "Before the *Christian Guardian*, American Methodist Periodicals in the Upper Canadian Backwoods, 1818-1829", *Papers of the Bibliographical Society of Canada*, vol. 49, no. 2, Fall 2014, 143-165.

3. Goldwin French, *Parsons & Politics, The role of the Wesleyan Methodists in Upper Canada and the Maritimes from 1730 to 1855* (Toronto: Ryerson Press, 1962)140-142. The reference to "a rather incongruous union" is strictly an assessment by the author based on the vast differences between the religious outlook and values of American evangelical Protestantism -- as espoused by the Upper Canadian Methodist preachers -- and the conservative evangelical Anglicanism of the English Wesleyan Methodists.

4. Egerton Ryerson, "Impressions made by our late Visit to England", *Christian Guardian*, 30 October 1833. The 'English Impressions' article is reprinted in Hodgins, ed., *'The Story of my Life, by the late Rev. Egerton Ryerson*, 122-124, and by Sissons, *Egerton Ryerson*, I, 194-197. The preachers of the Methodist Episcopal Church in Canada, inclusive of the Rev. Egerton Ryerson, imbibed their evangelical Protestant beliefs in 'religious equality', 'voluntaryism' and 'the separation of church and state' from the preaching and teachings of the American Methodists of the Genesee Conference of New York. On the self-righteous character of young Egerton Ryerson, and his tendency to go to extremes in denouncing those who opposed 'what he believed to be right', see: R.D. Gidney, "Ryerson, Egerton", *Dictionary of Canadian Biography*, XI.

Colonel Joseph Ryerson, an Anglican Tory Loyalist of Norfolk County, Upper Canada, had six sons – George, William, John, Egerton, Edwy and Samuel, of whom the five eldest sons were converted to Methodism by circuit-riding preachers after the War of 1812. Subsequently, all five of the converts were admitted as Methodist preachers. However, none of the Ryerson brothers who converted to Methodism, and received 'the call' to preach, was as openly hostile to the Church of England religious establishment in Upper Canada as was the zealous young convert, the Rev. Egerton Ryerson.

5. The withdrawal of the support of the Ultra-Tories for the Tory Government of the Duke of Wellington in 1829 -- over the issue of Catholic Emancipation -- was to have a major impact on Upper Canadian Anglican Toryism. The defection of the Ultra-Tories in Britain was a contributing factor to the subsequent defeat of the Wellington Tory Government in November 1830 that brought to power the liberal-Whig Reform Government of Earl Grey. It was a Reform Government that continually intervened in the politics of Upper Canada on behalf of the Reformers, and that appointed a radical-Whig, Lord Durham, to report on the affairs of the two Canadian provinces.

6. On the evolution of the theology and religious principles of American evangelical Protestantism, see "The Evangelical Sectarians" in the Conclusion to this book. That summary is based on close readings of Alan Heimert, *Religion and the American Mind* (1966), 1-236, and of Nathan O. Hatch, *The Democratization of American Christianity* (1989), 3-77.

7. Craig, *Upper Canada*, 216; and Gidney, "Ryerson, Egerton", *DCB*, XI. See also Sissons, *Egerton Ryerson*, vol. I, 198-199; and Hodgins, ed., *'The Story of My Life' by the late Rev. Egerton Ryerson*, 124-125. The quotation is from Hodgins, 125. The angry response of Mackenzie to the 'English Impressions' article was published in a *Colonial Advocate*, 30 October 1833, the same day the Ryerson article was published. Mackenzie had returned to Upper Canada earlier in the summer of 1833.

8. Craig, *Upper Canada*, 216, in quoting part of a letter from five Methodist preachers, David Wright et al to Egerton Ryerson, 21 November 1833. See also Sissons, *Egerton Ryerson*, I, 214-216, as well as 217-218, a private letter, Edwy Ryerson to Egerton Ryerson, 26 November 1833, which expresses the same sentiments.

9. The John Ryerson letter to Egerton Ryerson, November 15, 1833, is partially quoted by: Hodgins, ed., *'The Story of My Life' by the late Rev. Egerton Ryerson*, 127-128; by Sissons, *Egerton Ryerson*, I, 210-211; and by French, *Parsons & Politics*, 145. However, the quoted sentences vary slightly in phrasing in

the three different accounts and each quotation of the paragraph has missing sentences. The letter has been reconstructed from the several overlapping and partial reproductions in the three published sources.

10. Hodgins, ed., *'The Story of My Life' by the later Rev. Egerton Ryerson*, 125-126; and Gidney, "Ryerson, Egerton", *DCB*, XI. One can surmise, as well, that the earlier alignment of Egerton Ryerson with the democratic radicals was motivated, at a deeper level, by the evangelical belief in the need to take political action to facilitate the coming of the Millennium. In that framework of beliefs, the arrival of the rule of 'the saints' was to be hastened by destroying the established church and the authoritarian political order which was conceived as being an obstacle to the attainment of the millennial unity of Christian love and liberty in the 'kingdom of light'.

11. Sissons, *Egerton Ryerson*, I, 228. Dunham (*Political Unrest*, 145), interprets the 'English Impressions' article as constituting an announcement of the apostasy of Egerton Ryerson in abandoning the democratic radicalism of the Reformers for 'moderate toryism'. Dunham arrived at a similar conclusion in maintaining that the continued commitment of Ryerson to "his policy of secularizing the clergy reserves" was "the only modification of his toryism". However, as indicated by the above analysis, the author totally rejects any interpretation that sees the Rev. Egerton Ryerson as having become a moderate Tory.

12. For a summary of the arguments of William Paley in defence of the Church establishment in England, see, William Westfall, *Two Worlds, The Protestant Culture of Nineteenth-Century Ontario* (Montreal & Kingston: McGill-Queen's Press, 1989), 91-92.

Appendix B

The 'young Tories' of Upper Canada

On July 2, 1833, former pupils of the Cornwall District Grammar School (1803-1811) assembled to honour Archdeacon John Strachan, and to express their "esteem and affection" for their former teacher/headmaster. At the gathering, his former pupils expressed their gratitude to Archdeacon Strachan for his "unweared efforts to improve their minds, and to impress upon them sound moral and religious principles", and thanked him for his friendship and interest in their "progress through life". One of the organizers of the ceremony, the Chief Justice, John Beverley Robinson, gave an Address in which he expressed to Archdeacon Strachan the feelings of his former pupils:

> ... we have never ceased to reflect with gratitude upon your unwearied efforts to cultivate our minds and strengthen our understandings, and above all to implant in our hearts those principles which alone make us good Christians, faithful subjects of our King, and independent and upright members of society.

Following the Address, Archdeacon Strachan was presented with a silver epergne supported by four classical figures: Religion, History, Poetry and Geography. On the back of the pedestal were engraved the names and place of residence of "the gentlemen who presented the plate".

The ceremony and the Epergne were described years later by the Bishop Alexander Neal Bethune, a former pupil at the Cornwall school and theological student of Strachan, in a published memoir on the life of his mentor. In the memoir, the Rev. Bethune described the ceremony and the Epergne, as well as listed the name, place of residence, and on occasion the profession, of the 42 former pupils who had contributed to the gift of plate. (1) Among them were the leading young Anglican Tories of Upper Canada, as well as several of the leading young Presbyterian and Roman Catholic Scots tories of the Province.

The leadership role of the former Strachan pupils in the public life of Upper Canada, and their contribution to its professional life and economic development is attested to by the large number of the 'young Tories' who have merited an entry in the *Dictionary of Canadian Biography* (*) based on their outstanding achievements. (2)

The former pupils of Archdeacon Strachan

John B. [Beverley] Robinson*, York, Chief Justice of Upper Canada
John Bethune*, Montreal, Rector of Montreal
R.G. Anderson, York, Teller, Bank of Upper Canada
George Ridout*, York, Judge of District Court of Niagara
J.G. [James Grant] Chewett*, York, Senior Draftsman, Surveyor General's Department
Samuel P. [Peters] Jarvis*, York, Deputy Secretary and Registrar, U.C.
J.B. [James Buchanan] Macaulay*, York, Judge of King's Bench, U.C.
Thos. G. [Thomas Gibbs] Ridout*, York, Cashier, Bank of U.C.
Robert Stanton*, York, King's Printer
G.S. [George Strange] Boulton*, Cobourg, Barrister, M.P.
W. B. [William Benjamin] Robinson*, Newmarket, M.P.
Jonas Jones*, Brockville, Judge, District Court, Johnstown District
John Radenhurst, York, Surveyor General's Department
W. [William] Macaulay*, Picton, Rector of Picton
A. N. [Alexander Neil] Bethune*, Cobourg, Rector of Cobourg
Henry Ahern, Vaudreuil
John Crawford, England
James G. [Gray] Bethune*, Cobourg, Cashier, Branch Bank, U.C.
James Duncan Gibb, Montreal
George Gregory, Montreal.

Of the twenty persons on this initial list, fourteen attended the gathering with the others sending their regrets. In addition, another twenty-two former pupils are listed who contributed to the purchase of the plate and may, or may not, have been present at the presentation ceremony: viz.

Fred. Griffin, Montreal
A.B.C. Gugy, Quebec, Barrister, M.P.

A. Jones, Prescott
John Macaulay*, Kingston
J. McLean, Kingston, Sheriff, Mdld. District
Arch. [Archibald] McLean*, Cornwall, Speaker of House of Assembly
J. McDonell, Montreal
Duncan McDonell, Cornwal
Donald [Donald Aeneas] McDonell*, Cornwall
Alex. McLean, Cornwall
J.S. [James Simcoe] Macaulay*, Woolwich, Capt. R.E.
G.H. [George Herchmer] Markland*, York, Inspector General, U.C.
G. Mitchell, Penetanguishene
Thos. Richardson, India
Wm. Stanton, Africa, D.A. Com. Genl.
P. [Philip] Van Koughnet*, Cornwall, M.P.
I. Weatherhead, Brockville
G.C. Wood, Cornwall
A. Wilkinson, Cornwall, Barrister
D.J. Smith, Kingston
James Macaulay, Cornwall, M. D.
T. Pyke, Halifax.

Not all of the leading Anglican Tories of Upper Canada were educated by the Rev. John Strachan, and not all of his students were Anglicans, but most were. It was the Anglicans of Upper Canada who held a particularly strong belief in the importance of their children receiving a formal education. Not only did the young Tories who were educated by the Rev. Strachan, comprise a major part of the educated elite in postwar Upper Canada, but most were the sons of Loyalists, many were lawyers, and almost all had been active participants in the War of 1812, particularly in commanding militia companies. One singularly noteworthy Upper Canadian Anglican Tory who was not educated at the Cornwall District Grammar School was Christopher Alexander Hagerman* of Kingston. Hagerman served as Solicitor General (July 1829 - March 1837) and as Attorney General (March 1837 - February 1840), and was the *de* *facto* leader of the Tories in the House of Assembly during the 1830s, following the elevation of Attorney General John Beverley Robinson to the bench as Chief Justice of the Court of King's Bench.

Not all of the Anglican youth educated by the Rev. John Strachan became staunch Tories. A notably exception was young Robert Baldwin*. He was educated, following the War of 1812, at the Home District Grammar School in York where the Rev. Strachan served as the headmaster during the period 1812-1829. In his upbringing, young Robert was strongly influenced by his father, the Anglo-Irish Anglican immigrant, William Warren Baldwin*, an Old Whig. Robert became a liberal-Whig in politics and espoused Lockean-liberal beliefs and values as a leading member of the Reform Party during the 1830s in Upper Canada, and subsequently during his tenure as the joint leader of the Reform Party – with Louis Hippolyte Lafontaine – during the 1840s in the new United Province of Canada.

Where the influence of the Rev. John Strachan* is concerned, the late Canadian historian Syd Wise noted that "John Strachan, more than any other man, was responsible for the framing of Tory policy in Church and State, and for the rationale by which it was defended". (3) Professor Wise also wrote with respect to the Rev. Strachan that: "his impact upon the Ontario community in its formative stage was very great ... and yet it cannot be said that his ideas have ever been adequately analyzed". (4) That lacuna has been addressed by the author with the publication of: *The Upper Canadian Anglican Tory Mind, a Cultural Fragment* (Oakville: Rock's Mills Press, 2018).

Notes

1. *Memoir of the Right Reverend John Strachan, D.D., L.L.D., First Bishop of Toronto,* by A.N. Bethune (Toronto: Henry Rowsell, 1870), 146-152. The Robinson quotation is from page 148.

2. The *Dictionary of Canadian Biography* entries can be consulted online. One oddity is that the biographical entries rarely mention the religion of an individual, other than for the clergy.

3. S.F. Wise, "God's Peculiar People" in W.L. Morton, ed., *The Shield of Achilles, Aspects of Canada in the Victorian Age* (Toronto: McClelland & Stewart, 1968), 56.

4. S. F. Wise, "Sermon Literature and Canadian Intellectual History", *United Church of Canada Archives Bulletin*, XVII, 1965, 14. In this article, Professor Wise comments on the value of sermon literature as "a medium for the expression of conservative ideas" (page 5), and comments further on the vital role that the sermons of the conservative clergy played in "the formation of a conservative political ideology" in Upper Canada ('Sermon Literature', 6 & 8).

Appendix C
Terminology

During the research and writing of the new chapters comprising this book, the author began to discern more clearly the distinct character and beliefs of the various groups engaged in the political life of the Province of Upper Canada. It became evident that the Reform Party, as it evolved, had come to be composed of four major outgroups that embodied separate and distinct political ideas; that religion was a key factor in determining political allegiance on most political issues; and that even the Tory establishment was composed of two different Anglican groups. The following terms have been used as descriptors. They evolved from the author's study of Anglican Toryism, his broader readings in Canadian history and in Canadian historiography, and his readings in the history of political thought, as well as his musings on the politics of Upper Canada.

Tories, moderate Tories, and generic tories

In the terminology evolved by the author, the term 'tory' is used to refer to those who were opposed to American democratic republicanism and believed in loyalty to the King, the British constitution, the unity of the British Empire, and the union of church and state. Thus, the term 'tory' is used in a generic sense for conservatives who, based on their Christian religious beliefs, supported the preservation of the traditional political and social order. In Upper Canada, the term 'tory' comprehended a good many, but not all, Anglicans, Church of Scotland adherents, Wesleyan Methodists, Lutherans, and the Scottish and English Roman Catholics who upheld the established political, religious and social order and the balanced constitution and either accepted or tolerated the existing church-state polity, although they differed over the exclusive prerogatives and endowments that the Church of England enjoyed. The appellation 'Tory' is used by the author as a descriptor for the High Church Anglican Tories and, more particularly, for the Rev. John Strachan and his former students of the Cornwall District Grammar School (1803-1811) who formed the core of the social and political elite of Upper Canada following the War of 1812, and who lived and acted in accordance with Anglican Tory beliefs, principles and values.

The 'High Church Tories' were staunch supporters of the union of church and state and were committed defenders of the exclusive prerogatives and endowments of the established Church of England in Upper Canada. There were also Anglicans who were 'moderate Tories'. They shared with the High Church Tories a belief in government based on Christian principles, values and beliefs and in the principle of an established church, but were willing -- for the sake of social harmony – for all Protestant religious denominations to share in the endowments which the Crown had bestowed on the Church of England for the support of "a Protestant Clergy". Both the 'High Church Tories' and the 'moderate Tories' were strong defenders of the balanced British Constitution, 'the rights of Englishmen', the limited constitutional monarchy, the rule of law and the British Imperial connection, and were believers in a 'natural' hierarchical social order.

Conservatives

The term 'conservative' is used in a much more comprehensive manner to include all groups and individuals, regardless of their religious affiliation, who supported the retention of the balanced British Constitution and the unity of Empire, and who were opposed to American democratic republicanism. In sum, the term 'conservative' embraces High Church Anglican Tories and moderate Anglican Tories, as well as generic tories of various religious persuasions, and 'situational conservatives'. The latter category – which utilizes a term introduced by a political scientist, Samuel P. Huntington -- comprises those who supported the established social and political order of Upper Canada simply out of a force of habit and custom, or out of economic self-interest, rather than from any deeper philosophical or religious conviction. In Upper Canada, it was the merchants who comprised the principal group of situational conservatives. They supported the Tory establishment for its economic development policies, the provincial government investment in public works, and stable government, but were not defenders of the unity of church and state. As such, the merchants of Upper Canada were quick to support the new Governor-in-Chief, Charles Poulett Thomson, in his policy to unite the two Canadian provinces, to have the new united government absorb the public debt of Upper Canada, and to undertake public works with the aid of the British government £1.5 million loan interest guarantee.

Terminology

The opposition 'Outgroups'

In Upper Canada, the Tory provincial government administration was opposed by liberal-Whigs who were Lockean-liberals in their political beliefs and principles but otherwise were social conservatives, and by democratic radicals who demanded democratic elective institutions -- within the existing constitution -- to empower 'the people'. The Tory establishment was also under attack by evangelical sectarians who demanded a complete separation of church and state and, as of the early 1830s, by egalitarian democratic republicans who were admirers of the American Republic and Jacksonian democracy. All four outgroups were encompassed within the provincial Reform Party.

The various outgroups were united in their hostility to the Tory governing establishment, and in their support of the Reform Party in its demand for 'responsible government'. As expounded by the Reformers, it was a proposed new principle of government. It required that the Crown appoint executive councillors who could command the support of a majority of the elected representatives in the House of Assembly, and that the representative of the Crown – the Lieutenant Governor – must take the advice of his Executive Council on local provincial matters. On their part, the Tories feared that the principle of responsible government would result -- if implemented -- in the overthrow of the balanced British constitution through placing the majority party of the House of Assembly in control of the provincial government ministry, the provincial Crown revenues, and the distribution of Crown patronage. For the Tories of Upper Canada, the principle of 'responsible government' was equated with party government, partisan politics, and democracy (popular sovereignty).

The term 'outgroups' has been borrowed from Robert Kelley, *The Transatlantic Persuasion, The Liberal-Democratic Mind in the Age of Gladstone* (New York: Alfred A. Knopf, 1969). In studying the transatlantic community of the 19th Century, Kelley used the term 'outgroups' to describe the various groups who were divorced from "the real center of power and prestige in society" and who, following the Napoleonic Wars and throughout the 19th Century, aligned themselves together under "the Liberal and Democratic banners". These groups, he noted, were often mutually antagonistic, had a narrowness of outlook, and generally were focussed on very limited partisan interests or a single issue. Yet, they were united in their image of 'the enemy': the traditional Tory political and social elite. The outgroups were united in being opposed to the traditional social hierarchy, the concept and social status of a 'gentleman', and the whole "habit of authority" in their society.

The 'American Methodists'

The adherents of the Methodist Episcopal Church are referred to by the author as 'American Methodists' which is in keeping with the terminology used by the Upper Canadian Anglican Tories. It was a terminology which was based on a recognition that the religious principles of the adherents of the Upper Canadian Methodists – 'voluntaryism', 'religious equality', and the 'separation of church and state' -- were derived from American evangelical Protestantism, and were introduced into Upper Canada by American itinerant preachers and the American sectarians who settled in the Province during the two decades prior to the War of 1812. Contrary to the assertions of the evangelical religious sects -- and their leading polemicist, the Rev. Egerton Ryerson -- the Church of England was an established church in Upper Canada, and it has been so treated in this work.

Family Compact

This is a term that was, and is, commonly used by 'progressive historians' as a descriptor for the Tory governing elite of the Province of Upper Canada. It is a pejorative term that was first introduced into Canadian politics in 1828 by one of the leading radicals, Barnabas Bidwell – an American immigrant and Jeffersonian democrat -- in drawing on his familiarity with American political epithets. Thereafter, the Reformers popularized the term in using it, at every opportunity, to characterize the Tories as being a family group of selfish, reactionary and corrupt oligarchs. The so-called Family Compact Tories were even accused, by the Reformers, of being responsible for what was claimed to be the economic backwardness of Upper Canada vis-à-vis the American Republic.

The so-called 'Family Compact' was held to be reactionary for its opposition to the introduction of the Reform Party concept of 'responsible government', which involved the establishment of a democratic form of government based on popular sovereignty. However, the Tories were simply defending the status quo in upholding the balanced British Constitution and the sovereignty of the Crown. They were reactionaries only when viewed within the context of the Liberal ideology of political progress. Similarly, the charge of corruption needs to be qualified.

Historically, among the leading Reformers of Upper Canada, it was the radical William Lyon Mackenzie who continually accused the Tory political establishment of financial corruption. Long before Lord Acton expressed his dictum that "Power tends to corrupt, and absolute power corrupts absolutely. Great men are almost always bad men ...." (April 1887), Mackenzie held a similar view. He acted on his belief that the power to control government finances was corrupting, and on a concomitant belief that the peculation of public funds was, or must be, a real problem in Upper Canada. Hence his penchant for making unsubstantiated – utterly fallacious -- charges of financial corruption against the Tory governing establishment.

More generally, when the Reform Party leadership -- inclusive of Egerton Ryerson -- claimed that the Tory system of government was corrupt, they were referring to the workings of the Constitution. They maintained that the Tories had corrupted the Constitution through using their control of the Legislative Council to block House of Assembly bills that represented 'the will of the people'.

The highly-negative characterization of the so-called Family Compact Tories by the Upper Canadian Reformers entered into Canadian historiography subsequently when repeated in the *Durham Report* (1839) and by the Liberal journalist, John Charles Dent in his popular histories of the 1880s. A highly-partisan Reform Party sympathizer, Dent engaged in a blatant act of character assassination in categorizing the 'Family Compact' Tories as being a 'bastard aristocracy' of intolerant bigots who were "utterly out of keeping with the times in which they lived" (Dent, *The Story of the Upper Canadian Rebellion* (vol. I, 1885, 77 & 79).

The negative 'Family Compact' characterization of the governing Tories has long since been totally discredited by historians who have studied the political history of the Province of Upper Canada: viz. Aileen Dunham, *Political Unrest in Upper Canada, 1815-1836* (Toronto: McClelland & Stewart, 1963, 1st. ed. 1927), Gerald Craig, *Upper Canada the Formative Years, 1784-1841* (Toronto: McClelland & Steward, 1963), and Robert W. Saunders, "What was the Family Compact?", *Ontario History*, XLIX, No. 4, Autumn 1957, 169-178). They have attested that the Tories were 'a quasi-aristocracy of bureaucrats and professional men' of education and of a proven loyalty to the Crown. Rather than family ties, they were united by their cultural values, their superior education, their religious and constitutional beliefs, and their opposition to American democratic republicanism.

More recently, Denis McKim ("Upper Canadian Thermidor, The Family Compact & the Counter-revolutionary Atlantic", *Ontario History*, CVI, No. 2, 2014, 235-262) has totally dismissed the negative 'Tory family compact' characterization. Through examining Tory beliefs, values and principles, McKim has argued that the Tories were not selfish, reactionary oligarchs. They were like-minded individuals, with "a dynamic vision for the colony", who constituted the political, social, and economic elite of the Province of Upper Canada, and who offered "an alternative model for colonial development" – a path not taken.

In sum, the term, 'Family Compact', is a pejorative term that was employed by Upper Canadian Reformers to denigrate, denounce and discredit the Tories who governed the Province of Upper Canada. It is a highly-inaccurate descriptor that ought to be abandoned by historians in favour of a neutral descriptor such as 'the governing Tory elite', or 'the Tory establishment'. More generally, a more appropriate descriptor would be 'the tory gentry', or, more precisely -- where the Anglican Tories are concerned – 'High Church Tories'.

Democracy

In Upper Canada, the democratic radical demand for 'democracy' was not so much a demand for universal manhood suffrage – although that was part of the rhetoric -- as it was a demand for democratic institutions of government. In Upper Canada, land was readily available with free Crown land grants before 1826 and relatively cheap land prices thereafter. Almost every adult male who took the Oath of Allegiance, who completed the settlement duties and received title to his land and met the residency requirement, had the vote for electing representatives to the House of Assembly under the traditional 40-shilling franchise. What the democratic radicals wanted were an elective Legislative Council and elected sheriffs, magistrates, and judges within the existing Constitution.

For the egalitarian democratic republicans, the demand for 'democracy' and 'freedom' extended still further than the establishment of democratic institutions. It embraced social equality, the election of a Governor on a universal male suffrage, and the vesting of sovereignty in the people rather than the Crown. It was a transformation that could only be achieved through a declaration of independence from Britain.

Liberal-Whigs

In Britain, the Old Whig beliefs of the early 18th Century in man as a social being, in government having evolved from the family, in a natural social hierarchy, and in government by a landed aristocracy pursuing the common good of the nation and the promotion of social harmony were gradually transformed -- during the course of the later 18th Century -- into liberal-whiggism under the influence of the political philosophy of John Locke. In the American colonies, the transformation was quite rapid over the period of 1765-1776, and readily apparent, as attested to by a prominent American historian, Bernard Bailyn (*The Intellectual Origins of the American Revolution*, 1967). The new liberal-Whigs adhered to the Lockean-liberal, man-centred, political philosophy that was based on inalienable natural rights, individualism, popular sovereignty, the separation of church and state, and a right of rebellion, which ideas -- beliefs, values and principles -- were enunciated in the Declaration of Independence of the new American Republic.

In Britain, by the late 1830s, the Whigs who were of a Lockean-liberal persuasion – the liberal-Whigs --began to refer to themselves as 'Liberals'. Somewhat earlier, the moderate-Tories came to be called 'Conservatives' under the leadership of Sir Robert Peel, who defined the programme of the new 'Conservative Party' in his Tamsworth Manifesto of 1834. In the United Province of Canada, the various political factions among the English and the French members of the House of Assembly eventually coalesced into two major political parties: viz. a coalition 'Liberal-Conservative Party' formed in 1854, and a united 'Liberal Party' founded in 1861.

Whig History - liberal-Whig History

What has been termed 'Whig history' is a Liberal historiography that views history teleologically in terms of the progress of humanity towards enlightenment, rationalism, and the liberty of the individual. As attested by Herbert Butterfield (*The Whig Interpretation of History*, 1965), Whig history is characterized by presentism, a distinct historical methodology, and a strong historical bias.

Whig histories are present-oriented in studying the past from the concerns of the present, and in viewing the march of history as demonstrating the principles of 'progress' in the growth of the liberty of the individual and the establishment of constitutional government based on the concept of popular sovereignty. For Whig historians, history serves as an arbitrator for the making of moral judgements on past events and personages. However, the moral judgements are based on liberal political principles, rather than God's moral law. In Whig histories, there is no concept of studying history for its own sake; there is little historical understanding; and there is a complete lack of 'an imaginative sympathy for the past'.

In their historical methodology, Whig histories are highly selective, highly biased, and given to making self-evident judgements on political issues. They focus on a single line of causation and on identifying 'the agency' responsible for the origin of the successful struggle to attain modern liberty and a government responsible to the people. (In Britain, the purported agency of progress in Whig histories was generally either the Protestant Reformation, or the recovery of the knowledge of the ancient Anglo-Saxon liberties suppressed by the Normans.) Whatever is viewed as not being germane to the attainment of the liberty of the individual, and a liberal-democratic popular government in the present, is excluded from the history story.

Whig histories focus on 'the great men of history', and 'the great watershed events', and divide the leading historical personages of each era into progressives ("democratic radicals, Protestant sects, and Lockean-liberals") and reactionaries ("Anglican Tories and Roman Catholics") on the basis of their respective principles and actions in supporting or hindering the ultimate triumph of liberal principles and values. Prominent Tories, who were judged to have obstructed the progress of liberal-Whig principles and the attainment of individual liberty and a liberal-democratic popular government, are denigrated, disparaged, and denounced. They are treated as objects of opprobrium for having impeded the progress of the nation, but otherwise are excluded from the historical narrative.

In Canadian historiography, the Whig history template of interpretation became firmly established during the 1880s following the publication of the popular history works of a highly-partisan Liberal journalist, John Charles Dent (1841-1888). In two major historical publications -- *The Last Forty Years: Canada since the Union of 1841*, 2 vols. (Toronto: George Virtue, 1881), and *The Story of the Upper Canadian Rebellion; largely derived from original sources and documents*, 2 vols. (Toronto: C. Blackett Robinson, 1885), Dent applied the Whig history template to the interpretation of Canadian history in focusing on the political history of the United Province of Canada, and subsequently sought the origins of the demand for 'responsible government' in the political history of the Province of Upper Canada.

For Dent, the great historical theme was the attainment of self-government in local affairs through the achievement of 'responsible government', the agency was the liberal Reform Party, the watershed event was the Rebellion of 1837, and the heroic personages were Lord Durham and Robert Baldwin.

The Rebellion of December 1837 is depicted by Dent as fully justified in having been undertaken by a people desiring freedom from the suffering of a long train of abuses under the "tyranny and oppression" of a Tory oligarchy in an outdated colonial system; and the defeat of 'the insurgents' is ascribed to a failure of leadership, principally in the erratic behaviour and indecision of William Lyon Mackenzie. Yet, the Rebellion is held to have been a success in that it awakened the English people to "the reality of Canadian grievances", made the British government aware of the need for the introduction of "a broad and liberal policy" of reform, and resulted in the appointment Lord Durham. In that purview, the Rebellion was 'an ordeal' that Upper Canadians were compelled to pass through on the way to the achievement of 'liberty'.

Lord Durham is hailed by Dent as "a Liberal of Liberals", and a champion of "the cause of liberty and the rights of the common people", who in a "Masterly State document", the Durham Report (March 1839), recommended the constitutional changes that the Reform Party had been advocating for years -- inclusive of the introduction of 'the great principle' of responsible government -- to address long-standing grievances.

As the story unfolds, it is Robert Baldwin who is held up for admiration for his commitment to the principle of responsible government in the struggle against a recalcitrant British government, and who is credited with attaining the implementation of 'responsible government' that brought self-government for Canadians in local affairs. Baldwin is portrayed as "a man with political ideas in advance of his time and surroundings", as a man with a high sense of duty and of untarnished integrity, 'whom Canadians held in great esteem, respect and veneration'.

In the Whig history interpretation of John Charles Dent, there is a thinly-veiled regret that 'the insurgents' were unsuccessful in their attempt to overthrow the Tory establishment and to establish a liberal-democratic Reform government. Dent muses about the positive reception such a government would have received from 'the people', and about an expected acquiescence on the part of the British government in the establishment of a popular government. His writings convey an undercurrent of regret at a mission left incomplete in the failure to attain a complete self-government for Canadians in an independent republic.

The liberal-Whig progressive interpretation of history dominated the field of Canadian history well into the 20th Century in being written from a number of evolving 'present-day perspectives': e.g. constitutional history/rise of self government, 'progressive history/new history', and 'colony to nation' history. As late as the mid-century, a prominent

Liberal historian disparaged the Anglican Tories and dismissed them as irrelevant to the progress of Upper Canada and to Canadian history more generally. He wrote:

> "What, after all, of Bishop Strachan and the young Tories he schooled, what else of Strachan the politician can one say than that it is the most difficult thing in the world to imagine there ever was such a man. Politically, he believed (as Walter Bagot said of Lord Elton) in everything it is impossible to believe in." (William Kilbourn, *The Firebrand, William Lyon Mackenzie and the Rebellion in Upper Canada*, 1956, Introduction.)

Underlying the liberal-Whig interpretation of Canadian history is a conceit on the part of Liberals that they were, and are, the true representatives of 'the people', and a belief that, historically, it was the Reformers who alone were the defenders of 'the rights of the people' in what is viewed as an epic struggle for individual liberty and popular government against supposedly dictatorial royal governors (royal absolutism) and reactionary Tories. Given that the Anglican Tories of Upper Canada were not in accord with the partisan liberal-Whig concept of 'progress' – which is embodied in the triumph of rationalism, individualism, secularism, and popular sovereignty -- the Tories were simply dismissed from the historical record and characterized, in passing, as intolerant reactionaries who were supposedly self-serving and corrupt.

Index
Anglican Toryism in Upper Canada

Age of Delusion
    Tory view, 393-395
    vs Age of Reason, 394-395
    French Revolution, 394
    Post-War Europe, 395-396

Alien Question
    immigration policy, 101-102, 140-141
    Proclamation (Oct. 1815), 103-104
    immigration politics, 104-106, 126-127, 402-403
    Naturalization Act (1740), 105-106
    Tory view, 107-111, 129-132, 140-141
    Bidwell controversy, 111-116
    Law Officers' position, 116-117
    Tory position, 117-122
    Naturalization Bill (1825), 123-125
    radical position, 125-126, 129-132, 144
    British legislation, 127
    Naturalization Act (1827), 127-132, 147
    betrayal in Britain, 132
    Naturalization Act (1828), 132-135
    bittersweet settlement, 135-137, 140-141, 148
    control of immigration, 139

American Methodists
    Tory view of, 202-.205, 235
    religious principles, 205-206
    political activism, 205
    Loyalist experience, xiii
    Saddlebags parliament, 214
    education of preachers, 237, 457
    evangelical Protestantism, 239
    Americanizing influence, 396, 457
    political influence, 368-369
    transformation of, 388-390, 420-421

American Revolution (1776-1783)
    Tory view of, 29, 52, 377
    religious factor, 377
    role of evangelicals, 373-378
    John Locke influence, 397-398
    Thomas Paine, 398
    American exceptionalism, 398
    Declaration of Independence, 398-399
    Bernard Bailyn thesis, 397
    second coming in U.C., 18, 29

American Settlers
    wartime appeals to, 18-19
    disaffection, 218-219, 396, 402
    perversity, 232-233
    Reform Party, 260
    threat posed, 24-28, 52, 401-402
    Rebellion, 309, 311, 335-336, 338-339

American Threat
    American alien settlers, 8, 24-26, 28, 50-51, 121-122, 141
    evangelical Protestantism, xi, 93
    ideological, xi, 23-24 65-67, 93
    military imperialism, xi, 15, 63, 69-71, 77-83, 403-404
    American character, 79, 81

Anglican Toryism
    meritocracy, x
    church-state union, 14
    philosophical conservatism, x, xii
    loyalty concept, 26, 278-280, 404
    rule of law, 350-351
    religious toleration, 353

Anglican Tories
    view of Upper Canada, 19-21
    view of England, 6-7
    the young Tories, 10, 352, 460-462
    view of U.S., 68-69, 71-77, 82
    survival anxiety, 81-83
    fear of abandonment, 83-85, 89-90
    colonies: economic value, 85-86
    colonies: strategic value, 86-89
    defence strategy, 90-92
    nationalism, 99, 345
    view of demagogues, 131-132
    view of the Church, 149, 352-353
    Tory principles, 270, 345, 350
    conservative divisions, 346-349
    conservative supporters, 350
    on political parties, 350
    educated gentlemen, 351
    on public opinion, 369
    on electioneering, 369
    Rebellion role, 371
    Tory establishment, 372-374
    immigration policy, 401-403

Index

Anglican Toryism (book)
   historiographical context, ix
   concept, ix-x, xviii
   dissertation text, xv
   focus, x-xii
   'ideas influence actions', x-xii, xv
   outgroups, xi
   provenance, xv-xvi, xviii-xix
   sources, xvii-xviii

Bailyn, Bernard (1922-)
   on American Revolution, 397
   ideological origins, 397

Battles (1812-1814)
   taking of Michilimackinac, 29
   capture of Detroit, 29-30, 32
   Queenston Heights, 16, 30,32
   incursions at York, 34
   attack on Fort George, 34
   Stoney Creek (6 June 1813), 34
   Beaver Dams (24 June 1813), 34
   naval operations, 34-35, 38, 40, 46
   Moraviantown (5 Oct. 1813), 35, 40
   Châteauguay (26 Oct. 1813), 40-41
   Crysler's Farm (11 Nov. 1813), 41
   Chippawa (5 July 1814), 45
   Lundy's Lane (25 July 1814), 45-46
   Malcolm's Mills (6 Nov. 1814), 49

Baldwin, Wm. Warren (1775-1844)
   Friends of Religious Liberty, 226.
   Loyalty Election (1836), 259
   Toronto Political Union, 261
   Rebellion, 308
   Old Whig, 363
   political activity, 364

Baldwin, Robert (1804-1855)
   Friends of Religious liberty, 226
   Loyalty Election (1836), 259
   Rebellion, 294, 308
   responsible government, 258-259
   attainment of, 412-413

Bidwell, Barnabas (1763-1833)
   election/alien issue, 111-115

Bidwell, Marshall Spring (1799-1872)
   bye-election, 116
   naturalization bill, 134-135
   Reform Party leader, 141,225
   radicalism, 189, 366
   Bidwell Report, 187 207-208, 238
   Rebellion, 308, 375

Bonnycastle, Sir RichardLt. Col., Royal Engineers
   political analysis (1837), 330-331

British Constitutional Society
   founding, 249-250, 357
   Tory support, 250, 256
   political role, 250-251, 282
   Loyalty Election (1836), 253, 357, 360
   campaign effort, 254-255
   British immigration, 254
   electoral support, 255
   loyalty principle, 256-257
   Tory reservations, 261

British Empire
   family concept, 7
   Unity of the Empire, xi, 23, 28, 85
   dependence on, 81-85, 404
   trade value/colonies, 85-86
   strategic value/colonies, 87-88
   defence policy, 89-92
   Tory loyalty to, 23, 417

British immigrant radicals
   'spirit of the times', 137-138
   character of, 138
   Sedition Act (1804), 138-140

British National Character
   Tory view of, 23, 52, 204
   characteristics, 5

British North America
   confederation proposal, 8-9
   imperial federation, 8
   Imperial unity, 8

Brock, Major-General Sir Isaac (1769-1812)
   leadership, 27
   character of, 29
   Michilimackinac, 29
   capture of Detroit, 29-30
   Queenston Heights, 30

Canadian Alliance Society (1834)
   Reform founders, 247
   programme, 248-249

Index

Canadian Historiography
   liberal-Whig history, ix, 472-475
   'hollow at the core', ix-xx
   Tory role/nation building, xvii,
   Syd Wise, 11-12

Cartwright, Richard (1759-1815)
   Loyalist, xvii
   Alien Board, 36
   on American immigrants, 103

Census, Canada West
   religious (1842), 420

Church Establishment (Anglican)
   financial support, 159-160, 162, 231-232
   legal status, 392
   Presbyterian claim, 179, 195, 392
   radical view, 137, 186, 196-197
   comprehension policy, 162, 353, 389
   Rolph argument, 196-197
   Robinson response, 197-198
   tithe situation, 159
   Tithe Declaratory Act, 163-164, 222
   Ryerson denial of, 212, 391
   British immigrant role, 215-216
   Lord Goderich, 228-231

Church of Rome
   tithe rights, 159
   financial support of, 192, 229
   marriage law, 216
   endowments, 233
   politics, 374

Church of Scotland
   Tory view of, 170
   financial support, 192
   co-establishment claim, 179, 195, 392
   Morris resolutions, 194-195
   politics, 374

Clergy Reserves
   Tory Reserves strategy, 151, 353
   clerical salaries, 151-152
   procuring clergymen, 152-153
   native-born clergy, 153-154
   educating clergy, 155-156
   appeals for aid, 156-157
   State Christian duty, 157-158
   financial aid, 159-160, 162, 181
   independent clergy concept, 160-162
   Tory political strategy, 214-215
   'a Protestant Clergy', 391
   Tory view of opponents, 393

Clergy Reserves (management)
   leasing problem, 165-166, 177, 240
   managing the Reserves, 165-169, 177
   Clergy Corporation (1819), 166-169
   financial difficulties, 168-169
   proposed new Charter, 177-178
   proposed Board, 178
   Sales Act (July 1827), 200-201, 222-224, 231
   Instructions/Lord Goderich, 229-231

Clergy Reserves (attacks on)
   Scots Church claims, 169-172
   Tory response, 172-176, 179, 184-185
   Tory view of, 174-176, 179, 214-215
   Assembly Address, 190-191
   pamphlet war, 192-194
   John Rolph, 195-197
   Presbyterian claims, 171-172, 194-196, 199
   Tory response, 173-174
   Assembly debate, 194-196
   'Protestant clergy' phrase, 165, 170, 184, 208, 213
   Tory fears, 174-176
   Sectarian demands, 199-200, 213
   Tory view of, 197-199
   Social impact, 198
   Bidwell Report, 187, 207-208, 238
   sectarian rhetoric, 214
   Saddlebags Assembly, 214
   Egerton Ryerson, 213
   Strachan view of, 232-233, 240

Colonial Department/Britain
   liberal-Whigs, 11

Demise of the Tories
   political factors, 404-414
   Durham Report, 405-408
   Union of Canadas, 409-412
   Lord Sydenham system, 411, 424
   French-Canadian bloc, 411, 412-414
   Responsible Government, 412-414
   Ryerson appointment, 423
   return of the rebels, 414
   a lost Saturnia regna, 414-416

Democratic Radicals
   political views, 365-367

Index

British immigrants, 365-366
American settlers, 366
M.S. Bidwell, 366
Loyalty Election, 366
Rebellion, 366
Egerton Ryerson, 367-368

Ecclesiastical Chart (Strachan)
claims made, 202-205
Ryerson critique, 205-206
Bidwell Report, 206-208
British Parliament, 208-210
George Ryerson, 209

Egalitarian Republicanism
American influence, 369-370
political values, 370-371
emergence, 369-370, 375

Evangelical Protestantism
evolution of, 376-385
Tory view of, 376-377, 383-384
in American Revolution, 377-378
Great Awakening, 378-381, 420
millenarianism, 379-383
in American Revolution, 381-382
politicization, 382-383
'retributive justice', 381
Second Great Awakening, 382-383
egalitarianism, 382
Gnosticism, 383-385
religious principles, 378-385

Evangelical Sectarians (U.C.)
vs Clergy Reserves, 174-176, 179
American Methodists, 367-368
religious principles, 367
Saddlebags Parliament, 214-215
political role, 373
a gnostic mentality, 385-386
E. Ryerson rhetoric, 367, 386
a revolutionary movement, 386-387
political activism, 386-387
egalitarianism, 388
millenarianism, 388
transformation of, 388-390

Extra-Parliamentary Associations
Friends of Religious Liberty, 226-229, 233
Reform Party use, 245, 247
Tory view of, 246-247, 249-250
Canadian Alliance, 247-249
Central Political Union, 281

Toronto Political Union, 261
William W. Baldwin, 364

Family Compact,
concept, 419
refutation, 468-470

French Canadians
assimilation of, 8-9, 417
language rights, 413
Tory view of, 417

General Elections
1828 election, 214
1830 election, 225
1834 election, 247
1836 election. 260, 365

Grant, George (1918-1988)
ancient vs modern, 14

Head, Sir Francis Bond
Lt. Governor, U.C.
Ex. Council resignations, 251-253, 282
Reform demand, 252
Tory response, 252-253
Loyalty Election, 253-254

Heimert, Alan (1929-1999)
on evangelical Calvinism, 377-378

Hooker, Richard (1554-1600)
on English Puritanism, 384

Intellectual History
Collingwood, R.G., 1
ideas in history, 3-4
Miller, Perry, 1

Jackson, General Andrew
Florida invasion, 69-70
Jacksonian Democracy, 270
Mackenzie view, 270

King's College
Charter (1827), 201, 231
demand of Radicals, 227, 240
Lord Goderich, 231
1837 compromise, 347-348
vs Friends Religious Liberty, 347

Liberal-Whigs
Reform Party, 363
British immigrants, 364-365
Loyalty Election, 365

479

political views, 330
principles, 422

Liberal-Whig History
historians, 418
characteristics, 472-475

Loyalist Asylum
asylum concept, xi, xiv, 7
government of, xiii
survival threats, x
Tory defenders, x-xi
'the loyal' in power, 122
threats to, 396-401
Tory view of, 396-397, 401

Loyalty
concept, xi, 8
Loyalists, 18, 28-29, 371-372
impact of the war, 54
'the Loyal', 279, 286
principles, 279-280

Macaulay, John (1792-1857)
Loyalist son, xvii
view of U.S., 64
on radicals, 67
on democracy, 71-72

Mackenzie, William Lyon (1795-1861)
radicalism, 189
Friends of Religious Liberty, 226
Canadian Alliance, 248
on Loyalty Election, 262, 283
printing *Common Sense*, 266
Declaration of Reformers, 267-268
planned Toronto convention, 268
delegate selection, 268-269
egalitarian republicanism, 269-270
rebellion proposal, 270-271
coup d'état plan, 276-277
independence declaration, 290-291
egalitarian republicanism, 369-370
threats to Tories, 291-292
Tory view of, 370
Rebellion role, 289-293, 295-297
rebel demands, 294
appeal to Americans, 296
supporters, 372
defeat of, 298-300
rebel names, 299-300
return, 414

MacNab, Sir Allan Napier (1798-1862)
Mackenzie uprising, 295, 297
'the men of Gore', 295
Duncombe uprising, 300-345
pacification effort, 304-305, 307

Marriage Law
political issue, 216-222
1793 Act, 217
1798 Act, 217-218
no enforcement, 219
1831 Marriage Law, 220
Tory initiative, 220-221

Morris, William (1786-1858)
of Church of Scotland, 172
co-establishment claim, 172,191
Clergy Reserves claim, 172
Resolutions, 194-196, 199
vs Clergy Reserves, 191-195, 199

National Policy
origin, 4-5, 9-10
programme, 4-9
purpose, 4 & 9
French problem, 8-9
'the loyal' in power, 140
dependence on Britain, 404

Outgroups
analysis of, xi – xii, 345, 457-468
'battle of ideas', xi
democratic radicals, xi
evangelical sectarians, xi
liberal-Whig secularists, xi, 471-472
egalitarian republicans, xi
concept of, 375-376
resentment, 373
Reform supporters, 376

Paine, Thomas (1737-1809)
Common Sense, 266-267
influence, 398

Perry, Peter (1792-1851)
Reform leader, 335
Rebellion stance, 335

Political Conventions
Mackenzie: 'a right', 262
Tory rejection of, 262-264,270
Toronto Political Union, 268
takeover by radicals, 269
projected Convention, 268-269

Index

Randal, Robert (c.1766-1834)
- on alien question, 132-133
- visit to England, 134

Rebellion of 1837
- coup d'état plan, 276-277, 289-290
- Tory view of, 289
- Independence resolution, 290-291
- Mackenzie uprising, 292-297, 299-300
- John Rolph role, 292-293, 294
- death of Col. Moodie, 293
- Tory response, 289, 293-300, 371
- defeat of rebels, 297-300, 333-334
- rebel names, 299-300
- Clemency Proclamation, 300
- Duncombe uprising, 300-305
- rebel surrender, 304-305
- high treason, 287, 305
- indictments, 305-307, 340
- rebel prisoners, 307-309
- Reform rebels, 308-309
- cultural aspects, 309-311, 329, 337-338
- Tory view of, 311-315, 325-326, 328-329
- Divine Providence, 313-314
- lessons learned, 314-315
- rule of law, 315-317
- treason trials, 317-321
- sentencings, 321-325, 342
- liberal-Whig view, 326-327
- rebel motives, 334, 338-339
- American settlers, 309, 335-336, 338, 339
- Medical doctors, 337

Reform Party (U.C.)
- party discipline, 225, 261, 354
- leaders, 373
- on Clergy Reserves, 225
- vigilance committees, 247
- Grand Convention (1834), 247
- Loyalty Election (1836), 258-260, 358
- support groups, 260, 354-355
- agitations/petitions, 355-356
- associations, 354, 357
- vs church-state, 356
- responsible government, 225, 245, 252-253, 258-259, 269, 357, 361-362
- Declaration of Reformers, 267-268
- Draft Constitution, 271-273, 275-276, 286
- American values, 356
- Reform leaders, 360
- Reformers Declaration, 358-359
- Rebellion role, 308-309

Reform Party (Great Britain)
- political principles, 228, 356
- Lord Goderich, 228-231
- anti-Tory bias, 354

Responsible Government
- concept, 248-259
- legislative response, 264-265
- Ex. Council issue, 251-252
- Russell Resolutions, 265, 358
- Reform Party, 361-362
- Tory rejection of, 362-363
- attainment of, 413-414
- impact (Tory view), 414-415
- a new 'worldview', 415-416
- threat to Toryism, 415-416

Robinson, John Beverley (1791-1863)
- National Policy, 4, 7
- political role, 4, 9-10, 110
- wartime service, 32, 37
- Incorporated Militia Act, 33
- Sedition problem, 38-39, 139
- Ancaster treason trials, 44-45
- view of U.S., 78-79, 102-103, 146
- portrait, 100
- Attorney General, 110
- on alien question, 115, 118-120, 124
- "a free people", 243
- vs electioneering, 369

Rolph, Dr. John (1793-1870)
- radicalism, 189, 196-197
- on alien question, 125-127
- vs church establishment, 196-197
- rebellion role, 278, 293-294, 375
- flight, 308
- return, 414

Ryerson, Egerton (1803-1882)
- vs. church establishment, 205, 210-212
- religious principles, 205-206
- sectarian zealotry, 213-214, 457
- millenarianism, 385-386, 459
- Friends of Religious Liberty, 226
- Ryerson family, 237-238
- Loyalty Election (1836), 256-258
- vs responsible government, 257
- political activities, 367
- Methodist preacher, 367

Impressions article, 443-449
analysis of, 449-456
education superintendent, 411-412
transformation of Methodism, 390

Slavery
in United States, 70-71
Upper Canada, 273-274, 285
1793 Act against, 273
1819 Court abolition, 274
Black loyalties, 373-374

Strachan, Rev. John (1778-1867)
portrait, viii
National Policy, 4
aspirations for pupils, 4
Loyal & Patriotic Society, 31
significance, viii
political role, 10
wartime speeches, 28-30
praise of militia, 32, 33
counteracting treason, 36-38
impact of the War, 51
Archdeacon, 201
on marriage law, 221-222
on Tithe Act, 222
on Reserve sales, 222-223
on 'political dissenters', 240-241
students of Strachan, 460-463
influence of Strachan, 463

Terminology
High Church Tory, 465-466
conservatives, 466
'outgroups', 467
'American Methodists', 468
'Family Compact', 468-470
Democracy, 470-471
liberal-Whigs, 471-472
Whig History, 472-475.

Tory Governing Elite
composition, 10-11
education, 4, 54
positions of power, 4, 54
nationalism, 4
'veterans of War of 1812', 54
on Executive Council, 222

Tory Legacy
philosophical, 416-417
a national vision, 417
vs American assimilation, 417
a Christian worldview, 415-417

in Canadian historiography, 418

Voegelin, Eric (1901-1985)
on English Puritanism, 384-385
on Age of Delusion, 395

War of 1812 (1812-1814)
See also, Battles (1812-1814)
American Declaration of War, 17
Hull's Proclamation, 15, 25-27
Tory view of U.S., 17-19
a defensive war, 21, 22-23
Tory appeals to Canadians, 19-24
Christian patriotism appeal, 21-23
Christian war aims, 23
fear of Americanization, 23-24
Militia Act defeat, 25
desertion problem, 26, 29, 35
early defeatism in U.C., 27
Tory appeals to Loyalists, 28-29
deplorable defensive strategy, 30-31, 33
Loyal & Patriotic Society, 31
Tory praise of militia, 31-33
Incorporated Militia Act, 33
Disaffection, Sedition & Treason, 33-41
Response of York Magistrates, 36
Alien Boards, 36
civil vs. martial law, 38-39
renegade Volunteers, 39-40, 45
raids by marauders, 41, 46-50
Nanticoke skirmish, 41
Tory legislative acts, 43
Ancaster treason trials, 44-45
burning of Newark, 42
incendiary warfare, 42
burning of St. David's, 45
American military raids, 47-50
Treaty of Ghent, 50
Impact of the war, 51-55

Willcocks, Joseph (1773-1814)
political career, 39
wartime treason, 39, 42
Canadian Volunteers, 39-40
burning of Newark, 42

Wise, Sydney F. (1924-2007)
conservative & tory terms, 11
on Canadian conservativism, 11-12
on Tory national vision, 12
on Tory economic policies, 12
on democratic radicalism, 14

Robert W. Passfield is a history graduate of the University of Western Ontario (Honours History, 1968) and of McMaster University (M.A., 1969) where he pursued Ph.D. studies in Canadian history and three minor fields: political philosophy, modern European history, and diplomatic history. In graduate school, he undertook to prepare a dissertation on "The Upper Canadian Tory Mind", which was to focus on the Anglican Tories of the Province of Upper Canada (Ontario) in the post-War of 1812 period. After a forty-year hiatus, that abortive thesis text was incorporated into a book: *The Upper Canadian Anglican Tory Mind, A Cultural Fragment* (2018), to which this book is a supplement.

Passfield is an advocate of a cultural-values approach to the writing of history. To truly understand an historical event, the historian must enter the mind of the protagonists to comprehend their respective principles, values and beliefs within the context of their existing condition and circumstance, as it is the 'ideas' of the protagonists that informed their outlook and actions.

In Upper Canada, it was the Anglican Tories alone who articulated a national vision for the province, and who struggled to build and defend a traditional Church-State 'nation' in North America independent of the new United States of America. Had the Tories not acted on their beliefs, Upper Canada might well have succumbed to either conquest or absorption by the American republic or have become totally Americanized. In disparaging and denigrating the principles, beliefs and values of the Upper Canadian Anglican Tories, and in ignoring their achievements – while focussing on the supposedly progressive Reform Party and the purportedly liberal values of its component 'outgroups' – historians have produced a national history that is truly 'hollow at the core'.

The present study rejects the liberal-Whig (liberal-progressive) interpretation of the political history of Upper Canada in favour of an interactive intellectual-history approach that focusses on the interplay of ideas, conflicting ideologies, and the influence of ideas on historical events.

Also Available
The Upper Canadian Anglican Tory Mind: A Cultural Fragment

The Author

Robert W. Passfield is a history graduate of the University of Western Ontario (Honours History, 1968), and of McMaster University (M.A., 1969) where he pursued Ph.D. studies in Canadian History and three minor fields: political philosophy, modern European history, and diplomatic history. In graduate school, he undertook to prepare a dissertation on 'The Upper Canadian Tory Mind', which was to focus on the Anglican Tories of the Province of Upper Canada (Ontario) in the post-War of 1812 period. He did not complete the study at that time.

Passfield is an advocate of a cultural values approach to the writing of history, which involves much more than a recording of 'what happened'. To truly understand an historical event, the historian must enter the minds of the protagonists – whether religious or secular – to comprehend their respective principles, values and beliefs, and their particular condition and circumstance. In effect, 'ideas influence actions'. It was the cultural values of each party that guided and governed its response to historical events, and the expressed thought which reveals the deeper meaning of the event.

The Book

This book is a study of the values, principles and beliefs of the Anglican Tories who sought to maintain a conservative nation in North America distinct from the secular Lockean-liberal political culture of the new United States of America. It was a conservative nation that was to serve as a home for the Loyalists of the American Revolution and for British immigrants in a constitutional monarchy that was based on a loyalty to Crown and the British Empire, and that had a 'British national character' which was to be sustained by an established Anglican Church, the workings of the balanced British Constitution, and a 'national' education system under the direction of the Established Church.

The Tory effort to maintain a Christian church-state polity in the Province of Upper Canada evoked opposition from various 'outgroups' – democratic radicals, evangelical Protestant sectarians, secular liberal-Whigs, and egalitarian democratic republicans – who combined to overwhelm the Tory establishment. Today, it is the surviving Tory fragment in the political culture of Canada that distinguishes English Canadians from Americans.

www.ingramcontent.com/pod-product-compliance
Lightning Source LLC
Chambersburg PA
CBHW071801080526
44589CB00012B/633